# FIJI HANDBOOK

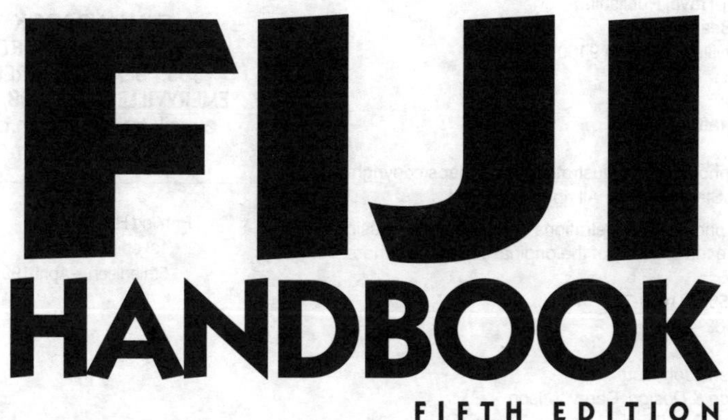


**FIFTH EDITION**

**DAVID STANLEY**

# FIJI HANDBOOK
## FIFTH EDITION

*Published by*
Avalon Travel Publishing
5855 Beaudry Street
Emeryville, California 94608, USA

*Printed by*
Colorcraft



*ISBN:* 1-56691-139-7
*ISSN:* 1082-4898

*Editor:* Asha Johnson
*Production & Design:* Carey Wilson
*Illustration:* Bob Race
*Cartography:* Eric Allen, Allen Leech
*Index:* Asha Johnson

*Front cover photo:* Kadavu, Fiji © Douglas Peebles Photography

Distributed in the United States and Canada by Publishers Group West

Printed in China



Please send all comments, corrections, additions, amendments, and critiques to:

**FIJI HANDBOOK**
**MOON TRAVEL HANDBOOKS**
**5855 BEAUDRY STREET**
**EMERYVILLE, CA 94608, USA**
**e-mail: travel@moon.com**
**www.moon.com**

Printing History
1st edition—1985
5th edition—April 1999
5 4 3 2 1

# CONTENTS

# MAPS



# MAP SYMBOLS

Primary Road
Secondary Road
Railroad
Ferry
Trail
Airfield/Airstrip
Capital City
City
Town
Accommodation
Sight
Golf Course
Mountain
Waterfall
Mangrove
Reef
Water

## CHARTS



## ABBREVIATIONS

A$—Australian dollars
a/c—air-conditioned
ATM—automated teller machine
C—Centigrade
C$—Canadian dollars
CDW—collision damage waiver
EEZ—Exclusive Economic Zone
E.U.—European Union
F$—Fiji dollars
4WD—four-wheel drive
G.P.O.—General Post Office
HI—Hosteling International
km—kilometer
kph—kilometers per hour
LDS—Latter-day Saints (Mormons)
LMS—London Missionary Society
mm—millimeters
MV—motor vessel
No.—number
N.Z.—New Zealand
pp—per person
P.W.D.—Public Works Department
SDA—Seventh-Day Adventist
SPF—South Pacific Forum
STD—sexually transmitted disease
tel.—telephone
U.S.—United States
US$—U.S. dollars
WW I—World War One
WW II—World War Two

## SPELLING AND PRONUNCIATION

When early British missionaries created a system of written Fijian they established a unique set of orthographic rules followed to this day. In an attempt to represent the sounds of spoken Fijian more precisely, they rendered "mb" as **b,** "nd" as **d,** "ng" as **g,** "ngg" as **q,** and "th" as **c.** Thus Beqa is pronounced *Mbengga,* Nadi is *Nandi,* Sigatoka is *Singatoka,* Cicia is *Thithia,* etc. In order to be able pronounce Fijian names and words correctly, visitors must take a few minutes to learn these pronunciation rules. Turn to Language in the Introduction for more information.

## ACCOMMODATION PRICE RANGES

Throughout this handbook, accommodations are generally grouped in the price categories that follow. Of course, currency fluctuations and inflation can lead to slight variations.

Shoestring. . . . . . . . under US$15 double
Budget . . . . . . . . . . . US$15-35 double
Inexpensive. . . . . . . . US$35-60 double
Moderate . . . . . . . . . . US$60-85 double
Expensive . . . . . . . . . US$85-110 double
Premium . . . . . . . . . US$110-150 double
Luxury . . . . . . . . . . . over US$150 double

# ACKNOWLEDGMENTS

The nationalities of those listed below are identified by the following signs which follow their names: at (Austria), au (Australia), ca (Canada), ch (Switzerland), dk (Denmark), es (Spain), fj (Fiji), gb (Great Britain), nc (New Caledonia), nl (Netherlands), nz (New Zealand), pt (Portugal), se (Sweden), and us (United States).

The antique engravings by M.G.L. Domeny de Rienzi are from the classic three-volume work *Oceanie ou Cinquième Partie du Monde* (Paris: Firmin Didot Frères, 1836).

Special thanks to Jack D. Haden (au) for a complete report on Rabi, to Gabriel Teoman (at) for a candid 59-page report on his many adventures in Fiji and Polynesia, to Armand Kuris (us) for a report on outer island snorkeling conditions, to Tatiana Blanc (nc) of the Secretariat of the Pacific Community for statistical support, to Asha Johnson (us) for maintaining communications at the publishers, and to my wife Ria de Vos for her continuing assistance, suggestions, and support.

Thanks too to the following readers who took the trouble to write us letters about their trips:

*Danielle Alvey (gb), Else Baker (us), Lauren Baldoni (au), Ann Bernsen (us), Roberta Blackburn (us), Claire Brenn (ch), Geoff Bourke (nz), T. Cardosa (us), Peter Christensen (us), John Davies (gb), Stefan Deneberg (se), Tania Dunnette (us), Richard Eastwood (au), Mary Graham (us), Sandy Gaudette (us), Lisanne Bruno Hansen (dk), Garry Hawkins (gb), Mark Henley (au), Kirk Huffman (es), Pat Kirikiti (us), José Emilio Lorente (es), John Maidment (gb), Bogumil Matijaca (ca), Joyce B. Moore (us), Marcia Ouellette (us), John Penisten (us), Leroy Lefty Pfistener (us), Paula Robertson (us), Doug Schrader (us), Rosie Simpson (gb), Chris Spoerri (ch), Stan Steele (us), Robert Steffen (ch), Bill Steinmetz (us), Antonio Trindade (pt), Bjorn Wahlin (se), and Arthur and Jane Zeeuw (nl).*

All their comments have been incorporated into the volume you're now holding. To have your own name included here next edition, write: David Stanley, c/o Moon Travel Handbooks, 5855 Beaudry Street, Emeryville, CA 94608, U.S.A. (e-mail: travel@moon.com).

**Attention Hotel Keepers, Tour Operators, and Divemasters**

The best way to keep your listing in *Fiji Handbook* up to date is to send us current information about your business. If you don't agree with what we've written, please tell us why—there's never any charge or obligation for a listing. Thanks to the following island tourism workers and government officials who *did* write in:

*Al Bakker (au), Elain Barrett-Power (fj), Peter Beer (fj), Kelly Bricker (fj), John Bullock (fj), Do Cammick (fj), Tony Cottrell (fj), Nancy Daniels (us), Margaret Davon (au), Mrs. Binesh Dayal (fj), James Di Giambattista (us), Lorna Eden (fj), Mary Farnworth (fj), Dallas Foon (fj), Bob Forster (fj), Carolyn Fotofili (fj), J.N. Godding (ca), John F. Goulding (au), John Gray (fj), Arlene Griffen (fj), Leyh Harness (fj), Tania de Hoon (fj), Arthur Jennings (fj), Yoko Jennings (fj), Ulrich Klose (fj), Jo Ann Kloss (us), Seini Korovou (fj), Armin Kullack (fj), Rob Kusters (nl), Ad Linkels (nl), Peter Lomas (fj), Aline Lyons (fj), Brenda McCroskey (us), Rob McLauchlan (fj), Lily Millar (fj), Anna Mohammed (fj), T. Nishida (fj), Jill Palise (fj), Vijen Prasad (us), Ulaiasi Rabua (fj), Laura Sanders (fj), Jim Selkin (us), Arvind Singh (fj), Hélène Tuwai (fj), Gayle Wade (fj), Tim Waters (ca), Jerry Wittert (us), Dulcie Wong (ca), Kevin Wunrow (us), and Randy Young (us).*

**From the Author**

While out researching my books I find it cheaper to pay my own way, and you can rest assured that nothing in this book is designed to repay freebies from hotels, restaurants, tour operators, or airlines. I prefer to arrive unexpected and uninvited, and to experience things as they really are. On the road I seldom identify myself to anyone. The essential difference between this book and the myriad travel brochures free for the taking in airports and tourist offices all across the region is that this book represents you, the traveler, while the brochures represent the travel industry. The companies and organizations included herein are there for information purposes only, and a mention in no way implies an endorsement.

## YOU WILL HAVE THE LAST WORD

Travel writing is among the least passive forms of journalism, and every time you use this book you become a participant. I've done my best to provide the sort of information I think will help make your trip a success, and now I'm asking for your help. If I led you astray or inconvenienced you, I want to know, and if you feel I've been unfair somewhere, don't hesitate to say. Some things are bound to have changed by the time you get there, and if you write and tell me I'll correct the new edition, which is probably already in preparation even as you are reading this.

Unlike many travel writers, this author doesn't accept hospitality from tourism businesses or obtain VIP treatment by announcing who he is to one and all. At times that makes it difficult to audit the expensive or isolated resorts, thus I especially welcome comments from readers who stayed at the upmarket places, particularly when the facilities didn't match the rates. If you feel you've been badly treated by a hotel, restaurant, car rental agency, airline, tour company, dive shop, or whoever, please let me know, and if it concurs with other information on hand, your complaint certainly will have an impact. Of course, we also want to hear about the things you thought were great. Reader's letters are examined during the concluding stages of editing the book, so you really will have the final say.

When writing, please be as precise and accurate as you can. Notes made on the scene are far better than later recollections. Write comments in your copy of *Fiji Handbook* as you go along, then send me a summary when you get home. If this book helped you, please help me make it even better. Address your feedback to:

David Stanley
c/o Moon Travel Handbooks
5855 Beaudry Street
Emeryville, CA 94608, U.S.A.
e-mail: travel@moon.com

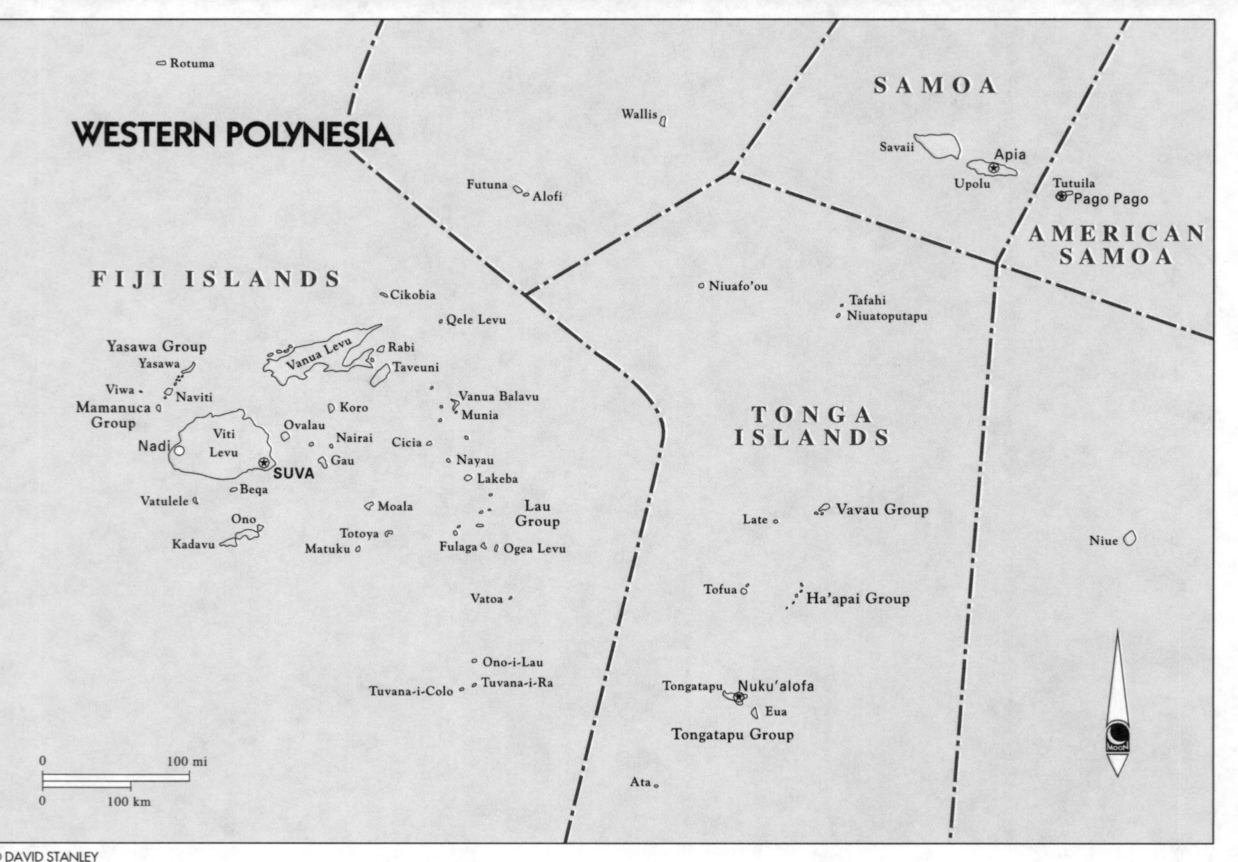
Rotuma
WESTERN POLYNESIA
Wallis
SAMOA
Savaii
Apia
Upolu
Tutuila
Pago Pago
AMERICAN SAMOA
Futuna
Alofi
FIJI ISLANDS
Cikobia
Qele Levu
Niuafo'ou
Tafahi
Niuatoputapu
Yasawa Group
Yasawa
Vanua Levu
Rabi
Taveuni
Viwa
Naviti
Mamanuca Group
Vanua Balavu
Munia
Koro
Ovalau
Viti Levu
Nadi
Nairai
Cicia
Gau
SUVA
Nayau
Lakeba
TONGA ISLANDS
Beqa
Vatulele
Moala
Lau Group
Ono
Totoya
Kadavu
Matuku
Fulaga
Ogea Levu
Late
Vavau Group
Niue
Vatoa
Tofua
Ha'apai Group
Ono-i-Lau
Tuvana-i-Ra
Tuvana-i-Colo
Tongatapu
Nuku'alofa
Eua
Tongatapu Group
0
100 mi
0
100 km
Ata
© DAVID STANLEY

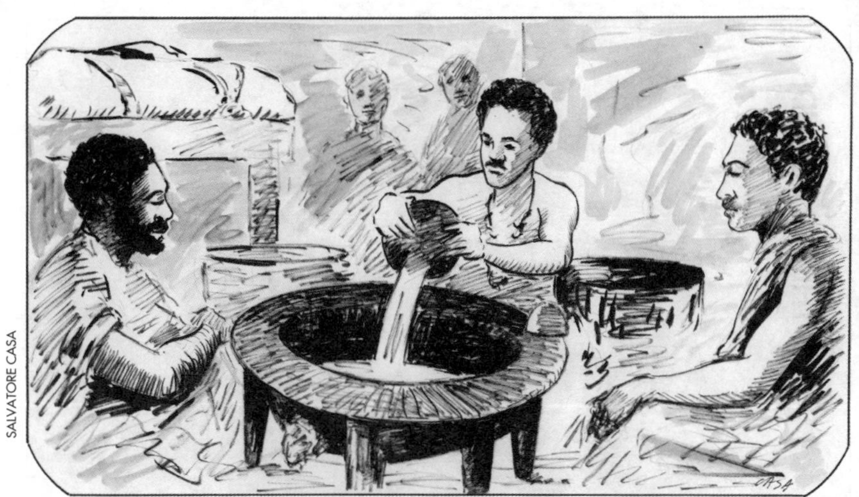

SALVATORE CASA

# INTRODUCTION

Once notorious as the "Cannibal Isles," Fiji is now the colorful crossroads of the South Pacific. Of the 322 islands that make up the Fiji Group, over 100 are inhabited by a rich mixture of vibrant, exuberant Melanesians, East Indians, Polynesians, Micronesians, Chinese, and Europeans, each with a cuisine and culture of their own. Here Melanesia mixes with Polynesia, ancient India with the Pacific, and tradition with the modern world in a unique blend.

Fiji preserves an amazing variety of traditional customs and crafts such as kava or *yaqona* (pronounced "yanggona") drinking, the presentation of the whale's tooth, firewalking, fish driving, turtle calling, tapa beating, and pottery making. Alongside this fascinating human history is a dramatic diversity of landforms and seascapes, all concentrated in a relatively small area. Fiji's sun-drenched beaches, blue lagoons, panoramic open hillsides, lush rainforests, and dazzling reefs are truly magnificent. Africa has such diversity, but there you'd have to travel weeks or months to see what you can see in Fiji in days.

Fiji offers posh resorts, good food and accommodations, nightlife, historic sites, outer-island living, hiking, kayaking, camping, surfing, snorkeling, and scuba diving. Traveling is easy by small plane, interisland ferry, copra boat, outboard canoe, open-sided bus, and air-conditioned coach. Even with a month at your disposal you'd barely scratch the surface of all there is to see and do.

Best of all, Fiji is a hassle-free country with uncrowded, inexpensive facilities available almost everywhere. You'll love the super-friendly people whose knowledge of English makes communicating a breeze. In a word, Fiji is a traveler's country *par excellence,* and whatever your budget, Fiji gives you good value for your money and plenty of ways to spend it. *Bula,* welcome to Fiji, everyone's favorite South Pacific country.

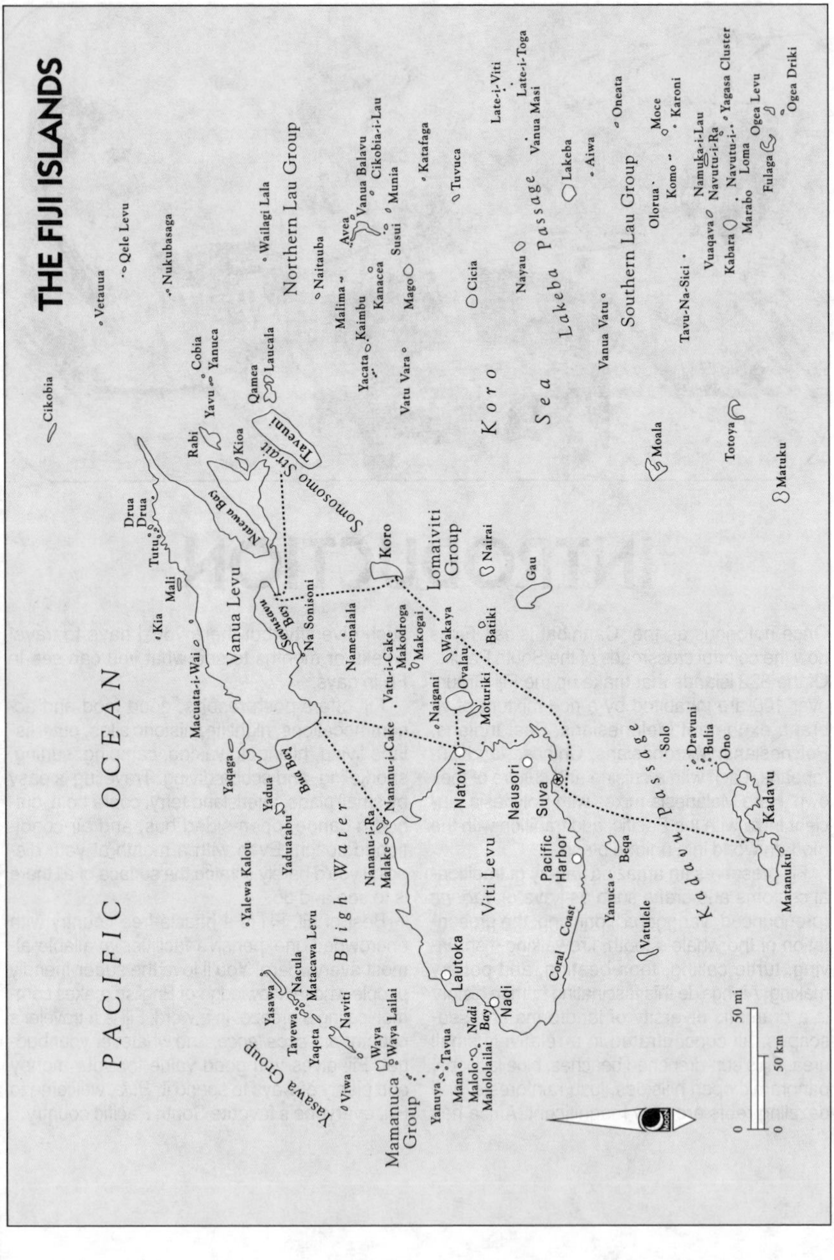

THE FIJI ISLANDS
PACIFIC OCEAN
Cikobia
Vetauua
Qele Levu
Nukubasaga
Wailagi Lala
Northern Lau Group
Naitauba
Avea
Vanua Balavu
Cikobia-i-Lau
Munia
Susui
Malima
Kanacea
Kaimbu
Yacata
Mago
Katafaga
Tuvuca
Vatu Vara
Cicia
Nayau
Lakeba
Lakeba Passage
Aiwa
Oneata
Vanua Masi
Late-i-Viti
Late-i-Toga
Koro Sea
Vanua Vatu
Southern Lau Group
Tavu-Na-Sici
Olorua
Komo
Moce
Karoni
Vuaqava
Kabara
Namuka-i-Lau
Navutu-i-Ra
Navutu-i-Loma
Yagasa Cluster
Marabo
Fulaga
Ogea Levu
Ogea Driki
Moala
Totoya
Matuku
Taveuni
Qamea
Laucala
Cobia
Yavu
Yanuca
Rabi
Kioa
Somosomo Strait
Natewa Bay
Drua Drua
Tutu
Mali
Kia
Vanua Levu
Macuata-i-Wai
Savusavu Bay
Na Sonisoni
Koro
Lomaiviti Group
Nairai
Gau
Batiki
Wakaya
Makodroga
Makogai
Namenalala
Vatu-i-Cake
Nananu-i-Cake
Nananu-i-Ra
Malake
Yaqaga
Bua Bay
Yadua
Yaduatabu
Bligh Water
Yalewa Kalou
Matacawa Levu
Nacula
Yasawa
Tavewa
Yaqeta
Naviti
Waya
Waya Lailai
Viwa
Yasawa Group
Mamanuca Group
Yanuya
Tavua
Mana
Malolo
Malololailai
Nadi Bay
Nadi
Lautoka
Viti Levu
Natovi
Ovalau
Moturiki
Naigani
Nausori
Suva
Pacific Harbor
Coral Coast
Beqa
Yanuca
Vatulele
Kadavu Passage
Solo
Dravuni
Bulia
Ono
Kadavu
Matanuku
0 50 mi
0 50 km

# THE LAND

Fiji lies 5,100 km southwest of Hawaii and 3,150 km northeast of Sydney, astride the main air route between North America and Australia. Nadi is the hub of Pacific air routes, while Suva is a regional shipping center. The 180th meridian cuts through Fiji, but the international dateline swings east so the entire group can share the same day.

The name Fiji is a Tongan corruption of the indigenous name "Viti." The Fiji Islands are arrayed in a horseshoe configuration with Viti Levu (great Fiji) and adjacent islands on the west, Vanua Levu (great land) and Taveuni to the north, and the Lau Group on the east. This upside-down-U-shaped archipelago encloses the Koro Sea, which is relatively shallow and sprinkled with the Lomaiviti, or central Fiji, group of islands. Together the Fiji Islands are scattered over 1,290,000 square km of the South Pacific Ocean.

If every single island were counted, the isles of the Fiji archipelago would number in the thousands. However, a mere 322 are judged large enough for human habitation and of these only 106 are inhabited. That leaves 216 uninhabited islands, most of them prohibitively isolated or lacking fresh water.

Most of the Fiji Islands are volcanic, remnants of a sunken continent that stretched through Australia. This origin accounts for the mineral deposits on the main islands. None of Fiji's volcanoes are presently active, though there are a few small hot springs. The two largest islands, Viti Levu and Vanua Levu, together account for 87% of Fiji's 18,272 square km of land. Viti Levu has 57% of the land area and 75% of the people, while Vanua Levu, with 30% of the land, has 18% of the population. Viti Levu alone is bigger than all five archipelagos of Tahiti-Polynesia; in fact, Fiji has more land and people than all of Polynesia combined.

### Viti Levu

The 1,000-meter-high Nadrau Plateau in central Viti Levu is cradled between Tomanivi (1,323 meters) on the north and Monavatu (1,131 meters) on the south. On different sides of this elevated divide are the Colo-East Plateau drained by the Rewa River, the Navosa Plateau drained by the Ba, the Colo-West Plateau drained by the Sigatoka, and the Navua Plateau drained by the Navua. Some 29 well-defined peaks rise above Viti Levu's interior; most of the people live in the river valleys or along the coast.

The Nadi River slices across the Nausori Highlands, with the Mount Evans Range (1,195 meters) towering above Lautoka. Other highland areas of Viti Levu are cut by great rivers like the Sigatoka, the Navua, the Rewa, and the Ba, navigable far inland by outboard canoe or kayak. Whitewater rafters shoot down the Navua and occasionally the Ba, while the lower Sigatoka flows gently through Fiji's market garden "salad bowl." Fiji's largest river, the Rewa, pours into the Pacific through a wide delta just below Nausori. After a hurricane the Rewa becomes a dark torrent worth a special visit to Nausori just to see. Sharks have been known to enter both the Rewa and the Sigatoka and swim far upstream.

### Vanua Levu

Vanua Levu has a peculiar shape, with two long peninsulas pointing northeastward. A mountain range between Labasa and Savusavu reaches 1,032 meters at Nasorolevu. Navotuvotu (842 meters), east of Bua Bay, is Fiji's best example of a broad shield volcano, with lava flows built up in layers. The mountains are closer to the southeast coast, and a broad lowland belt runs along the northwest. Of the rivers only the Dreketi, flowing west across northern Vanua Levu, is large; navigation on the Labasa is restricted to small boats. The interior of Vanua Levu is lower and drier than Viti Levu, yet scenically superb: the road from Labasa to Savusavu is a visual feast.

### Other Islands

Vanua Levu's bullet-shaped neighbor Taveuni soars to 1,241 meters, its rugged east coast battered by the southeast trades. Taveuni and Kadavu are known as the finest islands in Fiji for their scenic beauty and agricultural potential. Geologically, the uplifted limestone islands of the Lau Group have more in common with Tonga than with the rest of Fiji. Northwest of Viti Levu is the rugged limestone Yasawa Group.

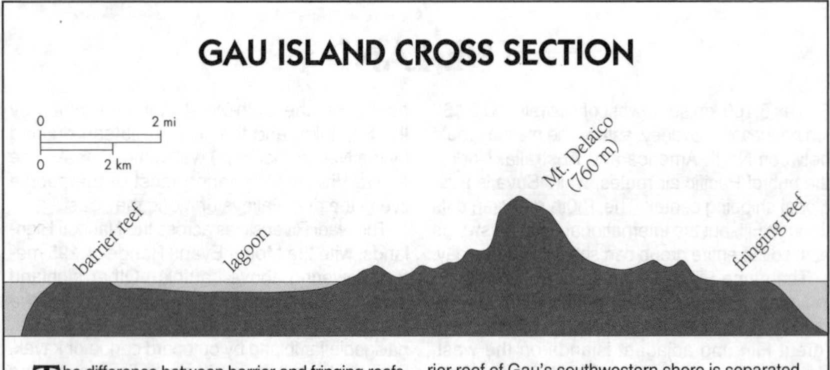


The difference between barrier and fringing reefs is illustrated in the southwest-northwest cross section of Gau Island (see the **Gau Island map**). The vertical scale has been exaggerated. The barrier reef of Gau's southwestern shore is separated from the main island's coast by a deep lagoon, while only a tidal flat lies between Gau's northeastern coast and the edge of the fringing reef.

### Coasts and Reefs

Fringing reefs are common along most of the coastlines, and Fiji is outstanding for its many barrier reefs. The Great Sea Reef off the north coast of Vanua Levu is the fourth-longest in the world, and the Astrolabe Reef north of Kadavu is one of the most colorful. Countless other unexplored barrier reefs are found off northern Viti Levu and elsewhere. The many cracks, crevices, walls, and caves along Fiji's reefs are guaranteed to delight the scuba diver.

The configuration of the Astrolabe Reef off Ono and Kadavu islands confirms Darwin's Theory of Atoll Formation. The famous formulator of the theory of natural selection surmised that atolls form as high volcanic islands subside into lagoons. The original island's fringing reef grows into a barrier reef as the volcanic portion sinks. When the last volcanic material finally disappears below sea level, the coral rim of the reef/atoll remains to indicate how big the island once was.

Of course, all this takes place over millions of years, but deep down below every atoll is the old volcanic core. Darwin's theory is well-illustrated here, where Ono and the small volcanic islands to the north remain inside the Astrolabe Reef. Return in 25 million years and all you'll find will be the reef itself.

## CORAL REEFS

Coral reefs cover some 200,000 square km worldwide, between 35 degrees north and 32 degrees south latitude. A reef is created by the accumulation of millions of calcareous skeletons left by myriad generations of tiny coral polyps, some no bigger than a pinhead. Though the skeleton is usually white, the living polyps are of many different colors. The individual polyps on the surface often live a long time, continuously secreting layers to the skeletal mass beneath the tiny layer of flesh.

Coral polyps thrive in clear salty water where the temperature never drops below 18° C. They must also have a base not over 50 meters below the water's surface on which to form. The coral colony grows slowly upward on the consolidated skeletons of its ancestors until it reaches the low-tide mark, after which development extends outward on the edges of the reef. Sunlight is critical for coral growth. Colonies grow quickly on the ocean side due to clearer water and a greater abundance of food. A strong, healthy reef can grow four to five centimeters a year. Fresh or cloudy water inhibits coral growth, which is why villages and ports all across the Pacific are located at the reef-free mouths of rivers. Hurricanes can kill coral by covering the reef with

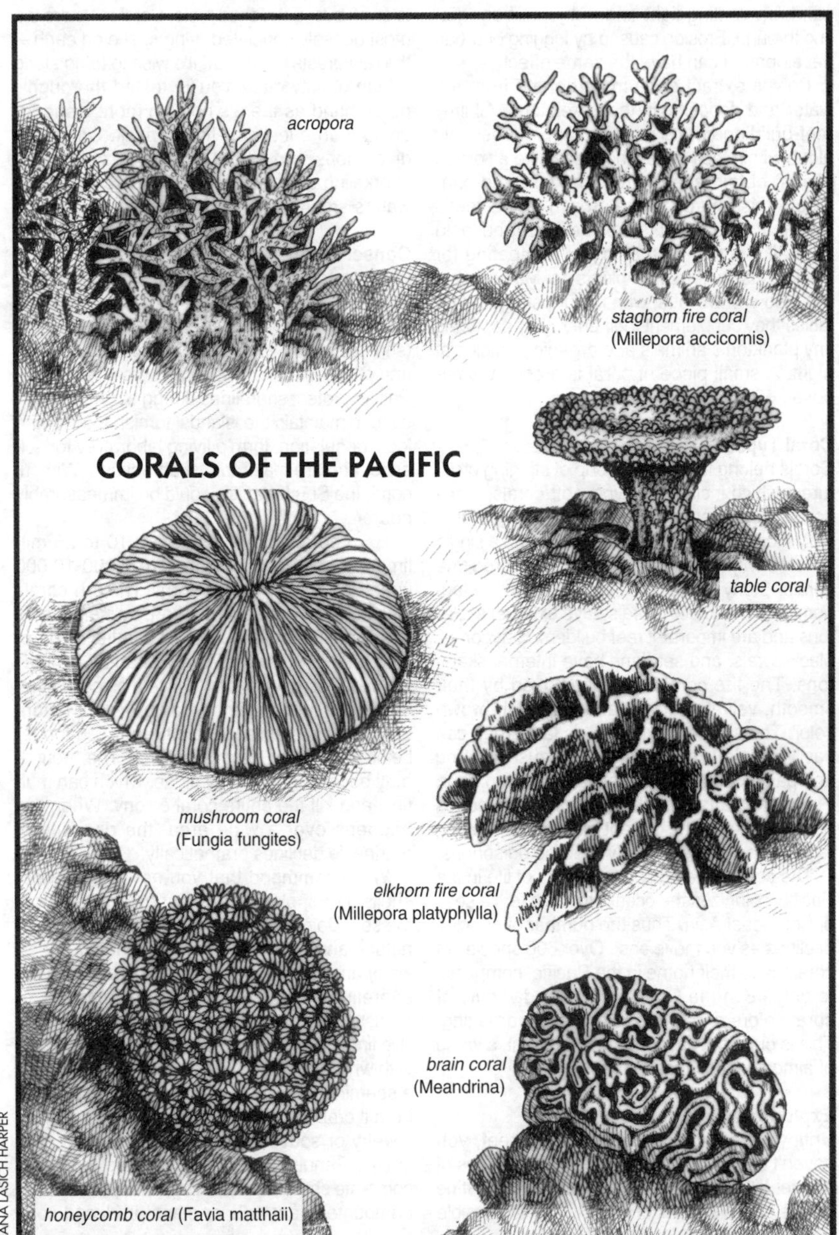
CORALS OF THE PACIFIC
acropora
staghorn fire coral
(Millepora accicornis)
table coral
mushroom coral
(Fungia fungites)
elkhorn fire coral
(Millepora platyphylla)
brain coral
(Meandrina)
honeycomb coral (Favia matthaii)
DIANA LASICH HARPER

sand, preventing light and nutrients from getting through. Erosion caused by logging or urban development can have the same effect.

Polyps extract calcium carbonate from the water and deposit it in their skeletons. All limy reef-building corals also contain microscopic algae within their cells. The algae, like all green plants, obtain energy from the sun and contribute this energy to the growth of the reef's skeleton. As a result, corals behave (and look) more like plants than animals, competing for sunlight just as terrestrial plants do. Many polyps are also carnivorous; with minute stinging tentacles they supplement their energy by capturing tiny planktonic animals and organic particles at night. A small piece of coral is a colony composed of large numbers of polyps.

## Coral Types

Corals belong to a broad group of stinging creatures, which includes polyps, soft corals, stony corals, sea anemones, sea fans, and jellyfish. Only those types with hard skeletons and a single hollow cavity within the body are considered true corals. Stony corals such as brain, table, staghorn, and mushroom corals have external skeletons and are important reef builders. Soft corals, black corals, and sea fans have internal skeletons. The fire corals are recognized by their smooth, velvety surface and yellowish brown color. The stinging toxins of this last group can easily penetrate human skin and cause swelling and painful burning that can last up to an hour. The many varieties of soft, colorful anemones gently waving in the current might seem inviting to touch, but beware: many are also poisonous.

The corals, like most other forms of life in the Pacific, colonized the ocean from the fertile seas of Southeast Asia. Thus the number of species declines as you move east. Over 600 species of coral make their home in the Pacific, compared to only 48 in the Caribbean. The diversity of coral colors and forms is endlessly amazing. This is our most unspoiled environment, a world of almost indescribable beauty.

## Exploring a Reef

Until you've explored a good coral reef, you haven't experienced one of the greatest joys of nature. While one cannot walk through pristine forests due to the lack of paths, it's quite possible to swim over untouched reefs. Coral reefs are the most densely populated living space on earth—the rainforests of the sea! It's wise to bring along a high quality mask you've tested thoroughly beforehand as there's nothing more disheartening than a leaky, ill-fitting mask. Otherwise dive shops throughout the region rent or sell snorkeling gear, so do get into the clear, warm waters around you.

## Conservation

Coral reefs are one of the most fragile and complex ecosystems on earth, providing food and shelter for countless species of fish, crustaceans (shrimps, crabs, and lobsters), mollusks (shells), and other animals. The coral reefs of the South Pacific protect shorelines during storms, supply sand to maintain the islands, furnish food for the local population, form a living laboratory for science, and are major tourist attractions. Without coral, the South Pacific would be immeasurably poorer.

Hard corals grow only about 10 to 25 millimeters a year and it can take 7,000-10,000 years for a coral reef to form. Though corals look solid they're easily broken; by standing on them, breaking off pieces, or carelessly dropping anchor you can destroy in a few minutes what took so long to form. Once a piece of coral breaks off it dies, and it may be years before the coral reestablishes itself and even longer before the broken piece is replaced. The "wound" may become infected by algae, which can multiply and kill the entire coral colony. When this happens over a wide area, the diversity of marinelife declines dramatically.

We recommend that you not remove seashells, coral, plantlife, or marine animals from the sea. Doing so upsets the delicate balance of nature, and coral is much more beautiful underwater anyway! This is a particular problem along shorelines frequented by large numbers of tourists, who can completely strip a reef in very little time. If you'd like a souvenir, content yourself with what you find on the beach (although even a seemingly empty shell may be inhabited by a hermit crab). Also think twice about purchasing jewelry or souvenirs made from coral or seashells. Genuine traditional handicrafts that incorporate shells are one thing, but by purchasing unmounted seashells or mass-produced coral

## THE GREENHOUSE EFFECT

The gravest danger facing the atolls and reefs of Oceania is the greenhouse effect, a gradual warming of Earth's environment due to fossil fuel combustion and the widespread clearing of forests. By the year 2030 the concentration of carbon dioxide in the atmosphere will have doubled from preindustrial levels. As infrared radiation from the sun is absorbed by the gas, the trapped heat melts mountain glaciers and the polar ice caps. In addition, seawater expands as it warms up, so water levels could rise almost a meter by the year 2100, destroying shorelines created 5,000 years ago.

A 1982 study demonstrated that sea levels had already risen 12 centimeters in the previous century; in 1995 2,500 scientists from 70 countries involved in an Intergovernmental Panel on Climate Change commissioned by the United Nations completed a two-year study with the warning that over the next century air temperatures may rise as much as 5° Celsius and sea levels could go up 95 centimeters. Not only will this reduce the growing area for food crops, but rising sea levels will mean salt water intrusion into groundwater supplies—a horrifying prospect if accompanied by the droughts that have been predicted. Coastal erosion will force governments to spend vast sums on road repairs and coastline stabilization.

Increasing temperatures may already be contributing to the dramatic jump in the number of hurricanes in the South Pacific. For example, Fiji experienced only 12 tropical hurricanes from 1941 to 1980 but 10 from 1981 to 1989, and in the face of devastating hurricanes, insurance companies are withdrawing coverage from some areas. In 1997 and 1998 the *El Niño* phenomenon brought with it another round of devastating hurricanes.

Coral bleaching occurs when the organism's symbiotic algae are expelled in response to environmental stresses, such as changes in water temperature, and widespread instances of bleaching and reefs being killed by rising sea temperatures have been confirmed around Tahiti and Cook Islands. To make matters worse, the coral-crunching crown-of-thorns starfish is again on the rise throughout the South Pacific (probably due to sewage and fertilizer runoff that nurture the starfish larvae). Reef destruction will reduce coastal fish stocks and impact tourism.

Unfortunately, those most responsible for the problem, the industrialized countries led by the United States (and including Australia) have strongly resisted taking any action to significantly cut greenhouse gas emissions, and new industrial polluters like India and China are sure to make matters much worse. And as if that weren't bad enough, the hydrofluorocarbons (HFCs) presently being developed by corporate giants like Du Pont to replace the ozone-destructive chlorofluorocarbons (CFCs) used in cooling systems are far more potent greenhouse gases than carbon dioxide. This is only one of many similar consumption-related problems, and it seems as if one section of humanity is hurtling down a suicidal slope, unable to resist the momentum, as the rest of our race watches the catastrophe approach in helpless horror. It will cost a lot to rewrite our collective ticket but there may not be any choice.

curios you are contributing to the destruction of the marine environment. The triton shell, for example, helps keep in check the reef-destroying crown-of-thorns starfish.

The anchors and anchor chains of private yachts can do serious damage to coral reefs. Pronged anchors are more environmentally friendly than larger, heavier anchors, and plastic tubing over the end of the anchor chain helps minimize the damage. If at all possible, anchor in sand. A longer anchor chain makes this easier, and a good windlass is essential for larger boats. A recording depth sounder will help locate sandy areas when none are available in shallow water. If you don't have a depth sounder and can't see the bottom, lower the anchor until it just touches the bottom and feel the anchor line as the boat drifts. If it "grumbles" lift it up, drift a little, and try again. Later, if you notice your chain grumbling, motor over the anchor, lift it out of the coral and move. Not only do sand and mud hold better, but your anchor will be less likely to become fouled. Try to arrive before 1500 to be able to see clearly where you're anchoring—Polaroid sunglasses make it easier to distinguish corals.

There's an urgent need for stricter government regulation of the marine environment, and in some places coral reefs are already protected. Appeals such as the one above have only limited impact—legislators must write stricter laws and impose

# FIJI CLIMATE CHART

| LOCATION | | JAN. | FEB. | MAR. | APRIL | MAY | JUNE | JULY | AUG. | SEPT. | OCT. | NOV. | DEC. | ALL YEAR |
|---|---|---|---|---|---|---|---|---|---|---|---|---|---|---|
| Nadi airport, | C | 27.0 | 26.9 | 26.7 | 26.2 | 25.0 | 24.0 | 23.3 | 23.8 | 24.5 | 25.2 | 25.9 | 26.6 | 25.4 |
| Viti Levu | mm | 294 | 291 | 373 | 195 | 99 | 78 | 51 | 62 | 88 | 73 | 137 | 181 | 1922 |
| Yasawa Island | C | 27.0 | 26.9 | 26.6 | 26.4 | 26.0 | 25.3 | 24.6 | 24.8 | 25.1 | 25.7 | 26.1 | 26.7 | 25.9 |
| | mm | 281 | 287 | 344 | 168 | 110 | 106 | 45 | 68 | 90 | 78 | 187 | 165 | 1929 |
| Ba, Viti Levu | C | 27.2 | 27.1 | 26.9 | 26.5 | 25.3 | 24.1 | 23.3 | 23.8 | 24.7 | 25.5 | 26.1 | 26.1 | 25.6 |
| | mm | 322 | 409 | 387 | 203 | 101 | 67 | 46 | 65 | 72 | 91 | 126 | 228 | 2117 |
| Nadarivatu, | C | 21.6 | 22.0 | 21.5 | 21.0 | 20.0 | 18.9 | 18.3 | 18.8 | 19.0 | 20.1 | 20.6 | 21.1 | 20.2 |
| Viti Levu | mm | 599 | 668 | 689 | 362 | 181 | 99 | 89 | 125 | 126 | 136 | 220 | 400 | 3694 |
| Rakiraki, | C | 27.6 | 27.6 | 27.3 | 26.8 | 25.9 | 24.9 | 24.2 | 24.6 | 25.1 | 25.9 | 26.6 | 27.1 | 26.2 |
| Viti Levu | mm | 307 | 371 | 372 | 236 | 122 | 66 | 47 | 68 | 74 | 83 | 140 | 221 | 2107 |
| Suva, Viti Levu | C | 26.8 | 26.9 | 26.8 | 26.1 | 24.8 | 23.9 | 23.1 | 23.2 | 23.7 | 24.4 | 25.3 | 26.2 | 25.1 |
| | mm | 314 | 299 | 386 | 343 | 280 | 177 | 148 | 200 | 212 | 218 | 268 | 313 | 3158 |
| Vunisea, | C | 26.4 | 26.8 | 26.1 | 25.4 | 24.2 | 23.2 | 22.4 | 22.6 | 23.1 | 23.9 | 24.7 | 26.1 | 24.6 |
| Kadavu I. | mm | 239 | 225 | 313 | 256 | 208 | 102 | 112 | 121 | 122 | 126 | 151 | 177 | 2152 |
| Nabouwalu, | C | 26.9 | 27.1 | 26.7 | 26.3 | 25.5 | 24.7 | 23.9 | 24.0 | 24.4 | 25.2 | 25.4 | 26.3 | 25.6 |
| Vanua Levu | mm | 328 | 354 | 352 | 275 | 198 | 130 | 96 | 114 | 139 | 164 | 208 | 279 | 2637 |
| Labasa, | C | 26.8 | 26.8 | 26.6 | 26.2 | 25.3 | 24.4 | 23.8 | 24.2 | 24.7 | 25.4 | 25.9 | 26.4 | 25.6 |
| Vanua Levu | mm | 449 | 457 | 465 | 236 | 97 | 86 | 38 | 60 | 77 | 96 | 210 | 263 | 2534 |
| Vunikodi, | C | 26.6 | 26.7 | 26.6 | 26.3 | 26.0 | 25.3 | 24.6 | 24.7 | 25.0 | 25.6 | 25.9 | 26.6 | 25.8 |
| Vanua Levu | mm | 302 | 377 | 409 | 225 | 143 | 131 | 92 | 90 | 114 | 132 | 264 | 220 | 2499 |
| Rotuma Island | C | 27.4 | 27.3 | 27.2 | 27.4 | 27.2 | 26.8 | 26.4 | 26.5 | 26.7 | 26.8 | 27.0 | 27.2 | 27.0 |
| | mm | 358 | 390 | 430 | 278 | 262 | 244 | 207 | 230 | 277 | 283 | 327 | 331 | 3617 |
| Matuku, | C | 26.8 | 27.0 | 26.8 | 26.3 | 25.1 | 24.1 | 23.1 | 23.6 | 24.2 | 25.0 | 25.7 | 26.4 | 25.3 |
| Lau Group | mm | 231 | 230 | 265 | 192 | 151 | 116 | 114 | 78 | 110 | 97 | 139 | 152 | 1875 |
| Ono-i-Lau, | C | 26.3 | 26.5 | 26.4 | 25.7 | 24.3 | 23.4 | 22.4 | 22.4 | 22.7 | 23.6 | 24.5 | 25.3 | 24.4 |
| Lau Group | mm | 201 | 199 | 266 | 196 | 144 | 109 | 90 | 94 | 106 | 114 | 128 | 145 | 1792 |

## A NOTE ON READING THE FIJI CLIMATE CHART

The top figure indicates the average monthly temperatures in degrees and tenths centigrade, while the monthly rainfall average in millimeters (mm) is given below. The last column gives the annual temperature and the total precipitation during the year. These figures have been averaged over a minimum of 10 years, in most cases much longer. Altitude is a factor at Nadarivatu (835 meters); all the others are very near sea level. You will notice that temperatures don't vary too much year-round, but there is a pronounced dry season midyear. Note, too, that some areas of Fiji are far drier than others.

fines. If you witness dumping or any other marine-related activity you think might be illegal, don't become directly involved but do take a few notes and calmly report the incident to the local authorities or police at the first opportunity. You'll learn something about their approach to these matters and make them aware of your concerns.

Resort developers can minimize damage to their valuable reefs by providing public mooring buoys so yachts don't have to drop anchor and pontoons so snorkelers aren't tempted to stand on coral. Licensing authorities can make such amenities mandatory whenever appropriate, and in extreme cases, endangered coral gardens should be declared off limits to private boats. As consumerism spreads, once-remote areas become subject to the problems of pollution and overexploitation: the garbage is visibly piling up on many shores. As a visitor, don't hesitate to practice your conservationist attitudes, and leave a clean wake.

## CLIMATE

Along the coast the weather is warm and pleasant, without great variations in temperature. The southeast trades prevail from June to October, the best months to visit. In February and March the wind often comes directly out of the east. These winds dump 3,000 mm of annual rainfall on the humid southeast coasts of the big islands, increasing to 5,000 mm inland. The drier northwest coasts, in the lee, get only 1,500-2,000 mm.

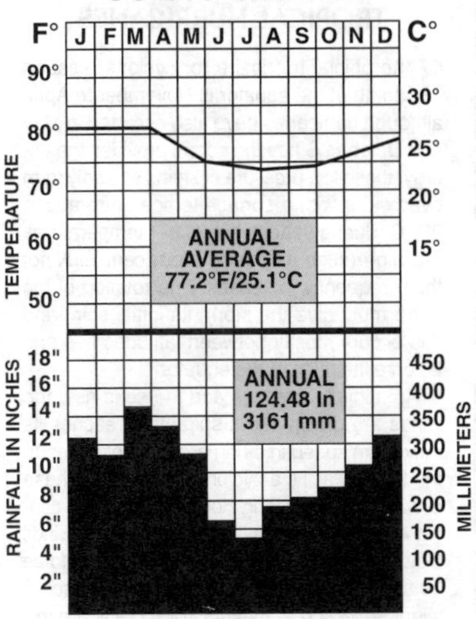


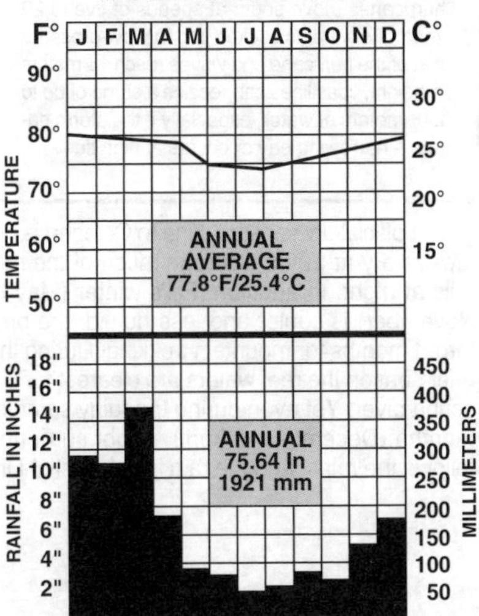

## TROPICAL HURRICANES

The official hurricane (or cyclone) season south of the equator is November to April, although hurricanes have also occurred in May and October. Since the ocean provides the energy, these low pressure systems can only form over water with a surface temperature above 27° C; during years when water temperatures are high (such as during the recent *El Niño*) their frequency increases. The rotation of the earth must give the storm its initial spin, and this occurs mostly between latitudes five and 20 on either side of the equator.

As rainfall increases and the seas rise, the winds are drawn into a spiral that reaches its maximum speed in a ring around the center. In the South Pacific a cyclone develops as these circular winds, rotating clockwise around a center, increase in velocity: force eight to nine winds blowing at 34 to 47 knots are called a gale, force 10 to 11 at 48 to 63 knots is a storm, force 12 winds revolving at 64 knots or more is a hurricane. Wind speeds can go as high as 100 knots with gusts to 140 on the left side of the storm's path in the direction it's moving.

The eye of the hurricane can be 10 to 30 kilometers wide and surprising clear and calm, although at sea contradictory wave patterns continue to wreak havoc. In the South Pacific most hurricanes move south at speeds of five to 20 knots. As water is sucked into the low-pressure eye of the hurricane and waves reach 14 meters in height, coastlines can receive a surge of up to four meters of water, especially if the storm enters a narrowing bay or occurs at high tide.

The official dry season (June to October) is not always dry at Suva, although much of the rain falls at night. In addition, Fiji's winter (May to November) is cooler and less humid, the preferred months for mountain trekking. During the drier season the reef waters are clearest for the scuba diver. Yet even during the rainy summer months (December to April), bright sun often follows the rains, and the rain is only a slight inconvenience. The refreshing trade winds relieve the high humidity. Summer is hurricane season, with Fiji, Samoa, and Tonga receiving up to five tropical storms annually.

In Fiji you can obtain prerecorded weather information by dialing 301-642.

### Currents and Winds

The Pacific Ocean has a greater impact on the world's climate than any other geographical feature on earth. By taking heat away from the equator and toward the poles, it stretches the bounds of the area in which life can exist. Broad circular ocean currents flow from east to west across the tropical Pacific, clockwise in the North Pacific, counterclockwise in the South Pacific. North and south of the "horse latitudes" just outside the tropics the currents cool and swing east. The prevailing winds move the same way: the southeast tradewinds south of the equator, the northeast tradewinds north of the equator, and the low-pressure "doldrums" in between. Westerlies blow east above the cool currents north and south of the tropics. This natural air-conditioning system brings warm water to Australia and Japan, cooler water to Peru and California.

The climate of the high islands is closely related to these winds. As air is heated near the equator it rises and flows at high altitudes toward the poles. By the time it reaches about 30 degrees south latitude it will have cooled enough to cause it to fall and flow back toward the equator near sea level. In the southern hemisphere the rotation of the earth deflects the winds to the left to become the southeast trades. When these cool moist tradewinds hit a high island, they are warmed by the sun and forced up. Above 500 meters elevation they begin to cool again and their moisture condenses into clouds. At night the winds do not capture much warmth and are more likely to discharge their moisture as rain. The windward slopes of the high islands catch the trades head-on and are usually wet, while those on the leeward side may be dry.

# FLORA AND FAUNA

## FLORA

The flora of Fiji originated in the Malaysian region; in the two regions, ecological niches are filled by similar plants. Over 3,000 species of plants grow in Fiji, a third of them endemic. Taveuni is known for its rare climbing *tagimaucia* flower. The absence of leaf-eating animals in Fiji allowed the vegetation to develop largely without the protective spines and thorns found elsewhere, and one of the only stinging plants is the *salato,* a shrub or tree bearing large, heart-shaped leaves with purple ribs and ragged edges that inflict painful wounds when touched. Hairs on the leaves break off in the skin and the intense stinging pain begins half a minute later. This soon diminishes into an itch that becomes painful again if scratched. The itch can recur weeks and even months later.

Patterns of rainfall are in large part responsible for the variety of vegetation here. The wetter sides of the high islands are heavily forested, with occasional thickets of bamboo and scrub. Natural forests cover 40% of Fiji's total land area and about a quarter of this is classified as production forest suitable for logging. The towering *dakua* or kauri tree, once carved into massive Fijian war canoes, has already disappeared from Viti Levu, and the last stands are now being logged on Vanua Levu. Since the 1960s much replanting has been done in mahogany, a hardwood originating in Central American. The native *yaka* is a conifer whose wood has an attractive grain.

Coconut groves fill the coastal plains. On the drier sides open savanna or *talasiga* of coarse grasses predominates where the original vegetation has been destroyed by slash-and-burn agriculture. Sugarcane is now cultivated in the lowlands here, and Caribbean pine has been planted in many dry hilly areas, giving them a Scandinavian appearance. Around Christmas poinciana or flame trees along the roads bloom bright red. The low islands of the Lau Group are restricted to a few hardy, drought-resistant species such as coconuts and pandanus. Well drained shorelines often feature ironwood or *nokonoko,* a casuarina appreciated by woodcarvers.

Mangroves can occasionally be found along some high island coastal lagoons. The cable roots of the saltwater-tolerant red mangrove anchor in the shallow upper layer of oxygenated mud, avoiding the layers of hydrogen sulfide below. The tree provides shade for tiny organisms dwelling in the tidal mudflats—a place for birds to nest and for fish or shellfish to feed and spawn. The mangroves also perform the same task as land-building coral colonies along the reefs. As sediments are trapped between the roots, the trees extend farther into the lagoon, creating a unique natural environment. The past decade has seen widespread destruction of the mangroves as land is reclaimed for agricultural use in northwest Viti Levu and around Labasa.

Many of Fiji's forest plants have medicinal applications which have recently attracted the attention of patent-hungry pharmaceutical giants such as SmithKline Beecham. The sap of the tree fern *(balabala)* was formerly used as a cure for headaches by Fijians and its heart was eaten in times of famine.

Though only introduced to Fiji in the late 1860s, sugarcane probably originated in the South Pacific. On New Guinea the islanders have cultivated the plant for thousands of years, selecting vigorous varieties with the most colorful stems. The story goes that two Melanesian fishermen, To-Kabwana and To-Karavuvu, found a piece of sugarcane in their net one day. They threw it away, but after twice catching it again they decided to keep it and painted the stalk a bright color. Eventually the cane burst and a woman came forth. She cooked food for the men but hid herself at night. Finally she was captured and became the wife of one of the men. From their union sprang the whole human race.

## FAUNA

Some Fijian clans have totemic relationships with eels, prawns, turtles, and sharks, and are able to summon these creatures with special chants. Red prawns are called on Vanua Vatu in Southern Lau, on a tiny island off Naweni in southern Vanua Levu, and on Vatulele Island. The Nasaqalau people of Lakeba in southern Lau call sharks, and villagers of Korolevu in central Viti Levu call eels. The women of Namuana on Kadavu summon giant sea turtles with their chants. Turtle calling is also practiced at Nacamaki village, in the northeast corner of Koro. Unfortunately sea turtles are becoming so rare that the turtle callers are having less and less success each year.

### Birds

Of the 70 species of land birds, 22 are endemic, including broadbills, cuckoos, doves, fantails, finches, flycatchers, fruitdoves, hawks, herons, honeyeaters, kingfishers, lorikeets, owls, parrots, pigeons, rails, robins, silktails, swallows, thrushes, warblers, whistlers, and white-eyes. The Fijian names of some of these birds, such as the *kaka* (parrot), *ga* (gray duck), and *kikau* (giant honey eater), imitate their calls. Red and green *kula* lorikeets are often seen in populated areas collecting nectar and pollen from flowering trees or feeding on fruit. Of the seabirds, boobies, frigate birds, petrels, and tropic birds are present. The best time to observe forest birds is in the very early morning—they move around a lot less in the heat of the day.

More in evidence is the introduced Indian mynah, with its yellow legs and beak, the Indian bulbul, and the Malay turtledove. The hopping Indian mynah bird *(Acridotheres tristis),* was introduced to many islands from Indonesia at the turn of the century to control insects, which were damaging the citrus and coconut plantations. The mynahs multiplied profusely and have become major pests, inflicting great harm on the very trees they were brought in to protect. Worse still, many indigenous birds are forced out of their habitat by these noisy, aggressive birds. This and rapid deforestation by man have made the South Pacific the region with the highest proportion of endangered endemic bird species on earth.

pink-billed parrot finch

LOUISE FOOTE

### Mammals

The first Fijians brought with them pigs, dogs, chickens, and gray rats. The only native mammals are the monkey-faced fruit bat or flying fox, called *beka* by the Fijians, and the smaller, insect-eating bat.

The Indian mongoose was introduced by planters in the 1880s to combat rats, which were damaging the plantations. Unfortunately, no one realized at the time that the mongoose hunts by day, whereas the rats are nocturnal; thus, the two seldom meet. Today, the mongoose is the scourge of chickens, native ground birds, iguanas, and other animals, though Kadavu, Koro, Gau, Ovalau, and Taveuni are mongoose-free (and thus the finest islands for birdwatching). Feral cats do the same sort of damage.

### Insects and Arachnids

Not to be confused with the inoffensive millipedes are the poisonous centipedes found in Fiji. While the millipede will roll up when touched the centipede may inflict a painful sting through its front legs. The two types are easily distinguished by the number of pairs of legs per body segment: centipedes one, millipedes two. Fiji's largest centipedes grow up to 18 centimeters long and can have anywhere from 15 to 180 pairs of legs. These nocturnal creatures feed on insects and may be found in houses while the two species of scorpions dwell only in the forest.

### Reptiles and Amphibians

Three of the world's seven species of sea turtles nest in Fiji: the green, hawksbill, and leatherback. Nesting occurs between November and February, at night when there is a full moon and a high tide. Sea turtles lay their eggs on the beach from which they themselves originally hatched. The female struggles up the beach and lays as many as 100 eggs in a hole, which she digs and then covers with her hind flippers. Female turtles don't commence this activity until they are 20 years old, thus a drop in numbers today has irreversible consequences a generation later. It's estimated that breeding females already number in the hundreds or low thousands, and all species of these magnificent creatures (sometimes erroneously referred to as "tortoises") now face extinction due to ruthless hunting, egg harvesting, and beach destruction. Turtles are often choked by floating plastic bags they mistake for food, or they drown in fishing nets. The turtles and their eggs are now protected by law in Fiji (maximum penalty of six months in prison for killing a turtle). Sadly, this law is seldom enforced.

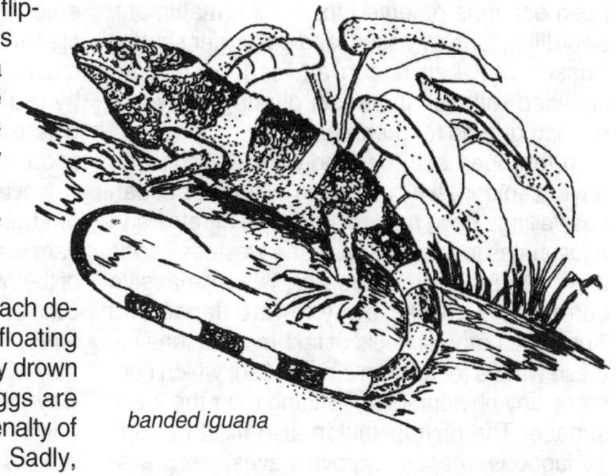
banded iguana

Geckos and skinks are small lizards often seen on the islands. The skink hunts insects by day; its tail breaks off if you catch it, but a new one quickly grows. The gecko is nocturnal and has no eyelids. Adhesive toe pads enable it to pass along vertical surfaces, and it changes color to avoid detection. Unlike the skink, which avoids humans, geckos often live in people's homes, where they eat insects attracted by electric lights. Its loud clicking call may be a territorial warning to other geckos.

One of the more unusual creatures found in Fiji and Tonga is the banded iguana, a lizard that lives in trees and can grow up to 70 centimeters long (two-thirds of which is tail). The iguanas are emerald green, and the male is easily distinguished from the female by his bluish-gray cross stripes. Banded iguanas change color to control their internal temperature, becoming darker when in the direct sun. Their nearest relatives are found in Central America, and how they could have reached Fiji remains a mystery. In 1979 a new species, the crested iguana, was discovered on Yaduataba, a small island off the west coast of Vanua Levu.

LOUISE FOOTE/2

tree frog

Two species of snakes inhabit Fiji: the very rare, poisonous *bolo loa,* and the harmless Pacific boa, which can grow up to two meters long. Venomous sea snakes are common on some coasts, but they're docile and easily handled. Fijians call the common banded black-and-white sea snake the *dadakulaci.* The land- and tree-dwelling native frogs are noteworthy for the long suction discs on their fingers and toes. Because they live deep in the rainforests and feed at night, they're seldom seen.

In 1936 the giant toad was introduced from Hawaii to control beetles, slugs, and millipedes. When this food source is exhausted, they tend to eat each other. At night gardens and lawns may be full of them.

## Fish

Fiji's richest store of life is found in the silent underwater world of the pelagic and lagoon fishes. It's estimated that half the fish remaining on our globe are swimming in the Pacific. Coral pinnacles on the lagoon floor provide a safe haven for angelfish, butterfly fish, damselfish, groupers, soldierfish, surgeonfish, triggerfish, trumpet fish, and countless more. These fish seldom venture more than a few meters away from the protective coral, but larger fish such as barracuda, jackfish, parrot fish, pike, stingrays, and small sharks range across lagoon waters that are seldom deeper than 30 meters. The external side of the reef is also home to many of the above, but the open ocean is reserved for bonito, mahimahi, swordfish, tuna, wrasses, and the larger sharks. Passes between ocean and lagoon can be crowded with fish in transit, offering a favorite hunting ground for predators.

In the open sea the food chain begins with phytoplankton, which flourish wherever ocean upswellings bring nutrients such as nitrates and phosphates to the surface. In the western Pacific this occurs near the equator, where massive currents draw water away toward Japan and Australia. Large schools of fast-moving tuna ply these waters feeding on smaller fish, which consume tiny phytoplankton drifting near the sunlit surface. The phytoplankton also exist in tropical lagoons where mangrove leaves, sea grasses, and other plant material are consumed by far more varied populations of reef fish, mollusks, and crustaceans.

**Sharks**

The danger from sharks has been greatly exaggerated. Of some 300 different species, only 28 are known to have attacked humans. Most dangerous are the white, tiger, and blue sharks. Fortunately, all of these inhabit deep water far from the coasts. An average of only 50 shark attacks a year occur worldwide, so considering the number of people who swim in the sea, your chances of being involved are about one in ten million. In the South Pacific shark attacks on snorkelers or scuba divers are extremely rare and the tiny mosquito is a far more dangerous predator.

Sharks are not aggressive where food is abundant, but they can be very nasty far offshore. You're always safer if you keep your head underwater (with a mask and snorkel), and don't panic if you see a shark—you might attract it. Even if you do, they're usually only curious, so keep your eye on the shark and slowly back off. The swimming techniques of humans must seem very clumsy to fish, so it's not surprising if they want a closer look.

Sharks are attracted by shiny objects (a knife or jewelry), bright colors (especially yellow and red), urine, blood, spearfishing, and splashing (divers should ease themselves into the water). Sharks normally stay outside the reef, but get local advice. White beaches are safer than dark, and clear water safer than murky. Avoid swimming in places where sewage or edible wastes enter the water, or where fish have just been cleaned. Slaughterhouses sometimes attract sharks to an area by dumping offal into the nearby sea. You should also exercise care in places where local residents have been fishing with spears or even hook and line that day.

Never swim alone if you suspect the presence of sharks. If you see one, even a supposedly harmless nurse shark lying on the bottom, get out of the water calmly and quickly, and go elsewhere. Studies indicate that sharks, like most other creatures, have a "personal space" around them that they will defend. Thus an attack could be a shark's way of warning someone to keep his distance, and it's a fact that over half the victims of these incidents are not eaten but merely bitten. Sharks are much less of a problem in the South Pacific than in colder waters because small marine mammals (commonly hunted by sharks) are rare here, so you won't be mistaken for a seal or an otter.

Let common sense be your guide, not irrational fear or carelessness. Many scuba divers come actually *looking* for sharks, and local divemasters seem able to swim among them with impunity. If you're in the market for some shark action, most dive shops can provide it. Just be aware that getting into the water with feeding sharks always entails some danger, and the divemaster who admits this and lays down some basic safety guidelines (such as keeping your hands clasped or arms folded) is probably a safer bet than the macho man who just says he's been doing it for years without incident. Never snorkel on your own (without the services of an experienced guide) near a spot where shark feeding is regularly practiced as you never know how the sharks will react to a surface swimmer without any food for them. Like all other wild animals, sharks deserve to be approached with respect.

**Sea Urchins**

Sea urchins (living pincushions) are common in tropical waters. The black variety is the most dangerous: their long, sharp quills can go right through a snorkeler's fins. Even the small ones, which you can easily pick up in your hand, can pinch you if you're careless. They're found on rocky shores and reefs, never on clear, sandy beaches where the surf rolls in.

Most sea urchins are not poisonous, though quill punctures are painful and can become infected if not treated. The pain is caused by an injected protein, which you can eliminate by holding the injured area in a pail of very hot water for about 15 minutes. This will coagulate the protein, eliminating the pain for good. If you can't heat water, soak the area in vinegar or urine for a quarter hour. Remove the quills if possible, but being made of calcium, they'll decompose in a couple of weeks anyway—not much of a consolation as you limp along in the meantime. In some places sea urchins are considered a delicacy: the orange or yellow urchin gonads are delicious with lemon and salt.

**Other Hazardous Creatures**

Although jellyfish, stonefish, crown-of-thorns starfish, cone shells, eels, and poisonous sea snakes are dangerous, injuries resulting from any of these are rare. Gently apply methylated spirit, alcohol, or urine (but not water, kerosene, or gasoline) to areas stung by jellyfish. Inoffensive sea cucumbers (bêche-de-mer) punctuate the lagoon shallows, but stonefish also rest on the bottom and are hard to see due to camouflaging; if you happen to step on one, its dorsal fins inject a painful poison, which burns like fire in the blood. Fortunately, stonefish are not common.

It's worth knowing that the venom produced by most marine animals is destroyed by heat, so your first move should be to soak the injured part in very hot water for 30 minutes. (Also hold an opposite foot or hand in the same water to prevent scalding due to numbness.) Other authorities claim the best first aid is to squeeze blood from a sea cucumber scraped raw on coral directly onto the wound. If a hospital or clinic is nearby, go there immediately.

Never pick up a live cone shell; some varieties have a deadly stinger dart coming out from the pointed end. The tiny blue-ring octopus is only five centimeters long but packs a poison that can kill a human. Eels hide in reef crevices by day; most are harmful only if you inadvertently poke your hand or foot in at them. Of course, never tempt fate by approaching them (fun-loving divemasters sometimes feed the big ones by hand and stroke their backs).

LOUISE FOOTE

kalahimu

# HISTORY AND GOVERNMENT

## HISTORY

### The Pre-European Period

The first people to arrive in Fiji were of a broad-nosed, light-skinned Austronesian-speaking race, probably the Polynesians. They originated in insular Southeast Asia and gradually migrated east past the already occupied islands of Melanesia. Distinctive *Lapita* pottery, decorated in horizontal geometric bands and dated from 1290 B.C., has been found in the sand dunes near Sigatoka, indicating they had reached here by 1500 B.C. or earlier. Much later, about 500 B.C., Melanesian people arrived, bringing with them their own distinct pottery traditions. From the fusion of these primordial peoples was the Fijian race born.

The hierarchical social structure of the early Fijians originated with the Polynesians. Status and descent passed through the male line, and power was embodied in the *turaga* (chief). The hereditary chiefs possessed the mana of an ancestral spirit or *vu*. Yet under the *vasu* system a chiefly woman's son could lay claim to the property of his mother's brothers, and such relationships combined with polygamy kept society in a state of constant strife. This feudal aristocracy combined in confederations, or *vanua,* which extended their influence through war. Treachery and cannibalism were an intrinsic part of these struggles; women were taken as prizes or traded to form alliances. For defense, villages were fortified with ring ditches, or built along ridges or terraced hillsides.

The native aristocracy practiced customs that today seem barbarous and particularly cruel. The skull cap of a defeated enemy might be polished and used as a *yaqona* (kava) cup to humiliate the foe. Some chiefs even took delight in cooking and consuming body parts as their agonized victims looked on. Men were buried alive to hold up the posts of new houses, war canoes were launched over the living bodies of young girls, and the widows of chiefs were strangled to keep their husbands company in the spirit world. The farewells of some of these women are remembered today in dances and songs known as *meke*.

These feudal islanders were, on the other hand, guardians of one of the highest material cultures of the Pacific. They built great ocean-going double canoes *(drua)* up to 30 meters long, constructed and adorned large solid thatched houses *(bures),* performed marvelous song-dances called *meke,* made tapa, pottery, and sennit (coconut cordage), and skillfully plaited mats. For centuries the Tongans came to Fiji to obtain great logs for canoe-making and sandalwood for carving.

### European Exploration

In 1643 Abel Tasman became the European discoverer of Fiji when he sighted Taveuni, although he didn't land. Tasman was searching for *terra australis incognita,* a great southern continent believed to balance the continents of the north. He also hoped to find new markets and trade routes. Unlike earlier Spanish explorers, Tasman entered the Pacific from the west rather than the east. He was the first European to see Tasmania, New Zealand, and Tonga, as well as Fiji. By sailing right around Australia from the Dutch East In-

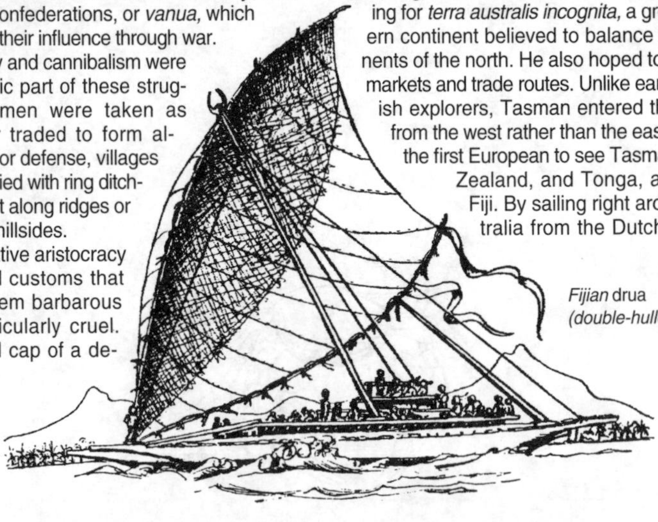

*Fijian* drua *(double-hulled canoe)*

# FIJI ISLANDS CHRONOLOGY

1500 B.C. Polynesians reach Fiji
500 B.C. Melanesians reach Fiji
1643 Abel Tasman sights Taveuni
1774 Captain Cook visits southern Lau
1789 Bligh and crew paddle past Yasawas
1800 sandalwood discovered on Vanua Levu
1820 bêche-de-mer trade begins
1827 Dumont d'Urville visits Bau
1830 Tahitian missionaries in southern Lau
1830 whalers begin using Levuka as a base
1835 Methodist missionaries arrive at Lakeba
1840 American Exploring Expedition visits Fiji
1846 John Brown Williams appointed U.S. agent in Fiji
1847 Tongan invasion of Lau led by Enele Ma'afu
1849 home of John Brown Williams burns
1851 first visit by hostile American gunboats
1853 King of Tonga appoints Ma'afu governor of Tongans in Lau
1854 Chief Cakobau accepts Christianity
1855 Cakobau puts down the Rewa revolt
1855 HMS *Herald* begins charting Fijian waters
1855 second visit by American gunboats
1858 first British consul arrives in Fiji
1860 founding of the town of Levuka
1862 Britain refuses to annex Fiji
1865 confederacy of Fijian chiefs formed
1867 American warship threatens to shell Levuka
1867 Rev. Baker killed and devoured by cannibals
1868 Polynesia Company granted the site of Suva
1871 Cakobau and Thurston form a government
1872 blackbirding of Melanesians to work on plantations halted
1874 Fiji becomes a British colony
1875 measles epidemic kills a third of Fijians
1876 British-led expedition subdues hill tribes
1877 Western Pacific High Commission established by British
1879 first indentured Indian laborers arrive
1881 first large sugar mill built at Nausori
1881 Rotuma annexed to Fiji
1882 capital moved from Levuka to Suva
1904 first elected Legislative Council
1916 Indian immigration ends
1920 indenture system terminated
1928 first flight from Hawaii lands at Suva
1932 gold discovered on Viti Levu
1935 Emperor Gold Mine opens at Vatukoula
1939 Nadi Airport built
1939 Government Building erected in Suva
1940 Native Land Trust Board established
1942 Fijian troops sent to the Solomons
1942 Rabi purchased for the Banabans
1951 Fiji Airways (later Air Pacific) formed
1953 Queen Elizabeth II visits Fiji
1954 first political party established
1963 women and indigenous Fijians granted the right to vote
1965 Constitutional Convention held in London
1966 internal self-government achieved
1967 first large tourist resort opens
1968 University of the South Pacific established
1970 Fiji's first constitution adopted
1970 Fiji becomes independent
1973 sugar industry nationalized
1973 first indigenous Fijian appointed governor-general
1977 governor-general overturns election results
1978 Fijian peacekeeping troops sent to Lebanon
1981 Fijian troops sent to the Sinai
1983 Monasavu Hydroelectric Project opens
1985 Fiji Labor Party formed
1986 Labor forms a coalition with main Indian-led party
1987 Labor defeats Alliance Party
1987 two military coups led by Lieutenant Colonel Rabuka
1987 Rabuka declares Fiji a republic
1987 Fiji expelled from British Commonwealth
1990 racially weighted constitution promulgated
1992 Rabuka elected under gerrymandered constitution
1994 Rabuka reelected with increased representation
1997 Fiji readmitted to the Commonwealth
1998 revised constitution comes into effect

## CANNIBALISM

It has been said that the Fijians were extremely hospitable to any strangers they did not wish to eat. Native voyagers who wrecked on their shores, who arrived "with salt water in their eyes," were liable to be killed and eaten, since all shipwrecked persons were believed to have been cursed and abandoned by the gods. Many European sailors from wrecked vessels shared the same fate. Cannibalism was a universal practice, and prisoners taken in war, or even women seized while fishing, were invariably eaten. Most of the early European accounts of Fiji emphasized this trait to the exclusion of almost everything else; at one time, the island group was even referred to as the "Cannibal Isles." By eating the flesh of the conquered enemy, one inflicted the ultimate revenge. One chief on Viti Levu is said to have consumed 872 people and to have made a pile of stones to record his achievement. The leaves of a certain vegetable *(Solanum uporo)* were wrapped around the human meat, and it was cooked in an earthen oven. Wooden forks such as the one pictured were employed at cannibal feasts by men who relied on their fingers for other food, but used these because it was considered improper to touch human flesh with fingers or lips. Present-day Fijians don't appreciate tourists who make jokes about cannibalism.

*cannibal fork*

LOUISE FOOTE

dies he proved New Holland (Australia) was not attached to the elusive southern continent.

In 1774, Captain Cook anchored off Vatoa (which he named Turtle Island) in southern Lau. Like Tasman he failed to proceed farther or land, and it was left to Capt. William Bligh to give Europeans an accurate picture of Fiji for the first time. After the *Bounty* mutiny in May 1789, Bligh and his companions were chased by canoeloads of Fijian warriors just north of the Yasawa Islands as they rowed through on their escape route to Timor. Some serious paddling, a timely squall, and a lucky gap in the Great Sea Reef saved the Englishmen from ending up as the main course at a cannibal feast. The section of sea where this happened is known as Bligh Water today. Bligh cut directly across the center of Fiji between the two main islands, and his careful observations made him the first real European explorer of Fiji, albeit an unwilling one. Bligh returned to Fiji in 1792, but once again he stayed aboard his ship.

### Beachcombers and Chiefs

All of these early explorers stressed the perilous nature of Fiji's reefs. This, combined with tales told by the Tongans of cannibalism and warlike Fijian natives, caused most travelers to shun the area. Then in 1800 a survivor from the shipwrecked American schooner *Argo* brought word that sandalwood grew abundantly along the Bua coast of Vanua Levu. This precipitated a rush of traders and beachcombers to the islands. A cargo of sandalwood bought from the islanders for $50 worth of trinkets could be sold to the Chinese at Canton for $20,000. By 1814 the forests had been stripped to provide joss sticks and incense, and the trade collapsed.

During this period Fiji was divided among warring chieftains. The first Europeans to actually mix with the Fijians were escaped convicts from Australia, who instructed the natives in the use of European muskets and were thus well received. White beachcombers such as the Swedish adventurer Charles Savage and the German Martin Bushart acted as middlemen between traders and Fijians and took sides in local conflicts. In one skirmish Savage was separated from his fellows, captured, and eaten. With help from the likes of Savage, Naulivou, the cannibal chief of tiny Bau Island just off eastern Viti Levu, and his brother Tanoa extended their influence over much of western Fiji.

In his book *Following the Equator,* Mark Twain had this to say about the beachcombers:

> *They lived worthless lives of sin and luxury, and died without honor—in most cases by violence. Only one of them had any ambition; he was an Irishman named Connor.*

*He tried to raise a family of fifty children and scored forty-eight. He died lamenting his failure. It was a foolish sort of avarice. Many a father would have been rich enough with forty.*

From 1820 to 1850 European traders collected bêche-de-mer, a sea cucumber which, when smoked and dried, also brought a good price in China. While the sandalwood traders only stayed long enough to take on a load, the bêche-de-mer collectors set up shore facilities where the slugs were processed. Many traders such as David Whippy followed the example of the beachcombers and took local wives, establishing the part-Fijian community of today. By monopolizing the bêche-de-mer trade and constantly warring, Chief Tanoa's son and successor, Ratu Seru Cakobau (pronounced Thakombau), became extremely powerful in the 1840s, proclaiming himself Tui Viti, or king of Fiji.

The beginnings of organized trade brought a second wave of official explorers to Fiji. In 1827 Dumont d'Urville landed on Bau Island and met Tanoa. The Frenchmen caused consternation and confusion by refusing to drink *yaqona* (kava), preferring their own wine. The American Exploring Expedition of 1840, led by Commodore Charles Wilkes, produced the first recognizable map of Fiji. When two Americans, including a nephew of Wilkes, were speared in a misunderstanding on a beach at Malolo Island, Wilkes ordered the offending fortified village stormed and 87 Fijians were killed. The survivors were made to water and provision Wilkes's ships as tribute. Captain H.M. Denham of the HMS *Herald* prepared accurate navigational charts of the island group in 1855-56, making regular commerce possible.

### European and Tongan Penetration

As early as the 1830s an assortment of European and American beachcombers had formed a small settlement at Levuka on the east coast of Ovalau Island just northeast of Bau, which whalers and traders used as a supply base. In 1846 John Brown Williams was appointed American commercial agent. On 4 July 1849 Williams's home on Nukulau Island near present-day Suva burned down. Though the conflagration was caused by the explosion of a cannon during Williams's own fervent celebration of his national holiday, he objected to the way Fijian onlookers carried off items they rescued from the flames. A shameless swindler, Williams had purchased Nukulau for only $30, yet he blamed the Tui Viti for his losses and sent Cakobau a $5,001.38 bill. American claims for damages eventually rose to $45,000, and in 1851 and 1855 American gunboats called and ordered Cakobau to pay up. This threat hung over Cakobau's head for many years, the 19th-century equivalent of 20th-century third world debt. Increasing American involvement in Fiji led the British to appoint a consul, W.T. Pritchard, who arrived in 1858.

The early 1830s also saw the arrival from Tonga of the first missionaries. Though Tahitian pastors were sent by the London Missionary Society to Oneata in southern Lau as early as 1830, it was the Methodists based at Lakeba after 1835 who made the most lasting impression by rendering the Fijian language into writing. At first Christianity made little headway among these fierce, idolatrous people, and only after converting the powerful chiefs were the missionaries successful. Methodist missionaries Cargill and Cross were appalled by what they saw during a visit to Bau in 1838. A white missionary, Rev. Thomas Baker, was clubbed and eaten in central Viti Levu by the *kai colo* (hill people) as late as 1867.

In 1847 Enele Ma'afu, a member of the Tongan royal family, arrived in Lau and began building a personal empire under the pretense of defending Christianity. In 1853 King George of Tonga made Ma'afu governor of all Tongans resident in Lau. Meanwhile, there was continuing resistance from the warlords of the Rewa River area to Cakobau's dominance. In addition the Europeans at Levuka suspected Cakobau of twice ordering their town set afire and were directing trade away from Bau. With his power in decline, in 1854 Cakobau accepted Christianity in exchange for an alliance with King George, and in 1855, with the help of 2,000 Tongans led by King George himself, Cakobau was able to put down the Rewa revolt at the Battle of Kaba. In the process, however, Ma'afu became the dominant force in Lau, Taveuni, and Vanua Levu.

During the early 1860s, as Americans fought their Civil War, the world price of cotton soared, and large numbers of Europeans arrived in Fiji hoping to establish cotton plantations. In 1867 the USS *Tuscaroga* called at Levuka and threatened to bombard the town unless the still-outstanding American debt was paid. The next year an enterprising Australian firm, the Polynesia Company, paid off the Americans in exchange for a grant from Cakobau of 80,000 hectares of choice land, including the site of modern Suva. The British government later refused to recognize this grant, though they refunded the money paid to the Americans and accepted the claims of settlers who had purchased land from the company. Settlers soon numbered around 2,000 and Levuka boomed.

It was a lawless era and a need was felt for a central government. An attempt at national rule by a confederacy of chiefs lasted two years until failing in 1867, then three regional governments were set up in Bau (western), Lau (eastern), and Bua (northern), but these were only partly successful. With prices for Fiji's "Sea Island" cotton collapsing as the American South resumed production, a national administration under Cakobau and planter John Thurston was established at Levuka in 1871.

However, Cakobau was never strong enough to impose his authority over the whole country, so with growing disorder in western Fiji, infighting between Europeans and Fijian chiefs, and a lack of cooperation from Ma'afu's rival confederation of chiefs in eastern Fiji, Cakobau decided he should cede his kingdom to Great Britain. The British had refused an invitation to annex Fiji in 1862, but this time they accepted rather than risk seeing the group fall into the hands of another power, and on 10 October 1874 Fiji became a British colony. A punitive expedition into central Viti Levu in 1876 brought the hill tribes *(kai colo)* under British rule. In 1877 the Western Pacific High Commission was set up to protect British interests in the surrounding unclaimed island groups as well. In 1881 Rotuma was annexed to Fiji. At first Levuka was the colony's capital, but in 1882 the government moved to a more spacious site at Suva.

### The Making of a Nation

The first British governor, Sir Arthur Gordon, and his colonial secretary and successor, Sir John Thurston, created modern Fiji almost single-handedly. They realized that the easiest way to rule was indirectly, through the existing Fijian chiefs. To protect the communal lands on which the chieftain system was based, they ordered that native land could not be sold, only leased. Not wishing to disturb native society, Gordon and Thurston ruled that Fijians could not be required to work on European plantations. Meanwhile the blackbirding of Melanesian laborers from the Solomons and New Hebrides had been restricted by the Polynesian Islanders Protection Act of 1872.

By this time sugar had taken the place of cotton and there was a tremendous labor shortage on the plantations. Gordon, who had previously served in Trinidad and Mauritius, saw indentured Indian workers as a solution. The first arrived in 1879, and by 1916, when Indian immigration ended, there were 63,000 present. To

CAINES JANIF LTD., SUVA

*Blackbirded Solomon Islanders, brought to work on European-owned plantations in Fiji, wait aboard ship off Levuka around the turn of the century. In 1910 the Melanesian labor trade was finally terminated by the British, but a few of the Solomon Islanders stayed on, and small communities of their descendants exist on Ovalau and near Suva.*

come to Fiji the Indians had to sign a labor contract *(girmit)* in which they agreed to cut sugarcane for their masters for five years. During the next five years they were allowed to lease small plots of their own from the Fijians and plant cane or raise livestock. Over half the Indians decided to remain in Fiji as free settlers after their 10-year contracts expired, and today their descendants form nearly half the population, many of them still working small leased plots.

Though this combination of European capital, Fijian land, and Indian labor did help preserve traditional Fijian culture, it also kept the Fijians backward—envious onlookers passed over by European and (later) Indian prosperity. The separate administration and special rights for indigenous Fijians installed by the British over a century ago continue in force today. In early 1875 Cakobau and two of his sons returned from a visit to Australia infected with measles. Though they themselves survived, the resulting epidemic wiped out a third of the Fijian population. As a response to this and other public health problems the Fiji School of Medicine was founded in 1885. At the beginning of European colonization there were about 200,000 Fijians, approximately 114,748 in 1881, and just 84,000 by 1921.

**The Colonial Period**

In 1912 a Gujerati lawyer, D.M. Manilal, arrived in Fiji from Mauritius to fight for Indian rights, just as his contemporary Mahatma Gandhi was doing in South Africa. Several prominent Anglican and Methodist missionaries also lobbied actively against the system. Indentured Indians continued to arrive in Fiji until 1916, but the protests led to the termination of the indenture system throughout the empire in 1920 (Manilal was deported from Fiji after a strike that year).

Although Fiji was a political colony of Britain, it was always an economic colony of Australia: the big Australian trading companies Burns Philp and W.R. Carpenters dominated business. (The ubiquitous Morris Hedstrom is a subsidiary of Carpenters.) Most of the Indians were brought to Fiji to work for the Australian-owned Colonial Sugar Refining Company, which controlled the sugar industry from 1881 right up until 1973, when it was purchased by the Fiji government for $14 million. After 1935, Fiji's gold fields were also exploited by Australians.

Under the British colonial system the Governor of Fiji had far greater decision-making authority than his counterparts in the French Pacific colonies. Whereas the French administrators were required to closely follow policies dictated from Paris, the governors of the British colonies had only to refer to the Colonial Office in London on special matters such as finance and foreign affairs. Otherwise they had great freedom to make policy decisions.

No representative government existed in Fiji until 1904, when a Legislative Council was formed with six elected Europeans and two Fijians nominated by the Great Council of Chiefs *(Bose Levu Vakaturaga),* itself an instrument of colonial rule. In 1916 the governor appointed an Indian member to the council. A 1929 reform granted five seats to each of the three communities: three elected and two appointed Europeans and Indians, and five nominated Fijians. The council was only an advisory body and the governor remained in complete control. The Europeans generally sided with the Fijians against any demands for equality from the Indians—typical colonial divide and rule.

During WW I an indigenous resistance movement to this colonial exploitation emerged in the form of the Viti Kabani, or Fiji Company, led by Apolosi Ranawai, a commoner from western Viti Levu. The company began as a reaction to profiteering by Fijian chiefs and white traders who bought and sold village products, but it soon moved beyond economic matters to question the whole eastern-dominated chiefly system, which allowed the British to rule so easily. The chiefs reacted by having the movement branded seditious and Apolosi Ranawai exiled.

Fijians were outstanding combat troops on the Allied side in the Solomon Islands campaign during WW II, and again in 1952-56 suppressing Malaya's national liberation struggle. So skilled were the Fijians at jungle warfare against the Japanese that it was never appropriate to list a Fijian as "missing in action"—the phrase used was "not yet arrived." The war years saw the development of Nadi Airport. Until 1952, Suva, the present Fijian capital, was headquarters for the entire British Imperial Administration in the South Pacific.

In 1963 the Legislative Council was expanded but still divided along racial lines; women and indigenous Fijians got the vote for the first time. Wishing to be rid of the British, whom they blamed for their second-class position, the Indians pushed for independence, but the Fijians had come to view the British as protectors and were somewhat reluctant. A Constitutional Convention was held in London in 1965 to move Fiji toward self-government, and after much discussion a constitution was adopted in 1970. Some legislature members were to be elected from a common roll (voting by all races), as the Indians desired, while other seats remained ethnic (voting in racial constituencies) to protect the Fijians. On 10 October 1970 Fiji became a fully independent nation and the first Fijian governor-general was appointed in 1973—none other than Ratu Sir George Cakobau, great-grandson of the chief who had ceded Fiji to Queen Victoria 99 years previously.

## SINCE INDEPENDENCE

### Political Development

During the 1940s Ratu Sir Lala Sukuna, paramount chief of Lau, played a key role in the creation of a separate administration for indigenous Fijians, with native land (83% of Fiji) under its jurisdiction. In 1954 he formed the Fijian Association to support the British governor against Indian demands for equal representation. In 1960 the National Federation Party (NFP) was formed to represent Indian cane farmers.

In 1966 the Alliance Party, a coalition of the Fijian Association, the General Electors' Association (representing Europeans, part-Fijians, and Chinese), and the Fiji Indian Alliance (a minority Indian group) won the legislative assembly elections. In 1970 Alliance Party leader Ratu Sir Kamisese Mara led Fiji into independence and in 1972 his party won Fiji's first post-independence elections. Ratu Mara served as prime minister almost continuously until the 1987 elections.

In 1975 Mr. Sakeasi Butadroka, a member of parliament previously expelled from the Alliance Party, presented a motion calling for all Indians to be repatriated to India at British expense. This was rejected but during the April 1977 elections Butadroka's Fijian Nationalist Party took enough votes away from the Alliance to allow the predominantly Indian NFP to obtain a majority in parliament. After a few days' hesitation, the governor-general reappointed Ratu Mara as prime minister, but his minority Alliance government was soon defeated. Meanwhile, Butadroka had been arrested for making racially inflammatory statements in violation of the Public Order Act, and in new elections in September 1977 the Alliance recovered its majority, due in part to a split of the NFP into Hindu and Muslim factions.

The formation of the Fiji Labor Party (FLP), headed by Dr. Timoci Bavadra, in July 1985 dramatically altered the political landscape. Fiji's previously nonpolitical trade unions had finally come behind a party that campaigned on bread-and-butter issues rather than race. Late in 1986 Labor and the NFP formed a coalition with the aim of defeating the Alliance in the next election. Dr. Bavadra, a former director of Primary and Preventive Health Services and president of the Fiji Public Service Association, was chosen as Coalition leader. In the 12 April 1987 elections the Coalition won 28 of 52 House of Representatives seats; 19 of the 28 elected Coalition members were Indians. What swung the election away from Alliance was not a change in Indian voting patterns but support for Labor from urban Fijians and part-Fijians, which cost Alliance four previously "safe" seats around Suva.

The Coalition cabinet had a majority of Indian members, but all positions of vital Fijian interest (Lands, Fijian Affairs, Labor and Immigration, Education, Agriculture and Rural Development) went to indigenous Fijian legislators, though none of them was a traditional chief. Coalition's progressive policies marked quite a switch from the conservatism of the Alliance—a new generation of political leadership dedicated to tackling the day-to-day problems of people of all races rather than perpetuating the privileges of the old chiefly oligarchy.

The new government also announced that nuclear warships would be banned from a nonaligned Fiji. Foreign Minister Krishna Datt said he would join Vanuatu and New Zealand in pressing for a nuclear-free Pacific at the 24 May 1987 meeting of the South Pacific Forum. Alleged corruption in the previous administration was also to be investigated. Given time the Coalition might have required the high chiefs to share the rental monies they received for leasing lands to Indians more fairly with ordinary Fijians. Most significant of all, the

Coalition would have transformed Fiji from a plural society where only indigenous Melanesian Fijians were called Fijians into a truly multiracial society where all citizens would be Fijians.

## The First Coup

After the election the extremist Fiji-for-Fijians Taukei (landowners) movement launched a destabilization campaign by throwing barricades across highways, organizing protest rallies and marches, and carrying out firebombings. On 24 April 1987 Senator Inoke Tabua and former Alliance cabinet minister Apisai Tora organized a march of 5,000 Fijians through Suva to protest "Indian domination" of the new government. Mr. Tora told a preparatory meeting for the demonstration that Fijians must "act now" to avoid ending up as "deprived as Australia's aborigines." (In fact, under the 1970 constitution the Coalition government would have had no way of changing Fiji's land laws without indigenous Fijian consent.) During the following weeks five gasoline bombs were thrown against government offices, though no one was injured. On 13 May 1987 Alliance Senator Jona Qio was arrested for arson.

At 1000 on Thursday 14 May 1987 Lt. Col. Sitiveni Rabuka (pronounced Rambuka), an ambitious officer whose career was stalled at number three in the Fiji army, and 10 heavily armed soldiers dressed in fatigues, their faces covered by gas masks, entered the House of Parliament in Suva. Rabuka ordered Dr. Bavadra and the Coalition members to follow a soldier out of the building, and when Dr. Bavadra hesitated the soldiers raised their guns. The legislators were loaded into army trucks and taken to Royal Fiji Military Forces headquarters. There was no bloodshed, though Rabuka later confirmed that his troops would have opened fire had there been any resistance. At a press conference five hours after the coup, Rabuka claimed he had acted to prevent violence and had no political ambitions of his own.

Australia and New Zealand promptly denounced the region's first military coup. Governor-General Ratu Sir Penaia Ganilau attempted to reverse the situation by declaring a state of emergency and ordering the mutineers to return to their barracks. They refused to obey. The next day the *Fiji Sun* ran a black-bordered editorial that declared, "Democracy died in Fiji yesterday. What right has a third-ranking officer to attack the sacred institutions of Parliament? What right has he to presume he knows best how this country shall be governed? The answer is none." Soon after, Rabuka's troops descended on both daily papers and ordered publication suspended. Journalists were evicted from the buildings.

Later that day Rabuka named a 15-member Council of Ministers, chaired by himself, to govern Fiji, with former Alliance prime minister Ratu Mara as foreign minister. Significantly, Rabuka was the only military officer on the council; most of the others were members of Ratu Mara's defeated administration. Rabuka claimed he had acted to "safeguard the Fijian land issue and the Fijian way of life."

On 19 May Dr. Bavadra and the other kidnaped members of his government were released after the governor-general announced a deal negotiated with Rabuka to avoid the possibility of foreign intervention. Rabuka's Council of Ministers was replaced by a 19-member caretaker Advisory Council appointed by the Great Council of Chiefs, which would govern until new elections could take place. The council would be headed by Ratu Ganilau, with Rabuka in charge of Home Affairs and the security forces. Only two seats were offered to Dr. Bavadra's government and they were refused.

The Sunday before the coup Ratu Mara was seen playing golf with Rabuka at Pacific Harbor. At the time of the coup he was at the Fijian Hotel chairing a meeting of the Pacific Democratic Union, a U.S.-sponsored grouping of ultra-right politicians from Australia, New Zealand, and elsewhere. Though Ratu Mara expressed "shock" at the coup, he accepted a position on Rabuka's Council of Ministers the next day, prompting New Zealand Prime Minister David Lange to accuse him of treachery under Fiji's constitution by acquiescing to military rule. Lange said Ratu Mara had pledged allegiance to the Queen but had brought about a rebellion in one of her countries. Ratu Ganilau was also strongly criticized for legitimizing a traitor by accepting Rabuka on his Advisory Council.

## Behind the Coup

In 1982 American interest in the South Pacific picked up after the U.S. ambassador to Fiji, William Bodde Jr., told a luncheon audience at the Kahala Hilton in Hawaii that the creation of a South Pacific nuclear-free zone would be "the most potentially disruptive development to U.S. relations with the region . . . I am convinced that the United States must do everything possible to counter this movement. It will not be an easy task, but it is one that we cannot afford to neglect." In 1983 Bodde's diplomacy resulted in the lifting of a ban on visits to Fiji by U.S. nuclear warships, and Fiji was soon rewarded by becoming the first South Pacific country to receive direct American aid. Substantial grants to the Fiji army for "weapons standardization" soon followed, and from 1984 to 1986 U.S. aid to Fiji tripled.

Immediately after the coup, rumors circulated throughout the South Pacific that the U.S. government was involved. On 16 June 1987 at a press conference at the National Press Club in Washington, D.C., Dr. Bavadra publicly accused the director of the South Pacific regional office of the U.S. Agency for International Development of channeling US$200,000 to right-winger Apisai Tora of the Taukei movement for destabilization purposes.

From 29 April to 1 May 1987 Gen. Vernon A. Walters, U.S. ambassador to the United Nations and a former CIA deputy director, visited Fiji. At a long meeting with Foreign Minister Datt, Walters tried to persuade the new government to give up its antinuclear stance. Walters told the Fiji press that the U.S. "has a duty to protect its South Pacific interests." Walters is believed to have been involved in previous coups in Iran (1953) and Brazil (1964), and during his stay in Fiji he also met with Rabuka and U.S. AID officials. During his 10-country Pacific trip Walters spread fanciful rumors of Libya subversion, diverting attention from what was about to happen in Fiji.

On 22 October 1987 the U.S. Information Service in New Zealand revealed that the amphibious assault ship USS *Belleau Wood* had been just west of Fiji immediately after the coup, supported by three C-130 Hercules transport planes, which staged through Nadi Airport 20-22 June. The same release mentioned four other C-130s at Nadi that month to support the gigantic hospital ship USNS *Mercy,* which was at Suva 23-27 June—an unprecedented level of U.S. military activity. By chance or design the U.S. would have been ready to intervene militarily within hours had anything gone wrong.

Yet direct American involvement in the coup has never been conclusively proven and the full story may never be told. Rabuka himself has always denied that the U.S. or any other foreign elements were involved. The events caught the Australian and New Zealand intelligence services totally by surprise, indicating that few knew of Rabuka's plans in advance.

Until the coup the most important mission of the Royal Fiji Defense Force was service in South Lebanon and the Sinai with peacekeeping operations. Half of the 2,600-member Fiji army was on rotating duty there, the Sinai force financed by the U.S., the troops in Lebanon by the United Nations. During WW II Fiji Indians refused to join the army unless they received the same pay as European recruits; indigenous Fijians had no such reservations and the force has been 95% Fijian ever since. Service in the strife-torn Middle East gave the Fiji military a unique preparation for its destabilizing role in Fiji itself. (Not many people outside Fiji realize that, after Australia and New Zealand, Lebanon is the foreign country indigenous Fijians know best.)

The mass media presented the coup in simplistic terms as a racial conflict between Indians and Fijians, though commentators with a deeper knowledge of the nature of power in Fiji saw it quite differently. Anthony D. van Fossen of Griffith University, Queensland, Australia, summed it up this way in the *Bulletin of Concerned Asian Scholars* (Vol. 19, No. 4, 1987):

> *Although the first coup has been most often seen in terms of ethnic tensions between indigenous Fijians and Fijian Indians, it may be more accurately seen as the result of tensions between aristocratic indigenous Fijians and their commoner allies defending feudalism, on the one hand, and the cause of social democracy, small-scale capitalism, and multi-ethnic nationalism represented by middle-class indigenous Fijian commoners and Hindus on the other.*

In their October 1987 issue, *Pacific Islands Monthly* published this comment by noted author Brij V. Lal of the Australia National University:

*More than anything else, the coup was about power. The emergence in an incipient form of a class-minded multi-racial politics, symbolized by the Labor Party and made possible by the support of many urban Fijians, posed a grave threat to the politics of race and racial compartmentalization preached by the Alliance and thus had to be nipped in the bud. The ascent of Dr. Bavadra, a chief from the long-neglected western Viti Levu, to the highest office in the land posed an unprecedented challenge to the traditional dominance of eastern chiefs, especially from Lau and Cakaudrove.*

The comments above have appeared in several editions of this book, and in early 1998 the author received a letter from the noted Cook Islands academic Dr. Ron Crocombe, who had this to say in part:

*I am saddened to see one who should be trying to give visitors balanced views, loading them with the biases of one side of a complex dispute. You speak of 83% of the land being owned by Fijians, but not that most of that is useless mountains, remote outer islands, or low fertility slopes, and that most of the top quality part of what is good agricultural land has been leased, against the owners' wishes in many cases, to Indian farmers and businessmen at rates fixed by law which are far below market value.*

*Labor as a "party that campaigned on bread and butter rather than race" is Labor ideology but not supported by facts. Labor was very much an Indian dominated and run party. Labor policy papers were prepared with minor exceptions by Indian and other non-Fijian persons. Tim Bavadra was a gentleman, but he always supported Alliance until he fell out with them and was chosen as the ideal front for an Indian dominated party in a context where the public was not yet ready for an Indian prime minister. Dr. Bavadra did not dare to stand for the Fijian seat in his electorate, and not only he, but every single Fijian who got in for the Coalition, got in on Indian and other non-Fijian votes through the cross-voting system of the time. With a cabinet held in place officially by its caucus (which was about three Indians to one Fijian) and unofficially by the people who provided the money and put them in power (almost totally Indian), it was indeed an Indian dominated cabinet, just as the former cabinets had been Fijian dominated.*

*The popular mythology put out by non-indigenous writers about the coup being nothing to do with race but about class to protect the chiefs is nonsense. Rabuka is from a low class and he toppled his high chiefly commander. He then neutralized the head of state who was his own personal high chief. The leading religious man for the Fijian ethnic nationalists was Manasa Lasaro, no high chief. The leading trade union man was Dan Veitata, a wharf laborer. The leading Fijian academic Asesela Ravuvu is no chief of any kind. Bavadra himself was a clan chief. Nobody seems to ask how the majority of Fijians feel, and I can assure you it is different from the vision portrayed. In your next edition do make it clear that this is a complex situation with many interest groups, and the basic issue is ethnicity, however unhappy that fact is these politically correct days.*

### The Second Coup

In July and August 1987 a committee set up by Governor-General Ganilau studied proposals for constitutional reform, and on 4 September talks began at Government House in Suva between Alliance and Coalition leaders under the chairmanship of Ratu Ganilau. With no hope of a consensus on a revised constitution the talks were aimed at preparing for new elections.

Then, on Friday, 26 September 1987, Rabuka struck again, just hours before the governor-general was to announce a government of national unity to rule Fiji until new elections could be held. The plan, arduously developed over four months and finally approved by veteran political leaders on all sides, would probably have resulted in Rabuka being sacked. Rabuka quickly threw out the 1970 constitution and pronounced himself "head of state." Some 300 prominent community leaders were arrested and Ratu Ganilau was confined to Government House. Newspapers were shut down, trade unions repressed, the judiciary suspended, the public service purged, the activities of political opponents restricted, a curfew imposed, and the first cases of torture reported.

At midnight on 7 October 1987 Rabuka declared Fiji a republic. Rabuka's new Council of Ministers included Taukei extremists Apisai Tora and Filipe Bole, Fijian Nationalist Party leader Sakeasi Butadroka, and other marginal figures. Rabuka appeared to have backing in the Great Council of Chiefs, which wanted a return to the style of customary rule threatened by the Indian presence and Western democracy. Regime ideologists trumpeted traditional culture and religious fundamentalism to justify their actions. Rabuka said he wanted Christianity adopted as Fiji's official religion and henceforth all trading (except at tourist hotels), sports, and public transport would be banned on Sunday. Rabuka even called for the conversion of Hindu and Muslim Indians to Christianity.

On 16 October Ratu Ganilau resigned as governor-general and two days later Fiji was expelled from the British Commonwealth. On 6 November Rabuka allowed *The Fiji Times* to resume publication after it pledged self-censorship, but the more independent *Fiji Sun* has never appeared again. Nobody accused the U.S. of having anything to do with Rabuka's second coup, and even Ratu Mara seemed annoyed that Rabuka had destroyed an opportunity to salvage the reputations of himself and Ratu Ganilau. Clearly Rabuka had become his own man.

### The Republic of Fiji

Realizing that Taukei/military rule was a recipe for disaster, on 5 December 1987 Rabuka appointed Ratu Ganilau president and Ratu Mara prime minister of his new republic. The 21-member cabinet included 10 members of Rabuka's military regime, four of them army officers. Rabuka himself (now a self-styled brigadier) was once again Minister of Home Affairs. This interim government set itself a deadline of two years to frame a new constitution and return Fiji to freely elected representative government. By mid-1988 the army had been expanded into a highly disciplined 6,000-member force loyal to Brigadier Rabuka, who left no doubt he would intervene a third time if his agenda was not followed. The Great Council of Chiefs was to decide on Fiji's republican constitution.

The coups transformed the Fijian economy. In 1987 Fiji experienced 11% negative growth in the gross domestic product. To slow the flight of capital the Fiji dollar was devalued 17.75% on 30 June 1987 and 15.25% on 7 October, and inflation, which had been under two percent before the coups, was up to 11.9% by the end of 1988. At the same time the public service (half the workforce) had to accept a 25% wage cut as government spending was slashed. Food prices skyrocketed, causing serious problems for many families. At the end of 1987 the per capita average income was 11% *below* what it had been in 1980. Between 1986 and 1996 some 58,300 Indians left Fiji for Australia, Canada, New Zealand, and the United States. Nearly three-quarters of Fiji's administrators and managers, and a quarter of all professional, technical, and clerical workers departed taking tens of millions of dollars with them, a crippling loss for a country with a total population of under 750,000.

On the other hand, the devaluations and wage-cutting measures, combined with the creation of a tax-free exporting sector and the encouragement of foreign investment, brought about an economic recovery by 1990. At the expense of democracy, social justice, and racial harmony, Fiji embarked on a standard IMF/World Bank-style structural readjustment program. In 1992 the imposition of a 10% value added tax (VAT) shifted the burden of taxation from rich to poor, standard IMF dogma. In effect, Rabuka and the old oligarchs have pushed Fiji squarely back into the third world, and even the Fiji Visitors Bureau had to set aside their former marketing slogan, "The Way the World Should Be."

### Interim Government

In May 1989 the interim government eased Sunday restrictions on work, trading, and sports.

This drew loud protests from Rev. Manasa Lasaro, fundamentalist general secretary of the Methodist Church of Fiji, who organized Sunday roadblocks in Labasa, leading to the arrest and conviction of himself and 56 others for unlawful obstruction. On 9 August Rabuka flew to Labasa by helicopter and arranged the release of Reverend Lasaro and the others on his own authority. On Sunday 15 October 1989 members of a Methodist youth group carried out firebombings against Hindu and Sikh temples and a Muslim mosque at Lautoka.

In November 1989 Dr. Bavadra died of spinal cancer at age 55 and 60,000 people attended his funeral at Viseisei, the largest such gathering in Fijian history. Foreign journalists were prevented from covering the funeral. The nominal head of the unelected interim government, Ratu Mara, considered Rabuka an unpredictable upstart and insisted that he choose between politics or military service. Thus in late 1989, the general and two army colonels were dropped from the cabinet, though Rabuka kept his post as army commander.

On 25 July 1990 President Ganilau promulgated a new constitution approved by the Great Council of Chiefs, which gave the chiefs the right to appoint the president and 24 of the 34 members of the Senate. The president had executive authority and appointed the prime minister from among the ethnic Fijian members of the House of Representatives. Under this constitution the 70-member House of Representatives was elected directly, with voting racially segregated. Ethnic Fijians were granted 37 seats from constituencies gerrymandered to ensure the dominance of the eastern chiefs. The constitution explicitly reserved the posts of president, prime minister, and army chief for ethnic Fijians. Christianity was made the official religion and Rabuka's troops were granted amnesty for any crimes committed during the 1987 coups. The Coalition promptly rejected this supremacist constitution as undemocratic and racist.

On 18 October 1990 a copy of the new constitution was burned during a nonviolent protest by a small group of academics and students. Six days later one of those involved, Dr. Anirudh Singh, a lecturer in physics at the University of the South Pacific, was abducted by five soldiers and taken to Colo-i-Suva where he was tortured with lit cigarettes and had his hands broken by an iron bar during "interrogation." Later he was released. On 29 October three journalists of the *Daily Post* were arrested for publishing a story suggesting that there might be a second constitution burning, and on 31 October Dr. Singh and six other alleged constitution burners were arrested and charged with sedition. After a public outcry the soldiers who had tortured Dr. Singh were turned over to police by the army, given a brief trial, fined F$340 each, and set free. Incredibly, just a few months later, the Fiji Army picked one of the convicted torturers, Capt. Sotia Ponijiase, to head Fiji's contingent in a United Nations observer team sent to Kuwait. When the story came to light, Captain Ponijiase was sent packing back to Fiji by the U.N.

Not satisfied with control of the Senate, in early 1991 the Great Council of Chiefs decided to project their power into the lower house through the formation of the Soqosoqo ni Vakavulewa ni Taukei (SVT), commonly called the Fijian Political Party. Meanwhile Fiji's multiethnic unions continued to rebuild their strength by organizing garment workers and leading strikes in the mining and sugar industries.

In June 1991 Major-General Rabuka rejected an offer from Ratu Mara to join the cabinet as Minister of Home Affairs and co-deputy prime minister, since it would have meant giving up his military power base. Instead Rabuka attempted to widen his political appeal by making public statements in support of striking gold miners and cane farmers, and even threatening a third coup.

By now Rabuka's ambition to become prime minister was obvious, and his new role as a populist rabble-rouser seemed designed to outflank both the Labor Party and the chiefs (Rabuka himself is a commoner). President Ganilau (Rabuka's paramount chief) quickly applied pressure, and in July the volatile general reversed himself and accepted the cabinet posts he had so recently refused. As a condition for reentering the government, Rabuka was forced to resign as army commander and the president's son, Major-Gen. Epeli Ganilau, was appointed his successor. With Rabuka out of the army everyone breathed a little easier, and the chiefs decided to co-opt a potential troublemaker by electing Rabuka president of the SVT.

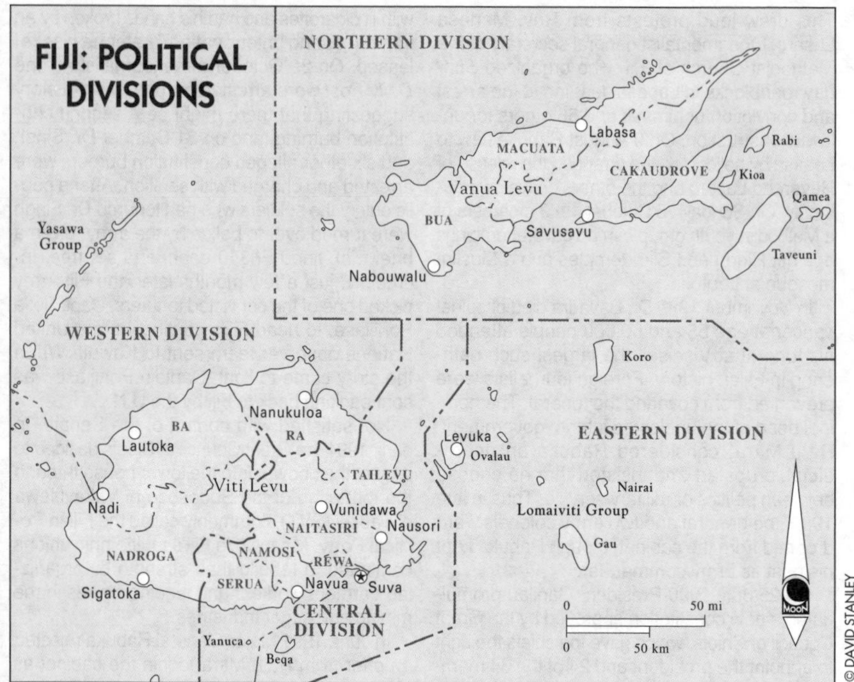


## Return to Democracy

The long-awaited parliamentary elections took place in late May 1992, and the SVT captured 30 of the 37 indigenous Fijian seats. Another five went to Fijian nationalists while the 27 Indian seats were split between the NFP with 14 and the FLP with 13. The five other races' seats went to the General Voters Party (GVP).

Just prior to the election, Ratu Mara retired from party politics and was named vice-president of Fiji by the Great Council of Chiefs. An intense power struggle then developed in the SVT between Ratu Mara's chosen successor as prime minister, former finance minister Josevata Kamikamica, and ex-general Rabuka. Since the SVT lacked a clear majority in the 70-seat house, coalition partners had to be sought, and in a remarkable turn of events populist Rabuka gained the support of the FLP by offering concessions to the trade unions and a promise to review the constitution and land leases. Thus Sitiveni Rabuka became prime minister thanks to the very party he had ousted from power at gunpoint exactly five years before!

The SVP formed a coalition with the GVP, but in November 1993 the Rabuka government was defeated in a parliamentary vote of no confidence over the budget, leading to fresh elections in February 1994. In these, Rabuka's SVT increased its representation to 31 seats. Many Indians had felt betrayed by FLP backing of Rabuka's prime ministership in 1992, and FLP representation dropped to seven seats, compared to 20 for the NFP.

Ratu Ganilau died of leukemia in December 1993, and Ratu Mara was sworn in as president in January 1994. Meanwhile, Rabuka cultivated a pragmatic image to facilitate his international acceptance in the South Pacific, and within Fiji itself he demonstrated his political prowess by holding out a hand of reconciliation to the Indian community. The 1990 constitution had called for a constitutional review before 1997, and in 1995 a three-member commission was appointed led by Sir Paul Reeves, a former governor-general of New Zealand, together with Mr. Tomasi Vakatora representing the Rabuka government and Mr. Brij Lal for the opposition.

The report of the commission titled *Towards a United Future* was submitted in September 1996. It recommended a return to the voting system outlined in the 1970 constitution with some members of parliament elected from racially divided communal constituencies and others from open ridings with racially mixed electorates. The commissioners suggested that the post of prime minister no longer be explicitly reserved for an indigenous Fijian but simply for the leader of the largest grouping in parliament of whatever race.

The report was passed to a parliamentary committee for study, and in May 1997 all sides agreed to a power-sharing formula to resolve Fiji's constitutional impasse. The number of guaranteed seats for indigenous Fijians in the lower house was reduced from 37 to 23, and voting across racial lines was instituted in another third of the seats. The prime minister was to be required to form a cabinet comprised of ministers from all parties in proportion to their representation in parliament—a form of power sharing unique in modern democracy. Nearly half the members of the senate and the country's president would continue to be appointed by the Great Council of Chiefs. Human rights guarantees were included. The Constitution Amendment Bill passed both houses of parliament unanimously, and was promulgated into law by President Mara on 25 July 1997. In July 1998 the new constitution formally took effect and the first election under it will be in 1999. In recognition of the rare national consensus that had been achieved, Fiji was welcomed back into the British Commonwealth in October 1997.

## FIJI AT A GLANCE

| DIVISION/ PROVINCE | HEADQUARTERS | AREA (square km) | POPULATION (1996) | PERCENT FIJIAN |
|---|---|---|---|---|
| Central Division | Suva | 4,293 | 297,255 | 59.5 |
| Naitasiri | Vunidawa | 1,666 | 126,441 | 56.1 |
| Namosi | Navua | 570 | 5,893 | 91.4 |
| Rewa | Nabalili | 272 | 101,193 | 58.6 |
| Serua | Navua | 830 | 15,495 | 55.1 |
| Tailevu | Nausori | 955 | 48,233 | 67.7 |
| **WESTERN DIVISION** | **LAUTOKA** | **6,360** | **295,891** | **39.4** |
| Ba | Lautoka | 2,634 | 211,080 | 33.2 |
| Nadroga | Sigatoka | 2,385 | 54,049 | 52.5 |
| Ra | Nanukuloa | 1,341 | 30,762 | 59.4 |
| **NORTHERN DIVISION** | **LABASA** | **6,198** | **138,754** | **46.9** |
| Macuata | Labasa | 2,004 | 80,151 | 28.2 |
| Bua | Nabouwalu | 1,378 | 14,977 | 73.6 |
| Cakaudrove | Savusavu | 2,816 | 43,626 | 72.0 |
| **EASTERN DIVISION** | **LEVUKA** | **1,422** | **40,755** | **89.4** |
| Kadavu | Vunisea | 478 | 9,539 | 99.2 |
| Lau | Lakeba | 487 | 12,203 | 98.6 |
| Lomaiviti | Levuka | 411 | 16,203 | 91.2 |
| Rotuma | Ahau | 46 | 2,810 | 5.8 |
| **TOTAL FIJI** | **SUVA** | **18,272** | **772,655** | **51.1** |

For many years it was unfashionable to look upon Fiji as a part of Melanesia and the Polynesian links were emphasized. The 1987 coups had a lot to do with rivalry between the eastward-looking chiefs of Bau and Lau and the Melanesian-leaning western Fijians. Ironically, some of the political friction between the dark-skinned commoner General Rabuka and the tall aristocrat Ratu Mara can also be seen in this light. The latter was always networking among Fiji's smaller Polynesian neighbors and it was only in 1996 that Prime Minister Rabuka brought Fiji into the Melanesian Spearhead grouping that had existed since 1988. Of course, the pragmatist Rabuka was merely acknowledging the vastly greater economic potential of Melanesia, but he was clearly much more comfortable socializing with the other Melanesian leaders at regional summits than Ratu Mara could ever have been. The events of 1987 only delayed a natural process that seems now to have resumed.

## GOVERNMENT

Fiji's constitution provides for a parliamentary system of government with a 71-seat House of Representatives or "lower house" consisting of 46 members from communal ridings and 25 from multiracial ridings with elections every five years. Twenty-three communal seats are reserved for indigenous Fijians, 19 for Fiji Indians, three for general electors (part-Fijians, Europeans, Chinese, etc.), and one for Rotumans. Voting is compulsory (F$50 fine for failing to vote). The 32-member "upper house" or Senate has 14 members appointed by the Great Council of Chiefs, nine by the prime minister, eight by the leader of the opposition, and one by the Council of Rotuma. Any legislation affecting the rights of indigenous Fijians must be approved by nine of the 14 senators appointed by the chiefs.

Aside from the national government, there's a well-developed system of local government. On the Fijian side, the basic unit is the village *(koro)* represented by a village herald *(turaga-ni-koro)* chosen by consensus. The 1,169 villages and 483 settlements are grouped into 189 districts *(tikina)*, the districts into 14 provinces *(yasana)*, the provinces into four administrative divisions: central, eastern, northern, and western. The executive head of a provincial council is known as a *roko tui*, and each division except eastern is headed by a commissioner assisted by a number of district officers. The Micronesians of Rabi and Polynesians of Rotuma govern themselves through island councils of their own. Ten city and town councils also function.

*Taro, which grows marvelously well in the rich soils of Fiji's bush gardens, is one of the staples of the Pacific and ensures a steady supply of nourishing food for the villagers.*

# ECONOMY

Fiji has a diversified economy based on tourism, sugar production, garment manufacturing, gold mining, timber, commercial fishing, and coconut products. Although eastern Viti Levu and the Lau Group have long dominated the country politically, western Viti Levu remains Fiji's economic powerhouse, with sugar, tourism, timber, and gold mining all concentrated there.

## Sugar

Almost all of Fiji's sugar is produced by small independent Indian farmers on contract to the government-owned Fiji Sugar Corporation, which took over from the Australian-owned Colonial Sugar Refining Company in 1973. Some 23,000 farmers cultivate cane on holdings averaging 4.5 hectares leased from indigenous Fijians. The corporation owns 595 km of 0.610-meter narrow-gauge railway, which it uses to carry the cane to the mills at Lautoka, Ba, Rakiraki, and Labasa. Nearly half a million metric tonnes of sugar are exported annually to Britain, Malaysia, Japan, and other countries, providing direct employment for 35,000 people. Workers cutting cane earn F$6 a day and two meals. A distillery at Lautoka produces rum and other liquors from the by-products of sugar. Over the next few years the viability of Fiji's sugar industry may be badly shaken as European Union import quotas are phased out (under the Lomé Convention, 163,000 metric tonnes of Fijian sugar are sold to the E.U. each year at fixed prices far above world market levels). If lease payments were concurrently increased, thousands of Fiji's cane growers would face bankruptcy.

### HOW A SUGAR MILL WORKS

The sugarcane is fed through a shredder toward a row of huge rollers that squeeze out the juice. The crushed fiber (bagasse) is burned to fuel the mill or is processed into paper. Lime is then added to the juice and the mixture is heated. Impurities settle in the clarifier and mill mud is filtered out to be used as fertilizer. The clear juice goes through a series of evaporators, in which it is boiled into steam under partial vacuum to remove water and create a syrup. The syrup is boiled again under greater pressure in a vacuum pan, and raw sugar crystals form. The mix then enters a centrifuge, which spins off the remaining syrup (molasses—used for distilling or cattle feed). The moist crystals are sent on to a rotating drum, where they are tumble-dried using hot air. Raw sugar comes out in the end.

## Timber

Timber is increasingly important as tens of thousands of hectares of softwood planted in western Viti Levu and Vanua Levu by the Fiji Pine Commission and private landowners in the late 1970s reach maturity. In addition, around 30,000 hectares of hardwood (74% of it mahogany) planted in southeastern Viti Levu after 1952 by the British is almost ready for harvesting (another 20,000 hectares in central Vanua Levu will be mature in a decade). The government-controlled Fiji Hardwood Corporation was set up in 1997 to manage this asset. Fiji already exports about F$40 million a year in sawed lumber and wood chips (the export of raw logs was banned in 1987). Yet Fiji's native forests outside the managed plantations are poorly protected from the greed of foreign logging companies and shortsighted local landowners, and each year large tracts of pristine rainforest are lost. Now that all of the lowland forests have been cleared, attention is turning to the highlands. The pine and mahogany projects have had the corollary benefit of reducing pressure on the natural forests to supply Fiji's timber needs.

## Fishing

Commercial fishing is important, with a government-subsidized tuna cannery at Levuka supplied in part by Fiji's own fleet of 17 longline vessels. The 15,000 metric tonnes of canned skipjack and albacore tuna produced each year comprise Fiji's fifth-largest export, shipped mostly to Britain and Canada (see **Ovalau** for more information). In addition, 3,000 tonnes of chilled yellowfin tuna is air freighted to Hawaii and Japan to serve the *sashimi* (raw fish) market.

**Mining**

Mining activity centers on gold from Vatukoula on northern Viti Levu and from Mount Kasi on Vanua Levu with other gold fields awaiting development (in 1998 Mount Kasi closed due to low world prices). Since 1984 Placer Pacific has spent US$10 million exploring the extensive low-grade copper deposits at Namosi, 30 km northwest of Suva, but in 1997, despite offers of near tax-free status from the government, the company put the US$1-billion project on hold as uneconomic.

**Rice**

Fiji now grows almost half its own rice needs and is trying to become self-sufficient. Much of the rice is grown around Nausori and Navua and on Vanua Levu. Most of Fiji's copra is produced in Lau, Lomaiviti, Taveuni, and Vanua Levu, half by European or part-Fijian planters and the rest by indigenous Fijian villagers. Copra production has slipped from 40,000 tonnes a year in the 1950s to about 10,000 tonnes today due to the low prices paid to producers.

**Garment Industry**

The garment industry employs 15,000, with female workers earning an average of F$30 a week. At peak periods the factories operate three shifts, seven days a week. Women working in the industry have complained of body searches and sexual harassment, with those who protest or organize industrial action fired and blacklisted. About 1,000 recently arrived Asian workers are also employed in the factories. The clothing produced by the 68 companies in the sector is exported mostly to Australia and New Zealand, where partial duty- and quota-free entry is allowed under the South Pacific Regional Trade and Economic Cooperation Agreement (SPARTECA) for products with at least 50% local content, and some manufacturers in those countries have moved their factories to Fiji to take advantage of the low labor costs. SPARTECA rules prevent local manufacturers from importing quality fabrics from outside the region, limiting them to the bottom end of the market.

**Other Manufacturing**

Food processors and furniture and toy makers are also prominent in the tax-free exporting sector. Until recently it was believed that manufacturing would overtake both sugar and tourism as the main source of income for the country, but the "globalization" of trade and progressive reduction of tariffs worldwide is cutting into Fiji's competitiveness. SPARTECA's local-content rule discourages local companies from reducing costs by introducing labor-saving technology, condemning them to obsolescence in the long term.

**Agriculture**

Aside from this cash economy, subsistence agriculture makes an important contribution to the life of indigenous Fijians in rural areas. Most are involved in subsistence agriculture, with manioc, taro, yams, sweet potato, and corn the principal subsistence crops. Kava is the fastest growing agricultural crop and in 1996 F$2.5 million worth of the roots was exported to Germany, the U.S., and other countries where they're used by major pharmaceutical firms to make antidepressants and muscle-relaxing drugs. Large European, American, and Japanese corporations have filed multiple patents in an attempt to monopolize the many uses of the plant. It's believed that kava could eventually overtake sugar as a moneymaker unless new plantations in Hawaii, Australia, and Mexico steal the market.

**Economic Problems**

Yet, in spite of all this potential, unemployment is a major social problem as four times more young people leave school than there are new jobs to take them. Immediately after the 1987 coups Fiji's currency was devalued 33% and in January 1998 the Fiji dollar was devalued another 20%. These moves increased the country's competitiveness by giving exporters more Fiji dollars for their products and encouraged tourism while lowering the real incomes of ordinary Fijians. To stimulate industry, firms that export 95% of their production are granted 13-year tax holidays, the duty-free import of materials, and freedom to repatriate capital and profits.

**Trade and Aid**

Fiji's balance of trade has improved in recent years, and although the country still imports 30%

more than it exports, much of the imbalance is resold to tourists and foreign airlines who pay in foreign exchange. Raw sugar is the nation's largest visible export earner, followed by garments, unrefined gold, canned fish, wood chips, molasses, sawed timber, and ginger, in that order. Yet trade imbalances still exist with Australia, Japan, and New Zealand.

Mineral fuels used to eat up much of Fiji's import budget, but this declined when the Monasavu Hydroelectric Project and other self-sufficiency measures came on-line in the 1980s. Manufactured goods, motor vehicles, food, petroleum products, and chemicals account for most of the import bill.

Fiji is the least dependent South Pacific nation. Overseas aid totals only US$50 million a year or about US$65 per capita (as compared to several thousand dollars per capita in Tahiti-Polynesia). Development aid is well diversified among over a dozen donors; the largest amounts come from the European Union (US$20.5 million), Australia (US$16.8 million), New Zealand (US$4.6 million), and Japan (US$3.8 million). Canadian and U.S. aid to Fiji is negligible. The New Zealand Government deserves a lot of credit for devoting much of its limited aid budget to the creation of national parks and reserves. Aside from conventional aid, in 1996 Fiji earned F$11.4 million from United Nations peacekeeping duties while the army's role in other multinational forces brought in further F$5.8 million (to date about 20 Fijian soldiers have been killed in Lebanon). Some 3,650 people serve in Fiji's military (800 of them overseas) costing the country over F$40 million a year.

In 1995 Fiji's financial standing was severely shaken when it was announced that the government-owned National Bank of Fiji was holding hundreds of millions of dollars in bad debts resulting from politically motivated loans to indigenous Fijian and Rotuman politicians and businesspeople. The subsequent run on deposits cost the bank another F$20 million, and the government was forced to step in to save the bank and cover its losses. In 1996 F$80 million was spent on the bailout and in 1997 another F$133 million (or 12% of the 1997 budget) was diverted from development projects to cover it. Rising public indebtedness and deficit spending are discouraging foreign investment, and Fiji's Customs and Excise Department is said to be riddled with corruption. The 1999 elections will bring in Fiji's first democratic government in a dozen years and it will have its hands full putting the country back on course.

### Law of the Sea

This treaty has changed the face of the Pacific. States traditionally exercised sovereignty over a

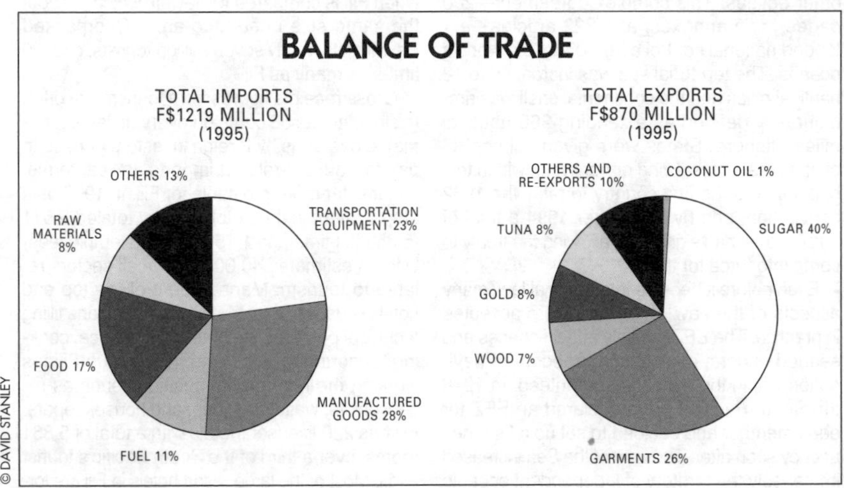

three-mile belt of territorial sea along their shores; the high seas beyond those limits could be freely used by anyone. Then on 28 September 1945, President Harry Truman declared U.S. sovereignty over the natural resources of the adjacent continental shelf. U.S. fishing boats soon became involved in an acrimonious dispute with several South American countries over their rich anchovy fishing grounds, and in 1952 Chile, Ecuador, and Peru declared a 200-nautical-mile exclusive economic zone along their shores. In 1958 the United Nations convened a Conference on the Law of the Sea at Geneva, which accepted national control over shelves up to 200 meters deep. Agreement could not be reached on extended territorial sea limits.

National claims multiplied so much that in 1974 another U.N. conference was convened, leading to the signing of the Law of the Sea convention at Jamaica in 1982 by 159 states and other entities. This complex agreement—200 pages, nine annexes, and 320 articles—extended national control over 40% of the world's oceans. The territorial sea was increased to 12 nautical miles and the continental shelf was ambiguously defined as extending 200 nautical miles offshore. States were given full control over all resources, living or nonliving, within this belt. Fiji was the first country to ratify the 1982 convention, and by November 1994 a total of 60 countries had signed up, allowing the treaty to come into force for them.

Even before it became international law, many aspects of the Law of the Sea were accepted in practice. The EEZs mainly affect fisheries and seabed mineral exploitation; freedom of navigation within the zones is guaranteed. In 1976 the South Pacific Forum declared an EEZ for each member and decided to set up a fisheries agency soon after. The Law of the Sea increased immensely the territory of independent oceanic states, giving them real political weight for the first time. The land area of the 23 separate entities in Micronesia, Melanesia, and Polynesia (excluding Hawaii and New Zealand) total only 550,361 square km, while their EEZs total 29,878,000 square km! It's known that vast mineral deposits are scattered across this seabed, though the cost of extraction (estimated at US$1.5 billion) has prevented their exploitation to date.

**Tourism**

Tourism is the leading money-maker, earning over F$500 million a year—more than sugar and gold combined. Tourism surpassed sugar in 1989 and in the five years that followed its contribution to the gross domestic product increased from 28% to 32%. In 1997 some 359,441 tourists visited Fiji—more than twice as many as visited Tahiti and 15 times as many as visited Tonga. Things appear in better perspective, however, when Fiji is compared to Hawaii, which is about the same size in surface area. Overpacked Hawaii gets nearly seven million tourists, over 20 times as many as Fiji.

Gross receipts figures from tourism are often misleading, as 56 cents on every dollar is repatriated overseas by foreign investors or used to pay for tourism-related imports. In real terms, sugar is far more profitable for Fiji. In 1997 paid employment in the hotel industry totaled 6,511 (5,358 full-time and 1,153 part-time employees) with an estimated 40,000 jobs in all sectors related to tourism. Management of the top end hotels is usually expatriate, with Fiji Indians filling technical positions such as maintenance, cooking, accounting, etc., and indigenous Fijians working the high-profile positions such as receptionists, waiters, guides, and housekeepers. Fiji has 220 licensed hotels with a total of 5,861 rooms, over a third of the South Pacific's tourist beds. Most of the large resort hotels in Fiji are foreign owned (although the Tanoa and Cathay hotel chains are local Fiji-based enterprises). The Fiji Government is doing all it can to promote luxury hotel development by offering 20-year tax holidays on new projects.

The main tourist resorts are centered along the Coral Coast of Viti Levu and in the Mamanuca Islands off Nadi/Lautoka. For years the Fiji government declared there would never be any hotel development in the Yasawa and Lau groups, but several resorts exist there now (including one owned by the president). Investment by the U.S. hotel chains is on the increase as Japanese firms pull out. In 1996 ITT-Sheraton bought two luxury hotels on Nadi's Denarau Island from a group of Japanese banks and about the same time Hyatt announced a multi-million dollar investment in a new hotel adjacent to the Sheratons. Outrigger Hotels of Hawaii is building a major resort on the Coral Coast. About 23% of Fiji's tourists come from Australia, 19% from New Zealand, 13% from Japan, 11% from the U.S., nine percent from continental Europe, eight percent from Britain, and four percent from Canada. The vast majority of visitors arrive in Fiji to/from Auckland, Sydney, Tokyo, Honolulu, Los Angeles, and Vancouver.

## Ecotourism

Recently "ecotourism" has become the thing, and with increasing concern in Western countries over the damaging impact of solar radiation, more and more people are looking for land-based activities as an alternative to lying on the beach. This trend is also fueled by the "baby boomers" who hitchhiked around Europe in the 1970s. Today they're looking for more exotic locales in which to practice "soft adventure tourism" and they've got a lot more disposable income to spend this time around. In the South Pacific the most widespread manifestation of the ecotourism/adventure phenomenon is the current scuba diving boom, and tours by chartered yacht, ocean kayak, surfboard, bicycle, or on foot are proliferating.

This presents both a danger and an opportunity. Income from visitors wishing to experience nature gives local residents and governments an incentive for preserving the environment, although tourism can quickly degrade that environment through littering, the collection of coral and shells, and the development of roads, docks, and resorts in natural areas. Means of access created for ecotourists often end up being used by local residents whose priority is not conservation. Perhaps the strongest argument in favor of the creation of national parks and reserves in the South Pacific is the ability of such parks to attract visitors from industrialized countries while at the same time creating a framework for the preservation of nature. For in the final analysis, it is governments that must enact regulations to protect the environment—market forces usually do the opposite.

Too often what is called ecotourism is actually packaged consumer tourism with a green coating, or just an excuse for high prices. Some four-wheel-drive jeep safaris and jet boat excursions have more to do with ecoterrorism than ecotourism. A genuine ecotourism resort will be built of local materials using natural ventilation. This means no air conditioning and only limited use of fans. The buildings will fit into the natural landscape and not restrict access to customary lands or the sea. Local fish and vegetables will have preference over imported meats on tourist tables, and wastes will be minimized. The use of aggressive motorized transport will be kept to an absolute minimum. Cultural sensitivity will be enhanced by profit sharing with the landowning clans and local participation in ownership. It's worth considering all of this as a flood of phony ecotourism facilities are popping up.

Through this handbook we've tried to encourage this type of people-oriented tourism, which we feel is more directly beneficial to the islanders themselves. Whenever possible we've featured smaller, family-operated, locally owned businesses. By patronizing these you'll not only get to meet the inhabitants on a person-to-person basis, but also contribute to local development. Guesthouse tourism offers excellent employment opportunities for island women as proprietors, *and* it's exactly what most visitors want. Appropriate tourism requires little investment, there's less disruption, and full control remains with the people themselves. Luxury a/c hotels are monotonously uniform around the world—the South Pacific's the place for something different.

# THE PEOPLE

## ETHNIC GROUPS

### The Fijians

Fiji is a transitional zone between Polynesia and Melanesia. Fijians bear a physical resemblance to the Melanesians, but like the Polynesians, they have hereditary chiefs, patrilineal descent, a love of elaborate ceremonies, and a fairly homogeneous language and culture. Fijians have interbred with Polynesians to the extent that they have lighter skin and larger stature than other Melanesians. In the interior and west of Viti Levu where the contact was less, the people tend to be somewhat darker and smaller than the easterners. Yet Fijians still have Melanesian frizzy hair, while most—but not all—Polynesians have straight hair.

The Fijians live in villages along the rivers or coast, with anywhere from 50 to 400 people led by a hereditary chief. To see a Fijian family living in an isolated house in a rural area is uncommon. The traditional thatched *bure* is fast disappearing from Fiji as villagers rebuild in tin and panel (often following destructive cyclones). Grass is not as accessible as cement, takes more time to repair, and is less permanent.

Away from the three largest islands the population is almost totally Fijian. *Mataqali* (clans) are grouped into *yavusa* of varying rank and function. Several *yavusa* form a *vanua,* a number of which make up a *matanitu.* Chiefs of the most important *vanua* are known as high chiefs. In western Viti Levu the groups are smaller, and outstanding commoners can always rise to positions of power and prestige reserved for high chiefs in the east.

Fijians work communal land individually, not as a group. Each Fijian is assigned a piece of native land. They grow most of their own food in village gardens, and only a few staples such as tea, sugar, flour, etc., are imported from Suva and sold in local coop stores. A visit to one of these stores will demonstrate just how little they import and how self-sufficient they are. Fishing, village maintenance work, and ceremonial presentations are done together. While village life provides a form of collective security, individuals are discouraged from rising above the group. Fijians who attempt to set up a business are often stifled by the demands of relatives and friends. The Fijian custom of claiming favors from members of one's own group is known as *kerekere.* This pattern makes it difficult for Fijians to compete with Indians, for whom life has always been a struggle. A Fijian will stand and wait his turn while an Indian will crowd and fight to be first.

**The Indians**

Most of the Indians now in Fiji are descended from indentured laborers recruited in Bengal and Bihar a century ago. In the first year of the system (1879) some 450 Indians arrived in Fiji to work in the cane fields. By 1883 the total had risen to 2,300 and in 1916, when the last indentured laborers arrived, 63,000 Indians were present in the colony. In 1920 the indenture system was finally terminated, the cane fields were divided into four-hectare plots, and the Indian workers became tenant farmers on land owned by Fijians. Indians continued to arrive until 1931, though many of these later arrivals were Gujerati or Sikh businesspeople.

In 1940 the Indian population stood at 98,000, still below the Fijian total of 105,000, but by the 1946 census Indians had outstripped Fijians 120,000 to 117,000—making Fijians a minority in their own home. In the wake of the coups the relative proportions changed as thousands of Indians emigrated to North America and Australia, and by early 1989 indigenous Fijians once again outnumbered Fiji Indians. The 1996 census reported that Fiji's total population was 772,655, of which 51.1% were Fijian while 43.6% were Indian (at the 1986 census 46% were Fijian and 48.7% Indian). Between 1986 and 1996 the number of Indians in Fiji actually decreased by 12,125 with the heaviest falls in rural areas. Aside from emigration, the more widespread use of contraceptives by Indian women has led to a lower fertility rate. The crude birth rate per 1,000 population is 28.4 for Fijians and 21.0 for Fiji Indians.

Unlike the village-based Fijians, a majority of Indians are concentrated in the cane-growing areas and live in isolated farmhouses, small settlements, or towns. Many Indians also live in Suva, as do an increasing number of Fijians. Within the Fiji Indian community there are divisions of Hindu (80%) versus Muslim (20%), north Indian versus south Indian, and Gujerati versus the rest. The Sikhs and Gujeratis have always been somewhat of an elite as they immigrated freely to Fiji outside the indenture system.

CAINES JANIF LTD., SUVA

*The descendants of late 19th-century arrivals, such as this characterful young woman, make up the majority of Fiji's population today. These indentured laborers faced many hardships and indignities, one of which stemmed from a British policy of allowing only 40 Indian women to be brought to the island for every 100 men.*

The different groups have kept alive their ancient religious beliefs and rituals. Hindus tend to marry within their caste, although the restrictions on behavior, which characterize the caste system in India, have disappeared. Indian marriages are often arranged by the parents, while the Fijians generally choose their own partners. Rural Indians still associate most closely with other members of their extended patrilineal family group, and Hindu and Muslim religious beliefs still restrict Indian women to a position subservient to men.

It's often said that Indians concentrate on accumulation while Fijians emphasize distribution. Yet Fiji's laws themselves encourage Indians to invest their savings in business by preventing them or anyone else from purchasing native communal land. High-profile Indian dominance of the retail sector has distorted the picture and the reality is that the per capita incomes of ordinary indigenous Fijians and Fiji Indians are not that different. The Fijians are not "poor" because they are exploited by Indians; the two groups simply amass their wealth in different ways. In large measure, Fiji's excellent service and retail industries exist thanks to the thrift and efficiency of the Indians. When you consider their position in a land where most have lived four generations and where they form almost half the population, where many laws are slanted against them, and where all natural resources are in the hands of others, their industriousness and patience are admirable.

### Other Groups

The 5,000 Fiji-born Europeans or *Kai Vavalagi* are descendants of Australians and New Zealanders who came to create cotton, sugar, or copra plantations in the 19th century. Many married Fijian women, and the 13,000 part-Fijians or *Kai Loma* of today are the result. There is almost no intermarriage between Fijians *(Kai Viti)* and Fiji Indians *(Kai India)*. Many other Europeans are present in Fiji on temporary contracts or as tourists.

Most of the 5,000 Chinese in Fiji are descended from free settlers who came to set up small businesses a century ago, although since 1987 there has been an influx of Chinese from mainland China who were originally admitted to operate market gardens but who have since moved into the towns. Fiji Chinese tend to intermarry freely with the other racial groups.

The people of Rotuma, a majority of whom now live in Suva, are Polynesians. On neighboring islands off Vanua Levu are the Micronesians of Rabi (from Kiribati) and the Polynesians of Kioa (from Tuvalu). The descendants of Solomon Islanders blackbirded during the 19th century still live in communities near Suva, Levuka, and Labasa. The Tongans in Lau and other Pacific islanders who have immigrated to Fiji make this an ethnic crossroads of the Pacific.

### Social Conditions

Some 98% of the country's population was born in Fiji. The partial breakdown in race relations after the Rabuka coups was a tragedy for Fiji, though racial antagonism has been exaggerated and the different ethnic groups have always gotten along remarkably well together, with little animosity. You may hear individuals make disparaging remarks about the other group, but it's highly unlikely you'll witness any real confrontations. Gabriel Teoman of Erl, Austria, who visited Fiji in early 1998, sent us this comment:

> *Concerning Fijian-Indian relations, I have to say that, all in all, I'm very impressed. Never did I hear any Fijian badmouth the Indians (and don't worry, I subtly tried to stir things up), and only occasionally did I hear Indians complain about Fijian laziness or drunkenness. Comments about land rights or politics always seemed to be directed towards the people in charge, not the next door neighbor. In three months I did not see one nasty incident, but many Fijians and Indians sharing grog, stories, wedding ceremonies, laughs. I know it's not a multicultural paradise, and there might very well be stronger tensions underneath the surface, but compared to so many other places, Europe included, the transcultural interaction seemed amazingly encouraging. I heard many anti-Indian prejudices before coming here (money-grabbing, etc.). But for me, they were just as friendly, funny, and hospitable as the Fijians.*

As important as race are the variations between rich and poor, or urban (46%) and rural (54%). Avenues for future economic growth are limited, and there's chronic unemployment. The lack of work is reflected in an increasing crime rate. Two-thirds of the rural population is without electricity. Although Fiji's economy grew by 25% between 1977 and 1991, the number of people living in poverty increased by two-thirds over the same period. The imposition in 1992 of a 10% value-added tax combined with reductions in income tax and import duties shifted the burden of taxation from the haves to the have nots. A quarter of the population now lives in poverty, and contrary to the myth of Indian economic domination, Fiji Indians are more likely to be facing poverty than members of other groups, as the beggars on the streets of Nadi and Suva attest. Single-parent urban families cut off from the extended-family social safety net are the group most effected, especially women trying to raise families on their own. As a Fijian woman on Taveuni said to the author: "Life is easy in Fiji, only money is a problem."

Literacy is high at 87%. Primary education is compulsory for all children aged six to 13 but many schools are still racially segregated. Over 100 church-operated schools receive government subsidies. The Fiji Institute of Technology was founded at Suva in 1963, followed by the University of the South Pacific in 1968. The university serves the 12 Pacific countries that contribute to its costs. Medical services in Fiji are heavily subsidized. The main hospitals are at

Labasa, Lautoka, and Suva, though smaller hospitals, health centers, and nursing stations are scattered around the country. The most common infectious diseases are influenza, gonorrhea, and syphilis. At birth male citizens of Fiji have a life expectancy of 72 years, the longest in the South Pacific, and women average 75 years.

## LAND RIGHTS

When Fiji became a British colony in 1874, the land was divided between white settlers who had bought plantations and the *taukei ni gele,* the Fijian "owners of the soil." The government assumed title to the balance. Today the alienated (privately owned) plantation lands are known as "freehold" land—about 10% of the total. Another seven percent is Crown land and the remaining 83% is inalienable Fijian communal land, which can be leased (about 30% is) but may never be sold. Compare this 83% (much of it not arable) with only three percent Maori land in New Zealand and almost zero native Hawaiian land. Land ownership has provided the Fijians with a security that allows them to preserve their traditional culture, unlike indigenous peoples in most other countries.

Communal land is administered on behalf of some 6,600 clan groups *(mataqali)* by the Native Land Trust Board, a government agency established in 1940. The NLTB retains 25% of the lease money to cover administration, and a further 10% is paid directly to regional hereditary chiefs. In 1966 the Agricultural Landlord and Tenant Act (ALTA) increased the period for which native land can be leased from 10 to 30 years. The 30-year leases began coming up for renewal in 1997, and from 2000 to 2005 28% of the leases will expire (another 19% will expire from 2006 to 2010). Many Fijian clans say they want their land back so they can farm it themselves, and Fiji's 23,000 Indian sugarcane farmers are becoming highly apprehensive. If rents are greatly increased or the leases terminated, Fiji's sugar industry could be badly damaged and an explosive social situation created. This whole question has become the single most important issue in Fiji politics and in late 1997 a Joint Parliamentary Select Committee began looking into ALTA and the possible resettlement of Indian farmers whose leases cannot be extended.

At the First Constitutional Conference in 1965, Indian rights were promulgated, and the 1970 independence constitution asserted that everyone born in Fiji would be a citizen with equal rights. These rights are reaffirmed in the 1997 constitution. But land laws, right up to the present, have very much favored "Fiji for the Fijians." Fiji Indians have always accepted Fijian ownership of the land, provided they are granted satisfactory leases. Now that the leases seem endangered, many Indians fear they will be driven from the only land they've ever known. The stifling of land development may keep Fiji quaint for tourists, but it also condemns a large portion of the population of both races to backwardness and poverty.

## GENDER ISSUES

### Women in Fiji

Traditionally indigenous Fijian women were confined to the home, while the men would handle most matters outside the immediate family. The clear-cut roles of the woman as homemaker and the man as defender and decision-maker gave stability to village life. Western education has caused many Fijian women to question their subordinate position and the changing lifestyle has made the old relationship between the sexes outmoded. Women's liberation has arrived! As paid employment expands and access to family planning allows women to hold jobs, they demand equal treatment from society. Fijian women are more emancipated than their sisters in the other Melanesian countries, though men continue to dominate public life throughout the region. Tradition is often manipulated to deny women the right to express themselves publicly on community matters.

Cultural barriers hinder women's access to education and employment, and the proportion of girls in school falls rapidly as the grade level increases. Female students are nudged into low-paying fields such as nursing or secretarial services; in Fiji and elsewhere, export-oriented garment factories exploit women workers with low wages and poor conditions. Levels of domestic violence vary greatly, though it's far less accepted among indigenous Fijians than it is among Fiji Indians, and in Fiji's Macuata Province women have a suicide rate seven times above the world average, with most of the victims being Indians. Those little signs on buses reading "real men don't hit women" suggest the problem. Travelers should take an interest in women's issues.

## RELIGION

The main religious groups in Fiji are Hindus (290,000), Methodists (265,000), Catholics (70,000), Muslims (62,000), Assemblies of God (33,000), and Seventh-Day Adventists (20,000). Around 40% of the total population is Hindu or Muslim due to the large Indian population, and only two percent of Indians have converted to Christianity despite Methodist missionary efforts dating back to 1884. About 78% of indigenous Fijians are Methodist, 8.5% Catholic.

The ecumenical **Pacific Conference of Churches** (Box 208, Suva, Fiji; tel. 311-277, fax 303-205) began in 1961 as an association of the mainstream Protestant churches, but since 1976 many Catholic dioceses have been included as well. Both the Pacific Theological College (founded in 1966) and the Pacific Regional Seminary (opened in 1972) are in southern Suva, and the South Pacific is one of the few areas of the world with a large surplus of ministers of religion.

Since the 1987 military coups, an avalanche of well-financed American fundamentalist missionary groups has descended on Fiji and membership in the Assemblies of God and some other new Christian sects is growing quickly at the expense of the Methodists. While the Methodist Church has long been localized, the new evangelical sects are dominated by foreign personnel, ideas, and money. The ultraconservative outlook of the new religious imperialists continues the tradition of allying Christianity with colonialism or neocolonialism.

The fundamentalists tend to portray God as a white man and discourage self-sufficiency by telling the islanders to await their reward in heaven. They stress passages in the Bible calling for obedience to authority and resignation, often providing the ideological justification for the repression of dissent, as happened immediately after the military coups in Fiji.

### Mormons

You don't have to travel far in the South Pacific to find the assembly-line Mormon chapels, schools, and sporting facilities, paid for by church members who are expected to tithe 10% of their incomes. The Mormon church spends over US$500 million a year on foreign missions and sends out almost 50,000 missionaries, more than any other American church by far. Like Thor Heyerdahl, Mormons believe that Polynesia was settled by American Indians, who were themselves descendants of the 10 lost tribes of Israel and must be reconverted to hasten the second coming of Christ. Thus the present church is willing to spend a lot of time and money

## HANNAH DUDLEY'S LEGACY

One of the few Methodist missionaries to achieve lasting success proselytizing among Fiji's Indian community was an Englishwoman named Hannah Dudley who had previously worked in India where she learned Hindustani. An individualist unwilling to follow the usual rules for white evangelists laid down by the male-managed mission of her day, "our Miss Dudley" (as her fellow missionaries called her) arrived in Suva in 1903 to work among the indentured Indian laborers. Hannah adopted vegetarianism as a step toward godliness and visited the Hindu and Muslim women in their own homes as only a woman could. Through the woman she made contact with the men, and her Bible classes soon created a circle of Indian converts in Suva. Although conditions for the Indians of her day were harsh, Hannah didn't protest to the colonial authorities as some other Methodist missionaries had, but gathered the needy and lost around her. Her own home became an orphanage and her Indian contacts and converts soon came to know her as *mataji,* the little mother. When Hannah returned to Calcutta in 1905 to work with the Bengali Mission, she took her orphans along. In 1934 members of the Indian Methodist congregation in Suva erected the Dudley Memorial Church on the spot where Hannah first preached. The white building, strongly influenced by Hindu architecture, can still be seen at the corner of Toorak Road and Amy Street, just up the hill from downtown Suva.

spreading the word. The Mormons are especially successful in countries such as Tonga and Samoa, which are too poor to provide public education for all. There's a strong link to Hawaii's Brigham Young University (www.byuh.edu), and many island students help pay for their schooling by representing their home country at the Mormon-owned Polynesian Cultural Center on Oahu.

In Fiji, Mormon missionary activity is a recent phenomenon, as prior to a "revelation" in 1978 blacks were barred from the Mormon priesthood. Due to a change in government policies, the number of Mormon missionaries granted Fijian visas has increased tenfold since 1987, and 90% of the money used to support Mormon activities in Fiji comes from the church headquarters in Utah. The pairs of clean-cut young Mormon "elders" seen on the outliers—each in shirt and tie, riding a bicycle or driving a minibus—are sent down from the States for two-year stays.

### Other Religious Groups

More numerous than the Mormons are adherents of the **Seventh-Day Adventist Church,** a politically ultra-conservative group that grew out of the 19th century American Baptist movement. This is the largest non-historical religious group in the South Pacific, and in Fiji they operate the Fulton Teacher Training College at Nakalawaca just south of Korovou in Tailevu Province. The SDA Church teaches the imminent return of Christ, and Saturday (rather than Sunday) is observed as the Sabbath. SDAs regard the human body as the temple of the Holy Spirit, thus much attention is paid to health matters. Members are forbidden to partake of certain foods, alcohol, drugs, and tobacco, and the church expends considerable energy on the provision of medical and dental services. They're also active in education and local economic development.

The **Assemblies of God** (AOG) is a Pentecostal sect founded in Arkansas in 1914 and presently headquartered in Springfield, Missouri. Although the AOG carries out some relief work, it opposes social reform in the belief that only God can solve humanity's problems. The sect is strongest in Fiji, where their numbers increased twelvefold between 1966 and 1992. A large AOG Bible College operates in Suva, and from Fiji the group has spread to other Pacific countries. Disgraced American tele-evangelists Jimmy Swaggart and Jim Bakker were both former AOG ministers.

The **Jehovah's Witnesses** originated in 19th century America and since 1909 their headquarters has been in Brooklyn, from whence their worldwide operations are financed. Jehovah's Witnesses' teachings against military service and blood transfusions have often brought them into conflict with governments, and they in turn regard other churches, especially the Catholic Church, as instruments of the Devil. Members must spread the word by canvassing their neighborhood door-to-door, or by standing on streetcorners offering copies of *The Watchtower.* This group focuses mostly on Christ's return, and since "the end of time" is fast approaching, it has little interest in relief work.

## LANGUAGE

Fijian, a member of the Austronesian family of languages spoken from Easter Island to Madagascar, has more speakers than any other indigenous Pacific language. Fijian vowels are pronounced as in Latin or Spanish, while the consonants are similar to those of English. Syllables end in a vowel, and the next-to-last syllable is usually the one emphasized. Where two vowels appear together they are sounded separately. In 1835 two Methodist missionaries, David Cargill and William Cross, devised the form of written Fijian used in Fiji today. Since all consonants in Fijian are separated by vowels, they spelled *mb* as *b, nd* as *d, ng* as *g, ngg* as *q,* and *th* as *c.*

Though Cargill and Cross worked at Lakeba in the Lau Group, the political importance of tiny Bau Island just off Viti Levu caused the Bauan dialect of Fijian to be selected as the "official" version of the language, and in 1850 a dictionary and grammar were published. When the Bible was translated into Bauan that dialect's dominance was assured, and it is today's spoken and written Fijian. From 1920 to 1970 the use of Fijian was discouraged in favor of English, but since independence there has been a revival.

Hindustani or Hindi is the household tongue of most Fiji Indians. Fiji Hindi has diverged from that spoken in India with the adoption of many words from English and other Indian languages such as Urdu. Though a quarter of Fiji Indians are descended from immigrants from southern India where Tamil and Telegu are spoken, few use those languages today, even at home. Fiji Muslims speak Hindi out of practical considerations, though they might consider Urdu their mother tongue. In their spoken forms, Hindi and Urdu are very similar. English is the second official language in Fiji and is understood by almost everyone. All schools teach exclusively in English after the fourth grade. Fiji Indians and indigenous Fijians usually communicate with one another in English. Gilbertese is spoken by the Banabans of Rabi.

See the Capsule Fijian Vocabulary and the Capsule Hindi Vocabulary for some useful words and phrases.

# CUSTOMS

Fijians and Fiji Indians are very tradition-oriented peoples who have retained a surprising number of their ancestral customs despite the flood of conflicting influences that have swept the Pacific over the past century. Rather than a melting pot where one group assimilated another, Fiji is a patchwork of varied traditions.

The obligations and responsibilities of Fijian village life include not only the erection and upkeep of certain buildings, but personal participation in the many ceremonies that give their lives meaning. Hindu Indians, on the other hand, practice firewalking and observe festivals such as Holi and Diwali, just as their forebears in India did for thousands of years.

### Fijian Firewalking

In Fiji, both Fijians and Indians practice firewalking, with the difference being that the Fijians walk on heated stones instead of hot embers. Legends tell how the ability to walk on fire was first given to a warrior named Tui-na-viqalita from Beqa Island, just off the south coast of Viti Levu, who had spared the life of a spirit god he caught while fishing for eels. The freed spirit gave to Tui-na-viqalita the gift of immunity to fire. Today his descendants act as *bete* (high priests) of the rite of *vilavilairevo* (jumping into the oven). Only members of his tribe, the Sawau, perform the ceremony. The Tui Sawau lives at Dakuibeqa village on Beqa, but firewalking is now only performed at the resort hotels on Viti Levu.

Fijian firewalkers (men only) are not permitted to have sex or to eat any coconut for two weeks prior to a performance. A man whose wife is pregnant is also barred. In a circular pit about four meters across, hundreds of large stones are first heated by a wood fire until they're white-hot. If you throw a handkerchief on the stones, it will burst into flames. Much ceremony and chanting accompanies certain phases of the ritual, such as the moment when the wood is removed to leave just the white-hot stones. The men psych themselves up in a nearby hut, then emerge, enter the pit, and walk briskly once around it. Bundles of leaves and grass are then thrown on the stones and the men stand inside the steaming pit again to chant a final song. They seem to have complete immunity to pain and there's no trace of injury. The men appear to fortify themselves with the heat, to gain some psychic power from the ritual.

### Indian Firewalking

By an extraordinary coincidence, Fiji Indians brought with them the ancient practice of religious firewalking. In southern India, firewalking occurs in the pre-monsoon season as a call to the goddess Kali (Durga) for rain. Fiji Indian firewalking is an act of purification, or fulfillment of a vow to thank the god for help in a difficult situation.

In Fiji there is firewalking in most Hindu temples once a year, at full moon sometime between May and September according to the Hindu calendar. The actual event takes place on a Sunday at 1600 on the Suva side of Viti Levu, and at 0400 on the Nadi/Lautoka side. In August firewalking takes place at the Sangam Temple on Howell Road, Suva. During the 10 festival days preceding the walk, participants remain in isolation, eat only unspiced vegetarian food, and spiritually prepare themselves. There are prayers at the temple in the early morning and a group singing of religious stories evenings from Monday through Thursday. The yellow-clad devotees, their faces painted bright yellow

THE FIJI TIMES

*Spikes piercing their cheeks, Fiji Indians walk over hot coals at a religious festival, to purify themselves or give thanks to Durga for assistance rendered.*

and red, often pierce their cheeks or other bodily parts with spikes or three-pronged forks as part of the purification rites. Their faith is so strong they feel no pain.

The event is extremely colorful; drumming and chanting accompany the visual spectacle. Visitors are welcome to observe the firewalking, but since the exact date varies from temple to temple according to the phases of the moon (among other factors), you just have to keep asking to find out where and when it will take place. To enter the temple you must remove your shoes and any leather clothing.

### The *Yaqona Ceremony*

*Yaqona* (kava), a tranquilizing, nonalcoholic drink that numbs the tongue and lips, comes from the *waka* (dried root) of the pepper plant *(Macropiper methysticum).* This ceremonial preparation is the most honored feature of the formal life of Fijians, Tongans, and Samoans. It is performed with the utmost gravity according to a sacramental ritual to mark births, marriages, deaths, official visits, the installation of a new chief, etc.

New mats are first spread on the floor, on which is placed a handcarved *tanoa* (wooden bowl) nearly a meter wide. A long fiber cord decorated with cowry shells leads from the bowl to the guests of honor. At the end of the cord is a white cowry, which symbolizes a link to ancestral spirits. As many as 70 men take their places before the bowl. The officiants are adorned with tapa, fiber, and croton leaves, their torsos smeared with glistening coconut oil, their faces usually blackened.

The guests present a bundle of *waka* to the hosts, along with a short speech explaining their visit, a custom known as a *sevusevu.* The *sevusevu* is received by the hosts and acknowledged with a short speech of acceptance. The *waka* are then scraped clean and pounded in a *tabili* (mortar). Formerly they were chewed. Nowadays the pulp is put in a cloth sack and mixed with water in the *tanoa.* In the chiefly ceremony the *yaqona* is kneaded and strained through *vau* (hibiscus) fibers.

The mixer displays the strength of the grog (kava) to the *mata ni vanua* (master of ceremonies) by pouring out a cupful into the *tanoa.* If the *mata ni vanua* considers the mix too strong, he calls for *wai* (water), then says *lose* (mix), and the mixer proceeds. Again he shows the consistency to the *mata ni vanua* by pouring out a cupful. If it appears right the *mata ni vanua* says *loba* (squeeze). The mixer squeezes the remaining juice out of the pulp, puts it aside, and announces, *sa lose oti saka na yaqona, vaka turaga* (the kava is ready, my chief). He runs both hands around the rim of the *tanoa* and claps three times.

The *mata ni vanua* then says *talo* (serve). The cupbearer squats in front of the *tanoa* with a *bilo* (half coconut shell), which the mixer fills. The cupbearer then presents the first cup to the guest of honor, who claps once and drains it, and everyone claps three times. The second cup goes to the guests' *mata ni vanua,* who claps once and drinks. The man sitting next to the mixer says *aa,* and everyone answers *maca* (empty). The third cup is for the first local chief, who claps once before drinking, and everyone claps three times after. Then the *mata ni vanua* of the first local chief claps once and drinks, and everyone says *maca.* The same occurs for the second local chief and his *mata ni vanua.*

After these six men have finished their cups, the mixer announces, *sa maca saka tu na yaqona, vaka turaga* (the bowl is empty, my chief), and the *mata ni vanua* says *cobo* (clap). The mixer then runs both hands around the rim of the *tanoa* and claps three times. This terminates the full ceremony, but then a second bowl is prepared and everyone drinks. During the drinking of the first bowl complete silence must be maintained.

### Social Kava Drinking

While the above describes one of several forms of the full *yaqona* ceremony, which is performed only for high chiefs, abbreviated versions are put on for tourists at the hotels. However, the village people have simplified grog sessions almost daily. Kava drinking is an important form of Fijian entertainment and a way of structuring friendships and community relations. Even in government offices a bowl of grog is kept for the staff to take as a refreshment at *yaqona* breaks. Some say the Fijians have *yaqona* rather than blood in their veins. Excessive kava drinking over a long period can make the skin scaly and rough, a condition known as *kanikani.*

Individual visitors to villages are invariably invited to participate in informal kava ceremonies, in which case it's customary to present a bunch of kava roots to the group. Do this at the beginning, before anybody starts drinking, and make a short speech explaining the purpose of your visit (be it a desire to meet the people and learn about their way of life, an interest in seeing or doing something in particular on their island, or just a holiday from work). Don't hand the roots to anyone, just place them on the mat in the center of the circle. The bigger the bundle of roots, the bigger the smiles. (The roots are easily purchased at any town market for about F$13 a half kilo.)

Clap once when the cupbearer offers you the *bilo,* then take it in both hands and say *"bula"* just before the cup meets your lips. Clap three times after you drink. Remember, you're a participant, not an onlooking tourist, so don't take photos if the ceremony is rather formal. Even though you may not like the appearance or taste of the drink, do try to finish at least the first cup. Tip the cup to show you're done.

It's considered extremely bad manners to turn your back on a chief during a kava ceremony, to walk in front of the circle of people when entering or leaving, or to step over the long cord attached to the *tanoa.*

### Presentation of the *Tabua*

The *tabua* is a tooth of the sperm whale. It was once presented when chiefs exchanged delegates at confederacy meetings and before conferences on peace or war. In recent times, the *tabua* is presented during chiefly *yaqona* cere-

*Draped in croton leaves, the cupbearer offers a bowl of* yaqona *to a visiting chief at a formal kava ceremony.*

MINISTRY OF INFORMATION, GOVERNMENT OF FIJI

## TABUA

*Yaqona* (or kava) the Fijians share with the Polynesians, but the *tabua,* or whale's tooth, is significant only in Fiji. The *tabuas* obtained from the sperm whale have always played an important part in Fijian ceremonies. During great festivals they were hung around the necks of warriors and chiefs in the 19th century; even today they are presented to distinguished guests and are exchanged at weddings, births, deaths, reconciliations, and also when personal or communal contracts or agreements are entered into. *Tabuas,* contrary to popular belief, have never been used as a currency and will not purchase goods or services. To be presented with a *tabua* is a great honor.

FIELD MUSEUM OF NATURAL HISTORY, CHICAGO

monies as a symbolic welcome for a respected visitor or guest or as a prelude to public business or modern-day official functions. On the village level, *tabuas* are still commonly presented to arrange marriages, to show sympathy at funerals, to request favors, to settle disputes, or simply to show respect.

Old *tabuas* are highly polished from continuous handling. The larger the tooth, the greater its ceremonial value. *Tabuas* are prized cultural property and may not be exported from Fiji. Endangered species laws prohibit their entry into the United States, Australia, and many other countries.

### Stingray Spearing and Fish Drives

Stingrays are lethal-looking creatures with caudal spines up to 18 centimeters long. To catch them, eight or nine punts are drawn up in a line about a kilometer long beside the reef. As soon as a stingray is sighted, a punt is paddled forward with great speed until close enough to hurl a spear.

Another time-honored sport and source of food is the fish drive. An entire village participates. Around the flat surface of a reef at rising tide, sometimes as many as 70 men and women group themselves in a circle a kilometer or more in circumference. All grip a ring of connected liana vines with leaves attached. While shouting, singing, and beating long poles on the seabed, the group slowly contracts the ring as the tide comes in. The shadow of the ring alone is enough to keep the fish within the circle. The fish are finally directed landward into a net or stone fish trap.

### The Rising of the *Balolo*

Among all the Pacific island groups, this event takes place only in Samoa and Fiji. The *balolo (Eunice viridis)* is a thin, segmented worm of the Coelomate order, considered a culinary delicacy throughout these islands—the caviar of the Pacific. It's about 45 cm long and lives deep in the fissures of coral reefs. Twice a year it releases an unusual "tail" that contains its eggs or sperm. The worm itself returns to the coral to regenerate a new reproductive tail. The rising of the *balolo* is a natural almanac that keeps both lunar and solar times, and has a fixed day of appearance—even if a hurricane is raging—one night in the last quarter of the moon in October, and the corresponding night in November. It has never failed to appear on time for over 100 years now, and you can even check your calendar by it.

Because this rising occurs with such mathematical certainty, Fijians are waiting in their boats to scoop the millions of writhing, reddish brown (male) and moss green (female) spawn

MINISTRY OF INFORMATION, GOVERNMENT OF FIJI

*closing the ring during a Beqa fish drive*

from the water when they rise to the surface before dawn. Within an hour after the rising, the eggs and sperm are released to spawn the next generation of *balolo*. The free-swimming larvae seek a suitable coral patch to begin the cycle again. This is one of the most bizarre curiosities in the natural history of the South Pacific, and the southeast coast of Ovalau is a good place to observe it.

## CONDUCT

Foreign travel is an exceptional experience enjoyed by a privileged few. Too often, tourists try to transfer their lifestyles to tropical islands, thereby missing out on what is unique to the region. Travel can be a learning experience if approached openly and with a positive attitude, so read up on the local culture before you arrive and become aware of the social and environmental problems of the area. A wise traveler soon graduates from hearing and seeing to listening and observing. Speaking is good for the ego and listening is good for the soul.

The path is primed with packaged pleasures, but pierce the bubble of tourism and you'll encounter something far from the schedules and organized efficiency: a time to learn how other people live. Walk gently, for human qualities are as fragile and responsive to abuse as the brilliant reefs. The islanders are by nature soft-spoken and reserved. Often they won't show open disapproval if their social codes are broken, but don't underestimate them: they understand far more than you think. Consider that you're only one of thousands of visitors to their country, so don't expect to be treated better than anyone else. Respect is one of the most important things in life and humility is also greatly appreciated.

If you're alone you're lucky, for the single traveler is everyone's friend. Get away from other tourists and meet the people. There aren't many places on earth where you can still do this meaningfully, but Fiji is one. If you do meet people with similar interests, keep in touch by writing. This is no tourist's paradise, though, and local residents are not exhibits or paid performers. They have just as many problems as you, and if you see them as real people you're less likely to be viewed as a stereotypical tourist. You may have come to escape civilization, but keep in mind that you're just a guest.

Most important of all, try to see things their way. Take an interest in local customs, values, languages, challenges, and successes. If things work differently than they do back home, give thanks—that's why you've come. Reflect on what you've experienced and you'll return home with a better understanding of how much we all have in common, outwardly different as we may seem. Do that and your trip won't have been wasted.

**Fijian Customs**

It's a Fijian custom to smile when you meet a stranger and say something like "Good morning," or at least "Hello." Of course, you needn't do this in large towns, but you should almost everywhere else. If you meet someone you know, stop for a moment to exchange a few words.

Fijian villages are private property and it's important to get permission before entering one. Of course it's okay to continue along a road that passes through a village, but do ask before leaving the road. It's good manners to take off your hat while walking through a village, where only the chief is permitted to wear a hat. Some villagers also object to sunglasses. Objects such as backpacks, handbags, and cameras are better carried in your hands rather than slung over your shoulders. Alcohol is usually forbidden. Don't point at people in villages.

If you wish to surf off a village, picnic on their beach, or fish in their lagoon, you should also ask permission. You'll almost always be made most welcome and granted any favors you request if you present a *sevusevu* of kava roots to the village headman or chief. If you approach the Fijians with respect you're sure to be so treated in return.

Take off your shoes before entering a *bure* and stoop as you walk around inside. Clap three times when you join people already seated on mats on the floor. Men should sit cross-legged, women with their legs to the side. Sitting with your legs stretched out in front is insulting. Fijian villagers consider it offensive to walk in front of a person seated on the floor (pass behind) or to fail to say *tulou* (excuse me) as you go by. Don't stand up during a *sevusevu* to village elders. When you give a gift hold it out with both hands, not one hand. Never place your hand on another's head and don't sit in doorways.

Fijian children are very well behaved, and there's no running or shouting when you arrive in a village, and they leave you alone if you wish. The Fijians love children, so don't hesitate to bring your own. You'll never have to worry about finding a baby-sitter. Just make sure your children understand the importance of being on their best behavior in the village. Do you notice how Fijians rarely shout? In Fiji, raising your voice is a sign of anger.

**Dress**

It's important to know that the dress code in Fiji is strict. Short shorts, halter tops, and bathing costumes in public shows a lack of respect, and in the context of a Fijian village it's considered offensive: a *sulu* wrapped around you solves this one. Men should always wear a shirt in town, and women should wear dresses that adequately cover their legs while seated. Nothing will mark you so quickly as a tourist nor make you more popular with street vendors than scanty dress. Of course, there *is* a place for it: on the beach in front of a resort hotel. In a society where even bathing suits are considered extremely risqué for local women, public nudity is unthinkable, and topless sunbathing by women is also banned in Fiji (except at isolated island resorts).

**Questions**

The islanders are eager to please, so phrase your questions carefully. They'll answer yes or no according to what they think you want to hear—don't suggest the answer in your question. Test this by asking your informant to confirm something you know to be incorrect. Also don't ask negative questions, such as "you're not going to Suva, are you?" Invariably the answer will be "yes," meaning "yes, I'm not going to Suva." It also could work like this: "Don't you have anything cheaper?" "Yes." "What do you have that is cheaper?" "Nothing." Yes, he doesn't have anything cheaper. If you want to be sure of something, ask several people the same question in different ways.

**Dangers and Annoyances**

In Suva, beware of the seemingly friendly Fijian men (usually with a small package or canvas bag in their hands) who will greet you on the street with a hearty *Bula!* These are "sword sellers" who will ask your name, quickly carve it on a mask, and then demand F$20 for a set that you could buy at a Nadi curio shop for F$5. Other times they'll try to engage you in conversation and may offer a "gift." Just say "thank you very much" and walk away from them quickly without accepting anything, as they can suddenly become unpleasant and aggressive. Their grotesque swords and masks themselves have nothing to do with Fiji.

Similarly, overly sociable people at bars may expect you to buy them drinks. In the main tourist centers such as Nadi and Suva, take care if a local invites you to visit his home as you may be seen mainly as a source of beer and other goods.

Although *The Fiji Times* is often full of stories of violent crimes including assaults, robberies, and burglaries, it's partly the very novelty of these events that makes them worth reporting. Fiji is still a much safer country than the U.S. and tourists are not specifically targeted for attack, but normal precautions should still be taken. Keep to well lit streets at night, take a taxi if you've had more than one drink, and steer clear of robust, poorly dressed Fijian men who may accost you on the street for no reason. Don't react if offered drugs. It's wise to keep valuables locked in your bag in hotel rooms.

Women should have few real problems traveling around Fiji on their own, so long as they're prepared to cope with frequent offers of marriage. Although a female tourist shouldn't have to face sexist violence the way a local woman might, it's smart to be defensive and to lie about where you're staying. If you want to be left alone, conservative dress and purposeful behavior will work to your advantage. In village situations seek the company of local women.

Littering is punished by a minimum F$40 fine and breaking bottles in public can earn six months in jail (unfortunately seldom enforced).

LOUISE FOOTE

M.G.L. DOMENY DE RIENZI

# ON THE ROAD

## Highlights

Fiji's many attractions are hard to shortlist but two outstanding natural features on the south side of Viti Levu are the Sigatoka Sand Dunes and the Navua River with its cliff-hugging rapids. Tavewa and Wayasewa in the Yasawa Group combine abundant natural beauty with budget accommodations.

Fiji's finest bus rides take you through open rolling countryside from Lautoka to Rakiraki, or across the mountains of Vanua Levu from Savusavu to Labasa. Without doubt, the most picturesque town is the old capital Levuka, and Suva has some of the South Pacific's most exciting nightlife. There are many candidates for best beach, reef, and outer island: all are tops. Two weeks is the absolute minimum amount of time required to get a feel for Fiji, and one month is much better.

## Parks and Reserves

The **National Trust for Fiji** (Box 2089, Government Buildings, Suva, Fiji; tel. 301-807, fax 305-092) administers eight national parks and historic sites. Of these the Sigatoka Sand Dunes National Park and the Waisali Nature Reserve near Savusavu both have visitor centers easily accessible by public bus. Koroyanitu National Park, inland from Lautoka, is also easily reached and has accommodations for hikers. Although not an official reserve, the forested area around Nadarivatu in central Viti Levu is similar. The nature reserves at Bouma and Lavena on the northeastern side of Taveuni feature unspoiled rainforests and waterfalls reached along hiking trails. Colo-i-Suva Forest Park behind Suva also beckons the ecotourist with quiet walks through a mahogany forest. Further information on all of these is provided later in this handbook.

# SPORTS AND RECREATION

## Hiking

All of the high islands offer hiking possibilities and many remote villages are linked by well-used trails. The most important hike described in this book is the two-day Sigatoka River Trek down the Sigatoka River from Nadarivatu. Levuka makes an excellent base with the trail to The Peak beginning right behind the town, and a challenging cross-island trail to Lovoni is nearby. More arduous is the all-day climb to Lake Tagimaucia on Taveuni. For some outer island hiking, you can walk right around Nananu-i-Ra in under a day, or across Waya or Wayasewa. Kadavu offers many hiking possibilities.

## Surfing

A growing number of surfing camps are off southern and western Viti Levu. The most famous is Tavarua Island in the Mamanuca Group, accessible only to American surfers on pre-packaged tours from the States. Other mortals can also use speedboats from Seashell Cove Resort to surf nearby reef breaks at far less expense, or stay at the new top-end surf resort on Namotu Island right next to Tavarua. Beach break surfing is possible at Club Masa near Sigatoka, and budget surfing camps have been built on Yanuca and Kadavu islands. Surfing is also possible at Suva and from the Waidroka Bay Resort on the Coral Coast. Few of Fiji's waves are for the beginner, especially the reef breaks, and of course, you must bring your own board(s). There's surf throughout the year with the best swells out of the south from March to October.

Fijian clans control the fishing rights on their reefs and on many islands they also claim to own the surfing rights. This can also apply at breaks off uninhabited islands and even ocean reefs. In past upmarket surfing camps like Tavarua, Marlin Bay, and Namotu have paid big bucks to try to corner the right to surf famous waves like Cloudbreak and Frigates, and they often attempt to keep surfers from rival resorts away. On Yanuca Island a couple of Americans put a lot of time and money into building a surf camp, only to have the waves pulled out from under them when the moneymaking potential of the activity became apparent. Although none of this is enshrined in law, it's wise to check whether you'll actually be allowed to surf the environs before booking into a surfing resort in Fiji as things change fast. Once there, you'll soon become acquainted with the current situation. When surfing in a remote area without facilities it's important to present a *sevusevu* to the local chief and be on your best behavior.

## Windsurfing

Windsurfing is possible at a much wider range of locales, and many upmarket beach hotels off southern and western Viti Levu include equipment in their rates. Windsurfing is possible at most of the Mamanuca resorts, including Castaway, Musket Cove, Naitasi Resort, Navini Island, Plantation Island, Tokoriki, and Treasure Island. Other offshore resorts around Fiji offering windsurfing are Kaimbu Island, Matana Resort, Naigani Island, Qamea Beach, Toberua Island, Turtle Island, and Vatulele. Almost all of the surfing camps also offer windsurfing. For those on a budget, check out the windsurfing at Nadi's Club Fiji.

## Boating

Exciting **whitewater rafting** on the Upper Navua River is offered. In central Viti Levu, villagers will pole you through the Waiqa Gorge on a bamboo raft from Naitauvoli to Naivucini villages.

In the past, organized **ocean kayaking** expeditions have been offered among the Yasawa Islands, around Kadavu, and in Vanua Levu's Natewa Bay (see "Getting There," below, for details of sea kayaking tours). Those who only want to dabble can hire kayaks at Kadavu, Taveuni, and Savusavu. Several upmarket Mamanuca Resorts loan kayaks to their guests.

Get in some **sailing** by taking one of the day cruises by yacht offered from Nadi. Yacht charters are offered at Musket Cove Resort in the Mamanuca Group.

## Golf

Golfers are well catered to in Fiji. The two most famous courses are the Denarau Golf Club, next to the two Sheraton hotels at Nadi, and the Pacific Harbor Country Club, one of the finest courses in the Pacific. Many tourist hotels have golf courses, including the Mocambo at Nadi; the Fijian Resort Hotel, Reef Resort, and Naviti Beach Resort on the south side of Viti Levu; Naigani Island Resort and Wakaya Club in Lomaiviti; and Taveuni Estates on Taveuni. More locally oriented are the city golf courses at Nadi Airport, Lautoka, and in Suva, and the company-run courses near Rakiraki and Labasa sugar mills and at the Vatukuola gold mine, all built to serve former expatriate staffs. All are open to the public and only the Sheraton course could be considered expensive.

### Team Sports

The soccer season in Fiji is February to November, while rugby is played almost year-round. The main rugby season is June to November when there are 15 players on each side. From November to March it's "sevens" with seven team members to a side. (The Fijians are champion sevens players, "wild, intuitive, and artistic," and in 1997 they defeated South Africa to take the Rugby World Cup Sevens in Hong Kong.) Rugby is played only by Fijians, while soccer teams are both Fijian and Indian. Cricket is played from November to March, mostly in rural areas. Lawn bowling is also popular. Saturday is the big day for team sports.

### Scuba Diving and Snorkeling

Fiji has been called "the soft coral capital of the world" and few experienced divers will deny that Fiji has some of the finest diving in the South Pacific with top facilities at the best prices. If in doubt, you won't go wrong choosing Fiji. The worst underwater visibility conditions here are the equivalent of the finest off Florida. In the Gulf of Mexico you've about reached the limit if you can see for 15 meters; in Fiji visibility begins at 15 meters and increases to 45 meters in some places.

Diving is possible year-round in Fiji, with the marinelife most profuse from July to November. Water temperatures vary from 24° C in June, July, and August to 30° C in December, January, and February. Many fantastic dives are just 10 or 15 minutes away from the resorts by boat (whereas at Australia's Great Barrier Reef the

## 10 SAFETY RULES OF DIVING

1. The most important rule in scuba diving is to BREATHE CONTINUOUSLY. If you establish this rule, you won't forget and hold your breath, and overexpansion will never occur.
2. COME UP AT A RATE OF 18 METERS PER MINUTE OR LESS. This allows the gas dissolved in your body under pressure to come out of solution safely and also prevents vertigo from fast ascents. Always make a precautionary decompression stop at a depth of five meters.
3. NEVER ESCAPE TO THE SURFACE. Panic is the diver's worst enemy.
4. STOP, THINK, THEN ACT. Always maintain control.
5. PACE YOURSELF. KNOW YOUR LIMITATIONS. A DIVER SHOULD ALWAYS BE ABLE TO REST AND RELAX IN THE WATER. Proper use of the buoyancy vest will allow you to rest on the surface and maintain control under water. A diver who becomes fatigued in the water is a danger to himself and his buddy.
6. NEVER DIVE WITH A COLD. Avoid alcoholic beverages but drink plenty of water. Get a good night's sleep and refrain from strenuous physical activities on the day you dive. Dive conservatively if you are overweight or more than 45 years of age. Make fewer dives the last two days before flying and no dives at all during the final 24 hours.
7. PLAN YOUR DIVE. Know your starting point, your diving area, and your exit areas. DIVE YOUR PLAN.
8. NEVER EXCEED THE SAFE SPORT DIVING LIMIT OF 30 METERS. Make your first dive the deepest of the day.
9. All equipment must be equipped with QUICK RELEASES.
10. WEAR ADEQUATE PROTECTIVE CLOTHING AGAINST SUN AND CORAL.

speedboats often have to travel over 60 km to get to the dive sites). Fiji is a relatively safe place to dive since one of the only recompression chambers in the South Pacific is at Suva (tel. 305-154 in Suva or 850-630 in Savusavu). A nationwide Medevac service is on 24-hour standby at tel. 362-172.

Facilities for scuba diving exist at most of the resorts in the Mamanuca Group, along Viti Levu's Coral Coast and at Pacific Harbor, on Kadavu, Leleuvia, Beqa, Nananu-i-Ra, Tavewa, and Wayasewa, at Nadi, Lautoka, and Savusavu, and on Taveuni and adjacent islands. Low-budget divers should turn to the Kadavu, Leleuvia, Taveuni, Tavewa, and Wayasewa sections in this book. Specialized non-hotel dive shops are found at Nadi, Pacific Harbor, Lautoka, Savusavu, and on Taveuni. Serious divers will bring along their own mask, buoyancy compensator, and regulator. If you've never dived before, Fiji is an excellent place to learn, and the Kadavu, Leleuvia, Nadi, Nananu-i-Ra, Pacific Harbor, Taveuni, Tavewa, and Wayasewa scuba operators offer certification courses taking four or five days from budget accommodations. Many of the scuba operators listed in this book also offer introductory "resort courses" for those who only want a taste of scuba diving. For information about live-aboard dive boats see "Scuba Cruises," which follows.

Even if you aren't willing to put the necessary money and effort into scuba diving, you'd be foolish not to check out the many snorkeling possibilities. Some dive shops take snorkelers out in their boats for a nominal rate, but there are countless places around Fiji where you can snorkel straight out to the reef for free, mostly on smaller outer islands. The beach snorkeling off Viti Levu and Vanua Levu is usually poor and a complete waste of time around Nadi, Lautoka, Pacific Harbor, Suva, and Labasa. The snorkeling along the Coral Coast is fair but only at high tide. Around Savusavu sharp rocks make it hard to get into the water at all (and the top beaches are private). On the other hand, you'll have no trouble finding fabulous reefs in the Mamanuca Group, the Yasawas, off Nananu-i-Ra, Kadavu, Ono, and Taveuni, and at the small resort islands near Ovalau.

Be careful, however, and know the dangers. Practice snorkeling in the shallow water; don't head into deep water until you're sure you've got the hang of it. Breathe easily; don't hyperventilate. When snorkeling on a fringing reef, beware of deadly currents and undertows in channels that drain tidal flows. Observe the direction the water is flowing before you swim into it. If you feel yourself being dragged out to sea through a reef passage, try swimming across the current rather than against it. If you can't resist the pull at all, it may be better to let yourself be carried out. Wait till the current diminishes, then swim along the outer reef face until you find somewhere to come back in. Or use your energy to attract the attention of someone onshore.

Snorkeling on the outer edge or drop-off of a reef is thrilling for the variety of fish and corals, but attempt it only on a very calm day. Even then it's wise to have someone stand onshore or paddle behind you in a canoe to watch for occasional big waves, which can take you by surprise and smash you into the rocks. Also, beware of unperceived currents outside the reef—you may not get a second chance.

A far better idea is to limit your snorkeling to the protected inner reef and leave the open waters to the scuba diver. Yet while scuba diving quickly absorbs large amounts of money, snorkeling is free and you can do it as often as you like. You'll encounter the brightest colors in shallow waters anyway as beneath six meters the colors blue out as short wavelengths are lost. By diving with a tank you trade off the chance to observe shallow water species in order to gain access to the often larger deep water species. The best solution is to do a bit of both. In any case, avoid touching the reef or any of its creatures as the contact can be very harmful to both you and the reef. Take only pictures and leave only bubbles.

# ENTERTAINMENT

It's cheap to go to the movies in towns such as Labasa, Lautoka, Ba, Nadi, Nausori, and Suva if a repertoire of romance, horror, or adventure is to your liking. These same towns have local nightclubs where you can enjoy as much drinking and dancing as you like without spending an arm and a leg. When there's live music, a cover charge is collected.

A South Pacific institution widespread in Fiji is the old colonial clubs that offer inexpensive beer in safe, friendly surroundings. Such clubs are found in Labasa, Lautoka, Levuka, Nadi, Savusavu, Sigatoka, Taveuni, and Tavua, and although they're all private clubs with Members Only signs on the door, foreign visitors are allowed entry (except at the pretentious Union Club in Suva). Occasionally the bartender will ask you to sign the guest book or tell you to request authorization from the club secretary. Many bars and clubs in Fiji refuse entry to persons dressed in flip-flops, boots, rugby jerseys, shorts, singlets, or T-shirts, and one must remove one's hat at the door.

RICHARD GOODMAN

*Grasping war clubs, Fijian men perform a* meke.

Fiji's one unique spectacle is the **Fijian firewalking** performed several times a week at the large hotels along the southwest side of Viti Levu: Sheraton Royal (Wednesday), Sheraton-Fiji (Thursday), Fijian Resort Hotel (Friday), Reef Resort (Friday), The Naviti (Wednesday), the Warwick (Friday), and Pacific Harbor (Tuesday and Saturday). A fixed admission price is charged but it's well worth going at least once. For more information on firewalking, see "Customs" in the Introduction. The same hotels that present firewalking usually stage a Fijian *meke* (described below) on an alternate night.

### Fijian Dancing *(Meke)*

The term *meke* describes the combination of dance, song, and theater performed at feasts and on special occasions. Brandishing spears, their faces painted with charcoal, the men wear frangipani leis and skirts of shredded leaves. The war club dance reenacts heroic events of the past. Both men and women perform the *vakamalolo,* a sitting dance, while the *seasea* is danced by women flourishing fans. The *tralala,* in which visitors may be asked to join, is a simple two-step shuffle danced side-by-side (early missionaries forbade the Fijians from dancing face-to-face). As elsewhere in the Pacific the dances tell a story, though the music now is strongly influenced by Christian hymns and contemporary pop. Less sensual than Polynesian dancing, the rousing Fijian dancing evokes the country's violent past. Fijian *meke* are often part of a *magiti* or feast performed at hotels. The Dance Theater of Fiji at Pacific Harbor is well regarded.

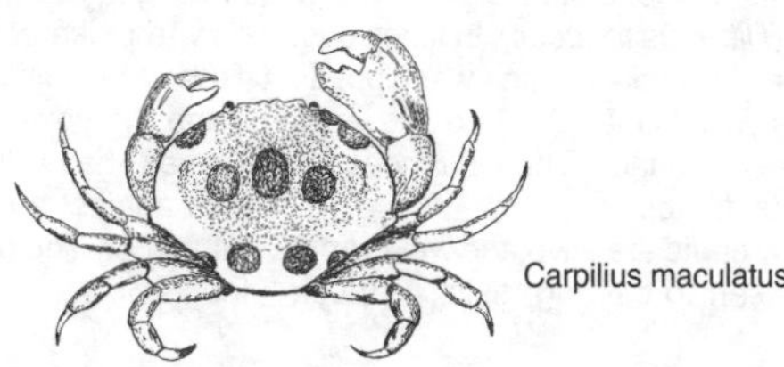

LOUISE FOOTE

Carpilius maculatus

# PUBLIC HOLIDAYS AND FESTIVALS

Public holidays in Fiji include New Year's Day (1 January), National Youth Day (a Friday in early March), Good Friday and Easter Monday (March/April), Ratu Sukuna Day (a Monday or Friday around 29 May), Queen Elizabeth's Birthday (a Monday or Friday around 14 June), Constitution Day (sometime around 27 July), Prophet Mohammed's Birthday (anytime from July to December), Fiji Day (a Monday around 10 October), Diwali (October or November), and Christmas Days (25 and 26 December).

Check with the Fiji Visitors Bureau to see if any festivals are scheduled during your visit. The best known are the Bula Festival in Nadi (July), the Hibiscus Festival in Suva (July or August), the Sugar Festival in Lautoka (September), and the Back to Levuka Festival (early October). Around the end of June there's the President's Cup yacht race at Nadi. Before Diwali, the Hindu festival of lights, Hindus clean their homes, then light lamps or candles to mark the arrival of spring. Fruit and sweets are offered to Lakshmi, goddess of wealth. Holi is an Indian spring festival in February or March.

One of the main sporting events of the year is the **International Bula Marathon** held in June. The main event involves a 42-km run from Lautoka to the Sheraton at Nadi. The **South Pacific Games,** the region's major sporting event, will be in Fiji in 2003.

### When to Go

Compared to parts of North America and Europe, the seasonal climatic variations in Fiji are not extreme. There's a hotter, more humid season from November to April and a cooler, drier time from May to October. Hurricanes can come during the "rainy" season but they only last a few days a year. The sun sets around 1800 year-round and there aren't periods when the days are shorter or longer.

Seasonal differences in airfares should be more influential in deciding when to go. On Air New Zealand flights from North America the low season is mid-April to August, the prime time in Fiji. Christmas is busy but in February and March many hotels stand half empty and special discounted rates are on offer. In short, there isn't really any one season which is the "best" time to go and every season has its advantages.

# ARTS AND CRAFTS

The traditional art of Fiji is closely related to that of Tonga. Fijian canoes, too, were patterned after the more advanced Polynesian type, although the Fijians were timid sailors. War clubs, food bowls, *tanoas* (kava bowls), eating utensils, clay pots, and tapa cloth *(masi)* are considered Fiji's finest artifacts.

There are two kinds of woodcarvings: the ones made from *vesi (Intsia bijuga)*—ironwood in English—or *nawanawa (Cordia subcordata)* wood are superior to those of the lighter, highly breakable *vau (Hibiscus tiliaceus).* In times past it often took years to make a Fijian war club, as the carving was done in the living tree and left to grow into the desired shape. The top *tanoas* are carved in the Lau Group.

Though many crafts are alive and well, some Fijians have taken to carving "tikis" or mock New Guinea masks smeared with black shoe polish to look like ebony for sale to tourists. Also avoid crafts made from endangered species such as sea turtles (tortoise shell) and marine mammals (whales' teeth, etc.). Prohibited entry into most countries, they will be confiscated by customs if found.

### Pottery Making

Fijian pottery making is unique in that it is a Melanesian artform. The Polynesians forgot how to make pottery thousands of years ago. Today the main center for pottery making in Fiji is the Sigatoka Valley on Viti Levu. Here, the women shape clay using a wooden paddle outside against a rounded stone held inside the future pot. The potter's wheel was unknown in the Pacific.

A saucerlike section forms the bottom; the sides are built up using slabs of clay, or coils and strips. These are welded and battered to shape. When the form is ready the pot is dried inside the house for a few days, then heated over an open fire for about an hour. Resin from the gum of the *dakua* (kauri) tree is rubbed on the outside while the pot is still hot. This adds a varnish that brings out the color of the clay and improves the pot's water-holding ability.

This pottery is extremely fragile, which accounts for the quantity of potsherds found on ancient village sites. Smaller, less breakable pottery products such as ashtrays are now made for sale to visitors.

### Weaving

Woven articles are the most widespread handicrafts. Pandanus fiber is the most common, but coconut leaf and husk, vine tendril, banana stem, tree and shrub bark, the stems and leaves of water weeds, and the skin of the sago palm leaf are all used. On some islands the fibers are passed through a fire, boiled, then bleached in the sun. Vegetable dyes of very lovely mellow tones are sometimes used, but gaudier store dyes are much more prevalent. Shells are occasionally utilized to cut, curl, or make the fibers pliable.

### Tapa Cloth

This is Fiji's most characteristic traditional product. Tapa is light, portable, and inexpensive, and a piece makes an excellent souvenir to brighten up a room back home. It's made by women on Vatulele Island off Viti Levu and on certain islands of the Lau Group.

To make tapa, the inner, water-soaked bark of the paper mulberry *(Broussonetia papyrifera)* is stripped from the tree and steeped in water. Then it's scraped with shells and pounded into a thin sheet with wooden mallets. Four of these sheets are applied one over another and pounded together, then left to dry in the sun.

While Tongan tapa is decorated by holding a relief pattern under the tapa and overpainting the lines, Fijian tapa *(masi kesa)* is distinctive for its rhythmic geometric designs applied with stencils made from green pandanus and banana leaves. The stain is rubbed on in the same manner in which temple rubbings are made from a stone inscription.

The only colors used are red, from red clay, and a black pigment obtained by burning candlenuts. Both powders are mixed with boiled gums made from scraped roots. Sunlight deepens and sets the colors. Each island group had its characteristic colors and patterns, ranging from plantlike paintings to geometric designs. Sheets of tapa feel like felt when finished. On some islands tapa is still used for clothing, bedding, and room dividers, and as ceremonial red carpets. Tablecloths, bedcovers, place mats, and wall hangings of tapa make handsome souvenirs.

*Fijian* masi *(tapa)*

# SHOPPING

Most large shops in Fiji close at 1300 on Saturday but smaller grocery stores are often open on Sunday. After the 1987 military coups most commercial business was suspended on Sunday but these restrictions were dropped in 1996 and you'll find many restaurants and bars now open on Sunday. Fiji Indians dominate the retail trade. If you're buying from an Indian merchant, always bargain hard and consider all sales final. Indigenous Fijians usually begin by asking a much lower starting price, in which case bargaining isn't so important. When bargaining for handicrafts at a market remember that an Indian seller's starting price could be 10 times the real price and that it will be hard to disengage once the bargaining has begun. Avoid the hassle by going straight to the Fijian sellers.

Fiji's "duty-free" shops such as Prouds or Tappoo are not really duty-free, as all goods are subject to various fiscal duties plus the 10% value-added tax. Bargaining is the order of the day, but to be frank, Americans can usually buy the sort of Japanese electrical merchandise sold "duty-free" in Fiji cheaper in the States, where they'll get more recent models. If you do buy something, get an itemized receipt and international guarantee, and watch that they don't switch packages and unload a demo on you. Once purchased, items cannot be returned, so don't let yourself be talked into anything. Camera film is inexpensive, however, and the selection good—stock up.

If you'd like to do some shopping in Fiji, locally made handicrafts such as tapa cloth, mats, kava bowls, war clubs, woodcarvings, etc., are a much better investment (see "Arts and Crafts," above). The four-pronged cannibal forks available everywhere make unique souvenirs, but avoid the masks which are made only for sale to tourists and have nothing to do with Fiji. If you're spending serious money for top-quality work, visit the Fiji Museum and the Government Handicraft Center in Suva beforehand to see what is authentic.

To learn what's available on the tourist market and to become familiar with prices, browse one of the half dozen outlets of **Jacks Handicrafts** around Viti Levu. You'll find them in downtown Nadi, Sigatoka, and Suva, and at the Sheraton-Fiji, Fiji Mocambo, and Warwick hotels. If the sales person is overenthusiastic and begins following you around too closely, just stop and say you're only looking today and they'll probably leave you alone.

*Grog (kava) is mixed in a* tanoa, *such as this fine example carved from a single block of* vesi *wood. It's said that Fijians have* yaqona *rather than blood in their veins.*

FIELD MUSEUM OF NATURAL HISTORY, CHICAGO

You can often purchase your souvenirs directly from the Fijian producers at markets, etc. Just beware of aggressive indigenous Fijian "sword sellers" on the streets of Suva, Nadi, and Lautoka who peddle fake handicrafts at high prices, or high-pressure duty-free touts who may try to pull you into their shops, or self-appointed guides who offer to help you find the "best price." If you get the feeling you're being hustled, walk away.

# ACCOMMODATIONS

With the *Fiji Handbook* in hand you're guaranteed a good, inexpensive place to stay on every island. Each and every hotel in the region is included herein, not just a selection. We consistently do this to give you a solid second reference in case your travel agent or someone else recommends a certain place. To allow you the widest possible choice, all price categories are included, and throughout we've tried to spotlight properties that offer value for money. If you think we're wrong or you were badly treated, be sure to send a us a written complaint. Equally important, let us know when you agree with what's here or if you think a place deserves a better rave. Your letter will have an impact!

We don't solicit freebies from the hotel chains; our only income derives from the price you paid for this book. So we don't mind telling you that, as usual, most of the luxury hotels are just not worth the exorbitant prices they charge. Many simply recreate Hawaii at twice the cost, offering far more luxury than you need. Even worse, they tend to isolate you in a American/Australian environment, away from the Fiji you came to experience. Most are worth visiting as sightseeing attractions, watering holes, or sources of entertainment, but unless you're a millionaire, sleep elsewhere. Plenty of middle-level hotels charge half what the top-end places ask, while providing adequate comfort.

## ACCOMMODATION PRICE RANGES

Throughout this handbook, accommodations are generally grouped in the price categories that follow. Of course, currency fluctuations and inflation can lead to slight variations.

| | |
|---|---|
| Shoestring | under US$15 double |
| Budget | US$15-35 double |
| Inexpensive | US$35-60 double |
| Moderate | US$60-85 double |
| Expensive | US$85-110 double |
| Premium | US$110-150 double |
| Luxury | over US$150 double |

Dormitory, "bunkroom," or backpacker accommodations are available on all of the main islands, with communal cooking facilities usually provided. If you're traveling alone, these are excellent since they're just the place to meet other travelers. Couples can usually get a double room for a price only slightly above two dorm beds. For the most part, the dormitories are safe and congenial for those who don't mind sacrificing their privacy to save money.

Needless to say, always ask the price of your accommodations before accepting them. In cases where there's a local and a tourist price, you'll always pay the higher tariff if you don't check beforehand. Asking first gives you the opportunity to bargain if someone quotes an absurdly high starting price. Otherwise, hotel prices are usually fixed and bargaining isn't the normal way to go.

Be aware that some of the low-budget places included in this book are a lot more basic than what is sometimes referred to as "budget" accommodations in the States. The standards of cleanliness in the common bathrooms may be lower than you expected, the furnishings "early attic," the beds uncomfortable, linens and towels skimpy, housekeeping nonexistent, and window screens lacking, but ask yourself, where in the U.S. are you going to find a room for a similar price? Luckily, good medium-priced accommodations are usually available for those unwilling to put up with Spartan conditions.

When picking a hotel, keep in mind that although a thatched bungalow is cooler and infinitely more attractive than a concrete box, it's also more likely to have insect problems. If in doubt check the window screens and carry mosquito coils and repellent. Hopefully there'll be a resident lizard or two to feed on the bugs. Always turn on a light before getting out of bed to use the facilities at night, as even the finest hotels in the tropics have cockroaches.

A room with cooking facilities can save you a lot on restaurant meals, and some moderately priced establishments have weekly rates. If you have to choose a meal plan, take only breakfast and dinner (Modified American Plan or MAP) and have fruit for lunch. As you check into your room, note the nearest fire exits. And don't automatically take the first room offered; if you're paying good money look at several, then choose.

A 10% government tax is added to all accommodations prices. Most hotels include the tax in their quoted rates, but some don't. You can often tell whether tax is included by looking at the amount: if it's F$33 tax is probably included, whereas if it's F$30 it may not be. When things are slow, specials are offered and some prices become negotiable, and occasionally you'll pay less than the prices quoted in this book. This is most likely to happen in February and March, the lowest tourist season.

### Reserving Ahead

Booking accommodations in advance usually works to your disadvantage as full-service travel agents will begin by trying to sell you their most expensive properties (which pay them the highest commissions) and work down from there. The quite adequate middle and budget places included in this handbook often aren't on their screens or are sold at highly inflated prices. Herein we provide the rates for direct local bookings, and if you book through a travel agent abroad you could end up paying considerably more as multiple commissions are tacked on. Thus we suggest you avoid making any hotel reservations at all before arriving in Fiji (unless you're coming for a major event).

There aren't many islands where it's to your advantage to book ahead in the medium to lower price range, but you can sometimes obtain substantial discounts at the luxury hotels by including them as part of a package tour. Even then, you'll almost always find medium-priced accommodations for less than the package price and your freedom of choice won't be impaired. If, however, you intend to spend most of your time at a specific first-class hotel, you'll benefit from bulk rates by taking a package tour instead of paying the higher "rack rate" the hotels charge to individuals who just walk in off the street. Call Air New Zealand's toll-free number and ask them to mail you their *Go As You Please* brochure, which lists deluxe hotel rooms in Fiji that can be booked on an individual basis at slightly reduced rates. Polynesian Airlines has a similar *Polypac Hotel Accommodation* brochure. Also call Discover Wholesale Travel and some of the other agents listed herein in "Getting There."

### Accommodation Categories

Fiji offers a wide variety of places to stay, from low-budget to world-class. Standard big-city international hotels are found in Nadi and Suva, while many of the upmarket beach resorts are on small islands in the Mamanuca Group off Nadi and along the Coral Coast on Viti Levu's sunny south side. The Mamanuca resorts are secluded, with fan-cooled *bure* accommodations, while at the Coral Coast hotels you often get an a/c room in a main building. The Coral Coast has more to offer in the way of land tours, shopping, and entertainment/eating options, while the offshore resorts are preferable if you want a rest or are into water sports. The Coral Coast beaches are only good at high tide and the reefs are degraded, while on the outer islands the reefs are usually pristine.

In recent years smaller luxury resorts have multiplied in remote locations, from the guest-accepting plantations near Savusavu and on Taveuni to isolated beach resorts on outlying islands such as Kaimbu, Kadavu (Matana), Laucala, Matangi, Beqa, Naigani, Namenalala, Nukubati, Qamea, Toberua, Turtle, Vatulele, Wakaya, and Yasawa. Prices at these begin at several hundred dollars a day and rise to four figures, so some care should be taken in selecting the right one. A few such as Beqa, Matana, and Matangi are marketed almost exclusively to scuba divers, and Namenalala is a good ecotourism choice. If you delight in glamorous socializing with other mixed couples, Turtle and Vatulele are for you. Families are welcome at Castaway, Matangi, Naigani, and Toberua, but children are generally not accepted at Kaimbu, Matamanoa, Nukubati, Nukuyaweni, Qamea, Turtle, Vatulele, Wakaya, and Yasawa. The very wealthy will feel at home on Kaimbu, Laucala, and Wakaya, whereas many of the Mamanuca resorts are designed for larger numbers of guests interested in intensive sporting and social activities.

However, unless you're feeling charitable to the transnational conglomerates that control many of the top hotels, you'll do better by focusing on the middle and bottom ends of the market, while using the big resorts as entertainment sources or sightseeing attractions. Like such places around the world, many of the deluxe hotels are boring, sterile enclaves of affluence carefully shielded from any type of spontaneity. They cater mostly to people on packaged holidays who book through travel agents abroad, while the budget places covered in this book but not in most agents computers go after a younger crowd who decide where they'll stay after reaching Fiji.

Low-budget accommodations are spread out, with concentrations in Korotogo, Nadi, Lautoka, Levuka, Suva, and Savusavu, and on Taveuni. Low-cost outer island beach resorts exist on Kadavu, Leleuvia, Mana, Nananu-i-Ra, Ono, Tavewa, Thaqalai, Waya, and Wayasewa. The largest budget chain in Fiji is Cathay Hotels with properties in Suva, Lautoka, and on the Coral Coast (visit their Fiji For Less website at www.fiji4less.com). At all of these, the easiest way to check on the availability of rooms is to call them up after you get to Fiji.

A few of the cheapies in Suva and Lautoka double as whorehouses, making them cheap in both senses of the word. Women should exercise care in the way they deal with the male staff at low-budget hostels as we've received a few complaints about characters who became a nuisance. Many hotels, both in cities and at the beach, offer dormitory beds as well as individual rooms. Most of the dorms are mixed. Women can sometimes request a women-only dorm when things are slow, but it's usually not guaranteed. Some city hotels lock their front doors at 2300, so ask first if you're planning a night on the town. Several islands with air service from Suva, including Koro, Moala, Gau, and Cicia, have no regular accommodations for visitors at all, so it's good to know someone before heading their way.

### Camping

Camping facilities (bring your own tent) are found at backpacker resorts on Kadavu, Leleuvia, Mana, Ono, Ovalau, Rotuma, Taveuni, Tavewa, Caqalai, Waya, Wayasewa, and Yanuca Lailai Islands. A few shoestring hostels in Nadi and Savusavu also allow it, as do Viti Levu beach resorts like Seashell Cove, The Beachouse, and the Coral Coast Christian Camp. On Vanua Levu, you can camp at Mumu Resort and at Buca Bay. Nature reserves where camping is possible include Colo-i-Suva Forest Park, Nukulau Island off Suva, and at Nadarivatu.

*Camping, Kadavu Island. Where hotels don't exist, your tent is your home away from home.*

Elsewhere, get permission before pitching your tent as all land is owned by someone and land rights are sensitive issues in Fiji. Some freelance campers on beaches such as Natadola near Nadi and around Pacific Harbor have had their possessions stolen, so take care.

In Fijian villages don't ask a Fijian friend for permission to camp beside his house. Although he may feel obligated to grant the request of a guest, you'll be proclaiming to everyone that his home isn't completely to your liking. If all you really want is to camp, make that clear from the start and get permission to do so on a beach or by a river, but *not* in the village. A *sevusevu* should always be presented in this case. There's really nowhere to camp totally for free. Never camp under a coconut tree, as falling coconuts are lethal (actually, coconuts have two eyes so they only strike the wicked).

**Staying in Villages**

The most direct way to meet the Fijian people and learn a little about their culture is to stay in a village for a few nights. A number of hiking tours offer overnighting in remote villages, and it's also possible to arrange it for yourself. If you befriend someone from an outlying island, ask them to write you a letter of introduction to their relatives back in the village. Mail a copy of it ahead with a polite letter introducing yourself, then start slowly heading that way.

In places well off the beaten track where there are no regular tourist accommodations, you could just show up in a village and ask permission of the *turaga-ni-koro* (village herald) to spend the night. Similarly, both Fiji Indians and native Fijians will spontaneously invite you in. The Fijians' innate dignity and kindness should not be taken for granted, however.

All across the Pacific it's customary to reciprocate when someone gives you a gift—if not now, then sometime in the future. Visitors who accept gifts (such as meals and accommodations) from islanders and do not reciprocate are undermining traditional culture and causing resentment, often without realizing it. It's sometimes hard to know how to repay hospitality, but Fijian culture has a solution: the *sevusevu.* This can be money, but it's usually a 500-gram "pyramid" of kava roots *(waka),* which can be easily purchased at any Fijian market for about F$13. *Sevusevus* are more often performed between families or couples about to be married, or at births or christenings, but the custom is certainly a perfect way for visitors to show their appreciation.

We recommend that travelers donate around F$20 pp per night to village hosts (carry sufficient cash in small denominations). The *waka* bundle is additional, and anyone traveling in remote areas of Fiji should pack some (take whole roots, not powdered kava). If you give the money up front together with the *waka* as a *sevusevu,* they'll know you're not a freeloader and you'll get VIP treatment, though in all cases it's absolutely essential to contribute something.

The *sevusevu* should be placed before (not handed to) the *turaga-ni-koro* or village herald so he can accept or refuse. If he accepts (by touching the package), your welcome is confirmed and you may spend the night in the village. It's also nice to give some money to the lady of the house upon departure, with your thanks. Just say it's your goodbye *sevusevu* and watch the smile. A Fijian may refuse the money, but he/she will not be offended by the offer if it is done properly. Of course, developing interpersonal relationships with your hosts is more important than money, and mere cash or gifts is no substitute for making friends.

If you're headed for a remote outer island without hotels or resorts you could also take some gifts along, such as lengths of material, T-shirts, badges, pins, knitting needles, hats, acoustic guitar strings, school books, colored pens, toys, playing cards, fishhooks, line, or lures, or a big jar of instant coffee. Keep in mind, however, that Seventh-Day Adventists are forbidden to have coffee, cigarettes, or kava, so you might ask if there are any SDAs around in order to avoid embarrassment. Uncontroversial food items to donate include sugar, flour, rice, corned beef, matches, chewing gum, peanuts, and biscuits. One thing *not* to take is alcohol, which is always sure to offend somebody.

Once you're staying with one family avoid moving to the home of another family in the same village as this would probably be seen as a slight to the first. Be wary of readily accepting invitations to meals with villagers other than your hosts as the offer may only be meant as a courtesy. Don't overly admire any of the possessions of your hosts or they may feel obligated to give them to you. If you are forced to accept something you know you cannot take, ask them to keep it there for you in trust.

When choosing your traveling companions for a trip that involves staying in Fijian villages, make sure you agree on these things before you set out. Otherwise you could end up subsidizing somebody else's trip, or worse, have to stand by and watch the Fijian villagers subsidize it. Never arrive in a village on a Sunday, and don't overstay your welcome.

A final note from Josje Hebbes of the Netherlands:

> *If people only meet Indians on the street or in tourist centers they will get a totally wrong idea of Indian culture. To appreciate their hospitality and friendliness one should also try to spend some time in rural Indian settlements. If you go on a day hike you might be invited for lunch. First they will serve you something sweet like juice or tea. That's their way. Make sure you don't leave Fiji with a mistaken impression of Fiji Indians!*

**Village Life**

When you enter a Fijian village, people will usually want to be helpful and will direct or accompany you to the person or place you seek. If you show genuine interest in something and ask to see how it is done, you'll usually be treated with respect and asked if there's anything else you'd like to know. Initially, Fijians may hesitate to welcome you into their homes because they may fear you will not wish to sit on a mat and eat native foods with your fingers. Once you show them this isn't true, you'll receive the full hospitality treatment.

Consider participating in the daily activities of the family, such as weaving, cooking, gardening, and fishing. Your hosts will probably try to dissuade you from "working," but if you persist you'll become accepted. Staying in a village is definitely not for everyone. Many houses contain no electricity, running water, toilet, furniture, etc., and only native food will be available. Water and your left hand serve as toilet paper.

You should also expect to sacrifice most of your privacy, to stay up far into the night drinking grog, and to sit in the house and socialize when you could be out exploring. On Sunday you'll have to stay put the whole day. The constant attention and lack of sanitary conditions may become tiresome, but it would be considered rude to attempt to be alone or refuse the food or grog.

With the proliferation of backpackers resorts around Fiji, staying in villages has become much less a part of visits to the remoter parts of Fiji than it was a decade ago, and relatively few travelers do it today. The Australian guidebooks also discourage going off the beaten travelers track. However, so long as you're prepared to accept all of the above and know beforehand that this is not a cheap way to travel, a couple of nights in an outlying village could easily be the highlight of your trip.

# FOOD AND DRINK

Unlike some other South Pacific nations, Fiji has many good, inexpensive eateries. The ubiquitous Chinese restaurants are probably your best bet for dinner and you can almost always get alcohol with the meal. At lunchtime look for an Indian place. Indian dishes are spicy, often curries with rice and *dhal* (lentil soup), but orthodox Hindus don't consume beef and Muslims forgo pork. Instead of bread Indians eat *roti,* a flat, tortilla-like pancake. *Puri* are small, deep-fried *rotis.* Baked in a stone oven *roti* becomes *naan,* a Punjabi specialty similar to pita bread. *Palau* is a main plate of rice and vegetables always including peas. *Samosas* are lumps of potato and other vegetables wrapped in dough and deep-fried. *Pakoras* are deep-fried chunks of dough spiced with chili and often served with a pickle chutney. Yogurt mixed with water makes a refreshing drink called *lassi.* If you have the chance, try South Indian vegetarian dishes like *iddili* (little white rice cakes served with *dhal)* and *masala dosai* (a rice potato-filled pancake served with a watery curry sauce called *sambar).*

Fijian food is usually steamed or boiled instead of fried, and dishes such as baked fish *(ika)* in coconut cream *(lolo)* with cassava *(tapioca),* taro *(dalo),* breadfruit *(uto),* and sweet potato *(kumala)* take a long time to prepare and must be served fresh, which makes it difficult to offer them in a restaurant. Don't miss an opportunity to try *duruka* (young sugar cane) or *vakalolo* (fish and prawns), both baked in *lolo. Kokoda* is an appetizing dish made of diced raw fish marinated in coconut cream and lime juice, while smoked octopus is *kuita.* Taro leaves are used to make a spinach called *palusami* (often stuffed with corned beef), which is known as *rourou* when soaked in coconut cream. Taro stems are cut into a marinated salad called *baba.* Seasoned "bird meat" (chicken) is wrapped and steamed in banana leaves to produce *kovu. Miti* is a sauce made of coconut cream, oranges, and chilies.

A good opportunity to taste authentic Fijian food and see traditional dancing is at a *lovo* or underground oven feast staged weekly at one of the large hotels around Nadi or on the Coral Coast for about F$40. These are usually accompanied by a Fijian *meke* or song and dance performance in which legends, love stories, and historical events are told in song and gesture. Alternatively, firewalking may be presented.

Many restaurants are closed on Sunday, and a 10% tax is added to the bill at some upmarket restaurants although it's usually included in the menu price. Fijians have their own pace and trying to make them do things more quickly is often counterproductive. Their charm and the friendly personal attention you receive more than make up for the occasionally slow service at restaurants.

The Hot Bread Kitchen chain of bakeries around Fiji serves fresh fruit loaves, cheese and onion loaves, muffins, and other assorted breads. The Morris Hedstrom supermarket chain is about the cheapest, and many have milk bars with ice cream and sweets.

The famous Fiji Bitter beer is brewed by Australian-owned Carlton Brewery Ltd., with breweries in Suva and Lautoka. South Pacific Distilleries Ltd. in Lautoka produces brandy, gin, rum, vodka, and whisky under a variety of brand names. What could be better than a vodka and tonic in the midday heat or a rum and coke at sunset? Supermarkets in Fiji usually only sell beer and other alcohol weekdays 0800-1800, Saturday 0800-1300. Licensed restaurants can only serve alcohol to those who order meals. Drinking alcoholic beverages on the street is prohibited. Unlike Australia and New Zealand, it's not customary to bring your own (BYO) booze into restaurants.

**Traditional Foods**

The traditional diet of the Fijians consists of root crops and fruit, plus lagoon fish and the occasional pig. The vegetables include taro, yams, cassava (manioc), breadfruit, and sweet potatoes. The sweet potato *(kumala)* is something of an anomaly—it's the only Pacific food plant with

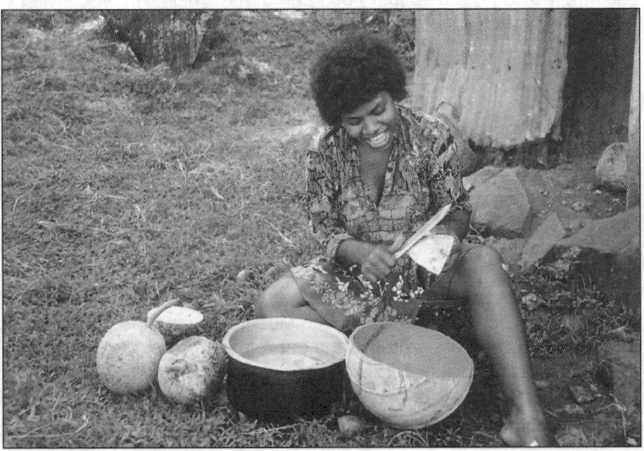

*slicing breadfruit*

DAVID STANLEY

## THE COCONUT PALM

Human life would not be possible on most of the Pacific's far-flung atolls without this all-purpose tree. It reaches maturity in eight years, then produces about 50 nuts a year for 60 years. Aside from the tree's esthetic value and usefulness in providing shade, the water of the green coconut provides a refreshing drink, and the white meat of the young nut is a delicious food. The harder meat of more mature nuts is grated and squeezed, which creates a coconut cream that is eaten alone or used in cooking. The oldest nuts are cracked open and the hard meat removed then dried to be sold as copra. It takes about 6,000 coconuts to make a ton of copra. Copra is pressed to extract the oil, which in turn is made into candles, cosmetics, and soap. Scented with flowers, the oil nurtures the skin.

The juice or sap from the cut flower spathes of the palm provides toddy, a popular drink; the toddy is distilled into a spirit called arrack, the whiskey of the Pacific. Otherwise the sap can be boiled to make candy. Millionaire's salad is made by shredding the growth cut from the heart of the tree. For each salad, a fully mature tree must be sacrificed.

The nut's hard inner shell can be used as a cup and makes excellent firewood. Rope, cordage, brushes, and heavy matting are produced from the coir fiber of the husk. The smoke from burning husks is a most effective mosquito repellent. The leaves of the coconut tree are used to thatch the roofs of the islanders' cottages or are woven into baskets, mats, and fans. The trunk provides timber for building and furniture. Actually, these are only the common uses: there are many others as well.

*Every part of the coconut tree* (Cocus nucifera) *can be used.*

a South American origin. How it got to the islands is not known.

Taro is an elephant-eared plant cultivated in freshwater swamps. Although yams are considered a prestige food, they're not as nutritious as breadfruit and taro. Yams can grow up to three meters long and weigh hundreds of kilos. Papaya (pawpaw) is nourishing: a third of a cup contains as much vitamin C as 18 apples. To ripen a green papaya overnight, puncture it a few times with a knife. Don't overeat papaya—unless you *need* an effective laxative.

The ancient Pacific islanders stopped making pottery over a millennium ago and instead developed an ingenious way of cooking in an underground earth oven known as a *lovo.* First a stack of dry coconut husks is burned in a pit. Once the fire is going well, coral stones are heaped on top, and when most of the husks have burnt away the food is wrapped in banana leaves and placed on the hot stones—fish and meat below, vegetables above. A whole pig may be cleaned, then stuffed with banana leaves and hot stones. This cooks the beast from inside out as well as outside in, and the leaves create steam. The food is then covered with more leaves and stones, and after about two and a half hours everything is cooked.

# VISAS AND OFFICIALDOM

Everyone needs a passport valid at least three months beyond the date of entry. No visa is required of visitors from 101 countries (including Western Europe, North America, Japan, Israel, most Commonwealth countries, and more) for stays of four months. Tickets to leave Fiji are officially required but usually not checked. The obligatory vaccination against yellow fever or cholera only applies if you're arriving directly from an infected area, such as the Amazon jungles or the banks of the Ganges River (no vaccinations necessary if you're arriving from North America, New Zealand, or Australia).

Fiji has diplomatic missions in Brussels, Canberra, Jakarta, Kuala Lumpur, London, New York, Ottawa, Port Moresby, Seoul, Taipei, Tokyo, Washington, Wellington, and Vancouver. The main ones are listed here.

Extensions of stay are given out by the immigration offices at Lautoka, Nadi Airport, Savusavu, and Suva. You must apply before your current permit expires. After the first four months, you can get another two months to bring your total stay up to six months by paying a F$55 fee. Bring your passport, onward or return ticket, and proof of sufficient funds. After six months you must leave but you can return the next day and start on another four months.

Work permits are difficult to obtain and the fastest means of achieving permanent residence is to put money into the country. For information on business opportunities in your field of expertise contact the **Fiji Trade and Investment Board** (tel. 315-988, fax 301-873). **Rolle Realty Ltd.** (tel. 304-544, www.fiji-online.com/rolle) in Nadi and Suva lists many investment properties in Fiji.

Fiji has four ports of entry for yachts: Lautoka, Levuka, Savusavu, and Suva. Calling at an outer island before clearing customs is prohibited. Levuka is the easiest place to check in or out, as all of the officials have offices right on the main wharf, and Savusavu is also convenient. To visit the outer islands, yachts require a letter of authorization from the Secretary for Fijian Affairs in Suva, or the commissioner (at Labasa, Lautoka, or Nausori) of the division they wish to visit. Yacht permits to visit the Lau Group must be obtained from the president's office (tel. 314-244) in Suva and they're hard to get due to a yacht drug bust in 1993.

## DIPLOMATIC OFFICES

Permanent Mission to the United Nations, 630 3rd Ave., 7th Floor, New York, NY 10017, New York, NY 10017, U.S.A. (tel. 212/687-4130, fax 212/687-3963)

Embassy of Fiji, 2233 Wisconsin Ave. NW, Suite 240, Washington, D.C. 20007, U.S.A. (tel. 202/337-8320, fax 202/337-1996)

High Commission of Fiji, Box 159, Queen Elizabeth Terrace, Canberra, ACT 2600, Australia (tel. 61-6/260-5115, fax 61-6/260-5105)

High Commission of Fiji, 31 Pipitea St., Thorndon, Wellington, New Zealand (tel. 64-4/473-5401, fax 64-4/499-1011)

High Commission of Fiji, Defense House, 4th Floor, Champion Parade, Port Moresby NCD, Papua New Guinea (tel. 675/321-1914, fax 675/321-7220)

High Commission of Fiji, 34 Hyde Park Gate, London SW3 5DN, United Kingdom (tel. 44-171/584-3661, fax 44-171/584-2838)

Embassy of Fiji, 66 avenue de Cortenberg, B.P. 7, 1040 Brussels, Belgium (tel. 32-2/736-9050, fax 32-2/736-1458)

Embassy of Fiji, Noa Building, 14th Floor, 3-5, 2-Chome, Azabudai, Minato-Ku, Tokyo 106, Japan (tel. 81-3/3587-2038, fax 81-3/3587-2563)

High Commission of Fiji, Level 2, Menara Chan, 138 Jalan Ampang, 50450 Kuala Lumpur, Malaysia (tel. 60-3/264-8422, fax 60-3/925-7555)

# MONEY

The currency is the Fiji dollar, which is about two to one to the U.S. dollar in value (US$1 = F$2). In January 1998 Fiji devalued its dollar 20% and in the months that followed it dropped another 10%. Despite this, tourism operators announced they would try to maintain their 1997 pricing through 1998, but substantial increases are to be expected in 1999 or 2000. Thus you may pay considerably more in Fiji dollars than the prices quoted herein, but still less than you would have paid in U.S. dollar terms in 1997.

The first Fijian coins were minted in London in 1934, but Fiji continued to deal in British pounds, shillings, and pence until 1969 when dollars and cents were introduced (at the rate of two Fiji dollars to one pound). There are coins of one, two, five, 10, 20, and 50 cents and one dollar, and bills of F$1, F$2, F$5, F$10, F$20, and F$50 (the F$5 and F$50 notes have confusingly similar colors and designs).

Banking hours are Mon.-Thurs. 0930-1500, Friday 0930-1600. Commercial banks operating in Fiji include the ANZ Bank, Indian-owned Bank of Baroda, Pakistani-owned Habib Bank, Bank of Hawaii, Merchant Bank, National Bank of Fiji, and Westpac Banking Corporation. There are bank branches in all the main towns, but it's usually not possible to change traveler's checks or foreign banknotes in rural areas or on outer islands. Take care when changing at the luxury hotels as they often give a rate much lower than the banks. Recent cases of stolen traveler's checks being changed in Fiji has caused many hotels and restaurants to begin refusing them. Thus it's a good idea to plan ahead and change enough at a bank to keep you going over weekends. Credit cards are strictly for the cities and resorts (the most useful cards to bring are American Express, Diners Club, JCB International, MasterCard, and Visa). The Westpac Bank gives cash advances on MasterCard and Visa, the ANZ Bank on JCB International. Many tourist facilities levy a 5% surcharge on credit card payments.

Many banks now have automated teller machines (ATMs) outside their offices and these provide local currency against checking account Visa and MasterCard at good rates without commission. Occasionally the machines don't work due to problems with the software, in which case you'll almost always be able to get a cash advance at the counter inside. To avoid emergencies, it's better not to be 100% dependent on ATMs. Ask your bank what fee they'll charge if you use an ATM abroad and find out if you need a special personal identification number (PIN).

The import of foreign currency is unrestricted, but only F$100 in Fijian banknotes may be exported. Avoid taking any Fijian banknotes out of the country at all, as Fiji dollars are difficult to change and heavily discounted outside Fiji. The Thomas Cook offices in Suva and Nadi will change whatever you have left into the currency of the next country on your itinerary (don't forget to keep enough local currency to pay your airport departure tax at the check-in counter).

For security the bulk of your travel funds should be in traveler's checks. American Express is probably the best kind to have, as they're represented by Tapa International in Suva (4th Floor, ANZ House, 25 Victoria Parade; tel. 302-333, fax 302-048) and Nadi (Nadi Airport Concourse; tel. 722-325). If your American Express checks or card are lost or stolen, contact either of these. Thomas Cook has offices of their own at 21 Thomson St., Suva (tel. 301-603, fax 300-304), and in Nadi (tel. 703-110).

If you need money sent, have your banker make a telegraphic transfer to any Westpac Bank branch in Fiji. Many banks will hold a sealed envelope for you in their vault for a nominal fee—a good way to avoid carrying unneeded valuables with you all around Fiji.

In 1992 Fiji introduced a 10% value added tax (VAT), which is usually (but not always) included in quoted prices. Among the few items exempt from the tax are unprocessed local foods and bus fares. Despite VAT, Fiji is one of the least expensive countries in the South Pacific, especially since the devaluation. Tipping isn't customary in Fiji, although some resorts do have a staff Christmas fund, to which contributions are welcome.

# POST AND TELECOMMUNICATIONS

### Post

Post offices are generally open weekdays 0800-1600 and they hold general delivery mail two months. Fiji's postal workers are amazingly polite and efficient, and postage is inexpensive, so mail all of your postcards from here! Consider using air mail for parcels, however, as surface mail takes up to six months. If time isn't important, however, most surface parcels do eventually arrive and small packets weighing less that one kilogram benefit from an especially low tariff. The weight limit for overseas parcels is 10 kilograms. Post Fiji's *fast* POST service guarantees that your letter or parcel will get on the first international airline connection to your destination for a small surcharge. Express mail service (EMS) is more expensive but faster and up to 20 kilograms may be sent (available to 28 countries). Post offices all around Fiji accept EMS mail.

When writing to Fiji, use the words "Fiji Islands" in the address (otherwise the letter might go to Fuji, Japan) and underline Fiji (so it doesn't end up in Iceland). Also include the post office box number as there's no residential mail delivery in Fiji. If it's a remote island or small village you're writing to, the person's name will be sufficient. Sending a picture postcard to an islander is a very nice way of saying thank you.

Aside from EMS, the other major courier services active in Fiji are **CDP** (tel. 313-077) at Labasa, Lautoka, Ba, Nadi, Sigatoka, and Suva, **DHL** (tel. 313-166) with offices at Labasa, Lautoka, Levuka, Nadi, Savusavu, and Suva, **TNT** (tel. 384-677) at Lautoka, Nadi, and Suva, and **UPS** (tel. 312-697) at Lautoka, Nadi, and Suva. To Europe or North America, DHL charges F$110 for a small box up to 10 kilograms or F$195 for a big box up to 25 kilograms, less than you would pay by EMS.

### Telecommunications

Card telephones are very handy and if you'll be staying in Fiji more than a few days and intend to make your own arrangements, it's wise to purchase a local telephone card right away. In this handbook we provide all the numbers you'll need to make hotel reservations, check restaurant hours, find out about cultural shows, and compare car rental rates, saving you a lot of time and inconvenience.

By using a telephone card to call long distance you limit the amount the call can possibly cost and won't end up overspending should you forget to keep track of the time. On short calls you avoid three-minute minimum charges. International telephone calls placed from hotel rooms are always much more expensive than the same calls made from public phones using telephone cards (ask the receptionist for the location of the nearest card phone). What you sacrifice is your privacy as anyone can stand around and listen to your call, as often happens. Card phones are usually found outside post offices or large stores. Check that the phone actually works before bothering to arrange your numbers and notes, as it seems over half the 500 card phones in Fiji are out of order at any given time.

Magnetic telephone cards are sold at all post offices and in many shops in denominations of F$3, F$5, F$10, and F$20 (foreign phone cards cannot be used in Fiji). It's probably wiser to get a F$3 or F$5 card rather than one of the higher values in case you happen to leave it behind in the phone (easy to do). Since local telephone rates are very inexpensive in Fiji, even the F$3 card lasts for ages (local calls are 20 cents each). Domestic long-distance calls from public telephones are half price 1800-0600, and all day on Saturday, Sunday, and public holidays. Fiji domestic directory assistance is 011, international directory assistance 022, the domestic operator 010, the international operator 012. In emergencies, dial 000.

Fiji's international access code from public telephones is 05, so insert your card, dial 05, the country code, the area code, and the number (to Canada and the U.S. the country code is always 1). To call overseas collect (billed to your party at the higher person-to-person rate), dial 031, the country code, the area code, and the number. If calling Fiji from abroad, dial your own international access code, Fiji's telephone code **679.** There are no area codes in Fiji. If the line is inaudible, hang up immediately and try again later.

The basic long-distance charge for three minutes is F$5.28 to Australia or New Zealand, F$8.91 to North America, Europe, or Japan. All operator-assisted international calls have a three-minute minimum charge and additional time is charged per minute, whereas international calls made using telephone cards have no minimum and the charges are broken down into flat six-second units (telephone cards with less than F$3 credit on them cannot be used for international calls). Calls to Australia and New Zealand are 25% cheaper 2300-0600.

If you have a "calling card" or phone pass issued by your own telephone company you can access an operator or automated voice prompt in your home country by dialing a "country direct" number from any touch-tone phone in Fiji. Such calls are billed to your home telephone number at the full non-discounted rate an operator-assisted call to Fiji would cost from your country, which in Fiji works out about 50% more expensive than using a local telephone card for international calls as described above (don't be fooled by misleading telephone company advertising that implies that calling "direct" is cheaper). Still, if don't mind paying extra for the convenience, the "country direct" numbers to dial include TNZ New Zealand 004-890-6401, Telstra Australia 004-890-6101, Optus Australia 004-890-6102, AT&T United States 004-890-1001, MCI United States 004-890-1002, Sprint United States 004-890-1003, Telecom Hawaii 004-890-1004, Teleglobe Canada 004-890-1005, and BT United Kingdom 004-890-4401. The service is also available to Hong Kong, Japan, Korea, Singapore, and Taiwan. Even though the phone companies have the cheek to suggest it, never use a "direct" number to place a domestic call within a single foreign country or an international call to a country other than your own as the call will be routed through your home country and you'll be shocked when you see the bill.

### Fax

Faxes can be sent from the post offices in Labasa, Lautoka, Ba, Nadi, Sigatoka, and Suva. Outgoing faxes cost F$5.50 a page to regional countries, F$7.70 to other countries, both plus a F$3.30 handing fee. You can also receive faxes at these post offices for F$1.10 a page. The numbers you'll probably use are fax 702-467 at Nadi Airport Post Office, fax 702-166 at Nadi Town Post Office, and fax 302-666 at Suva General Post Office.

If a fax you are trying to send to Fiji from abroad doesn't go through smoothly on the first or second try, wait and try again at another time of day. If it doesn't work then, stop trying as the fax machine at the other end may not be able to read your signal, and your telephone company will levy a minimum charge for each attempt. Call the international operator to ask what is going wrong.

### The Internet
An increasing number of tourism-related businesses in Fiji have e-mail addresses, which makes communicating with them from abroad a lot cheaper and easier. When sending e-mail to Fiji, never include a large attached file with your message unless it has been specifically requested as the recipient may have to pay US$1 a minute in long distance telephone charges to download it. To allow ourselves the flexibility of updating our listings more frequently, we have committed most Fiji e-mail and website addresses to this book's backmatter (overseas electronic addresses meant to be used prior to arrival in Fiji are embedded in this introduction). If you use the web, have a look at that part of the appendix now, if you haven't already done so. If an e-mail address provided anywhere in this book doesn't work, check www.is.com.fj or www.bulafiji.com for an update. In Fiji, public internet access is offered by Telecom Fiji opposite the post office in Suva, a chance to catch up on your e-mail. Fiji's first internet cafe opened in Lautoka in January 1998 at The Last Call Italian Restaurant, 21 Tui Street.

# TIME AND MEASUREMENTS

### Time
The international dateline generally follows 180 degrees longitude and creates a difference of 24 hours in time between the two sides. It swings east at Tuvalu to avoid slicing Fiji in two. Everything in the Eastern Hemisphere west of the date line is a day later, everything in the Western Hemisphere east of the line is a day earlier (or behind). Air travelers lose a day when they fly west across the date line and gain it back when they return. Keep track of things by repeating to yourself, *If it's Sunday in Samoa, it's Monday on Malolo.*

You're better calling from North America to Fiji in the evening as it will be mid-afternoon in the islands (plus you'll probably benefit from off-peak telephone rates). From Europe, call very late at night. In the other direction, if you're calling from Fiji to North America or Europe, do so in the early morning as it will already be afternoon in North America and evening in Europe.

In this book all clock times are rendered according to the 24-hour system, i.e. 0100 is 1:00 a.m., 1300 is 1:00 p.m., 2330 is 11:30 p.m. There isn't much twilight in the tropics and when the sun begins to go down, you have less than half an hour before darkness. The islanders operate on "coconut time"—the nut will fall when it is ripe. In the languid air of the South Seas punctuality takes on a new meaning. Appointments are approximate and service relaxed. Even the seasons are fuzzy: sometimes wetter, sometimes drier, but almost always hot. Slow down to the island pace and get in step with where you are. You may not get as much done, but you'll enjoy life a lot more.

### Measurements
The metric system is used in Fiji. Study the conversion table at the back of this handbook if you're not used to thinking metric. Most distances herein are quoted in kilometers—they become easy to comprehend when you know than one km is the distance a normal person walks in 10 minutes. A meter is slightly more than a yard and a liter is just over a quart.

Unless otherwise indicated, north is at the top of all maps in this handbook. When using official topographical maps you can determine the scale by taking the representative fraction (RF) and dividing by 100. This will give the number of meters represented by one centimeter. For example, a map with an RF of 1:10,000 would represent 100 meters for every centimeter on the map.

### Electric Currents
If you're taking along a plug-in razor, radio, computer, electric immersion coil, or other electrical appliance, be aware that Fiji uses 240 AC voltage, 50 cycles. Most appliances require a converter to change from one voltage to another. You'll also need an adapter to cope with different socket types, which vary between flat two-pronged plugs in American Samoa, round two-pronged plugs in the French territories, and three-pronged plugs with the two on top at angles almost everywhere else. Pick up both items before you leave home, as they're hard to find in the islands. Remember voltages if you buy duty-free appliances: dual voltage (110/220 V) items are best.

**Videos**
Commercial travel video tapes make nice souvenirs, but always keep in mind that there are three incompatible video formats loose in the world: NTSC (used in North America), PAL (used in Britain, Germany, Japan, Australia, New Zealand, and Fiji), and SECAM (used in France and Russia). Don't buy prerecorded tapes abroad unless they're of the system used in your country.

# INFORMATION

## MEDIA

### Print Media
The *Fiji Times* (Box 1167, Suva; tel. 304-111, fax 302-011), "the first newspaper published in the world today," was founded at Levuka in 1869 but is now owned by publishing mogul Rupert Murdoch's estate. The *Daily Post* (Box 7010, Valelevu, Nasinu; tel. 313-342, fax 313-363) is a morning newspaper mostly owned by Colonial Mutual Insurance and the government-run Fiji Development Bank. The *Times* has a daily print run of 37,000, the *Post* about 10,000.

Two excellent regional newsmagazines are published in Suva: *Pacific Islands Monthly* (tel. 304-111, fax 303-809), also part of the Murdoch empire, and *Islands Business* (Box 12718, Suva; tel. 303-108, fax 301-423), owned by local European businessmen. As well, there's a monthly Fijian business magazine called *The Review* (Box 12095, Suva; tel. 305-700, fax 301-930), owned by Fiji journalist Yashwant Gaunder. Copies of these are well worth picking up during your trip, and a subscription will help you keep in touch. Turn to Resources at the end of this book for more Pacific-oriented publications.

### TV
Television broadcasting only began in Fiji in 1991, and Fiji TV is on the air Mon.-Sat. 1400-2300 and Sunday 1000-2300 with one free and two paid channels. The Fiji Government owns 65% of the company and another 15% is owned by TV New Zealand, which manages the station.

### Radio
A great way to keep in touch with world and local affairs is to take along a small AM/FM shortwave portable radio. Your only expense will be the radio itself and batteries. Below we provide the names and frequencies of the local stations, so set your tuning buttons to these as soon as you arrive in an area.

Try picking up the BBC World Service on your shortwave receiver at 5.98, 7.15, 9.66, 9.74, 11.77, 11.96, 12.08, or 15.36 MHz (15.36 MHz generally works best). For Radio Australia try 6.08, 7.24, 9.66, 11.88, 12.08, 15.51, and 17.71 MHz. Look for Radio New Zealand International at 6.10, 6.14, 9.87, 11.69, 11.73, and 17.67 MHz. These frequencies vary according to the time of day and usually work best at night. (Sadly both RNZI and Radio Australia have recently faced cutbacks that could impact their services.) Also check Radio Vanuatu at 3945 MHz and the Solomon Islands Broadcasting Corporation at 5020 MHz (a strong signal often heard in Fiji).

Unfortunately Fiji doesn't have a shortwave broadcaster of its own but privately owned **Communications Fiji Ltd.** (Private Mail Bag, Suva; tel. 314-766, fax 303-748) rebroadcasts the BBC World Service over 106.8 MHz FM 24 hours a day (available around Suva only). Communications Fiji Ltd. also operates three lively commercial FM stations, which broadcast around the clock: FM 96 in English, Viti FM in Fijian, and Radio Navtarang in Hindi.

In addition, the quasi-official **Island Network Ltd.** (Box 334, Suva; tel. 314-333, fax 301-643), formerly the Fiji Broadcasting Corporation, operates five AM/FM radio stations: Radio Fiji Gold (RFG) in English, RF1 in Fijian for older listeners, Bula FM in Fijian for younger listeners, RF2 in Hindi for older listeners, and 98 FM in Hindi for younger listeners.

At Suva you can pick up the local stations at the following frequencies: RFG at 100.4 MHz, FM 96 at 96.0 MHz, RF1 at 107.6 MHz FM or at 558 kHz AM, Bula FM at 102.0 MHz, Viti FM at 102.8 MHz, RF2 at 105.2 MHz FM or at 774 kHz AM, 98 FM at 98.0 MHz, and Navtarang at 98.8 MHz.

At Nadi and Lautoka check the following frequencies: RFG at 94.2 MHz, FM 96 at 95.4 MHz, RF1 at 639 kHz AM, Bula FM at 91.0 MHz, Viti FM at 99.6 MHz, RF2 at 891 kHz AM, 98 FM at 88.6 MHz, and Navtarang at 97.4 MHz.

On the Coral Coast it's FM 96 at 99.0 MHz, RFG at 100.6 MHz, Navtarang at 102.2 MHz, Bula FM at 103.0 MHz, and Viti FM at 107.8 MHz. At Levuka pick up RFG at 90.6 MHz. Around Rakiraki look for RF1 at 1152 kHz AM, RF2 at 1467 kHz AM, and FM 96 at 98.8 MHz. Elsewhere in northern Viti Levu, you can get RFG at 94.6 MHz, FM 96 at 99.2 MHz, Navtarang at 101.6 MHz, and Viti FM at 103.2 MHz in Tavua and Ba.

On Vanua Levu, check the following frequencies at Labasa: RFG at 90.6 MHz, FM 96 at 95.4 MHz, RF1 at 684 kHz AM, Viti FM at 99.6 MHz, RF2 at 810 kHz AM, and Navtarang at 97.4 MHz. At Savusavu it's RF1 at 684 kHz AM and RF2 at 810 kHz AM. Reception of any station is difficult at Taveuni.

The local stations broadcast mostly pop music and repetitive advertising with very little news or commentary (the presenters sometimes get things hilariously mixed up). Radio Fiji Gold broadcasts local news and a weather report on the hour weekdays 0600-2200 (weekends every other hour) with a special news of the day report at 1745, followed by the BBC world news just after 1800. The BBC news is also broadcast on RFG at 1900 and 2100. Radio FM 96 broadcasts news and weather on the hour weekdays 0600-1800, Saturday at 0700, 1000, 1300, and 1800, Sunday at 0800, 1300, 1800.

## TOURIST INFORMATION

### Information

The government-funded **Fiji Visitors Bureau** (Box 92, Suva; tel. 302-433, fax 300-970, www.bulafiji.com) mails out general brochures and a list of hotels with current prices free upon request. In Fiji they have walk-in offices at Nadi Airport and in Suva. They also maintain a local toll-free information number at tel. 0800-721-721.

The **Fiji Hotel Association** (Private Mail Bag, Suva; tel. 302-975, fax 300-331) will mail you a brochure listing all upmarket hotels with specific prices, although low-budget accommodations are not included.

The free ***Fiji Magic*** magazine (Box 12095, Suva; tel. 305-916, fax 301-930) is very useful to get an idea of what's on during your visit.

Also browse the local **bookstores,** Desai Bookshops, Zenon Bookshops, and Sigatoka Stationary Supplies, with branches all over Fiji. The bookcenters at the University of the South Pacific in Suva have the widest selection of books.

### TOURIST OFFICES

Fiji Visitors Bureau, Box 92, Suva, Fiji Islands (tel. 679/302-433, fax 679/300-970; www.bulafiji.com; e-mail: infodesk@fijifvb.gov.fj)

Fiji Visitors Bureau, Box 9217, Nadi Airport, Fiji Islands (tel. 679/722-433, fax 679/720-141, e-mail: fvbnadi@is.com.fj)

Fiji Visitors Bureau, Suite 220, 5777 West Century Blvd., Los Angeles, CA 90045, U.S.A. (tel. 310/568-1616 or 800/932-3454, fax 310/670-2318, e-mail: fiji@primenet.com)

Fiji Visitors Bureau, Level 12, St. Martin's Tower, 31 Market St., Sydney, NSW 2000, Australia (tel. 61-2/9264-3399, fax 61-2/9264-3060, e-mail: fijiau@ozemail.com.au)

Fiji Visitors Bureau, Box 1179, Auckland, New Zealand (tel. 64-9/373-2133, fax 64-9/309-4720, e-mail: office@fijinz.co.nz)

Fiji Visitors Bureau, 14th floor, NOA Bldg., 3-5, 2-Chome, Azabudai, Minato-ku, Tokyo 106, Japan (tel. 81-3/3587-2038, fax 81-3/3587-2563)

Fiji Embassy, 34 Hyde Park Gate, London SW7 5DN, United Kingdom (tel. 44-171/584-3661, fax 44-171/584-2838)

**Travel Agencies**

If you like the security of advance reservations but aren't interested in joining a regular packaged tour, several local companies specialize in booking cruises, hotel rooms, airport transfers, sightseeing tours, rental cars, etc. Only the Blue Lagoon and Captain Cook mini-cruises mentioned in "Getting There" really need to be booked from abroad; upon arrival you'll have dozens of hotels and resorts competing for your business at prices much lower than you'd pay your friendly travel agent back home. Thus it's smart to wait and make most of your ground arrangements upon arrival at Nadi Airport, rather than risk being exiled to one of Fiji's most expensive resorts by some agent only interested in a commission.

Fiji's largest travel agency is **Rosie The Travel Service** (Box 9268, Nadi Airport; tel. 722-935, fax 722-607, e-mail: rosiefiji@is.com.fj), with a 24-hour office in the arrivals arcade at Nadi Airport and 14 branches around Viti Levu. This handbook will give you an idea what's out there, and upon arrival Rosie or one of the other agents at Nadi Airport will be able to explain current prices and check availability. In Australia advance bookings can be made through Rosie The Travel Service (Level 5, Ste. 505, East Towers, 9 Bronte Rd., Bondi Junction, Sydney, NSW 2022, Australia; tel. 61-2/9389-3666, fax 61-2/9369-1129). This locally owned business has provided efficient, personalized service since 1974.

Numerous other private travel agencies have offices at Nadi Airport and in Nadi Town, many of them oriented toward backpacker or budget travel. These are discussed in this book's Nadi chapter. Also check the "Bula Fiji Starter Packs" described in "Getting There."

# HEALTH

Fiji's climate is a healthy one, and the main causes of death are noncommunicable diseases such as heart disease, diabetes, and cancer. The sea and air are clear and usually pollution-free. The humidity nourishes the skin and the local fruit is brimming with vitamins. If you take a few precautions, you'll never have a sick day. The information provided below is intended to make you knowledgeable, not fearful. If you have access to the internet, check www.cdc.gov/travel/index.htm for up-to-the-minute information.

Health care is good, with an abundance of hospitals, health centers, and nursing stations scattered around the country. The largest hospitals are in Labasa, Lautoka, Levuka, Ba, Savusavu, Sigatoka, Suva, and Taveuni. The crowded government-run medical facilities provide free medical treatment to local residents but have special rates for foreigners. It's usually no more expensive to visit a private doctor or clinic where you'll receive much faster service since everyone is paying. We've tried to list local doctors and dentists throughout the handbook, and in emergencies and outside clinic hours, you can always turn to the government-run facilities. Unfortunately, very few facilities are provided for travelers with disabilities.

To call an ambulance dial 000. In case of scuba diving accidents, an operating dive recompression chamber (tel. 305-154 in Suva or 850-630 in Savusavu) is available at the Gordon Street Medical Center in Suva. The 24-hour recompression medical evacuation number is tel. 362-172.

**Travel Insurance**

The sale of travel insurance is big business but the value of the policies themselves is often questionable. If your regular group health insurance also covers you while you're traveling abroad it's probably enough as medical costs in Fiji are generally low. Most policies only pay the amount above and beyond what your national or group health insurance will pay and are invalid if you don't have any health insurance at all. You may also be covered by your credit card company if you paid for your plane ticket with the card. Buying extra travel insurance is about the same as buying a lottery ticket: there's always the chance it will pay off, but it's usually money down the drain.

If you do opt for the security of travel insurance, make sure emergency medical evacuations are covered. Some policies are invalid if you engage in any "dangerous activities," such as scuba diving, parasailing, surfing, or even riding a motor scooter, so be sure to read the fine print. Scuba divers may find it comforting to know that a recompression chamber is available at Suva, but even then an emergency medical evacuation by helicopter might be required and there isn't any point buying a policy that doesn't cover it. Some companies will pay your bills directly while others require you to pay and collect receipts that may be reimbursed later.

Some policies also cover travel delays, lost baggage, and theft. In practice, your airline probably already covers the first two adequately and claiming something extra from your insurance company could be more trouble than it's worth. Theft insurance never covers items left on the beach while you're in swimming. All this said, you should weigh the advantages and decide for yourself if you want a policy. Just don't be too influenced by what your travel agent says as they'll only want to sell you coverage in order to earn another commission.

**Acclimatizing**

Don't go from winter weather into the steaming tropics without a rest before and after. Minimize jet lag by setting your watch to local time at your destination as soon as you board the flight. Westbound flights into the South Pacific from North America or Europe are less jolting since you follow the sun and your body gets a few hours extra sleep. On the way home you're moving against the sun and the hours of sleep your body loses cause jet lag. Airplane cabins have low humidity, so drink lots of juice or water instead of carbonated drinks, and don't overeat in-flight. It's also wise to forgo coffee, as it will only keep you awake, and alcohol, which will dehydrate you.

Scuba diving on departure day can give you a severe case of the bends. Before flying there should be a minimum of 12 hours surface interval after a non-decompression dive and a minimum of 24 hours after a decompression dive. Factors contributing to decompression sickness include a lack of sleep and/or the excessive consumption of alcohol before diving.

If you start feeling seasick onboard a ship, stare at the horizon, which is always steady, and stop thinking about it. Anti-motion-sickness pills are useful to have along; otherwise, ginger helps alleviate seasickness. Travel stores sell acubands that find a pressure point on the wrist and create a stable flow of blood to the head, thus miraculously preventing seasickness!

Frequently the feeling of thirst is false and only due to mucous membrane dryness. Gargling or taking two or three gulps of warm water should be enough. Keep moisture in your body by having a hot drink like tea or black coffee, or any kind of slightly salted or sour drink in small quantities. Salt in fresh lime juice is remarkably refreshing.

The tap water in Fiji is usually drinkable except immediately after a cyclone or during droughts, when care should be taken. If in doubt, boil it or use purification pills. Tap water that is uncomfortably hot to touch is usually safe. Allow it to cool in a clean container. Don't forget that if the tap water is contaminated, the local ice will be too. Avoid brushing your teeth with water unfit to drink, and wash or peel fruit and vegetables if you can. Cooked food is less subject to contamination than raw.

**Sunburn**

Though you may think a tan will make you look healthier and more attractive, it's actually very damaging to the skin, which becomes dry, rigid, and prematurely old and wrinkled, especially on the face. Begin with short exposures to the sun, perhaps half an hour at a time, followed by an equal time in the shade. Avoid the sun from 1000 to 1500, the most dangerous time. Clouds and beach umbrellas will not protect you fully. Wear a T-shirt while snorkeling to protect your back. Drink plenty of liquids to keep your pores open. Sunbathing is the main cause of cataracts to the eyes, so wear sunglasses and a wide-brimmed hat, and beware of reflected sunlight.

Use a sunscreen lotion containing PABA rather than oil, and don't forget to apply it to your nose, lips, forehead, neck, hands, and feet. Sunscreens protect you from ultraviolet rays (a leading cause of cancer), while oils magnify the sun's effect. A 15-factor sunscreen provides 93% protection (a more expensive 30-factor sunscreen is only slightly better at 97% protection). Apply the lotion *before* going to the beach to avoid being burned on the way, and reapply every couple of hours to replace sunscreen washed away by perspiration. Swimming also washes away your protection. After sunbathing take a tepid shower rather than a hot one, which would wash away your natural skin oils. Stay moist and use a vitamin E evening cream to preserve the youth of your skin. Calamine ointment soothes skin already burned, as does coconut oil. Pharmacists recommend Solarcaine to soothe burned skin. Rinsing off with a vinegar solution reduces peeling, and aspirin relieves some of the pain and irritation. Vitamin A and calcium counteract overdoses of vitamin D received from the sun. The fairer your skin, the more essential it is to take care.

As earth's ozone layer is depleted due to the commercial use of chlorofluorocarbons (CFCs) and other factors, the need to protect oneself from ultraviolet radiation is becoming more urgent. In 1990 the U.S. Centers for Disease Control and Prevention in Atlanta reported that deaths from skin cancer increased 26% between 1973 and 1985. Previously the cancers didn't develop until age 50 or 60, but now much younger people are affected.

### Ailments

Cuts and scratches infect easily in the tropics and take a long time to heal. Prevent infection from coral cuts by immediately washing wounds with soap and fresh water, then rubbing in vinegar or alcohol (whiskey will do)—painful but effective. Use an antiseptic like hydrogen peroxide and an antibacterial ointment such as neosporin, if you have them. Islanders usually dab coral cuts with lime juice. All cuts turn septic quickly in the tropics, so try to keep them clean and covered.

For bites, burns, and cuts, an antiseptic such as Solarcaine speeds healing and helps prevent infection. Pure aloe vera is good for sunburn, scratches, and even coral cuts. Bites by sand flies itch for days and can become infected. Not everyone is affected by insect bites in the same way. Some people are practically immune to insects, while traveling companions experiencing exactly the same conditions are soon covered with bites. You'll soon know which type you are.

Prickly heat, an intensely irritating rash, is caused by wearing heavy clothing that is inappropriate for the climate. When sweat glands are blocked and the sweat is unable to evaporate, the skin becomes soggy and small red blisters appear. Synthetic fabrics like nylon are especially bad in this regard. Take a cold shower, apply calamine lotion, dust with talcum powder, and take off those clothes! Until things improve, avoid alcohol, tea, coffee, and any physical activity that makes you sweat. If you're sweating profusely, increase your intake of salt slightly to avoid fatigue, but not without concurrently drinking more water.

Use antidiarrheal medications such as Lomotil or Imodium sparingly. Rather than take drugs to plug yourself up, drink plenty of unsweetened liquids like green coconut or fresh fruit juice to help flush yourself out. Egg yolk mixed with nutmeg helps diarrhea, or have a rice and tea day. Avoid dairy products. Most cases of diarrhea are self-limiting and require only simple replacement of the fluids and salts lost in diarrheal stools. If the diarrhea is persistent or you experience high fever, drowsiness, or blood in the stool, stop traveling, rest, and consider seeing a doctor. For constipation eat pineapple or any peeled fruit.

If you're sleeping in villages or with the locals you may pick up head or body lice. Pharmacists and general stores usually have a remedy that will eliminate the problem in minutes (pack a bottle with you if you're uptight). You'll know you're lousy when you start to scratch: pick out the little varmints and snap them between your thumbnails for fun. The villagers pluck the creatures out of each other's hair one by one, a way of confirming friendships and showing affection. Intestinal parasites (worms) are also widespread. The hookworm bores its way through the soles of your feet, and if you go barefoot through moist gardens and plantations you may pick up something.

### AIDS

In 1981 scientists in the United States and France first recognized the Acquired Immune Deficiency Syndrome (AIDS), which was later discovered to be caused by a virus called the Human Immuno-deficiency Virus (HIV). HIV breaks down the body's immunity to infections leading to AIDS. The virus can lie hidden in the body for up to 10 years without producing any obvious symptoms or before developing into the AIDS disease and in the meantime the person can unknowingly infect others.

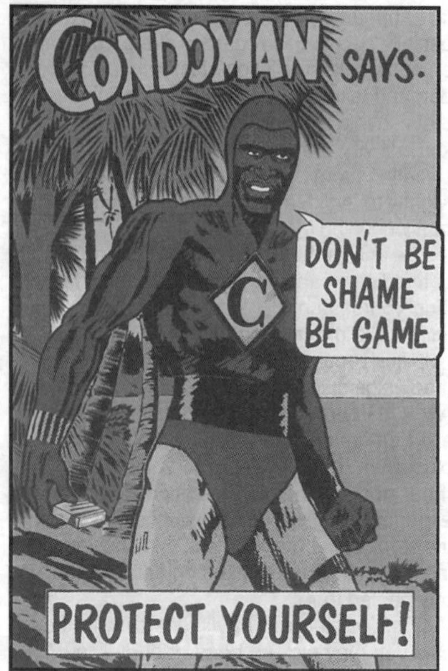


HIV lives in white blood cells and is present in the sexual fluids of humans. It's difficult to catch and is spread mostly through sexual intercourse, by needle or syringe sharing among intravenous drug users, in blood transfusions, and during pregnancy and birth (if the mother is infected). Using another person's razor blade or having your body pierced or tattooed are also risky, but the HIV virus cannot be transmitted by shaking hands, kissing, cuddling, fondling, sneezing, cooking food, or sharing eating or drinking utensils. One cannot be infected by saliva, sweat, tears, urine, or feces; toilet seats, telephones, swimming pools, or mosquito bites do not cause AIDS. Ostracizing a known AIDS victim is not only immoral but also absurd.

Most blood banks now screen their products for HIV, and you can protect yourself against dirty needles by only allowing an injection if you see the syringe taken out of a fresh unopened pack. The simplest safeguard during sex is the proper use of a latex condom. Unroll the condom onto the erect penis; while withdrawing after ejaculation, hold onto the condom as you come out. Never try to recycle a condom, and pack a supply with you as it's a nuisance trying to buy them locally.

HIV is spread more often through anal than vaginal sex because the lining of the rectum is much weaker than that of the vagina, and ordinary condoms sometimes tear when used in anal sex. If you have anal sex, only use extra-strong condoms and special water-based lubricants since oil, Vaseline, and cream weaken the rubber. During oral sex you must make sure you don't get any semen or menstrual blood in your mouth. A woman runs 10 times the risk of contracting AIDS from a man than the other way around, and the threat is always greater when another sexually transmitted disease (STD) is present.

The very existence of AIDS calls for a basic change in human behavior. No vaccine or drug exists that can prevent or cure AIDS, and because the virus mutates frequently, no remedy may ever be totally effective. Other STDs such as syphilis, gonorrhea, chlamydia, hepatitis B, and herpes are far more common than AIDS and can lead to serious complications such as infertility, but at least they can usually be cured.

The euphoria of travel can make it easier to fall in love or have sex with a stranger, so travelers must be informed of these dangers. As a tourist you should always practice safe sex to prevent AIDS and other STDs. You never know who is infected or even if you yourself have become infected. It's important to bring the subject up *before* you start to make love. Make a joke out of it by pulling out a condom and asking your new partner, "Say, do you know what this is?" Or perhaps, "Your condom or mine?" Far from being unromantic or embarrassing, you'll both feel more relaxed with the subject off your minds and it's much better than worrying afterwards if you might have been infected. The golden rule is safe sex or no sex.

By the end of 1999 an estimated 33 million people worldwide were HIV carriers, and millions of others had already died of AIDS. In the South Pacific, the number of cases is still extremely small compared to the 650,000 confirmed HIV infections in the United States. Tahiti-Polynesia, New Caledonia, Papua New Guinea, and Guam are the most affected countries, yet it's worth noting that other STDs have already reached epidemic proportions in the urban areas of Fiji, demonstrating that the type of behavior leading to the rapid spread of AIDS is present.

An HIV infection can be detected through a blood test because the antibodies created by the body to fight off the virus can be seen under a microscope. It takes at least three weeks for the antibodies to be produced and in some cases as long as six months before they can be picked up during a screening test. If you think you may have run a risk, you should discuss the appropriateness of a test with your doctor. It's always better to know if you are infected so as to be able to avoid infecting others, to obtain early treatment of symptoms, and to make realistic plans. If you know someone with AIDS you should give them all the support you can (there's no danger in such contact unless blood is present).

**Toxic Fish**

Over 400 species of tropical reef fish, including wrasses, snappers, groupers, jacks, moray eels, surgeonfish, shellfish, and especially barracudas are known to cause seafood poisoning (ciguatera). There's no way to tell if a fish will cause ciguatera: a species can be poisonous on one side of the island, but not on the other.

In 1976 French and Japanese scientists working in the Gambier Islands southeast of Tahiti determined that a one-celled dinoflagellate or plankton called *Gambierdiscus toxicus* was the cause. Normally these microalgae are found only in the ocean depths, but when a reef ecosystem is disturbed by natural or human causes they can multiply dramatically in a lagoon. The dinoflagellates are consumed by tiny herbivorous fish and the toxin passes up through the food chain to larger fish where it becomes concentrated in the head and guts. The toxins have no effect on the fish that feed on them.

The symptoms (numbness and tingling around the mouth and extremities, reversal of hot/cold sensations, prickling, itching, nausea, vomiting, erratic heartbeat, joint and muscle pains) usually subside in a few days. Induce vomiting, take castor oil as a laxative, and avoid alcohol if you're unlucky. Symptoms can recur for up to a year, and victims may become allergic to all seafoods. In the Marshall Islands, an injected drug called Mannitel has been effective in treating ciguatera, but as yet little is known about it.

Avoid biointoxication by cleaning fish as soon as they're caught, discarding the head and organs, and taking special care with oversized fish caught in shallow water. Small fish are generally safer. Whether the fish is consumed cooked or raw has no bearing on this problem. Local residents often know from experience which species may be eaten.

**Other Diseases**

Infectious hepatitis A (jaundice) is a liver ailment transmitted person to person or through unboiled water, uncooked vegetables, or other foods contaminated during handling. The risk of infection is highest among those who eat village food, so if you'll be spending much time in rural areas consider getting an immune globulin shot, which provides six months protection. Better is a vaccine called Havrix, which provides up to 10 years protection (given in two doses two weeks apart, then a third dose six months later). If you've ever had hepatitis A in your life you are already immune. Otherwise, you'll know you've got the hep when your eyeballs and urine turn yellow. Time and rest are the only cure. Viral hepatitis B is spread through sexual or blood contact.

Cholera is rare in the South Pacific but there have been sporadic outbreaks in Micronesia. Cholera is acquired via contaminated food or water, so in the improbable event that you arrive in an infected area avoid uncooked foods, peel your own fruit, and drink bottled drinks. Typhoid fever is also caused by contaminated food or water, while tetanus (lockjaw) occurs when cuts or bites become infected. Horrible disfiguring diseases such as leprosy and elephantiasis are hard to catch, so it's unlikely you'll be visited by one of these nightmares of the flesh.

There's no malaria here, but a mosquito-transmitted disease known as dengue fever is endemic. In early 1998 a major outbreak in Fiji resulted in an estimated 25,000 cases and 11 deaths. Signs are headaches, sore throat, pain in the joints, fever, chills, nausea, and rash. This painful illness also known as "breakbone fever" can last anywhere from five to 15 days. Although you can relieve the symptoms somewhat, the only real cure is to stay in bed, drink lots of water, and wait it out. Avoid aspirin as this can lead to complications. No vaccine exists, so just try to avoid getting bitten (the *Aedes aegypti* mosquito bites only during the day). Dengue fever can kill infants so extra care must be taken to protect them if an outbreak is in progress.

### Vaccinations

Most visitors are not required to get any vaccinations at all before coming to Fiji. Tetanus, diphtheria, and typhoid fever shots are not required and only worth considering if you're going far off the beaten track. Tetanus and diphtheria shots are given together, and a booster is required every 10 years. The typhoid fever shot is every three years. Polio is believed to have been eradicated from the region.

The cholera vaccine is only 50% effective and valid just six months, and bad reactions are common, which explains why most doctors in developed countries won't administer it. Just forget it unless you're sure you're headed for an infected area. If you'll be visiting Tuvalu, Nauru, Kiribati, or anywhere in Micronesia before Fiji, ask Air Marshall Islands or Air Nauru if a cholera vaccination is required. In that case you'll be able to obtain it locally without difficulty.

A yellow-fever vaccination is required if you've been in an infected area within the six days prior to arrival. Yellow fever is a mosquito-borne disease that only occurs in Central Africa and northern South America (excluding Chile), places you're not likely to have been just before arriving in the South Pacific. Since the vaccination is valid 10 years, get one if you're an inveterate globe-trotter.

Immune globulin (IG) and the Havrix vaccine aren't 100% effective against hepatitis A, but they do increase your general resistance to infections. IG prophylaxis must be repeated every five months. Hepatitis B vaccination involves three doses over a six-month period (duration of protection unknown) and is recommended mostly for people planning extended stays in the region.

## WHAT TO TAKE

### Packing

Assemble everything you simply must take and cannot live without—then cut the pile in half. If you're still left with more than will fit into a medium-size suitcase or backpack, continue eliminating. You have to be tough on yourself and just limit what you take. Now put it all into your bag. If the total (bag and contents) weighs over 16 kg, you'll sacrifice much of your mobility. If you can keep it down to 10 kg, you're traveling *light*. Categorize, separate, and pack all your things into clear plastic bags or stuff sacks for convenience and protection from moisture. Items that might leak should be in resealable bags. In addition to your principal bag, you'll want a day pack or flight bag. When checking in for flights, carry anything that cannot be replaced in your hand luggage.

### Your Luggage

A soft medium-size backpack with a lightweight internal frame is best. Big external-frame packs are fine for mountain climbing but get caught in airport conveyor belts and are very inconvenient on public transport. The best packs have a zippered compartment in back where you can tuck in the hip belt and straps before turning your pack over to an airline or bus. This type of pack has the flexibility of allowing you to simply walk when motorized transport is unavailable or unacceptable; and with the straps zipped in it looks like a regular suitcase, should you wish to go upmarket for a while.

Make sure your pack allows you to carry the weight on your hips, has a cushion for spine support, and doesn't pull backwards. The pack should strap snugly to your body but also allow ventilation to your back. It should be made of a water-resistant material such as nylon and have a Fastex buckle.

Look for a pack with double, two-way zipper compartments and pockets you can lock with miniature padlocks. They might not *stop* a thief, but they will deter the casual pilferer. A 60-cm length of lightweight chain and another padlock will allow you to fasten your pack to something. Keep valuables locked in your bag, out of sight, as even upmarket hotel rooms aren't 100% safe.

### Clothing and Camping Equipment

For clothes take loose-fitting cotton washables, light in color and weight. Synthetic fabrics are hot and sticky, and most of the things you wear at home are too heavy for the tropics—be prepared for the humidity. Dress is casual, with slacks and a sports shirt okay for men even at dinner parties. Local women often wear long colorful dresses in the evening, but respectable shorts are okay in daytime. If in doubt, bring the minimum with you and buy tropical garb upon arrival. Stick to clothes you can rinse in your room sink. In midwinter (July and August) it can be cool at night, so a light sweater or windbreaker may come in handy. (Reader Claire Brenn writes: "If you have some good but unfashionable clothes you don't wish to take home, just leave them behind in your hotel room with a small thank you note. The locals will gladly have them but to offer them directly might be embarrassing.")

The *sulu* is a bright two-meter piece of cloth both men and women wrap about themselves as an all-purpose garment. Any islander can show you how to wear it. Missionaries taught the South Sea island women to drape their attributes in long, flowing gowns, called muumuus in Hawaii. In the South Pacific, the dress is better known as a Mother Hubbard for the muumuu-attired nursery rhyme character who "went to the cupboard to fetch her poor dog a bone."

Take comfortable shoes that have been broken in. Running shoes and rubber thongs (flip-flops) are handy for day use but will bar you from nightspots with strict dress codes. Scuba divers' wetsuit booties are lightweight and perfect for both crossing rivers and lagoon walking, though an old pair of sneakers may be just as good (never use the booties to walk on breakable coral).

A small nylon tent guarantees backpackers a place to sleep every night, but it *must* be mosquito- and waterproof. Get one with a tent fly, then waterproof both tent and fly with a can of waterproofing spray. You'll seldom need a sleeping bag in the tropics, so that's one item you can easily cut. A youth hostel sleeping sheet is ideal—all HI handbooks give instructions on how to make your own or buy one at your local hostel. You don't really need to carry a bulky foam pad, as the ground is seldom cold.

Below we've provided a few checklists to help you assemble your gear. The listed items combined weigh well over 16 kg, so eliminate what doesn't suit you:

- pack with internal frame
- day pack or airline bag
- sun hat or visor
- essential clothing only
- bathing suit
- sturdy walking shoes
- rubber thongs
- rubber booties
- nylon tent and fly
- tent-patching tape
- mosquito net
- sleeping sheet

**Accessories**

Bring some reading material, as good books can be hard to find in resort areas. A mask and snorkel are essential equipment—you'll be missing half of Fiji's beauty without them. Scuba divers will bring their own regulator, buoyancy compensator, and gauges to avoid rental fees and to eliminate the possibility of catching a transmissible disease from rental equipment. A lightweight three-mm Lycra wetsuit will provide protection against marine stings and coral.

Neutral gray eyeglasses protect your eyes from the sun and give the least color distortion. Take an extra pair (if you wear them).

Also take along postcards of your hometown and snapshots of your house, family, workplace, etc; islanders love to see these. Always keep a promise to mail islanders the photos you take of them.

- portable shortwave radio
- camera and 10 rolls of film
- compass
- pocket flashlight
- extra batteries
- candle
- pocket alarm calculator
- extra pair of eyeglasses
- sunglasses
- mask and snorkel
- padlock and lightweight chain
- collapsible umbrella
- string for a clothesline
- powdered laundry soap
- universal sink plug
- mini-towel
- silicon glue
- sewing kit

- mini-scissors
- nail clippers
- fishing line for sewing gear
- plastic cup and plate
- can and bottle opener
- corkscrew
- penknife
- spoon
- water bottle
- matches
- tea bags

**Toiletries and Medical Kit**
Since everyone has his/her own medical requirements and brand names vary from country to country, there's no point going into detail here. Note, however, that even the basics (such as aspirin) are unavailable on some outer islands, so be prepared. Bring medicated powder for prickly heat rash. Charcoal tablets are useful for diarrhea and poisoning (they absorb the irritants). Bring an adequate supply of any personal medications, plus your prescriptions (in generic terminology) as American-made medications may by unobtainable in the islands. Antibiotics should only be used to treat serious wounds, and only after medical advice.

High humidity causes curly hair to swell and bush, straight hair to droop. If it's curly have it cut short or keep it long in a ponytail or bun. A good cut is essential with straight hair. Water-based makeup is preferable, as the heat and humidity cause oil glands to work overtime. High-quality locally made shampoo, body oils, and insect repellent are sold on all the islands, and the bottles are conveniently smaller than those sold in Western countries. See "Health," above, for more ideas.

- wax earplugs
- soap in plastic container
- soft toothbrush
- toothpaste
- roll-on deodorant
- shampoo
- comb and brush
- skin creams
- makeup
- tampons or napkins
- white toilet paper
- vitamin/mineral supplement
- insect repellent
- PABA sunscreen
- lip balm
- a motion-sickness remedy
- contraceptives
- iodine
- water-purification pills
- delousing powder
- a diarrhea remedy
- Tiger Balm
- a cold remedy
- Alka-Seltzer
- aspirin
- antihistamine
- antifungal
- Calmitol ointment
- antibacterial ointment
- antiseptic cream
- disinfectant
- simple dressings
- adhesive bandages (like Band-Aids)
- painkiller
- prescription medicines

**Money and Documents**
All post offices have passport applications. If you lose your passport you should report the matter to the local police at once, obtain a certificate or receipt, then proceed to your embassy for a replacement. If you have your birth certificate with you it expedites things considerably. Don't bother getting an international driver's license as your regular license is all you need to drive here.

Traveler's checks in U.S. dollars are recommended, and in the South Pacific, American Express is the most efficient company when it comes to providing refunds for lost checks. Bring along a small supply of US$1 and US$5 bills to use if you don't manage to change money immediately upon arrival or if you run out of local currency and can't get to a bank.

Carry your valuables in a money belt worn around your waist or neck under your clothing; most camping stores have these. Make several photocopies of the information page of your passport, personal identification, driver's license, scuba certification card, credit cards, airline tickets, receipts for purchase of traveler's checks, etc.—you should be able to get them all on one page. On the side, write the phone numbers you'd need to call to report lost documents. A brief medical history with your blood type, allergies, chronic or special health problems, eyeglass and medical prescriptions, etc., might also come in handy. Put these inside plastic bags to protect them from moisture, then carry the lists in different places, and leave one at home.

- passport
- airline tickets
- scuba certification card
- driver's license
- traveler's checks
- some U.S. cash
- credit card
- photocopies of documents
- money belt
- address book
- notebook
- envelopes
- extra ballpoints

## FILM AND PHOTOGRAPHY

Scan the ads in photographic magazines for deals on mail-order cameras and film, or buy at a discount shop in any large city. Run a roll of film through your camera to be sure it's in good working order; clean the lens with lens-cleaning tissue and check the batteries. Remove the batteries from your camera when storing it at home for long periods. Register valuable cameras or electronic equipment with customs before you leave home so there won't be any argument over where you bought the items when you return, or at least carry a copy of the original bill of sale.

The type of camera you choose could depend on the way you travel. If you'll be staying mostly in one place, a heavy single-lens reflex (SLR) camera with spare lenses and other equipment won't trouble you. If you'll be moving around a lot for a considerable length of time, a 35-mm automatic compact camera will be better. The compacts are mostly useful for close-up shots; landscapes will seem spread out and far away. A wide-angle lens gives excellent depth of field, but hold the camera upright to avoid converging verticals. A polarizing filter prevents reflections from glass windows and water, and makes the sky bluer.

Although film is cheap and readily available in Fiji, you never know if it's been spoiled by an airport X-ray on the way there. On a long trip, mailers are essential as exposed film shouldn't be held for long periods. Choose 36-exposure film over 24-exposure to save on the number of rolls you have to carry. When purchasing film in the islands take care to check the expiration date.

Films are rated by their speed and sensitivity to light, using ISO numbers from 25 to 1600. The higher the number, the greater the film's sensitivity to light. Slower films with lower ISOs (like 100-200) produce sharp images in bright sunlight. Faster films with higher ISOs (like 400) stop action and work well in low-light situations, such as in dark rainforests or at sunset. If you have a manual SLR you can avoid overexposure at midday by reducing the exposure half a stop, but *do* overexpose when photographing dark-skinned Fijians. From 1000 to 1600 the light is often too bright to take good photos, and panoramas usually come out best early or late in the day.

Wayne J. Andrews of Eastman Kodak offers the following suggestions for enhanced photography. Keep your photos simple with one main subject and an uncomplicated background. Get as close to your subjects as you can and lower or raise the camera to their level. Include people in the foreground of scenic shots to add interest and perspective. Outdoors a flash can fill in unflattering facial shadows caused by high sun or backlit conditions. Most of all, be creative. Look for interesting details and compose the photo before you push the trigger. Instead of taking a head-on photo of a group of people, step to one side and ask them to face you. The angle improves the photo. Photograph subjects coming toward you rather than passing by. Ask permission before photographing people. If you're asked for money (rare) you can always walk away—give your subjects the same choice. There is probably no country in the world where the photographer will have as interesting and willing subjects as in Fiji.

When packing, protect your camera against vibration. Checked baggage is scanned by powerful airport X-ray monitors, so carry both camera and film aboard the plane in a clear plastic bag and ask security for a visual inspection. Some airports will refuse to do this, however. A good alternative is to use a lead-laminated pouch. The old high-dose X-ray units are seldom seen these days but even low-dose inspection units can ruin fast film (400 ASA and above). Beware of the cumulative effect of X-ray machines.

Store your camera in a plastic bag during rain and while traveling in motorized canoes, etc. In the tropics the humidity can cause film to stick to itself; silica-gel crystals in the bag will protect film from humidity and mold growth. Protect camera and film from direct sunlight and load the film in the shade. When loading, check that the takeup spool revolves. Never leave camera or film in a hot place like a car floor, glove compartment, or trunk.

# GETTING THERE

Fiji's geographic position makes it the hub of transport for the entire South Pacific, and Nadi is the region's most important international airport, with long-haul services to points all around the Pacific Rim. Eleven international airlines fly into Nadi: Aircalin, Air Marshall Islands, Air Nauru, Air New Zealand, Air Pacific, Air Vanuatu, Canada 3000, Polynesian Airlines, Qantas Airways, Royal Tongan Airlines, and Solomon Airlines. Air Marshall Islands and Air Pacific also use Suva's Nausori Airport.

Fiji's national airline, **Air Pacific,** was founded in 1951 as Fiji Airways by Harold Gatty, a famous Australian aviator who had set a record with American Willy Post in 1931 by flying around the world in eight days. In 1972 the airline was reorganized as a regional carrier and the name changed to Air Pacific. Thanks to careful management, the Nadi-based company has made a profit every year since 1985. The carrier arrives at Nadi from Apia, Auckland, Brisbane, Christchurch, Honiara, Honolulu, Los Angeles, Melbourne, Port Vila, Sydney, Tokyo, Tongatapu, and Wellington, and at Suva from Apia, Auckland, and Sydney. Qantas owns 46% of Air Pacific (the Fiji government owns the rest) and most Qantas flights to Fiji are actually code shares with the Fijian carrier. Qantas is Air Pacific's general sales agent in Europe, North America, and Australia, and you'll probably fly Air Pacific if you booked with Qantas. Air Pacific code shares with Solomon Airlines when going to Honiara, and with Aircalin to Papeete.

### Preparations

First decide when you're going and how long you wish to stay away. Your plane ticket will be your biggest single expense, so spend some time considering the possibilities. Read this entire chapter right through before going any further. If you're online check the internet sites of the airlines, then call them up directly over their toll-free 800 numbers to get current information on fares. The following airlines have flights from North America:

**Air New Zealand:** tel. 1-800/262-1234, www.airnz.co.nz

**Air Pacific:** tel. 1-800/227-4446, www.bulafiji.com/airlines/airpac/htm

**Canada 3000:** tel. 1-416/674-0257, www.canada3000.com

Sometimes Canada and parts of the U.S. have different toll-free numbers, so if a number given in this chapter doesn't work, dial 800 information at 1-800/555-1212 (all 800 and 888 numbers are free). In Canada, Air New Zealand's toll-free number is tel. 1-800/663-5494.

Call both Air New Zealand and Air Pacific and say you want the *lowest possible fare*. Cheapest are the excursion fares but these usually have limitations and restrictions, so be sure to ask. Some have an advance-purchase deadline, which means it's wise to begin shopping early. If you're not happy with the answers you get, call the number back later and try again. Many different agents take calls on these lines, and some are more knowledgeable than others. The numbers are often busy during peak business hours, so call first thing in the morning, after dinner, or on the weekend. *Be persistent.*

After you're heard what the airlines have to say, try the "discounters," specialist travel agencies that deal in bulk and sell seats and rooms at wholesale prices. Many airlines have more seats than they can market through normal channels, so they sell their unused long-haul capacity to "consolidators" or "bucket shops" at discounts of 40-50% off the official tariffs. The discounters buy tickets on this gray market and pass the savings along to you. Many such companies run ads in the Sunday travel sections of newspapers like the *San Francisco Examiner, New York Times,* and *Toronto Star,* or in major entertainment weeklies.

Despite their occasionally shady appearance, most discounters and consolidators are perfectly legitimate, and your ticket will probably be issued by the airline itself. Most discounted tickets look and are exactly the same as regular full-fare tickets but they're usually nonrefundable. There may also be penalties if you wish to change your routing or reservations, and other restrictions not associated with the more expensive tickets. Rates are competitive, so allow yourself time to shop around. A few hours spent on the phone, doing time on hold and asking questions, will save you money.

## Seasons

The month of outbound travel from the U.S. determines which seasonal fare you'll pay, and inquiring far in advance could allow you to reschedule your vacation slightly to take advantage of a lower fare.

Air New Zealand and Air Pacific have their low (or "basic") season on flights to Fiji from mid-April to August, shoulder season from September to November and in March, and high (or "peak") season from December to February. They've

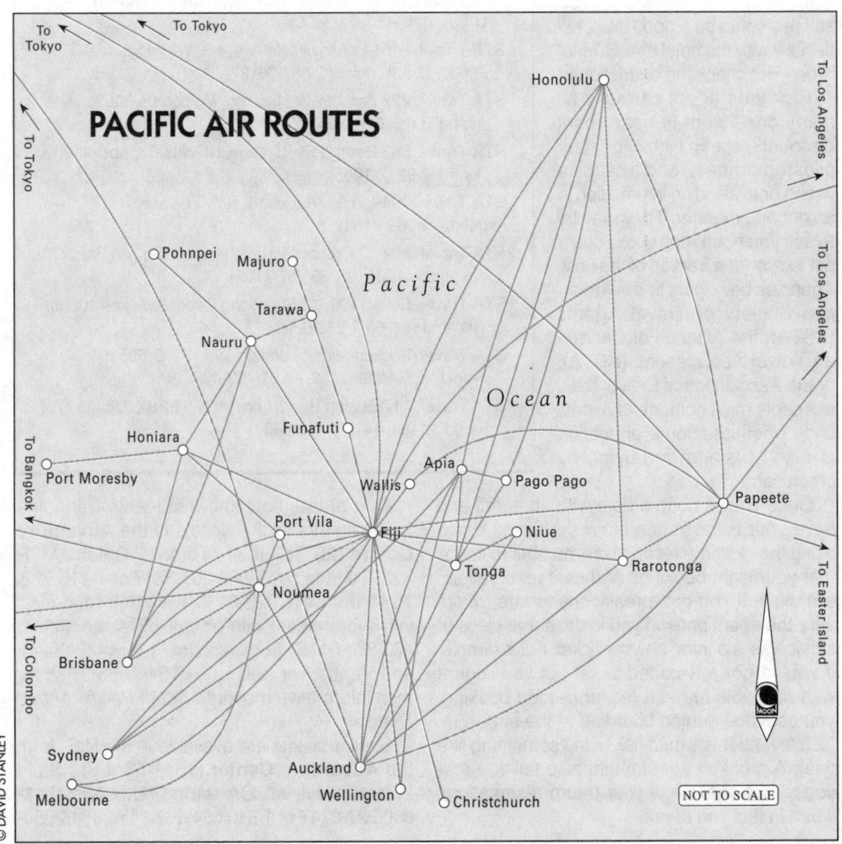

made April to November—the top months in Fiji—their off-season because that's winter in Australia and New Zealand. If you're only going to the islands and can make it at that time, it certainly works to your advantage.

### Travel Agents

Be aware that any travel agent worth his/her commission will probably want to sell you a package tour, and it's a fact that some vacation packages actually cost less than regular roundtrip airfare! If they'll let you extend your return date to give you some time to yourself this could be a good deal, especially with the hotel thrown in for "free." But check the restrictions.

Pick your agent carefully as many don't want to hear about discounts, cheap flights, or complicated routes, and will give wrong or misleading information in an offhand manner. They may try to sell you hotel rooms you could get locally for a fraction of the cost. Agencies belonging to the American Society of Travel Agents (ASTA), the Alliance of Canadian Travel Associations (ACTA), or the Association of British Travel Agents must conform to a strict code of ethics. Some protection is also obtained by paying by credit card.

Once you've done a deal with an agent and have your ticket in hand, call the airline again using their toll-free reservations number to check that your flight bookings and seat reservations are okay. If you got a really cheap fare, make sure the agent booked you in the same class of service as is printed on your ticket. For example, if you've got a K-coded ticket but your agent was only able to get a higher B-code booking, you could be denied boarding at the airport (in fact, few agents would risk doing something like this). A crooked agent might also tell you that you're free to change your return reservations when in fact you're not.

One of the most knowledgeable Canadian travel agents for Fiji tickets is the **Adventure Centre** (25 Bellair St., Toronto, Ontario M5R 3L3, Canada; tel. 1-800/267-3347 or 1-416/922-7584, fax 1-416/922-8136, www.trek.ca, e-mail: info@tor.trek.ca) with offices in Calgary (tel. 1-403/283-6115), Edmonton (tel. 1-403/439-0024), and Vancouver (tel. 1-604/734-1066). Ask for their informative brochure *South Pacific Airfare Specials.*

Similar tickets are available in the U.S. from the **Adventure Center** (1311 63rd St., Suite 200, Emeryville, CA 94608, U.S.A.; tel. 1-800/227-8747 or 1-510/654-1879, fax 1-510/654-

## STUDENT TRAVEL OFFICES

STA Travel, 297 Newbury St., Boston, MA 02115, U.S.A (tel. 617/266-6014)

STA Travel, 429 S. Dearborn St., Chicago, IL 60605, U.S.A. (tel. 312/786-9050)

STA Travel, 920 Westwood Blvd., Los Angeles, CA 90024, U.S.A. (tel. 310/824-1574)

STA Travel, 10 Downing St. (6th Ave. and Bleecker), New York, NY 10014, U.S.A. (tel. 212/627-3111)

STA Travel, 3730 Walnut St., Philadelphia, PA 19104, U.S.A. (tel. 215/382-2928)

STA Travel, 51 Grant Ave., San Francisco, CA 94108, U.S.A. (tel. 415/391-8407)

STA Travel, 4341 University Way NE, Seattle, WA 98105, U.S.A. (tel. 206/633-5000)

STA Travel, 2401 Pennsylvania Ave. #G, Washington, DC 20037, U.S.A. (tel. 202/887-0912)

STA Travel, 222 Faraday St., Carlton, Melbourne 3053, Australia (tel. 61-3/9349-2411)

STA Travel, 855 George St., Sydney, NSW 2007, Australia (tel. 61-2/9212-1255)

STA Travel, 10 High St., Auckland, New Zealand (tel. 64-9/309-0458)

STA Travel, #02-17 Orchard Parade Hotel, 1 Tanglin Road, Singapore 1024 (tel. 65/737-7188)

STA Travel, Suite 1406, 33 Surawong Road, Bangkok 10500, Thailand (tel. 66-2/236-0262)

STA Travel, Bockenheimer Landstrasse 133, D-60325 Frankfurt, Germany (tel. 49-69/703-035)

STA Travel, 117 Euston Road, London NW1 2SX, United Kingdom (tel. 44-171/465-0484)

4200, e-mail: tripinfo@adventure-center.com).

**Discover Wholesale Travel** (2192 Dupont Dr., Suite 116, Irvine, CA 92612, U.S.A.; tel. 1-800/576-7770, 1-800/759-7330, or 1-949/833-1136, fax 1-949/833-1176) sells discounted air tickets and offers rock-bottom rates on rooms at the top hotels. They sometimes have significantly lower fares for passengers booking within two weeks of departure ("distressed seats"). President Mary Anne Cook claims everyone on her staff has 10 years experience selling the South Pacific and "most importantly, we all love the area!"

Some of the cheapest return tickets to Fiji are sold by **Fiji Travel** (8885 Venice Blvd., Suite 202, Los Angeles, CA 90034, U.S.A.: tel. 1-800/500-3454 or 1-310/202-4220, fax 1-310/202-8233, www.fijitravel.com). They make their money through high volume, and to attract customers they keep their profit margins as low as possible. Thus you should absorb the airline's time with all your questions about fare seasons, schedules, etc., and only call consolidators like Fiji Travel and Discover Wholesale Travel after you know exactly what you want and how much everybody else is charging.

One U.S. agent willing to help you work out a personalized itinerary is Rob Jenneve of **Island Adventures** (574 Mills Way, Goleta, CA 93117, U.S.A.; tel. 1-800/289-4957 or 1-805/685-9230, fax 1-805/685-0960, e-mail: motuman@aol.com). Rob can put together flight and accommodation packages that are only slightly more expensive than the cheapest return airfare, and it's often possible to extend your return date to up to 30 days on the lowest fares or up to 90 days for a bit more. This option combines the benefits of packaged and independent travel, and you could end up spending a week at a medium-priced hotel with transfers for only US$50-100 more than you'd have to spend anyway just to get to the islands! Rob also books complex circle-Pacific routes and can steer you toward deluxe resorts that offer value for money.

### Student Fares

If you're a student, recent graduate, or teacher, you can sometimes benefit from lower student fares by booking through a student travel office. There are two rival organizations of this kind: Council Travel Services, with offices in college towns across the U.S. and a sister organization

## COUNCIL TRAVEL OFFICES

Council Travel, 2486 Channing Way, Berkeley, CA 94704, U.S.A. (tel. 510/848-8604)

Council Travel, 273 Newbury St., Boston, MA 02115, U.S.A. (tel. 617/266-1926)

Council Travel, 1153 N. Dearborn St., 2nd Floor, Chicago, IL 60610, U.S.A. (tel. 312/951-0585)

Council Travel, 10904 Lindbrook Dr., Los Angeles, CA 90024, U.S.A. (tel. 310/208-3551)

Council Travel, One Datran Center, Suite 220, 9100 S. Dadeland Blvd., Miami, FL 33156, U.S.A. (tel. 305/670-9261)

Council Travel, 205 East 42nd St., New York, NY 10017-5706, U.S.A. (tel. 212/822-2700)

Council Travel, 1430 SW Park Ave., Portland, OR 97201, U.S.A. (tel. 503/228-1900)

Council Travel, 953 Garnet Ave., San Diego, CA 92109, U.S.A. (tel. 619/270-6401)

Council Travel, 530 Bush St., San Francisco, CA 94108, U.S.A. tel. 415/421-3473)

Council Travel, 1314 N.E. 43rd St., Suite 210, Seattle, WA 98105, U.S.A. (tel. 206/632-2448)

Travel Cuts, 187 College St., Toronto, ON M5T 1P7, Canada (tel. 416/979-2406)

Travel Cuts, 567 Seymour St., Vancouver, BC V6B 3H6, Canada (tel. 604/681-9136)

SYFS, 102/12-13 Koasan Road, Banglumpoo, Bangkok 10200, Thailand (tel. 66-2/282-0507)

HKST, 921a Star House, Tsimshatsui, Kowloon, Hong Kong (tel. 852/2730-3269)

CIEE, Cosmos Aoyoma, B1, 5-53-67 Jingumae, Shibuya-ku, Tokyo, Japan (tel. 81-3/5467-5501)

Council Travel, 18 Graf Adolph Strasse, D-40212 Düsseldorf 1, Germany (tel. 49-211/363-030)

Council Travel, 22 rue des Pyramides, 75001 Paris, France (tel. 33-1/4455-5544)

Council Travel, 28A Poland St., near Oxford Circus, London W1V 3DB, United Kingdom (tel. 44-171/437-7767)

in Canada known as Travel Cuts; and STA Travel (Student Travel Australia) with a wholesale division known as the Student Travel Network. Both organizations require you to pay a nominal fee for an official student card, and to get the cheapest fares you have to prove you're really a student. Slightly higher fares on the same routes are available to nonstudents, so they're always worth checking.

**STA Travel** (www.sta-travel.com) offers special airfares for students and young people under 26 years old with minimal restrictions. Their prices on roundtrip fares to Fiji are competitive, but they don't sell more complicated tickets to a number of points (standard routings like Los Angeles-Fiji-Auckland-Sydney-Bangkok-London-Los Angeles are their style). Call their toll-free number (tel. 1-800/777-0112) for the latest information.

Different student fares are available from **Council Travel Services,** a division of the nonprofit Council on International Educational Exchange (CIEE). Both they and **Travel Cuts** (tel. 1-800/667-2887) in Canada are stricter about making sure you're a "real" student: you must first obtain the widely recognized International Student Identity Card (US$20) to get a ticket at the student rate. Some fares are limited to students and youths under 26 years of age, but part-time students and teachers also qualify. Circle-Pacific and round-the-world routings are also available from Council Travel Services and there are special connecting flights to Los Angeles from other U.S. points.

### Bula Fiji Starter Packs

If you book air only and would like the security of a reserved room in which to recover from jetlag and get your bearings, **Fiji For Less** (www.fiji4less.com) offers a variety of "starter packs" that provide a transfer from Nadi Airport plus two nights accommodations at a budget Lautoka area or Coral Coast hotel such as Saweni Beach Apartments or Tubakula Beach Resort. Both resorts offer cooking facilities, and a few basic groceries are included to allow you to prepare your own breakfast without having to go out shopping. They'll even change money at bank rates without commission, and free luggage storage is available.

Since Fiji For Less only accepts direct bookings over the internet or by fax, and pays no commissions to wholesalers or travel agents, they're able to keep their prices low. Two-night transfer/bed packages to Tubakula cost US$34 pp in a dormitory, US$50/78 single/double in a private room, or US$100 double in an ocean-view bungalow. Prices at Saweni are slightly cheaper and the same deal is offered to the Cathay Hotel in Lautoka, if you'd rather be in town. These resorts organize a/c transfers back to the airport or on to Suva at prices only slightly above public transportation.

To book, send a fax to 308-646 in Fiji or 1-310/362-8493 in the U.S. stating your name, address, and contact information (phone, fax, or e-mail) a few days before you leave for Fiji. Say which type of accommodations you prefer and give your flight details (remember the international dateline). In order have a driver waiting at the airport, they'll need a credit card authorization. Confirmation will be faxed or e-mailed to you within 48 hours. Better yet, check their website or fax one of the numbers above in advance for current information.

### Current Trends

High operating costs have caused the larger airlines to switch to wide-bodied aircraft and long-haul routes with less frequent service and fewer stops. In the South Pacific this works to your disadvantage, as many islands get bypassed. Most airlines now charge extra for stopovers that once were free, or simply refuse to grant any stopovers at all on the cheapest fares.

Increasingly airlines are combining in global alliances to compete internationally. Thus Air Pacific is part of a family comprising Qantas, American Airlines, Canadian Airlines, British Airways, and Japan Airlines, while Air New Zealand has close ties to Ansett Australia, United Airlines, Lufthansa, and Singapore Airlines. This is to your advantage as within the different blocks frequent flier programs are often interchangeable, booking becomes easier, flight schedules are coordinated, and through fares exist. They also have special air passes and round-the-world deals combining the networks of a variety of affiliated carriers, several of which are discussed below.

### Circular Tickets

If you plan a wide-ranging trip with stops on several continents, the **Global Explorer** may be the ticket for you. This fare allows six free stops selected from over 400 destinations on 28,500 miles of routes. You can use the services of any of these airlines: Air Liberté, Air Pacific, American Airlines, British Airways, Canadian Airlines, Deutsche Airlines, and Qantas. This pass costs US$3,089 and additional stops after the first six are US$100 each. You must purchase the pass a week in advance and it's valid one year. Date changes and the first rerouting is free (additional reroutings US$100). Ask Qantas or Air Pacific about this ticket.

A similar fare available only in the South Pacific and Europe is the **World Navigator,** which encompasses the networks of Aircalin, Air New Zealand, Air UK, Ansett Australia, Emirates, KLM Royal Dutch Airlines, Northwest Airlines, and South African Airways. From London, the World Navigator costs £1,099/1,199/1,299 in the low/shoulder/peak seasons (the low season is April to June only). From Australia, it's A$2,569/2,779/2,979/3,189 according to season with the lowest seasons running from mid-January to February and October to mid-November.

In North America, Air New Zealand sells a **World Escapade** valid for a round-the-world journey on Air New Zealand, Ansett Australia, and Singapore Airlines. You're allowed 29,000 miles with unlimited stops at US$2,799. One transatlantic and one transpacific journey must be included, but the ticket is valid one year and backtracking is allowed.

Air New Zealand's **Pacific Escapade** allows a circle-Pacific trip on the same three airlines. With this one you get 22,000 miles at US$2,600 with all the stops you want (maximum of three each in Australia and New Zealand). You'll have to transit Singapore at least once and travel must begin in either Los Angeles or Vancouver (no add-ons). On both Escapades, should you go over the allowable mileage, 4,500 extra miles are US$300. Reservation changes are free the first time but extra after that.

Northwest Airlines in conjunction with Air New Zealand offers a **Circle-Pacific fare** of US$2,650 from Los Angeles with add-on airfares available from other North American cities. This ticket allows four free stopovers in Asia and the South Pacific, additional stops US$50 each. To reissue the ticket also costs US$50. It's valid six months and date changes are free. You must travel in a continuous circle without any backtracking. Air Pacific also has a Circle-Pacific fare, so compare.

## AIR SERVICES

### From North America

Air New Zealand and Air Pacific are the major carriers serving Fiji out of Los Angeles, Honolulu, and Vancouver. **Air Pacific** flies a Boeing 747 flight from Los Angeles to Nadi nonstop four times a week and from Honolulu weekly. If you have to fly via Hawaii on Air New Zealand, it's a five-and-a-half-hour flight from California to Honolulu, then another six and a half hours from Honolulu to Fiji. The four nonstop Air Pacific flights from Los Angeles take only 10 hours total as you save all the time Air New Zealand spends on the ground in Hawaii.

From Los Angeles, a 30-day return ticket to Fiji on Air Pacific is US$888/1,048/1,298 low/shoulder/high season. From Honolulu it's US$688/848/1,098. These are the midweek fares—weekend departures are US$60 more expensive—and some restrictions apply. When booking, ask for a flight that arrives at Nadi in the early morning to avoid the expensive hassle of arriving late at night. Flying Air Pacific means you enjoy the friendly flavor of Fiji from the moment you leave the ground.

From November to April **Canada 3000** operates direct weekly charter flights from Vancouver via Honolulu with connections to/from Toronto. **Canadian Airlines International** and Air Pacific operate a code-share service between Vancouver/Toronto and Fiji via Honolulu. Air New Zealand passengers originating in Canada must change planes in Honolulu or Los Angeles.

### Air New Zealand

In the 1950s Air New Zealand pioneered its "Coral Route" using Solent flying boats, and today the carrier has achieved a death grip over long-haul air routes into the region by allowing stopovers in Tahiti, Cook Islands, Fiji, Samoa, and Tonga as part of through services between North America and New Zealand. Air New Zealand also arrives in Fiji from Nagoya, Japan. Yet despite Air New Zealand's frequent services, travelers in Europe and North America often

## AIRPORT CODES

| | | |
|---|---|---|
| AKL—Auckland | LEV—Levuka | SEA—Seattle |
| APW—Apia/Faleolo | LKB—Lakeba | SFO—San Francisco |
| BNE—Brisbane | MEL—Melbourne | SIN—Singapore |
| CHC—Christchurch | MFJ—Moala | SUV—Suva |
| FGI—Apia/Fagalii | MNF—Mana | SVU—Savusavu |
| FUN—Funafuti | NAN—Nadi | SYD—Sydney |
| HIR—Honiara | NGI—Gau | TBU—Tongatapu |
| HNL—Honolulu | NOU—Nouméa | TRW—Tarawa |
| ICI—Cicia | OSA—Osaka | TVU—Taveuni |
| INU—Nauru | POM—Port Moresby | TYO—Tokyo |
| IPC—Easter Island | PPG—Pago Pago | VBV—Vanua Balavu |
| IUE—Niue | PPT—Papeete | VLI—Port Vila |
| KDV—Kadavu | PTF—Malololailai | WLG—Wellington |
| KXF—Koro | RAR—Rarotonga | WLS—Wallis |
| LAX—Los Angeles | RTA—Rotuma | YVR—Vancouver |
| LBS—Labasa | SCL—Santiago | YYZ—Toronto |

have difficulty booking seats and it's advisable to reserve well ahead.

Return tickets to Fiji on Air New Zealand usually cost exactly the same as on Air Pacific. Ask for the "No Stop Apex," which is US$888/1,048/1,298 if you leave Los Angeles at the beginning of the week (US$200 cheaper from Honolulu). To set out on Thursday, Friday, Saturday, or Sunday costs US$60 more. The maximum stay is one month and you must pay at least 21 days before departure (50% cancellation penalty).

If you want to include a bit more of the South Pacific in your trip, consider Air New Zealand's "Coral Experience," which allows one stop plus your destination with additional stops available at US$145 each. Thus you can fly Los Angeles-Tahiti-Rarotonga-Fiji-Los Angeles for US$1,143/1,343/1,593 low/shoulder/high season if you leave at the beginning of the week for a trip of three months maximum. Add US$150 if wish to extend your period of stay to six months, plus another US$60 if you'd like to set out on Thursday, Friday, Saturday, or Sunday. Drop either Tahiti or Rarotonga from your itinerary and you'll save US$145. Trips originating in Honolulu are US$200 cheaper in all cases. Remember that the "Coral Experience" must be purchased 14 days in advance and there's a US$75 penalty to change your flight dates after your initial purchase. A 35% cancellation fee also applies after the 14-day ticket deadline.

For a more wide-ranging trip with fewer restrictions, check out Air New Zealand's "Coral Explorer Airpass," which costs US$1,758/2,008/2,258 low/shoulder/high season. This worthwhile ticket allows you to fly Los Angeles-Tahiti-Rarotonga-Fiji-Auckland-Tongatapu/Apia-Honolulu-Los Angeles or vice versa. Extend the ticket to Australia for US$100 more; eliminate Auckland-Tongatapu/Apia and it's about US$100 less. Begin in Honolulu and it's US$200 less again. You can stay up to one year but rerouting costs US$75 (date changes are free). There's no advance purchase requirement and you can fly any day. To follow exactly the same routing minus one stop on a six-month "Coral Experience" with all its restrictions costs US$1,633/1,883/2,133.

In Canada, Air New Zealand calls the same fares by different names: the "No Stop Apex" is the "Shotover Fare" while the "Coral Experience" is the "Bungy Fare" (but the "Explorer" is still the "Explorer"). The cheaper "Backpacker Downunder" fare from Canada must be purchased 14 days in advance and does not cover hotel expenses due to flight misconnections. On most Air New Zealand tickets special "add-on" fares to Los Angeles or Vancouver are available from cities right across the U.S. and Canada—be sure to ask about them.

Air New Zealand's cabin service is professional, and you'll like the champagne breakfasts and outstanding food with complimentary beer and wine. Another plus are the relaxing seats with adjustable head rests and lots of leg room. The *Blue Pacific* videos about their destinations are entertaining the first time you see them, but after a while you get bored. The only reading material provided is the *Pacific Wave* inflight magazine, the *Skyshop* duty free catalog, and the *Primetime* entertainment magazine. These are unlikely to hold your attention for long, so bring along a book or magazine of your own (the daily newspaper is provided only to passengers in first class).

**From Australia**

**Air Pacific** offers nonstop flights to Nadi from Brisbane, Melbourne, and Sydney (most Qantas flights to Fiji are now operated by Air Pacific planes). From Sydney, Air Pacific also has direct flights to Suva. In November 1998 **Ansett Australia** also began twice-weekly service to Fiji. Since the Australian government sold Qantas and deregulated airfares, the cost of flying out of Australia has dropped dramatically. Now you can often find much better deals than the published Apex fares, especially during off months.

Air New Zealand is competing fiercely in the Australian market, and they offer competitive fares to many South Pacific points via Auckland. You can usually buy such tickets for a lower price than you'd pay at the airline office itself by working through an agent specializing in bargain airfares. The airlines sometimes offer specials during the off months, so check the travel sections in the weekend papers and call Flight Centres International. For information on slightly reduced fares available from STA Travel, see Student Fares, above.

The Circle-Pacific and round-the-world fares described above are also available here. Apex (advance purchase excursion) tickets must be bought 14 days in advance and heavy cancellation penalties apply. The low season ex-Australia is generally mid-January to May and October to November.

**From New Zealand**

Both Air New Zealand and Air Pacific fly to Nadi from Auckland, and Air Pacific also flies from Christchurch and Wellington to Nadi and from Auckland to Suva. Unrestricted low airfares to Fiji can be hard to come by and some tickets have advance purchase requirements, so start shopping well ahead. Ask around at a number of different travel agencies for special unadvertised or under-the-counter fares. Agents to call include STA Travel and Flight Centres International.

Air New Zealand offers reduced excursion fares from Auckland to Fiji with a maximum stay of 90 days at NZ$822 from January to June and mid-October to mid-December, and NZ$983 the

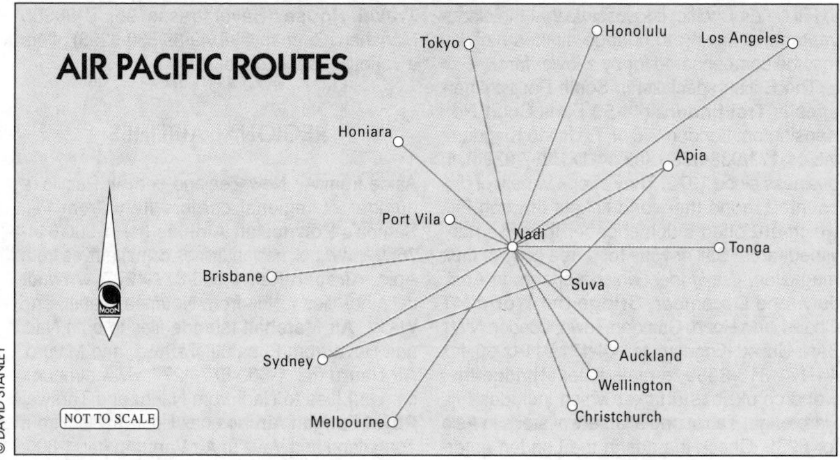


© DAVID STANLEY

other months. It's often cheaper to buy a package tour to the islands with airfare, accommodations, and transfers all included, but these are usually limited to seven nights on one island and you're stuck in a boring touristic environment. Ask if you can extend your return date.

### From Europe

Since no European carriers reach Fiji, you'll have to use a gateway city such as Sydney, Honolulu, or Los Angeles. **Air New Zealand** offers nonstop flights London-Los Angeles five times a week and Frankfurt-Los Angeles three times a week, with connections in L.A. direct to Fiji. In April 1998 Air New Zealand launched a weekly nonstop flight between Nadi and Los Angeles, allowing European passengers to fly to Fiji from Frankfurt or London with only one change of aircraft at Los Angeles.

Air New Zealand reservations numbers around Europe are tel. 03/202-1355 (Belgium), tel. 0800/907-712 (France), tel. 01/3081-7778 (Germany), tel. 1678-76126 (Italy), tel. 08-002527 (Luxembourg), tel. 06/022-1016 (Netherlands), tel. 900/993241 (Spain), tel. 020/792-939 (Sweden), tel. 0800/557-778 (Switzerland), and tel. 44-181/741-2299 (United Kingdom). Ask about their Coral Route fares. Be aware that Air New Zealand flights from Europe are heavily booked and reservations should be made far in advance.

Also call your local British Airways or Qantas office and ask what connections they are offering to Fiji on Air Pacific. It's possible that the disadvantage of having to change airlines halfway may be compensated for by a lower fare.

The British specialist in South Pacific itineraries is **Trailfinders** (44-50 Earls Court Rd., Kensington, London W8 6FT, United Kingdom; tel. 44-171/938-3366, fax 44-171/937-9294), in business since 1970. They offer a variety of discounted round-the-world tickets through Fiji, which are often much cheaper than the published fares. Call or write for a free copy of their magazine, *Trailfinder,* which appears in April, July, and December. **Bridge the World** (47 Chalk Farm Road, Camden Town, London NW1 8AN, United Kingdom; tel. 44-171/911-0900, fax 44-171/813-3350, e-mail: sales@bridge-the-world.co.uk) has a ticket which includes Fiji, Rarotonga, Tahiti, and a variety of stops in Asia for £935. Check the ads in the London entertainment magazines for other such companies.

In Holland **Pacific Island Travel** (Herengracht 495,1017 BT Amsterdam, the Netherlands; tel. 31-20/626-1325, fax 31-20/623-0008, e-mail: pitnet@xs4all.nl) sells most of the air passes and long-distance tickets mentioned in this section, plus package tours. **Barron & De Keijzer Travel** (Herengracht 340, 1016 CG Amsterdam, the Netherlands; tel. 31-20/625-8600, fax 31-20/622-7559) sells Air New Zealand's Coral Route with travel via London. Also in Amsterdam, **Reisbureau Amber** (Da Costastraat 77, 1053 ZG Amsterdam, the Netherlands; tel. 31-20/685-1155, fax 31-20/689-0406) is one of the best places in Europe to pick up books on Fiji.

In Switzerland try **Globetrotter Travel Service** (Rennweg 35, CH-8023 Zürich, Switzerland; tel. 41-1/213-8080, fax 41-1/213-8088), with offices in Baden, Basel, Bern, Luzern, St. Gallen, Thun, Winterthur, Zug, and Zürich. Their quarterly newsletter, *Ticket-Info,* lists hundreds of cheap flights, including many through Fiji.

Bucket shops in Germany sell a "Pacific Airpass" on Air New Zealand from Frankfurt to the South Pacific that allows all the usual Coral Route stops and is valid six months. All flights must be booked prior to leaving Europe, and there's a charge to change the dates once the ticket has been issued. One agency selling such tickets is **Walther-Weltreisen** (Hirschberger Strasse 30, D-53119 Bonn, Germany; tel. 49-228/661-239, fax 49-228/661-181). The **Pacific Travel House** (Bayerstrasse 95, D-80335 München, Germany; tel. 49-89/530-9293) offers a variety of package tours.

## REGIONAL AIRLINES

Aside from Air New Zealand and Air Pacific, a number of regional carriers fly to/from Fiji. Samoa's **Polynesian Airlines** (tel. 1-800/644-7659, www.polynesianairlines.co.nz) arrives from Apia. **Aircalin** (tel. 1-800/677-4277, www.aircalin.nc) flies to Fiji from Nouméa, Tahiti, and Wallis. **Air Marshall Islands** flies to both Nadi and Suva from Funafuti, Tarawa, and Majuro. **Air Nauru** (tel. 1-800/677-4277, www.airnauru.com.au) flies to Nadi from Nauru and Tarawa. **Royal Tongan Airlines** has flights to Nadi from Tongatapu and Vava'u. **Air Vanuatu** (tel. 1-800/

677-4277) flies from Port Vila. **Solomon Airlines** (tel. 1-800/677-4277) links Fiji to Honiara and Port Vila. Keep in mind that few regional flights operate daily and quite a few are only once or twice a week.

### Regional Air Passes

In 1995 the Association of South Pacific Airlines introduced a **Visit South Pacific Pass** to coincide with "Visit South Pacific Year" and the pass has been so successful that the Association decided to extend it indefinitely. This pass allows travelers to include the services of 10 regional carriers in a single ticket. The initial two-leg air pass has to be purchased in conjunction with an international ticket into the region, but additional legs up to a maximum of eight can be purchased after arrival. Only the first sector has to be booked ahead.

The flights are priced at three different levels. For US$175 per sector you can go Fiji-Apia/Nauru/Tongatapu/Port Vila/Vava'u/Funafuti, Apia-Tongatapu, Nouméa-Port Vila, Nauru-Pohnpei/Tarawa, Niue-Tongatapu, or Funafuti-Tarawa. For US$220 you have a choice of Honiara-Nadi/Port Vila/Port Moresby, Nouméa/Tahiti-Nadi, Funafuti-Majuro, Fiji-Tarawa, or a variety of flights from Australia and New Zealand to the islands. For US$320 there's Honiara-Auckland, Tahiti-Nouméa, Sydney-Tongatapu, and Fiji-Majuro. It's a great way of getting around the South Pacific.

Air New Zealand calls this ticket the "Pacifica Airpass" and it can only be purchased in North or South America, Europe, or Asia. One North American agent selling the Visit South Pacific Pass is **Air Promotions Systems** (5757 West Century Blvd., Suite 660, Los Angeles, CA 90045-6407, U.S.A.; tel. 1-800/677-4277 or 1-310/670-7302; fax 1-310/338-0708, www.pacificislands.com). They handle the pass for flights on Aircalin, Air Nauru, Air Vanuatu, and Solomon Airlines. For information on using the pass on Air Pacific, Polynesian Airlines, Qantas, or Royal Tongan Airlines, call the toll-free 800 numbers of those airlines provided earlier. For Air Marshall Islands or Air Niugini, try Air Pacific.

### Air Pacific

Air Pacific has two different **Pacific Triangle Fares,** good ways to get around and experience the region's variety of cultures: Fiji-Apia-Tonga-Fiji (F$724) and Fiji-Nouméa-Port Vila-Fiji (F$809). Both are valid for one year and can be purchased at any travel agency in Fiji or direct from the airline. They're usually good only for journeys commencing in Fiji. Flight dates can be changed at no charge. When booking these circular tickets, be aware that it's much better to go Fiji-Apia-Tonga-Fiji than vice versa, because the flights between Apia and Fiji are often fully booked while it's easy to get on between Tonga and Fiji. Also obtainable locally are Air Pacific's special 28-day roundtrip excursion fares from Fiji to Apia (F$561), Tonga (F$469), Port Vila (F$579), and Honiara (F$1,045). Some of these fares have seasonal variations.

A **Pacific Air Pass** allows 30 days travel (on Air Pacific flights only) from Fiji to Apia, Tonga, and Port Vila (US$462). This pass can only be purchased from Qantas Airways offices in North America and Europe, or from Air Pacific's U.S. office (Suite 475, 841 Apollo St., El Segundo, CA 90245-4741, U.S.A.; tel. 1-800/227-4446 or 1-310/524-9350, fax 1-310/524-9356, www.bulafiji.com/airlines/airpac/htm). Available in North America only is the **Fiji/Vanuatu/Solomons Triangle Fare,** which gives you 60 days to go around this circuit at US$617. The 30-day Nadi-Honiara excursion fare is US$514 if purchased in North America.

### Polynesian Airlines

Polynesian Airlines offers a **Polypass** valid for 45 days unlimited travel between Nadi, Tongatapu, Apia, and Pago Pago, plus one roundtrip from Sydney, Melbourne, Auckland, or Wellington for US$999. From Honolulu the pass costs US$1,149, from Los Angeles US$1,399. Restrictions are that your itinerary must be worked out in advance and can only be changed once. Thus it's important to book all flights well ahead. A 20% penalty is charged to refund an unused ticket (no refund after one year).

Also ask about Polynesian's **Pacific Triangle Fare** (US$450), which allows one a full year to complete the Apia-Tongatapu-Nadi loop.

### Air Nauru

Air Nauru (www.airnauru.com.au), flag carrier of the tiny phosphate-rich Republic of Nauru in Micronesia, has flights from Nadi to Nauru

(A$486) twice a week, to Tarawa weekly. From Nauru there are onward connections to Pohnpei (A$499), Guam (A$585), and Manila (A$941) twice a week. Cheaper 28-day roundtrip excursion fares are available from Fiji. Their "Pacific Explorer Pass" allows you to do a Fiji-Tarawa-Nauru-Fiji circle trip for US$450 (available from Air Promotions Systems, mentioned above). In Suva their office is in Ratu Sakuna House, Macarthur St. and Victoria Parade.

**Important Note**

Airfares, rules, and regulations tend to fluctuate a lot, so some of the information above may have changed. This is only a guide; we've included a few fares to give you a rough idea how much things might cost. Your travel agent will know what's available at the time you're ready to travel, but if you're not satisfied with his/her advice, keep shopping around. The biggest step is deciding to go—once you're over that, the rest is easy!

## PROBLEMS

When planning your trip allow a minimum two-hour stopover between connecting flights at U.S. airports, although with airport delays on the increase even this may not be enough. In the islands allow at least a day between flights. In some airports flights are not called over the public address system, so keep your eyes open. Whenever traveling, always have a paperback or two, some toiletries, and a change of underwear in your hand luggage.

If your flight is canceled due to a mechanical problem with the aircraft, the airline will cover your hotel bill and meals. If they reschedule the flight on short notice for reasons of their own or you're bumped off an overbooked flight, they should also pay. They may not feel obligated to pay, however, if the delay is due to weather conditions, a strike by another company, national emergencies, etc., although the best airlines still pick up the tab in these cases.

It's an established practice among airlines to provide light refreshments to passengers delayed two hours after the scheduled departure time and a meal after four hours. Don't expect to get this from a computer airline on an outer island, but politely request it if you're at a gateway airport. If you are unexpectedly forced to spend the night somewhere, an airline employee may hand you a form on which they offer to telephone a friend or relative to inform them of the delay. Don't trust them to do this, however. Call your party yourself if you want to be sure they get the message.

**Overbooking**

To compensate for no-shows, most airlines overbook their flights. To avoid being bumped, ask for your seat assignment when booking, check in early, and go to the departure area well before flight time. Of course, if you *are* bumped by a reputable international airline at a major airport you'll be regaled with free meals and lodging and sometimes even free flight vouchers (don't expect anything like this from Air Fiji or Sunflower Airlines).

Whenever you break your journey for more than 72 hours, always reconfirm your onward reservations and check your seat assignment at the same time. Get the name of the person who takes your reconfirmation so they cannot later deny it. Failure to reconfirm could result in the cancellation of your complete remaining itinerary. This could also happen if you miss a flight for any reason. If you want special vegetarian or kosher food in-flight, request it when buying your ticket, booking, and reconfirming.

When you try to reconfirm your Air New Zealand flight the agent will tell you that this formality is no longer required. Theoretically this is true, but unless you request your seat assignment in advance, either at an Air New Zealand office or over the phone, you could be "bumped" from a full flight, reservation or no reservation. Air New Zealand's ticket cover bears this surprising message:

> *. . . no guarantee of a seat is indicated by the terms "reservation," "booking," "O.K." status, or the times associated therewith.*

They do admit in the same notice that confirmed passengers denied seats may be eligible for compensation, so if you're not in a hurry, a night or two at an upmarket hotel with all meals courtesy of Air New Zealand may not be a hardship. Your best bet if you don't want to get "bumped" is to request seat assignments for your entire itinerary before you leave home, or at least at the Air New Zealand office in Nadi or Suva. Any good travel agent selling tickets on Air New Zealand should know enough to automatically request your seat assignments as they make your bookings. In Fiji Air New Zealand offices will still accept a local contact telephone number from you. Check Air New Zealand's reconfirmation policy as it could change.

**Baggage**

International airlines allow economy-class passengers either 20 kilos of baggage or two pieces not over 32 kilos each (ask which applies to you). Under the piece system, neither bag must have a combined length, width, and height of over 158 centimeters (62 inches) and the two pieces together must not exceed 272 centimeters (107 inches). On most long-haul tickets to/from North America or Europe, the piece system applies to all sectors, but check this with the airline. The frequent flier programs of some major airlines allow participants to carry up to 10 kilos of excess baggage free of charge. Both commuter carriers in Fiji restrict you to 20 kilos total, so it's better to pack according to the lowest common denominator.

Bicycles, folding kayaks, and surfboards can usually be checked as baggage (sometimes for an additional US$50-100 charge), but sailboards may have to be shipped airfreight. If you do travel with a sailboard, be sure to call it a surfboard at check-in.

Tag your bag with name, address, and phone number inside and out. Stow anything that could conceivably be considered a weapon (scissors, penknife, toy gun, mace, etc.) in your checked luggage. One reason for lost baggage is that some people fail to remove used baggage tags after they claim their luggage. Get into the habit of tearing off old baggage tags, unless you want your luggage to travel in the opposite direction! As you're checking in, look to see if the three-letter city codes on your baggage tag receipt and boarding pass are the same. If you're headed to Nadi the tag should read NAN (Suva is SUV).

If your baggage is damaged or doesn't arrive at your destination, inform the airline officials *immediately* and have them fill out a written report; otherwise future claims for compensation will be compromised. Airlines usually reimburse out-of-pocket expenses if your baggage is lost or delayed over 24 hours. The amount varies from US$25 to US$50. Your chances of getting it are better if you're polite but firm. Keep receipts for any money you're forced to spend to replace missing articles.

Claims for lost luggage can take weeks to process. Keep in touch with the airline to show your concern and hang on to your baggage tag until the matter is resolved. If you feel you did not receive the attention you deserved, write the airline an objective letter outlining the case. Get the names of the employees you're dealing with so you can mention them in the letter. Of course, don't expect any pocket money or compensation on a remote outer island. Report the loss, then wait till you get back to their main office. Whatever happens, try to avoid getting angry. The people you're dealing with don't want the problem any more than you do.

## BY BOAT

Even as much Pacific shipping was being sunk during WW II, airstrips were springing up on all the main islands. This hastened the inevitable replacement of the old steamships with modern aircraft, and it's now extremely rare to arrive in Fiji by boat (private yachts excepted). Most islands export similar products and there's little interregional trade; large container ships headed for Australia, New Zealand, and Japan don't usually accept passengers.

Those bitten by nostalgia for the slower prewar ways may like to know that a couple of passenger-carrying freighters do still call at Fiji, though their fares are much higher than those charged by the airlines. A specialized agency booking such passages is **TravLtips** (Box 188, Flushing, NY 11358, U.S.A.; tel. 1-800/872-8584 or 1-718/939-2400, fax 1-718/939-2047, www.TravLtips.com, e-mail: info@travltips.com). They can place you aboard a British-registered **Bank Line** container ship on its way around the world from Europe via the Panama Canal, Papeete, Nouméa, Suva, Lautoka, Port Vila, Santo, Honiara, and Papua New Guinea. A round-the-world ticket for the four-month journey is US$12,125, but segments are sold if space is available 30 days before sailing. Similarly, TravLtips books German-registered

**Columbus Line** vessels, which make 45-day roundtrips between Los Angeles and Australia via Suva. These ships can accommodate only about a dozen passengers, so inquire well in advance. Also ask about passenger accommodation on cargo vessels of the **Blue Star Line,** which call at Suva and Nouméa between Los Angeles and Auckland.

### Tourist Cruises

**Blue Lagoon Cruises Ltd.** (Box 130, Lautoka, Fiji; tel. 661-622, fax 664-098) has been offering upmarket minicruises from Lautoka to the Yasawa Islands since its founding in 1950 by Captain Trevor Withers. The three-night trips (from F$957) leave daily, while the six-night cruise (from F$1,716) is weekly. Four and seven-night cruises are also possible. Prices are per person, double occupancy, and include meals (excluding alcohol), entertainment, shore excursions, and tax (no additional "port charges" and no tipping). "A" deck is about 15% more expensive than "B" deck but you have the railing right outside your cabin door instead of a locked porthole window. On the three-night cruises they use older three-deck, 40-passenger vessels, while larger four-deck, 60-passenger mini-cruise ships are used on the six-night (and some of the three-night) voyages. In 1996 the 72-passenger, US$8-million luxury cruiser *Mystique Princess* began operating three-night trips from F$1,419. The meals are often beach barbecue affairs, with Fijian dancing. You'll have plenty of opportunities to snorkel in the calm, crystal-clear waters (bring your own gear). Though a bit expensive, these trips have a good reputation. There are daily departures, but reservations are essential, as they're usually booked solid months ahead. (We've heard recently that Blue Lagoon has been having problems with the Yasawas chiefs who figured they were being taken for granted and that a few shore excursions have been stopped. Ask if they're still going to the Sawa-i-Lau cave, for example.)

**Captain Cook Cruises** (Box 23, Nadi, Fiji; tel. 701-823, fax 702-045, www.captcookcrus.com.au), on Narewa Road near the bridge into Nadi town, is an Australian company whose Fiji operation is 50% owned by Qantas Airways. Like Blue Lagoon Cruises they offer unpretentious three/four-night cruises to the Yasawa Islands aboard the 68-meter MV *Reef Escape,* departing Nadi Tuesday and Saturday. The 60 double-occupancy cabins begin at F$979/1,315 pp twin with bunk beds or F$1,216/1,623 with normal beds. The two itineraries vary somewhat and there's a discount if you do both in succession. The *Reef Escape* is the largest cruise ship based in Fiji and it's worth considering as a change of pace. Until recently it was used for cruises along Australia's Great Barrier Reef. The food is good, cabins bright, activities and entertainment fun, and there's even a miniature swimming pool and spa! Most of your fellow passengers will be Australians, which can be stimulating, and the Fijian staff will spoil you silly.

In addition, Captain Cook Cruises operates two/three-night cruises to the southern Yasawas on the square-rigged brigantine *Ra Marama*—a more romantic choice than the mini-cruise ships. These trips depart Nadi every Monday and Thursday morning and cost F$475/595 pp (children under 12 not accepted). You sleep ashore in double *bures,* the food is good with lots of fresh vegetables and salads, and the staff friendly and well organized. Your biggest disappointment will probably be that they have the diesel engine on all the time and don't bother trying to use the sails. Still, the 34-meter *Ra Marama* is a fine vessel built for a former governor-general of Fiji of teak planks at Singapore in 1957. These trips can be booked through most travel agents in Fiji or via the numbers above; readers who've gone report having a great time.

### Scuba Cruises

Four **live-aboard dive boats** ply Fiji waters. A seven-night stay on one of these vessels could run as high as F$5,000 pp (airfare, alcohol, and tax extra), but the boat anchors right above the dive sites, so no time is wasted commuting back and forth. All meals are included and the diving is unlimited. Singles are usually allowed to share a cabin with another diver to avoid a single supplement. Bookings can be made through any of the scuba wholesalers listed under Scuba Tours below.

The five-stateroom *Sere Ni Wai* (or "song of the sea") is a 30-meter boat based at Suva and operating around Beqa, Kadavu, Lomaiviti, and northern Lau. Captain Greg Lawlor's family has been in Fiji for four generations but his boat is new, launched in 1995. If you're already in Fiji, try calling **Mollie Dean Cruises** (Box 3256, Lami, Fiji; tel. 361-174, fax 361-137), which books divers on the *Sere Ni Wai* locally.

Another famous boat is the 34-meter, eight-cabin *Nai'a* which does seven-day scuba cruises to Lomaiviti and northern Lau at F$3,460, or 10 days for F$4,950, tax included. Captain Bob Barrel has a longstanding interest in dolphins and whales, and whalewatching expeditions to Tonga are organized annually. Local bookings are accepted when space is available and you might even be able to swing a discount. Call **Nai'a Cruises** (Box 332, Pacific Harbor, Fiji; tel. 450-382, fax 450-566, www.naia.com.fj).

In 1998 the American-owned, 32-meter dive boat *Fiji Aggressor* (tel. 361-382, fax 362-930, www.pac-aggressor.com) was deployed to the Cousteau Fiji Islands Resort near Savusavu. The *Aggressor's* jet-driven launch zips divers to scuba sites at 30 knots, providing unlimited diving for 16 divers flown in on packages from the States. Unlike the eco-friendly *Nai'a,* which uses sails to cruise at night, this powerful catamaran projects an image of brute force.

The *Matangi Princess II,* a 26-meter cruise vessel with six a/c cabins, operates around Taveuni from their base at Maravu Plantation (Tropical Dive, tel./fax 880-660). In North America, information on the *Matangi Princess II* can be obtained by calling 1-888/234-5447 (www.Tropicalinspirations.com). We've heard this boat doesn't match the standards of the other three.

## ORGANIZED TOURS

### Packaged Holidays

While packaged travel certainly isn't for everyone, reduced group airfares and hotel rates make some tours worth considering. For two people with limited time and a desire to stay at a first-class hotel, this is the cheapest way to go. The "wholesalers" who put these packages together get their rooms at rates far lower than what individuals pay. Special-interest tours are very popular among sportspeople who want to be sure they'll get to participate in the various activities they enjoy. The main drawback to the tours is that you're on a fixed itinerary in a touristic environment, out of touch with local life. Singles pay a healthy supplement. Some of the companies mentioned below do not accept consumer inquiries and require you to work through a travel agent.

A company dealing with all aspects of travel to Fiji is **Fiji Reservations and Travel** (2439 S. Kihei Road, Suite 204A, Kihei, Maui, HI 96753, U.S.A.; tel. 1-800/588-3454 or 1-808/879-1598, fax 1-808/879-6274, www.fijireservations.com, e-mail: fiji@maui.net). Check their website for surfing, kayaking, and diving tours, plus discounted packages to all the top resorts. They also arrange house rentals and land purchases. **Islands in the Sun** (2381 Rosecrans Ave. #325, El Segundo, CA 90245-4913, U.S.A.; tel. 1-800/828-6877, fax 1-310/536-6266) has a useful brochure describing many package tours to Fiji.

**Fiji Travel** (8885 Venice Blvd., Suite 202, Los Angeles, CA 90034, U.S.A.; tel. 1-800/500-3454 or 1-310/202-4220, fax 1-310/202-8233, www.fijitravel.com) sells all-inclusive tours to Fiji's top resorts, books Blue Lagoon cruises, and has surfing/scuba packages. Their cheapest packages are lower than regular airfare, such as US$860 for six nights (double occupancy) at Sandalwood Inn or Seashell Cove including return flights from Los Angeles and transfers. If they'll let you extend your return date to allow some time on your own, it's a deal.

**Sunspots International** (1918 N.E. 181st, Portland, OR 97230, U.S.A.; tel. 1-800/334-5623 or 1-503/666-3893, fax 1-503/661-7771, www.sunspotsintl.com) has an informative color brochure on Fiji, plus a good website. **Sunmakers** (100 West Harrison, South Tower, Suite 350, Seattle, WA 98119, U.S.A.; tel. 1-800/359-4359 or 1-206/216-2900, fax 1-206/216-2906) books customized itineraries in Fiji. **Travel Arrangements Ltd.** (1268 Broadway, Sonoma, CA 95476, U.S.A.; tel. 1-800/392-8213 or 1-707/938-1118, fax 1-707/938-1268) also has a color brochure depicting upmarket accommodations in Fiji.

In Canada the Fiji specialist is **Goway Travel** (3284 Yonge St., Suite 300, Toronto, Ontario M4N 3M7, Canada; tel. 1-800/387-8850, fax 1-416/322-1109, www.goway.com, e-mail: res@goway.com) with a second office in Vancouver. Their U.S. branch is **Goway Travel** (6762A Centinela Ave., Culver City, CA 90230, U.S.A.; tel. 1-800/387-8850, fax 1-800/665-4432, e-mail: res@goway.

com). Goway's Fiji brochure is one of the most detailed you'll find.

**From Australia and New Zealand**

**Hideaway Holidays** (Val Gavriloff, 994 Victoria Rd., West Ryde, NSW 2114, Australia; tel. 61-2/9807-4222, fax 61-2/9808-2260, www.hideawayholidays.com.au, e-mail: sales@hideawayholidays.com.au) specializes in off-the-beaten-track packages to every part of Fiji and can organize complicated itineraries.

**Qantas Jetabout Holidays** (Level 6, 141 Walker St., North Sydney, NSW 2060, Australia; tel. 1-300/360-347 or 61-2/9957-0538, fax 61-2/9957-0393, www.qantas.com.au) offers a variety of standard package tours to Fiji. In Europe these trips can be booked through Jetabout Holidays (Sovereign House, 361 King St., Hammersmith, London W6 9NJ, United Kingdom; tel. 44-181/748-8676, fax 44-181/748-7236).

The **Pacific and International Travel Company** (Level 1, 91 York St., Sydney, NSW 2000, Australia; tel. 61-2/9244-1811, fax 61-2/9262-6318, e-mail: andrewc@pitc.com.au) books package tours to Fiji and Blue Lagoon Cruises. Also check **Adventure World** (Box 480, North Sydney, NSW 2059, Australia; tel. 61-2/9223-7966, fax 61-2/9956-7707, www.adventureworld.com.au, e-mail: syd@adventureworld.com.au), and **Goway Travel** (350 Kent St., 8th floor, Sydney, NSW 2000, Australia; tel. 61-2/9262-4755, fax 61-2/9290-1905).

From New Zealand **ASPAC Vacations Ltd.** (Box 4330, Auckland, New Zealand; tel. 64-9/623-0259, fax 64-9/623-0257, e-mail: southpacific@aspac-vacations.co.nz) has packaged tours and cruises to Fiji. **Travel Arrangements Ltd.** (Box 297, Auckland, New Zealand; tel. 64-9/379-5944, fax 64-9/373-2369) offers sailing holidays and package tours.

**Scuba Tours**

Fiji is one of the world's prime scuba locales, and most of the islands have excellent facilities for divers. Although it's not that difficult to make your own arrangements as you go, you should consider joining an organized scuba tour if you want to cram in as much diving as possible. To stay in business, the dive travel specialists mentioned below are forced to charge prices similar to what you'd pay on the beach, and the convenience of having everything prearranged is often worth it. Before booking, find out exactly where you'll be staying and ask if daily transfers and meals are provided. Diver certification is mandatory.

Consider the live-aboard dive boats previously mentioned. They're a bit more expensive than hotel-based diving, but you're offered up to five dives a day and a total experience. Some repeat divers won't go any other way.

One of the top American scuba wholesalers selling Fiji is **Poseidon Ventures Tours** (359 San Miguel Dr., Newport Beach, CA 92660, U.S.A.; tel. 1-800/854-9334 or 1-949/644-5344, fax 1-949/644-5392, www.poseidontours.com, e-mail: poseidon@fea.net; or 3724 FM 1960 West, Suite 114, Houston, TX 77068, U.S.A.; tel. 1-281/586-7800, fax 1-281/586-7870). They offer seven-night diving tours beginning at US$2,129 including five days of two-tank diving, airfare from Los Angeles, double-occupancy hotel accommodations, meals, taxes, and transfers. They also sell live-aboard diving.

**Tropical Adventures Travel** (Box 4337, Seattle, WA 98104-0337, U.S.A.; tel. 1-800/247-3483 or 1-206/441-3483, fax 1-206/441-5431,

BOB HALSTEAD

*feeding fish*

www.divetropical.com, e-mail: dive@divetropical.com) also specializes in booking live-aboard diving with three boats to choose from. Expect to pay about US$300 a night all-inclusive and singles are expected to share (no supplement). Airfare is extra. Ask for Tropical's Fiji specialist, Geoff Hynes. Over 6,000 divers a year book through this company, which has been in business since 1973.

In 1998 the noted underwater photographer and author, Carl Roessler, closed down See & Sea Travel Service, which he'd founded in 1966, and became an independent consultant providing advice on scuba facilities and sites worldwide. He makes his money out of "finder fees" paid by selected island suppliers, and his 35 years of experience leading dive tours around the Pacific costs nothing extra to you. Check out his website at www.divxprt.com/see&sea and if you like what you see get in touch with him at **Sea Images** (Box 471899, San Francisco, CA 94147, U.S.A.; tel. 1-415/922-5807, fax 1-415/922-5662, e-mail: divxprt@ix.netcom.com).

Another Fiji specialist is **Aqua-Trek** (110 Sutter St., Suite 205, San Francisco, CA 94104, U.S.A.; tel. 1-800/541-4334 or 1-415/398-8990, fax 1-415/398-0479, www.aquatrek.com, e-mail: info@aquatrek.com). **Adventure Express** (650 5th St., Suite 505, San Francisco, CA 94107, U.S.A.; tel. 1-800/443-0799 or 1-415/442-0799, fax 1-415/442-0289, www.AdventureExpress.com) offers "shoestring" diving at Kadavu, Suva, or Taveuni from US$1,852 pp including return airfare from Los Angeles, transfers, double-occupancy accommodations, meals, and six days of diving. They also book the live-aboards and more upmarket land-based diving.

Jean-Michel Cousteau's **Project Ocean Search** offers all-inclusive two-week programs based at the Cousteau Fiji Islands Resort near Savusavu for serious scuba divers. For information contact **Cousteau Productions** (tel. 1-805/899-8899, fax 1-805/899-8898, www.jmcfir.com, e-mail: jmcousteau@aol.com) in Santa Barbara, California.

In Australia try **Dive Adventures** (Level 9, 32 York St., Sydney, NSW 2000, Australia; tel. 61-2/9299-4633, fax 61-2/9299-4644, www.diveadventures.com.au, e-mail: advnture@magna.com.au), a scuba wholesaler with packages to Fiji. **Allways Dive Expeditions** (168 High St., Ashburton, Melbourne, Victoria 3147, Australia: tel. 61-3/9885-8863, fax 61-3/9885-1164, www.allwaysdive.com.au, e-mail: allways@netlink.com.au) organizes dive expeditions to all the Melanesian countries.

**Dive 'N Fishing Travel** (15E Vega Pl., Mairangi Bay, Auckland 10, New Zealand; tel. 64-9/479-2210, fax 64-9/479-2214, e-mail: divefish@ihug.co.nz) arranges scuba and game fishing tours to Fiji at competitive rates.

Alternatively, you can make your own arrangements directly with island dive shops. Information about these operators is included under the heading Sports and Recreation in the respective chapters of this book.

### Tours for Children

About the only packages to Fiji especially designed for families traveling with children are the "Rascals in Paradise" programs offered by **Adventure Express** (650 5th St., Suite 505, San Francisco, CA 94107, U.S.A.; tel. 1-800/872-7225 or 1-415/978-9800, fax 1-415/442-0289, www.AdventureExpress.com). Special "family week" group tours to Fiji's Matangi Island Resort are operated in late March. The price is based on two adults with one or two children aged 2-11, and international airfares and transfers to Vatulele are additional. A single parent with child would have to pay two adult fares. Adventure Express also books regular scuba diving tours and upmarket hotel rooms.

### Tours for Naturalists

Perhaps the most rewarding way to visit the South Seas is with **Earthwatch** (Box 9104, Watertown, MA 02272, U.S.A.; tel. 1-800/776-0188 or 1-617/926-8200, fax 1-617/926-8532, www.earthwatch.org, e-mail: info@earthwatch.org), a nonprofit organization founded in 1971 to serve as a bridge between the public and the scientific community. The programs vary from year to year, but in past they've sent teams to study the coral reefs and rainforests of Fiji. These are not study tours but opportunities for amateurs to help out with serious work, a kind of short-term scientific Peace Corps. As a research volunteer, a team member's share of project costs is tax-deductible in the U.S. and some other countries. For more information contact Earthwatch at the address above, or 126 Bank St., South Melbourne, Victoria 3205, Australia (tel. 61-3/9682-6828, fax 61-3/9686-3652), or Belsyre Court, 57 Woodstock

Rd., Oxford OX2 6HU, United Kingdom (tel. 44-1865/311-600, fax 44-865/311-383), or Technova Inc., Imperial Tower, 13 F Uchisaiwai-Cho 1-1-1, Chiyoda-Ku, Tokyo 100-0011, Japan (tel. 81-3/3508-2280, fax 81-3/3508-7578).

### Tours for Seniors

Since 1989, the **Pacific Islands Institute** (Box 1926, Kailua, HI 96734, U.S.A.; tel. 1-808/262-8942, fax 1-808/263-0178, www.pac-island.com, e-mail: info@pac-island.com) has operated educational tours to Fiji and Polynesia in cooperation with Hawaii Pacific University. Their **Elderhostel** people-to-people study programs designed for those aged 55 or over (younger spouses welcome) last two or three weeks. For example, the 24-day tour of Fiji, Tonga, and Samoa offered about 10 times a year costs US$4,400 from Los Angeles or US$4,771 from Boston including airfares, meals, double-occupancy accommodations, transfers, excursions, admissions, tips, taxes, and insurance (singles pay US$435 extra). A full week is spent at Savusavu. These culturally responsible trips are highly recommended.

### Kayak Tours

Among the most exciting tours to Fiji are the nine-to 11-day kayaking expeditions offered from May to November by **Southern Sea Ventures** (Suite 263, 184 Blues Point Rd., McMahons Point, NSW 2060, Australia; tel. 61-2/9460-3375, fax 61-2/9460-3376, www.evo.com.au/cventure, e-mail: cventure@tpg.com.au). Their groups of 12 persons maximum paddle stable two-person sea kayaks through the sheltered tropical waters of the Yasawa chain. Accommodations are tents on the beach, and participants must be in reasonable physical shape, as three or four hours a day are spent on the water. The price ranges A$1,400-2,700 and doesn't include airfare. In North America you can book through Quest Nature Tours (36 Finch Ave. West, Toronto, Ontario M2N 2G9, Canada; tel. 1-800/387-1483 or 1-416/221-3000, fax 1-416/221-5730, e-mail: travel@worldwidequest.com). In New Zealand contact Adventure South (Box 33-153, Christchurch, New Zealand; tel. 64-3/332-1222, fax 64-3/332-4030, e-mail: geoff@advsouth.co.nz).

**Mountain Travel/Sobek Expeditions** (6420 Fairmount Ave., El Cerrito, CA 94530, U.S.A.; tel. 1-800/227-2384 or 1-510/527-8100, fax 1-510/525-7710, www.mtsobek.com, e-mail: info@mtsobek.com) runs a 13-day combination hiking/sea kayaking tour to Fiji four times a year at US$1,990 plus airfare. Participants combine trekking through central Viti Levu with kayaking the Yasawas. They're usually sold out well ahead.

Deluxe kayak tours to Kadavu, Fiji, are offered from May to December by Michael and Melissa McCoy of **Kayak Kadavu** (www.fiji-kayak-kadavu.com). Their seven/nine-night trips are US$1,325/1,675 pp. An escort boat carries all the heavy gear, allowing participants the luxury of paddling a lightweight sit-on-top kayak around some really breathtaking locations. In North America book through Fiji Reservations and Travel (address above). Other kayaking trips to Ono and Kadavu are organized by **Tamarillo** (Box 9869, Wellington, New Zealand; tel. 64-4/239-9990, fax 64-4/239-9789, www.tamarillo.co.nz/tamarillo.html, e-mail: enquiries@tamarillo.co.nz). There are four one-week trips in August and September at NZ$1,735 from Nadi or NZ$2,590 from Auckland.

### Surfing Tours

The largest operator of surfing tours to the South Pacific is **The Surf Travel Company** (Box 446, Cronulla, NSW 2230, Australia; tel. 61-2/9527-4722, fax 61-2/9527-4522, www.surftravel.com.au, e-mail: surftrav@ozemail.com.au) with packages to Frigates Pass and Seashell Cove. In New Zealand book through Mark Thompson (7 Danbury Dr., Torbay, Auckland, New Zealand; tel./fax 64-9/473-8388). **Waterways Travel** (15145 Califa St., Ste. 1, Van Nuys, CA 91411, U.S.A,; tel. 1-800/928-3757 or 1-818/376-0341, fax 1-818/376-0353, www.waterwaystravel.com) offers a variety of surfing tours to Fiji.

For information on tours to Tavarua Island and the famous Cloudbreak contact **Tavarua Island Tours** (Box 60159, Santa Barbara, CA 93160, U.S.A.; tel. 1-805/686-4551, fax 1-805/683-6696, e-mail: tavarua@is.com.fj). Tavarua's neighbor, **Namotu Island Resort** (Box 531, Nadi, Fiji; tel. 706-439, fax 706-039, e-mail: namotu@is.com.fj), is similar. Additional information on these is provided in the Mamanucas chapter.

### Hiking Tours

From May to October **Adventure Fiji,** a division of Rosie The Travel Service (Box 9268, Nadi

Airport, Fiji; tel. 722-935, fax 722-607, e-mail: rosiefiji@ is.com.fj), runs adventuresome five-night hiking trips in the upper Wainibuka River area of central Viti Levu south of Rakiraki. Horses carry trekkers' backpacks, so the trips are feasible for almost anyone in good condition. The F$600 pp price includes transport to the trailhead, food and accommodations at a few of the 11 Fijian villages along the way, guides, and a bamboo raft ride on the Wainibuka River. Trekkers only hike about five hours a day, allowing lots of time to get to know the village people. These tours begin from Nadi every Monday. In Australia bookings can be made through Rosie The Travel Service (Level 5, Ste. 505, East Towers, 9 Bronte Rd., Bondi Junction, Sydney, NSW 2022, Australia; tel. 61-2/9389-3666, fax 61-2/9369-1129).

**Yacht Tours and Charters**

If you were planning on spending a substantial amount to stay at a luxury resort, consider chartering a yacht instead! Divided up among the members of your party the per-person charter price will be about the same, but you'll experience much more of Fiji's beauty on a boat than you would staying in a hotel room. All charterers visit remote islands accessible only by small boat and thus receive special insights into island life unspoiled by normal tourist trappings. Of course, activities such as sailing, snorkeling, and general exploring by sea and land are included in the price.

Yacht charters are available either "bareboat" (for those with the skill to sail on their own) or "crewed" (in which case charterers pay a daily fee for a skipper plus his/her provisions). On a "flotilla" charter a group of bareboats follows an experienced lead yacht.

Due to the riskiness of navigating Fiji's poorly marked reefs, yacht charters aren't as common in Fiji as they are in Tonga or Tahiti. All charter boats are required by law to carry a Fijian guide.

**Musket Cove Yacht Charters** (Private Mail Bag NAP 0352, Nadi Airport, Fiji; tel./fax 666-710) offers bareboat yacht charters among the Mamanuca and Yasawa islands from their base at the Musket Cove Marina on Malololailai Island in the Mamanuca Group. Some are exclusive crewed charters, others bareboat with the mandatory Fijian guide, others surfing charters.

Larger groups could consider the 27-meter ketch *Tau* at the Raffles Tradewinds Hotel, Suva, which costs F$2,550/16,500 a day/week plus 10% tax for up to six persons, including all meals, drinks, and an experienced crew (scuba diving is extra). It's available year-round. For full information contact Bilo Ltd., Box 3084, Lami, Fiji; tel. 361-057, fax 362-177.

In the U.S. charters are arranged by **Ocean Voyages Inc.** (1709 Bridgeway, Sausalito, CA 94965, U.S.A.; tel. 1-800/299-4444 or 1-415/332-4681, fax 1-415/332-7460, www.crowleys.com/links.htm, e-mail: voyages@ix.netcom.com). Unlike their competitors, Ocean Voyages can sometimes organize "shareboat" charters in which singles and couples book a cabin instead of an entire yacht. Shorter trips are usually around Fiji only while longer journeys encompassing several island groups are possible. Shareboat prices average US$100-250 pp a day, and scuba diving is possible at extra cost on some boats (ask). They also arrange charters on sailboats such as the *Golden Opus,* which can handle extended cruises from Fiji to Tonga, Vanuatu, or the Solomons at US$15,500/16,500/ 17,500 a week for two/four/ six persons all inclusive except drinks and communications. The *Tau* is cheaper at US$11,750 a week for up to six persons.

One of the classic "tall ships" cruising the South Pacific is the two-masted brigantine *Soren Larsen,* built in 1949. From May to November this 42-meter square rig vessel operates 10-19 day voyages to Tonga, Fiji, Vanuatu, and New Caledonia costing NZ$2,500-3,680. The 12-member professional crew is actively assisted by 22 voyage participants. For information contact **Square Sail Pacific** (Box 310, Kumeu, Auckland 1250, New Zealand; tel. 64-9/411-8755, fax 64-9/411-8484). Ocean Voyages handles bookings in North America. In the U.K. contact **Explore Worldwide** (1 Frederick St., Aldershot, Hants GU11 1LQ, United Kingdom; tel. 44-1252/319-448, fax 44-1251/343170, www.explore.co.uk).

A few private brokers arranging bareboat or crewed yacht charters are **Sun Yacht Charters** (Box 737, Camden, ME 04843, U.S.A.; tel. 1-800/772-3500, fax 1-207/236-3972, www.sunyachts.com), **Charter World Pty. Ltd.** (23 Passchendaele St., Hampton, Melbourne 3188, Australia; tel. 61-3/9521-0033, fax 61-3/9521-0081), **Sail Connections Ltd.** (Box 3234, Auckland 1015, New Zealand; tel. 64-9/358-0556, fax 64-9/358-4341, e-mail: jeni@sailconnections.co.nz),

**Yachting Partners International** (28-29 Richmond Pl., Brighton, Sussex, BN2 2NA, United Kingdom; tel. 44-1273/571-722, fax 44-1273/571-720, e-mail: ypi@ypi.co.uk), and **Crestar Yachts Ltd.** (125 Sloane St., London SW1X 9AU, United Kingdom; tel. 44-171/730-9962, fax 44-171/824-8691).

## BY SAILING YACHT

### Getting Aboard

Hitch rides into the Pacific on yachts from California, Panama, New Zealand, and Australia, or around the yachting triangle Papeete-Suva-Honolulu. At home, scrutinize the classified listings of yachts seeking crews, yachts to be delivered, etc., in magazines like *Yachting, Cruising World, Sail,* and *Latitude 38.* You can even advertise yourself for about US$25 (plan to have the ad appear three months before the beginning of the season). Check the bulletin boards at yacht clubs. The **Seven Seas Cruising Association** (1525 South Andrews Ave., Suite 217, Fort Lauderdale, FL 33316, U.S.A.; tel. 1-954/463-2431, fax 1-954/463-7183, www.ssca.org, e-mail: SSCA1@ibm.net) is in touch with yachties all around the Pacific, and the classified section "Crew Exchange" in their monthly *Commodores' Bulletin* contains ads from captains in search of crew.

Cruising yachts are recognizable by their foreign flags, wind-vane steering gear, sturdy appearance, and laundry hung out to dry. Put up notices on yacht club and marine bulletin boards, and meet people in bars. When a boat is hauled out, you can find work scraping and repainting the bottom, varnishing, and doing minor repairs.

## MARITIME COORDINATES

| ISLAND GROUP/ ISLAND | LAND AREA (SQ KM) | HIGHEST POINT (METERS) | LATITUDE | LONGITUDE |
|---|---|---|---|---|
| **VITI LEVU GROUP** | | | | |
| Beqa | 36.0 | 439 | 18.40°S | 178.13°E |
| Vatulele | 31.6 | 34 | 18.50°S | 177.63°E |
| Viti Levu | 10,429.0 | 1,323 | 17.80°S | 178.00°E |
| **YASAWA GROUP** | | | | |
| Naviti | 34.0 | 388 | 17.13°S | 177.25°E |
| Yasawa | 32.0 | 244 | 16.80°S | 177.50°E |
| **KADAVU GROUP** | | | | |
| Dravuni | 0.8 | 40 | 18.78°S | 178.53°E |
| Kadavu | 411.0 | 838 | 19.05°S | 178.25°E |
| Ono | 30.0 | 354 | 18.88°S | 178.50°E |
| **LOMAIVITI GROUP** | | | | |
| Gau | 140.0 | 747 | 18.00°S | 179.30°E |
| Koro | 104.0 | 522 | 17.30°S | 179.40°E |
| Makogai | 8.4 | 267 | 17.43°S | 178.98°E |
| Ovalau | 101.0 | 626 | 17.70°S | 178.80°E |
| Wakaya | 8.0 | 152 | 17.65°S | 179.02°E |
| **VANUA LEVU GROUP** | | | | |
| Namenalala | 0.4 | 105 | 17.11°S | 179.10°E |
| Qamea | 34.0 | 304 | 16.77°S | 179.77°W |
| Rabi | 69.0 | 463 | 16.50°S | 180.00°E |

It's much easier, however, to crew on yachts already in the islands. In Tahiti, for example, after a month on the open sea, some of the original crew may have flown home or onward, opening a place for you. Pago Pago, Vava'u, Suva, Musket Cove, and Port Vila are other places to look for a boat.

If you've never crewed before, it's better to try for a short passage the first time. Once at sea on the way to Tahiti, there's no way they'll turn around to take a seasick crew member back to Hawaii. Good captains evaluate crew on personality, attitude, and a willingness to learn more than experience, so don't lie. Be honest and open when interviewing with a skipper—a deception will soon become apparent.

It's also good to know what a captain's *really* like before you commit yourself to an isolated month with her/him. To determine what might happen should the electronic gadgetry break down, find out if there's a sextant aboard and whether he/she knows how to use it. A run-down-looking boat may often be mechanically unsound too. Also be concerned about a skipper who doesn't do a careful safety briefing early on, or who seems to have a hard time hanging onto crew. If the previous crew have left the boat at an unlikely place, there must have been a reason. Once you're on a boat and part of the yachtie community, things are easy. (P.S. from veteran yachtie Peter Moree: "We do need more ladies out here—adventurous types naturally.")

### Time of Year

The weather and seasons play a deciding role in any South Pacific trip by sailboat and you'll have to pull out of many beautiful places, or be unable to stop there, because of bad weather. The

| ISLAND GROUP/ ISLAND | LAND AREA (SQ KM) | HIGHEST POINT (M) | LATITUDE | LONGITUDE |
|---|---|---|---|---|
| **VANUA LEVU GROUP** *(continued)* | | | | |
| Taveuni | 470.0 | 1,241 | 16.85°S | 179.95°E |
| Vanua Levu | 5,556.0 | 1,032 | 16.60°S | 179.20°E |
| Yaduataba | 0.7 | 100 | 16.84°S | 178.28°E |
| **LAU GROUP** | | | | |
| Cicia | 34.0 | 165 | 17.75°S | 179.33°W |
| Fulaga | 18.5 | 79 | 19.17°S | 178.65°W |
| Kabara | 31.0 | 143 | 18.95°S | 178.97°W |
| Kanacea | 13.0 | 259 | 17.25°S | 179.17°W |
| Lakeba | 54.0 | 215 | 18.20°S | 178.80°W |
| Ogea Levu | 13.3 | 82 | 19.18°S | 178.47°W |
| Ono-i-Lau | 7.9 | 113 | 20.80°S | 178.75°W |
| Vanua Balavu | 53.0 | 283 | 17.25°S | 178.92°W |
| Vuaqava | 7.7 | 107 | 18.83°S | 178.92°W |
| Wailagi Lala | 0.3 | 5 | 16.75°S | 179.18°W |
| **MOALA GROUP** | | | | |
| Matuku | 57.0 | 385 | 19.18°S | 179.75°E |
| Moala | 62.5 | 468 | 18.60°S | 179.90°E |
| Totoya | 28.0 | 366 | 18.93°S | 179.83°W |
| **RINGGOLD ISLES** | | | | |
| Qelelevu | 1.5 | 12 | 16.09°S | 179.26°W |
| **ROTUMA GROUP** | | | | |
| Conway Reef | 0.1 | 2 | 21.77°S | 174.52°E |
| Rotuma | 47.0 | 256 | 12.50°S | 177.13°E |

favorite season for rides in the South Pacific is May to October; sometimes you'll even have to turn one down. Around August or September start looking for a ride from the South Pacific to Hawaii or New Zealand.

Be aware of the hurricane season: November to March in the South Pacific, July to December in the northwest Pacific (near Guam), and June to October in the area between Mexico and Hawaii. Few yachts will be cruising those areas at these times. A few yachts spend the winter at Pago Pago and Vava'u (the main "hurricane holes"), but most South Pacific cruisers will have left for hurricane-free New Zealand by October.

Also, know which way the winds are blowing; prevailing trade winds in the tropics are from the northeast north of the equator, from the southeast south of the equator. North of the tropic of Cancer and south of the tropic of Capricorn winds are out of the west. Due to the action of prevailing southeast tradewinds boat trips are smoother from east to west than west to east throughout the South Pacific, so that's the way to go.

### Yachting Routes

The South Pacific is good for sailing; there's not too much traffic and no piracy like you'd find in the Mediterranean or in Indonesian waters. The common yachting route or "Coconut Milk Run" across the South Pacific utilizes the northeast and southeast trades: from California to Tahiti via the Marquesas or Hawaii, then Rarotonga, Vava'u, Suva, and New Zealand. Some yachts continue west from Fiji to Port Vila. In the other direction, you'll sail on the westerlies from New Zealand to a point south of the Australs, then north on the trades to Tahiti.

Some 300 yachts leave the U.S. west coast for Tahiti every year, almost always crewed by couples or men only. Most stay in the South Seas about a year before returning to North America, while a few continue around the world. About 60-80 cross the Indian Ocean every year (look for rides from Sydney in May, Cairns or Darwin from June to August, Bali from August to October, Singapore from October to December); around 700 yachts sail from Europe to the Caribbean (from Gibraltar and Gran Canaria from October to December).

Cruising yachts average about 150 km a day, so it takes about a month to get from the U.S. west coast to Hawaii, then another month from Hawaii to Tahiti. To enjoy the finest weather conditions many yachts clear the Panama Canal or depart California in February to arrive in the Marquesas in March. From Hawaii, yachts often leave for Tahiti in April or May. Many stay on for the *Heiva i Tahiti* festival, which ends on 14 July, at which time they sail west to Vava'u or Suva, where you'll find them in July and August. In mid-September the yachting season culminates with a race by about 40 boats from Musket Cove on Fiji's Malololailai Island to Port Vila (it's very easy to hitch a ride at this time). By late October the bulk of the yachting community is sailing south via New Caledonia to New Zealand or Australia to spend the southern summer there. In April or May on alternate years (1999, 2001, etc.) there's a yacht race from Auckland and Sydney to Suva, timed to coincide with the cruisers' return after the hurricane season.

**Blue Water Rallies** (Peter Seymour, Windsor Cottage, Chedworth, Cheltenham, Gloucestershire GL54 4AA, United Kingdom; tel./fax 44-1285/720-904) organizes annual round-the-world yachting rallies, departing Europe each October. Inquiries from both owners and potential crew members are welcome for these 20-month circumnavigations that visit Galapagos, the Marquesas, Tahiti, Tonga, and Fiji. Blue Water's professional support services will help make that "voyage of a lifetime" a reality! Similar events are organized by Jimmy Cornell's **World Cruising** (Box 165, London WC1B 3XA, United Kingdom; tel. 44-171/405-9905, fax 44-171/831-0161), departing Fort Lauderdale, Florida, in February.

Be aware that a law enacted in New Zealand in 1995 requires foreign yachts departing New Zealand to obtain a "Certificate of Inspection" from the New Zealand Yachting Federation prior to customs clearance. This regulation has led to a 30% decline in the number of yachts visiting New Zealand, and it's wise to consider alternative summer anchorages before sailing into a situation where some clerk may force you to spend of thousands of dollars upgrading safety standards on your boat before you'll be permitted to leave.

### Life Aboard

To crew on a yacht you must be willing to wash and iron clothes, cook, steer, keep watch at night, and help with engine work. Other jobs might include changing and resetting sails, cleaning the boat, scraping the bottom, pulling up the anchor, and climbing the main mast to watch for reefs. Do more than is expected of you. A safety harness must be worn in rough weather. As a guest in someone else's home you'll want to wash your dishes promptly after use and put them, and all other gear, back where you found them. Tampons must not be thrown in the toilet bowl. Smoking is usually prohibited as a safety hazard.

You'll be a lot more useful if you know how to tie knots like the clove hitch, rolling hitch, sheet bend, double sheet bend, reef knot, square knot, figure eight, and bowline. Check your local library for books on sailing or write away for the comprehensive free catalog of nautical books available from International Marine Publishing (Box 548, Black Lick, OH 43004, U.S.A.; tel. 1-800/262-4729, fax 1-614/759-3641, www.pbg.mcgraw-hill.com/im).

Anybody who wants to get on well under sail must be flexible and tolerant, both physically and emotionally. Expense-sharing crew members pay US$50 a week or more per person. After 30 days you'll be happy to hit land for a freshwater shower. Give adequate notice when you're ready to leave the boat, but *do* disembark when your journey's up. Boat people have few enough opportunities for privacy as it is. If you've had a good trip, ask the captain to write you a letter of recommendation; it'll help you hitch another ride.

**Food for Thought**

When you consider the big investment, depreciation, cost of maintenance, operating expenses, and considerable risk (most cruising yachts are not insured), travel by sailing yacht is quite a luxury. The huge cost can be surmised from charter fees (US$500 a day and up for a 10-meter yacht). International law makes a clear distinction between passengers and crew. Crew members paying only for their own food, cooking gas, and part of the diesel are very different from charterers who do nothing and pay full costs. The crew is there to help operate the boat, adding safety, but like passengers, they're very much under the control of the captain. Crew has no say in where the yacht will go.

The skipper is personally responsible for crew coming into foreign ports: he's entitled to hold their passports and to see that they have onward tickets and sufficient funds for further traveling. Otherwise the skipper might have to pay their hotel bills and even return airfares to the crew's country of origin. Crew may be asked to pay a share of third-party liability insurance. Possession of dope can result in seizure of the yacht. Because of such considerations, skippers often hesitate to accept crew. Crew members should remember that at no cost to themselves they can learn a bit of sailing and visit places nearly inaccessible by other means. Although not for everyone, it's *the* way to see the real South Pacific, and folks who arrive by yacht are treated differently than other tourists.

*Fijian* bure

# GETTING AROUND

## BY AIR

While most international flights are focused on Nadi, Fiji's domestic air service radiates from Suva and two local airlines compete fiercely. **Air Fiji** (Box 1259, Suva, Fiji; tel. 313-666, fax 300-771, www.airfiji.net) flies their fast Brazilian-made Bandeirantes (15 seats), sturdy Canadian-made Twin Otters, pocket-size Britten Norman Islanders, and exotic Chinese-made Y12 Harbins from Suva's Nausori Airport six times a day to Labasa (F$138) and Nadi (F$114), twice a day to Kadavu (F$92), Levuka (F$54), Savusavu (F$118), and Taveuni (F$150), five times a week to Gau (F$76), four times a week to Koro (F$104) and Moala (F$136), three times a week to Lakeba (F$150), and Vanua Balavu (F$150), and twice a week to Cicia (F$138). Savusavu to Taveuni (F$82) is twice daily (all fares one-way). The 30-day "Discover Fiji Air Pass" (US$236) must be purchased prior to arrival in Fiji and it's only valid on flights to Kadavu, Nadi, Savusavu, Suva, and Taveuni.

**Sunflower Airlines** (Box 9452, Nadi Airport, Fiji; tel. 723-016, fax 723-611, www.fiji.to) bases much of its domestic network at Nadi, with four flights a day to Labasa (F$180), three a day to Suva (F$120) and Taveuni (F$222), two a day to Savusavu (F$180), and daily to Kadavu (F$126). From Suva, Sunflower has flights to Labasa (twice daily, F$148), Nadi

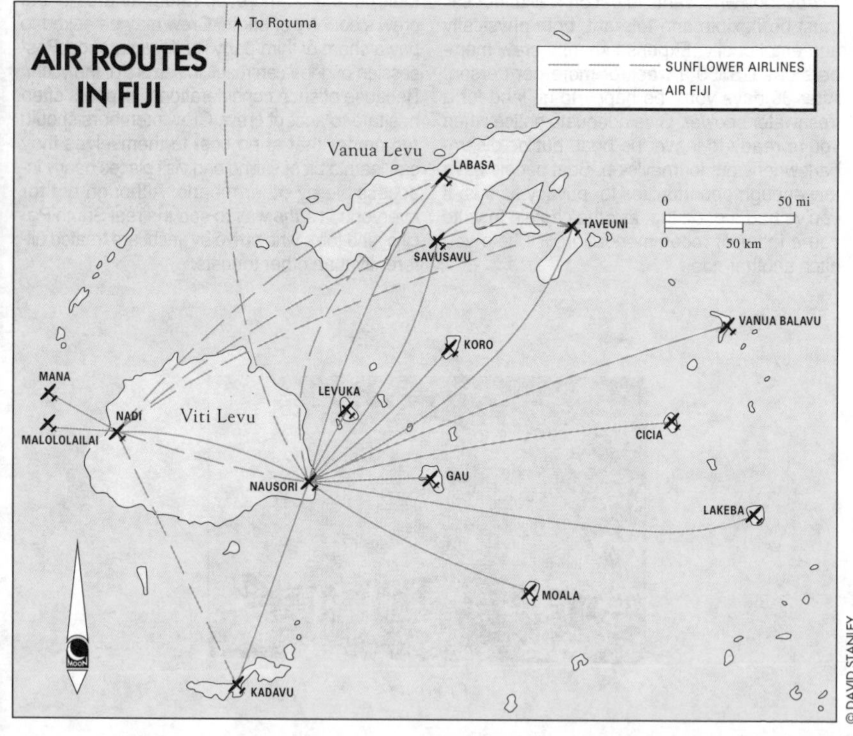

(three daily, F$120), and Rotuma (twice weekly, F$376). From Taveuni, they go to Savusavu (twice daily, F$82) and Labasa (three weekly, F$82). Flying in their 10-seat Britten Norman Islanders, versatile, 20-seat Twin Otters, or the coffin-like, 35-seat Short 330 is sort of fun.

From Nadi, the busy little resort island of Malololailai gets 10 flights a day by Sunflower Airlines and six by Air Fiji (F$54). Mana Island is visited eight times a day by Sunflower and four times by Air Fiji (F$66).

**Turtle Airways Ltd.** (Private Mail Bag, NAP 0355, Nadi Airport, Fiji; tel. 722-988, fax 720-346) flies their five Cessna floatplanes three times a day from Nadi to Castaway and Mana Islands (F$95 one-way, F$190 roundtrip).

Because only Nadi and Nausori airports have electric lighting on their runways all flights are during daylight hours. Always reconfirm your return flight upon arrival at an outer island, as the reservation lists are sometimes not sent out from Suva. Failure to do this could mean you'll be "bumped" without compensation. Student discounts are for local students only and there are no standby fares. Children aged 12 and under pay 50%, infants two and under carried in arms pay 10%. Sunflower Airlines and Air Fiji allow 20 kilograms of baggage, but only 15 kilograms is allowed on Turtle Airways (overweight costs one percent of the full one-way fare per kilogram with a F$5 minimum).

## BY BOAT

Since most shipping operates out of Suva, passenger services by sea both within Fiji and to neighboring countries are listed in the Suva section. Ferries to the Mamanuca Group are covered under Nadi, those to the Yasawas under Lautoka, those between Vanua Levu and Taveuni under Buca Bay and Taveuni.

The largest company is **Patterson Brothers Shipping,** set up by Levuka copra planter Reg Patterson and his brother just after WW I. Patterson's three Japanese-built car ferries, the *Jubilee, Ovalau,* and *Princess Ashika,* are usually used on the Tuesday to Saturday Buresala-Natovi-Nabouwalu-Ellington Wharf run. The barge *Yaubula* shuttles between Natuvu and Taveuni. Delays due to mechanical failures on Patterson's aging fleet are routine.

**Consort Shipping Line** runs the large car ferry *Spirit of Free Enterprise* from Suva to Koro, Savusavu, and Taveuni twice a week. The ferry *Adi Savusavu* of **Beachcomber Cruises** also visits Savusavu and Taveuni from Suva two or three times a week.

Other regular boat trips originating in Suva include the competing Patterson Brothers and Emosi Ferry Services shuttles to Levuka and the weekly ferries to Kadavu.

### By Ocean Kayak

Ocean kayaking is experiencing a boom in Fiji with kayaking tours now offered in the Yasawas, Kadavu, and Vanua Levu. Most islands have a sheltered lagoon ready-made for the excitement of kayak touring, and this effortless transportation mode can make you a real independent 20th-century explorer! Many international airlines accept folding kayaks as checked baggage at no charge.

For a better introduction to ocean kayaking than is possible here, check at your local public library for sea kayaking manuals. Noted author Paul Theroux toured the entire South Pacific by kayak, and his experiences are recounted in *The Happy Isles of Oceania: Paddling the Pacific* (London: Hamish Hamilton, 1992).

## BY BUS

Scheduled bus service is available all over Fiji, and fares are low. If you're from the States you'll be amazed how accessible, inexpensive, and convenient the bus service is. Most long-distance bus services operate several times a day and bus stations are usually adjacent to local markets. Buses with a signboard in the window reading Via Highway are local "stage" buses that will stop anywhere along their routes and can be excruciatingly slow on a long trip. Express buses are much faster but they'll only stop in a few towns and won't let you off at resorts along the way. Unfortunately the times of local buses are not posted at the bus stations and it's often hard to find anyone to ask about buses to remote locations. The people most likely to know are other bus drivers but you'll often receive misleading or incorrect information about local buses. Express bus times *are* posted at the stations and it's often possible to pick up printed express bus timetables at tourist offices.

On Viti Levu, the most important routes are between Lautoka and Suva, the biggest cities. If you follow the southern route via Sigatoka you'll be on Queens Road, the smoother and faster of the two. Kings Road via Tavua is longer and can be rough and dusty, but you get to see a little of the interior. Fares from Suva are F$2.12 to Pacific Harbor, F$5.30 to Sigatoka, F$7.77 to Nadi, F$8.12 to Nadi Airport, F$8.95 to Lautoka, and F$10.36 to Ba. Fares average about F$2 for each hour of travel. Express buses are 22 cents extra and to reserve a seat on a bus costs another 50 cents (usually unnecessary).

**Pacific Transport Ltd.** (Box 1266, Suva, Fiji; tel. 304-366) has 11 buses a day along Queens Road, with expresses leaving Suva for Lautoka at 0645, 0830, 0930, 1210, 1500, and 1730 (five hours). Eastbound, the expresses leave Lautoka for Suva at 0630, 0700, 1210, 1550, and 1730. An additional Suva-bound express leaves Nadi at 0900. These buses stop at Navua, Pacific Harbor, Sigatoka (coffee break), Nadi, and Nadi Airport *only.* The 1500 bus from Suva continues on to Ba. If you want off at a Coral Coast resort or some other smaller place, you must take one of the five local "stage" buses, which take six hours to reach Lautoka via Queens Road. The daily **Sunset Express** (tel. 322-811) leaves Suva for Sigatoka, Nadi, and Lautoka at 0845 and 1600 (four hours).

**Sunbeam Transport Ltd.** (tel. 382-122) services the northern Kings Road from Suva to Lautoka four or five times a day, with expresses leaving Suva at 0645, 1200, 1330, and 1715 (six hours). Another local Sunbeam bus leaves Suva for Vatukoula via Tavua daily at 0730 (seven hours). From Lautoka, they depart at 0615, 0630, 0815, 1215, and 1630. A Sunbeam express bus along Kings Road is a comfortable way to see Viti Levu's picturesque back side. These expresses only stop at Nausori, Korovou, Vaileka (Rakiraki), Tavua, and Ba. If you want off anywhere else you must take one of the two local buses, which take nine fun-filled hours to reach Lautoka via Kings Road. **Reliance Transport** (tel. 382-296) also services Kings Road.

**K.R. Latchan's Ltd.** (tel. 477-268) also runs express buses around Viti Levu. Their buses often run about 30 minutes ahead of the scheduled Sunbeam or Pacific Transport services and scoop all their passengers.

There are many other local buses, especially closer to Suva or Lautoka. The a/c tourist expresses such as UTC's "Fiji Express" cost twice as much as the services just described and are not as much fun as the ordinary expresses, whose big open windows with roll-down canvas covers give you a panoramic view of Viti Levu. Bus service on Vanua Levu and Taveuni is also good. Local buses often show up late, but the long-distance buses are usually right on time. Passenger trucks serving as "carriers" charge set rates to and from interior villages.

Shared "running" taxis and minibuses also shuttle back and forth between Suva, Nadi, and Lautoka, leaving when full and charging only a little more than the bus. Look for them in the markets around the bus stations. They'll often drop you exactly where you want to go; drawbacks include the less safe driving and lack of insurance coverage (in 1997 three Japanese tourists were killed in a collision caused by a speeding minibus). In a speeding minibus you also miss out on much of the scenery. It's possible to hire a complete taxi from Nadi Airport to Suva for about F$50 for the car, with brief stops along the way for photos, resort visits, etc.

Often the drivers of private or company cars and vans try to earn a little money on the side by stopping to offer lifts to persons waiting for buses beside the highway. They ask the same as you'd pay on the bus but are much faster and will probably drop you off exactly where you want to go. Many locals don't really understand hitchhiking, and it's probably only worth doing on remote roads where bus service is inadequate. In such places almost everyone will stop. Be aware that truck drivers who give you a lift may also expect the equivalent of bus fare; locals pay this without question. It's always appropriate to offer the bus fare and let the driver decide.

## TAXIS

Fijian taxis are plentiful and among the cheapest in the South Pacific, usable even by low-budget backpackers. Only in Suva do the taxis have meters but everywhere it's usually easier to ask the driver for a flat rate before you get in. If the first price you're quoted is too high you can often bargain (although bargaining is much more accepted by Fiji Indian than by ethnic Fijian drivers). A short ride across town can cost F$1-2, a longer trip into a nearby suburb about F$3. Taxis parked in front of luxury hotels will expect much more than this and it may be worth walking a short distance and flagging one down on the street. Taxis returning to their stand after a trip will pick up passengers at bus stops and charge the regular bus fare (ask if it's the "returning fare").

Don't tip your driver; tips are neither expected nor necessary. And don't invite your driver for a drink or become overly familiar with him as he may abuse your trust. If you're a woman taking a cab alone in the Nadi area, don't let your driver think there is any "hope" for him, or you could have problems (videos often portray Western women as promiscuous, which leads to mistaken expectations).

## CAR RENTALS

Rental cars are expensive in Fiji, due in part to high import duties on cars and a 10% government tax, so with public transportation as good as it is here, you should think twice before renting a car. By law, third-party public liability insurance is compulsory for rental vehicles and is included in the basic rate, but collision damage waiver (CDW) insurance is F$12-20 per day extra. Even with CDW, you're often still responsible for a "nonwaivable excess," which can be as high as the first F$2,000 in damage to the car! Many cars on the road have no insurance, so you could end up paying even if you're not responsible for the accident.

Your home driver's license is recognized for your first six months in Fiji, and driving is on the left (as in Britain and Japan). Get an automatic if you don't care to have to shift gears with your left hand. Seat belts must be worn in the front seat and the police are empowered to give roadside breath-analyzer tests. The police around Viti Levu occasionally employ hand-held radar. Speed limits are 50 kph in towns, 80 kph on the highway. Pedestrians have the right of way at crosswalks.

Unpaved roads can be very slippery, especially on inclines. Fast-moving vehicles on the gravel roads throw up small stones which can smash your front window (and you'll have to pay the damages). As you pass oncoming cars, hold your hand against the windshield just in case. When approaching a Fijian village slow right down, as there may be poorly marked speed humps in the road. Also beware of narrow bridges, and take care with local motorists, who sometimes stop in the middle of the road, pass on blind curves, and drive at high speeds. Driving can be an especially risky business at night. Many of the roads are atrocious (check the spare tire), although the 486-km road around Viti Levu is now fully paved except for a 62-km stretch on the northeast side which is easily passable if you go slowly. Luckily, there isn't a lot of traffic.

If you plan to use a rental car to explore the rough country roads in Viti Levu's mountainous interior, think twice before announcing your plans to the agency, as they may suddenly decline your business. The rental contracts all contain clauses stating that the insurance coverage is not valid under such conditions. However, some companies offer four-wheel-drive Suzukis just made for mountain roads. Tank up on Saturday, as many gas stations are closed on Sunday, and always keep the tank over half full. If you run out of gas in a rural area, small village stores sometimes sell fuel from drums.

Several international car rental chains are represented in Fiji, including Avis, Budget, Hertz, and Thrifty. Local companies like Bula Rental Cars, Central Rent-a-Car, Dove Rent-a-Car, Kenns Rent-a-Car, Khan's Rental Cars, Roxy Rentals, Satellite Rentals, Sharmas Rental Cars, and Tanoa Rent-a-Car are often cheaper, but check around as prices vary. The international companies rent only new cars, while the less expensive local companies may offer secondhand vehicles. If in doubt, check the vehicle carefully before driving off. The international franchises generally provide better support should anything go wrong. Budget, Central, and Khan's won't rent to persons under age 25, while most of the others will so long as you're over 21.

A dozen companies have offices in the arrivals concourse at Nadi Airport and three are also at Nausori Airport. Agencies with town offices in Suva include Avis, Budget, Central, Dove, Hertz, and Thrifty. In Lautoka you'll find Budget and Central. Avis and Thrifty also have desks in many resort hotels on Viti Levu. On Vanua Levu, Avis and Budget are at Savusavu and Labasa. The other islands, including Taveuni, do not have rental cars.

Both unlimited-kilometer and per-kilometer rates are available. **Thrifty** (tel. 722-935), run by Rosie The Travel Service, offers unlimited-kilometer prices from F$95/570 daily/weekly, which include CDW (F$700 nonwaivable) and tax, but there's a 150-km limit on one-day rentals. **Budget** (tel. 722-636) charges F$69/414 for their cheapest mini but F$18 a day insurance (F$500 nonwaivable) is extra. **Avis** begins at F$88/462 plus $20 a day insurance (F$500 nonwaivable). Hertz is a lot more expensive. Prices with Avis and Budget may be lower if you book ahead from the U.S. The insurance plans used by all of the local companies have nonwaivable excess fees of F$1,500-2,000, which makes renting from them more risky. Also beware of companies like Central whose brochures advertise their off-season rates in large typeface (period not specified), or Satellite and Tanoa which add the 10% tax later (most of the others include it in the quoted price). Of the local companies, **Sharmas Rental Cars** (tel. 701-055), at Nadi Airport and near the ANZ Bank in Nadi town, offers unlimited-kilometer rates of F$385 a week or F$1,209 for 31 days, plus F$12.50 a day insurance. On a per-kilometer basis, **Khan's Rental Cars** (tel. 701-009) in Nadi charges F$15 a day plus 17 cents per kilometer and F$16 CDW (F$2,000 nonwaivable). **Roxy Rentals** (tel. 722-763) is similar.

Many of the local car rental agencies at Nadi Airport offer substantial discounts on their brochure prices for weekly rentals, and you can often get a car for F$350-400 a week with kilometers, tax, and insurance included. Ask how many kilometers are on the speedometer and beware of vehicles above 50,000 as they may be unreliable. On a per-kilometer basis, you'll only want to use the car in the local area. Some companies advertise low prices with the qualification in fine print that these apply only to rentals of three days or more. Most companies charge a F$30 delivery fee if you don't return the vehicle to the office where you rented it. If you want the cheapest economy subcompact, reserve ahead.

If you do rent a car, remember those sudden tropical downpours and don't leave the windows open. Also avoid parking under coconut trees (a falling nut might break the window), and never go off and leave the keys in the ignition.

# AIRPORTS

### Nadi International Airport

Nadi Airport (NAN) is between Lautoka and Nadi, 22 km south of the former and eight km north of the latter. There are frequent buses to these towns until around 2200. To catch a bus to Nadi (54 cents), cross the highway; buses to Lautoka (F$1.18) stop on the airport side of the road. A few express buses drop passengers right outside the international departures hall. A taxi from the airport should be F$6 to downtown Nadi or F$20 to Lautoka.

As you come out of customs a uniformed representative of the Fiji Visitors Bureau will ask you where you intend to stay in order to be helpful and to direct you to a driver from that hotel. Most Nadi hotels offer free transfers (ask) but you ought to change a bit of money before going. Agents of other hotels will also accost you and try to sign you up for the commission they'll earn. Be polite but defensive in dealing with them. The people selling stays at the outer island backpacker resorts can be especially aggressive. Most of the resorts have offices in the airport concourse in front of you—the upmarket places downstairs, the backpackers camps upstairs—and it's better to head straight for them rather than to deal with intermediaries.

The actual office of the Fiji Visitors Bureau (tel. 722-433) is beside the bank to the left as you come out of customs. They open for all international arrivals and can advise you on accommodations (and tell you if your resort of choice has an office at the airport). Pick up their brochures, hotel lists, and free tourist magazines (especially *Fiji Magic*).

There's a 24-hour ANZ Bank (F$2 commission) beside the Visitors Bureau and another bank in the departure lounge. Their rates are about 1% worse than the banks in town. The airport banks don't stock Tongan pa'anga,

Samoan tala, French Pacific francs, or other regional currencies, so buy these at Thomas Cook in Nadi or Suva before coming to the airport.

Many travel agencies and car rental companies are also located in the arrivals arcade. The rent-a-car companies you'll find here are Avis, Budget, Central, Hertz, Kenns, Khan's, Roxy, Satellite, Sharmas, Tanoa, and Thrifty. All of the international airlines flying into Nadi have offices in this same arcade (Air Fiji represents Air Vanuatu).

The post office is across the parking lot from the arrivals hall (ask). The airport cafe just before the security check at departures serves inexpensive light meals. The luggage storage service, near the snack bar in the domestic departures area, is open 24 hours (bicycles or surfboards F$6 a day, bags larger that 75 by 50 centimeters F$4 a day, other luggage F$3 a day). Most hotels around Nadi will also store luggage. There's zero tolerance for drugs in Fiji and a three-dog sniffer unit checks all baggage passing through NAN. One reader said the airport security officers allowed him to pitch his tent in the airport parking lot.

Duty-free shops are found in both the departure lounge and in the arrivals area just before the baggage claim area. If you're arriving for a prebooked stay at a deluxe resort, grab a bottle or two of cheap Fiji rum as drink prices at the resort bars are high (you can usually get mix at the hotel shops). You can use leftover Fijian currency to stock up on cheap film and cigarettes just before you leave (film prices here are the lowest in the South Pacific). Prices vary slightly at the different duty-free shops and it's worth comparing before buying.

A departure tax of F$20 in cash Fijian currency is payable on all international flights, but transit passengers connecting within 12 hours and children under the age of 16 are exempt (no airport tax on domestic flights). Have a look at the museum exhibits near the departures gates upstairs as you're waiting for your flight. The airport never closes. NAN's 24-hour flight arrival and departure information number is 722-076.

### Nausori Airport

Nausori Airport (SUV) is on the plain of the Rewa River delta, 23 km northeast of downtown Suva. After Hurricane Kina in January 1993 the whole terminal was flooded by Rewa water for several days. There's no special airport bus and a taxi direct to/from Suva will run about F$20. You can save money by taking a taxi from the airport only as far as Nausori (four km, F$3), then a local bus to Suva from there (19 km, with services every 10 minutes until 2100 for 90 cents). Airport-bound, catch a local bus from Suva to Nausori, then a taxi to the airport (only F$2 in this direction). It's also possible to catch a local bus to Nausori from the highway opposite the airport about every 15 minutes (40 cents).

Avis, Budget, and Hertz all have car rental offices in the terminal, and a lunch counter provides light snacks. You're not allowed to sleep overnight at this airport. The departure tax is F$20 on all international flights, but no tax is levied on domestic flights. The airport information number is tel. 478-799.

BOB RACE

# NADI AND THE MAMANUCAS

## NADI

At 10,429 square km, Viti Levu is the eighth largest island in the South Pacific, only a shade smaller than the Big Island of Hawaii. This 1,323-meter-high island accounts for over half of Fiji's land area and dominates the country in almost every respect. Nadi International Airport facing Nadi Bay on the west side of Viti Levu has long been the main gateway to the Fiji Islands and the South Pacific. The airport itself sits in the center of an ancient volcano the west side of which has fallen away.

A small airstrip existed at Nadi even before WW II, and after Pearl Harbor the Royal New Zealand Air Force began converting it into a fighter strip. Before long the U.S. military was there, building a major air base with paved runways for bombers and transport aircraft serving Australia and New Zealand. In the early 1960s, Nadi Airport was expanded to accommodate jet aircraft, and today the largest jumbo jets can land here. This activity has made Nadi what it is today.

All around Nadi are cane fields worked by the predominantly Indian population. There aren't many sandy, palm-fringed beaches on the western side of Viti Levu—for that you have to go to the nearby Mamanuca Group where a string of sun-drenched "Robinson Crusoe" resorts soak up vacationers in search of a place to relax. The long gray mainland beaches near Nadi face shallow murky waters devoid of snorkeling possibilities but fine for windsurfing and water-skiing. Fiji's tropical rainforests are on the other side of Viti Levu as this is the dry side of the island.

In recent years Nadi (pronounced "Nandi") has grown into Fiji's third largest town, with a mixed population of 32,000. The town center's main feature is a kilometer of restaurants and shops with high-pressure sales staffs peddling mass-produced souvenirs. It's easily the most touristy place in Fiji, yet there's also a surprisingly colorful market (especially on Saturday morning) and the road out to the airport is flanked by a multitude of places to stay. Still, if you're not that exhausted after your transpacific flight you'd do better to head for Lautoka (see the separate Lautoka chapter later in this handbook). All of the hotels around Nadi tend to experience quite a bit of aircraft/traffic/disco noise, while those at Lautoka are out of range of such noise pollution.

### Sights

Nadi's only substantial sight is the **Sri Siva Subrahmaniya Swami Temple** at the south entrance to town, erected by local Hindus in 1994 after the lease on their former temple property expired. This colorful South Indian-style temple, built by craftspeople flown in from India itself, is the largest and finest of its kind in the South Pacific. Sober visitors may enter the temple, but shoes must be removed at the entrance, and smoking and photography are prohibited inside the compound (open daily 0500-1330/1530-2000, admission free).

M.E. DE VOS

*Sri Siva Subramaniya Swami Temple, Nadi.*

### Sports and Recreation

**Aqua-Trek** (Dave Dickinson, Box 10215, Nadi Airport; tel. 702-413, fax 702-412), located at 465 Queens Rd., opposite the Mobil station in Nadi town, is the only full-service dive shop in western Fiji. They also run a dive shop on Mana Island. Aqua-Trek charges F$80/160 for one/two boat dives with gear or F$520 for PADI open-water certification (medical examination required). Shark feeding is offered.

**Dive Tropex** (Eddie Jennings, Box 10522, Nadi Airport; tel. 703-944, fax 703-955), in the beach hut at the Sheraton, offers scuba diving at F$99/141/462 one/two/eight tanks including gear. When space is available snorkelers can go along for F$40. A four-day PADI certification course is F$614 for one to three students, or F$404 pp for four students of more. For an introductory dive it's F$135. Several Japanese instructors are on the staff.

Much less expensive diving is offered by **Inner Space Adventures** (Box 9535, Nadi Airport; tel./fax 723-883), between the Horizon and Travellers beach resorts at Wailoaloa Beach. They go out daily at 0900, charging F$60/77/105 for one/two/three tanks, equipment and pickup anywhere around Nadi included. Snorkelers are welcome to tag along at F$25 pp, gear included. Their four-day open-water PADI certification course costs F$320—good value.

The **New Town Beach Pony Club** (Box 9299, Nadi Airport; tel. 724-449) at Wailoaloa Beach offers one-hour beach rides at F$15, 1.5 hours crosscountry at F$20, or a two-hour combination at F$25. Longer rides can be arranged.

The 18-hole, par-71 **Nadi Airport Golf Club** (Box 9015, Nadi; tel. 722-148) is pleasantly situated between the airport runways and the sea at Wailoaloa Beach. Green fees are F$15, plus F$20 for clubs. There's a bar and pool table in the clubhouse (tourists welcome). It's busy with local players on Saturday but quiet during the week.

Other golf courses are available at the Fiji Mocambo Hotel (green fees F$11, clubs F$11) and at the Sheratons. The 18-hole, par-72 course at the **Denarau Golf & Racquet Club** (Box 9081, Nadi Airport; tel. 750-477, fax 750-484) opposite the Sheratons was designed by Eichi Motohashi. The course features bunkers shaped like a marlin, crab, starfish, and octopus, and water shots across all four par-three

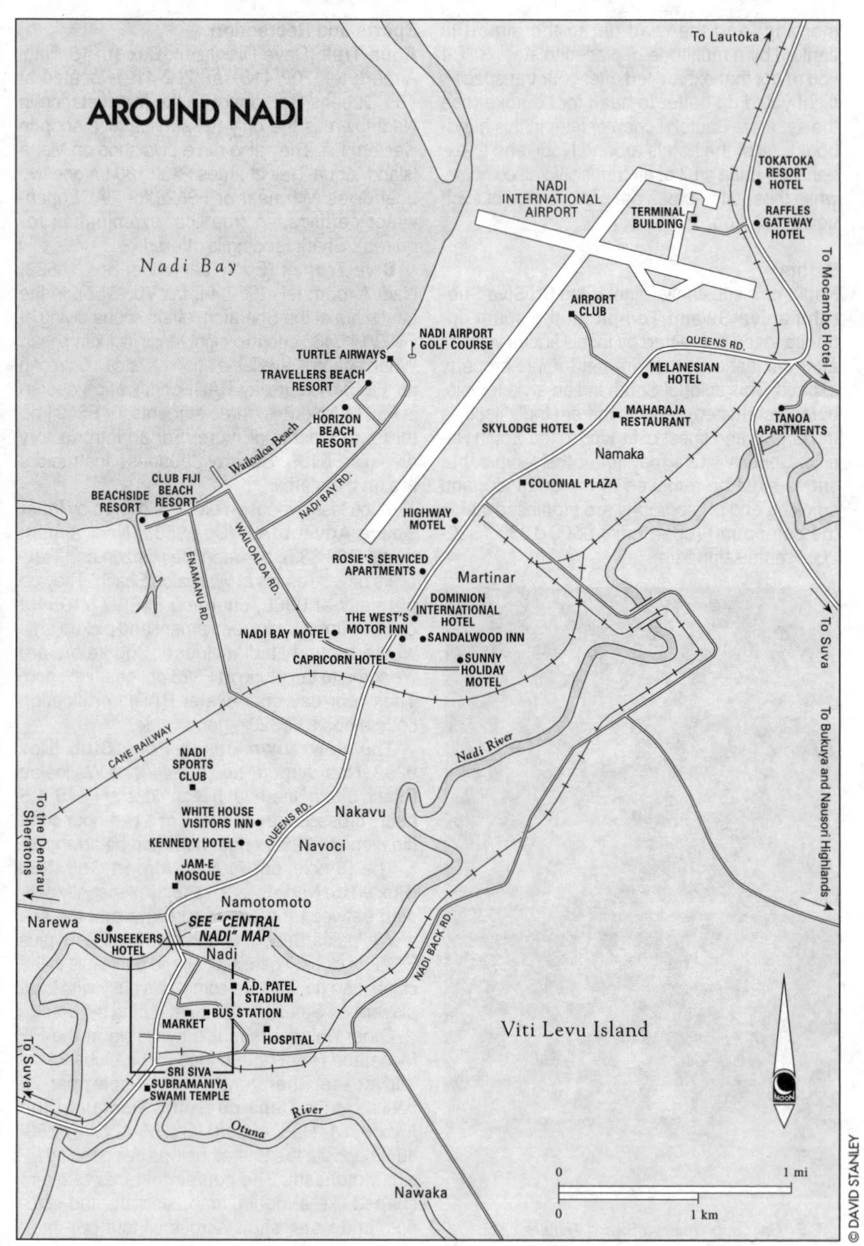
AROUND NADI
To Lautoka
NADI INTERNATIONAL AIRPORT
TERMINAL BUILDING
TOKATOKA RESORT HOTEL
RAFFLES GATEWAY HOTEL
To Mocambo Hotel
Nadi Bay
AIRPORT CLUB
NADI AIRPORT GOLF COURSE
TURTLE AIRWAYS
QUEENS RD.
MELANESIAN HOTEL
TRAVELLERS BEACH RESORT
HORIZON BEACH RESORT
MAHARAJA RESTAURANT
SKYLODGE HOTEL
TANOA APARTMENTS
Wailoaloa Beach
Namaka
NADI BAY RD.
CLUB FIJI BEACH RESORT
BEACHSIDE RESORT
COLONIAL PLAZA
HIGHWAY MOTEL
WAILOALOA RD.
ENAMANU RD.
ROSIE'S SERVICED APARTMENTS
Martinar
DOMINION INTERNATIONAL HOTEL
THE WEST'S MOTOR INN
NADI BAY MOTEL
SANDALWOOD INN
To Suva
CAPRICORN HOTEL
SUNNY HOLIDAY MOTEL
CANE RAILWAY
Nadi River
To Bukuya and Nausori Highlands
NADI SPORTS CLUB
QUEENS RD.
To the Denarau Sheratons
WHITE HOUSE VISITORS INN
Nakavu
KENNEDY HOTEL
Navoci
JAM-E MOSQUE
Namotomoto
Narewa
SEE "CENTRAL NADI" MAP
SUNSEEKERS HOTEL
Nadi
NADI BACK RD.
A.D. PATEL STADIUM
BUS STATION
MARKET
HOSPITAL
Viti Levu Island
To Suva
SRI SIVA SUBRAMANIYA SWAMI TEMPLE
Otuna River
Nawaka
0
1 mi
0
1 km
MOON
© DAVID STANLEY

holes (the average golfer loses four balls per round). Green fees are F$85 for those staying at one of the Sheratons or F$94 for other mortals. Golfers are not allowed to walk around the course and a shared electric cart is included. Clubs can be rented at F$30 a set. A better deal is their "sunset golf" package, which allows you to do nine holes beginning at 1600 for only F$38 including happy hour drinks at the clubhouse bar after your round. On Fridays this "chook run" begins at 1500. Call ahead to reconfirm as their specials vary from time to time and ask about the dress code. Ten tennis courts are available here at F$12/18 day/night per hour.

During the June-to-March sports season, see rugby or soccer on Saturdays at the A.D. Patel Stadium, near Nadi Bus Station.

## ACCOMMODATIONS

### Budget Accommodations in Town

Most of the hotels offer free transport from the airport, which is lucky because there aren't any budget places within walking distance of the terminal itself. As you leave customs you'll see a group of people representing the hotels to the right. If you know which hotel you want, call out the name and if a driver from that hotel is there, you should get a free ride (ask). If not, the Fiji Visitors Bureau (tel. 722-433) to the left will help you telephone them for a small fee. (There have been reports of nocturnal muggings along the road from the bridge on the north side of Nadi town to the Sunseekers and Kennedy hotels, as well as on the isolated roads to Wailoaloa Beach. After dark a bus or taxi would be advisable, especially if you're carrying a backpack.)

There are three budget choices in the downtown area, two with confusingly similar names but under separate managements. The seedy **Nadi Town Motel** (Box 1326, Nadi; tel. 700-600, fax 701-541), also known as the "Downtown Backpackers Inn", occupying the top floor of an office building opposite the BP service station in the center of Nadi, is a bit of a dive and the only attraction here is the shoestring price: F$20 single or double with fan, F$35 with a/c, both with private bath. The five-bed dormitory is just F$5 pp and basic rooms with shared bath are F$15. Breakfast is supposed to be included in all rates but don't be surprised if they try to charge extra. Definitely ask to see the room before accepting, expect dirty sheets, and, if you're a woman, don't tolerate any nonsense from the male motel staff. The adjacent Seventh Heaven Night Club sends out a steady disco beat well into the morning. The travel agency below the motel arranges transport to Nananu-i-Ra Island at F$20 pp.

Around the corner on Koroivolu Street is the two-story, 31-room **Nadi Hotel** (Box 91, Nadi; tel. 700-000, fax 700-280). Spacious rooms with private bath begin at F$22/28 single/double standard with fan, F$33/39 superior with a/c, or F$10 pp in an 10-bed dorm. Deluxe rooms with fridge are F$44/50/60 single/double/triple. The neat courtyard with a swimming pool out back makes this a pleasant, convenient place to stay. Some rooms are also subjected to nightclub noise though, so ask for a superior room in the block farthest away from Seventh Heaven. The restaurant has three-course meals at F$10.

The two-story **Coconut Inn Hotel** (Box 2756, Nadi; tel. 701-169, fax 700-616), 37 Vunavau St., is a block from the Nadi Hotel and the Nadi Town Motel. The 22 rooms with private bath upstairs begin at F$33/43 single/double (plus F$10 for a/c), and downstairs is a F$11 dorm (three beds). Beware of rooms without windows.

On Narewa Road at the north edge of Nadi town is the **Sunseekers Hotel** (Box 100, Nadi; tel. 700-400, fax 702-047). The 20 rooms here are F$50 double with fan but shared bath, F$55 with a/c and private bath, or F$11 for a bunk in the six-bed dorm. There's a bar on the large deck out back which overlooks the swimming pool (often dry) and surrounding countryside. Bicycle rentals are F$3.50 an hour or F$11 a day (0800-1600). Despite the sign, this is not an approved Hosteling International associate. Airport pickups are free but to return to the airport you must take a taxi (F$6).

Better is the two-story **White House Visitors Inn** (Box 2150, Nadi; tel. 700-022, fax 702-822), at 40 Kennedy Ave., up Ray Prasad Road just off Queens Road, a 10-minute walk north of central Nadi. The 12 fan-equipped rooms are F$27 double with shared bath, F$33/38 single/double with private bath, or F$12 pp in the dorm. Rooms with a/c cost F$8 extra. The beds are comfortable, and a weight-watchers' toast-and-coffee breakfast is included in the price. You can cook your own meals in the communal kitchen, and there's a grocery store across the street. This small hotel is a fairly peaceful place to stay with a small swimming pool, video lounge, and free airport pickups. Baggage storage is F$1 per day (but only if you make your outer island bookings through them). Though you'll hear a bit of traffic and animal noise, you won't be bothered by disco music. It's very popular and might be full.

Half a block up Kennedy Avenue from the White House is the three-story **Kennedy Hotel** (Box 9045, Nadi Airport; tel. 702-360, fax 702-218), the highest-priced hotel in this category. The 16 a/c rooms with private bath, TV, and coffee-making facilities are F$47 single or double without fridge, F$57 with fridge, tax included. Beds in the four fan-cooled, four-bed dormitory blocks cost F$11 pp, or F$15 for a bed in the eight-bed a/c dorm. Deluxe two-bedroom apartments with cooking facilities are F$95. A plus are the spacious gardenlike grounds with a large swimming pool, and there's a restaurant/bar on the premises. The Kennedy is quite popular and but some of the rooms are rather small and shabby so have a look before committing yourself.

### Budget Airport Hotels

The listings below are arranged from the airport into town. The budget hotel closest to the terminal is the **Kon Tiki Private Hotel** (Box 10463, Nadi Airport; tel. 722-836), set in cane fields a 15-minute walk in from Queens Road, past the Fiji Mocambo Hotel. The 18 rooms go for F$19/25/33 single/double/triple with private bath and fan, F$28/33 with a/c, F$8 pp dormitory (six beds). Some hard drinking goes on at the bar, so don't accept a room near it. Kon Tiki is all by itself down a side road, so you're dependent on the hotel restaurant for food, although a small breakfast is included and you may be able to use their kitchen. They arrange daily transfers to Nananu-i-Ra Island at F$25 each way.

The Chinese-operated **Westgarden Hotel** (Box 9968, Nadi Airport; tel. 721-788, fax 721-790), on the 3rd floor above Chopsticks Restaurant at Namaka, has nine a/c rooms with bath at F$50 single or double, F$55 triple, F$60 family.

The **Melanesian Hotel** (Box 10410, Nadi Airport; tel. 722-438, fax 720-425), near the Westgarden but a bit farther off the road, has 16 rooms with bath beginning at F$38/45 single/double, F$10 extra for a/c. A mixed five-bed dorm (F$15 pp) is also available. The new management has picked the Melanesian up and it's now a pleasant place to stop, with a swimming pool, bar, and restaurant.

More basic is the **Highway Motel** (Box 9282, Nadi; tel. 723-761), a single-story block with rooms at F$27/40 single/double, all with private facilities. Rooms with a/c are sometimes more. The Highway offers shared cooking facilities and luggage storage. You can bargain for a discount when things are slow.

Across the street from the Shell service station in Martintar is **Mountainview Apartments** (Box 1476, Nadi; tel. 721-880, fax 721-800), above the Bounty Restaurant and near the Dominion International Hotel, with 10 fan-cooled rooms with bath at F$30/33 single/double. The one a/c room is F$39 single or double, and if you want cooking facilities it's an extra F$5 a day for the stove and gas tank.

The two-story **Sandalwood Inn** (John and Ana Birch, Box 9454, Nadi Airport; tel. 722-044, fax 720-103), on Ragg Street beside the Dominion International Hotel, is F$26/32/38 single/double/triple plus tax for one of the five rooms with shared bath in the old wing, or F$32/34/40 for one of the seven standard rooms with fridge and private bath in the new wing (the 13 a/c rooms are F$48/54/60). The atmosphere is pleasant and the layout attractive with a pool, a bar, and a medium-priced restaurant serving authentic Fijian dishes! A cooked breakfast and three-course dinner are F$24 plus tax. Avoid the rooms facing the swimming pool if you plan to go to bed early. Two hundred meters inland from the Inn is the two-story **Sandalwood Lodge** (same management) with 24 a/c rooms with bath, fridge, and cooking facilities in two blocks facing a swimming pool at F$64/70/76. Add 10% tax to all prices.

Close by is the 14-room **Sunny Holiday Motel** (Box 1326, Nadi Airport; tel. 722-158, fax 701-541), on Northern Press Road behind Hamacho Japanese Restaurant—the cheapest place to stay around Nadi. It's F$15/20 single/double with shared bath, F$22/27 with private bath, or F$6 in the four-bed dorm. Self-contained apartments with cooking facilities are F$35. Inveterate campers may like to know that this is about the only place in this area where you're allowed to unroll your tent (F$2.50 pp). There's a pool table, TV room, bar, and luggage storage. It's all a little run-down, but friendly, uncrowded, and fine for those on shoestring budgets. They book the daily shuttle to Nananu-i-Ra Island (F$22 one-way).

A few hundred meters down Wailoaloa Beach Road off the main highway, in the opposite direction from the Sunny Holiday, is the **Nadi Bay Motel** (Bryan and Victoria Curran, Private Mail Bag, NAP 0359, Nadi; tel. 723-599, fax 720-092), a two-story concrete edifice enclosing a swimming pool. The 25 rooms are F$27/37 single/double with fan, F$7 extra for private bath, F$16 extra for private bath and a/c. An apartment with cooking facilities is F$53/63 single/double. There's also a F$10 dorm. Washing machines are available, plus a congenial bar, inexpensive restaurant, and luggage room. The airport flight path passes right above the Nadi Bay and the roar of jets on the adjacent runway can be jarring. If you take any scuba lessons in the motel swimming pool, be prepared for a steady stream of wisecracks from the jerks lounging by the pool.

### Budget Beach Hotels

There are six budget or inexpensive places to stay on Wailoaloa Beach, also known as Newtown Beach, on the opposite side of the airport runway from the main highway. The first four places are near the seaplane base and golf club, a dusty three-km hike from the Nadi Bay Motel, so ask for their free shuttle buses at the airport or take a taxi (F$6). The Wailoaloa Newtown bus from Nadi market also passes nearby four times a day. These places are probably your best bet on the weekend, and sporting types can play a round of golf on the public course or go jogging along the beach (the swimming in the knee-deep water isn't great). The main base of Inner Space Adventures is here, with scuba diving and horseback riding on offer.

The most popular of the lot is the **Horizon Beach Resort** (Box 1401, Nadi; tel. 722-832, fax 720-662), a large wooden two-story house just across a field from the beach. The 14 rooms with shared bath begin at F$30 single or double with fan, F$38 with a/c. Horizon's 10-bed dormitory is F$6 pp. No cooking facilities are provided but there's a medium-priced restaurant/bar. To use the washer/drier is F$10 a load.

A hundred meters inland from the Horizon is the friendly two-story **Newtown Beach Motel** (Box 787, Nadi; tel. 723-339, fax 720-087). The seven clean rooms with fan are F$33 single or double (or F$11 pp in the five-bed dorm). There's no cooking, but a huge dinner is offered for F$7.

A hundred meters along the beach from the Horizon is **Travelers Beach Resort** (Box 700, Nadi; tel. 723-322, fax 720-026). The 12 fan-cooled standard rooms with private bath are F$33/39 single/double, the eight a/c rooms F$39/50, the two a/c beachfront rooms F$55 single or double, and the 13 villas with kitchenette F$66/77/88 single/double/triple. Four four-bed dorms are provided at F$11 pp. The villas are tightly packed in a compound a block back from the beach. There's an expensive restaurant/bar and a swimming pool, but many other facilities listed in their brochure seem to have vanished. The management style leaves a lot to be desired and credible complaints have been received.

Ratu Kini Boko has a large modern house at Wailoaloa Beach opposite the Travelers Beach Resort villas called **Mana Rose Apartments** (tel. 723-333) where he puts up guests in transit to his backpacker resort on Mana Island. The three four-bed dorms are F$15 pp including breakfast, double rooms are F$40, and there's a plush lounge where you can relax.

Also on Wailoaloa Beach, a km southwest of the places just mentioned and three km off Queens Road from McDonald's Restaurant (F$3 one way by taxi), is **Club Fiji Beach Resort** (John and Elly Bullock, Box 9619, Nadi Airport; tel. 720-150, fax 720-350). The 24 thatched duplex bungalows, all with veranda, private bath, solar hot water, and fridge, are priced according to location: F$60 single or double for a garden unit, F$78 oceanview. The eight a/c beachfront suites in a two-story building are F$110/123 double/triple. One duplex has been converted into a pair of six-bunk, 12-person dormitories at F$10 pp, with a small discount if you have a youth hostel card. Add 10% tax to all rates. Club Fiji's staff does its utmost to keep the accommodations and grounds spotless. The atmosphere is friendly and relaxed, and you'll meet other travelers at the bar. Tea- and coffee-making facilities are provided but there's no cooking. The Club's restaurant serves authentic Fijian food and a variety of dishes (F$35 breakfast and dinner plan). Special evening events include the *lovo* on Thursday and the beach barbecue on Saturday night. Horseback riding is F$15 an hour, the Hobie cat is F$15 an hour, and windsurfing and paddle boats are complimentary. A two-hour snorkeling trip by boat is F$20 pp. The day tour to Natadola Beach and the two-island boat trip each cost F$50 with lunch. At low tide the beach resembles a tidal flat, but there's a small clean swimming pool, and the location is lovely—the equivalent of the Sheratons at a fifth the price and without the stuffy upmarket atmosphere. Club Fiji is recommended as your top choice in this price range, but call ahead as they're often full.

Also good is the **Beachside Resort** (Box 9883, Nadi Airport; tel. 703-488, fax 703-688), next to Club Fiji at Wailoaloa Beach. The five a/c rooms on the ground floor of the main building are F$68/78 double/triple, while the 10 rooms on the second and third floors are F$88/98 (reduced rates often available). These rooms have fridges but no cooking facilities. However, seven new *bures* adjacent to the main building do have kitchens and run F$600 double a week. A three-course dinner at the resort's thatched restaurant is F$17.50. Despite the name the Beachside isn't right on the beach although it does have a swimming pool. A timeshare condo development called "Fantasy Beach Estate" is going up just beyond the Beachside and beach access should be possible through the Fantasy complex. There will also be a yacht marina. Although the accommodations are of a high standard there's less atmosphere here than at Club Fiji, which makes it very much a second choice.

### Inexpensive

The three medium-priced selections that follow are highly competitive and often run specials that reduce the quoted rates. **Rosie's Deluxe Serviced Apartments** (Box 9268, Nadi Airport; tel. 722-755, fax 722-607), in Martintar near Ed's Bar, offers studio apartments accommodating four at F$60, one-bedrooms for up to five at F$80, and two-bedrooms for up to seven at F$106. All eight a/c units have cooking facilities, fridge, and private balcony. The walls are not completely soundproof and the units facing the highway get considerable traffic noise, but they're still good value. You may use the communal washer and drier free. Rosie The Travel Service office at the airport is the place to check current prices and availability. Free airport transfers are provided in both directions, even in the middle of the night.

**The West's Motor Inn** (Peter Beer, Box 10097, Nadi Airport; tel. 720-044, fax 720-071) is next to the Dominion International, not far from Rosie's Apartments. The 62 a/c rooms with private bath and fridge begin at F$88 single or double standard (or F$99 for a larger deluxe room). Their 50% day-use rate can extend your occupancy from 1030 until 1800 if you have a late flight. The name really doesn't do justice to this pleasant two-story hotel with its courtyard swimming pool, piano bar, restaurant, conference room, secretarial services, and Rosie tour desk.

The **Capricorn International Hotel** (Box 9043, Nadi Airport; tel. 720-088, fax 720-522), between The West's Motor Inn and Hamacho Japanese Restaurant, consists of two-story blocks surrounding a swimming pool. The 62 small a/c rooms with fridge begin at F$75 single or double. Cooking facilities are not provided, but there's a restaurant/bar on the premises. Dove Rent-a-Car has a desk here.

### Moderate

The two-story, colonial-style **Raffles Gateway Hotel** (Box 9891, Nadi Airport; tel. 722-444, fax 720-620) is just across the highway from the airport terminal, within easy walking distance. Its 92 a/c rooms begin at F$105 single or double. Happy hour at the poolside bar is 1800-1900 (half-price drinks)—worth checking out if you're stuck at the airport waiting for a flight.

Several km southwest of the airport is the **Skylodge Hotel** (Box 9222, Nadi Airport; tel. 722-200, fax 724-330), which was constructed in the early 1960s as Nadi Airport was being expanded to take jet aircraft. Airline crews on layovers originally stayed here, and business travelers still make up 50% of the clientele. The 53 a/c units begin at F$114 single or double; children under 16 are free, provided the bed configurations aren't changed. It's better to pay F$32 more here and get a room with cooking facilities in one of the four-unit clusters well-spaced among the greenery, rather than a smaller room in the main building or near the busy highway. If you're catching a flight in the middle of the night there's a F$66 "day use" rate valid until 2300. Pitch-and-putt golf, half-size tennis facilities, and a swimming pool are on the premises. Airport transfers are free.

The **Dominion International Hotel** (Box 9178, Nadi Airport; tel. 722-255, fax 720-187), halfway between the airport and town, is one of Nadi's nicest top end hotels. This appealing three-story building was built in 1973, and they've done their best to keep the place up. The 85 a/c rooms with balcony or terrace are F$110/115/125 single/double/triple, plus F$20 extra if you want a "deluxe" with a TV and a bath tub instead of a shower. Their 60% "extended stay rate" allows you to keep your room until 2200. If you stay six nights, the seventh is free. Lots of well shaded tables and chairs surround the swimming pool, and the nearby hotel bar has a happy hour 1800-1900 daily. On Saturday night you'll be treated to a *meke.* There's a Rosie The Travel Service desk in the Dominion and a barber shop/beauty salon. The hotel bottle shop facing the highway is open Mon.-Fri. 1100-2100, Saturday 1100-1400/1600-2100, should you wish to stock your fridge. The tennis court is free for guests (day use only). It's all very relaxed and not at all pretentious.

### Expensive

The **Tokatoka Resort Hotel** (Box 9305, Nadi Airport; tel. 720-222, fax 720-400), right next to the Raffles Gateway Hotel a short walk from the airport terminal, caters to families with young children by offering 116 a/c villas and rooms with cooking facilities, mini-fridge, and video for F$130/140 single/double and up. Eight special rooms for guests with disablities are available. Anyone planning a business meeting in Nadi should inquire about the 200-seat conference room that is provided free when at least 10 hotel rooms are booked. A small supermarket and a large designer swimming pool with water slide are on the premises. A different buffet is mounted every night (F$24 including tea/coffee)—Friday it's a Pacific feast and *meke.*

### Premium

People on brief prepaid stopovers in Fiji are often accommodated at one of three hotels off Votualevu Road, a couple of km inland from the airport (take a taxi). The closest to the terminal is **Tanoa Apartments** (Box 9211, Nadi Airport; tel. 723-685, fax 721-193), on a hilltop overlooking the surrounding countryside. The 23 self-catering apartments begin at F$164 (weekly and monthly rates available). Facilities include a swimming pool, spa pool, and sauna. First opened in 1965, this property was the beginning of today's locally owned Tanoa hotel chain.

A few hundred meters inland from Tanoa Apartments is the Malaysian-owned **Fiji Mocambo Hotel** (Box 9195, Nadi Airport; tel. 722-000, fax 720-324), a sprawling two-story hotel with mountain views from the spacious grounds. The 128 a/c rooms with patio or balcony and fridge begin at F$213/225/265 single/double/triple including breakfast. Secretarial services can be arranged for businesspeople, conference facilities and swimming pool are available, and there's a par-27, nine-hole executive golf course on the adjacent slope (free for guests). Lots of in-house entertainment is laid on, including a *meke* once a week. A live band plays in the Vale ni Marau Lounge Thursday, Friday, and Saturday 2100-0100.

Across the street from the Fiji Mocambo is the two-story **Tanoa International Hotel** (Box 9203, Nadi Airport; tel. 720-277, fax 720-191), formerly the Nadi Travelodge Hotel and now owned by local businessman Yanktesh Permal Reddy. The 133 superior a/c rooms with fridge are F$180 single or double, F$220 suite, and children under 16 may stay free. They have a half-price day-use rate, which gives you a room from noon until midnight if you're leaving in the middle of the night (airport transfers are free). The hotel coffee shop is open 24 hours a day, and a swimming pool, fitness center, and floodlit tennis courts are on the premises.

### Luxury

Nadi's two big transnational hotels, the Sheraton Royal and the Sheraton Fiji, are on Denarau Beach opposite Yakuilau Island, seven km west of the bridge on the north side of Nadi town and a 15-minute drive from the airport. These are Nadi's only upmarket hotels right on the beach, although the gray sands here can't match those of the Mamanuca Islands. The murky waters lapping Sheraton shores are okay for swimming, and two pontoons are anchored in deeper water, but there'd be no point in snorkeling here. Windsurfing, water-skiing, and sailboating are more practicable activities.

Sidestepping the Waikiki syndrome, neither hotel is taller than the surrounding palms, though the manicured affluence has a dull Hawaiian neighbor-island feel. In 1993 a F$15-million championship golf course opened on the site of a former mangrove swamp adjacent to the resort. In 1996 ITT-Sheraton bought both resorts from the Japanese interests that had controlled them since 1988. Two-thirds of the hotel staff and all of the taxi drivers based here belong to the landowning clan.

Almost all the tourists staying at these places are on package tours and they pay only a fraction of the rack rates quoted below. If you call direct upon arrival in Fiji (instead of booking through a travel agent abroad) you may be offered a 50% discount on the published rates. Ask if there are any "specials" going. Both hotels are rather isolated, and restaurant-hopping possibilities are restricted to the pricey hotel restaurants, so you should take the meal package if you intend to spend most of your time here. Also bring insect repellent unless you yourself want to be on the menu!

The pretentious **Sheraton Royal Denarau Resort** (Box 9081, Nadi Airport; tel. 750-000, fax 750-259) opened in 1975 as The Regent of Fiji. This sprawling series of two-story clusters with traditional touches between the golf course and the beach contains 285 spacious a/c rooms beginning at F$345 single or double plus tax. Facilities include an impressive lobby with shops to one side, a thatched pool bar you can swim right up to, and 10 floodlit tennis courts.

The Sheraton Royal's neighbor, the modern-style **Sheraton Fiji Resort** (Box 9761, Nadi Airport; tel. 750-777, fax 750-818), has 300 a/c rooms that begin at F$448 single or double plus tax but including a buffet breakfast. This $60-million two-story hotel complex opened in 1987, complete with a 16-shop arcade and an 800-seat ballroom.

There's no bus service to either Sheraton. A taxi to/from Nadi town should be around F$6, though the cabs parked in front of the hotels will expect much more—perhaps as much as F$20 to the airport. Avis Rent A Car has a desk in each of the hotels. If your travel agent booked you into either of these, you'll only be exposed to Fiji on the short walk from the plane to your a/c car before being wrapped in North American safety again (the Mamanuca resorts like Naitasi are better value).

A 302-room **Grand Hyatt Fiji Hotel** is to be built next to the Sheraton Royal as a joint venture between Hyatt and Air Pacific.

## FOOD

### Downtown Restaurants

Several excellent places to eat are opposite the Mobil service station on Queens Road at the north end of Nadi town. For Cantonese and European food try the upstairs dining room at **Poon's Restaurant** (tel. 700-896; Mon.-Sat. 1000-2200, Sunday 1200-1400 and 1800-2200), which is recommended for its filling meals at reasonable prices, pleasant atmosphere, and friendly service. **Mama's Pizza Inn** (tel. 700-221), just up the road from Poon's, serves pizzas big enough for two or three people for F$8-23. Mama's has a second location in Colonial Plaza halfway out toward the airport. A number of other pricey Asian restaurants are between Mama's and the bridge.

The package tour buses often park in front of **Chefs The Corner** (tel. 703-131), Sangayam and Queens Roads opposite Morris Hedstrom.

JOHN PENISTEN

*A Fiji Indian family enjoys watermelon.*

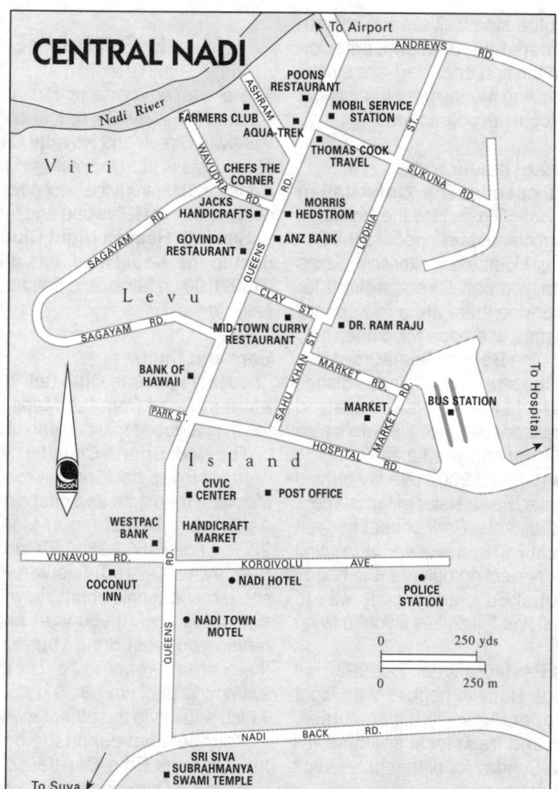

This rather expensive self-service restaurant does have some of the favorite ice cream in town (F$2-4). Just down Sangayam Road are **The Edge Cafe** and **Chefs Restaurant,** both very upmarket and also run by two former Sheraton chefs, Josef and Eugene. All are closed on Sunday.

Fewer tourists stray into **Govinda Vegetarian Restaurant and Coffee Lounge** (tel. 702-445; Mon.-Fri. 0800-1900, Saturday 0800-1700), on Queens Road almost opposite the ANZ Bank. It's the equivalent of the famous Hare Krishna Restaurant in Suva with only pure vegetarian food on offer. Govinda's set Indian meal of two rotis, rice, two vegetable curries, dhal, papadam, samosa, and chutney is F$4.50. They also have ice cream for half the price of Chefs just up the street.

Probably the number one low-budget eatery in Nadi is the basic **Mid-Town Curry Restaurant** (tel. 700-536; closed Sunday), around the corner from Govinda on Clay Street. They serve real Fiji Indian dishes instead of the usual tourist fare, which means *very spicy.* Come early as they close at 1800.

**Chopsticks Restaurant** (tel. 700-178), upstairs from the Bank of Baroda on the main street, offers Chinese dishes, curries, and seafood.

About the top place to try real Fijian dishes like *palusami* and *kokoda* is at the seafood buffet served daily 1200-1400 (F$7) at the **Coconut Tree Restaurant** (tel. 701-169) below the Coconut Inn Hotel, 37 Vunavau St., down the side street opposite the Nadi Handicraft Market.

Be aware that the sidewalk terrace restaurants near the Tourist Information Center on the main street in the center of Nadi are strictly designed for extracting money from tourists not familiar with the local price structure.

### Restaurants toward the Airport

Luigi and Carla operate **The Only Italian Restaurant** (tel. 724-590), next to the Shell service station in Martintar almost opposite the Dominion International Hotel. Their excellent pizzas average F$16, or you can take spaghetti for about F$12. Otherwise there are a few special meat and fish dishes. It's open for dinner only from about 1800. The **Bounty Restaurant** (tel. 720-840) across the street has Chinese dishes and hamburgers for lunch, steaks and seafood for dinner, all at reasonable prices. There's also a good bar here if you only want a drink.

**RJ's for Ribs** (tel. 722-900), directly behind Ed's Bar at Martintar, has a sister establishment in Beverly Hills, California. Pork or beef ribs run F$12, fillet mignon F$18, a skewer of prawns F$22. RJ's is the perfect complement to happy hour (1730-2000) at Ed's, and a tasty way to polish off those leftover Fiji dollars if you're flying out the next day.

The **Maharaja Restaurant** (tel. 722-962), out near the Skylodge Hotel is popular with flight crews who come for the spicy Indian curries, tandoori dishes, and fresh local seafood. It's open daily but on Sunday for dinner only—a bit expensive but very good.

## ENTERTAINMENT

There are two movie houses in Nadi: **Jupiter Cinema** (tel. 703-950), next to the Coconut Inn on Vunavau Street, and **Novelty Cinema** (tel. 700-155), upstairs from the mall next to the Nadi Civic Center, not far from the post office. Both show an eclectic mix of Hollywood and Indian films.

**Seventh Heaven Night Club** (tel. 703-188), next to the Nadi Hotel, has a live rock band 2100-0100 on Friday and Saturday nights. Locals call it "the zoo."

### Bars and Clubs

The **Nadi Farmers Club** (tel. 700-415), just up Ashram Road from the Mobil station in Nadi town, is a good local drinking place.

The **Nadi Sports Club** (tel. 700-239) is a km north of town, back on the road beside Jame Mosque, then right and past a garment factory. Aside from the bar (open Mon.-Thurs. 1600-2200, Friday 1600-2300, Saturday 1200-2300, Sunday 1200-2100) this very smart club has squash and tennis courts, lawn bowling, and a swimming pool. If you wish to play squash or tennis you must bring your own racquets as there are no rentals. To use the competition swimming pool is F$3.30 a day, the same fee which applies to the other facilities.

Your best bet out on the hotel strip toward the airport is **Ed's Bar** (tel. 720-373), a little north of the Dominion International Hotel. Happy

*handicraft seller, Nadi*

DOUG HANKIN

hour is 1730-2000 daily with live music Friday and Saturday nights. It's a safe local place not only for tourists with a friendly young staff.

The **Airport Club** (Mon.-Thurs. 1100-2300, Friday and Saturday 1100-0200), in the Airport Housing Area down the road past Namaka Police Station and almost underneath the airport control tower, is an old-fashioned colonial club with tables overlooking the runways. It's an interesting place to sit and drink draft beer as the planes soar above the swimming pool.

### Cultural Shows for Visitors

The **Sheraton Fiji** (tel. 750-777) has a free *meke* Tuesday and Saturday at 2100. Thursday at 1900 Fijian firewalking comes with the *meke* and a F$11 fee is charged. The *meke* and *magiti* (feast) at the **Sheraton Royal** (tel. 750-000) happen Monday and Friday at 2000 (F$45).

You can also enjoy a *lovo* feast and *meke* at the **Fiji Mocambo Hotel** (tel. 722-828) on Monday (F$25), at the **Tokatoka Resort Hotel** (tel. 720-222) on Friday (F$24), and at the **Dominion International Hotel** (tel. 722-255) on Saturday.

### Shopping

The **Nadi Handicraft Market,** opposite the Nadi Hotel just off Queens Road, is worth a look. Before going there, have a look around **Jack's Handicrafts** (tel. 700-744), opposite Morris Hedstrom on the main street, to get an idea what's available and how much things should cost. Just beware the friendly handshake in Nadi, for you may find yourself buying something you neither care for nor desire.

If you have an interest in world literature, you can buy classical works of Indian literature and books on yoga at very reasonable prices at the **Ramakrishna Mission** (Box 716, Nadi; tel. 702-786), across the street from the Farmers Club. It's open Mon.-Fri. 0900-1300 and 1500-1700, Saturday 0900-1300.

## SERVICES

### Money

The **Westpac Bank** opposite the Nadi Handicraft Market, the **ANZ Bank** near Morris Hedstrom, and the **Bank of Hawaii** between these two, change traveler's checks without commission. They're open Mon.-Thurs. 0930-1500, Friday 0930-1600. The Bank of Hawaii has a Visa ATM.

**Money Exchange** (tel. 703-366; Mon.-Fri. 0830-1700, Saturday 0830-1600), between the ANZ Bank and Morris Hedstrom, changes cash and traveler's checks without commission at a rate just slightly lower than the banks.

**Thomas Cook Travel** (tel. 703-110; Mon.-Fri. 0830-1700, Saturday 0830-1200), across from the Mobil station on Queens Road, is a good source of the banknotes of other Pacific countries—very convenient if you'll be flying to Australia, New Caledonia, New Zealand, Samoa, Solomon Islands, Tonga, or Vanuatu and don't want the hassle of having to change money at a strange airport upon arrival. They'll also change the banknotes of these countries into Fijian.

**Tapa International** (tel. 722-325), in the concourse at Nadi Airport, is the American Express representative. If you buy traveler's checks from them using a personal check and your American Express card, you'll have to actually pick up the checks at the ANZ Bank in Nadi town, so go early.

### Post

There are two large post offices, one next to the market in central Nadi, and another between the cargo warehouses directly across the park in front of the arrivals hall at Nadi Airport. Check both if you're expecting general delivery mail. Nadi Town Post Office near the market receives faxes sent to 702-166. At the Nadi Airport Post Office the public fax number is 720-467. Both post offices are open Mon.-Fri. 0800-1700, Saturday 0800-1100.

### Consulates

The **Canadian Honorary Consul** can be reached at tel./fax 721-936. For the **Italian Honorary Consul** call Mediterranean Villas (tel. 664-011).

### Toilets

Public toilets are at the corner of Nadi Market closest to the post office, at the bus station, and in the Nadi Civic Center.

## INFORMATION

The **Fiji Visitors Bureau** office (Box 9217, Nadi Airport; tel. 722-433, fax 720-141) is in the arrivals concourse at the airport. There is no tourist information office in downtown Nadi although a certain travel agency masquerades as such.

The **Nadi Town Council Library** (Box 241, Nadi; tel. 700-606; Mon.-Fri. 0900-1700, Saturday 0900-1300) is in the shopping mall at the Nadi Civic Center on Queens Road.

### Travel Agents

The deceptively named **Tourist Information Center** (Box 251, Nadi; tel. 700-243 or 721-295, fax 702-746; Mon.-Sat. 0730-1830, Sunday 0930-1500), with offices in central Nadi and opposite the Dominion International Hotel, is a commercial travel agency run by Victory Inland Safaris. Also known as "Fiji Island Adventures," they offer a variety of 4WD and trekking excursions into the Nausori Highlands, and book low-budget beach resorts on Mana, Tavewa, Waya, Leleuvia, and Kadavu islands.

**PVV Tours** (tel. 700-600) at the Nadi Town Motel is similar (their specialty is Nananu-i-Ra bookings and transfers).

**Tourist Travel and Tours Fiji** (tel. 700-199), in the courtyard between R.B. Patel Supermarket and Thomas Cook, makes the same sort of bookings as the Tourist Information Center. Many others are around town, including the **Swiss Tourist Center** (tel./fax 703-930) and **Bayrisches Tourist** (tel./fax 703-922), both near the bridge into Nadi.

Out at the airport there's **Rabua's Travel Agency** (Box 10385, Nadi Airport; tel./fax 724-364), Office No. 23, upstairs in the arcade at international arrivals. The manager Ulaiasi "Rambo" Rabua books Dive Trek on Wayasewa (his home island) and most other offshore resorts. He shares an office with Ecotouring Fiji Ltd. (Box 2212, Nadi; tel./fax 724-364), which takes bookings of this kind from abroad. **Margaret Travel Service** (Box 9831, Nadi Airport; tel. 721-988, fax 721-992), upstairs in the airport arcade, also does outer island bookings. We've received several complaints about a company called Fiji Holiday Connections, also at the airport.

**Rosie The Travel Service** (tel. 722-935), at Nadi Airport and opposite the Nadi Handicraft Market in town, is a conventional travel agency that books somewhat more upmarket tours, activities, and accommodations.

There's little or no government regulation of the Nadi travel agencies, and some are quite unreliable. To increase their business they often promise things the managers of the resorts may be unwilling or unable to supply. Cases of travelers who reserved and prepaid a double room ending up in the dormitory are not unknown. Other times you'll be assured that the boat of one resort will drop you off at another, only to have the boatkeeper refuse to do so. If you prepay the return boat trip, the resort people won't have much incentive to bring you back to Nadi or Lautoka exactly on schedule.

For this reason it's better to avoid prepaying too much at the travel agencies, so as to retain some bargaining leverage. This is especially true when planning an itinerary that involves staying at more than one resort. If you can manage to pay the boat fare one way only (instead of roundtrip) it'll be a lot easier to switch resorts, or just to walk out if the place you booked in Nadi isn't as nice as they said it would be. These agents take as much as 30% commission from the resorts and you can often get a better deal by booking direct (the Nadi agents are unable to give you discounts, no matter what they say). Most of the necessary phone numbers are provided in this book and a telephone card is all you need to get in touch. Remember too that these agents only promote properties that pay them commissions that are passed along to you in the end.

### Airline Offices

Reconfirm your flight, request a seat assignment, and check the departure time by calling your airline: Aircalin (tel. 722-145), Air Marshall Islands (tel. 722-192), Air Nauru (tel. 722-795), Air New Zealand (tel. 722-955), Air Pacific (tel. 720-888), Air Vanuatu (tel. 722-521), Qantas Airways (tel. 722-880), Royal Tongan Airlines (tel. 724-355), and Solomon Airlines (tel. 722-831). All these offices are at the airport.

## HEALTH

The outpatient department at **Nadi District Hospital** (tel. 701-128), inland from Nadi Bus Station, is open Mon.-Thurs. 0800-1630, Friday 0800-1600, Saturday 0800-1200.

You'll save time by visiting Dr. Ram Raju (tel. 701-375; Mon.-Fri. 0830-1630, Saturday and Sunday 0900-1230), Lodhia and Clay Streets, a family doctor specializing in travel health. Dr. Adbul Gani (tel. 703-776; Mon.-Fri. 0800-1700, Saturday 0800-1300) has his dental surgery nearby on Lodhia Street.

Dr. Uma D. Sharma (tel. 700-718; Mon.-Fri. 0800-1700, Saturday 0800-1300) operates a dental clinic in the mall at the Nadi Civic Center near the post office. Two medical doctors have a clinic with similar hours a few shops away in the same mall.

Dr. A. Narayan runs the Namaka Medical Center (tel. 722-288) on Queens Road, about two km from Nadi Airport on the way into town. After hours press the bell for service.

## TRANSPORTATION

See "Getting Around by Air" in the main introduction for information on regular Air Fiji and Sunflower Airlines flights to Malololailai and Mana islands and other parts of Fiji.

**Turtle Airways** (Private Mail Bag NAP 0355, Nadi Airport; tel. 722-988, fax 720-346), next to the golf course at Wailoaloa Beach, runs a seaplane shuttle to the offshore resorts at F$95 oneway, F$190 roundtrip (baggage limited to one 15-kg suitcase plus one carry-on). Scenic flights with Turtle are F$55 pp for 10 minutes, F$120 for 30 minutes (minimum of three persons).

**South Sea Cruises** (Box 718, Nadi; tel. 722-988, fax 720-346) operates a catamaran shuttle to the offshore island resorts on the 25-meter, 300-passenger *Island Express*. The boat leaves from Nadi's Port Denarau daily at 0900 and 1330 for Malololailai (F$33 each way), Malolo (F$36), Castaway (F$40), and Mana (F$40). With a connection to Matamanoa or Tokoriki, it's F$67. Interisland hops between the resorts themselves are F$30 each. Be prepared to wade on and off the boat at all islands except Mana. If all you want is a glimpse of the lovely Mamanuca Group, a four-island, four-hour, nonstop roundtrip cruise on is F$35. Catamaran bookings can be made at any travel agency around Nadi, and transfers from the main Nadi hotels to the wharf are free.

**Pacific Transport** (tel. 701-386) has express buses to Suva via Queens Road daily at 0720, 0750, 0900, 1300, 1640, and 1820 (four hours, F$8). The 0900 bus is the most convenient, as it begins its run at Nadi (the others all arrive from Lautoka). Five other "stage" buses also operate daily to Suva (five hours). The daily **Sunset Express** (tel. 720-266) leaves Nadi for Sigatoka and Suva at 1010 and 1555. Nadi's bus station adjoining the market is an active place.

Local buses to Lautoka, the airport, and everywhere in between pick up passengers at the bus stop on Queens Road opposite Morris Hedstrom.

You can bargain for fares with the collective taxis cruising the highway from the airport into Nadi. They'll usually take what you'd pay on a bus, but ask first. Collective taxis and minibuses parked in a corner of the bus station take passengers nonstop from Nadi to Suva in three hours for F$10 pp.

For information on car rentals, turn to "Getting Around" in this book's introduction.

### Local Tours

Many day cruises and bus tours that operate in the Nadi area are listed in the free tourist magazine *Fiji Magic*. Reservations can be made through hotel reception desks or at Rosie The Travel Service, with several offices around Nadi. Bus transfers to/from your hotel are included in the price, though some trips are arbitrarily canceled when not enough people sign up.

The "road tours" offered by **Rosie The Travel Service** (tel. 722-935), at Nadi Airport and opposite the Nadi Handicraft Market in town, are cheaper than those of other companies because lunch isn't included (lunch is included on all the cruises and river trips). Their day-trips to Suva (F$46) involve too much time on the bus, so instead go for the Sigatoka Valley/Tavuni Hill Fort (F$45 including entry fees) or Emperor Gold Mine (F$44) full-day tours. If you're looking for a morning tour around Nadi, sign up for the four-hour Vuda Lookout/Viseisei Village/Garden of the Sleeping Giant tour, which costs F$45 pp, including admission to the garden; other than Viseisei, these places are not accessible on public transport. These trips only operate Mon.-Sat., but on Sunday Rosie offers a half-day drive to the Vuda Lookout and Lautoka for F$33 pp. Also ask about the full-day hiking tours to the Nausori Highlands (daily except Sunday, F$58), the easiest way to see this beautiful area.

The **United Touring Company** (Box 9172, Nadi Airport; tel. 722-811, fax 720-107), or UTC, offers the same kind of day tours as Rosie at higher prices with lunch included.

**Peni's Waterfall Tours** (Box 1842, Nadi; tel. 703-801), in the Westpoint Arcade off Queens Road in central Nadi, promises three nights of "genuine Fijian lifestyle" at Bukuya, a mountain village in the Nausori Highlands, for F$160 pp including meals, activities, and *bure* accommodations. The **Tourist Information Center** (tel. 700-243) offers "Sleeping Giant Safari Treks" with stays at different villages at F$169/190/210 for two/three/four night, plus tax. Hiking trips offered by Adventure Fiji, a division of Rosie The Travel Service, are more expensive than these but the quality is more consistent (see "Hiking Tours" in the main introduction).

Should you not wish to join an organized bus tour from Nadi, you can easily organize your own day tour by taking a local bus (not an express) to the Sigatoka Sand Dunes National Park visitor center on Queens Road. After a hike over the dunes, catch another bus on to Sigatoka town for lunch at the Sigatoka Club, some shopping and sightseeing, and perhaps a taxi visit to the Tavuni Hill Fort. Plenty of buses run back to Nadi from Sigatoka until late. All this will cost you far less than the cheapest half-day tour and you'll be able to mix freely with the locals.

### Day Cruises

Food and accommodations at the Mamanuca island resorts are expensive and a much cheaper way to enjoy the islands—for a day at least—is by booking a full-day cruise to Plantation (F$66), Castaway (F$70), or Mana (F$79) on the catamaran *Island Express,* operated by **South Sea Cruises** (tel. 722-988). The price includes transfers from most Nadi hotels, the boat trip, a buffet lunch on the island of your choice, nonmotorized sporting activities, and a day at the beach. Bookings can be made through Rosie The Travel Service or any other Nadi travel agent.

South Sea Cruises also has day-trips to Plantation Island Resort on the two-masted schooner *Seaspray* (F$66 including lunch). A "combo cruise" to Plantation has you go out on the *Island Express* and return on the *Seaspray* or *Stardust II* (F$63 with lunch). By taking this option you'll see more resorts and experience another boat, but have less time on Plantation. By flying to Malololailai from Nadi Airport you get the most time at Plantation for the lowest price (F$50 day return), but lunch won't be included.

**Captain Cook Cruises** (tel. 701-823) runs day cruises to Tivua Island aboard the MV *Lady Geraldine* for F$73 including a picnic lunch. Starlight dinner cruises on a tall ship are F$75 (dinner served at a restaurant ashore).

The **Oceanic Schooner Co.** (Box 9625, Nadi Airport; tel. 722-455, fax 720-134) does more upscale cruises on the 30-meter schooner *Whale's Tale,* built at Suva's Whippy Shipyard in 1985. You get a champagne breakfast and gourmet lunch served aboard ship, an open bar, and sunset cocktails in the company of a limited number of fellow passengers for F$160 pp.

Guests staying at one of the Sheratons can take the **Bounty Island Day Cruise** (tel./fax 650-200) to tiny Bounty Island on the MV *TJ Blue* (F$39/66 for a half/full day). Other companies offer day cruises to imaginatively named specks of sand such as Aqualand (tel. 722-988), Daydream Island (tel. 724-597), Fantasy Island (tel. 723-314), and Malamala Island (tel. 702-443), costing anywhere from F$55 to F$69, always including lunch and Nadi hotel pickups, and sometimes drinks and nonmotorized sporting activities as well. These are fine if all you want is a day at the beach, otherwise you'll find them a colossal bore. Any hotel tour desk can book them.

Younger travelers will enjoy a day cruise to **Beachcomber Island** (tel. 661-500), Fiji's unofficial Club Med for the under 35 set. Operating daily, the F$60 pp fare includes bus transfers from Nadi hotels, a return boat ride via Lautoka, and a buffet lunch. Large families should consider Beachcomber because after two full adult fares are paid, the first child under 16 is half price and additional children are quarter price; kids under two are free.

Thirty-minute jet boat rides around the mouth of the Nadi River are offered by **Shotover Jet** (Box 1932, Nadi; tel. 750-400, fax 750-666) about every half hour from Port Denarau (adults F$59, children under 16 years F$29). It's fairly certain the birds and fish of this mangrove area are less thrilled by these gas-guzzling, high-impact craft than the tourists seated therein.

## SOUTH OF NADI

### Sonaisali Island Resort

Opened in 1992, this luxury resort (Box 2544, Nadi; tel. 720-781, fax 706-092), down Nacobi

Road from Queens Road, is on Naisali, a long, low island in Momi Bay, just 300 meters off the coast of Viti Levu. The 32 a/c rooms with fridge in several main two-story buildings are F$231 single or double, and there are 21 thatched two-bedroom *bures* at F$330 (no cooking facilities). The full meal plan is F$59 pp and guests are expected to dress up for dinner in the restaurant. The resort features a full-service marina, a swimming pool with swim-up bar, tennis courts, a children's program, and free nonmotorized water sports, but the snorkeling off their beach is poor. The resort's scuba diving operation takes guests out to unique locations such as Kingfisher Reef at F$95/125 one/two tanks including equipment. PADI open-water certification is F$575 for one or F$475 pp for two. Rosie The Travel Service has a desk at Sonaisali. A taxi from the airport might cost F$20 and a shuttle boat provides free access to the island 24 hours a day.

### Momi Bay

On a hilltop overlooking Momi Bay, 28 km from Nadi, are two **British six-inch guns,** one named Queen Victoria (1900), the other Edward VIII (1901). Both were recycled from the Boer War and set up here by the New Zealand army's 30th Battalion in 1941 to defend the southern approach to Nadi Bay. The only shots fired in anger during the war were across the bow of a Royal New Zealand Navy ship that forgot to make the correct signals as it entered the passage. It quickly turned around, made the correct signals, and reentered quietly. To get reach the battery, take a bus along the old highway to Momi, then walk three km west. The Nabilla village bus runs directly there from Nadi four times a day. This historic site is managed by the National Trust for Fiji and open daily 0800-1700 (admission F$2).

### Seashell Cove

**Seashell Cove Surf and Dive Resort** (Box 9530, Nadi Airport; tel. 706-100, fax 706-094), on Momi Bay, 37 km southwest of Nadi, is a laid-back surfing/diving backpacker camp with hotel facilities. They have 11 duplex *bures* with fans, fridge, and cooking facilities at F$90 single or double, and 16 clean rooms with lumpy beds and shared bath in the lodge at F$45 single or double. Larger units are available for families at F$110 for up to six, and baby-sitters are provided. The big 25-bed dormitory above the bar is divided into five-bed compartments for F$15 pp. Otherwise, pitch your own tent beside the volleyball court for F$8 per tent. Cooking facilities are not provided for campers, lodge, or dormitory guests, although a good-value meal plan is offered at F$30 pp and there's a small grocery store just outside the camp. A *meke* and Fijian feast (F$16) occurs on Friday. Seashell's coffee shop is open until midnight, with a pool table and table tennis. Some surfers stay up all night drinking kava with the friendly staff, a great opportunity to get to know them. Baggage storage is available free of charge.

The beach here isn't exciting and at low tide it's a 10-minute trudge across the mudflats to the water. Amenities and activities include a swimming pool, day-trips to Natadola Beach (F$28 including lunch), tennis (free), and volleyball (free). There's a horse that's used to carry kids under 10 around the resort, but skip the kayaks as they leak and become unstable after 20 minutes in the water.

At F$25 pp, Seashell has two boats to shuttle surfers out to the reliable left at Namotu Island breakers or long hollow right at Wilkes Passage; the famous Cloudbreak lefthander at Navula Reef (F$35 pp) is between Wilkes and Seashell. (Recently only Seashell Cove and Tavarua Island were permitted to surf Cloudbreak through an exclusive arrangement with the traditional Fijian owners of the surf. Even then, expect crowds of 25 guys in the water—all other spots are uncrowded.) There's also an offshore right at the Momi Bay Lighthouse. This type of reef break surfing can be dangerous for the inexperienced.

In 1995 the well-organized scuba diving operation, **Scuba Bula,** run by Steve and Nicky Henderson, was upgraded with new equipment and a new boat but the cost is still reasonable at F$60/100 for one/two tanks plus F$10 for gear and F$440 for a PADI certification course. Seashell divers experience lots of fish/shark action at Navula Lighthouse, and there's great drift diving at Canyons (the guides really know their spots). When there's space, snorkelers are welcome to go along at F$15 pp.

Airport transfers are F$10 pp each way. Dominion Transport (tel. 701-505) has buses direct to Seashell from Nadi bus station at 0745, 1215, 1430, and 1600, and there are good onward connections from the resort by public bus to Sigatoka weekdays. A taxi from Nadi town might cost F$20.

# THE MAMANUCA GROUP

The Mamanuca Group is a paradise of eye-popping reefs and sand-fringed isles shared by traditional Fijian villages and jet-age resorts. The white coral beaches and super snorkeling grounds attract visitors aplenty; boats and planes arrive constantly, bringing folks in from nearby Nadi or Lautoka. These islands are in the lee of big Viti Levu, which means you'll get about as much sun here as anywhere in Fiji. Some of the South Pacific's finest skin diving, surfing, game fishing, and yachting await you, and many nautical activities are included in the basic rates. The Mamanucas are fine for a little time in the sun, though much of it is a tourist scene irrelevant to the rest of Fiji.

Almost all of the regular tourist resorts described below are in the luxury price category, with Plantation Island Resort offering the least expensive regular rooms and Beachcomber Island providing dormitories with meals included in the rates. Among the top resorts, self-catering facilities are only provided at Musket Cove and Naitasi. Low-budget backpacker accommodations are on Mana and Malolo, the only islands permanently inhabited by Fijian villagers. If the beach and beyond are your main focus of interest you won't mind staying on a tiny coral speck like Tavarua, Namotu, Navini, Matamanoa, Beachcomber, and Treasure, but if hiking and land-based exploring are on your agenda pick a bigger island such as Malololailai, Malolo, Castaway, Mana, or Tokoriki.

### Dive Sites

Some of the most exhilarating diving is on the Malolo Barrier Reef and the passages around tiny **Namotu** or "Magic Island" where nutrients for the marinelife and corals are swept in by strong currents. Both pelagic and reef fish abound in the canyons, caves, and coral heads around Namotu, but in some places the action has been distorted by scuba operators who regularly feed the fish. The outer slopes of Namotu, where the reef plunges 1,000 meters into the Pacific abyss, feature turtles, reef sharks, and vast schools of barracuda, with visibility up to 50 meters. Dolphins also frequent this area.

Bigger fish, manta rays, and ocean-going sharks are often seen at **The Big W** on the outer edge of the Malolo Barrier Reef. Susie, the friendly bronze whale shark, happens by from time to time. Vertical walls drop 70 meters at this spectacular site.

In another passage in the outer barrier reef are the pinnacles of **Gotham City,** so called for the batfish seen here, along with brilliantly colored soft corals and vast schools of tropical fish.

One of the world's most famous reef shark encounter venues is **Supermarket,** a 30-meter wall just west of Mana Island. Grays, white tips, and black tips are always present, and you might even see a tiger shark. Divemasters hand feed sharks over two meters long on this exciting dive.

Shallow Kaka Reef north of Mana Island is known as **The Circus** for the myriad clown fish and colorful corals. Eagle rays sometimes frequent the **South Mana Reef** straight out from the island's wharf. Other well-known Mamanuca dive sites include Japanese Gardens, Lobster Caves, the Pinnacles (near Malolo), Sunflower Reef, The Barrel Head, The Fingers, Jockie's Point, a B-26 bomber dating from WW II, and the wreck of the *Salamanda,* a decommissioned Blue Lagoon cruise ship.

### Malololailai Island

Malololailai, or "Little Malolo," 22 km west of Nadi, is the first of the Mamanuca Group. It's a 216-hectare island eight km around (a nice walk). In 1880 an American sailor named Louis Armstrong bought Malololailai from the Fijians for one musket; in 1964 Dick Smith purchased it for many muskets. You can still be alone at the beaches on the far side of the island, but with two growing resorts, a marina, and projects for a golf course and lots more time-share condominiums in the pipeline it's becoming overdeveloped. An airstrip across the island's waist separates its two resorts; inland are rounded, grassy hills.

**Plantation Island Resort** (Box 9176, Nadi Airport; tel. 669-333, fax 669-200), on the southwest side of Malololailai, is one of the largest of the resorts off Nadi. The 110 rooms (beginning at

F$190 single or double plus tax but including breakfast) are divided between 40 a/c hotel rooms in a two-story building and 70 individual *bures.* Add F$37 pp for lunch and dinner, as no cooking facilities are provided. Snorkeling gear, rowboats, and windsurfing are free, but boat trips cost extra. Coral viewing on Plantation's 30-passenger, glass-bottom "yellow submarine" is F$12 (free for guests). Plantation is a popular day-trip destination from Nadi.

Also on Malololailai Island is **Musket Cove Resort** (Dick and Carol Smith, Private Mail Bag NAP 0352, Nadi Airport; tel. 662-215, fax 662-633), which opened in 1977. The eight seaview *bures* and four garden *bures,* all with kitchenettes, are F$260 single or double. Cooking facilities are also provided in the six villas at F$395 single or double, plus F$15 per extra adult to a maximum of six. However, the 12 two-story beachfront *bures* and six lagoon *bures* at F$320 single or double only have a breakfast bar. A well-stocked grocery store selling fresh fruit and vegetables is on the premises. **Dick's Place Restaurant and Bar** by the pool has a F$55 pp three meal plan available. Entertainment is provided at the Thursday night pig roast. All drinks are F$2 at the bar on Ratu Nemani Island, a tiny coral islet connected to the marina by a floating bridge. Yachties are the main customers.

Activities at Musket Cove such as snorkeling, windsurfing, water-skiing, line fishing, and village boat trips are free for guests. Paid activities include the Hobie cats (F$25 an hour), kayaks (F$25 a half day), and mountain bikes (F$5 an hour). The launch *Anthony Star* is available for deep-sea game-fishing charters at F$50 pp for four hours with a four-person minimum (the catch belongs to the boat). The 10-meter cruiser *Dolphin Star* can be chartered for longer fishing trips at F$100 an hour. The 17-meter ketch *Dul-*

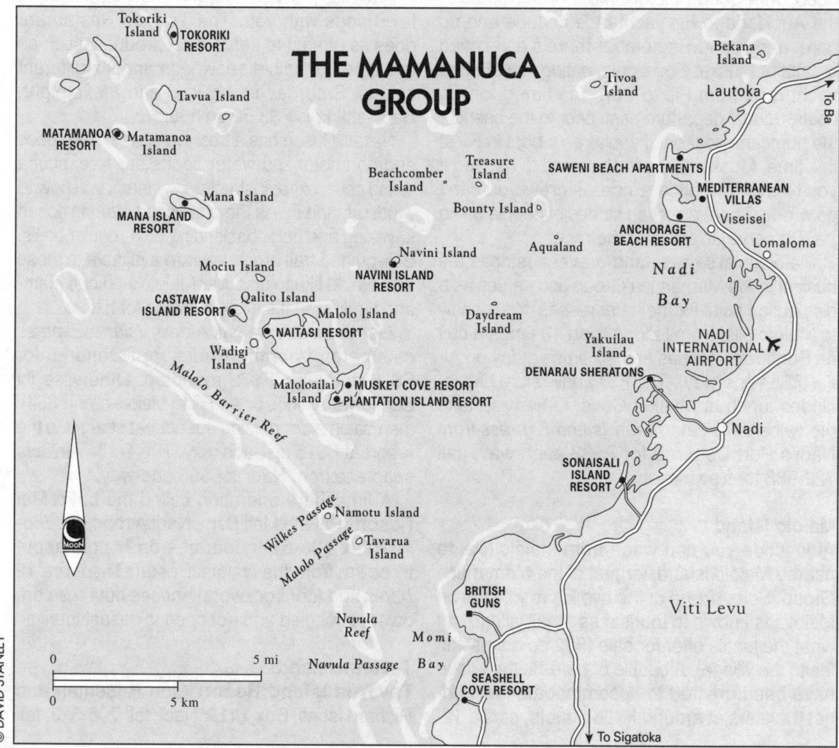

*cinea* does cruises for snorkeling (F$35 pp without lunch), dolphin watching (F$32 pp), and sunset viewing (F$22 pp). "Discover Sailing" lessons are F$100 pp.

Scuba diving with **Mamanuca Diving** (tel. 650-926, fax 662-633) at the marina costs F$75/105 one/two tanks including equipment, shark encounters cost F$85, or pay F$400 for the four-day PADI certification course (minimum of two persons). They operate daily trips to Sunflower Reef and The Three Sisters. **Musket Cove Yacht Charters** (tel./fax 666-710) has a small fleet of charter yachts stationed at Musket Cove. The compulsory Fijian guide is included in all charter rates.

Malololailai is a favorite stopover for cruising yachts with water and clean showers at the marina (mooring is F$5/30/100 a day/week/month). Fuel and groceries are also available. The marked anchorage is protected and 15 meters deep, with good holding. Most of the boats in the Auckland to Fiji yacht race in June end up here, and in mid-September there's a yachting regatta at Musket Cove, culminating in a 965-km yacht race from Fiji to Port Vila timed for the boats' annual departure east, prior to the onset of the hurricane season. If you're on a boat in Fiji at this time, Musket Cove is *the* place to be, and if you're trying to hitch a ride as crew you can't go wrong. There are even stories of people being *paid* to serve as crew for the race!

Malololailai's grass-and-gravel airstrip is the busiest in the Mamanuca Group and serves as a distribution point for the other resorts. You can fly to Malololailai from Nadi Airport 10 times a day on Sunflower Airlines and six times a day on Air Fiji (F$54 one-way). The F$75 day return fare includes lunch at Musket Cove. Otherwise take the twice-daily catamaran *Island Express* from Nadi's Port Denarau for F$33 each way; call 722-988 for free pickup.

### Malolo Island

At low tide you can wade from Malololailai to nearby Malolo Island, largest of the Mamanuca Group. Solevu, one of the two Fijian villages on Malolo, is known to tourists as "shell village" for what the locals offer for sale (F$2 pp admission fee to the village). A couple of *bures* in the village have been erected to accommodate low-budget travelers at around F$66 double, plus a 12-bed dorm at F$25 pp and camping at F$18 pp, all including meals. Transfers from Nadi are F$30/41 each way in a small/large boat. Bookings can be made through the Tourist Information Center in central Nadi. A stay here can be combined with a sojourn at the backpacker places on Mana Island, but only prepay your boat fare one way in this case (they'll want you to pay for the roundtrip). A boat between Malolo and Mana costs F$15 pp each way.

The **Naitasi Resort** (Box 10044, Nadi Airport; tel. 669-178, fax 669-197), at Malolo's western tip, offers 28 one-bedroom bungalows with fan at F$295 for up to three adults, and 10 two-bedroom family villas at F$425 for up to six. Naitasi Resort's Nadi airport office offers special reduced rates when things are slow. The family units are privately owned by 10 individuals, and each is decorated differently. The Island Store sells basic groceries that allow you to make use of the cooking facilities provided, but you should also bring a few things with you. The Terrace Restaurant does its utmost to serve local produce, such as five types of edible seaweeds and six different salads. Saturday is the *lovo* and *meke* night. Baby-sitting is F$3.50 an hour.

Naitasi Resort has a freshwater swimming pool, and nonmotorized water sports are free; scuba diving costs extra. Instructors will teach you how to windsurf, and this is the only resort offering ocean kayaking and horseback riding on a regular basis. Self-guided trail brochures are available to those who would like to discover Malolo's unique plant- and birdlife, so it's a good choice for hikers.

Get there on the twice-daily *Island Express* catamaran from the Nadi's Port Denarau for F$36 one-way, F$72 roundtrip. Otherwise fly Sunflower Airlines or Air Fiji to Malololailai (F$54), then catch a connecting speedboat straight to the resort at F$15 pp each way. The Turtle Airways seaplane from Nadi is F$95 one-way.

A timeshare operation called the **Lako Mai Resort** (Private Mail Bag , Nadi Airport; tel. 706-101, fax 706-017) operates on Malolo about three km from the Naitasi Resort. There are 12 *bures* and four Lockwood houses but these are owner-occupied and not open to casual tourists.

### Tavarua Island

**Tavarua Island Resort** (Jon Roseman and Richard Isbell, Box 1419, Nadi; tel. 706-513, fax

706-395), just south of Malololailai, operates as a surfing base camp. The guests are accommodated in 12 beach *bures,* and Tavarua caters to older, more affluent surfers than places like Seashell Surf and Dive on Viti Levu. A one/two week package from Los Angeles could cost US$2,151/3,240 including airfare, plus US$20 for transfers. Though the price may suggest it, one should not expect luxurious facilities here. Rather, it's the exclusivity you pay for, as Tavarua has negotiated sole access to some of Fiji's finest waves. There are both lefts and rights in Malolo Passage at Tavarua, although the emphasis is usually on the lefts. When the swell is high enough you'll have some of the best surfing anywhere. On the off days you can get in some deep-sea fishing, windsurfing, snorkeling, or scuba diving (extra charge). Surfing guests are expected to have had at least three years experience in a variety of conditions. Bookings must be made in advance through Tavarua Island Tours (Box 60159, Santa Barbara, CA 93160, U.S.A.; tel. 1-805/686-4551, fax 1-805/683-6696)—local bookings from within Fiji are not accepted. They're usually sold out, especially in June, July, and August (US$250 deposit to get on the waiting list).

### Namotu Island

Just across Malolo Passage from Tavarua Island on tiny Namotu Island is **Namotu Island Resort** (Box 531, Nadi; tel. 706-439, fax 706-039), a "Blue Water Sports Camp" for surfers. They have four beach *bures* at F$500 pp, plus two deluxe *bures* at F$1,250 double, 10% tax additional. The dormitory has closed and children under 12 are not accepted but meals are included. The minimum stay is three nights and boat transfers are free if you stay over a week. Otherwise it's F$80 pp return (the boat leaves Namotu at 1000 sharp). You must bring your own surfboards and sailboards as none are available here (currents in the channel often carry lost boards far out to sea). Fishing is free for the first hour, F$30 pp per additional hour. Scuba diving is F$75 and up (all motorized activities cost extra). As at Tavarua, Namotu's market is mostly upmarket American surfers and sailors who fly down from Hawaii to ride Fiji's spectacular waves. The famous Namotu Left peels off directly in front of their bar, and from your stool you can look across the channel to the more challenging Wilkes Right. Swimming Pools is off the southeastern corner of Namotu.

### Wadigi Island

In 1998 **Wadigi Island Lodge** (Ross and Jeni Allen, Box 9274, Nadi Airport; tel./fax 720-901) opened on tiny Wadigi Island off the west end of Malolo. Each group gets the entire three-suite resort, costing F$1,420 for a couple or F$613 pp for up to six persons (children under 12 not accepted). Included in the tariff are all meals, drinks, transfers from Malolo, and sporting equipment such as kayaks, windsurfers, spy boards, fishing rods, and snorkeling gear. Only deep sea fishing and scuba diving cost extra.

### Castaway Island

**Castaway Island Resort** (Private Mail Bag 0358, Nadi Airport; tel. 661-233, fax 665-753), on 174-hectare Qalito Island just west of Malolo and 15 km from Nadi, was built by Dick Smith in 1966 as Fiji's first outer-island resort. The 66 tastefully decorated thatched *bures* sleep four—F$410 and up including a buffet breakfast. No cooking facilities are provided but the all-meal plan is F$50 pp. The *lovo* and *meke* are on Monday night, the beach barbecue on Saturday. Among the free water sports are sailing, windsurfing, paddle boats, tennis, and snorkeling, but game fishing and scuba diving are extra. One/two tank dives with shark feeding are F$70/110, plus F$20 for gear. Their PADI certification course is F$600 for one or F$450 pp for two or more, and several other courses are also available. A swimming pool is available. Many Australian holidaymakers return to Castaway year after year; families with small children are welcome. A free "kids club" operates from 0900-1600 and 1900-2100 daily with lots of fun activities for those aged three and over, while mom and dad have some time to themselves. There's the daily catamaran *Island Express* from Nadi's Port Denarau (F$40 one-way, F$70 roundtrip), and Turtle Airways has three seaplane flights a day from Nadi for F$95. Castaway has a booking office opposite the Capricorn International Hotel in Nadi.

### Navini Island

**Navini Island Resort** (Box 9445, Nadi Airport; tel. 662-188, fax 665-566) is the smallest of Mamanuca resorts, a tiny coral isle with only nine thatched *bures.* Rates vary from F$320 double for a fan-cooled beachfront unit to F$460 for the honeymoon *bure* with spa and enclosed courtyard. Discounts are available for stays over a week. The two/three meal package is F$57/65 pp a day (no cooking facilities). Everyone gets to know one another by eating at a long table (private dining is also possible). Complimentary morning boat trips are offered, as are snorkeling gear, windsurfers, and kayaks. Car/boat transfers from Nadi via the Vuda Point Marina are arranged anytime upon request (F$120 return). Only overnight guests are accepted.

**Mana Island**

Mana Island, 32 km northwest of Nadi, is well known for its scuba diving facilities and jumbo luxury resort, but in recent years a whole slew of backpackers hostels have sprouted in the Fijian village on the eastern side of the island. There's much bad blood between the Japanese investors who run the resort and the Fijian villagers who accommodate the backpackers, and a high fence has been erected down the middle of the island to separate the two ends of the market. Uniformed security guards patrol the perimeter and shoestring travelers are most unwelcome anywhere in the resort, including the restaurants, bars, and watersports huts. Even the scuba diving facilities are segregated.

Although this situation does poison the atmosphere on Mana Island slightly, there are lots of lovely beaches all around the island, most of them empty because the packaged tourists seldom stray far from their resort. The long white beach on the northeast side of the island is deserted. At the resort, the snorkeling is better off South Beach at low tide, off North Beach at high tide, but the nicest beach is Sunset Beach at the western end of the island. There's a great view of the Mamanucas and southern Yasawas from the highest point on Mana, a 15-minute hike from the backpacker camps, and splendid snorkeling on the reef. The Mana Main Reef is famous for its drop-offs with visibility never less than 25 meters, and you'll see turtles, fish of all descriptions, and the occasional crayfish.

The presence of the resort supports the frequent air and sea connections from Nadi, and the budget places allow you to enjoy Mana's stunning beauty at a fraction of the price tourists at the Japanese resort are paying. But to be frank, some of the backpacker camps on Mana are rather squalid and the places on Tavewa Island in the Yasawas offer better accommodations for only a bit more money.

Right up against the security fence near an enclosed sentry box is **Mereani's Backpackers Inn** (Box 10486, Nadi Airport; tel. 663-099, fax 702-840), a large house with dormitories of four, six, and eight bunks at F$30 pp, and four double rooms at F$35 pp. When the main hostel fills up they open a 12-bed overflow dormitory next to the staff quarters, but this arrangement should be avoided. All rates include three generous

*Dream Beach, Mana Island*

meals served to your table (breakfast is a buffet). It's possible to knock about F$11 pp off the price by cooking your own food in their kitchen, but only very basic tinned foods are available on Mana so it's better to take the meal plan unless saving a few dollars is crucial. You can get drinks at their bar all day. Activities include deep-sea fishing trips (F$20 an hour) and a four-island boat excursions (F$20). Those staying two weeks get an extra night free and several complimentary trips. To book call 703-466 in Nadi, at which time launch transfers on the *Shining Princess,* also known as the *Adi Neinoka,* will be organized.

**Ratu Kini Boko's Village Hostel** or "Mana Backpackers" (Box 5818, Lautoka; tel. 669-143) has their dining area alongside the resort fence right next to Mereani's Inn but the large accommodations building is 100 meters back in the village. The concrete main house has one big 20-bunk dorm, another four-bunk dorm in the corridor, and two thatched dormitory *bures* with seven and 14 bunks in the backyard, all at F$30 pp including buffet-style meals. The main house also contains two double rooms with shared bath at F$66 double and two better rooms with private bath and outside entrance at F$100 double, buffet meals included. One other large thatched *bure* in the backyard is F$77 double or F$100 for four. A full-day boat trip to other resort islands is F$25 pp, snorkeling on the reef F$15. For current information, call their Lautoka office (tel. 723-333) or the hostel. People on their way to Ratu Kini's often stay at Mana Rose Apartments near Travelers Beach Resort at Wailoaloa Beach in Nadi. Both Ratu Kini's and Mereani's have generators that only work at lunchtime and from 1700 until after midnight, at which time the fans go off. Expect water shortages, overcrowding, rather messy conditions, and a total lack of privacy in the mixed dorms of both hostels.

Ratu Kini Boko is a colorful character. He's the chief of 20 islands in the Mamanuca Group, but years ago he leased the western half of Mana Island to an Australian company, which sublet their property to the Japanese who now run Mana Island Resort. The resort's founder, Errol Fifer, still has a house at Sunset Beach, in case you bump into him. Mereani's is run by another branch of Ratu Kini's family and they compete fiercely.

In 1997 a new backpacker hostel called **Dream Beach** (tel. 931-022) opened on a splendid beach on the north side of Mana Island, across the hill from Ratu Kini's. Two seven-bunk and one eight-bunk houses cost F$30 pp including meals. One private room with bath is available at F$77 double. If you have your own tent you can pitch it right on their beach at F$27 pp including three meals. There's a 5% discount if you stay four nights. Dream Beach is operated by Pastor Aisake Kabu and it's certainly your best bet at the moment, nicely secluded from the village and resort. Because of this, it could be full and you should book ahead either by calling them directly or through Cecilia Travel Services (Box 10725, Nadi Airport; tel. 724-033), upstairs in the airport arcade at arrivals. If you're willing to camp (own tent), just show up.

Juxtaposed against the backpacker camps is **Mana Island Resort** (Box 610, Lautoka; tel. 661-455, fax 661-562), by far the biggest of the tourist resorts off Nadi. This opulent establishment boasts 128 tin-roofed bungalows clustered between the island's grassy rounded hilltops, white sandy beaches, and crystal-clear waters, and 32 hotel rooms in a pair of two-story blocks facing North Beach. The 90 standard bungalows are F$235 single or double, F$275 triple, while the 32 deluxe beachfront bungalows are F$380 single or double, F$425 triple. The six executive bungalows cost F$450 single or double, and the hotel rooms are F$350, breakfast included in all rates but add tax. Cooking facilities are not provided, so you'll have to patronize either the Mamanuca Restaurant, the North Beach Barbecue Buffet, or the South Beach A La Carte Restaurant (entrees F$20-31). Live entertainment is presented nightly, and three nights a week there's a Fijian or Polynesian floor show. The room rates include nonmotorized water sports, although water-skiing, para-flying, water scooters, game fishing, scuba diving, and the 45-minute semisubmersible rides (F$33 pp) are extra.

Resort guests may patronize **Aqua-Trek** (tel. 669-309) which offers boat dives at F$60 for one tank plus F$20 for equipment or F$330 for a six-dive package. Night dives are F$90. They run a variety of dive courses, beginning with a four-day PADI open-water certification course (F$520). Divemaster Apisi Bati specializes in underwater shark feeding.

Aqua Trek doesn't accept divers from the backpacker camps who must dive with **Indigenous Scuba Service** (Mr. Valu Tamanivalu, Box 1809, Nadi Airport; tel. 997-795, fax 702-336), which has a dive shop adjacent to Mereani's Inn. Their prices are a bit lower than those of Aqua-Trek at F$50 a dive plus F$20 for gear, F$270 for six dives, or F$450 for PADI open-water certification (four days). If you'd just like to try scuba, ask for a F$80 resort course. They'll take you out snorkeling for F$10 including mask and snorkel.

In 1995 an airstrip opened on Mana, and Sunflower Airlines now has eight flights a day from Nadi; Air Fiji has four flights (F$66 each way). The terminal is a seven-minute walk west of the resort (to get to the backpacker camps head for the wharf from which the security fence is visible). If you're already staying in Nadi it's just as easy to arrive on the twice-daily *Island Express* catamaran from Port Denarau (F$40 each way including Nadi hotel pickups). The *Island Express* ties up to the wharf at South Beach and Mana is the only Mamanuca island with a wharf, so you don't need to take off your shoes.

Any Nadi travel agency or hotel can book these transfers but only buy a one-way ticket so you'll have the freedom to return by another means (a roundtrip is no cheaper anyway). By taking the *Island Express* or plane to Mana you won't have to commit yourself to one backpacker hostel or another and can size up the situation when you get there. Ratu Kini's and Mereani's also have their own shuttle boats, which cost F$30 each way including bus transfers from Nadi hotels.

### Matamanoa Island

**Matamanoa Sunrise Resort** (Box 9729, Nadi Airport; tel. 660-511, fax 661-069), to the northwest of Mana Island, has 11 a/c hotel rooms at F$210 single or double, or F$360 for one of the 20 fan-cooled beachfront *bures* sleeping four, plus tax. Slightly reduced rates are available from October to April except during the two weeks before and after new years. Children under 12 are not accepted but the first two aged 12-16 sharing with their parents sleep free. Breakfast is included and it's F$56 extra for lunch and dinner (no cooking facilities). Complimentary afternoon tea is served in the bar, followed by happy hour 1730-1830. The tiny island's fine white beach and blue lagoon are complemented by a swimming pool and lighted tennis court. Boat transfers from Nadi are F$67 pp each way with a change of boats at Mana Island. No daytrippers get this far.

### Tokoriki Island

**Tokoriki Sunset Resort** (Box 10547, Nadi Airport; tel. 721-619, fax 721-620) is the farthest Mamanuca resort from Nadi. There are 19 spacious fan-cooled *bures* at F$374 for four adults and two children (no cooking facilities). The resort faces west on a kilometer-long beach and water sports such as reef fishing, windsurfing, and Hobie cats are free (water-skiing and sportfishing available at additional charge). Dive Tropex runs the scuba operation on the island, charging F$80/140 for one/two tanks including gear. At the center of the island is a 94-meter-high hill offering good views of the Yasawa and Mamanuca groups. As on Matamanoa, you must take the catamaran to Mana, then a launch to Tokoriki (F$67 pp each way). The regular launch to Matamanoa and Tokoriki leaves Mana daily at 1100. Turtle Airways charges F$116 pp to fly from Nadi to either Matamanoa or Tokoriki.

### Vomo Island

Standing alone midway between Lautoka and Wayasewa Island (see the Yasawa Islands map), 91-hectare Vomo is a high volcanic island with a white beach around its west side. Since 1993 the coral terrace and slopes behind this beach have been the site of the **Vomo Island Resort** (Box 9650, Lautoka; tel. 667-955, booking office tel. 666-111, fax 667-997). The 30 large a/c villas run F$627 pp double occupancy, including all meals, plus tax. Although more expensive than the two Sheratons at Nadi, the swimming and snorkeling are infinitely better. Helicopter transfers from Nadi Airport cost F$479 pp return, launch transfers from Nadi's Port Denarau are F$363 pp return, but you can also arrive on a Turtle Airways seaplane for F$116 pp each way.

### Beachcomber Island

Beachcomber Island (Dan Costello, Box 364, Lautoka; tel. 661-500, fax 664-496), 18 km west of Lautoka, is Club Med at a fraction of the price. Since the 1960s this famous resort has received many thousands of young travelers, and it's still a super place to meet the opposite sex. You'll like the informal atmosphere and late-night parties; there's a sand-floor bar, dancing, and floor shows four nights a week. The island is so small you can stroll around it in 10 minutes, but there's a white sandy beach and buildings nestled among coconut trees and tropical vegetation. This is one of the few places in Fiji where both sexes might be able to sunbathe topless. A beautiful coral reef extends far out on all sides and scuba diving is available with Subsurface Fiji (F$70/130 for one/two tanks, PADI certification F$495). A full range of other sporting activities is also available at an additional charge (parasailing F$48, windsurfing F$20 an hour, water-skiing F$28, jet skis F$40 for 15 minutes).

Accommodations include all meals served buffet style. Most people opt for the big, open mixed dormitory where the 42 double-decker bunks (84 beds) cost F$69 each a night, but you can also get one of 20 thatched beachfront *bures* with ceiling fan and private facilities for F$250/300/369 single/double/triple. Small families should ask for a *bure* as children 6- 15 are half price, under six free. The 14 lodge rooms with shared bath at F$165/220 single/double (fridge and fan provided) are a good compromise for the budget-conscious traveler. Former water problems have been solved by laying pipes from the mainland and installing solar water heating.

Of course, there's also the F$60 roundtrip boat ride from Lautoka to consider, but that includes lunch on arrival day. You can make a day-trip to Beachcomber for the same price if you only want a few hours in the sun. There's a free shuttle bus from all Lautoka/Nadi hotels to the wharf; the connecting three-master ferry *Tui Tai* leaves daily at 1000. Faster access is possible on the twin-hulled *Drodolagi* from Port Denarau at 0900. Beachcomber has been doing it right since the 1960s, and the biggest drawback is its very popularity, which makes it crowded and busy. Reserve well ahead at their Lautoka or Nadi Airport offices, or at any travel agency.

### Treasure Island Resort

Beachcomber's little neighbor, **Treasure Island** (Box 2210, Lautoka; tel. 661-599, fax 663-577), caters to couples and families less interested in an intense singles' social scene. It's extremely popular among New Zealand and Australian holidaymakers and occupancy levels seldom drop below 80%. The resort is half owned by the Tokatoka Nakelo land-owning clan, which also supplies most of the workers, although the management is European. At Treasure, instead of helping yourself at a buffet and eating at a long communal picnic table as you would at Beachcomber, you'll be fed regular meals in a restaurant (meal plan F$57 pp daily). Cooking facilities are not provided. The 67 units, each with three single beds (F$350 single or double), are contained in 34 functional duplex bungalows packed into the greenery behind the island's white sands. Some nautical activities such as windsurfing, sailing, canoes, and spy board, which cost extra on Beachcomber, are free on Treasure Island. Several Dive Tropex personnel are based on Treasure Island, offering diving at F$70/125 including gear for one/two-tank boat dives. Unlike Beachcomber, Treasure doesn't accept any day-trippers. Guests arrive on the shuttle boat *Stardust II,* which departs Nadi's Port Denarau daily at 0945 and 1400 (F$30 each way, half price under age 16). There's no wharf here, so be prepared to wade ashore.

SALVATORE CASA

# SOUTHERN VITI LEVU

The southwest side of Viti Levu along the Queens Road is known as the Coral Coast for the fringing reef along this shore. Sigatoka and Navua are the main towns in this area with most accommodations between them at Korotogo and Korolevu. This shoreline is heavily promoted as one of the top resort areas in Fiji, probably because of its convenient location along the busy highway between Nadi and Suva, but to be frank, the beaches here are second rate, with good swimming and snorkeling conditions only at high tide. Much of the coral has been destroyed by hurricanes. To compensate, most of the hotels have swimming pools and in some places you can go reef walking at low tide. Top sights include the Sigatoka sand dunes and the impressive gorge of the Navua River. The possibility of rainfall and lushness of the vegetation increases as you move east.

### Scuba Diving

**Sea Sports Ltd.** (Denis Beckmann, Box 688, Sigatoka; tel. 500-225, fax 520-239) offers scuba diving from its dive shops at The Fijian, Reef, and Tubakula resorts. Its free red-and-blue minibus picks up clients at all the other Coral Coast resorts just after 0700 (just after 0900 on Sunday) The charge is F$68 for one tank, F$99 for two tanks (both on the same morning), plus equipment. Night dives are possible. A 10-dive package is F$435. Sea Sports runs four-day PADI/NAUI open-water certification courses (F$485, medical examination required). Otherwise an introductory dive is F$104. Most dive sites are within 15 minutes of the resort jetties, so you don't waste much time commuting. Snorkelers can go along when things are slow at F$10 pp including a mask and snorkel.

### Getting Around

An easy way to get between the Coral Coast resorts and Nadi/Suva is on the a/c **Fiji Express** shuttle bus run by United Touring Company (tel. 722-811). The bus leaves the Travelodge, Berjaya Inn and other top hotels in Suva (F$27) at 0800 and calls at the Centra Resort Pacific Harbor (F$24), Warwick Hotel (F$19), Naviti Resort, Hideaway, Tabua Sands, Reef Resort (F$18), Fijian Hotel (F$15), most Nadi hotels, and the Sheratons (F$6), arriving at Nadi Airport at 1230 (quoted fares are to the airport). It leaves Nadi Airport at 1330 and returns along the same route, reaching Suva at 1800. Bookings can be made at the UTC office in the airport arrival concourse or at hotel tour desks.

Also ask about the a/c **Queen's Deluxe Coach,** which runs in the opposite direction, leaving The Fijian Hotel for Suva at 0910, the Warwick and Naviti at 1030, and Pacific Harbor at 1100. The return trip departs the Suva Travelodge around 1600.

Many less expensive non-a/c buses pass on the highway, but make sure you're waiting somewhere they'll stop. Pacific Transport's "stage" or "highway" buses between Lautoka/Nadi and Suva will stop at any of the Coral Coast resorts, but the express buses call only at Sigatoka, Pacific Harbor, and Navua. If you're on an eastbound express, get a ticket to Sigatoka and look for a local bus (or taxi) from there.

**Coral Coast Tours** (Box 367, Sigatoka; tel. 500-314 or 500-646, fax 520-688) offers four-hour morning and afternoon Sigatoka Valley tours to the Tavuni Hill Fort at F$33. Pickups are offered at all hotels between The Warwick and Shangri-La's Fijian Resort. Their 11-hour around-the-island tour is F$120 including breakfast and lunch. There's also a 4WD highlands tour to Bukuya at F$94 including lunch. These trips offer a good introduction to Fiji if you've only limited time at your disposal.

## NATADOLA AND THE FIJIAN

### Natadola Beach

The long, white sandy beach here is the best on Viti Levu and a popular picnic spot with day-trippers arriving on the sugar train from The Fijian Hotel on the Coral Coast. The small left point break at Natadola is good for beginning surfers but one must always be aware of the currents and undertow. Very few facilities are available here, although the local villagers offer horseback riding. In past travelers have camped freelance on Natadola Beach, but theft is a problem here. Don't leave valuables unattended. It may be possible to rent a *bure* in Sanasana village at the south end of the beach at F$25 pp including meals.

The luxury-category **Natadola Beach Resort** (Box 10123, Nadi Airport; tel./fax 721-000) offers one block of three rooms, another block of four rooms, and two individual units at F$250 single or double (minimum stay three nights). Children under 16 are not accepted. Each of the nine fan-cooled units has a fridge but no cooking facilities are provided so you must use their restaurant. Day-trippers cannot order drinks here without having lunch. The long swimming pool winds between the palms.

**Paradise Transport** (tel. 500-028 or 500-011) has six buses a day on weekdays from Sigatoka to Vusama village about three km from the beach (call for times). Otherwise get off any Nadi bus at the Maro School stop on Queens Road and hitch 10 km to the beach. It's also possible to hike to Natadola in three hours along the coastal railway line from opposite Shangri-La's Fijian Resort Hotel.

### The Fijian

**Shangri-La's Fijian Resort** (Private Mail Bag NAPO 353, Nadi Airport; tel. 520-155, fax 500-402) occupies all 40 hectares of Yanuca Island, not to be confused with another island of the same name west of Beqa. This Yanuca Island is connected to the main island by a causeway 10 km west of Sigatoka and 61 km southeast of Nadi Airport. President Mara's wife is the main landowner of the island although the resort is Malaysian owned. Opened in 1967, the 436-room complex of three-story Hawaiian-style buildings was Fiji's first large resort and is still Fiji's biggest hotel, catering to a predominantly Japanese clientele. The a/c rooms begin at F$295 single or double, or F$865 for a deluxe beach *bure,* plus tax. There's no charge for two children 15 or under sharing their parents' room so this resort is a good choice for families. The Fijian offers a nine-hole golf course (par 31), five tennis courts, four restaurants and five bars, two swimming pools, and a white sandy beach. Weekly events include a *meke* on Tuesday and firewalking on Friday night. Scuba diving is arranged by Sea Sports Limited. Avis Rent A Car has a desk in The Fijian. Luxury.

A local attraction is the Fijian Princess, a restored narrow-gauge railway originally built to haul sugarcane but that now runs 16-km day-trips to Natadola Beach daily at 1000. The train station is on the highway opposite the access road to The Fijian Hotel, and the ride costs F$59 pp including a barbecue lunch. For information

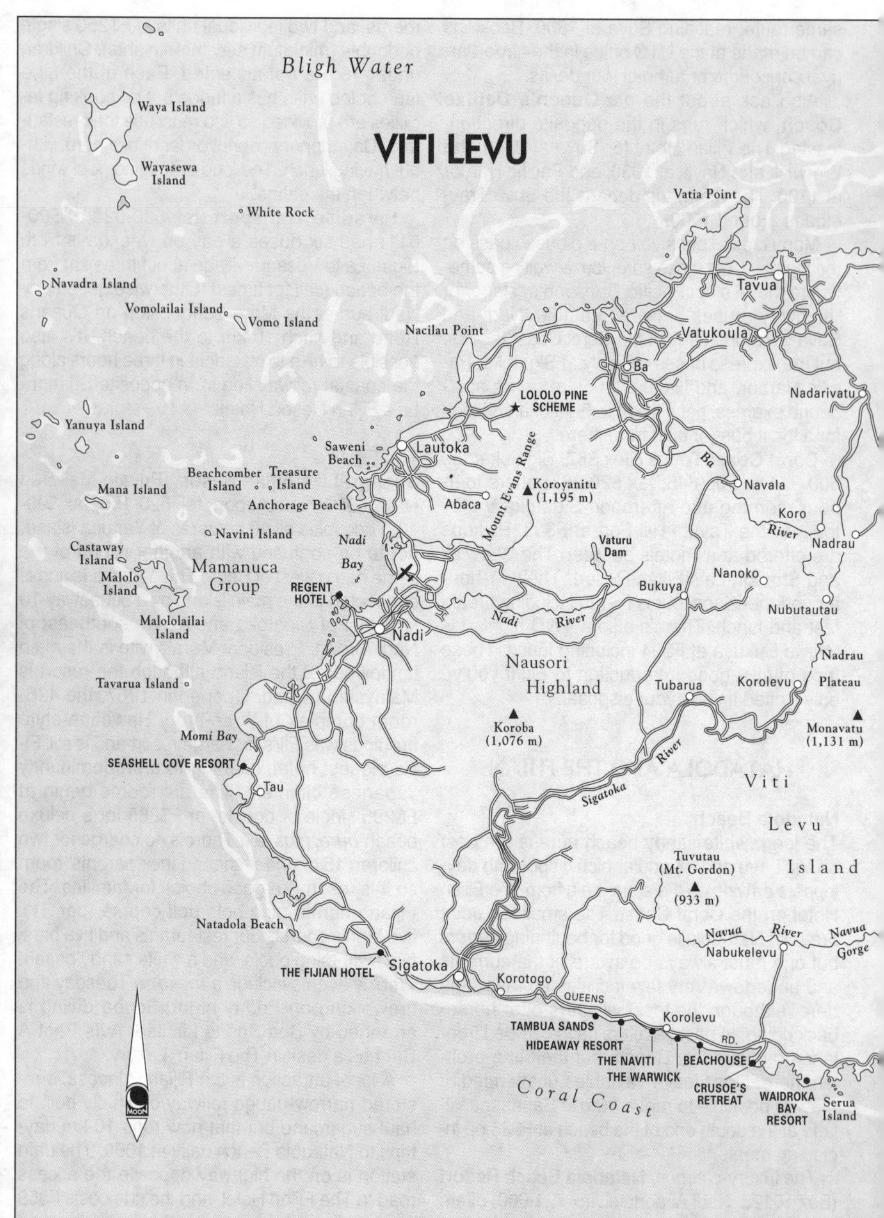
Bligh Water
VITI LEVU
Waya Island
Wayasewa Island
White Rock
Navadra Island
Vomolailai Island
Vomo Island
Nacilau Point
Vatia Point
Tavua
Vatukoula
Ba
Nadarivatu
LOLOLO PINE SCHEME
Yanuya Island
Saweni Beach
Lautoka
Mount Evans Range
Ba River
Navala
Beachcomber Island
Treasure Island
Koroyanitu (1,195 m)
Mana Island
Anchorage Beach
Abaca
Koro River
Navini Island
Nadrau
Castaway Island
Nadi Bay
Vaturu Dam
Malolo Island
Mamanuca Group
REGENT HOTEL
Nanoko
Bukuya
Nubutautau
Malololailai Island
Nadi
Nadi River
Nausori Highland
Nadrau Plateau
Tavarua Island
Tubarua
Korolevu
Momi Bay
Koroba (1,076 m)
Monavatu (1,131 m)
SEASHELL COVE RESORT
Sigatoka River
Tau
Viti Levu Island
Tuvutau (Mt. Gordon) (933 m)
Natadola Beach
Navua River
Navua Gorge
Nabukelevu
Sigatoka
THE FIJIAN HOTEL
Korotogo
QUEENS RD.
TAMBUA SANDS
HIDEAWAY RESORT
Korolevu
THE NAVITI
THE WARWICK
BEACHOUSE
CRUSOE'S RETREAT
WAIDROKA BAY RESORT
Serua Island
Coral Coast
MOON

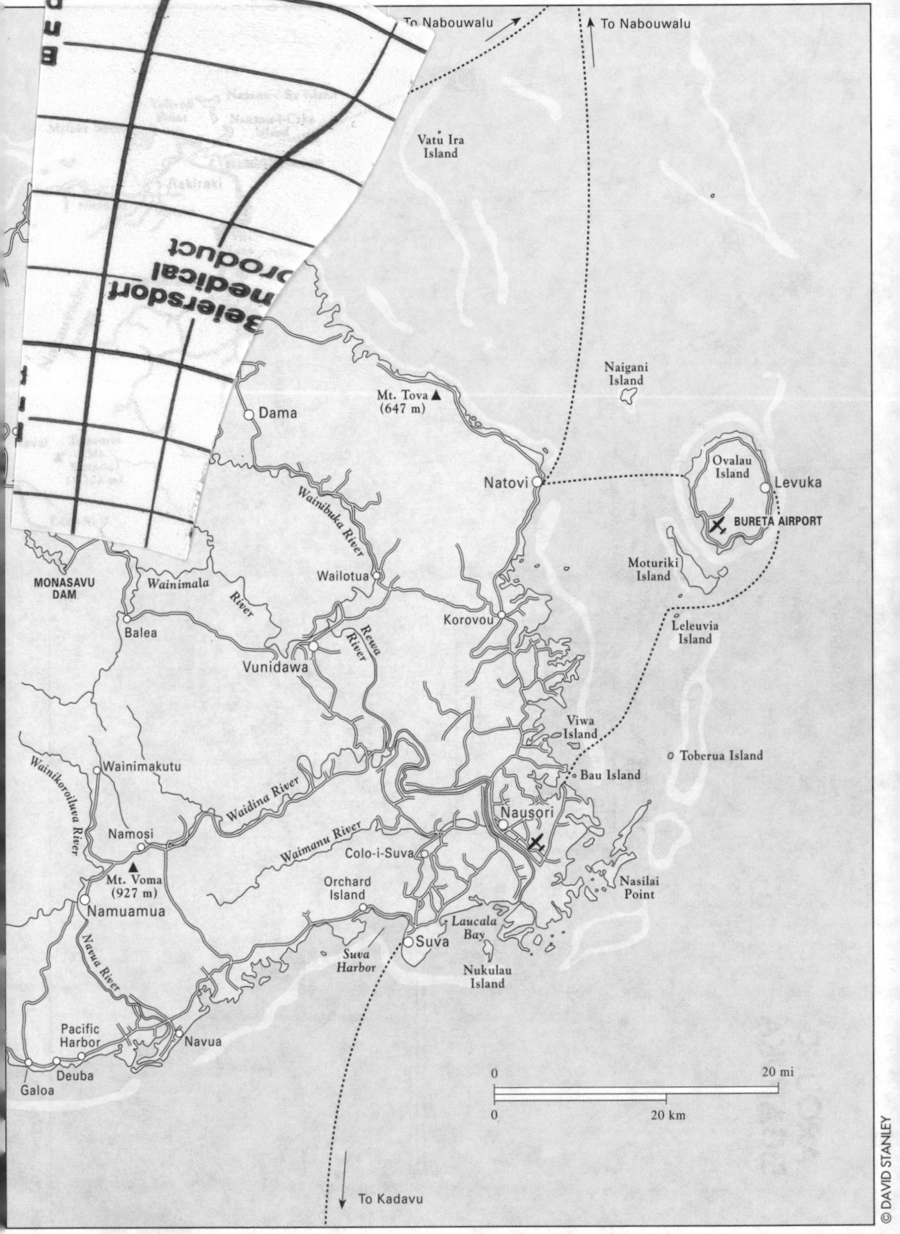

To Nabouwalu
To Nabouwalu
Vatu Ira Island
Mt. Tova (647 m)
Dama
Naigani Island
Ovalau Island
Natovi
Levuka
BURETA AIRPORT
Wainibuka River
Moturiki Island
MONASAVU DAM
Wainimala River
Wailotua
Balea
Korovou
Leleuvia Island
Rewa River
Vunidawa
Viwa Island
Toberua Island
Wainimakutu
Bau Island
Wainikoroiluva River
Waidina River
Nausori
Namosi
Waimanu River
Colo-i-Suva
Mt. Voma (927 m)
Orchard Island
Nasilai Point
Namuamua
Laucala Bay
Suva
Navua River
Suva Harbor
Nukulau Island
Pacific Harbor
Navua
Deuba
Galoa
0 20 mi
0 20 km
To Kadavu

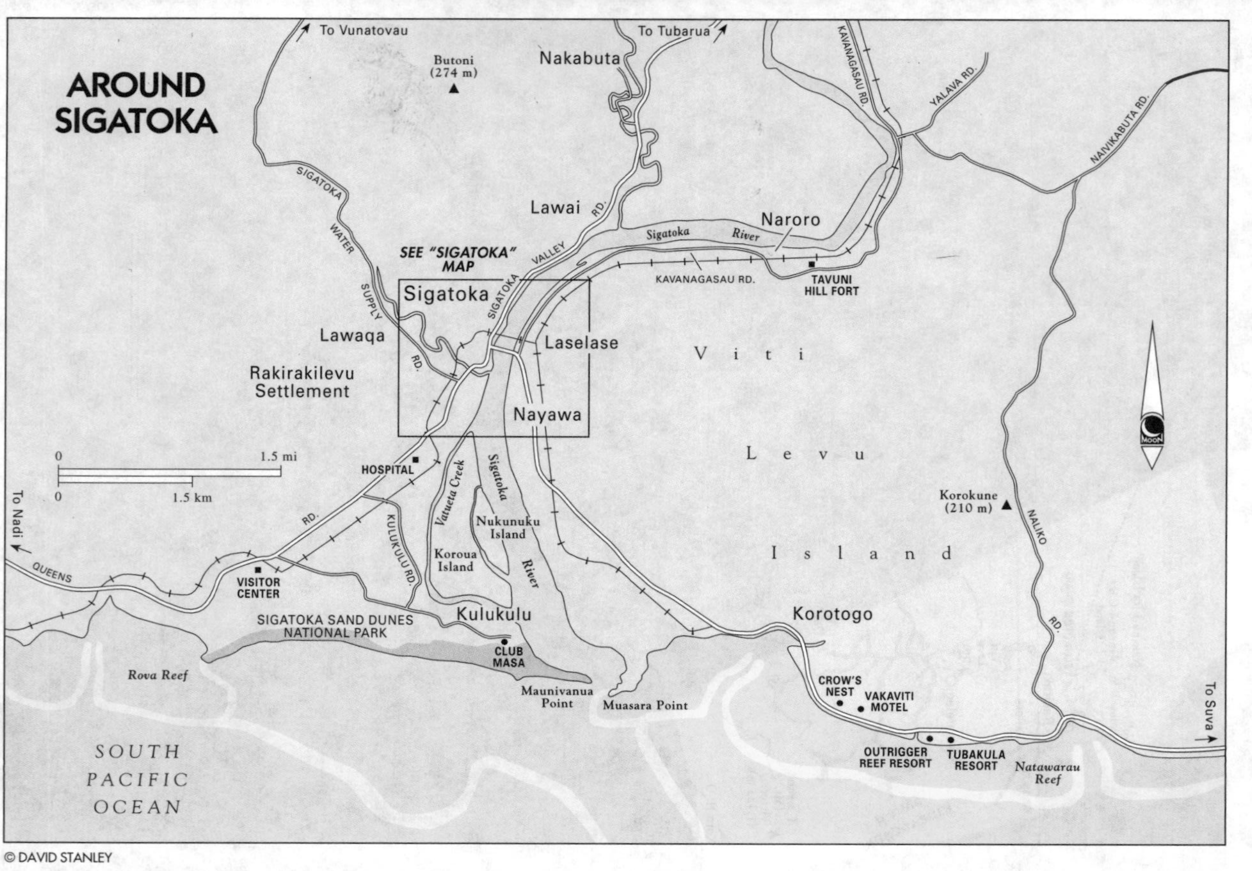
AROUND SIGATOKA
To Vunatovau
Butoni (274 m)
Nakabuta
To Tubarua
KAVANAGASAU RD.
YALAVA RD.
NAIVIKABUTA RD.
SIGATOKA WATER SUPPLY RD.
Lawai
SIGATOKA VALLEY RD.
Naroro
Sigatoka River
SEE "SIGATOKA" MAP
KAVANAGASAU RD.
TAVUNI HILL FORT
Sigatoka
Lawaqa
Laselase
Viti Levu Island
Rakirakilevu Settlement
Nayawa
0 1.5 mi
0 1.5 km
HOSPITAL
Vatueta Creek
Sigatoka River
Korokune (210 m)
NALIKO RD.
To Nadi
Nukunuku Island
Koroua Island
KULUKULU RD.
QUEENS RD.
VISITOR CENTER
Kulukulu
Korotogo
SIGATOKA SAND DUNES NATIONAL PARK
CLUB MASA
Rova Reef
Maunivanua Point
Muasara Point
CROW'S NEST
VAKAVITI MOTEL
To Suva
OUTRIGGER REEF RESORT
TUBAKULA RESORT
Natawarau Reef
SOUTH PACIFIC OCEAN

call the **Coral Coast Railway Co.** (Box 571, Sigatoka; tel. 520-434). Across the road from the train station is the **Ka Levu Cultural Center,** a mock-Fijian village dispensing instant Fijian culture to tourists for F$10 pp admission.

### Sigatoka Sand Dunes

From the mouth of the Sigatoka River westward, five kilometers of incredible 20-meter-high sand dunes separate the cane fields from the beach, formed over millennia as the southeast tradewinds blew sediments brought down by the river back up onto the shore. The winds sometimes uncover human bones from old burials, and potsherds lie scattered along the seashore—these fragments have been carbon dated at up to 3,000 years old. Giant sea turtles come ashore here now and then to lay their eggs. It's a fascinating, evocative place, protected since 1989 as a national park through the efforts of the National Trust for Fiji. The **Visitors Center** (tel. 520-343; admission F$5 pp) is on Queens Road, about four km west of Sigatoka. Exhibits outline the ecology of the park and park wardens lead visitors along a footpath over the dunes that reach as high as 50 meters in this area. It's well worth a visit to experience this unique environment. Any local bus between Nadi and Sigatoka will drop you at the Sand Dunes Visitors Center on the main highway (the express buses won't stop here).

## KULUKULU

Fiji's superlative surfing beach is near Kulukulu village, five km south of Sigatoka, where the Sigatoka River breaks through Viti Levu's fringing reef to form the Sigatoka sand dunes. The surf is primarily a rivermouth point break with numerous beachbreaks down the beach. It's one of the only places for beach break surfing on Viti Levu, and unlike most other surfing locales around Fiji, no boat is required here. The windsurfing in this area is fantastic, as you can either sail "flat water" across the rivermouth or do "wave jumping" in the sea (all-sand bottom and big rollers with high wind). The surfing is good all the time, but if you want to combine it with windsurfing, it's good planning to surf in the morning and windsurf in afternoon when the wind comes up. Be prepared, however, as these waters are treacherous for novices. You can also bodysurf here. There's a nice place nearby where you can swim in the river and avoid the currents in the sea.

American surfer Marcus Oliver runs a small budget resort behind the dunes called **Club Masa** (Box 710, Sigatoka; no telephone), also known as Oasis Budget Lodge, "a licensed private hotel for nomads of the winds and surf." The rates including two good meals are F$40 pp in the 10-bed dormitory or F$50 pp in the two double rooms and two four-bed rooms (two-night minimum stay). Camping is not allowed. There's no electricity, but the layout is attractive and the location excellent. Have a beer on their pleasant open porch. Food and drinks are unavailable during the day, so you should bring something for snacks. Sporting equipment is not provided, and ask what time they plan to lock the gate before going out for an evening stroll. When Marcus is away the Club is managed by his father Gordon Oliver and it's important to make a good impression when you first arrive as he doesn't accept just anybody as a guest. It's a good base from which to surf this coast.

Sunbeam Transport (tel. 500-168) has buses from Sigatoka to Kulukulu village seven times a day on Wednesday and Saturday, five times on other weekdays, but none on Sunday and holidays. Taxi fare to Club Masa should be around F$4, and later you may only have to pay 50 cents for a seat in an empty taxi returning to Sigatoka.

## SIGATOKA

Sigatoka (pronounced "Singatoka") is the main center for the Coral Coast tourist district and headquarters of Nadroga/Navosa Province with a racially mixed population of 8,000. A new bridge over the Sigatoka River opened here in 1997, replacing an older bridge that was damaged during a 1994 hurricane but is still used by pedestrians. The town has a picturesque riverside setting and is pleasant to stroll around. You'll find the ubiquitous souvenir shops and a colorful local market (especially on Wednesday and Saturday) with a large handicraft section. **Jack's Handicrafts** (tel. 500-810) facing the river is also worth a look.

Strangely, the traditional handmade **Fijian pottery** for which Sigatoka is famous is not available here. Find it by asking in Nayawa (where the clay originates), Yavulo, and Nasama villages near Sigatoka. Better yet, take the **Bounty Cruise** (tel. 500-963) up the river from Sigatoka to Nakabuta and Lawai villages, where the pottery is displayed for sale. Cruises leave daily except Sunday at 1000 (F$48 including lunch).

Upriver from Sigatoka is a wide valley known as Fiji's "salad bowl" for its rich market gardens by Fiji's second-largest river. Vegetables are grown in farms on the west side of the valley, while the lands on the east bank are planted with sugarcane. Small trucks use the good dirt road up the west side of the river to take the produce to market, while a network of narrow-gauge railways collects the cane from the east side. You can drive right up the valley in a normal car. The locals believe that Dakuwaqa, shark god of the Fijians, dwells in the river.

The valley also supplies a fruit juice cannery at Sigatoka that processes bananas, pineapples, mangos, guava, papayas, oranges, and tomatoes purchased from villagers who harvest fruit growing wild on their land (the creation of large plantations is inhibited by the threat of hurricanes). South Pacific Foods Ltd. sells mostly to the U.S. where their canned juice and pulp has secured a niche in the organic food market. Owned by the French transnational Pernod Ricard, the company's entire production is usually secured by advance orders a year ahead.

Also near Sigatoka, five km up the left (east) bank of the river from the bridge, is the **Tavuni Hill Fort** on a bluff at Naroro village. The fort was established by the 18th-century Tongan chief Maile Latemai and destroyed by native troops under British control in 1876. An interpretive center and walkways have been established, and admission is F$6 for adults or F$3 for children (closed Sunday). There's a good view of the river and surrounding countryside from here. Those without transport could take a taxi from Sigatoka to the reception area (about F$5), then walk back to town in an hour or so. Otherwise the Mavua bus will bring you here from Sigatoka.

### Accommodations

The budget-priced **Riverview Hotel** (Box 22, Sigatoka; tel. 520-544, fax 520-200), above a restaurant facing the new bridge in town, has seven rooms with bath and balcony at F$40/45 single/double.

LOUISE FOOTE

*The original explorers of Oceania, the Polynesians, left distinctive* lapita pottery*, decorated in horizontal bands, scattered across the Pacific. Around 500 B.C. the art was lost and no more pottery was made in Polynesia. Melanesian pottery stems from a different tradition. This antique water pot was shaped and decorated by hand, as are those made in the Sigatoka Valley today.*

The **Sigatoka Club** (Box 38, Sigatoka; tel. 500-026), across the traffic circle from the Riverview, has four fan-cooled rooms with private bath at F$28/38 single/double and a five-bed dorm at F$15 pp. Check that there's water before checking in and bring mosquito coils. The rooms are often full but the Club's bar is always perfect for a beer or a game of pool (three tables). The bar is open Mon.-Sat. 1000-2200, Sunday 1000-2100. Meals at the Club are good. Budget

The basic **Sigatoka Accommodations** (Box 35, Sigatoka; tel. 520-965), opposite the BP service station on Queens Road, has three shoestring rooms with bath at F$25 single or double. Camping on the back lawn is possible.

### Food

The **Oriental Pacific Restaurant** (tel. 520-275) in front of the bus station dispenses greasy fast food to bus passengers during their 15-minute stop here.

The **Rattan Restaurant** (tel. 500-818), further along the row of shops beside the market, has inexpensive chicken, fish, sausage, and chip meals in the warmer behind the front counter. More expensive a la carte dishes are served in the dark dining room in back.

If you have the time, it's better to head over to the **Sigatoka Club** near the new bridge where meals average F$4 at lunchtime (listed on a blackboard) but are much more expensive at dinner (printed menu). The **Sea Palace Restaurant** (tel. 500-648), near Jack's Handicrafts, is a bit more upmarket. One reader recommended **Le Cafe** (tel. 520-877), up the riverside road from the old bridge.

### Services and Transportation

Of the four **banks** in Sigatoka, the Westpac is the most convenient since they have a separate overseas section at the back and you don't have to join the long queue of local customers.

The **District Hospital** (tel. 500-455) is just southwest of Sigatoka, out on the road to Nadi.

**Pacific Transport** (tel. 500-676) express buses leave Sigatoka for Suva at 0845, 0910, 1025, 1425, 1800, and 1945 (3.5 hours, F$6), for Nadi Airport at 0935, 1115, 1220, 1500, 1800, and 2020 (1.5 hours, F$3.23). The daily **Sunset Express** leaves for Suva at 1120 and 1705, for Nadi and Lautoka at 1110 and 1825. Many additional local services also operate to/from Nadi. (Beware of taxi drivers hustling for passengers in the bus station who may claim there's no bus going where you want to go.)

Weekdays the 0900 bus operated by **Paradise Transport** (tel. 500-028 or 500-011) up the west side of the Sigatoka Valley to Tubarua offers a 4.5-hour roundtrip valley tour for F$5.40. Carriers to places far up the valley like Korolevu (F$6) and Namoli (F$7) leave weekdays just after noon.

## KOROTOGO

A cluster of self-catering budget places is at Korotogo, eight km east of Sigatoka, with only the Reef Resort, Sandy Point Beach Cottages, and Tubakula Beach Resort right on the beach itself. Most of the places farther east at Korolevu are quite upmarket. East of Korotogo the sugar fields of western Viti Levu are replaced by coconut plantations merging into rainforests on the green slopes behind.

A road through the Reef Resort Golf Course almost opposite Sandy Point Beach Cottages leads to a commercial bird park called **Kula Eco Park** (tel. 500-505; open daily 1000-1630, admission F$12, children under 12 half price).

**Independent Tours** (Box 1147, Sigatoka; tel./fax 520-678) at Tom's Restaurant in Korotogo rents mountain bikes at F$8/15 for a half/full day. They also offer a variety of bicycle tours costing F$79 for one day or F$299 for three days and two nights (minimum of two persons).

### Accommodations

The first place you reach as you enter Korotogo from Sigatoka is **Korotogo Lodge** (tel. 500-733, fax 520-182), next to Tom's Restaurant at the west end of Korotogo. They have two family rooms at F$22/33 single/double and one smaller room at F$27 single or double. It's F$15 pp in the 10-bed dorm or you can hire the entire dorm for F$49. Rooms by the hour are F$10. You can use the communal kitchen, but it's all rather basic and not on the beach. This place has been around for quite a while, and it shows. Budget.

The **Crow's Nest Motor Lodge** (Charlie Wang, Box 270, Sigatoka; tel. 500-513, fax 520-354), 500 meters east of Korotogo Lodge, offers 18 split-level duplex bungalows with cooking facilities and verandah at F$75/99 single/double. The Crow's Nest Dormitory at the bottom of the hill is F$11 pp for the 10 beds. The nautical touches in the excellent moderately priced restaurant behind the swimming pool spill over into the rooms. The nicely landscaped grounds are just across the highway from the beach and good views over the lagoon are obtained from the Crow's Nest's elevated perch. Unfortunately the new management seems to be letting maintenance slide. There's an Avis Rent A Car desk here. Moderate.

The **Vakaviti Motel and Dorm** (Arthur Jennings, Box 5, Sigatoka; tel. 500-526, fax 520-424), next to the Crow's Nest, has three self-catering units at F$45/55 single/double, and a five-bed family *bure* at F$65 double, plus F$6 per additional person. There are two six-bed dormitories, one with a nice ocean view at F$15 pp and another with no fan at F$12 pp. Facilities include a swimming pool and a large lending library/book exchange at the reception. The manager's half dozen dogs greet newcomers enthusiastically. It's often full. Budget to inexpensive.

The **Casablanca Hotel** (tel. 520-600, fax 520-616), next door to Vakaviti, is a two-story hillside building on the inland side of Queens Road. Its eight a/c rooms with cooking facilities and arched balconies begin at F$45/55 single/double. Inexpensive.

A more upmarket place to stay is **Bedarra House** (Box 1213, Sigatoka; tel. 500-476, fax 520-116), with four bath-equipped rooms facing the spacious restaurant/bar on the main floor and a *bure* out back for honeymooners, each F$132 double. A new two-story block with 10 additional rooms is planned. It's all tastefully decorated but cooking facilities are not provided in all rooms. This spacious two-story hotel prides itself on the personalized service, and a swimming pool, video room, and upstairs lounge round out their facilities. Expensive.

Just a few hundred meters east near the Reef Resort is **Waratah Lodge** (Box 86, Sigatoka; tel. 500-278, fax 520-616), with three large A-frame bungalows at F$44 double, plus F$5 per additional person up to six maximum. The two rooms below the reception in the main building are F$33/44 single/double. Cooking facilities are available and a grocery store is right next door.

The swimming pool and charming management add to the allure. It's good value and recommended. Budget.

The **Reef Resort** (Box 173, Sigatoka; tel. 500-044, fax 520-074), about a kilometer east of the Crow's Nest, is a three-story building facing right onto a white sandy beach (no road in between). The 72 a/c rooms are F$180 for up to three persons, family suites F$230—the most upmarket hotel of this stretch of the Coral Coast. Most nonmotorized recreational activities are free, and the hotel tennis courts, nine-hole par-31 golf course, and horses are available to both guests and nonguests at reasonable rates (golf is free for guests, F$10 for others). Even if you're not staying there, check out the Asian buffet (F$21) on Wednesday, the Fijian feast (F$23) on Friday, the firewalking (F$12) also on Friday, and the Fijian dancing (F$3) on Saturday night. Meals in the hotel restaurant are prepared to please the mostly Australian clientele with special attention to the kids. Thrifty Car Rental, Rosie The Travel Service, and Sea Sports Ltd. have desks here. By the time you get there all of the above may be history as plans call for the Reef Resort to be redeveloped by Outrigger Hotels of Hawaii as the **Outrigger Reef Resort,** opening in late 1999. The 208 a/c rooms in four terraced buildings and 47 *bures* should be top of the line, and you'll doubtless hear all about it. To provide more building space the road is to be rerouted away from the coast. Premium.

**Sandy Point Beach Cottages** (Box 23, Sigatoka; tel. 500-125, fax 520-147) shares the same beach with the adjacent Reef Resort. Three fan-cooled double units with full cooking facilities are offered at F$60 single, F$80 double or triple, and a five-bed cottage is F$130. Set in spacious grounds right by the sea, Sandy Point has its own freshwater swimming pool. The five huge satellite dishes you see on their lawn allow you to pick up eight channels on the TV in your room. It's a good choice for families or small groups, but it's often full so you must reserve well ahead. Inexpensive.

A bit east again is **Tubakula Beach Resort** (Box 2, Sigatoka; tel. 500-097, fax 500-201). The 23 pleasant A-frame bungalows with fan, cooking facilities, and private bath, each capable of sleeping three, vary in price from F$50 in the garden to F$68 facing the beach. Superior bungalows are F$70 poolside or F$86 beachfront. One bungalow has three rooms with shared bath at F$30/36/39 single/double/triple. Their "Beach Club" dormitory consists of eight rooms, each with three or four beds at F$14 a bed. Small discounts are available to youth hostel, VIP, and Nomads card holders, and if you stay a week you'll get 10% off. Late readers will like the good lighting. A communal kitchen is available to all, plus a swimming pool, games room, nightly videos, and minimarket. The snorkeling here is good, there's surfing and scuba diving nearby, and bus excursions are available. What more do you want? Basically, Tubakula is a quiet, do-your-own-thing kind of place for people who don't need lots of organized activities. Seated on your terrace watching the sky turn orange and purple behind the black silhouettes of the palms along the beach, a bucket of cold Fiji Bitter stubbies close at hand, you'd swear this was paradise! It's one of the most popular backpacker's resorts in Fiji and well worth a couple of nights. Budget.

### Food

Opposite the Reef Resort is a grocery store and **Fasta Food** (tel. 520-619) with a variety of inexpensive dishes listed on a blackboard. It caters mostly to hungry tourists staying at the Reef who don't have access to cooking facilities. For something better walk 800 meters west to the more atmospheric **Crow's Nest Restaurant** (tel. 500-230).

**Tom's Restaurant** (Tom Jacksam, tel. 520-238; open Mon.-Sat. 1200-1500 and 1800-2200, Sunday 1800-2200), at the west entrance to Korotogo, specializes in Chinese dishes, but there are several vegetarian items on the menu and grilled choices such as steaks. To date all reviews have been good.

## VATUKARASA

This small village between Korotogo and Korolevu is notable for its quaint appearance and the **Baravi Handicraft Boutique** (tel. 520-364), which carries a wide selection of Fijian handicrafts at fixed prices. They buy directly from the craftspeople themselves and add only a 20% markup, plus tax. It's a good place to get an idea of how much things should cost and is worth an outing by local bus if you're staying at one of the Coral Coast resorts.

## KOROLEVU

At Korolevu, east of Korotogo, the accommodations cater to a more upscale crowd, and cooking facilities are not provided for guests. These places are intended primarily for people on package holidays who intend to spend most of their time unwinding on the beach. Distances between the resorts are great, so for sightseeing you'll be dependent on your hotel's tour desk. An exception is the celebrated Beachouse, which only opened in 1996. The Coral Village Resort and Waidroka Bay Resort farther east also accommodate budget travelers, but they're both far off the highway.

### Accommodations

The **Tambua Sands Beach Resort** (Box 177, Sigatoka; tel. 500-399, fax 520-265), in an attractive location facing the sea about 10 km east of the Reef Resort, has 32 beach bungalows at F$77/88 single/double. Ask for a unit near the beach—they all cost the same (no cooking facilities). There's a very nice swimming pool, live music most evenings, and a *meke* on Friday night. Thrifty Car Rental and Rosie The Travel Service share a desk in this hotel. Inexpensive.

The 85-room **Hideaway Resort** (Box 233, Sigatoka; tel. 500-177, fax 520-025) at Korolevu, is three km east of Tambua Sands and 20 km east of Sigatoka. Set on a palm-fringed beach before a verdant valley, the smaller fan-cooled *bures* begin at F$180/200/215 single/double/triple; larger units suitable for up to six people go for F$264, breakfast included (no cooking facilities). Not all rooms have a/c. Hideaway's dormitory has closed. A five-day, five-dinner plan is F$109. This resort provides entertainment nightly, including a *meke* on Tuesday and Friday, and an all-you-can-eat Fijian feast Sunday night (F$25). An afternoon excursion to a rainforest waterfall departs at 1330 on Tuesday and Saturday (F$25). The Rosie The Travel Service desk arranges other trips and Thrifty Car Rental bookings. Surfing is possible on a very hollow right in the pass here (not for beginners), and scuba diving can be arranged. Expensive.

**The Naviti Resort** (Box 29, Korolevu; tel. 530-444, fax 530-343), just west of Korolevu and 100 km from Nadi Airport, has 140 spacious a/c rooms in a series of two-story blocks beginning at F$263/372 single/double including all meals plus unlimited wine or beer and many activities. The "all inclusive" pricing allows you to relax and enjoy your holiday without worrying about mounting bills (a room alone is F$231 single or double). There's firewalking on Wednesday and a *lovo* on Friday night. The five tennis courts are floodlit at night. Nonguests may use the nine-hole golf course for F$10 and scuba diving is possible. A fun park contains children's rides and games. Rosie The Travel Service has

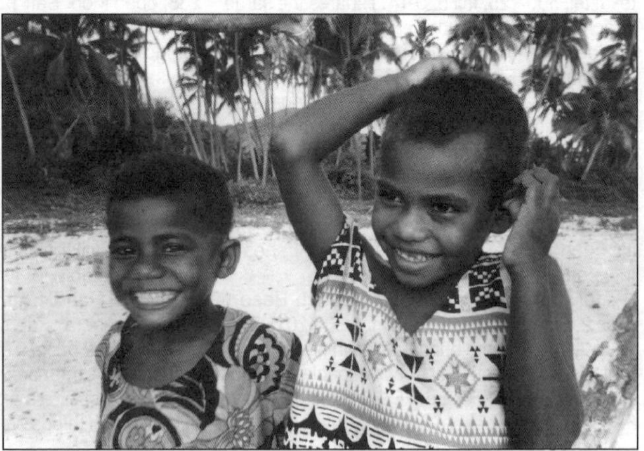

*two children near Hideaway Resort*

DAVID STANLEY

DAVID STANLEY

*Myriad hermit crabs crawl for the money at Hideaway's weekly crustacean caper.*

a desk at The Naviti. The resort shares its beach with a Fijian village, and the World Wide Fund for Nature is assisting with an ecotourism project called Tokolavo in this area—you might ask about it if you're staying here. Luxury.

**The Warwick Fiji** (Box 100, Korolevu; tel. 530-555, fax 530-010; warwick@is.com.fj), on the Queens Road just east of Korolevu, 107 km from Nadi Airport, is the second-largest hotel on the Coral Coast (after The Fijian). Erected in 1979 and part of the Hyatt Regency chain until 1991, it's now owned by the same Singapore-controlled company as The Naviti and there's a shuttle bus between the two. The 250 a/c rooms in three-story wings running east and west from the lobby begin at F$260/295 double/triple, and rise to F$400 for a club suite. The Wicked Walu seafood restaurant on a small offshore islet connected to the main beach by a causeway serves large portions but is expensive (dinner only). The other hotel restaurants could be crowded with Australian families and you might even end up waiting in a long line (F$55 meal plan). If you'd rather eat out, Vilisite's Restaurant (tel. 530-054), by the lagoon between The Warwick and The Naviti, offers medium-priced seafood. There's live music in the Hibiscus Lounge nightly until 0100 and disco dancing on Sunday. The firewalking is on Friday. This plush resort is very much oriented toward organized activities with a complete sports and fitness center. Avis Rent A Car has a desk in the Warwick. Luxury.

One of the South Pacific's best budget resorts, **The Beachouse** (Box 68, Korolevu; tel. 530-500, fax 530-400; beachouse@is.com.fj), is on a very nice palm-fringed white beach just off Queens Road, between Navola and Namatakula villages, about five km east of The Warwick. It's 35 km east of Sigatoka and 43 km west of Pacific Harbor—keep in mind that only local buses will stop here. Their slogan is "low cost luxury on the beach" and the whole project was specially designed to serve the needs of backpackers (and not as an upmarket hotel with a dormitory tacked on as an afterthought). The two wooden accommodation blocks each have four four-bunk dorms downstairs (F$17 pp) and four double fan-cooled loft rooms upstairs (F$39 double). When all of the dorms are full an overflow cabin with four bunks and six mattresses on the floor is opened (also F$17 pp—call ahead to find out if you'll have to stay there). Campers are allowed to pitch their tents on the wide lawn between the rooms and the beach at F$8 pp. Separate toilet/shower facilities for men and women are just behind the main buildings, and nearby is a communal kitchen and dining area. It's all very clean and pleasant. Breakfast in their beachfront lounge consists of all the tea, bread, and jam you want for F$3. Fish and chips or lasagna for lunch costs around F$8, and there's also a dinner menu. If you wish to cook for yourself you should bring food as the closest grocery store is in Korolevu (there's only a tiny cooperative store in Namatakula). Not only is the ocean swimming good at high tide (unlike the situation at many other Coral Coast hotels where you end up using the pool) but they'll take you out to the nearby reef in their launch for snorkeling at F$3 pp. Ask about currents before going far off on your own. Other trips include a minibus tour to Vasevu Falls (F$2 for transportation, plus F$5 admission to the falls) and a shopping/shuttle to Suva on Tuesday (F$10 return). Canoes, surf-skis, and bicycles are loaned for free, and there's a bush tack up into the hills behind the resort. The lending library serves those who only came to relax. Budget.

**Crusoe's Retreat** (Box 20, Korolevu; tel. 500-185, fax 520-666), formerly known as Man Friday Resort, is right by the beach, six km off Queens Road at Naboutini—the most secluded place to stay on the Coral Coast. The 27 large thatched *bures* are F$160 double including all meals served at a common table. The name alludes to Daniel Defoe's novel *Robinson Crusoe,* and the footprint-shaped freshwater swimming pool symbolizes Man Friday. This resort is being upgraded by a new management team. Premium.

**Coral Village Resort** (Margaret and Tony Davon, Box 104, Korolevu; tel. 500-807, fax 308-383), previously known as Gaia Beach Resort, is on a lovely beach 4.5 km off Queens Road down the same access road as Crusoe's Retreat. The eight fan-cooled bungalows are F$65/75/85 single/double/triple with fridge, and there are three six-bed dorms at F$33 pp including two meals. Cooking your own food is impossible, so you must patronize their restaurant (F$26 pp meal plan). Scuba diving is offered. This secluded, peaceful place in harmony with nature is a good spot to relax. If you call ahead they'll pick you up from the bus stop on Queens Road. Inexpensive.

The **Waidroka Bay Resort** (Box 323, Pacific Harbor; tel. 304-605, fax 304-383) is up the road leading to the Dogowale Radio Tower between Korovisilou and Talenaua, four km off Queens Road. Accommodations range from a 12-bed dormitory at F$12 pp, three lodge rooms at F$48 for up to four, and four neat little oceanfront bungalows with bath and fan at F$75/110 double/triple. The meal plan is F$30 pp a day (cooking facilities not provided). Waidroka caters mostly to the scuba/surfing crowd, and diving is F$50/95 for one/two tanks, plus F$15 for equipment. There are three surf breaks just a five-minute boat ride from the resort, and they'll ferry you out at F$10 pp for two hours. Snorkeling trips cost the same. To surf on Frigates Passage is F$35 pp with a F$135 minimum charge for the boat. Call ahead and they'll pick you up from the bus stop and Queens Road. Budget.

# PACIFIC HARBOR AND VICINITY

## PACIFIC HARBOR

Southeastern Viti Levu from Deuba to Suva is wetter and greener than the coast to the west, and the emphasis changes from beach life to cultural and natural attractions. Pacific Harbor satisfies both sporting types and culture vultures, while Fiji's finest river trips begin at Navua. Here scattered Fiji Indian dwellings join the Fijian villages that predominate farther west. All of the places listed below are easily accessible on the fairly frequent Galoa bus from Suva market.

Pacific Harbor is a sprawling, misplaced south Florida-style condo development and instant culture village, 152 km east of Nadi Airport and 44 km west of Suva. Begun in the early 1970s by Canadian developer David Gilmour (the current owner of Wakaya Island) and his father Peter Munk, good paved roads meander between the landscaped lots with curving canals to drain what was once a swamp. If it weren't for the backdrop of deep green hills you'd almost think you were in some Miami suburb. In 1988 a Japanese corporation purchased Pacific Harbor, and many of the 180 individual villas are owned by Australian or Hong Kong investors.

### Sights

Pacific Harbor's imposing **Cultural Center** (Box 74, Pacific Harbor; tel. 450-177, fax 450-083) offers the chance to experience some freeze-dried Fijian culture. This recreated Fijian village on a small "sacred island" is complete with a 20-meter-tall temple and natives attired in jungle garb. Visitors tour the island hourly, seated in a double-hulled *drua* with a tour guide "warrior" carrying a spear, and at various stops village occupations such as canoe making, weaving, tapa, and pottery are demonstrated for the canoe-bound guests. At 1100 there are one-hour performances by the Dance Theater of Fiji (Monday, Wednesday, Thursday, and Friday) and Fijian firewalking (Tuesday and Saturday), and if you want to see one of the shows it's best to arrive with the tour buses in the morning. Ad-

*a model of a fortified village at the Pacific Harbor Cultural Center*

mission is F$18 pp for the village tour (Mon.-Sat. 0900-1500), then another F$18 to see the dancing or firewalking, or F$33 for village tour and show combined. Rosie The Travel Service runs full-day bus tours to the Cultural Center from Nadi at F$73 pp including the tour and show but not lunch. The Dance Theater has an international reputation, with several successful North American tours to their credit.

Entry to the Waikiki-style **Marketplace of Fiji** at the Cultural Center, made up of mock-colonial boutiques and assorted historical displays, is free of charge. If you arrive here after 1500, all of the tourist buses will have left, and you'll be able to see quite a bit of the Cultural Center for nothing from the Flame Tree Restaurant. The main Pacific Harbor post office is next to the Cultural Center.

### Sports and Recreation

**Beqa Divers** (Box 777, Suva; tel. 450-323 or 361-088, fax 361-047), based at Pacific Harbor, is a branch of Suva's Scubahire. Their three boats and professional team of instructors head south for diving in the nearby Beqa Lagoon daily at 0900 (F$143 with two tanks and a mediocre lunch). They pioneered diving on sites just north of Yanuca Island such as Side Streets, Soft Coral Grotto, Caesar's Rocks, and Coral Gardens. The *Tasu No. 2,* a Taiwanese fishing boat intentionally sunk near Yanuca in 1994, is a great wreck dive.

**Dive Connections** (Leyh and Edward Harness, Box 14869, Suva; tel. 450-541, fax 450-539) at 16 River Drive, just across the bridge from the Sakura Japanese Restaurant, also does diving at F$65/100 for one/two tank dives (plus F$15 a day for gear), or F$400 for a 10-dive package. Night dives are F$70. The four-day PADI open water certification is F$395 (medical examination not required), otherwise there's an introductory two-dive package for F$130. Fishing charters (F$440/660 a half/full day) and picnic excursions to Yanuca Island (F$45 pp including lunch and snorkeling) can be arranged on their 12-meter dive boat *Scuba Queen.* One American reader said she'd had the finest diving in her life with them. They'll pick up anywhere within eight kilometers of the Pacific Harbor bridge.

In early 1999 the American scuba wholesaler **Aqua-Trek** set up a new dive base at the Centra Resort Pacific Harbor's marina. They cater mostly to divers on prepaid packages and individuals may be better off with the other operators.

Serious divers also have at their disposal the 18-meter live-aboard *Beqa Princess,* based at The Pub across the river from the Centra Resort Pacific Harbor. The *Beqa Princess* specializes in three-night scuba cruises to the islands south of Viti Levu and day-trips to the Beqa Lagoon. Two-tank day trips are F$100 including lunch or the boat may be chartered. Call **Tropical Expeditions** (Box 271, Pacific Harbor; tel. 450-767, fax 450-757) for the scoop on scuba or snorkeling day trips on the *Beqa Princess.*

**Baywater Charters** (Box 137, Pacific Harbor; tel. 450-235, fax 450-606) has two game-fishing boats based here, the nine-meter catamaran *Marau II* and the 14-meter monohull *Commander One.* Charter prices are F$400/750 for a half/full day including lunch for four to six anglers.

Aside from the Cultural Center, Pacific Harbor's main claim to fame is its 18-hole, par-72 championship course at the **Pacific Harbour Golf and Country Club** (Box 144, Pacific

PACIFIC HARBOUR GOLF AND COUNTRY CLUB ★ FIJI ★

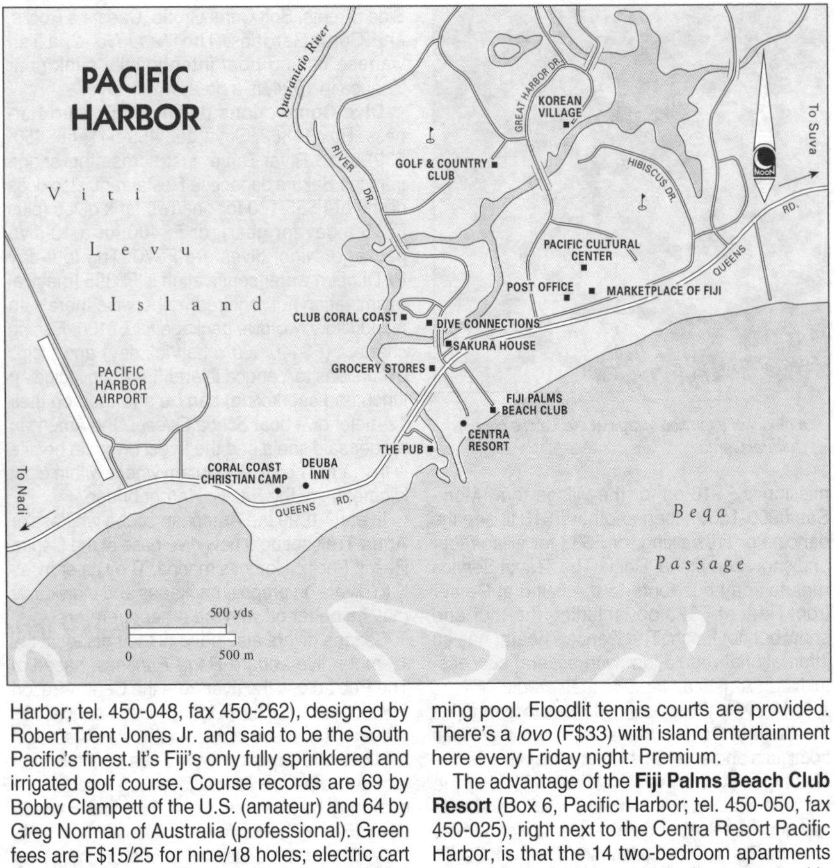

Harbor; tel. 450-048, fax 450-262), designed by Robert Trent Jones Jr. and said to be the South Pacific's finest. It's Fiji's only fully sprinklered and irrigated golf course. Course records are 69 by Bobby Clampett of the U.S. (amateur) and 64 by Greg Norman of Australia (professional). Green fees are F$15/25 for nine/18 holes; electric cart rental is F$15/25 for nine/18 holes and club hire is a further F$15/20. You'll find a restaurant and bar in the clubhouse, about two km inland off Queens Road.

### Upscale Accommodations

The 84 a/c rooms at the three-story **Centra Resort Pacific Harbor** (Box 144, Pacific Harbor; tel. 450-022, fax 450-262) are F$160/180/200 single/double/triple plus tax. Built in 1972 and formerly known as the Pacific Harbor International Hotel, the Centra Resort is now Japanese-owned. It's at the mouth of the Qaraniqio River, between Queens Road and a long sandy beach, on attractive grounds and with a nice deep swimming pool. Floodlit tennis courts are provided. There's a *lovo* (F$33) with island entertainment here every Friday night. Premium.

The advantage of the **Fiji Palms Beach Club Resort** (Box 6, Pacific Harbor; tel. 450-050, fax 450-025), right next to the Centra Resort Pacific Harbor, is that the 14 two-bedroom apartments have cooking facilities, which allows you to skip the many expensive restaurants in these parts. The first night is F$150 for up to six people, but the second night is F$135, and a week costs F$900 for the unit. Many of the apartments have been sold as part of a timeshare scheme. Expensive.

**Club Coral Coast** (Tak Hasegawa, Box 303, Pacific Harbor; tel. 450-421, fax 450-900) offers quality rooms with shared cooking facilities and fridge in large modern villas at Pacific Harbor. It's on Belo Circle near Dive Connections, across the small bridge from Sakura House Restaurant and left. There are four a/c rooms with bath in one villa and two in another at F$70/80/90 single/double/triple. Budget accommodation with shared bath is F$25/35 single/double. Facilities include a 20-meter swimming pool, jacuzzi, tennis, and many other sporting facilities. Inexpensive.

**Villa Services Ltd.** (Box 331, Pacific Harbor; tel./fax 450-959), with an office at the Marketplace of Fiji, rents out 24 of the Pacific Harbor villas at F$85/95 double/triple. All villas have kitchens, lounge, and washing machine, and most also have a pool. The minimum stay is three nights and there's a slight reduction after a week. Inexpensive

The pink-painted **Korean Village** (Box 11, Pacific Harbor; tel. 450-100, fax 450-153), formerly the Atholl Hotel, is beautifully set between the river and the golf course, a 10-minute walk from the clubhouse. The 22 plush rooms are officially F$350 double but ask for room for the F$75 "local rate." In 1998 the hotel was closed due to the suspension of Korean Airlines flights to Fiji. It's inland a couple of kilometers behind the Cultural Center, so take a taxi. Inexpensive to expensive.

### Budget Accommodations

For a cheaper room you must travel one km west of the bridge at Pacific Harbor. The friendly **Coral Coast Christian Camp** (Box 36, Pacific Harbor; tel./fax 450-178), at Deuba 13 km west of Navua, offers four five-bed Kozy Korner rooms with a good communal kitchen and cold showers at F$14/22/32 single/double/triple. The five adjoining motel units go for F$22/44/61, complete with private bath, kitchen, fridge, and fan. Camping costs F$6 pp. A good selection of groceries is sold at the office. No dancing or alcoholic beverages are permitted on the premises; on Sunday at 1930 you're invited to the Fellowship Meeting in the manager's flat. The Camp is just across the highway from long golden Loloma Beach, the closest public beach to Suva, but watch your valuables if you swim here. Guests can obtain vouchers from the manager that allow a 20% discount on Cultural Center tours. The Christian Camp is also useful as a base for trips up the Navua River—the managers will help organize the contacts. You might meet other travelers with whom to share the hire of a boat. It's also a good place to spend the night while arranging to get out to the surfers' camps on Yanuca Island. Just avoid arriving on a weekend as it's often fully booked by church groups from Friday afternoon until Monday morning.

Right next door to the Christian Camp is the **Deuba Inn** (Loraini Jones, Box 132, Pacific Harbor; tel. 450-544, fax 450-818), which opened in 1994. They have 10 rooms with shared bath at F$22/32/38 single/double/triple and five self-catering units at F$40/60/65/70 single/double/triple/quad. Camping is F$8 pp. The Inn's main drawback is that you can't cook your own food in the cheaper rooms and meals at the restaurant add up. However, inexpensive snacks are available at the takeaway counter at lunchtime and the Inn is a useful backup if you happen to arrive on a day when the Camp is full. Their bar is also handy if you're staying at the "dry" Christian Camp (happy hour 1700-1900).

### Food

**Kumarans Restaurant** (tel. 450-294; daily until 2000), across the highway from the Centra Resort Pacific Harbor, has some cheap curries at lunchtime, but the dinner menu is pricey.

The **Oasis Restaurant** (tel. 450-617), in the Marketplace of Fiji, has a fairly reasonable sandwich, salad, and burger menu at lunchtime and more substantial blackboard specials for dinner. A pot of coffee is F$3.

There are three small grocery stores beside Kumarans by the bridge at Pacific Harbor, and the self-service Trading Post Supermarket at the Marketplace of Fiji has a good selection. For fruit and vegetables you must go to Navua.

### Transportation

Only charter flights from Nadi Airport land at Pacific Harbor's airstrip, but all of the Queens Road express buses stop here. If coming to Pacific Harbor from Suva by express bus, you'll be dropped near the Centra Resort Pacific Harbor, a kilometer from the Cultural Center. The slower Galoa buses will stop right in front of the Cultural Center itself (advise the driver beforehand).

The a/c Queens Deluxe Coach leaves from the front door of the Centra Resort Pacific Harbor for Suva (F$12) at 1100, for Nadi at 1700 (F$25). The a/c Fiji Express leaves the resort for Nadi at 0900 and for Suva at 1700. Much cheaper and just as fast are the regular Pacific Transport express buses which stop on the highway: to Nadi Airport at 0750, 0930, 1035, 1315, 1605, and 1835 (three hours, F$7); to Suva at 1015, 1100, 1155, 1555, 1930, 2115 (one hour, F$2.50).

**Rosie The Travel Service** (tel. 450-655) in the Marketplace of Fiji can make any required hotel or tour bookings.

## NAVUA

The bustling river town of Navua (pop. 4,500), 39 km west of Suva, is the market center of the mostly Indian-inhabited rice-growing delta area near the mouth of the Navua River. It's also the headquarters of Serua and Namosi provinces. If low-grade copper deposits totaling 900 million metric tonnes located just inland at Namosi are ever developed, Navua will become a major mining port, passed by four-lane highways, ore conveyors, and a huge drain pipe for copper tailings. For at least 30 years millions of tonnes of waste material a year will be dumped into the ocean by an operation consuming more fossil fuel energy than the rest of the country combined. The present quiet road between Navua and Suva will bustle with new housing estates and heavy traffic, Fiji's social and environmental balance will be turned on its head, and the change from today will be total!

DR. NIELSEN

*The tortuous Navua River drains much of central Viti Levu.*

### Transportation

All of the express buses between Suva and Nadi stop at Navua. Village boats leave from the wharf beside Navua market for Beqa Island south of Viti Levu daily except Sunday, but more depart on Saturday. Flat-bottomed punts to **Namuamua** village, 25 km up the Navua River, depart on Thursday, Friday, and Saturday afternoons, but almost anytime you can charter an outboard from Navua wharf to Namuamua at F$50 for the boat roundtrip. The hour-long ride takes you between high canyon walls and over boiling rapids with waterfalls on each side. Above Namuamua is the fabulous **Upper Navua,** accessible only to intrepid river-runners in rubber rafts. It's also possible to reach the river by road at Nabukelevu.

### River Tours

An easy way to experience the picturesque lower Navua is with **Wilderness Ethnic Adventure Fiji** (Box 1389, Suva; tel. 315-730, fax 300-584), which runs full-day motorized boat trips 20 km up the river from Navua to Nukusere village, where lunch is taken and visitors get an introduction to Fijian culture. Any travel agent in Suva can make the bookings (adults F$54, children F$33). The same company also has more canoe and rubber raft trips down the same river at F$59. In Nadi, book through Rosie The Travel Service.

**Discover Fiji Tours** (Box 171, Navua; tel. 450-180, fax 450-549) also offers trips up the Navua River, leaving Navua at 1030 daily and returning at 1630. They take you upriver to a waterfall by motorized canoe and after a swim you go to Nakavu village where there's a welcoming kava ceremony and you have lunch. In the afternoon you float down the river on a bamboo raft (on Sunday the village visit is replaced by a riverside picnic). The cost is F$55 pp from Pacific Harbor or F$65 from Suva (minimum of two). Call to book.

Mr. Sakiusa Naivalu (tel. 460-641) of Navua also organizes upriver boat trips to Namuamua at F$50 with the possibility of spending the night there.

The brochures of some of the Navua River tour companies promise a kava ceremony and other events, but these are only organized for groups. If only a couple of you are going that day, nothing much of the kind is going to happen. Ask when booking, otherwise just relax and enjoy the boat ride and scenery, and wait to see your dancing at the Cultural Center. (If saving money is a priority and you can get a small group together, it's much cheaper to go to Navua by public bus and hire a market boat from there.)

Exciting whitewater rafting trips on the Upper Navua River west of Namuamua are offered by **Rivers Fiji** (Box 307, Pacific Harbor; tel. 450-147, fax 450-148). You're driven over the mountains to a remote spot where you get in a rubber raft and shoot through a narrow gorge inaccessible by motorized boat. Due to the class III rapids involved, children under 12 are not accepted, but for others it's F$250 including lunch. Rivers Fiji also does a less strenuous run down the Luva River north of Namuamua on which it's possible to paddle your own inflatable kayak. This costs F$168 for children 7-11 and F$216 for others. On both trips you finish the day by boarding a motorized punt at Namuamua and cruising down the main river to Nakavu village where you reboard the van to your hotel. Prices include pick-ups at Coral Coast and Suva hotels (F$15 extra for Nadi pickups). If you're really keen, ask about overnight camping expeditions even farther up the Navua where class IV whitewater is found.

### Toward Suva

The **Ocean Pacific Club** (Box 3229, Lami; tel. 304-864, fax 361-577), near Nabukavesi village on a hillside between Navua and Suva, 3.5 km off Queens Road (and 25 km west of Suva), has eight duplex bungalows at F$35 single or double. You can use the common kitchen. At last report the Club was for sale so call ahead.

# ISLANDS OFF SOUTHERN VITI LEVU

## VATULELE ISLAND

This small island, 32 km south of Viti Levu, reaches a height of only 34 meters on its north end; there are steep bluffs on the west coast and gentle slopes facing a wide lagoon on the east. Both passes into the lagoon are from its north end. Five different levels of erosion are visible on the cliffs from which the uplifted limestone was undercut. There are also rock paintings, but no one knows when they were executed. Vatulele today is famous for its tapa cloth.

Other unique features of 31-square-km Vatulele are the sacred **red prawns,** which are found in tidal pools at Korolamalama Cave at the foot of a cliff near the island's rocky north coast. These scarlet prawns with remarkably long antennae are called *ura buta,* or cooked prawns, for their color. The red color probably comes from iron oxide in the limestone of their abode. It's strictly *tabu* to eat them or remove them from the pools. If you do, it will bring ill luck or even shipwreck. The story goes that a princess of yesteryear rejected a gift of cooked prawns from a suitor and threw them in the pools, where the boiled-red creatures were restored to life. Villagers can call the prawns by repeating a chant.

The 950 inhabitants live in four villages on the east side of Vatulele. Village boats from Viti Levu leave Paradise Point near Korolevu Post Office on Tuesday, Thursday, and Saturday if the weather is good. Sunflower Airlines flies to Vatulele from Nadi daily (F$616 pp return). The island's small private airstrip is near the villages, six km from the resort described below, to which tourists are transferred by bus.

In 1990 Vatulele got its own luxury resort, the **Vatulele Island Resort** (Box 9936, Nadi Airport; tel. 550-300, fax 550-062) on Vatulele's west side. The 12 futuristic villas in a hybrid Fijian/New Mexico style sit about 50 meters apart on a magnificent white sand beach facing a protected lagoon. The emphasis is on luxurious exclusivity: villas cost F$1,342/1,936 single/double, including all meals and tax. The minimum stay is four nights, and children are only accepted at certain times of the year. To preserve the natural environment, motorized water sports are not offered, but there's lots to do, including sailing, snorkeling, windsurfing, paddling, tennis, and hiking, with guides and gear provided at no additional cost. The only thing you'll be charged extra for is scuba diving (F$132 a tank). This world-class resort is a creation of Australian TV producer Henry Crawford and local promoter Martin Livingston, a former manager of Turtle Island Resort in the Yasawas.

## YANUCA ISLAND

In 1994 a surfers' camp opened on a splendid beach on little Yanuca Island, to the west of Beqa (not to be confused with the Yanuca Island on which Shangri-La's Fijian Resort is found). **Frigate Surfriders** (Ratu Penaia Drekeni, Box 39, Pacific Harbor; tel. 450-801) offers cots in two four-person dormitory *bures* and five double tents at F$65 pp for surfers, F$30 pp for non-surfers, plus tax. Included are accommodations and all meals, windsurfing, surfing, and sport-fishing. For information ask at the video rental shop in the Marketplace of Fiji at Pacific Harbor. Boat transfers are F$20 pp return.

A 10-minute walk from Frigate Surfriders is a second surfing camp called **Batiluva Beach Resort** (Box 149, Pacific Harbor; tel. 450-019 or 450-202, fax 450-067) which offers dormitory accommodations at F$75 pp, including meals, surfing, snorkeling, and fishing (transfers F$40 return). It's run by an American and information should be available from Rosie Delai at Alamanda Tours (Box 111, Pacific Harbor; tel. 450-330) opposite the Marketplace of Fiji video rental shop.

The lefthander in Frigate Passage southwest of Yanuca has been called the most underrated wave in Fiji: "fast, hollow, consistent, and deserted." The Frigate Surfriders leaflet describes it thus:

> *Frigate Passage, out on the western edge of the Beqa Barrier Reef, is a sucking, often barreling photocopy of Cloudbreak near Nadi. The wave comprises three sections that often join up. The outside section presents a very steep take-off as the swell begins to draw over the reef. The wave then starts to bend and you enter a long walled speed section with stand-up tubes. This leads to a pitching inside section that breaks onto the reef, and if your timing is right you can backdoor this part and kick out safely in deep water.*

Just be aware that there's an ongoing dispute over who holds the "rights" to surf here, so check the current situation before booking or you could get caught up in their squabbles. All surfing is banned on Sunday. Yet even without the surfing, Yanuca is still worth a visit (great beach-based snorkeling). As at neighboring Beqa, Fijian firewalking is a tradition here. Village boats to the one Fijian village on Yanuca depart on Tuesday and Saturday afternoons from the bridge near the Centra Resort Pacific Harbor.

## BEQA ISLAND

Beqa (pronounced "Mbengga") is the home of the famous Fijian firewalkers; Rukua, Naceva, and Dakuibeqa are firewalking villages. Nowadays, however, they only perform at the hotels on Viti Levu. At low tide you can hike the 27 km around the island: the road only goes from Waisomo to Dakuni. Malumu Bay, between the two branches of the island, is thought to be a drowned crater. Climb Korolevu (439 meters), the highest peak, from Waisomo or Lalati. Kadavu Island is visible to the south of Beqa.

It's quite possible to stay in any of the Fijian villages on Beqa by following the procedure outlined in "Staying in Villages" in the main introduction. Ask around the wharf at Navua around noon any day except Sunday and you'll soon find someone happy to take you. Alcohol is not allowed in the villages on Beqa, so if you're

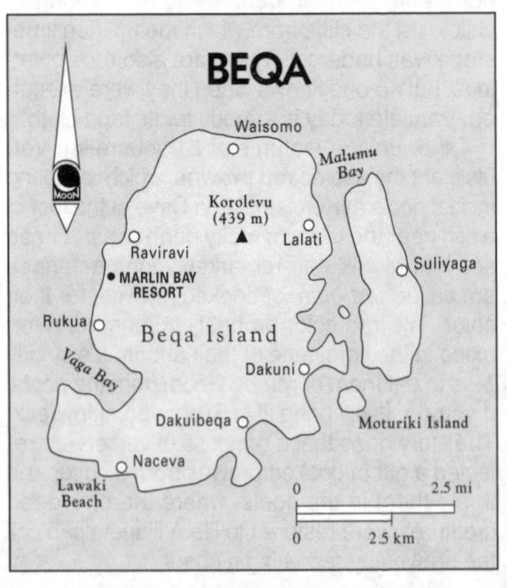

asked to buy a case of beer, politely decline and offer to buy other groceries instead. The number one beach is Lawaki to the west of Naceva. Present the village chief of Naceva with a nice bundle of *waka* if you want to camp there.

Mikaele Funaki's **Island and Village Concept Tours** (Box 14328, Suva; tel. 307-951) organizes three-night homestays at Naceva or another village at F$98 pp including food and shared accommodations, local sightseeing and snorkeling tours, and return boat transfers from Navua. The packages begin every Tuesday and Friday. Call for information.

The **Marlin Bay Resort** (Box 112, Deuba; tel. 304-042, fax 304-028) opened in 1991 on a golden beach between Raviravi and Rukua villages on the west side of Beqa. It's expensive because all prices are based on U.S. dollars. The 16 luxurious *bures* go for F$360 single or double, F$395 triple. The five-star meal plan is F$110 pp a day (no cooking facilities). Most guests are scuba divers who come to dive on spots like Soft Coral Plateau, Fan Reef, and Joe's Best. It's F$160 for a two-tank boat dive (plus F$60 for equipment, if required), and unlimited shore diving is free. There's a swimming pool and surfing runs to Frigate's Pass are arranged at F$100 pp for two sessions. Boat pickups for the Marlin Bay Resort take place at The Pub Restaurant, Pacific Harbor, and cost F$100 return.

The 65 km of barrier reef around the 390-square-km Beqa Lagoon features multicolored soft corals and fabulous sea fans at Side Streets, and an exciting wall and big fish at Cutter Passage. Aside from its surfing potential, **Frigate Passage** on the west side of the barrier reef is one of the top scuba diving sites near Suva. A vigorous tidal flow washes in and out of the passage, which attracts large schools of fish, and there are large coral heads. **Sulfur Passage** on the east side of Beqa is equally good.

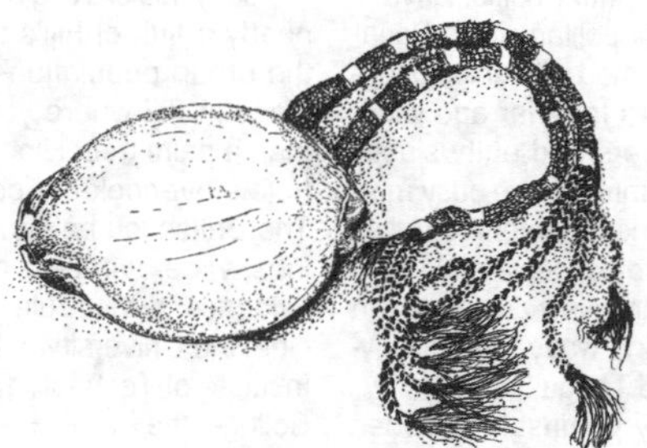

LOUISE FOOTE

*The golden cowry* (Cypraea aurantium), *which the Fijians call* buli kula, *is one of the rarest of all seashells. On important ceremonial occasions, a high chief would wear the shell pendant around his neck as a symbol of the highest authority.*

SALVATORE CASA

# SUVA AND VICINITY

The pulsing heart of the South Pacific, Suva is the largest and most cosmopolitan city in Oceania. The port is always jammed with ships bringing goods and passengers from far and wide, and busloads of commuters and enthusiastic visitors constantly stream through the busy market bus station. In the business center are Indian women in saris, large sturdy chocolate-skinned Fijians, expat Australians and New Zealanders in shorts and knee socks, and wavy-haired Polynesians from Rotuma and Tonga.

Suva squats on a hilly peninsula between Laucala Bay and Suva Harbor in the southeast corner of Viti Levu. The verdant mountains north and west catch the southeast trades, producing damp conditions year-round. Visitors sporting a sunburn from Fiji's western sunbelt resorts may appreciate Suva's warm tropical rains (most of which fall at night). In 1870 the Polynesia Company sent Australian settlers to camp along mosquito-infested Nubukalou Creek on land obtained from High Chief Cakobau. When efforts to grow sugarcane in the area failed, the company convinced the British to move their headquarters here, and since 1882 Suva has been the capital of Fiji.

Today this exciting multiracial city of 170,000—nearly a fifth of Fiji's total population and half the urban population—is also about the only place in Fiji where you'll see a building taller than a palm tree. High-rise office buildings and hotels overlook the compact downtown area. The British left behind imposing colonial buildings, wide avenues, and manicured parks as evidence of their rule. The Fiji School of Medicine, the University of the South Pacific, the Fiji Institute of Technology, the Pacific Theological College, the Pacific Regional Seminary, and the headquarters of many regional organizations and diplomatic missions have been established here. In addition, the city offers some of the most brilliant nightlife between Kings Cross (Sydney) and North Beach (San Francisco), plus shopping, sightseeing, and many good-value places to stay and eat.

Keep in mind that on Sunday most shops will be closed, restaurants keep reduced hours, and fewer taxis or buses will be on the road. In short, the city will be quiet—a good time to wander around in relative peace. If you decide to catch the Friday or Saturday bus/boat service to Leleuvia or Levuka and spend the weekend there,

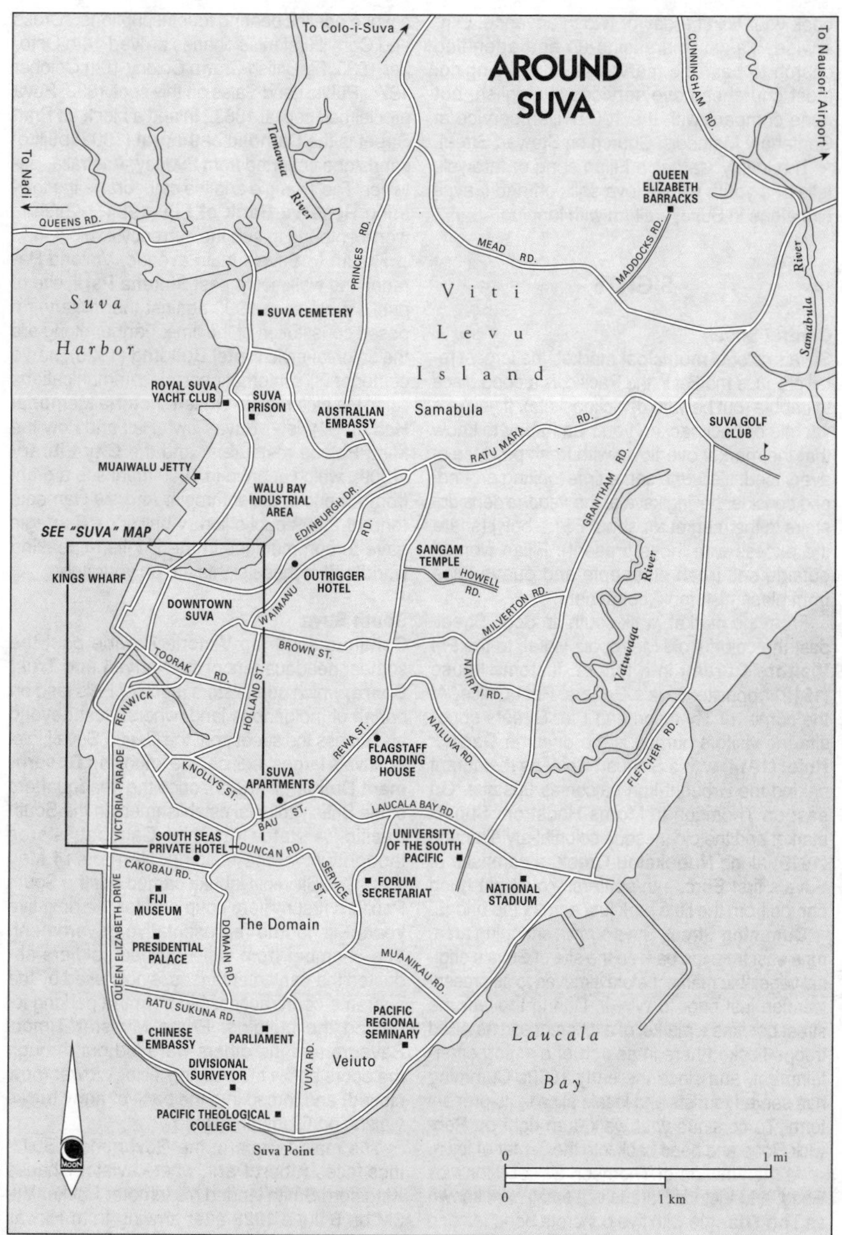
AROUND SUVA
To Colo-i-Suva
To Nausori Airport
To Nadi
CUNNINGHAM RD.
QUEEN ELIZABETH BARRACKS
QUEENS RD.
Tamavua River
PRINCES RD.
MEAD RD.
MADDOCKS RD.
Samabula River
Viti Levu Island
Suva Harbor
SUVA CEMETERY
ROYAL SUVA YACHT CLUB
SUVA PRISON
AUSTRALIAN EMBASSY
Samabula
RATU MARA RD.
SUVA GOLF CLUB
GRANTHAM RD.
MUAIWALU JETTY
WALU BAY INDUSTRIAL AREA
EDINBURGH DR.
SEE "SUVA" MAP
SANGAM TEMPLE
HOWELL RD.
KINGS WHARF
OUTRIGGER HOTEL
Vatuwaqa River
MILVERTON RD.
DOWNTOWN SUVA
WAIMANU RD.
BROWN ST.
TOORAK RD.
NAIRAI RD.
RENWICK
HOLLAND ST.
FLAGSTAFF BOARDING HOUSE
REWA ST.
NAILUVA RD.
VICTORIA PARADE
KNOLLYS ST.
SUVA APARTMENTS
FLETCHER RD.
BAU ST.
LAUCALA BAY RD.
SOUTH SEAS PRIVATE HOTEL
DUNCAN RD.
UNIVERSITY OF THE SOUTH PACIFIC
CAKOBAU RD.
SERVICE ST.
FORUM SECRETARIAT
NATIONAL STADIUM
FIJI MUSEUM
The Domain
PRESIDENTIAL PALACE
DOMAIN RD.
QUEEN ELIZABETH DRIVE
MUANIKAU RD.
RATU SUKUNA RD.
PACIFIC REGIONAL SEMINARY
CHINESE EMBASSY
PARLIAMENT
Laucala Bay
VUYA RD.
Veiuto
DIVISIONAL SURVEYOR
PACIFIC THEOLOGICAL COLLEGE
Suva Point
MOON
0
1 mi
0
1 km

book your ticket a day or two in advance. Otherwise, it's worth dressing up and attending church to hear the marvelous choral singing. Most churches have services in English, but none compare with the 1000 Fijian service at Centenary Methodist Church on Stewart Street.

The lovely *Isa Lei,* a Fijian song of farewell, tells of a youth whose love sails off and leaves him alone in Suva, smitten with longing.

## SIGHTS

### Central Suva

Suva's colorful **municipal market,** the largest retail produce market in the Pacific, is a good place to dabble (but beware of pickpockets). If you're a yachtie or backpacker, you'll be happy to know that the market overflows with fresh produce of every kind. It's worth some time looking around, and consider having kava at the *yaqona* dens upstairs in the market for about F$1 a bowl (share the excess with those present). Fijian women outside sell fresh pineapple and guava juice from glass "fish tank" containers.

From the market, walk south on Scott Street, past the colorful old Metropole Hotel, to the **Fiji Visitors Bureau** in a former customs house (1912) opposite Suva's General Post Office. At the corner of Thomson and Pier Streets opposite the visitors bureau is the onetime **Garrick Hotel** (1914) with a Sichuan Chinese restaurant behind the wrought-iron balconies upstairs. Go east on Thomson to Morris Hedstrom Supermarket and the picturesque colonial-style arcade (1919) along **Nubukalou Creek,** a campsite of Suva's first European settlers. You'll get good photos from the little park just across the bridge.

**Cumming Street,** Suva's main shopping area, runs east from the park on the site of Suva's original vegetable market before it moved to its present location just prior to WW II. During the war the street became a market of a different sort as Allied troops flocked here in search of evening entertainment, and since the early 1960s Cumming has served tourists and locals alike in its present form. To continue your walk, turn right on Renwick Road and head back into the center of town.

At the junction of Thomson Street, Renwick Road, and Victoria Parade is a small park known as **The Triangle** with five concrete benches and a white obelisk bearing four inscriptions: "Cross and Cargill first missionaries arrived 14th October 1835; Fiji British Crown Colony 10th October 1874; Public Land Sales on this spot 1880; Suva proclaimed capital 1882." Inland a block on Pratt Street is the **Catholic cathedral** (1902) built of sandstone imported from Sydney, Australia. Between The Triangle and the cathedral is the towering **Reserve Bank of Fiji** (1984), which is worth entering to see the currency exhibition.

Return to Suva's main avenue, Victoria Parade, and walk south past **Sukuna Park,** site of public protests in 1990 against the military-imposed constitution of the time. Farther along are the colonial-style **Fintel Building** (1926), nerve center of Fiji's international telecommunications links, the picturesque **Queen Victoria Memorial Hall** (1904), later Suva Town Hall and now the Ming Palace restaurant, and the **City Library** (1909), which opened in 1909 thanks to a grant from American philanthropist Andrew Carnegie (one of 2,509 public library buildings Carnegie gave to communities in the English-speaking world). All of these sights are on your right.

### South Suva

Continue south on Victoria Parade past the somber headquarters of the **Native Land Trust Board,** which administers much of Fiji's land on behalf of indigenous landowners. Just beyond and across the street from the Centra Suva Hotel is Suva's largest edifice, the imposing **Government Buildings** (1939), once the headquarters of the British colonial establishment in the South Pacific. A statue of Chief Cakobau stares thoughtfully at the building. Here on 14 May 1987 Col. Sitiveni Rabuka carried out the South Pacific's first military coup and for the next five years Fiji had no representative government. The chamber from which armed soldiers abducted the parliamentarians is now used by the supreme court, accessible from the parking lot behind the building. Prime Minister Timoci Bavadra and the others were led out through the doors below the building's clock tower (now closed) and forced into the back of army trucks waiting on Gladstone Road.

The main facade of the Government Buildings faces **Albert Park,** where aviator Charles Kingsford Smith landed his trimotor Fokker VII-3M on 6 June 1928 after arriving from Hawaii on the first-ever flight from California to Australia. (The first commercial flight to Fiji was a Pan Am flying boat, which landed in Suva Harbor in October 1941.) Facing the west side of the park is the elegant, Edwardian-style **Grand Pacific Hotel,** built by the Union Steamship Company in 1914 to accommodate its transpacific passengers. The 75 rooms were designed to appear as shipboard staterooms, with upstairs passageways surveying the harbor, like the promenade deck of a ship. For decades the Grand Pacific was the social center of the city, but it has been closed since 1992. The building is owned by the phosphate-rich Republic of Nauru, and in 1998 Outrigger Hotels of Hawaii announced that the Grand Pacific would be renovated and expanded into a 136-room luxury hotel, opening in late 1999.

South of Albert Park are the pleasant **Thurston Botanical Gardens,** opened in 1913, where tropical flowers such as cannas and plumbagos blossom. The original Fijian village of Suva once stood on this site. (It's fun to observe the young Indian couples enjoying brief moments away from the watchful eyes of their families.) On the grounds of the gardens is a clock tower dating from 1918 and the **Fiji Museum** (Box 2023, Government Buildings, Suva; tel. 315-944, fax 305-143), founded in 1904 and the oldest in the South Pacific. The first hall deals in archaeology, with much information about Fiji's unique pottery. Centerpiece of the adjacent maritime exhibit is a double-hulled canoe made in 1913, plus five huge *drua* steering oars each originally held by four men, several large sail booms, and a bamboo house raft *(bilibili).* The cannibal forks near the entrance are fascinating, as are the whale tooth necklaces and the large collection of Fijian war clubs and spears. The history gallery beyond the museum shop has a rich collection of 19th century exhibits with items connected with the many peoples who have come to Fiji, including Tongans, Europeans, Solomon Islanders, and Indians. Notice the rudder from HMS *Bounty.* An a/c room upstairs contains a display of tapa cloth. You can ask to watch a video on Pacific themes in the museum theater. The museum shop sells an illustrated catalog titled *Yalo i Viti* and copies of the museum journal, *Domodomo,* plus other interesting books. Visiting hours are Mon.-Fri. 0930-1600, Saturday and Sunday 1300-1630, admission F$3.30. Plans exist for a National Center for Culture and the Arts to be built adjacent to the existing museum.

South of the gardens is **Presidential Palace,** formerly called Government House, the residence of the British governors of Fiji. The original building, erected in 1882, burned after being hit by lightning in 1921. The present edifice, which dates from 1928, is a replica of the former British governor's residence in Colombo, Sri Lanka. The grounds cannot be visited but you're welcome to take a photo of the sentry on ceremonial guard duty in his belted red tunic and immaculate white *sulu* (kilt). The changing of the guard takes place daily at noon with an especially elaborate ceremony the first Friday of every month to the accompaniment of the military band.

From the seawall south of Government House you get a good view across Suva Harbor to Beqa Island (to the left) and the dark, green mountains of eastern Viti Levu punctuated by Joske's Thumb, a high volcanic plug (to the right). Follow the seawall south past a few old colonial buildings, and turn left onto Ratu Sukuna Road, the first street after the Police Academy.

About 500 meters up this road is the **Parliament of Fiji** (1992), an impressive, traditional-style building with an orange pyramid-shaped roof. The main entrance is around the corner off Battery Road. If you want a complete tour, call the parliamentary library the day before at tel. 305-811, otherwise ask the librarians if they can admit you to the main chamber (weekdays only). When parliament is in session you may enter the public gallery. The top time to be there is for the debate on the budget in November, but you might need to arrive at 0800 to get a seat that day. Other sittings are poorly attended by both the public and members. Thirteen huge tapa banners hang from the walls, and skillfully plaited coconut fiber ropes from the Lau Group and a pair of *tabuas* complete the decor. The location is spectacular with scenic sea and mountain views.

From Parliament it's a good idea to catch a taxi to the University of the South Pacific. The Nasese bus does a scenic loop through the beautiful garden suburbs of South Suva: just flag it down if you need a ride back to the market. Both Protestants and Catholics have their most important regional training facilities for ministers and priests in South Suva.

*Fiji's emerald green banded iguana is the most striking reptile of the Pacific.*

THE FIJI TIMES

**University of the South Pacific**

A frequent bus from near the Bank of Hawaii on Victoria Parade will bring you direct to the University of the South Pacific (ask the driver to let you know where to get out). Founded in 1968, this beautiful 72.8-hectare campus on a hilltop overlooking Laucala Bay is jointly owned by 12 Pacific countries. Although over 70% of the almost 2,000 full-time and more than 600 part-time students are from Fiji, the rest are on scholarships from every corner of the Pacific.

The site of the USP's Laucala Campus was a Royal New Zealand Air Force seaplane base before the land was turned over to USP. As you enter from Laucala Bay Road you'll pass the Botanical Garden (1988) on the right, then the British-built Administration Building on the left. Next comes the $3.5-million university library (1988), erected with Australian aid. The design of the Student Union Building (1975), just across a wooden bridge from the library, was influenced by traditional Pacific building motifs of interlocking circles. Look for the pleasant canteen in the Student Union (open Mon.-Sat. 0800-2030 during the school year). There's a choice of Indian or island food.

Several buildings south of this, past the university bookstore and a traditional Fijian *bure,* is the **Institute of Pacific Studies** (Box 1168, Suva; tel. 313-632), housed in the former RNZAF officers' mess. Every available space on the walls of the IPS building has been covered with murals by Pacific painters. This Institute is a leading publisher of insightful books written by Pacific islanders; these books may be perused and purchased at their bookroom inside the building.

Students from outside the Pacific islands pay about F$8,200 a year tuition to study at USP. Room and board are available at around F$3,162 and books will run another F$400. There are academic minimum-entry requirements and applications must be received by 31 December for the following term. The two semesters are late February to the end of June, and late July until the end of November. Many courses in the social sciences have a high level of content pertaining to Pacific culture, and postgraduate studies in a growing number of areas are available. To obtain a calendar (F$20), send a Visa or MasterCard authorization to: The Manager, Book Center, University of the South Pacific, Box 1168, Suva, Fiji Islands (tel. 313-900, fax 303-265, www.usp.ac.fj/~bookcentre).

The USP is always in need of qualified staff, so if you're from a university milieu and looking for a chance to live in the South Seas, this could be it. If your credentials are impeccable you should write to the registrar from home. On the spot it's better to talk to a department head about his/her needs before going to see the registrar.

**Northwest of Suva**

The part of Suva north of Walu Bay accommodates much of Suva's shipping and industry. Carlton Brewery on Foster Road cannot be visited. About 600 meters beyond the brewery is the vintage **Suva Prison** (1913), a fascinating colonial structure with high walls and barbwire. Opposite is the **Royal Suva Yacht Club,** where you can sign in and buy a drink, meet some yachties, and maybe find a boat to crew on. In the picturesque **Suva Cemetery,** just to the north, the Fijian graves are wrapped in colorful *sulus* and tapa cloth, and make good subjects for photographers.

Catch one of the frequent Shore, Lami, or Galoa buses west on Queens Road, past **Suvavou** village, home of the Suva area's original Fijian inhabitants, and past Lami town to the **Raffles Tradewinds Hotel,** seven km from the market. Many cruising yachts tie up here, and the view of the Bay of Islands from the hotel is good.

**Orchid Island**

Seven km northwest of Suva is the **Orchid Island Cultural Center** (Box 1018, Suva; tel. 361-128). In the past it offered a good synopsis of Fijian customs through demonstrations, dancing, and historical exhibits, affording a glimpse into traditions such as the kava ceremony, tapa and pottery making, etc. At the miniature zoo you could see and photograph Fiji's rare banded iguanas and snakes up close. Replicas of a Fijian war canoe and thatched temple *(bure kalou)* were on the grounds. We've used the past tense here because Orchid Island has gone downhill and now looks abandoned, although some readers report being admitted and shown around the empty, decaying buildings by residual staff who were only too happy to pocket their F$10 pp admission fee. You might check Orchid Island's current status at the Fiji Visitors Bureau (and don't bother going on a Sunday). The Shore and Galoa buses pass this way.

**Colo-i-Suva Forest Park**

This lovely park, at an altitude of 122-183 meters, offers 6.5 km of trails through the lush forest flanking the upper drainage area of Waisila Creek. The mahogany trees you see here are natives of Central America and were planted after the area was logged in the 1950s. Enter from the Forestry Station along the Falls Trail. A half-km nature trail begins near the Upper Pools, and aside from waterfalls and natural swimming pools there are thatched pavilions with tables at which to picnic. With the lovely green forests behind Suva in full view, this is one of the most breathtaking places in all of Fiji and you may spot a few native butterflies, birds, reptiles, and

MINISTRY OF INFORMATION, GOVERNMENT OF FIJI

*A good cross-section of Fiji's flora can be seen in Colo-i-Suva Forest Park near Suva.*

frogs. The park is so unspoiled it's hard to imagine you're only 11 km from Suva.

When the park first opened in 1973, camping was allowed near the upper and lower pools. Then in the mid-1980s the rangers were forced to prohibit camping due to thefts from both campers and swimmers. Recently security patrols have been stepped up and camping is once again allowed, but someone must still keep watch over the campsite at all times, especially on weekends. You must also keep an eye on your gear if you go swimming (valuables can be left at the visitors center). The park (tel. 361-128) is open daily 0800-1600, and there's a F$5 pp entry fee (under age 12 F$1, under six free) to cover park maintenance and management. Get there on the Sawani or Serea buses (61 cents), which leave from Lane No. 3 at Suva Bus Station every hour (Sunday every two hours), but come on a dry day as it's even rainier than Suva and the creeks are prone to flooding.

On your way back to Suva from Colo-i-Suva ask the bus driver to drop you at Wailoku Road, just past the Fiji School of Medicine in Tamavua Heights. Every half hour the Wailoku bus runs down the hill: stay on till the bus stops and turns around, then continue down the road a few hundred meters to a bridge. Take the trail on the left just across the bridge and hike about five minutes upstream to **Wailoku Falls,** where you can swim in a deep pool of cold, clear water amid the idyllic verdant vegetation. This nice picnic spot is on government land and no admission is charged. The nearby Wailoku Settlement is inhabited by descendants of blackbirded Solomon Islanders. If you only want to visit the falls, look for the Wailoku bus at the harbor end of Lane No. 2 at the market bus station.

### Hiking

For a bird's-eye view of Suva and the entire surrounding area, spend a morning climbing to the volcanic plug atop **Mt. Korobaba** (429 meters), the highest peak around. Take a Shore bus to the cement factory beyond the Tradewinds Hotel at Lami, then follow the dirt road past the factory

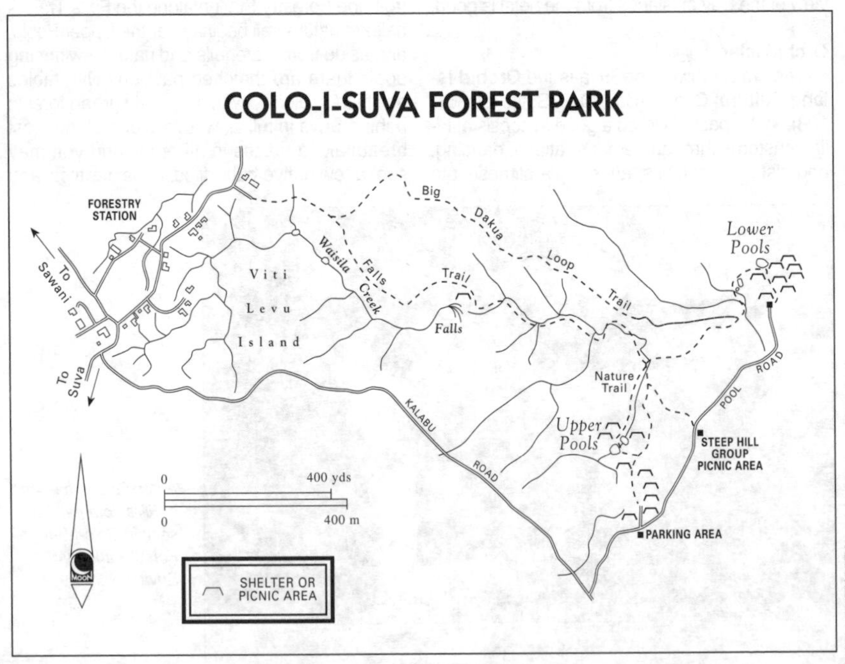

DAVID STANLEY

*Wailoku Falls*

up into the foothills. After about 45 minutes on the main track, you'll come to a fork just after a sharp descent. Keep left and cross a small stream. Soon after, the track divides again. Go up on the right and look for a trail straight up to the right where the tracks rejoin. It's a 10-minute scramble to the summit from here.

There's a far more challenging climb to the top of **Joske's Thumb,** a volcanic plug 15 km west of Suva. Take a bus to Naikorokoro Road, then walk inland 30 minutes to where the road turns sharply right and crosses a bridge. Follow the track straight ahead and continue up the river till you reach a small village. Request permission of the villagers to proceed. From the village to the Thumb will take just under three hours, and a guide might be advisable. The last bit is extremely steep, and ropes may be necessary. It even took Sir Edmund Hillary two tries to climb the Thumb.

### Sports and Recreation

**Scubahire** (Box 777, Suva; tel. 361-088, fax 361-047), 75 Marine Dr., opposite the Lami Shopping Center, is the country's oldest dive shop (established by Dave and Lorraine Evans in 1970) and one of the only PADI five-star dive centers in Fiji. Their four-day PADI certification course (F$495) involves six boat dives and Fiji's only purpose-built diver training pool is on their Lami premises. You'll need to show a medical certificate proving you're fit for diving. An introductory dive is F$154. Scubahire arranges full-day diving trips to the Beqa Lagoon with Beqa Divers at their Pacific Harbor base for F$143, including two tanks, weight belt, backpack, and lunch. Other equipment can be rented. Scubahire will also take snorkelers out on their full-day dive trips for F$66 pp, snorkeling gear and lunch included. When things are slow they may offer a "special" reduced rate for the all-day scuba trip, if you ask. All diving is out of Pacific Harbor—the Suva office only takes bookings, does certification courses, and sells equipment.

**Dive Center Ltd.** (Box 3066, Lami; tel. 300-599, fax 302-639), 4 Matua St., Walu Bay (opposite Carlton Brewery), also rents and sells scuba gear at daily and weekly rates, and fills tanks.

Surfers should call Matthew Light (tel. 361-560 or 998-830), who runs a shuttle out to Sandspit Lighthouse where there's good surfing on a southwest swell at high tide (F$15 pp roundtrip). He picks up at the Raffles Tradewinds Hotel in Lami.

At the 18-hole, par-72 **Fiji Golf Club** (tel. 382-872), 15 Rifle Range Rd., Vatuwaqa, the course record is 65. Green fees are F$15/20 for nine/18 holes, club hire F$10/20 for a half/full set, plus trolley hire at F$3. Call ahead to ask if any competitions are scheduled as the course may be closed to the public at those times. (Prime Minister Rabuka and President Mara are regulars).

The **Olympic Swimming Pool,** 224 Victoria Parade, charges F$1.10 admission. It's open Mon.-Fri. 1000-1800, Saturday 0800-1800 (April-Sept.), or Mon.-Fri. 0900-1900, Saturday 0600-1900 (Oct.-March). Lockers are available.

The Fijians are a very muscular, keenly athletic people who send champion teams far and wide in the Pacific. You can see rugby (April-Sept.) and soccer (March-Oct.) on Saturday afternoons at 1500 at the **National Stadium** near the University of the South Pacific. Rugby and soccer are also played at Albert Park on Saturday, and you could also see a cricket game here (mid-October to Easter).

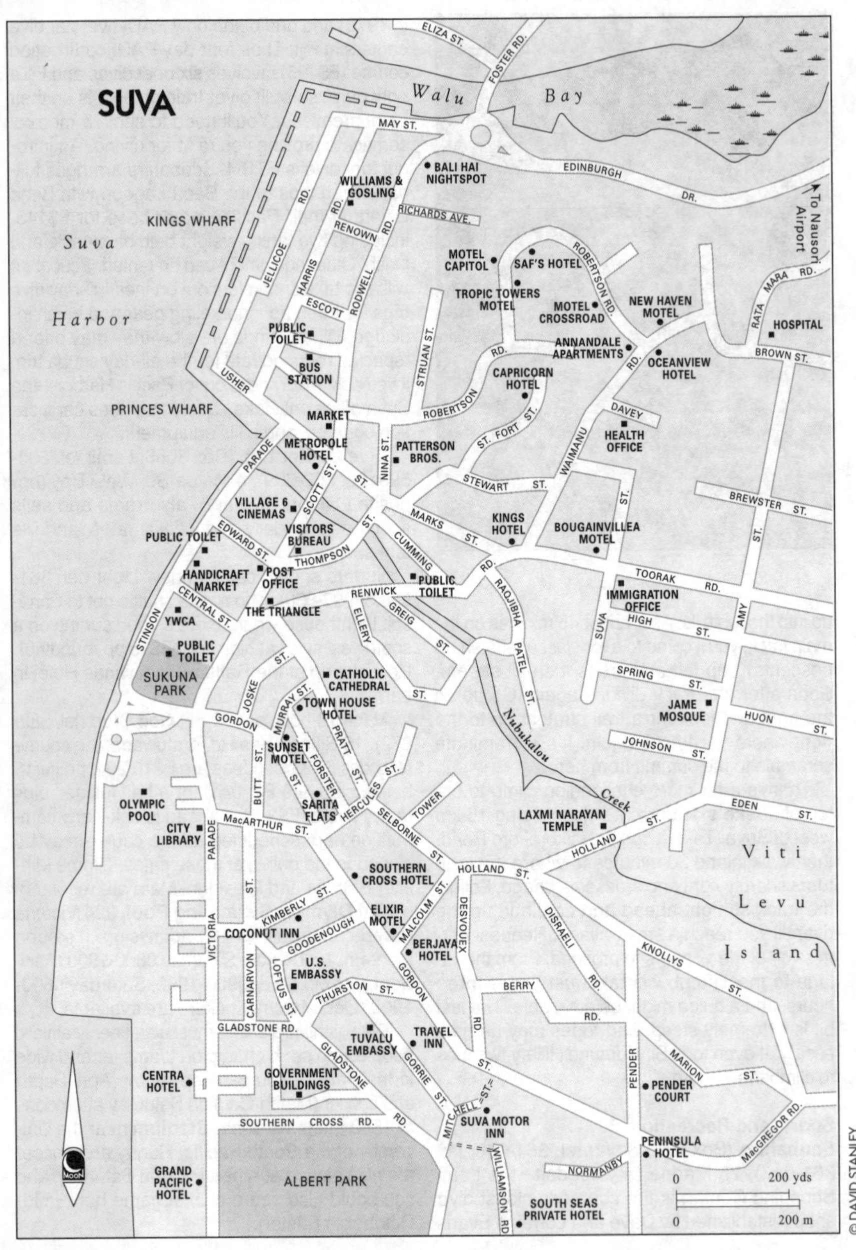
SUVA
Walu Bay
Suva Harbor
Viti Levu Island
KINGS WHARF
PRINCES WHARF
BALI HAI NIGHTSPOT
WILLIAMS & GOSLING
MOTEL CAPITOL
SAF'S HOTEL
TROPIC TOWERS MOTEL
MOTEL CROSSROAD
NEW HAVEN MOTEL
HOSPITAL
ANNANDALE APARTMENTS
OCEANVIEW HOTEL
CAPRICORN HOTEL
PUBLIC TOILET
BUS STATION
MARKET
METROPOLE HOTEL
PATTERSON BROS.
HEALTH OFFICE
VILLAGE 6 CINEMAS
VISITORS BUREAU
KINGS HOTEL
BOUGAINVILLEA MOTEL
HANDICRAFT MARKET
POST OFFICE
IMMIGRATION OFFICE
YWCA
THE TRIANGLE
SUKUNA PARK
CATHOLIC CATHEDRAL
TOWN HOUSE HOTEL
JAME MOSQUE
SUNSET MOTEL
SARITA FLATS
OLYMPIC POOL
CITY LIBRARY
LAXMI NARAYAN TEMPLE
SOUTHERN CROSS HOTEL
ELIXIR MOTEL
COCONUT INN
BERJAYA HOTEL
U.S. EMBASSY
TUVALU EMBASSY
TRAVEL INN
CENTRA HOTEL
GOVERNMENT BUILDINGS
PENDER COURT
SUVA MOTOR INN
PENINSULA HOTEL
GRAND PACIFIC HOTEL
ALBERT PARK
SOUTH SEAS PRIVATE HOTEL
To Nausori Airport
ELIZA ST.
FOSTER RD.
MAY ST.
EDINBURGH DR.
RICHARDS AVE.
RENOWN RD.
JELLICOE RD.
HARRIS RD.
RODWELL RD.
ESCOTT
ROBERTSON RD.
RATA MARA RD.
BROWN ST.
STRUAN ST.
USHER
ROBERTSON RD.
ST. FORT ST.
DAVEY
WAIMANU RD.
NINA ST.
PARADE
SCOTT ST.
STEWART ST.
BREWSTER ST.
MARKS ST.
CUMMING ST.
EDWARD ST.
THOMPSON ST.
RENWICK RD.
RAOJIBHA PATEL ST.
TOORAK RD.
CENTRAL ST.
ELLERY ST.
GREIG ST.
SUVA ST.
HIGH ST.
AMY ST.
STINSON PARADE
SPRING ST.
JOSKE ST.
MURRAY ST.
HUON ST.
GORDON ST.
PRATT ST.
JOHNSON ST.
BUTT ST.
FORSTER ST.
Nubukalou Creek
EDEN ST.
HERCULES ST.
TOWER ST.
SELBORNE ST.
MacARTHUR ST.
HOLLAND ST.
KIMBERLY ST.
MALCOLM ST.
DESVOUEX RD.
DISRAELI RD.
GOODENOUGH ST.
VICTORIA PARADE
KNOLLYS ST.
CARNARVON ST.
LOFTUS ST.
THURSTON ST.
BERRY RD.
GLADSTONE RD.
GORRIE ST.
PENDER ST.
MARION ST.
MITCHELL ST.
WILLIAMSON RD.
MacGREGOR RD.
SOUTHERN CROSS RD.
NORMANBY
0 200 yds
0 200 m
MOON

## ACCOMMODATIONS

There's a wide variety of places to stay and the low-budget accommodations can be divided into two groups. The places on the south side of the downtown area near Albert Park are mostly decent and provide communal cooking facilities to bona fide travelers. However, many of those northeast of downtown are dicey and cater mostly to "short-time" guests; few of these bother providing cooking facilities. Many of the medium-priced hotels and self-catering apartments are along Gordon Street and its continuation MacGregor Road. If you want to spend some time in Suva to take advantage of the city's good facilities and varied activities, look for something with cooking facilities and weekly rates.

### Budget Accommodations around Albert Park

The high-rise **YWCA** (Box 534, Suva; tel. 304-829, fax 303-004) on Sukuna Park has two singles and one double available for female foreign visitors only (F$10 pp).

Suva's original backpacker's oasis is the **Coconut Inn** (Box 14598, Suva; tel. 305-881, fax 700-616), 8 Kimberly St., which charges F$9 per bunk in the two four-bed dormitories. The four private rooms with shared bath are F$20/25 single/double, and a small flat upstairs with private bath is F$40 for up to three. The Inn offers cooking facilities and luggage storage (definitely, watch your gear). It's convenient to town and right on the fringe of the nightclub quarter (ask what time they lock the door if you might be returning late). It's far less crowded now than it was back in the days when it was the only cheap place to stay, and some of the long-term residents are real characters.

The 42-room **South Seas Private Hotel** (Box 2086, Government Buildings, Suva; tel. 312-296, fax 308-646), 6 Williamson Rd., one block east of Albert Park, really conveys the flavor in its name. The building originally housed workers involved in laying the first telecommunications cable across the Pacific and until 1983 it served as a girl's hostel. Things changed when backpackers took over the dormitories (and break-ins through the floorboards by amorous young men came to an end). Today you can get a bed in a five-bed dorm for F$10, a fan-cooled room with shared bath at F$16/24 single/double, or a better room with private bath at F$36 double—good value. You'll get a F$1 discount if you have a youth hostel, VIP, or Nomads card. This quiet hotel has a pleasant veranda and a large communal kitchen that may be used 0700-2000 only. For a refundable F$10 deposit, you may borrow a plate, mug, knife, fork, and spoon, but there's a longstanding shortage of pots and pans (blankets in the rooms are also in short supply). It's possible to leave excess luggage at the South Seas for free while you're off visiting other islands, but lock your bag securely with a padlock that can't be picked. The staff changes money at bank rates. It's always crowded with travelers (not all of them friendly), and you may arrive to find it full. Catch a taxi here from the market the first time (F$2). The staff can arrange daily express bus transfers from the hotel door to Tubakula Beach Resort (F$6) and Nadi (F$10).

**Travel Inn** (Box 2086, Government Buildings, Suva; tel. 304-254, fax 308-646), formerly known as Loloma Lodge and Pacific Grand Holiday Apartments, an older two-story building at 19 Gorrie St., is owned by the same company as the South Seas Private Hotel. There are 16 fan-cooled rooms with shared bath at F$19/27 single/double, all with access to communal cooking facilities, and four self-contained apartments for F$44 triple daily. A small discount is offered to youth hostel, VIP, and Nomads card holders. There are plenty of blankets and good locks on the doors. Visitors from other Pacific islands often stay here, as this is one of Suva's better buys.

For a longer stay check **Nukurua Apartments** (GPO Box 1109, Suva; tel. 312-343, fax 305-644), nearby at 25 Gorrie Street. The eight furnished a/c apartments cost F$650-750 a month (F$250 refundable cleaning deposit).

### Budget Accommodations Northeast of Downtown

The **Metropole Hotel** (Box 404, Suva; tel. 304-112), on Scott Street opposite the market, is an old-fashioned British pub gone native. There are five rooms with shared bath at F$20/28 single/double. The bars next to and below the hotel section are extremely noisy, but they close at 2100.

The **Kings Suva Hotel** (Box 15748, Suva; tel. 304-411, fax 300-103) on Waimanu Road is rougher, and the four noisy bars make it more appealing to tramps than travelers. The 27 rooms are F$20/25 single/double without bath, F$28/33 with bath, but have a look beforehand as quality varies. In short, this place is a dive.

The friendly **Bougainvillea Motel** (Box 15030, Suva; tel. 303-522, fax 303-289), 55 Toorak Rd., has 12 spacious self-contained rooms with balcony, phone, fridge, sofa, table and chairs, and coffee-making facilities at F$35 double with fan, F$45 with a/c and TV. One room has been converted into a seven-bunk dorm at F$8 pp. It's convenient to the shopping district. Don't be put off by the acid pink exterior: despite the noisy nightclubs just down the road it's surprisingly peaceful here at night.

The colorful, 44-room **Oceanview Hotel** (Box 16037, Suva; tel. 312-129), 270 Waimanu Rd., has two singles at F$20, 33 doubles at F$25, and nine four-person family rooms at F$35. It has a pleasant hillside location, but avoid staying in the noisy rooms over the reception area and bar. The new management has tried to clean the place up, and security has improved. It's one of the only "lowlife" hotels in this area with any atmosphere.

If your main interest is Suva's seedier side, two shoestring establishments are just down Robertson Road from the Oceanview. The 15-room **Motel Crossroad** (tel. 313-820), 124 Robertson Rd., is cheap at F$20 single or double, but only hookers and johns ever stay there. Similar is the 23-room **Motel Capitol** (tel. 313-246), 91 Robertson Rd., with seven rooms with shared bath at F$20 single or double, and 16 with private bath at F$25.

It's hard to place the clientele at **Saf's Apartment Hotel** (Box 3985, Samabula; tel. 301-849), on Robertson between the Crossroad and Capitol. The 40 bare rooms with bath are F$20/25 single/double downstairs, F$30/35 upstairs, or F$35/45 with TV and cooking facilities (F$10 extra for a/c). A bed in an eight-bed dorm is F$7 pp. Nice views are obtained from the upper balconies of this three-story concrete building, but it's noisy and security could be a concern.

Just up Waimanu Road from the Oceanview is the 14-room **New Haven Motel** (Box 992, Suva; tel. 315-220), which is rather dirty and used mostly for one purpose. It's F$20 single or double upstairs for all night or F$12 downstairs for a short time.

Up the hill beyond the hospital is the two-story **Outrigger Hotel** (Box 750, Suva; tel. 314-944, fax 302-944), near the hospital at 349 Waimanu Road. The 20 a/c rooms with bath and fridge are F$49/54/60 single/double/triple and there's a F$16 pp dorm (six beds). Continental breakfast is included. Most of the rooms have a good view of Suva Harbor. There's a swimming pool and Papa La Pizza is on the premises. Unfortunately, feedback about the Outrigger is mixed.

The **Tanoa House Private Hotel** (Box 704, Suva; tel. 381-575), 5 Princes Rd. in Samabula South, is a totally respectable guesthouse run by an ex-colonial from the Gilberts. The place has a garden with a view, and you meet genuine island characters. The 10 rooms with shared bath are F$20/25/30 single/double/triple; breakfast is F$5 extra, and other meals are available. It's situated across from the Fiji Institute of Technology near the end of Waimanu Road, too far to walk from downtown, but you can get there easily on the Samabula bus.

The 23 units at **Amy Apartments Motel** (Box 3985, Samabula; tel. 315-113), at 98 Amy St. several blocks east of Waimanu Road, are F$33 single or double with fan, F$48 with a/c. Many of the people staying here seem to have more on their minds than sleep, and it can be rather noisy with shouts and laughter echoing through the halls.

Another place to avoid is the **Flagstaff Boarding House** (Box 1328, Suva; tel. 313-873), 62 Rewa St., which is also well frequented by "short time" guests (F$25 single or double).

### Apartment Hotels

Several apartment hotels behind the Central Police Station are worth a try. The congenial **Town House Apartment Hotel** (Box 485, Suva; tel. 300-055, fax 303-446), 3 Forster St., is a five-story building with panoramic views from the rooftop bar (happy hour 1700-1900). The 28 a/c units with cooking facilities and fridge are good value at F$47/59/80 single/double/triple and up. Inexpensive.

Nearby and under the same ownership is the four-story **Sunset Apartment Motel** (Box 485, Suva; tel. 301-799, fax 303-446), corner of Gordon and Murray Streets. Avoid the four rooms without cooking facilities that go for F$42/46 single/double, and ask for one of the 10 two-bedroom apartments with kitchens and fridge at

F$50/64, or the deluxe apartment at F$77. The two-bedroom apartments cost F$70/88/99 for three/four/five persons. A place in their 12-bed dorm is F$9 (no cooking). Some of the cheaper rooms are noisy and have uncomfortably soft beds. Weekly rates are available. The friendly manageress, Violet, owns a fleet of taxis. Budget to inexpensive.

The Town House reception also handles bookings at **Sarita Flats** (tel. 300-084), nearby at 39 Gordon St., where a bed-sitting room apartment with cooking facilities will be F$55 single or double. This two-story building lacks the balconies and good views of the Town House. Inexpensive.

Four-story **Elixir Motel Apartments** (Box 2347, Government Buildings, Suva; tel. 303-288, fax 303-383), on the corner of Gordon and Malcolm Streets, has 14 two-bedroom apartments with cooking facilities and private bath at F$55 without a/c for up to three people, F$66 with a/c. Weekly and monthly rates are 10% lower. Inexpensive.

The **Suva Motor Inn** (Box 2500, Government Buildings, Suva; tel. 313-973, fax 300-381), a three-story complex near Albert Park, corner of Mitchell and Gorrie Streets, has 37 a/c studio apartments with kitchenette at F$99 single or double, F$119 triple (25% discount by the week). The seven two-bedroom apartments capable of accommodating five persons are F$154 for the first two, plus F$20 for each extra person. A courtyard swimming pool with waterslide and cascade faces the restaurant/bar. This new building is generally more luxurious and expensive than the others in this category, but well worth considering by families who want a bit of comfort. Moderate.

Cheaper are the apartments with fan at **Pender Court** (GPO Box 14590, Suva; tel. 314-992, fax 387-840), 31 Pender Street. The 13 studios with kitchenettes begin at F$40 single or double (10% reduction by the week), and there are also six one-bedroom apartments with kitchens for F$50 (reduced rates possible). It's sometimes a little noisy but good value. Budget.

Eleven better self-catering units owned by the National Olympic Committee are available at **Suva Apartments** (Box 12488, Suva; tel. 304-280, fax 301-647), 17 Bau St., a block or two east of Pender Court. They're F$30/35/47 single/double/triple daily, with 10% off on weekly rentals. Be prepared for traffic noise. Budget.

Up in the Waimanu Road area, the **Capricorn Apartment Hotel** (Box 1261, Suva; tel. 303-732, fax 303-069), 7 St. Fort St., has 34 spacious a/c units with cooking facilities, fridge, and TV beginning at F$85 single or double, F$95 triple, plus tax. The three- and four-story apartment blocks edge the swimming pool, and there are good views of the harbor from the individual balconies. Inexpensive.

**Tropic Towers Apartment Motel** (Box 1347, Suva; tel. 304-470, fax 304-169), 86 Robertson Rd., has 34 a/c apartments with cooking facilities in a four-story building starting at F$60/72/83 single/double/triple. Ask about the 13 "budget" units in the annex, which are F$33/44 single/double with shared bath. Washing machines (F$9) and a swimming pool are available for guests; screened windows or mosquito nets are not. This and the Capricorn are good choices for families. Budget to inexpensive.

One of the best deals up this way is the **Annandale Apartments** (Box 12818, Suva; tel. 311-054), 265 Waimanu Road opposite the Oceanview Hotel. The 12 spacious two-bedroom apartments are F$45/200/600 a day/week/month for up to three or four people. A fridge, kitchen, sitting room, and balcony are provided in each. Budget.

### Upmarket Hotels

Suva's largest hotel is the **Centra Suva** (Box 1357, Suva; tel. 301-600, fax 300-251), formerly the Travelodge, on the waterfront opposite the Government Buildings. It's a big American-style place with 130 a/c rooms with fridge and TV beginning at F$135 single or double plus tax. The swimming pool behind the two-story buildings compensates for the lack of a beach. Special events here include "island night" on Wednesday with a *meke* at 2000, and the Sunday poolside barbecue lunch. Expensive.

Your best bet if you want to go upmarket are the Southern Cross, Berjaya, and Peninsula International hotels, all within minutes of one another along Gordon Street. You can save money by calling ahead to all three to inquire about that day's "local rate," then take a taxi to the place of your choice. When things are slow, the receptionist may also agree to upgrade you to deluxe at no additional charge if you agree to stay for a few days. Of course, these deals don't apply to overseas bookings.

Suva's Grand Pacific Hotel in its heyday

OUTRIGGER HOTELS

The **Southern Cross Hotel** (Box 1076, Suva; tel. 314-233, fax 302-901) is a high-rise concrete building at 63 Gordon Street. The 35 a/c rooms are F$69/79/88 single/double/triple. Beware of rooms on the lower floors, which are blasted by band music six nights a week. The hotel restaurant on the 6th floor serves delicious Fijian and Korean dishes. Inexpensive.

The nine-story **Berjaya Hotel** (Box 112, Suva; tel. 312-300, fax 301-300), part of the Best Western chain, at the corner of Malcolm and Gordon Streets, is the tallest hotel in Fiji. The 48 a/c rooms with fridge and TV all face the harbor. It's F$134 single or double on the lower floors or F$146 on the upper floors and on those days when they're giving the reduced "local rate" the Berjaya becomes the best value top end hotel in Suva. This Malaysian-owned hotel hosts Suva's only Malaysian restaurant. Moderate to expensive.

The **Peninsula International Hotel** (Box 888, Suva; tel. 313-711, fax 314-473), at the corner of MacGregor Road and Pender Street, is a stylish four-floor building with swimming pool. The 39 a/c rooms begin at F$55/72 single/double, while the eight suites with kitchenettes run F$72/89. Inexpensive.

The 108-room **Raffles Tradewinds Hotel** (Box 3377, Lami; tel. 362-450, fax 361-464), at Lami on the Bay of Islands seven km west of Suva, includes a 500-seat convention center and floating seafood restaurant. Rates are F$132/149/172 single/double/triple with private bath, fridge, and a/c, breakfast included but plus tax. Many cruising yachts anchor here. Though bus service into Suva is good, the location is inconvenient for those without a car. Moderate.

### Camping

Nukulau, a tiny reef island southeast of Suva, was the site of the residence of the first U.S. consul to Fiji, John Brown Williams, and the burning of the house on 4 July 1849 set in motion a chain of events that led to Fiji becoming a British colony. Later Nukulau was used as the government quarantine station, and most indentured Indian laborers spent their first two weeks in Fiji here. Today it's a public park where camping is allowed.

Free three-day camping permits are available during office hours from the Divisional Surveyor (tel. 315-836), Central/Eastern Office, Lands and Surveys Department, Suva Point. Take a taxi to the office or the Nasese bus from the market.

There's a caretaker and toilets on the island and drinking water is available, but you must take your own food. The swimming is good. Matthew Light (tel. 361-560 or 998-830) ferries groups back and forth from Nukulau in his speedboat at F$50 return for the boat.

## FOOD

### Downtown Eateries

One of the few places serving a regular cooked breakfast is the **Palm Court Bistro** (tel. 304-

662; Mon.-Fri. 0700-1700, Saturday 0700-1430) in the Queensland Insurance Arcade behind Air New Zealand on Victoria Parade. Their burgers and sandwiches are good at lunchtime.

**Judes** (tel. 315-461; closed Sunday), in the arcade opposite Sukuna Park, also has good sandwiches at lunchtime and reasonable coffee. An inexpensive snack bar with concrete outdoor picnic tables is at the back side of the Handicraft Market facing the harbor (the "long soup" is a bargain).

Economical snacks are also served at **Donald's Kitchen** (tel. 315-587), 103 Cumming Street. One block over on Marks Street are cheaper Chinese restaurants, such as **Kim's Cafe** (tel. 313-252), 128 Marks St., where you can get a toasted egg sandwich and coffee for about a dollar fifty. There are scores more cheap milk bars around Suva, and you'll find them for yourself as you stroll around town.

An Austrian reader sent us this:

*Why didn't you mention the market stalls? Burgers for F$1, yummy cakes for 50 cents, curry wrapped up in* roti *also 50 cents, juices (not only guava and pineapple, but all kinds) for 20 cents, lots of* ivi *(chestnuts) for F$1, etc. It's the budget place to eat, and nice social surroundings too.*

### Fijian

A popular place to sample Fijian food is the **Old Mill Cottage Cafe** (tel. 312-134; closed Sunday and evenings), 49 Carnarvon St.—the street behind the Golden Dragon nightclub. Government employees from nearby offices descend on this place at lunchtime for the inexpensive curried freshwater mussels, curried chicken livers, fresh seaweed in coconut milk, taro leaves creamed in coconut milk, and fish cooked in coconut milk. It's great, but don't come for coffee as it's cold and overpriced.

### Indian

The **Hare Krishna Vegetarian Restaurant** (tel. 314-154; closed Sunday), at the corner of Pratt and Joske Streets, serves ice cream (12 flavors), sweets, and snacks downstairs, main meals upstairs (available Mon.-Sat. 1100-1430, Friday also 1900-2100). If you want the all-you-can-eat vegetarian *thali* (F$6.50), just sit down and they'll bring it to you. But if you're not that starved, go up to the self-service counter and pick up a couple of vegetable dishes, which you can have with one or two rotis. This will cost about half as much as the full meal, though ordering individual dishes can be unexpectedly expensive, so unless you want the full meal it's better to look elsewhere. No smoking or alcohol are allowed.

Another laudable Indian place is the **Curry House** (tel. 313-000 or 313-756; closed Sunday) at two locations: 87 Cumming St., and next to the Ming Palace in the old town hall on Victoria Parade. Their special vegetarian *thali* (F$3) is an exceptional lunch and they also have quality meat curries from F$5. Try the takeaway *rotis*.

The **Top Taste Cafe de Curry** (Mon.-Sat. 0830-1730), just across Nubukalou Creek from Morris Hedstrom Supermarket, around the corner from Cumming St., has a large selection of Indian curry dishes and a nice covered terrace on which to eat them.

### Chinese

Not many Indian restaurants in Suva are open at night or on Sunday, so this is when you should turn to the many excellent, inexpensive Chinese restaurants. Most serve beer while the Indian restaurants are usually "dry."

The **Diamond Palace Restaurant** (tel. 303-848), upstairs at 30 Cumming St., serves generous portions, and the staff and surroundings are pleasant. **Geralyne's Restaurant** (tel. 311-037; closed Sunday), 160 Renwick Rd., is similar.

Also try the good-value **Lantern Palace Restaurant** (tel. 314-633) at 10 Pratt St. near Hare Krishna. The **Guang Wha Restaurant** next door to the Lantern Palace is cheaper and more likely to be open on holidays.

The more expensive **Sichuan Pavilion Restaurant** (tel. 315-194), upstairs in the old Garrick Hotel building at 6 Thomson St., is perhaps Suva's finest Asian restaurant. Employees of the Chinese Embassy frequent it for the spicy-hot Chinese dishes (though they're not as hot as Sichuan food elsewhere). Weather permitting, sit outside on the balcony and watch all Suva go by.

The **Phoenix Restaurant** (tel. 311-889), 165 Victoria Parade, has inexpensive Chinese dishes like red pork with fried rice (F$6) and big bottles of beer. Just ignore the horrific green painted walls and the odd cockroach running around.

The popular **Peking Restaurant** (tel. 312-714; daily 1130-2230), 195 Victoria Parade, is only a bit more expensive than the Chinese places with their dishes in warmers at the entrance but the atmosphere is nicer and the meals are individually prepared. Small parties of four or more can order set dinner menus served in the traditional Chinese banquet manner (F$8.50 pp and up). To sample all the specialties of the house, eight hours advance notice and a group of at least six is required (F$18 pp).

Suva's most imposing Chinese restaurant by far is the 250-seat **Ming Palace** (tel. 315-111) in the old town hall next to the public library on Victoria Parade.

**Fong Lee Seafood Restaurant,** 293 Victoria Parade, is more expensive than the Peking Restaurant and the dining area isn't as agreeable but the food is said to be the tastiest in Suva (notice the many affluent local Chinese having dinner there). Lunch is cheaper than dinner at the Fong Lee, or you can eat at the **Zifu Restaurant** (tel. 313-988) next door for a third the price (the Zifu is highly recommended for lunch).

The top place to eat Chinese style near the Raffles Tradewinds Hotel yacht anchorage is the **Castle Restaurant** (tel. 361-223; closed Sunday) in the Lami Shopping Center.

### Better Restaurants

**Tiko's Floating Restaurant** (tel. 313-626; dinner only) is housed in the MV *Lycianda,* an ex-Blue Lagoon cruise ship launched at Suva in 1970 and now anchored off Stinson Parade behind Sukuna Park. Their steaks and seafood are good for a splurge and there's a bar called the Engineroom.

**Cardo's Chargrill** (tel. 314-330), in Regal Lane around behind the Qantas and Air Pacific offices, is run by descendants of Espero Cardo, an Argentine gaucho said to have arrived on a Koro Sea cruise in the early 1800s only to have his cattle rustled from belowdecks by Fijian warriors. What's known for sure is that today you can sit at a table with a view of Suva Harbor and consume steaks of 250, 300, or 450 grams priced from F$13-25. Fancier dishes on the main menu cater to other tastes.

**JJ's Bar & Grill** (tel. 305-005), at 10 Gordon St. just up from Sukuna Park, is a smart yuppie place with daily specials listed on blackboards. Soups, salads, and sandwiches are available at lunch, and if you don't want any of the main courses it's just as good to order a couple of appetizer dishes (the calamari friti come recommended).

Two trendy upmarket restaurants are at Flagstaff, halfway out to the university (take a taxi). The **Great Wok of China** (tel. 301-285), corner of Bau St. and Laucala Bay Rd., features spicy Sichuan food, while the **Blue Palm** (tel. 314-998) on Rewa St. just opposite has a steak and seafood menu as well as more Chinese food.

## ENTERTAINMENT AND EVENTS

In 1996 **Village Six Cinemas** (tel. 306-006) opened on Scott St. and you now have a choice of six Hollywood films several times a day. Regular admission is F$4, reduced to F$3 on Tuesday. The air conditioning is a relief on a hot day. Most of Suva's other cinemas show Asian karate films or Indian movies in Hindi, and it's much easier to check their listings in the *Fiji Times* than to make the rounds in person. The films change every three days at downmarket cinemas like the Century (tel. 311-641), 67 Marks St., Lilac (tel. 311-411), 10 Waimanu Rd., and the Phoenix (tel. 300-094), 192 Rodwell Road north of the bus station. Admission there is F$2 for a hard seat or F$3 for a soft seat.

The only regular cultural show in Suva is "island night" at the Centra Suva (tel. 301-600) Wednesday at 1900, which features Polynesian dancing at 2000.

The **Fiji Indian Cultural Center** (tel. 300-050), 271 Toorak Rd., offers classes in Indian music, dancing, art, etc. It's well worth calling to find out if any public performances are scheduled during your visit.

The top time to be in Suva is in August during the **Hibiscus Festival** fills Albert Park with stalls, games, and carnival revelers.

### Nightclubs

There are many nightclubs, all of which have nominal weekend cover charges and require neat dress, although nothing much happens until after 2200, and women shouldn't enter alone.

Late at night, it's wise to take a taxi back to your hotel. Suva is still a very safe city, but nasty, violent robberies do occur.

Gays will feel comfortable at **Lucky Eddie's** (tel. 312-884; daily after 2000), 217 Victoria Parade, but it's not really a gay bar, as the Fijian women present try to prove.

**Signals Night Club** (tel. 313-590; Mon.-Sat. 1800-0100), at 255 Victoria Parade opposite the Suva City Library, charges F$3 cover after 2000 Thurs.-Sat. only.

A shade rougher but also very popular is the **Golden Dragon** (tel. 311-018; open Mon.-Sat. 1930-0100), 379 Victoria Parade.

**Birdland Jazz Club** (tel. 303-833), 6 Carnarvon St., back behind the Shell service station on Victoria Parade, is open Tues.-Sun. from 1800 with outstanding live rhythm and blues from 2230 on Thursday, Saturday, and Sunday (F$3 cover). Other nights there's recorded jazz. It's a late night place where people come after they've been to the others. **Bojangles Night Club,** adjacent to Birdland, is a disco open nightly from 1800 (F$3 cover after 2200).

**The Barn** (tel. 307-845), 54 Carnarvon St., is a popular country and western club open Mon.-Thurs. 1900-0100, Friday 1800-0100, Saturday 1930-0100 (live entertainment and a F$5 cover from 2100).

The most interracial of the clubs is **Chequers Nightspot** (tel. 313-563), 27 Waimanu Rd., which has live music nightly except Sunday. Hang onto your wallet here.

For real earthy atmosphere try the **Bali Hai** (tel. 315-868), at 194 Rodwell Rd., the roughest club in Suva. Friday and Saturday nights the place is packed with Fijians (no Indians) and tourists are rare, so beware. If you're looking for action, you'll be able to pick a partner within minutes, but take care with aggressive males. The dance hall on the top floor is the swingingest, with body-to-body jive—the Bali Hai will rock you.

### Bars

**O'Reilly's Pub** (tel. 312-968), 5 MacArthur St., just around the corner from Lucky Eddie's, has a happy hour with local beer at F$1 a mug weekdays 1700-1945, Saturday 1800-1945. It's a nice relaxed way to kick off a night on the town, and with the big sports screen and canned music it's super. They're open Sunday from 1800.

The **Bad Dog Cafe,** next door to O'Reilly's, is a trendy wine bar with a whimsical name serving margaritas, sangria, and a dozen imported beers. Mexican dishes are on the food menu and for F$6 corkage you may BYO bottle of wine from the adjacent Victoria Wines shop. A back door from Bad Dog leads into the **Wolfhound Bar,** Suva's second mock Irish pub.

**Traps Bar** (tel. 312-922; Mon.-Sat. from 1800), at 305 Victoria Parade next to the Shell service station, is a groupie Suva social scene with a happy hour until 2000 (drunks are unwelcome here). There's live music on Wednesday.

**Shooters Bar,** at 58 Carnarvon St. next to The Barn, has a happy hour Mon.-Sat. 1700-

DAVID STANLEY

*Suva Bowling Club*

2000. They play harder rock music than the others and the atmosphere is somewhere between O'Reilly's and Traps.

The bar at the **Suva Lawn Bowling Club** (tel. 302-394), facing the lagoon opposite Thurston Botanical Gardens and just off Albert Park, is a very convenient place to down a large bottle of Fiji Bitter—the perfect place for a cold one after visiting the museum. You can sit and watch the bowling, or see the sun set over Viti Levu. Foreign tourists are welcome.

Those in search of more subdued drinking should try the **Piano Bar** at the Centra Suva, which often presents rather good jazz singers, or the **Rooftop Garden Bar** at the Town House Motel (tel. 300-055) which has a happy hour 1700-1900.

## SHOPPING

The **Government Handicraft Center** (tel. 211-306) behind Ratu Sukuna House, MacArthur and Carnarvon Streets, is a low-pressure place to familiarize yourself with what is authentic, though prices are high here, making it better to do your buying elsewhere. **Jacks Handicrafts,** Renwick Road and Pier St., has a representative selection of Fijian crafts with prices clearly marked.

The large **Curio and Handicraft Market** (Mon.-Sat. 0800-1700) on the waterfront behind the post office is a good place to haggle over crafts, so long as you know what is really Fijian (avoid masks and "tikis"). Unfortunately many of the vendors are rather aggressive and it's not possible to shop around in peace. Never come here on the day when a cruise ship is in port—prices shoot up. And watch out for the annoying "sword sellers" mentioned under "Dangers and Annoyances" in the main introduction as they could accost you anywhere in Suva.

For clothing see the fashionable hand-printed shirts and dresses at **Tiki Togs** (tel. 304-381), 38 Thomson St. across from the General Post Office, and at 199 Victoria Parade next to Pizza Hut. You could come out looking like a real South Seas character at a reasonable price. Also check **Sogo Fiji** (tel. 315-007), on Cumming Street and on Victoria Parade next to the Bank of Hawaii.

Cumming Street is Suva's busiest shopping street. Expect to receive a 10-40% discount at the "duty-free" shops by bargaining, but *shop around* before you buy. Be especially wary when purchasing gold jewelry, as it might be fake. And watch out for hustlers who will try to show you around and get you a "good price." The large **Morris Hedstrom** store across Nubukalou Creek from Cumming Street has a good selection of sunscreens.

**J.R. White & Co.** (tel. 302-325), in the mall behind Air New Zealand, has all kinds of sporting equipment (but not camping gear or backpacks). They can repair worn-out zippers.

**Sumit Cycles** (tel. 300-135), 41 Toorak Road, sells new and used bicycles and does repairs.

The **Philatelic Bureau** (Box 100, Suva; tel. 312-928) at the General Post Office sells the stamps of Niue, Pitcairn, Samoa, Solomon Islands, Tuvalu, and Vanuatu, as well as those of Fiji. To place a standing order from overseas, send a credit card authorization for F$30 deposit.

## SERVICES

### Money

Rates at the banks vary slightly and you might get a dollar or two more on a large exchange by checking the Westpac Bank, ANZ Bank, and Bank of Hawaii before signing your checks. All of them have branches on Victoria Parade near The Triangle (several have ATMs).

**Thomas Cook Travel** (tel. 301-603), opposite the General Post Office, changes foreign currency Mon.-Fri. 0830-1700, Saturday 0830-1200, at competitive rates, and sells the banknotes of neighboring countries like New Caledonia, Samoa, Solomon Islands, Tonga, and Vanuatu—convenient if you're headed for any of them.

On Sunday and holidays changing money is a problem (try your hotel if you get stuck).

### Telecommunications

Fintel, the **Fiji International Telecommunications** office (tel. 312-933, fax 301-025), 158 Victoria Parade, is open Mon.-Sat. 0800-2000 for long-distance calls and telegrams. The six private card phone booths here are the most convenient place in Suva to place either local or inter-

DAVID STANLEY

Parliament building, Suva, Viti Levu

national calls. The basic charge for three minutes is F$4.74 to Australia or New Zealand, F$8.01 to North America and Europe (no minimum when using card phones). There's a 25% discount on international calls from card phones daily 2200-0600 and all day on weekends.

The public fax at Suva General Post Office is fax 302-666 should you need to receive a fax from anyone.

Internet access is available at the **Telecom Fiji Customer Care Center** (tel. 311-342; www.is.com.fj; Mon.-Fri. 0800-1630), opposite the General Post Office and Fiji Visitors Bureau. The charge is F$3.30 for the first 15 minutes, then 22 cents each additional minute, and it's possible to book ready access at a set time by calling ahead or dropping in.

**Immigration**

The **Immigration Office** (tel. 312-622; Mon.-Fri. 0830-1300/1400-1500) for extensions of stay, etc., is at the corner of Toorak Road and Suva Street.

Cruising yachts wishing to visit the outer islands must first obtain a free permit from the Provincial Development Unit at the **Ministry for Fijian Affairs** (Box 2100, Government Buildings, Suva; tel. 304-200), 61 Carnarvon Street. They'll want to see the customs papers for the boat and all passports but the procedure is fast and friendly. (Yachties anchoring off a Fijian village should present a *sevusevu* of kava to the chief.)

**Consulates**

The following countries have diplomatic missions in Suva: **China** (tel. 300-215), 147 Queen Elizabeth Dr., Suva Point; **Chile** (tel. 300-433), Asgar & Co., Queensland Insurance Arcade behind Air New Zealand, Victoria Parade; **European Union** (tel. 313-633), 4th floor, Development Bank Center, 360 Victoria Parade; **Federated States of Micronesia** (tel. 304-566), 37 Loftus St.; **France** (tel. 312-233), 1st floor, Dominion House, Scott St.; **Germany** (tel. 315-000), 4th floor, Dominion House, Scott St.; **Japan** (tel. 304-633), 2nd floor, Dominion House, Scott St.; **Korea** (tel. 300-977), Vanua House, Victoria Parade; **Malaysia** (tel. 312-166), 5th floor, Pacific House, Butt and MacArthur Streets; **Marshall Islands** (tel. 387-899), 41 Borron Rd., Samabula; **Nauru** (tel. 313-566), 7th floor, Ratu Sukuna House, Victoria Parade and MacArthur; **New Zealand** (tel. 311-422), 10th floor, Reserve Bank Building, Pratt St.; **Papua New Guinea** (tel. 304-244), 3rd floor, Credit Corporation Building, Gordon and Malcolm Streets; **Taiwan** (tel. 315-922), 6th floor, Pacific House, Butt and MacArthur Streets; **Tuvalu** (tel. 301-355), 16 Gorrie St.; **United Kingdom** (tel. 311-033), 47 Gladstone Rd.; and the **U.S.A.** (tel. 314-466, fax 300-081), 31 Loftus Street. Canada and Italy have honorary consuls at Nadi.

Everyone other than New Zealanders requires a visa to visit Australia, and these are readily available free of charge at the **Australian Embassy** (Box 214, Suva; tel. 382-219; Mon.-Fri.

0830-1200), 10 Reservoir Rd., off Princes Road, Samabula. You can also sit and read week-old Australian newspapers here. To get there it's probably easier to take a taxi, then return to town on the Samabula bus.

### Public Toilets

Public toilets are just outside the Handicraft Market on the side of the building facing the harbor; beside Nubukalou Creek off Renwick Road; and between the vegetable market and the bus station. Some are free, others charge five cents a visit. The public toilets in Sukuna Park are 24 cents.

### Yachting Facilities

The **Royal Suva Yacht Club** (Box 335, Suva; tel. 312-921, fax 304-433, channel 16), on Foster Road between Suva and Lami, offers visiting yachts such amenities as mooring privileges, warm showers, laundry facilities, cheap drinks, and the full use of club services by the whole crew for F$30 a week. Tuesday and Friday nights there are barbecues (F$6.50). There have been reports of thefts from boats anchored here, so watch out. Many yachts anchor off the Raffles Tradewinds Hotel on the Bay of Islands, a recognized hurricane anchorage.

## INFORMATION

The **Fiji Visitors Bureau** (tel. 302-433; Mon.-Fri. 0800-1630, Saturday 0800-1200) is on Thomson Street across from the General Post Office.

The **Tourism Council of the South Pacific** (tel. 304-177, fax 301-995), FNPF Plaza, 3rd Floor, 343-359 Victoria Parade at Loftus St., provides general brochures on the entire South Pacific. Ask for a copy of their free guidebook *The South Pacific Islands Travel Planner.*

The **Bureau of Statistics** (Box 2221, Suva; tel. 315-144, fax 303-656), 4th floor, Ratu Sukuna House, Victoria Parade and MacArthur, has many interesting technical publications on the country and a library where you may browse.

The **Maps and Plans Room** (tel. 211-395; Mon.-Thurs. 0900-1300 and 1400-1530, Friday 0900-1300 and 1400-1500) of the Lands and Survey Department, Ground Floor, Government Buildings, sells excellent topographical maps of Fiji.

**Carpenters Shipping** (tel. 312-244), 4th Floor, Neptune House, Tofua Street, Walu Bay, sells British navigational charts (F$43 each). Nearby is the **Fiji Hydrographic Office** (tel. 315-457; Mon.-Fri. 0830-1300 and 1400-1600), Top Floor, Freeston Rd., Walu Bay, with local navigational charts at F$16.50 a sheet.

### Bookstores

Suva's number one bookstore is the **USP Book Center** (tel. 313-900, fax 303-265; Mon.-Thurs 0830-1615, Friday 0830-1545) at the Laucala Bay university campus. Not only do they have one of the finest Pacific sections in the region, but they stock the publications of some 20 occasional publishers affiliated with the university and you can turn up some intriguing items. Also visit the Book Display Room in the **Institute of Pacific Studies** building, not far from the Book Center. They sell assorted books by local authors published by the IPS itself.

The **Methodist Book Center** (tel. 311-466), 11 Stewart St. adjacent to Centenary Methodist Church, has a good selection of local books on Fiji and the Pacific.

The **Desai Bookshop** (tel. 314-088), on Thomson Street opposite the General Post Office, has a shelf of books on Fiji. The **Fiji Museum** shop sells a few excellent books at reasonable prices.

**Missions to Seamen** (tel. 300-911; Mon.-Fri. 0900-1300 and 1330-1600), on the main wharf (inside—go through the security gate), trades used paperback books one for one.

### Libraries

The **Suva City Library** (Box 176, Suva; tel. 313-433, extension 241; Monday, Tuesday, Thursday, Friday 0930-1800, Wednesday 1200-1800, Saturday 0900-1300), at 196 Victoria Parade, allows visitors to take out four books upon payment of a refundable F$20 deposit. Ask if they have any old paperbacks for sale.

The library at the Laucala Campus of the **University of the South Pacific** (tel. 212-402) is open Mon.-Fri. 0800-1600 year-round. During semesters they also open the library on Saturday, Sunday afternoon, and in the evening. A library tour is offered Friday at 0900. You'll find the reading room with international newspapers downstairs.

The **Alliance Française** (Box 14548, Suva; tel. 313-802, fax 313-803), 77 Cakobau Rd., has an excellent selection of French books, magazines, and newspapers. You're welcome to peruse materials in the reading room Mon.-Fri. 0830-1200 and 1300-1700. Ask about their video and film evenings.

**Ecology Groups**

The **Greenpeace Pacific Campaign** headquarters (tel. 305-031, fax 312-784) is above the Ming Palace Restaurant in the old town hall on Victoria Parade.

The **Pacific Concerns Resource Center** (tel. 304-649, fax 304-755), 83 Amy St. off Toorak Road (enter from the rear of the building), sells a number of issue-related books and booklets on social and political questions in the South Pacific. The Center is the directing body of the Nuclear-Free and Independent Pacific (NFIP) movement, a grassroots coalition opposing colonialism.

The **South Pacific Action Committee for Human Ecology and Environment** or SPACHEE (Box 16737, Suva; tel. 312-371, fax 303-053; Mon.-Fri. 0830-1630) has a resource center at the junction of Ratu Cakobau, Domain, and Denison Roads, a block back from the South Seas Private Hotel.

The **National Trust for Fiji** (Box 2089, Government Buildings, Suva; tel. 301-807, fax 305-092), 3 Ma'afu St., manages eight nature reserves and historic sites around Fiji. Their neighbor, the **World Wide Fund for Nature** (Private Mail Bag, GPO Suva; tel. 315-533, fax 315-410), 4 Ma'afu St., assists various projects around the country for the support of wildlife and wild habitats.

**Travel Agents**

**Hunts Travel** (Box 686, Suva; tel. 315-288, fax 302-212), in the Dominion House arcade behind the Fiji Visitors Bureau, is the place to pick up air tickets. They often know more about Air Pacific flights than the Air Pacific employees themselves!

Also compare **Travelworld Services** (tel. 315-870, fax 303-729), 18 Waimanu Rd., which gives five percent discounts on plane tickets to other Pacific countries.

**Rosie The Travel Service** (tel. 314-436), 46 Gordon St., books tours and accommodations all around Fiji.

**Airline Offices**

Reconfirm your onward flight reservations at your airlines' Suva office: **Aircalin** (tel. 302-133), Provident Plaza One, Ellery St.; **Air Fiji** (tel. 313-666), 185 Victoria Parade (also represents Air Vanuatu and Polynesian Airlines); **Air Marshall Islands** (tel. 303-888), Vanua Arcade, Victoria Parade; **Air Nauru** (tel. 312-377), Ratu Sukuna House, 249 Victoria Parade; **Air New Zealand** (tel. 313-100), Queensland Insurance Center, Victoria Parade; **Air Pacific** (tel. 304-388), CML Building, Victoria Parade; **Qantas Airways** (tel. 311-833), CML Building, Victoria Parade; **Solomon Airlines** (tel. 315-889), Global Air Service, 3 Ellery St., and **Sunflower Airlines** (tel. 315-755), Honson Arcade on Thompson St. opposite the Fiji Visitors Bureau (also represents Royal Tongan Airlines). While you're there, check your seat assignment.

## HEALTH

Suva's **Colonial War Memorial Hospital** (tel. 313-444), on Waimanu Rd. about a kilometer northeast of the center, is available 24 hours a day in emergencies. The hospital charges commercial rates to nonresidents so in non-life-threatening situations you're better off seeing a private doctor.

The poorly marked **Health Office** (tel. 314-988; open Mon.-Fri. 0800-1630), on Davey Ave. off Waimanu Road near the YMCA, gives tetanus, polio, and yellow fever vaccinations Tuesday and Friday 0800-1000. They're free, except yellow fever, which is F$16.

You'll receive good attention at the **Gordon St. Medical Center** (tel. 313-355, fax 302-423), Gordon and Thurston Streets (basic consultations F$15). There's a female doctor there. The **Fiji Recompression Chamber Facility** (tel. 305-154 or 850-630) is adjacent to this clinic (donated by the Cousteau Society in 1992).

The **J.P. Bayly Clinic** (tel. 315-888, weekdays 0800-1600), 190 Rodwell Rd. opposite the Phoenix Cinema, accommodates four doctors and a female dentist (Dr. Satya Khan).

Two other dentists are Dr. David M. Charya (tel. 302-160), The Dental Center, 59 Cumming St.; and Dr. Abdul S. Haroon (tel. 313-870), Suite 12, Epworth House off Nina Street (just down the hall from Patterson Brothers). Dr. Haroon has treated many visitors, including me.

## TRANSPORTATION

Although nearly all international flights to Fiji arrive at Nadi, Suva is still the most important transportation center in the country. Interisland shipping crowds the harbor, and if you can't find a ship going precisely your way at the time you want to travel, Air Fiji and Sunflower Airlines fly to all the major Fiji islands, while Air Pacific serves New Zealand, Tonga, and Samoa—all from Nausori Airport. Make the rounds of the shipping offices listed below, then head over to Walu Bay to check the information. Compare the price of a cabin and deck passage, and ask if meals are included. Start checking early, as many domestic services within Fiji are only once a week and trips to other countries are far less frequent.

A solid block of buses awaits your patronage at the market bus station near the harbor, with continuous local service, and frequent long-distance departures to Nadi and Lautoka. Many of the points of interest around Suva are accessible on foot, but if you wander too far, jump on any bus headed in the right direction and you'll end up back in the market. Taxis are also easy to find and relatively cheap.

Suva's bus station can be a little confusing as there are many different companies, and time tables are not posted. Most drivers know where a certain bus will park, so just ask. For information on bus services around Viti Levu and domestic flights from Nausori Airport, see "Getting Around" in the main introduction. Shipping services from Suva are covered below.

### Ships to Other Countries

The Wednesday issue of the *Fiji Times* carries a special section on international shipping, though most are container ships that don't accept passengers. Most shipping is headed for Tonga and Samoa—there's not much going westward, and actually getting on any of the ships mentioned below requires considerable persistence. It's often easier to sign on as crew on a yacht. Try both yacht anchorages in Suva: put up a notice, ask around, etc.

**Carpenters Shipping** (tel. 312-244, fax 301-572), 4th Floor, Neptune House, Tofua Street, Walu Bay, is an agent for the *Moana,* which sails occasionally from Suva to Wallis and Futuna, then on to Nouméa. This ship *does* accept passengers, although Carpenters may advise otherwise. If you get this story just find out when the ship will arrive at Suva, then go and see the captain. This is a beautiful trip, not at all crowded between Fiji and Wallis. Book a cabin, however, if you're going right through to Nouméa.

Carpenters is also an agent for the monthly **Bank Line** service to Lautoka, Port Vila, Luganville, Honiara, Papua New Guinea, and on to Great Britain. Again, they cannot sell you a passenger ticket and will only tell you when the ship is due in port and where it's headed. It's up to you to make arrangements personally with the captain, and the fare won't be cheap.

The **Pacific Forum Line** (tel. 315-444, fax 302-754), 187 Rodwell Rd., will know about container ships from Suva to Apia, Pago Pago, and Nuku'alofa, such as the Samoan government-owned *Forum Samoa* (every three weeks) and the Tongan government-owned *Fua Kavenga* (monthly service). The office doesn't sell passenger tickets, so just ask when these ships will be in port, then go and talk to the captain, who is the only one who can decide if you'll be able to go.

The **Tuvalu Embassy** (Box 14449, Suva; tel. 301-355, fax 301-023), 16 Gorrie St., runs the *Nivaga II* to Funafuti about four times a year, but the dates are variable. Tickets are F$124 without meals or F$200 with meals second class, F$139 without meals or F$215 with meals first class, F$70 deck. They only know approximately a week beforehand when the ship may sail. After reaching Funafuti, the ship cruises the Tuvalu Group.

**Williams & Gosling Ltd. Ships Agency** (Box 79, Suva; tel. 312-633, fax 307-358), 80 Harris Rd. near the market bus station, books passengers on the Kiribati Shipping Services vessel *Nei Matangare,* which leaves Suva for Funafuti and Tarawa about once a month. The three-day trip to Funafuti costs A$95/190 deck/cabin one way, otherwise the seven-day journey Suva-Tarawa with a day at Funafuti is A$184/368, meals included. The ship spends a week at Tarawa before returning to Fiji, so on a single roundtrip journey you could either have a week at Tarawa or two weeks at Funafuti.

**Ferries to Ovalau Island**

Air Fiji flies from Suva to Levuka (F$54) two or three times a day, but the most popular ways to go are the bus/launch/bus combinations via Natovi or Bau Landing. Two different companies operate these trips, which take four or five hours right through. Reservations are recommended on Saturday and public holidays.

The **Patterson Brothers** service (book at their Suva office mentioned below) leaves from the Western Bus Stand in Suva Mon.-Sat. at 1400 (F$24). This express bus goes from Suva to Natovi (67 km), where it drives onto a ferry to Buresala on Ovalau, then continues to Levuka, where it arrives around 1745. For the return journey you leave the Patterson Brothers office in Levuka Mon.-Sat. at 0500, arriving in Suva at 0800. Bus tickets must be purchased in advance at the office—no exceptions. Bicycles are carried free on the ferry.

The second option is the ***Emosi Express,*** departing Suva Monday, Wednesday, and Friday at 1200 for Bau Landing, where you board a speedboat powered by two 40-horsepower Yamaha engines to Leleuvia Island and Levuka (four hours, F$21.50 one-way). A free stopover on Leleuvia is possible. To book this, go to Emosi's Ferry Service (tel. 313-366), 35 Gordon Street. There's a two-room dormitory at the Gordon Street office where backpackers headed for Leleuvia can spend the night at F$5 pp (the cheapest beds in Fiji).

For variety and the most convenient timings, we recommend traveling with Patterson northbound and Emosi southbound. In good weather Emosi's boat is a lot more fun and follows a much more scenic route, with a cruise past Bau and a stop at Leleuvia. It's also slightly cheaper going with Emosi, but he only uses a small 15-person launch with a roof, so on a stormy day the much larger Patterson Brothers car ferry would be preferable. It's a beautiful circle trip, not to be missed.

**Ships to Northern Fiji**

Quite a few ships leave Suva on Saturday, but none depart on Sunday. **Patterson Brothers Shipping** (Private Mail Bag, Suva; tel. 315-644, fax 301-652), Suite 1, 1st Floor, Epworth Arcade off Nina Street, takes obligatory reservations for the Suva-Natovi-Nabouwalu-Labasa "Sea-Road" ferry/bus combination, which departs Suva's Western Bus Stand Tues.-Sat. at 0500. Fares from Suva are F$39 to Nabouwalu or F$43 right through to Labasa, an excellent 10-hour trip. There are special trips to Savusavu on holidays. Forthcoming departures are listed on a blackboard in their Suva office and the schedule varies slightly each week. Patterson Brothers also has offices in Labasa, Lautoka, Levuka, Savusavu, and Taveuni.

**Taina's Travel Services** (tel. 307-889, fax 306-189), upstairs in Epworth House opposite Patterson Brothers, handles bookings on the 65-meter MV *Adi Savusavu,* a former Swedish Scarlett Line ferry used on the Landskrona-Copenhagen run. Now operated by **Beachcomber Cruises,** this ferry generally leaves Suva northbound for Savusavu and Taveuni Tuesday at 1000; Thursday at 1800 the ship goes only to Savusavu; Saturday at 1100 a special bus departs Suva for Natovi where it connects with the *Adi Savusavu* to Savusavu at 1400. Fares from Walu Bay, Suva, are F$34/42 economy/first class to Savusavu or F$38/44 to Taveuni. A bus connection from Savusavu to Labasa is an extra F$5. The a/c first-class lounge contains 30 airline-style seats, plus six long tables with chairs. If you're fast it's possible to rent a mattress in first class at F$5 pp for the trip. Downstairs in economy are another 246 padded seats and space in which to spread a mat. The *Adi Savusavu* also carries 12 cars and 15 trucks.

**Consort Shipping Line** (Box 152, Suva; tel. 313-344, fax 303-389), in the Dominion House arcadé on Thomson Street, operates the MV *Spirit of Free Enterprise* (popularly known as the "Sofe"), a 450-passenger car ferry that formerly shuttled between the north and south islands of New Zealand. The "Sofe" leaves Suva on Tuesday at 2100 for Koro (nine hours, F$25), Savusavu (14 hours, F$32), and Taveuni (23 hours, F$34/68 deck/cabin). On Saturday night there's a trip from Suva to Koro and Savusavu only. The Tuesday northbound voyage spends all day Wednesday tied up at Savusavu and Taveuni passengers can get off and walk around. The two-berth cabins of the "Sofe" are quite comfortable and excellent value at F$55 pp to Savusavu or F$66 pp to Taveuni. For a refundable F$20 deposit the purser will give you the key to your cabin, allowing you to wander around

## ISA LEI (THE FIJIAN SONG OF FAREWELL)

| | |
|---|---|
| *Isa, isa vulagi lasa dina,*<br>*Nomu lako, au na rarawa kina?*<br>*Cava beka, ko a mai cakava,*<br>*Nomu lako, au na sega ni lasa.* | Isa, isa, you are my only treasure,<br>Must you leave me, so lonely and forsaken?<br>As the roses will miss the sun at dawning,<br>Every moment, my heart for you is yearning. |
| *Isa lei, na noqu rarawa,*<br>*Ni ko sana vodo e na mataka.*<br>*Bau nanuma, na nodatou lasa,*<br>*Mai Suva nanuma tikoga.* | Isa lei, the purple shadows falling,<br>Sad the morrow will dawn upon my sorrow.<br>Oh! Forget not, when you are far away,<br>Precious moments beside Suva Bay. |
| *Vanua rogo, na nomuni vanua,*<br>*Kena ca, ni levu tu na ua.*<br>*Lomaqu voli, me'u bau butuka,*<br>*Tovolea, ke balavu na bula.* | Isa lei, my heart was filled with pleasure,<br>From the moment, I heard your tender greeting.<br>'Mid the sunshine, we spent the hours together,<br>Now so swiftly those happy hours are fleeting. |
| *Isa lei, na noqu rarawa,*<br>*Ni ko sana vodo e na mataka.*<br>*Bau nanuma, na nodatou lasa,*<br>*Mai Suva nanuma tikoga.* | Isa lei, the purple shadows fall,<br>Sad the morrow will dawn upon my sorrow.<br>Oh! Forget not, when you are far away,<br>Precious moments beside Suva Bay. |
| *Domoni dina, na nomu yanuyanu,*<br>*Kena kau, wale na salusalu,*<br>*Mocelolo, bua, na kukuwalu,*<br>*Lagakali, baba na rosidamu.* | O'er the ocean your island home is calling,<br>Happy country where roses bloom in splendor,<br>Oh, I would but journey there beside you,<br>Then forever my heart would sing in rapture. |
| *Isa lei, na noqu rarawa,*<br>*Ni ko sana vodo e na mataka.*<br>*Bau nanuma, na nodatou lasa,*<br>*Mai Suva nanuma tikoga.* | Isa lei, the purple shadows fall,<br>Sad the morrow will dawn upon my sorrow.<br>Oh! Forget not, when you are far away,<br>Precious moments beside Suva Bay. |

the ship without worrying about your luggage. Another advantage of taking a cabin is that you're able to order meals in the pleasant first-class restaurant. Only cabin passengers may do this and the meals are excellent value at F$3. If you're traveling deck, take along something to eat, as the snack bar on board is unreliable. Readers have questioned safety standards on the "Sofe"—use it at your own risk.

**Ships to Kadavu**

**Whippys Shipping Co.** (Box 9, Suva; tel. 311-507 or 340-015, fax 302-545), in an unmarked office hidden behind Galilee Church at Miller's Wharf, Muaiwalu, Walu Bay, operates the MV *Gurawa* to Kadavu weekly. It departs Suva Friday at 0600 for northern Kadavu (Jona's, Nukubalavu, Albert's), charging F$37 to Jona's, F$40 to Albert's, or F$42 to Matana Resort. Every two weeks they go as far as Great Astrolabe Hideaway Resort (ask). The return to Suva from Kadavu is on Saturday morning. Monday at 2200 the *Gurawa* leaves Suva for Gau (F$40) and Nairai (F$40). This 15-meter cruiser accommodates 43 passengers on long padded benches (no cabins). Check with them the day before to find out which wharf the boat will be using (it's usually Miller's Wharf).

**Kadavu Shipping Co.** (tel. 311-766, fax 312-987), in the Ports Authority office building, Rona Street, Walu Bay, runs the MV *Bulou-ni-ceva* to Kadavu once or twice a week. The boat should leave Suva Monday and Thursday at midnight, with the Monday trip going to Vunisea and not calling at Jona's, Albert's, or Nukubalavu. The Thursday boat reaches Albert's Place around 1400. Saturday around 1000 they pick up passengers to return to Suva, arriving at 1700. Both trips call at Matana Resort. Fares are F$39/50 deck/cabin, but only the cabin fare includes meals. There are only two four-berth cabins, so early booking is advised. Otherwise you could ask for a place in the salon which costs F$45 to/from Kadavu including meals. Deck passengers can stretch out on long benches on the middle deck when it isn't crowded. Once a month this ship sails to Rotuma, a two-day journey costing F$90/140 deck/cabin. The *Bulou-ni-ceva* is a former Chinese riverboat now owned by Kadavu Province (the entire crew is from Kadavu).

### Ships to Other Islands

Ask on the smaller vessels tied up at Muaiwalu Jetty, Walu Bay, for passage to Nairai, Gau, Koro, Lau, etc. Don't believe the first person who tells you there's no boat going where you want—*ask around.* Food is included in the price and on the outward journey it will probably be okay, but on the return don't expect much more than rice and tea. If you're planning a long voyage by interisland ship, a big bundle of kava roots to captain and crew as a token of appreciation for their hospitality works wonders.

Keep in mind that all of the ferry departure times mentioned above and elsewhere in this book are only indications of what was true in the past. It's essential to check with the company office for current departure times during the week you wish to travel.

### Taxis

Taxi meters are set at level one daily 0600-2200 with 50 cents charged at flagfall and about 50 cents a km. From 2200 to 0600 the flagfall is F$1 plus 50 cents a km. You have to insist that they use their meter and it's a good idea if you'll be going far and aren't sure of the fare. Otherwise, just ask for a flat rate, which shouldn't be over F$2 in the city center or F$3 to the suburbs.

### Car Rentals

Car rentals are available in Suva from **Avis** (tel. 313-833) behind Asco Motors, Foster Road, Walu Bay, **Budget** (tel. 315-899), 123 Forster Rd., Walu Bay, **Central** (tel. 311-866), 293 Victoria Parade, **Dove** (tel. 311-755), Harifam Center, Greig Street, **Hertz** (tel. 302-186), 173 Victoria Parade, and **Thrifty** (tel. 314-436), 46 Gordon Street.

### Tours

For information on day-trips from Suva offered by **Wilderness Ethnic Adventure Fiji** (Box 1389, Suva; tel. 315-730, fax 300-584), turn to the Navua and Nausori sections in this book. Wilderness also runs two-hour city sightseeing tours three times a day (adults F$30, children under 12 years F$15). These trips can be booked through any travel agency in Suva.

Ask **Air Fiji** (tel. 313-666), 185 Victoria Parade, about day tours to Levuka, which include airfare from Nausori to Ovalau, ground transfers to/from Levuka, sightseeing tours, and breakfast, lunch, and afternoon tea at F$149 for adults, F$114 for children 12 and under. It's possible to spend the night in Levuka for an additional F$25 pp.

# NAUSORI AND VICINITY

## NAUSORI

In 1881 the Rewa River town of Nausori, 19 km northeast of Suva, was chosen as the site of Fiji's first large sugar refining mill, which operated until 1959. In those early days it was incorrectly believed that sugarcane grew better on the wetter eastern side of the island. Today cane is grown only on the drier, sunnier western sides of Viti Levu and Vanua Levu. The old sugar mill is now converted to use as a rice mill and storage depot, as the Rewa Valley has become a major rice-producing area.

Nausori is Fiji's fifth-largest town (population 22,000) and the headquarters of Central Division and Tailevu Province. The Rewa is Fiji's largest river and the nine-span bridge here was erected in 1937. The town is better known for its large international airport three km southeast, built as a fighter strip to defend Fiji's capital during WW II. There are several banks in Nausori. The population is predominantly Indian.

### Accommodations and Food

The budget-priced **Kings Nausori Hotel** (Box 67, Nausori; tel./fax 478-833), 99 Kings Rd., beside the chickenfeed mill, has three grubby rooms with private bath and hot water at F$25/30 single/double. The rooms are attached to the noisy bar and are rented mostly for "short times"—only of interest to people on the make. Due to licensing restrictions, women are not admitted to the hotel bar.

A far nicer drinking place is the **Whistling Duck Pub,** a block from the bus station in the center of town (ask directions). Upstairs in the adjacent building is **Prasad's Wine and Dine** restaurant where you can get cold beer with your inexpensive curries.

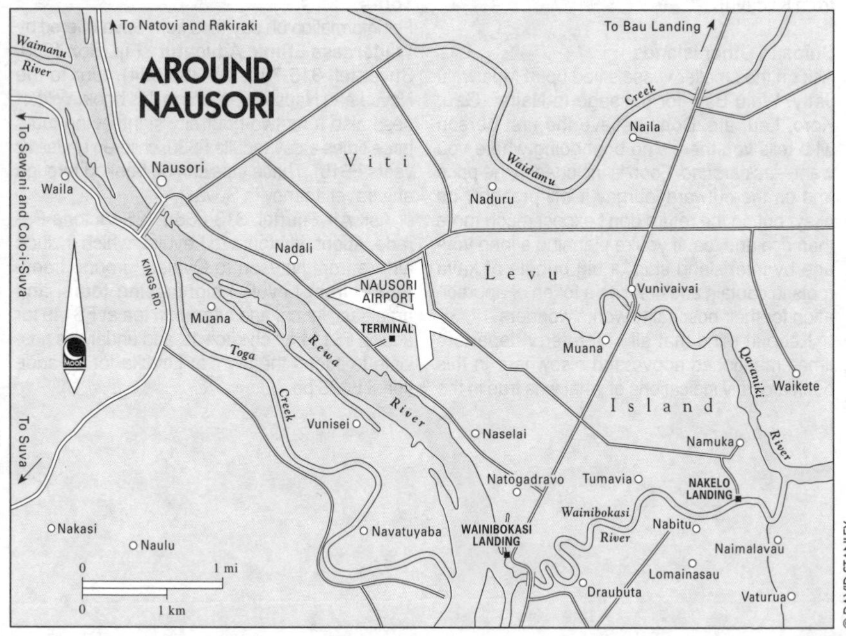

## TANOA~CANNIBAL KING OF BAU

Tanoa was about 65 years old in 1840 when the United States Exploring Expedition, under Lt. Charles Wilkes, toured Fiji. His rise to power threw the island into several years of strife, as Tanoa had to do away with virtually every minor chief who challenged his right to rule. With long colorful pennants playing from the mast and thousands of *Cypraea ovula* shells decorating the hull, his 30-meter outrigger canoe was the fastest in the region. One of Tanoa's favorite sports was overtaking and ramming smaller canoes at sea. The survivors were then fair game for whoever could catch and keep them. At feasts where most nobles were expected to provide a pig, Tanoa always furnished a human body. Wilkes included this sketch of Tanoa in volume three of the Expedition's monumental *Narrative,* published in 1845.

MERIAM LIBRARY, CSU CHICO

### From Nausori

Local buses to the airport (40 cents) and Suva (90 cents) are fairly frequent, but the last bus to Suva is at 2100. You can also catch Sunbeam Transport express buses to Lautoka from Nausori at 0715, 1240, 1400, and 1745 (5.5 hours).

## AROUND NAUSORI

### Rewa Delta

Take a bus from Nausori to Nakelo Landing to explore the heavily populated Rewa River Delta. Many outboards leave from Nakelo to take villagers to their riverside homes and passenger fares are under a dollar for short trips. Larger boats leave sporadically from Nakelo for Levuka, Gau, and Koro, but finding one would be pure chance. Some also depart from nearby Wainibokasi Landing.

At **Naililili** in the delta French Catholic missionaries built St. Joseph's Church of limestone in 1905 complete with stained glass windows. **Wilderness Ethnic Adventure Fiji** (Box 1389, Suva; tel. 315-730, fax 300-584) runs half-day boat tours of the Rewa Delta, with stops at Naililili, and at Nasilai village, where Fijian pottery is still made. The tour leaves twice daily at 0930 and 1300, and the F$35 pp price includes minibus transfers from Suva hotels (it only operates if at least four people sign up). A full-day delta trip with lunch at Nasilai village is F$49 (F$25 for children). This is a refreshing change of pace.

### Bau Island

Bau, a tiny, eight-hectare island just east of Viti Levu, has a special place in Fiji's history as this was the seat of High Chief Cakobau, who used European cannons and muskets to subdue most of western Fiji in the 1850s. At its pinnacle Bau had a population of 3,000, hundreds of war canoes guarded its waters, and over 20 temples stood on the island's central plain. After the Battle of Verata on Viti Levu in 1839, Cakobau and his father, Tanoa, presented 260 bodies of men, women, and children to their closest friends and allied chiefs for gastronomical purposes. Fifteen years after this slaughter, Cakobau converted to Christianity and prohibited cannibalism on Bau. In 1867 he became a sovereign, crowned by European traders and planters desiring a stable government in Fiji to protect their interests.

### Sights of Bau

The great stone slabs that form docks and seawalls around much of the island once accommodated Bau's fleet of war canoes. The graves of the Cakobau family and many of the old chiefs lie on the hilltop behind the school. The large, sturdy stone church located near the provincial offices was the first Christian church in Fiji. Inside its nearly one-meter-thick walls, just in front of the altar, is the old sacrificial stone once used for human sacrifices, today the baptismal font. Now painted white, this font was once known as King Cakobau's "skull crusher" and it's said a thousand brains were splattered against it. Across from the church are huge ancient trees and the thatched Council House on the site of the onetime temple of the war god Cagawalu. The family of the late Sir George Cakobau, governor-general of Fiji from 1973-82, has a large traditional-style home on the island. You can see everything on the island in an hour or so.

### Getting There

Take the Bau bus (five daily, 50 cents) from Nausori to Bau Landing where there are outboards to cross over to the island. Be aware that Bau is not considered a tourist attraction, and from time to time visitors are prevented from going to the island. It's important to get someone to invite you across, which they'll do willingly if you show a genuine interest in Fijian history. Like most Fijians, the inhabitants of Bau are friendly people. Bring a big bundle of *waka* for the *turaga-ni-koro,* and ask permission very politely to be shown around. There could be some confusion about who's to receive the *sevusevu,* however, as everyone on Bau's a chief! The more respectable your dress and demeanor, the better your chances of success. If you're told to contact the Ministry of Fijian Affairs in Suva, just depart gracefully as that's only their way of saying no. After all, it's up to them. Alternatively, you get a good close look at Bau from the *Emosi Express* ferry service to/from Levuka via Leleuvia.

### Viwa Island

Before Cakobau adopted Christianity in 1854, Methodist missionaries working for this effect resided on Viwa Island, just across the water from Bau. Here the first Fijian New Testament was printed in 1847; Rev. John Hunt, who did the translation, lies buried in the graveyard beside the church that bears his name.

Viwa is a good alternative if you aren't invited to visit Bau itself. To reach the island, hire an outboard at Bau Landing. If you're lucky, you'll be able to join some locals who are going. A single Fijian village stands on the island.

### Toberua Island

**Toberua Island Resort** (Michael Dennis, Box 567, Suva; tel. 479-177 or 302-356, fax 302-215), on a tiny reef island off the east tip of Viti Levu, caters to upmarket honeymooners, families, and professionals (George Harrison of the Beatles was there recently). Built in 1968, this was one of Fiji's first luxury outer-island resorts. The 14 thatched *bures* are designed in the purest Fijian style, yet it's all very luxurious and the small size means peace and quiet. The tariff is F$344/373/416 single/double/triple plus F$87 pp for three gourmet meals and F$55 for boat transfers. Two children under 16 sharing with adults are accommodated free and they're fed for half price or less. Baby-sitters are F$24 a day or F$9 an evening. Toberua is outside eastern Viti Levu's wet belt, so it's not as prone to rain as nearby Suva, and weather permitting, meals are served outdoors.

Don't expect tennis courts or a golf course at Toberua, though believe it or not, there's tropical golfing on the reef at low tide! (Nine holes from 90-180 meters, course par 27, clubs and balls provided free.) Deep-sea fishing is F$50 an hour and scuba diving F$70 a dive. All other activities are free, including snorkeling, sailing, windsurfing, and boat trips to a bird sanctuary or mangrove forest. Launch transfers are from Nakelo landing.

SALVATORE CASA

# NORTHERN VITI LEVU

## NORTHWEST OF NAUSORI

**Vunidawa**

If you have a few days to spare, consider exploring the river country northwest of Nausori. The main center of Naitasiri Province is Vunidawa on the Wainimala River, a big village with four stores, a hospital, a post office, a police station, two schools, and a provincial office. There are five buses a day except Sunday from Suva to Vunidawa, but no bus connection to Korovou or Monasavu.

Go for a swim in the river or borrow a horse to ride around the countryside. Stroll two km down the road to Waidawara, where there's a free hourly punt near the point where the Wainibuka and Wainimala rivers unite to form the mighty Rewa River. Take a whole day to hike up to Nairukuruku and Navuniyasi and back.

**River-Running**

There's an exciting bamboo raft *(bilibili)* trip through the Waiqa Gorge between Naitauvoli and Naivucini, two villages on the Cross-Island Highway west of Vunidawa. Two men with long poles guide each raft through the frothing rapids as the seated visitor views towering boulders enveloped in jungle. Reservations for the two-hour ride must be made in advance because an individual *bilibili* will have to be constructed for you. (There's no way to get a used *bilibili* back up to Naitauvoli.)

Write Turaga-ni-koro, Naitauvoli village, Wainimala, Naitasiri, P.A. Naikasaga, Fiji Islands, at least two weeks ahead, giving the exact date of your arrival in the village and the number in your party. Mr. Ilai Naibose (tel. 361-940) in Suva may be able to help you arrange this trip (and if not, ask at the Fiji Visitors Bureau). No trips are made on Sunday. If you plan to spend the night at Naitauvoli, specify whether you require imported European-style food or will be satisfied with local village produce. If you stay overnight, a *sevusevu* and monetary contribution to your hosts are expected in addition to the fee for the raft trip. One bus a day (except Sunday) departs Suva for Naivucini at 1455 (F$2.70); once there you'd have to look for a carrier on to Naitauvoli. There's no bus service on the Cross-Island Highway to Monasavu beyond Naivucini.

# THE TRANS-VITI LEVU TREK

For experienced hikers there's a rugged two-day trek from the Cross-Island Highway to Wainimakutu, up and down jungle river valleys through the rainforest. It will take a strong, fast hiker about three hours from Balea on the highway to Nasava, then another four over the ridge to Wainimakutu. The Trans-Viti Levu Trek passes through several large Fijian villages and gives you a good cross section of village life.

On this traditional route, you'll meet people going down the track on horseback or on foot. Since you must cross the rivers innumerable times, the trek is probably impossible for visitors during the rainy season (December to April), although the locals still manage to do it. If it's been raining, sections of the trail become a quagmire, stirred up by horses' hooves. Hiking boots aren't much use here; you'd be better off with shorts and an old pair of running shoes in which to wade across the rivers. There are many refreshing places to swim along the way. Some of the villages have small trade stores, but you're better off carrying your own food. Pack some *yaqona* as well. You can always give it away if someone invites you in.

But remember, you are not the first to undertake this walk; the villagers have played host to trekkers many times and some previous hikers have not shown much consideration to local residents along the track. Unless you have been specifically invited, do not presume automatic hospitality. If a villager provides food or a service, be prepared to offer adequate payment. This applies equally to the Sigatoka River Trek. Camping is a good alternative, so take your tent if you have one.

### The Route

Bus service on the Cross-Island Highway from Suva to Nadarivatu was interrupted in 1993 by Hurricane Keno, which destroyed the bridge at Lutu just beyond **Balea,** the Trans-Viti Levu trailhead. Buses now go only as far as Lutu, leaving Suva Mon.-Sat. at 1330 (F$2.92). For information on this bus or the one to Naivucini, call 312-230. The Lutu bus could drop you at Balea, otherwise large carrier trucks to Namosi and Lutu (F$3-4 pp) park near Foodtown, corner of Robertson Road and Struan Street near Suva Market, and most depart around midday.

From Balea walk down to the Wainimala River, which must be crossed three times before you reach the bank opposite Sawanikula. These crossings can be dangerous and well-nigh impossible in the rainy season, in which case it's better to stop and wait for some local people who might help you across. From Sawanikula it's not far to **Korovou,** a fairly large village with a clinic and two stores. Between Korovou and **Nasava** you cross the Wainimala River 14 times, but it's easier because you're farther upstream. Try to reach Nasava on the first day. If you sleep at Korovou you'll need an early start and a brisk pace to get to the first village south of the divide before nightfall on the second day.

From Nasava, follow the course of the Waisomo Creek up through a small gorge and past a waterfall. You zigzag back and forth across the creek all the way up almost to the divide.

DAVID STANLEY

*village on the trans-Viti Levu trek*

After a steep incline you cross to the south coast watershed. There's a clearing among the bamboo groves on top where you could camp, but there's no water. Before **Wainimakutu** (Nasau) the scenery gets better as you enter a wide valley with Mt. Naitaradamu (1,152 meters) behind you and the jagged outline of the unscaled Korobasabasaga Range to your left. Wainimakutu is a large village with two stores and bus service to Suva twice a day, Mon.-Fri. at 0600 and 1300 only. This fact makes it wise to begin your trek early in the week in order not to get stuck here on a weekend.

### Namosi

The bus from Wainimakutu to Suva goes via Namosi, spectacularly situated below massive Mt. Voma (927 meters), with sheer stone cliffs on all sides. You can climb Mt. Voma in a day from Namosi for a sweeping view of much of Viti Levu. It's steep but not too difficult. Allow at least four hours up and down (guides can be hired at Namosi village). Visit the old Catholic church at Namosi.

There are low-grade copper deposits estimated at one-half million tonnes situated at the foot of the Korobasabasaga Range, which Rupert Brooke called the "Gateway to Hell," 14 km north of Namosi by road. No mining has begun due to depressed world copper prices and the high initial cost of getting the mines into production, but feasibility studies continue. A 1979 study indicated that an investment of F$1 billion would be required.

# NORTHERN VITI LEVU

Northern Viti Levu has far more spectacular landscapes than the southern side of the island, and if you can only travel one way by road between Suva and Nadi, you're better off taking the northern route. Kings Road is now paved from Suva north to Korovou, then again from Dama to Lautoka, and between Korovou and Dama the 62-km gravel road is smooth. Since Kings Road follows the Wainibuka River from Wailotua village almost all the way to Viti Levu Bay, you get a good glimpse of the island's lush interior, and the north coast west of Rakiraki is breathtaking. Many visitors stop for a few days at Nananu-i-Ra Island off Rakiraki, and intrepid hikers can trek south down the Sigatoka River from the hill station of Nadarivatu.

### Korovou and Beyond

A good paved highway runs 31 km north from Nausori to Korovou, a small town of around 350 souls on the east side of Viti Levu at the junction of Kings Road and the road to Natovi, terminus of the Ovalau and Vanua Levu ferries. Its crossroads position in the heart of Tailevu Province makes Korovou an important stop for buses plying the northern route around the island. Sunbeam Transport express buses leave Korovou for Lautoka at 0800, 1325, 1500, and 1830 (five hours), with local buses departing at 0920, 0950, and 1015 (7.5 hours). (Be aware that because "korovou" means "new village," there are many places called that in Fiji—don't mix them up.)

The **Tailevu Hotel** (Box 189, Korovou; tel. 430-028, fax 430-244), on a hill overlooking the river just across the bridge from Korovou, has 14 rooms with bath and fridge at F$28/45 single/double including breakfast, and four cottages with cooking facilities at F$50 for up to four persons. Cheaper backpacker accommodation may be available if you call and ask, otherwise camping is F$8 a night. This colonial-style hotel features a large bar and restaurant, and a dance band plays on Friday and Saturday nights. The Tailevu makes a good base for visiting the surrounding area. Budget.

For a sweeping view of the entire Tailevu area, climb **Mt. Tova** (647 meters) in a day from Silana village, eight km northwest of Naqatawa.

The large dairy farms along the highway just west of Korovou were set up after WW I. **Dorothy's Waterfall** on the Waimaro River, a kilometer east of Dakuivuna village, is 10 km west of Korovou. Uru's Snack Bar overlooks the falls and it's a nice picnic spot if you have your own transportation. At Wailotua No. 1, 20 km west of Korovou, is a large **snake cave** right beside the village and easily accessible from the road. One stalactite in the cave is shaped like a six-headed snake (admission F$5). At Dama the paved road starts again and continues

45 km northwest to Rakiraki. (As you drive along this road you may be flagged down by Fijians emphatically inviting you to visit their village. At the end of the tour you'll be asked to sign the visitors book and make a financial contribution. If you decide to stop, don't bother trying to present anyone with kava roots as hard cash is all they're after.)

### Ra Province

The old Catholic Church of St. Francis Xavier at **Naiserelagi,** on a hilltop above Navunibitu Catholic School, on Kings Road about 25 km southeast of Rakiraki, was beautifully decorated with frescoes by Jean Charlot in 1962-63. Typical Fijian motifs such as the *tabua, tanoa,* and *yaqona* blend in the powerful composition behind the altar. Father Pierre Chanel, who was martyred on Futuna Island between Fiji and Samoa in 1841, appears on the left holding the weapon that killed him, a war club. Christ and the Madonna are portrayed in black. The church is worth stopping to see, and provided it's not too late in the day, you'll find an onward bus. Flying Prince Transport (tel. 694-346) runs buses between Naiserelagi and Vaileka five times a day (F$1.50), otherwise all of the local Suva buses stop there. At **Nanukuloa** village just north of here is the headquarters of Ra Province.

## RAKIRAKI

This part of northern Viti Levu is known as Rakiraki but the main town is called **Vaileka** (population 5,000). The Penang Sugar Mill was erected here in 1881. The mill is about a kilometer from the main business section of Vaileka. The sugar is loaded aboard ships at Ellington Wharf, connected to the mill by an 11-km cane railway. There are three banks and a large produce market in Vaileka, but most visitors simply pass through on their way to Nananu-i-Ra Island. A taxi from Vaileka to Ellington Wharf where the resort launches pick up guests will run F$8. Otherwise take a local bus east on Kings Road to the turnoff and walk two km down to the wharf. The express buses don't stop at the turnoff, but all buses from Lautoka (F$4) and Suva (F$7) stop in Vaileka.

### Accommodations and Food

The **Rakiraki Hotel** (Box 31, Rakiraki; tel. 694-101, fax 694-545), on Kings Road a couple of kilometers north of Vaileka, has 36 a/c rooms with fridge and private bath at F$99 single or double, F$123 triple, and 10 fan-cooled rooms at F$35/40/48 single/double/triple. Reduced rates are sometimes offered. There are no communal cooking facilities. The reception area and restaurant occupy the core of the original hotel dating back to 1945; the two-story accommodations blocks were added much later. Extensive gardens surround the hotel and the Rakiraki's outdoor bowling green draws middle-aged lawn bowling enthusiasts from Australia and New Zealand, and those folks like old-fashioned "colonial" touches like the typed daily menu featuring British-Indian curry dishes, and gin and tonic in the afternoon. Ask the manager if he can arrange a round for you at the nearby golf course owned by the Fiji Sugar Corporation. Only the local or "stage" buses will drop you off on Kings Road right in front of the hotel (the express buses will take you to Vaileka). Budget to inexpensive.

The upmarket **Wananavu Beach Resort** (John Gray, Box 305, Rakiraki; tel. 694-433, fax 694-499), on Volivoli Point facing Nananu-i-Ra Island, four km off Kings Road, is at Viti Levu's northernmost tip. There are 15 self-contained bungalows beginning at F$195 single or double, tropical breakfast included. No cooking facilities are provided, but each room does have a fridge. Stay four nights and the fifth is free. Ra Divers offers scuba diving from the resort, and a variety of other water sports are available. The resort has a swimming pool and tennis court, and the snorkeling off their beach is wonderful. Expensive.

A number of restaurants near the bus station at Vaileka serve Chinese meals, including **Gafoor & Sons, Vaileka Restaurant,** and **Rakiraki Lodge.** The "wine and dine" sections at Gafoor & Sons and Rakiraki Lodge are your best bets if you have time on your hands. The **Cosmopolitan Club** (tel. 694-330), a block from Vaileka bus station, is the local drinking place.

### West of Rakiraki

Right beside Kings Road, just a hundred meters west of the turnoff to Vaileka, is the grave of **Ratu Udreudre,** the cannibal king of this region who is alleged to have consumed 872 corpses. **Navatu Rock,** a few kilometers west of Vaileka, was the jumping-off point for the disembodied spirits of the ancient Fijians. A fortified village once stood on its summit. Navatu's triangular shape is duplicated by a small island just offshore.

The **Nakauvadra Range,** towering south of Rakiraki, is the traditional home of the Fijian serpent-god Degei, who is said to dwell in a cave on the summit of Mt. Uluda (866 meters). This "cave" is little more than a cleft in the rock. To climb the Nakauvadra Range, which the local Fijians look upon as their primeval homeland, permission must be obtained from the chief of Vatukacevaceva village who will provide guides. A *sevusevu* should be presented.

# NANANU-I-RA ISLAND

This small 355-hectare island, three km off the northernmost tip of Viti Levu, is a good place to spend some time amid tranquility and beauty. The climate is dry and sunny, and there are great beaches, reefs, snorkeling, walks, sunsets, and moonrises over the water—only roads are missing.

Seven or eight separate white sandy beaches lie scattered around the island, and it's big enough that you won't feel confined. In the early 19th century Nananu-i-Ra's original Fijian inhabitants were wiped out by disease and tribal warfare, and an heir sold the island to the Europeans whose descendants now operate small family-style resorts and a 219-hectare plantation on the island.

The northern two-thirds of Nananu-i-Ra Island, including all of the land around Kontiki Island Lodge, is owned by Mrs. Louise Harper of southern California, who bought it for a mere US$200,000 in 1966 (she also owns a sizable chunk of Proctor & Gamble back in the States). Today some 22 head of Harper cattle graze beneath coconuts on the Harper Plantation, and the plantation management actively discourages trespassing by tourists. The manager lives in a house adjoining Kontiki, and it's common courtesy to ask his permission before climbing the hill behind the lodge.

To hike right around Nananu-i-Ra on the beach takes about four hours of steady going, or all day if you stop for picnicking and snorkeling. The thickest section of mangroves is between Kontiki and Mokusigas Island Resort, on the west side of the island, and this stretch should be covered at low tide. However you do it, at some point you'll probably have to take off your shoes and wade through water just over your ankles or scramble over slippery rocks, but it's still a very nice walk. The entire coastline is public, but only as far as two meters above the high tide line. Avoid becoming stranded by high tide and forced to cut across Harper land.

An American couple, Edward and Betty Morris, have lived next to Nananu Beach Cottages since 1970. They spend four or five months a year on Nananu-i-Ra, otherwise they're in San Francisco. Ed is a former president of the International Brotherhood of Magicians and he doesn't mind sharing his magic with visitors, when he feels like it.

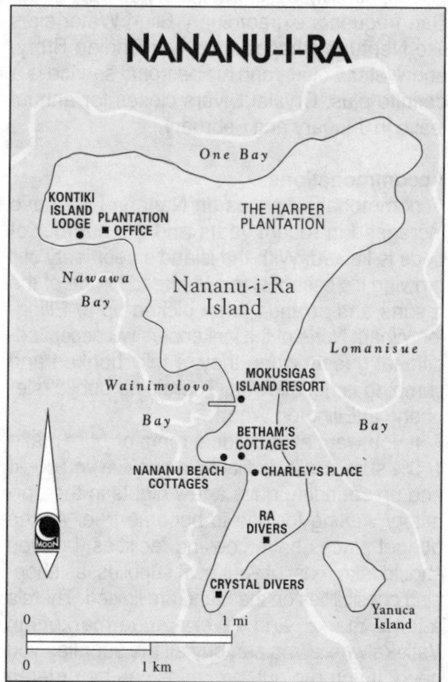

### Scuba Diving

**Ra Divers** (Papu Pangalu, Box 417, Rakiraki; tel. 694-511, fax 694-611), based on Nananu-i-Ra, offers scuba diving at F$65/120 for one/two tanks plus F$15 for gear. A 10-dive package is F$525, night diving F$85. If you need equipment, it's $75 for five days. Snorkelers can go along for F$20, if space is available (mask and snorkel supplied). Ra Diver's resort course costs F$120; full four-day PADI or NAUI certification is F$450 if you're alone or F$390 pp for two or more. They pick up clients regularly from all of the resorts. Some of Papu's favorite sites are Breathtaker, Dreammaker, Pinnacles, and Maze.

In 1998 Dan Grenier, formerly of the Lomaloma Resort on Vanua Balavu, opened a new dive shop at the south end of Nananu-i-Ra called **Crystal Divers** (Box 705, Rakiraki; tel./fax 694-747). Many of Dan's clients book from overseas via his internet site, paying F$70/130/650 for one/two/12 tank dives, plus F$29 for full gear (if required). Snorkelers can go along for F$20 if space is available (bring your own mask). His five-day PADI or NAUI certification course is F$495, otherwise an introductory dive is F$130. Dan frequents extraordinary Bligh Water sites like Neptune Rhapsody, Never Ending Story, and Water Colors, and his personal service is a definite plus. Crystal Divers closes for annual leave in January and February.

### Accommodations

Accommodation prices on Nananu-i-Ra have increased in recent years and the number of beds is limited. With the island's popularity still growing it's essential to call ahead to one of the resorts and arrange to be picked up at Ellington Wharf. None of the innkeepers will accept additional guests when they're fully booked and camping is not allowed. There's no public telephone at Ellington Wharf.

If you want an individual room or *bure* make 100% sure one is available, otherwise you could end up spending quite a few nights in the dormitory waiting for one to become free. All the budget places have cooking facilities, but you should take most of your own supplies, as shopping possibilities on the island are limited. There's a large market and several supermarkets in Vaileka where you can buy all the supplies you need. If you run out, groceries can be ordered from Vaileka for a small service charge, and Betham's Bungalows runs a minimarket with a reasonable selection of groceries (including beer). They also serve hot dogs and other snacks. Also bring enough cash, as only the Mokusigas Island Resort accepts credit cards.

Of all the places on Nananu-i-Ra, **Kontiki Island Lodge** (Box 87, Rakiraki; tel. 694-290) has more of the feeling of a low-budget resort, with ample opportunity for group activities. Because they cater mostly to backpackers, the dormitory guests are treated the same as everyone else, and the atmosphere is congenial. It's also ideal if you want to do your own thing, as the long deserted beach facing One Bay is just a 20-minute walk away. Kontiki is at the unspoiled north end of the island, with no other resorts or houses (except the Harper caretaker) nearby. It's quite popular and on Saturday night they're always full. Reservations are essential, and call again the morning before you'll arrive to make sure they haven't forgotten you.

Kontiki offers three modern self-catering bungalows, each with two double rooms at F$35 double and four dorm beds at F$16.50 pp plus tax. If you want privacy ask for one of the four rooms in the two thatched duplex *bures,* which are F$48 double. Check your mosquito net for holes when you arrive. All guests have access to fridges and cooking facilities, but take groceries as only a few very basic supplies are sold, including cold beer. In the evening the generator runs until 2200. (We've received some rather mixed feedback about Kontiki recently.) Budget.

At the other end of Nananu-i-Ra, a one-hour walk along the beach at low tide, are three other inexpensive places to stay, all offering cooking facilities. They experience more speedboat noise than Kontiki but are less crowded and perhaps preferable for a restful holiday. They almost always have a few free beds in the dorms but advance bookings are strongly recommended.

**MacDonald's Nananu Beach Cottages** (Box 140, Rakiraki; tel. 694-633) offers three individual houses with fridge at F$61 single or double, plus F$9 pp for additional persons, rooms with shared bath at F$44 double, and two five-bunk dormitory rooms at F$17 pp. Cooking facilities are provided in the dorm and a three-meal package is available at F$25 pp. Their snack bar sells sandwiches and pizzas as well as groceries, and a Fijian *lovo* feast is arranged once a week. It's peaceful and attractive with a private wharf and pontoon off their beach. Budget to inexpensive.

Right next to MacDonald's is friendly **Betham's Beach Cottages** (Peggy and Oscar Betham, Box 5, Rakiraki; tel. 694-132, fax 694-132) with four cement-block duplex houses at F$70 single or double, F$79 triple, plus two mixed dormitories, one with 10 beds and another with eight beds, at F$17 pp. It can get a bit crowded but cooking facilities and a fridge are provided. Budget to inexpensive.

Sharing the same high sandy beach with MacDonald's and Betham's is **Charley's Place** (Charley and Louise Anthony, Box 407, Rakiraki; tel. 694-676) run by a delightful, friendly family. The dormitory building has six beds (F$22 each) in the same room as the cooking facilities, plus one double room (F$45). The adjacent bungalow can sleep up to six people at F$60 for two, plus F$9 for each additional person. Both buildings are on a hill and you can watch the sunrise on one side and the sunset on the other. Charley's also rents two other houses further down the beach, each F$50 double. Budget.

The **Mokusigas Island Resort** (Box 268, Rakiraki; tel. 694-449, fax 694-404) opened on Nananu-i-Ra in 1991. The 20 comfortable bungalows with fridge are the same and each accommodates three adults. The price varies according to the location with the ocean panorama units costing F$270 while lagoon vista units are F$250 with continental breakfast included in these. The four "economy" bungalows up on the hill near the restaurant/bar are only F$200, but no breakfast is included. Add 10% tax to all rates. Cooking facilities are not provided and but you can buy a F$52 pp meal plan. The resort's dive shop offers scuba diving at F$55 from a boat or F$36 from shore. A five-day PADI certification course costs F$440. To create a diving attraction, the 43-meter *Papuan Explorer* was scuttled in 25 meters of water, 60 meters off the 189-meter Mokusigas jetty, which curves out into the sheltered lagoon. The snorkeling off the wharf is good, especially at low tide, with lots of coral and fish. Don't be disappointed by the skimpy little beach facing a mudflat you see when you first arrive: the mile-long picture-postcard beach in their brochure is a few minutes away over the hill on the other side of the island. All the resort facilities, including the restaurant, bar, and dive shop, are strictly for house guests only. Luxury.

### Getting There

Boat transfers from Ellington Wharf to Nananu-i-Ra are about F$18 pp return (20 minutes), though the resorts may levy a surcharge for one person alone. Check prices when you call to make your accommodation booking. A taxi to Ellington Wharf from the express bus stop in Vaileka is F$8 for the car. Several budget hotels in Nadi (including the Nadi Town Motel, Sunny Holiday Motel, and Kon Tiki Private Hotel) arrange minibus rides from Nadi direct to Ellington Wharf at F$20-25 pp, though it's cheaper to take an express bus from Lautoka to Vaileka, then a taxi to the landing. Coming from Nadi, you will have to change buses in Lautoka.

As you return to Ellington Wharf from Nananu-i-Ra, taxis will be waiting to whisk you to Vaileka where you'll connect with the express buses (share the F$8 taxi fare with other travelers to cut costs). You could also hike two km out to the main highway and try to flag down a bus, but only local buses will stop at this junction.

**Patterson Brothers** operates a car ferry service between Ellington Wharf and Nabouwalu on Tuesday, Thursday, and Saturday, a great shortcut to/from Vanua Levu (F$33 one-way). The ferry leaves Ellington Wharf at the difficult hour of 0630, so it's more useful as a way of coming here from Vanua Levu since it departs Nabouwalu at 1030. There's a connecting bus to/from Labasa (112 km). Often you'll be allowed to spend the night on the boat at Ellington Wharf.

# NORTHWESTERN VITI LEVU

## TAVUA

West of Rakiraki, Kings Road passes the government-run Yaqara Cattle Ranch where Fijian cowboys keep 5,500 head of cattle and 200 horses on a 7,000-hectare spread enclosed by an 80-km fence. At Tavua (population 2,500), an important junction on the north coast, buses on the north coast highway meet the daily service to Nadarivatu. Catching a bus from Tavua to Vaileka, Vatukoula, or Lautoka is no problem, but the green Tavua General Transport bus from Tavua to Nadrau (F$3.50) via Nadarivatu (F$2) leaves only from Mon.-Sat. at 1500. There are three banks in Tavua.

The two-story **Tavua Hotel** (Box 81, Tavua; tel. 680-522, fax 680-390), an old wooden colonial-style building on a hill, a five-minute walk from the bus stop, has 11 rooms with bath at F$33/44 single/double (the one a/c room is F$66). The seven-bed dorm is F$11 pp. Meals are about F$7 here. This hotel looks like it's going to be noisy due to the large bar downstairs, but all is silent after the bar and restaurant close at 2100. It's a bit rundown but okay for

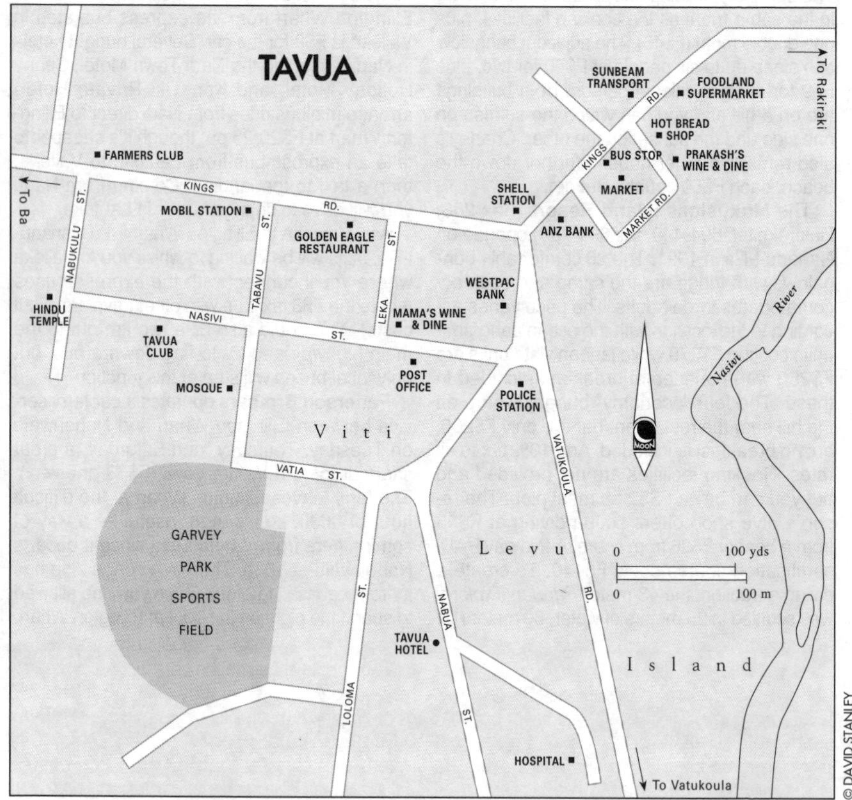

one night and a good base from which to explore Vatukoula. Budget.

The **Golden Eagle Restaurant** (tel. 680-635) on Kings Road in Tavua serves standard Indian curries. Socialize at the **Tavua Farmers Club** (tel. 680-236) on Kings Road toward Ba, or the more elitist **Tavua Club** (tel. 680-265) on Nasivi Street.

## VATUKOULA

In 1932 an old Australian prospector named Bill Borthwick discovered gold at Vatukoula, eight km south of Tavua. Two years later Borthwick and his partner, Peter Costello, sold their stake to an Australian company, and in 1935 the **Emperor Gold Mine** opened. In 1977 there was a major industrial action at the mine and the government had to step in to prevent it from closing. In 1983 the Western Mining Corporation of Australia bought a 20% share and took over management. Western modernized the facilities and greatly increased production, but after another bitter strike in 1991 they sold out and the mine is now operated by the Emperor Gold Mining Company once again. The 700 miners who walked out in 1991 have been replaced by nonunion labor.

The ore comes up from the underground area through the Smith Shaft near "Top Gate." It's washed, crushed, and roasted, then fed into a flotation process and the foundry where gold and silver are separated from the ore. Counting both underground operations and an open pit, the mine presently extracts 125,000 ounces of gold annually from 600,000 metric tonnes of ore. A tonne of silver is also produced each year and waste rock is crushed into gravel and sold. Proven recoverable ore reserves at Vatukoula are sufficient for another decade of mining, and in 1985 additional deposits were discovered at nearby Nasomo, where extraction began in 1988. Since 1935 the Emperor has produced five million ounces of gold worth over a billion U.S. dollars at today's prices. Low world gold prices in the late 1990s have forced the mine to cut costs.

Vatukoula is a typical company town of 7,000 inhabitants, with education and social services under the jurisdiction of the mine. The 1,650 miners employed here, most of them indigenous Fijians, live in WW II-style Quonset huts in racially segregated ghettos. In contrast, tradespeople and supervisors, usually Rotumans and part-Fijians, enjoy much better living conditions, and senior staff and management live in colonial-style comfort. Sensitive to profitability, the Emperor has tenaciously resisted the unionization of its workforce. Women are forbidden by law from working underground.

To arrange a guided tour of the mine you must contact the Public Relations Officer, Emperor Gold Mining Co. Ltd. (tel. 680-477, fax 680-779), at least one week in advance (although at last report the tours were suspended). It's not possible to just show up and be admitted. There's bus service from Tavua to Vatukoula every half hour, and even if you don't get off, it's well worth making the roundtrip to "Bottom Gate" to see the varying classes of company housing, to catch a glimpse of the golf course and open pit, and to enjoy the lovely scenery. Rosie The Travel Service in Nadi runs gold mine tours (F$44 without lunch), but these do not enter the mine itself and you can see almost as much from the regular bus for 50 cents each way. Cold beer is available at the **Bowling Club** (weekdays 1600-2300, Saturday 1000-2300, Sunday 1600-2100) near Bottom Gate, where meals are served Mon.-Sat. 1600-2100.

## BA

The large Indian town of Ba (population 15,000) on the Ba River is seldom visited by tourists. As the attractive mosque in the center of town suggests, nearly half of Fiji's Muslims live in Ba Province. Small fishing boats depart from behind the Shell service station opposite the mosque, and it's fairly easy to arrange to go along on all-night trips. A wide belt of mangroves covers much of the river's delta. Ba is better known for the large Rarawai Sugar Mill, opened by the Colonial Sugar Refining Co. in 1886.

The **Ba Hotel** (Box 29, Ba; tel. 674-000, fax 670-559), 110 Bank St., has 13 a/c rooms with bath at F$45/57 single/double—very pleasant with a functioning swimming pool, bar, and restaurant. Inexpensive.

Of the many places along Kings Road serving Indian and Chinese meals your best choice is

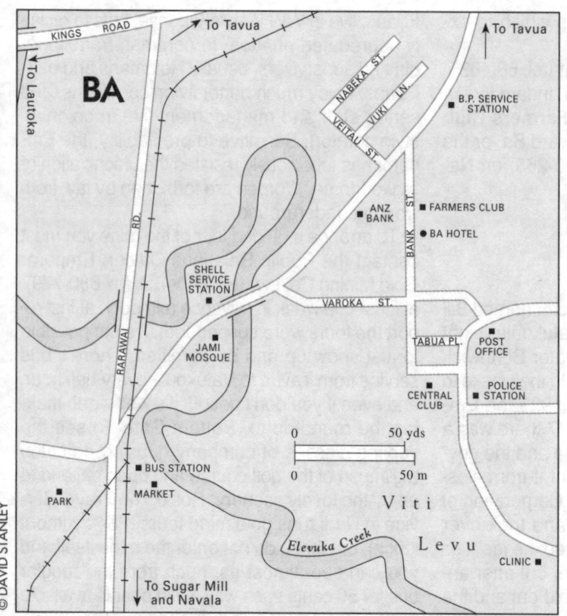


which has a proper dining room upstairs and a fast food center downstairs. **Vikan's Upper Restaurant** (tel. 674-426), Kings Road at Veitau St., has cheaper Indian food.

If you're spending the night here check out **Venus Cinema** beside the Ba Hotel, and the **Civic Cinema** on Tabua Place just up the hill. For drinks it's the **Farmers Club,** between Venus Cinema and the Ba Hotel, or the **Central Club** (tel. 674-348) on Tabua Place. Four banks have branches in Ba.

Important express buses leaving Ba daily are the Pacific Transport bus to Suva via Sigatoka at 0615 (six hours, F$10.30), and the Sunbeam Transport buses to Suva via Tavua at 0655, 0715, 0915, 1300, and 1715 (five hours). Local buses to Tavua and Lautoka are frequent. Buses to Navala and Bukuya are at 1200, 1635, and 1715 (except Sunday).

probably **Chand's Restaurant** (tel. 670-822), near the ANZ Bank and a bit toward the mosque,

*The surgeonfish gets its name from the knife-like spines just in front of its tail. Extreme care must be taken in handling the fish to avoid severe cuts.*

# INTO THE INTERIOR

### Nausori Highlands

A rough unpaved road runs 25 km southeast from Ba to Navala, a large traditional village on the sloping right bank of the Ba River. It then climbs another 20 km south to Bukuya village in the Nausori Highlands, from whence other gravel roads continue south into the Sigatoka Valley and 40 km due west to Nadi. The Nadi road passes Vaturu Dam, which supplies Nadi with fresh water. Gold strikes near Vaturu may herald a mining future for this area. The powerful open scenery of the highlands makes a visit well worthwhile.

**Navala** is one of the last fully thatched villages remaining on Viti Levu, its *bures* standing picturesquely against the surrounding hills. When water levels are right, whitewater rafters shoot the rapids through the scenic Ba River Gorge near here, and guided hiking or horseback riding can also be arranged. Sightseers are welcome, and it's possible to spend the night in the village for a reasonable amount, but one must take along a *sevusevu* for the *turaga-ni-koro* and pay a F$10 pp admission/photography fee toward village development. Access is fairly easy on the three buses a day that arrive from Ba. By rental vehicle you'll probably need a 4WD.

**Bukuya** in the center of western Viti Levu's highland plateau is less traditional than Navala and some of the only thatched *bures* in the village are those used by visitors on hiking/village stay tours organized by Peni's Waterfall Tours (Box 1842, Nadi; tel. 703-801) in Nadi. Packages including transportation to/from Nadi, *bure* accommodations, local meals, and activities cost F$110/130/160/165 pp for one/two/three/four nights. Camping is F$15 pp with a three-night minimum and all activities and transfers extra. A day tour from Nadi is F$66 pp and trekking expeditions can be arranged. We've received varying reports about Peni's trips, which seem to be a mixture of good and bad. Reader Andy Bray of Hampshire, England, sent us this:

> *Peni's tour is very much what you make of it. We got three good meals a day, transportation, a wild pig hunt, eel fishing, a waterfall trip, visits to neighboring villages, and various river and jungle treks. If you're content to settle into the typically slow Fijian pace and be satisfied with maybe one good activity a day, you'll enjoy it. If you're used to hot running water, electricity, and constant activity, it's not for you. I found it helped to gently badger the hosts so they wouldn't forget we had activities in mind.*

### Nadarivatu

An important forestry station is at Nadarivatu, a small settlement above Tavua. Its 900-meter altitude means a cool climate and a fantastic panorama of the north coast from the ridge. Beside the road right in front of the Forestry Training Center is **The Stone Bowl,** official source of the Sigatoka River, and a five-minute walk from the Center is the **Governor General's Swimming Pool** where a small creek has been dammed. Go up the creek a short distance to the main pool, though it's dry much of the year and the area has not been maintained. The trail to the fire tower atop **Mt. Lomalagi** (Mt. Heaven) begins nearby, a one-hour hike each way. The tower itself has collapsed and is no longer climbable, but the forest is lovely and you may see and hear many native birds. Pine forests cover the land.

In its heyday Nadarivatu was a summer retreat for expatriates from the nearby Emperor Gold Mine at Vatukoula, and their large bungalow still serves as a **Mine Resthouse.** The resthouse is only rented out to the public in exceptional circumstances and there's a charge of F$100 a night for the whole house (up to 10 people). For information contact the Public Relations Officer (tel. 680-477, fax 680-779) at Vatukoula. Visitors with tents are allowed to camp at the Forestry Training Center. Ask permission at the Ministry of Forests office as soon as you arrive. Some canned foods are available at the canteen opposite the Mine Resthouse, but bring food from Tavua. Cabin crackers are handy.

There's only one bus a day (excluding Sunday) between Tavua and Nadarivatu, leaving

Tavua at 1500, Nadarivatu at 0700—a spectacular one-and-a-half-hour bus ride (F$2). Arrive at the stop in Tavua at least 30 minutes ahead, as this bus does fill up. It originates/terminates in Nadrau village where you might also be able to stay (take along a *sevusevu* if you're thinking of this). It's also quite easy to hitch.

**Mount Victoria**

The two great rivers of Fiji, the Rewa and the Sigatoka, originate on the slopes of Mt. Victoria (Tomanivi), highest mountain in the country (1,323 meters). The climb begins near the bridge at Navai, 10 km southeast of Nadarivatu. Turn right up the hillside a few hundred meters down the jeep track, then climb up through native bush on the main path all the way to the top. Beware of misleading signboards. There are three small streams to cross; no water after the third. On your way down, stop for a swim in the largest stream. There's a flat area on top where you could camp—if you're willing to take your chances with Buli, the devil king of the mountain. Local guides (F$10) are available, but allow about six hours for the roundtrip. Bright red epiphytic orchids *(Dendrobium moh-li-anum)* are sometimes in full bloom. Mount Victoria is on the divide between the wet and dry sides of Viti Levu, and from the summit you should be able to distinguish the contrasting vegetation in these zones.

**Monasavu Hydroelectric Project**

The largest development project ever undertaken in Fiji, this massive F$300 million scheme at Monasavu, on the Nadrau Plateau near the center of Viti Levu, took 1,500 men and six years to complete. An earthen dam, 82 meters high, was built across the Nanuku River to supply water to the four 20-megawatt generating turbines at the Wailoa Power Station on the Wailoa River, 625 meters below. The dam forms a lake 17 km long, and the water drops through a 5.4-km tunnel at a 45-degree angle, one of the steepest engineered dips in the world. Overhead transmission lines carry power from Wailoa to Suva and Lautoka. At present Monasavu is filling 95% of Viti Levu's needs, representing huge savings on imported diesel oil, but by the year 2000 the project will have reached maximum capacity.

The Cross-Island Highway that passes the site was built to serve the dam project. Bus service ended when the project was completed and the construction camps closed in 1985. Traffic of all kinds was halted in 1993 when a hurricane took out the bridge at Lutu, although 4WD vehicles can still ford the river when water levels are low. At the present time buses go only from Tavua to Nadrau and from Suva to Naivucini, although occasional carriers go farther. In June 1998 there were tense scenes near the dam as landowners set up roadblocks to press claims of F$35 million for land flooded in the early 1980s.

## THE SIGATOKA RIVER TREK

One of the most rewarding trips you can make on Viti Levu is the three-day hike south across the center of the island from Nadarivatu to Korolevu on the Sigatoka River. Northbound the way is much harder to find. Many superb campsites can be found along the trail, and luckily this trek is not included in the Australian guidebooks, so the area isn't overrun by tourists. Have a generous bundle of *waka* ready in case you're invited to stay overnight in a village. (Kava for presentations on subsequent days can be purchased at

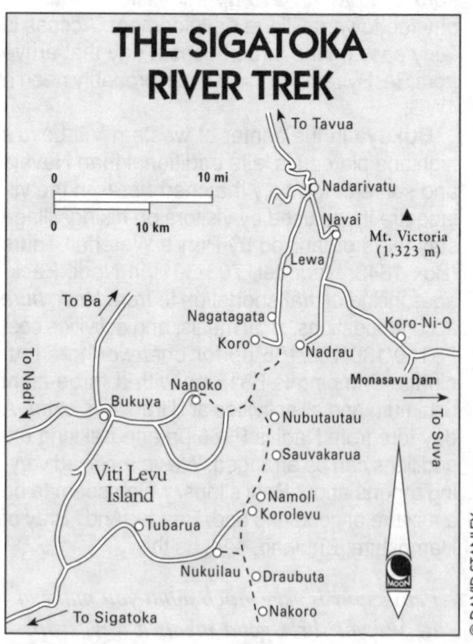

villages along the way.) Set out from Nadarivatu early in the week, so you won't suffer the embarrassment of arriving in a village on Sunday. Excellent topographical maps of the entire route can be purchased at the Lands and Survey Department in Suva and Lautoka.

Follow the dirt road south from Nadarivatu to **Nagatagata** where you should fill your canteen as the trail ahead is rigorous and there's no water to be found. From Nagatagata walk south about one hour. When you reach the electric high-power line, where the road turns right and begins to descend toward Koro, look for the well-worn footpath ahead. The trail winds along the ridge, and you can see as far as Ba. The primeval forests that once covered this part of Fiji were destroyed long ago by the slash-and-burn agricultural techniques of the Fijians.

When you reach the pine trees the path divides, with Nanoko to the right and Nubutautau down to the left. During the rainy season it's better to turn right and head to Nanoko, where you may be able to find a carrier to Bukuya or all the way to Nadi. Buses run between Bukuya and Ba three times a day (except Sunday). If you do decide to make for Nanoko, beware of a very roundabout loop road on the left. Another option is to skip all of the above by staying in the bus from Tavua right to the end of the line at Nadrau, from whence your hike would then begin.

Reverend Thomas Baker, the last missionary to be clubbed and devoured in Fiji (in 1867), met his fate at **Nubutautau.** Jack London wrote a story, "The Whale Tooth," about the death of the missionary, and the ax that brought about Reverend Baker's demise is still kept in the village. You should be able to stay in the community center in Nubutautau. The Nubutautau-Korolevu section of the trek involves 22 crossings of the Sigatoka River, which is easy enough in the dry season (cut a bamboo staff for balance), but almost impossible in the wet (December to April). Hiking boots will be useless in the river, so wear a pair of old running shoes.

It's a fantastic trip down the river to **Korolevu** if you can make it. The Korolevu villagers can call large eels up from a nearby pool with a certain chant. A few hours' walk away are the pottery villages, Draubuta and Nakoro, where traditional, long Fijian pots are still made. From Korolevu you can take a carrier to Tubarua, where there are two buses a day to Sigatoka. A carrier leaves Korolevu direct to Sigatoka every morning except Sunday, departing Sigatoka for the return around 1400 (if you want to do this trip in reverse). Reader Bruce French of Edgewood, Kentucky, wrote that "this trek was a big highlight of my South Pacific experience."

LOUISE FOOTE

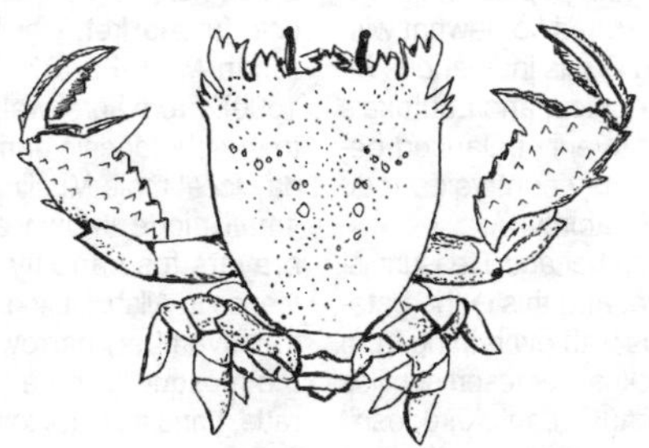

Ranina ranina

SALVATORE CASA

# LAUTOKA AND VICINITY

## LAUTOKA

Fiji's second city, Lautoka (population 45,000), is the focus of the country's sugar and timber industries, a major port, and the Western Division and Ba Province headquarters. It's an likable place with a row of towering royal palms along the main street. Though Lautoka grew up around the Fijian village of Namoli, the temples and mosques standing prominently in the center of the city reflect the large Indian population. In recent years things have changed somewhat with many Indians abandoning Fiji as indigenous Fijians move in to take their place, and Lautoka's population is now almost evenly balanced between the groups. Yet in the countryside Indians still comprise a large majority.

Shuttle boats to Beachcomber and Treasure islands depart from Lautoka, and this is the gateway to the Yasawa Islands with everything from Blue Lagoon cruises to backpacker resort shuttles and village boats. Yet because Lautoka doesn't depend only on tourism, you get a truer picture of ordinary life, and the city has a rambunctious nightlife. There's some duty-free shopping, but mainly this is just a nice place to wander around. Unless you're hooked on tourist-oriented activities, Lautoka is a good alternative to Nadi.

### SIGHTS OF LAUTOKA AND VICINITY

#### South of the Center

Begin next to the bus station at Lautoka's big, colorful **market,** which is busiest on Saturday (open Mon.-Fri. 0700-1730, Saturday 0530-1600). From here, walk south on Yasawa Street to the photogenic **Jame Mosque.** Five times a day local male Muslims direct prayers toward a small niche known as a *mihrab,* where the prayers fuse and fly to the *Kabba* in Mecca, thence to Allah. During the crushing season (June to November) narrow-gauge trains rattle past the mosque along a line parallel to Vitogo Parade, bringing cane to Lautoka's large sugar mill.

Follow the line east a bit to the **Sikh Temple,** rebuilt after a smaller temple burned down in 1989. To enter you must wash your hands and cover

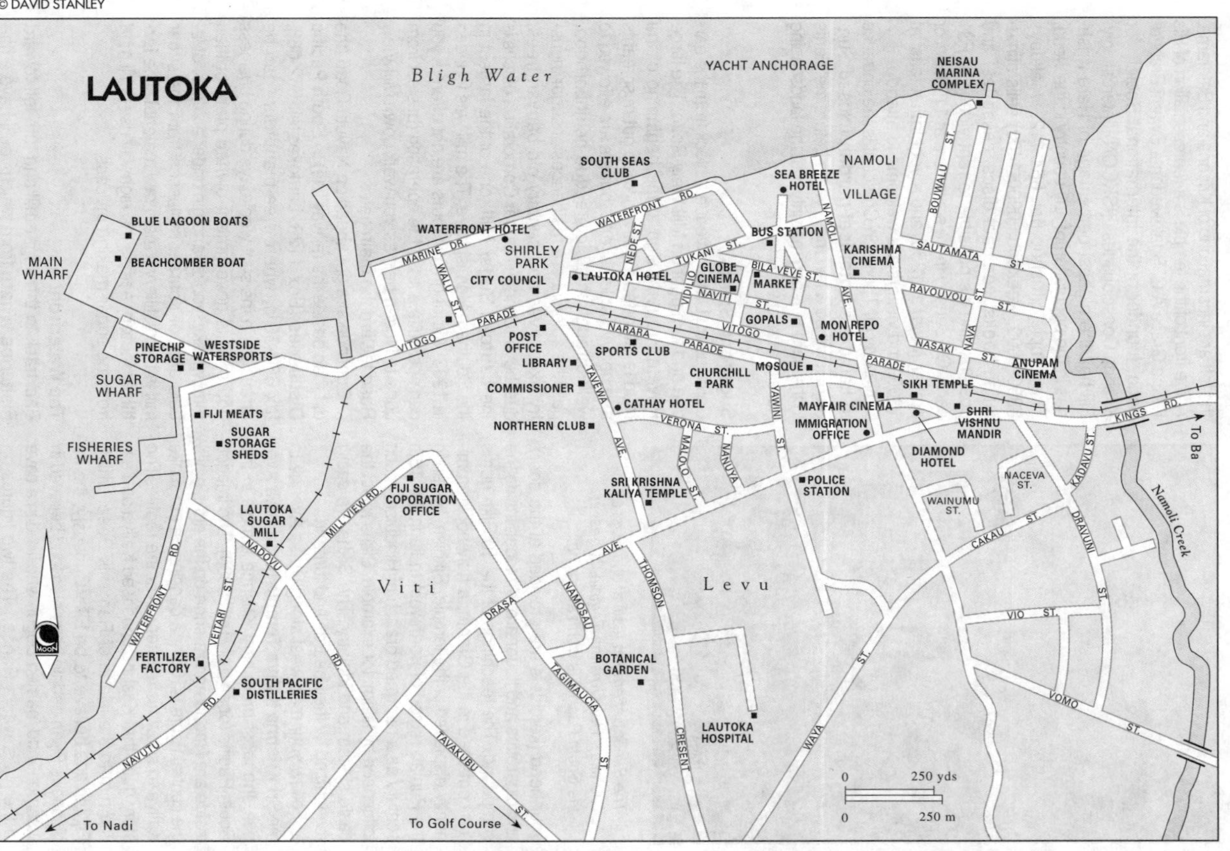
LAUTOKA
Bligh Water
YACHT ANCHORAGE
NEISAU MARINA COMPLEX
SOUTH SEAS CLUB
NAMOLI VILLAGE
SEA BREEZE HOTEL
WATERFRONT RD.
BOUWALU ST.
BLUE LAGOON BOATS
BEACHCOMBER BOAT
MAIN WHARF
WATERFRONT HOTEL
MARINE DR.
SHIRLEY PARK
NEDE ST.
BUS STATION
NAMOLI AVE.
TUKANI ST.
KARISHMA CINEMA
SAUTAMATA ST.
LAUTOKA HOTEL
GLOBE CINEMA
BILA VEVE ST.
MARKET
CITY COUNCIL
WALU ST.
VIDILIO
NAVITI ST.
RAVOUVOU ST.
GOPALS
MON REPO HOTEL
PARADE
VITOGO PARADE
NARARA PARADE
POST OFFICE
SPORTS CLUB
NASAKI ST.
NAVA
ANUPAM CINEMA
PINECHIP STORAGE
WESTSIDE WATERSPORTS
LIBRARY
MOSQUE
SUGAR WHARF
CHURCHILL PARK
COMMISSIONER
TAVEWA AVE.
SIKH TEMPLE
CATHAY HOTEL
YAVINI ST.
MAYFAIR CINEMA
SHRI VISHNU MANDIR
FIJI MEATS
KINGS RD.
NORTHERN CLUB
VERONA ST.
IMMIGRATION OFFICE
To Ba
SUGAR STORAGE SHEDS
MALOLO ST.
NANUYA
DIAMOND HOTEL
FISHERIES WHARF
KADAVU ST.
NACEVA ST.
POLICE STATION
FIJI SUGAR COPORATION OFFICE
SRI KRISHNA KALIYA TEMPLE
Namoli Creek
MILL VIEW RD.
WAINUMU ST.
LAUTOKA SUGAR MILL
CAKAU ST.
DRAVUNI ST.
NADOVU
WATERFRONT RD.
VEITARI ST.
Viti
Levu
THOMSON AVE.
DRASA
NAMOSAU
VIO ST.
FERTILIZER FACTORY
BOTANICAL GARDEN
TAGIMAUCIA ST.
WAYA ST.
SOUTH PACIFIC DISTILLERIES
VOMO ST.
NAVUTU RD.
TAVAKUBU ST.
LAUTOKA HOSPITAL
CRESENT
0 250 yds
0 250 m
To Nadi
To Golf Course
MOON

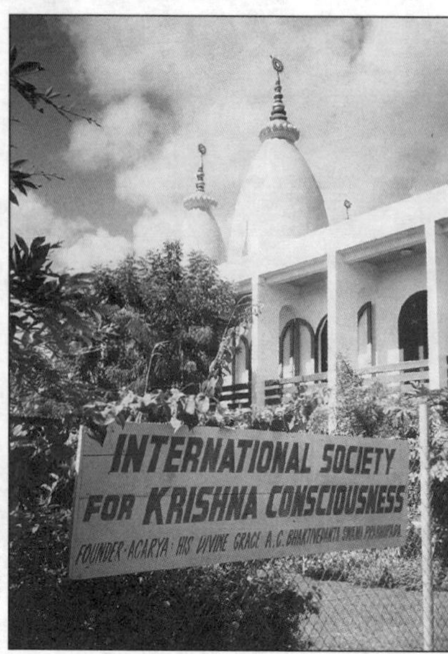


DAVID STANLEY

*The Sunday afternoon festival and feast at Lautoka's Hare Krishna Temple, largest in the South Pacific, is worth attending.*

your head (kerchiefs are provided at the door), and cigarettes and liquor are forbidden inside the compound. The teachings of the 10 Sikh gurus are contained in the Granth, a holy book prominently displayed in the temple. Sikhism began in the Punjab region of northwest India in the 16th century as a reformed branch of Hinduism much influenced by Islam: for example, Sikhs reject the caste system and idolatry. The Sikhs are easily recognized by their beards and turbans.

Follow your map west along Drasa Avenue to the **Sri Krishna Kaliya Temple** on Tavewa Avenue, the most prominent Krishna temple in the South Pacific (open daily until 2030). The images inside are Radha and Krishna on the right, while the central figure is Krishna dancing on the snake Kaliya to show his mastery over the reptile. The story goes that Krishna chastised Kaliya and exiled him to the island of Ramanik Deep, which Fiji Indians believe to be Fiji. (Curiously, the indigenous Fijian people have also long believed in a serpent-god, named Degei, who lived in a cave in the Nakauvadra Range.) The two figures on the left are incarnations of Krishna and Balarama. At the front of the temple is a representation of His Divine Grace A.C. Bhaktivedanta Swami Prabhupada, founder of the International Society for Krishna Consciousness (ISKCON). Interestingly, Fiji has the highest percentage of Hare Krishnas in the population of any country in the world. The temple gift shop (tel. 664-112; weekdays 0900-1600, weekends 0900-1400) sells stimulating books, compact discs, cassettes, and posters, and it's possible to rent videos at F$1 each. On Sunday there's a lecture at 1100, *arti* or prayer *(puja)* at 1230, and a vegetarian feast at 1300, and visitors are welcome to attend.

Nearby off Thomson Crescent is the entrance to Lautoka's **botanical garden** (closed Sunday). It will be a few more years before the plants in the garden reach maturity, but the landscaping here is attractive.

### Sugar and Spirits

Continue up Drasa Avenue a block from the garden and turn right on Mill View Road. The large Private Property sign at the beginning of the road is intended mostly to keep out miscreants and heavy vehicles, and tourists are allowed to walk through this picturesque neighborhood, past the colonial-era residences of sugar industry executives and century-old banyan trees. Just beyond the Fiji Sugar Corporation offices is the **Lautoka Sugar Mill,** one of the largest in the Southern Hemisphere. The mill was founded in 1903. Although mill tours are not offered, you can see quite a lot of the operation (busiest from June to November) as you walk down Mill View Road toward the main gate.

Continue straight ahead on Navutu Road (the dirt road beside the railway line) to **South Pacific Distilleries** (Box 1128, Lautoka; tel. 662-088, fax 664-361), where free plant tours can be arranged on the spot weekdays during business hours. This government-owned plant bottles rum, whisky, vodka, and gin under a variety of labels and, of course, molasses from the sugar mill is the distillery's main raw material. The **fertilizer factory** across the highway uses mill mud from the sugar-making process.

### The Waterfront

Backtrack to the sugar mill and turn left toward **Fisheries Wharf,** from which you'll have a fine view of the huge sugar storage sheds next to the mill and many colorful fishing boats. If you were thinking of visiting the Yasawa Islands, this is where you'll board your boat.

To the north, just beyond the conveyor belts used to load raw sugar onto the ships, is a veritable mountain of **pine chips** ready for export to Japan where they are used to make paper. Forestry is becoming more important as Fiji attempts to diversify its economy away from sugar. The **Main Wharf** behind the chips is the departure point for the famous Blue Lagoon Cruises to the Yasawa Islands, plus the 39-meter Beachcomber Island shuttle boat *Tui Tai.* As you return to central Lautoka, turn left onto **Marine Drive** for its view of the harbor, especially enchanting at sunset.

### North of Lautoka

One of the largest reforestation projects yet undertaken in the South Pacific is the **Lololo Pine Scheme,** eight km off Kings Road between Lautoka and Ba. The logs are sawn into timber if straight or ground into chip if twisted and then exported from Lautoka. There's a shady picnic area along a dammed creek at the forestry station where you could swim, but even if you don't stop, it's worthwhile taking the one-and-a-half-hour roundtrip bus ride from Lautoka to see this beautiful area and to learn how it's being used. The buses follow a circular route, returning by a different road.

### South of Lautoka

A popular legend invented in 1893 holds that **Viseisei village,** on the old road between Lautoka and Nadi, is the oldest settlement in Fiji. It's told how the first Fijians, led by Chiefs Lutunasobasoba and Degei, came from the west, landing their great canoe, the *Kaunitoni,* at Vuda Point, where the oil tanks are now. A Centennial Memorial (1835-1935) in front of the church commemorates the arrival of the first Methodist missionaries in Fiji, and opposite the memorial is a traditional Fijian *bure*—the residence of the present Tui Vuda.

Near the back of the church is another monument topped by a giant war club, the burial place of the village's chiefly family. The late Dr. Timoci Bavadra, the former prime minister of Fiji who was deposed by the Rabuka coup in 1987, hailed from Viseisei and is interred here. Dr. Bavadra's traditional-style home faces the main road near the church. His son presently lives there, and with his permission you'll be allowed to enter to see the photos hanging from the walls.

All this is only a few minutes' walk from the bus stop, but you're expected to have someone accompany you through the village. Ask permission of anyone you meet at the bus stop and they will send a child with you. As you part, you could give the child a pack of chewing gum (give something else if your escort is an adult). Nearby is a **Memorial Cultural Center,** where souvenirs

M.E. DE VOS

*near Lautoka, Fiji*

*the guns of Lomolomo on a hilltop between Lautoka and Nadi*

DAVID STANLEY

are sold to passengers on the bus tours that often stop here. There's a fine view of Nadi Bay from the Center. It's better not to come on a Sunday. A new bypass on Queens Road avoids Viseisei and only local buses between Lautoka and Nadi take the old road past the village.

A couple of kilometers from the village on the airport side of Viseisei, just above Lomolomo Public School, are two **British six-inch guns** set up here during WW II to defend the north side of Nadi Bay. It's a fairly easy climb from the main highway, and you get an excellent view from the top.

**Abaca**

An ecotourism project supported by New Zealand aid money has been established at Abaca (pronounced "Ambatha") village directly below the Mount Evans or Koroyanitu Range, 15 km east of Lautoka. **Koroyanitu National Heritage Park** is intended to support the preservation of Fiji's only unlogged cloud forest by creating a small tourism business for the locals. The village carrier used to transport visitors also carries the local kids to and from school. Four waterfalls are near the village, and Table Mountain, with sweeping views of the coast and Yasawas, is only an hour away. More ambitious hikes to higher peaks are possible. The landscape of wide green valleys set against steep slopes is superb.

The **Nase Forest Lodge,** 500 meters from the village, is a six-bunk guesthouse with cooking facilities at F$15 pp (take food as there's no shop). Camping by the lodge is F$10 per tent. Otherwise you can sleep on a mat in a village home at F$30 pp including meals. The park entry fee is F$5 pp. Guided hiking trips include a two-hour walk to Savione Falls at F$5 pp or a full-day hike to Batilamu at F$10 pp. Three-day, two-night treks to Navilawa via Batilamu can be arranged for small groups but arrangements should be made in advance. Sweeping views of the Yasawas and western side of Viti Levu are obtained from Batilamu and various archaeological sites are seen.

You can call Abaca directly by radio telephone at tel. 666-644 (wait for two beeps, then dial 1234). You may get an answering machine and they sometimes don't check for messages for a week at a time, in which case the receptionists at the Cathay or Lautoka hotels in Lautoka may be able to help you. You can get there on an official village carrier, which leaves these hotels Mon.-Fri. around 0900, charging F$8 pp. The closest public bus stop is Abaca Junction on the Tavakuba bus route, but it's 10 km from the village. It's also possible to hire a carrier direct to Abaca from Lautoka on Yasawa Street next to Lautoka market at about F$20 each way for the vehicle. Otherwise, the Lautoka hotels run daytrips at F$43 pp including lunch and the guided hike to the waterfuall. It's an outstanding opportunity to see a bit of this spectacular area, just don't go on a Sunday, the traditional day of worship and rest.

**Sports and Recreation**

**Westside Watersports** (Lance Millar, Box 7136, Lautoka; tel./fax 661-462), on Wharf Road, organizes scuba diving trips, fills tanks, and does Yasawa island transfers. Diving is F$88/132/450 for one/two/10 tanks including gear, night diving is F$110. PADI open-water certification is F$430 (five days), an introductory dive is F$110. They'll take snorkelers out in the boat for F$10 if space is available. Westside operates a dive shop on Tavewa Island.

**Subsurface Fiji** (Tony Cottrell, Box 1626, Lautoka; tel. 666-738, fax 669-955), at the corner of Nede and Naviti Streets near the Lautoka Hotel, also arranges scuba diving at F$77/140/320 for one/two/six tanks, plus $11 for equipment. They'll sometimes takes snorkelers along for F$25. A four-day PADI certification course is F$495, otherwise an introductory dive is F$105. Divers should call for a free hotel pickup. Tank air fills at offshore islands can also be arranged. Subsurface handles all scuba diving at Beachcomber Island.

The **Lautoka Golf Club** (tel. 661-384), a nine-hole course, charges F$15 green fees plus F$20 club rentals. A taxi from the market should cost around F$2.50.

All day Saturday you can catch exciting rugby (April to September) or soccer (September to May) games at the stadium in Churchill Park (admission is F$3-5). Information on upcoming games should be available to the adjacent Lautoka Sports and Social Club. Ask about league games.

## ACCOMMODATIONS

**Budget**

A good choice is the clean, quiet, three-story **Sea Breeze Hotel** (Box 152, Lautoka; tel. 660-717, fax 666-080), at 5 Bekana Ln. on the waterfront near the bus station. They have 26 rooms with private bath from F$25/35 single/double (rooms with a/c F$28/42). A larger family room accommodating four adults is F$50. A good breakfast is F$3-6 extra. A very pleasant lounge has a color TV, and a swimming pool overlooks the lagoon. Few backpackers stay here for some reason.

To be closer to the action, stay at the 38-room **Lautoka Hotel** (Box 51, Lautoka; tel. 660-388, fax 660-201), 2 Naviti St., which has a good restaurant and nightclub on the premises. There's also a nice swimming pool. Room prices vary from F$25/30 single/double for a spacious fan-cooled room with shared bath to F$46 single or double for a/c and private bath, F$70 for a/c, private bath, fridge, and waterbed, or F$10 pp in the dorm.

Also good are the 40 rooms at the friendly **Cathay Hotel** (Box 239, Lautoka; tel. 660-566, fax 660-136) on Tavewa Avenue, which features a swimming pool, TV room, and bar. The charge is F$29/39 single/double with fan and private bath, F$40/47 with a/c. Some of the rooms in less desirable locations have been divided into dormitories with two to five beds or bunks. Each dorm has its own toilet and shower at F$10 pp (F$1 discount for youth hostel, VIP, or Nomads card holders). The dorms here are the best deal in the city, otherwise take one of the superior a/c rooms upstairs. The Cathay offers free luggage storage for guests and the notice board at the reception often has useful information on travel to Fijian villages and the outer islands. Beer is available at the hotel bar, and there's also the Sportsman's Bar outside and adjacent to the hotel.

The 18-room **Diamond Hotel** (Box 736, Lautoka; tel. 661-920) on Nacula Street charges F$10 pp in the dorm (three beds), or F$20/25 single/double for a room with fan. Though plain and basic, it's okay for one night if everything else is full.

Another step down is the **Mon Repo Hotel** (Box 857, Lautoka; tel. 661-595), 75 Vitogo Parade, at F$18/25 single/double with shared bath. This building is a former police station and hookers on the beat outside are still brought in (peep holes between rooms). After a night of revelry be prepared for the muezzin of the mosque across the street who calls the faithful to prayer at the crack of dawn.

**Saweni Beach Apartments** (Box 239, Lautoka; tel. 661-777, fax 660-136), a kilometer off the main highway south of Lautoka, offers a row of 12 self-catering apartments with fan and hot water at F$42 for up to three persons, plus several F$9 pp dormitories in the annex with two to four beds. You can pitch your own tent here at F$6 pp and still use the dorm's communal kitchen. A small discount is offered if you show a youth hostel, VIP, or Nomads card, and there's 10% off on weekly stays. It's a fine place to hang out. The Nadi travel agents don't promote this place because the owners won't pay them commissions, which makes it all the cheaper and less crowded for you. Fishermen on the beach sell fresh fish every morning, and cruising yachts often anchor off Saweni Beach. It's quiet and the so-so beach only comes alive on weekends when local picnickers arrive. A local company called **First Divers** (fax 651-571) offers scuba diving and snorkeling trips from Saweni. A bus runs right to the hotel from Lautoka five times a day. Otherwise any of the local Nadi buses will drop you off a 10-minute walk away (taxi from Lautoka F$6).

### Inexpensive

Lautoka's top hotel is the **Waterfront Hotel** (Box 4653, Lautoka; tel. 664-777, fax 665-870), a two-story building erected in 1987 on Marine Drive. The 43 waterbed-equipped a/c rooms are F$111 single or double, F$135 triple (children under 16 are free if no extra bed is required). Weekly events include the Indian curry buffet on Friday night and the Sunday evening poolside barbecue (each F$16.50). There's a swimming pool, and members of tour groups departing Lautoka booked on Blue Lagoon cruises often stay here.

### Near Viseisei

**Mediterranean Villas** (Box 5240, Lautoka; tel. 664-011, fax 661-773), on Vuda Hill overlooking Viseisei village just off the old highway, has six individually decorated villas with fridge beginning at F$90 single or double. Cooking facilities are not provided, but a licensed Italian seafood restaurant is on the premises. The beach is far from here but the hotel has a private island for guests. This hotel acts as the honorary Italian consulate in Fiji. Moderate.

**First Landing Resort** (Box 348, Lautoka; tel. 666-171, fax 668-882) is next to the new Vuda Point Marina yacht harbor, but otherwise not a very convenient spot. It's three km down the road from Mediterranean Villas and left past the oil tanks. There are five cottages at F$135/160 double/triple including breakfast (F$185/210 with a/c). The units have a fridge but no cooking facilities. The large garden restaurant on the premises bakes pizza, seafood, and bread in a wood-fired stone oven. Tour groups often eat here. Moderate.

In the same general area, a 15-minute walk along the beach from Viseisei, the **Anchorage Beach Resort** (Box 9203, Nadi Airport; tel. 662-099, fax 665-571), which has gone upmarket since being taken over by the Tanoa Group in 1996. The nine garden-view rooms are F$132 single or double, the seven ocean view or "panoramic" rooms F$143, and the only two rooms with cooking facilities F$167 (other guests must use the restaurant). Each room has a fridge and balcony. A swimming pool is on the premises. Inexpensive.

For information on Beachcomber Island and Treasure Island resorts, both accessible from Lautoka, turn to **The Mamanuca Group.**

## FOOD

Several inexpensive local restaurants are near the bus station. The **Pacific Restaurant** (tel. 661-836; Mon.-Sat. 0700-1830, Sunday 0800-1500), on Yasawa Street near the Sigatoka Bookshop, has some of the hottest (spiciest) food you'll find anywhere in the Pacific.

**Jolly Good Fast Food** (tel. 669-980), Vakabale and Naviti Streets opposite the market, is a great place to sit and read a newspaper over a Coke. Eating outside in their covered garden is fun, and their "made to order" menu at the counter puts McDonald's to shame. The only drawback is the lack of beer.

The Foodcourt at back of **Morris Hedstrom Supermarket** (tel. 662-999; Mon.-Fri. 0830-1800, Saturday 0830-1600), Vidilio and Tukani Streets, offers fish or chicken and chips, hot pies, ice cream, and breakfast specials. It's a clean and only a bit more expensive than the market places.

Eat Italian at the **Pizza Inn** (tel. 660-388) in the Lautoka Hotel, 2 Naviti Street.

**The Last Call** (tel./fax 650-525; closed Sunday), a more upscale Italian restaurant at 21 Tui St. near the Waterfront Hotel, has an internet service for visitors costing 44 cents a minute (technical help free). Their homemade ice cream and imported cappuccino are also good.

### Indian

**Naran Ghela & Sons Milk Bar** (tel. 667-502; Mon.-Fri. 0800-1800, Saturday 0800-1630), 85

Vitogo Parade, is a good place for an Indian-style breakfast of spicy snacks, samosas, and sweets with coffee.

For the finest vegetarian food in Lautoka, head for **Gopal's** (tel. 662-990; Mon.-Fri. 0830-1730, Saturday 0830-1630), on the corner of Naviti and Yasawa Streets near the market. This is the Lautoka equivalent of Suva's Hare Krishna Restaurant. It's best at lunch with an all-you-can-eat vegetarian *thali* plate for F$6.50 but the selection declines toward closing. Come anytime for ice cream and sweets.

The unpretentious **Hot Snax Shop** (tel. 661-306), 56 Naviti St., may be the number one place in Fiji to sample South Indian dishes, such as *masala dosai,* a rice pancake with coconut chutney that makes a nice light lunch, or *samosas, iddili, puri,* and *palau.* The deep-fried *puri* are great for breakfast.

### Chinese

**Yangs Restaurant** (tel. 661-446; Mon.-Thurs. 0800-1745, Friday 0800-1830, Saturday 0800-1700), 27 Naviti St, is an excellent breakfast or lunch place with inexpensive Chinese specialties.

Enjoy ample servings of Cantonese food at the a/c **Sea Coast Restaurant** (tel. 660-675; closed Sunday) on Naviti St. near the Lautoka Hotel.

## ENTERTAINMENT

Four movie houses offer several showings daily except Sunday.

The disco scene in Lautoka centers on the **Hunter's Inn** at the Lautoka Hotel (tel. 660-388; open Friday and Saturday 2100-0100 only; F$5 cover). There's also **Coco's** (tel. 667-900) at 21 Naviti St., above the Great Wall of China Restaurant, but you won't be admitted if you're wearing a T-shirt or flip-flops.

The roughest place in town is **Lady Touch Disco** (tel. 666-677), above Gopal's in the city center. It's open Thurs.-Sat. 2000-0100, but nothing much happens before 2200. The cover charge is F$5 (ladies free), and flip-flop shoes aren't allowed. They also open for happy hour Saturday 1200-1430.

Lautoka's old colonial club is the **Northern Club** (tel. 662-469) on Tavewa Avenue opposite the Cathay Hotel. The sign outside says Members Only, but the club secretary is usually willing to sign in foreign visitors. Lunch and dinner are available here Mon.-Sat.; there's tennis and a swimming pool.

The **Lautoka Club** (tel. 660-637), behind the Sea Breeze Hotel, is another good drinking place with a sea view. The **Sports and Social Club** (tel. 660-837), on Narara Parade near Churchill Park, is another good local drinking place.

LOUISE FOOTE

### Sunday *Puja*

The big event of the week is the Sunday *puja* (prayer) at the **Sri Krishna Kaliya Temple** (tel. 664-112) on Tavewa Avenue at 1230, followed by a vegetarian feast at 1300. Visitors may join in the singing and dancing, if they wish. Take off your shoes and sit on the white marble floor, men on one side, women on the other. Bells ring, drums are beaten, conch shells blown, and stories from the Vedas, Srimad Bhagavatam, and Ramayana are acted out as everyone chants, *"Hare Krsna, Hare Krsna, Krsna Krsna, Hare Hare, Hare Rama, Hare Rama, Rama, Rama, Hare, Hare."* It's a real celebration of joy and a most moving experience. At one point children will circulate with small trays covered with burning candles, on which it is customary to place a donation; you may also drop a dollar or two in the yellow box in the center of the temple. You'll be readily invited to join the vegetarian feast later, and no more money will be asked of you.

## OTHER PRACTICALITIES

### Services

The ANZ Bank, Bank of Hawaii, Merchant Bank, and Westpac Bank are all on Naviti Street near the market. There's also an ANZ Bank branch diagonally opposite the post office, and a Westpac Bank branch a little west on Vitogo Parade beyond the Shell station. The ANZ Bank closer to the market has an ATM machine.

The **Immigration Department** (tel. 661-706) is at the corner of Namoli and Drasa Avenues.

Public toilets are on the back side of the bus station facing the market.

**Yachting Facilities**

The **Neisau Marina Complex** (Box 3831, Lautoka; tel. 664-858, fax 663-807), at the end of Bouwalu Street, provides complete haul-out facilities for yachts in need of repair. A berth begins at F$7 a day, while to anchor offshore and use the facilities (showers, etc.) is F$15 a week. There's also a **laundromat** (F$3 to wash, F$2 to dry). Spencer's Bar here opens at 1800 daily except Sunday with special happy hour prices until 2000 (no T-shirts or flip-flops).

**Information**

The **Department of Lands and Survey** (tel. 661-800; Mon.-Thurs. 0800-1300 and 1400-1530, Friday 0800-1300 and 1400-1500), behind the Commissioner Western Division office near the Cathay Hotel, sells excellent topographical maps of all of Fiji at F$5 a sheet.

The **Book Exchange** (tel. 665-625), 19 Yasawa St., trades and sells used books.

The **Western Regional Library** (tel. 660-091) on Tavewa Avenue is open Mon.-Fri. 1000-1700, Saturday 0900-1200.

**Sunflower Airlines** (tel. 664-753) is at 27 Vidilio St., while **Air Pacific** (tel. 664-008) is at 159 Vitogo Parade diagonally opposite the post office. **Rosie The Travel Service** (tel. 660-311) is next to Air Pacific.

**Health**

The emergency room at the **Lautoka Hospital** (tel. 660-399), off Thomson Crescent south of the center, is open 24 hours a day.

Vaccinations for tetanus, diphtheria, polio, and rubella are available at the **Health Office** (tel. 660-815) on Naviti Street opposite the Lautoka Hotel.

The privately operated **Vakabale Street Medical Center** (tel. 661-961; Mon.-Fri. 0830-1300 and 1400-1700, Saturday 0830-1300), near the corner of Vakabale and Naviti Streets not far from the market, includes a general medical practitioner and a dental surgeon on their roster.

## TRANSPORTATION

**Patterson Brothers** (tel. 661-173), at 15 Tukani Street opposite the bus station, runs a bus/ferry/bus service between Lautoka, Ellington Wharf, Nabouwalu, and Labasa (F$43), departing Lautoka on Tuesday, Thursday, and Saturday around 0400.

Buses, carriers, taxis—everything leaves from the bus stand beside the market. **Pacific Transport** (tel. 660-499) has express buses to Suva daily at 0630, 0700, 1210, 1550, and 1730 (five hours, F$8.95) via Sigatoka (Queens Road). Five other "stage" buses also operate daily along this route (six hours).

The daily **Sunset Express** (tel. 668-276) leaves for Suva via Sigatoka at 0930 and 1515 (four hours, F$9). **Sunbeam Transport** (tel. 662-822) has expresses to Suva at 0615, 0630, 0815, 1215, and 1630 (six hours, F$11.05) via Tavua (Kings Road), plus two local buses on the same route (nine hours). The northern route is more scenic than the southern. Local buses to Nadi (F$1.36) and Ba (F$1.48) depart every half hour or so.

Car rentals are available in Lautoka from **Budget** (tel. 666-166) on Walu St. and **Central** (tel. 664-511) at 73 Vitogo Parade.

Day cruises to Beachcomber Island (F$60 pp including lunch, reductions for children) depart Lautoka daily at 1000—a great way to spend a day. Any travel agency can book them.

SALVATORE CASA

# THE YASAWA ISLANDS

The Yasawas are a chain of 16 main volcanic islands and dozens of smaller ones, stretching 80 km in a north-northeast direction, roughly 35 km off the west coast of Viti Levu. In the lee of Viti Levu, the Yasawas are dry and sunny, with beautiful, isolated beaches, cliffs, bays, and reefs. The waters are crystal clear and almost totally shark-free. The group was romanticized in two movies about a pair of child castaways who eventually fall in love on a deserted isle. The original 1949 version of *The Blue Lagoon* starred Jean Simmons while the 1980 remake featured Brooke Shields. (A 1991 sequel *Return to the Blue Lagoon* with Milla Jovovich was filmed on Taveuni.)

It was from the north end of the Yasawas that two canoe-loads of cannibals sallied forth in 1789 and gave chase to Capt. William Bligh and his 18 companions less than a week after the famous mutiny. Two centuries later, increasing numbers of mini-cruise ships ply the chain, but there are still almost no motorized land vehicles or roads. The backpackers' usual routine is to head for Tavewa or Wayasewa while the thousand-dollar-a-day crowd is flown to Turtle Island. If you'll be trekking or kayaking, you should take along a good supply of *yaqona* (which doesn't grow in the Yasawas) for use as a *sevusevu* to village chiefs. All access to the Yasawas is via Lautoka. In the local dialect called Vuda, *bula* is *cola* (hello) and *vinaka* is *vina du riki* (thank you).

**Important:** When booking at one of the Yasawa backpacker resorts, don't prepay your return boat fare if there's any chance you'll wish to move to a different resort after arriving, as each place has its own boat and a roundtrip is the same price as two one-ways. Don't believe anyone who tells you that the Tavewa boats will drop you on Waya or Wayasewa on their way back to Lautoka as the decision to do so is strictly up to the captain at the moment you wish to travel and your bargaining position will be much stronger if you haven't paid in advance.

## WAYASEWA ISLAND

**Dive Trek Nature Lodge** (Box 6353, Lautoka; tel. 669-715, fax 724-363), also known as Wayalailai Eco Haven, is on the south side of Wayasewa adjacent to Namara village. In 1972 most of the villagers moved to the northwest side of

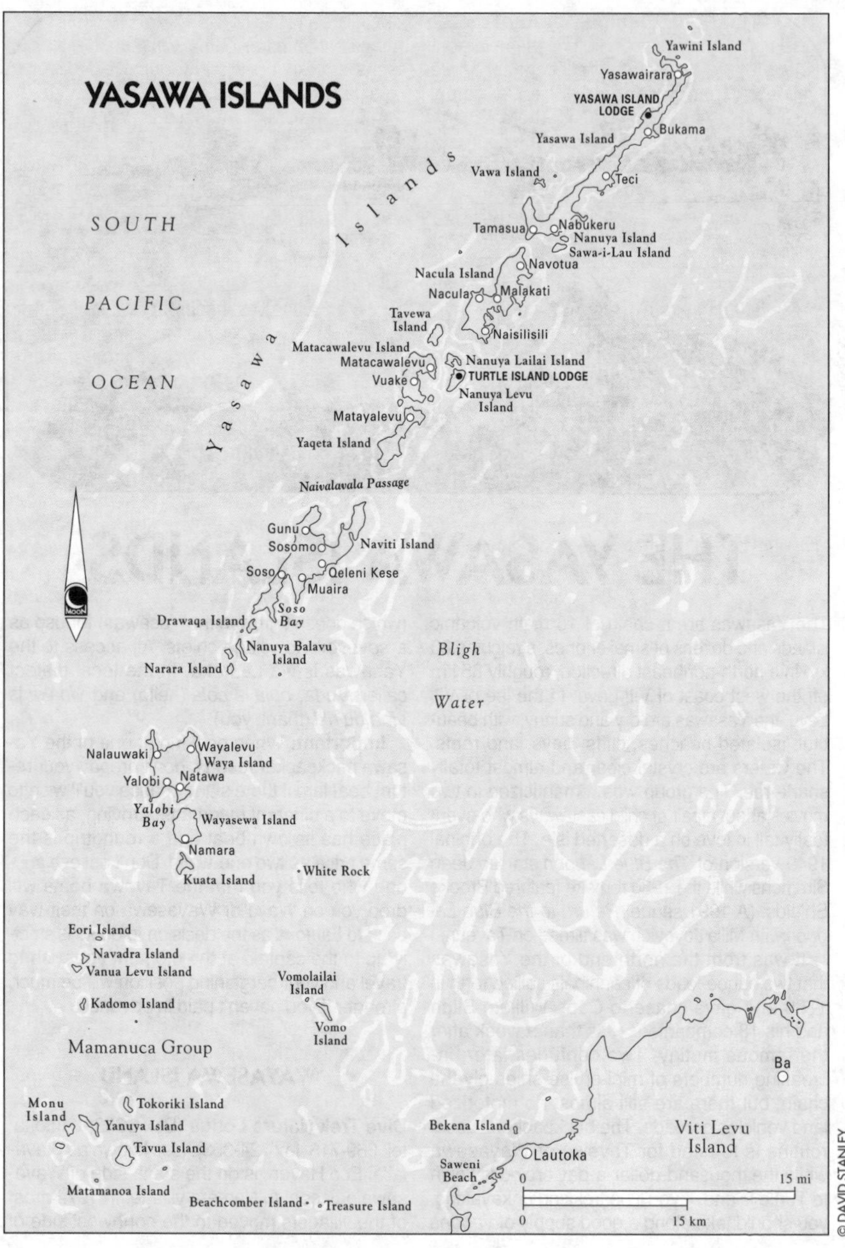
YASAWA ISLANDS
SOUTH
PACIFIC
OCEAN
Yasawa Islands
Yawini Island
Yasawairara
YASAWA ISLAND LODGE
Bukama
Yasawa Island
Vawa Island
Teci
Tamasua
Nabukeru
Nanuya Island
Sawa-i-Lau Island
Navotua
Nacula Island
Nacula
Malakati
Tavewa Island
Naisilisili
Matacawalevu Island
Matacawalevu
Nanuya Lailai Island
TURTLE ISLAND LODGE
Vuake
Nanuya Levu Island
Matayalevu
Yaqeta Island
Naivalavala Passage
Gunu
Sosomo
Naviti Island
Soso
Qeleni Kese
Muaira
Soso Bay
Drawaqa Island
Nanuya Balavu Island
Bligh
Water
Narara Island
Nalauwaki
Wayalevu
Waya Island
Yalobi
Natawa
Yalobi Bay
Wayasewa Island
Namara
Kuata Island
White Rock
Eori Island
Navadra Island
Vanua Levu Island
Vomolailai Island
Kadomo Island
Vomo Island
Mamanuca Group
Ba
Monu Island
Tokoriki Island
Yanuya Island
Bekena Island
Viti Levu Island
Tavua Island
Lautoka
Saweni Beach
0
15 mi
Matamanoa Island
Beachcomber Island
Treasure Island
0
15 km
MOON

the island, and since 1994 the east side of the village has been developed into one of the largest backpacker camps in Fiji. The location is spectacular, opposite Kuata Island directly below Wayasewa's highest peak (349 meters), with Viti Levu clearly visible to the east behind Vomo Island. Photos don't do this place justice.

The resort is built on two terraces, one 10 meters above the beach and the other 10 meters above that. The lower terrace has the double, duplex, and dormitory *bures,* while the upper accommodates the former village schoolhouse, now partitioned into 14 tiny double rooms, and the restaurant/bar. Rooms with shared bath and open ceiling in the school building are F$35 pp, while the five individual *bures* with private bath and a small porch are F$50 pp. One duplex *bure* with four beds on each side serves as an eight-bed dormitory or *burebau* at F$30 pp. The camping space nearby is F$22 pp. If you pay seven nights the eight is free. The minimum stay is three nights.

Three ample Fijian meals are included in all rates and the food is good with second helpings allowed (free tea and coffee throughout the day). Breakfast is served at 0700 to give you an early start. A barbecue and bonfire are held on Wednesday night, and Sunday afternoon a *lovo* is prepared. There's no shortage of water. The electric generator goes off at 2200 and disturbances in the double rooms or dorm (if any) are most likely to come in the early morning as people get up to see the sunrise or to do a pre-breakfast hike. Dive Trek appeals to all ages—even those who might normally opt for one of the more upmarket Mamanuca resorts will find the double *bures* quite acceptable. The extraordinary mix of guests is also due to the emphasis on scuba diving. Informal musical entertainment occurs nightly, and because this resort is owned by the village, the staff is like one big happy family.

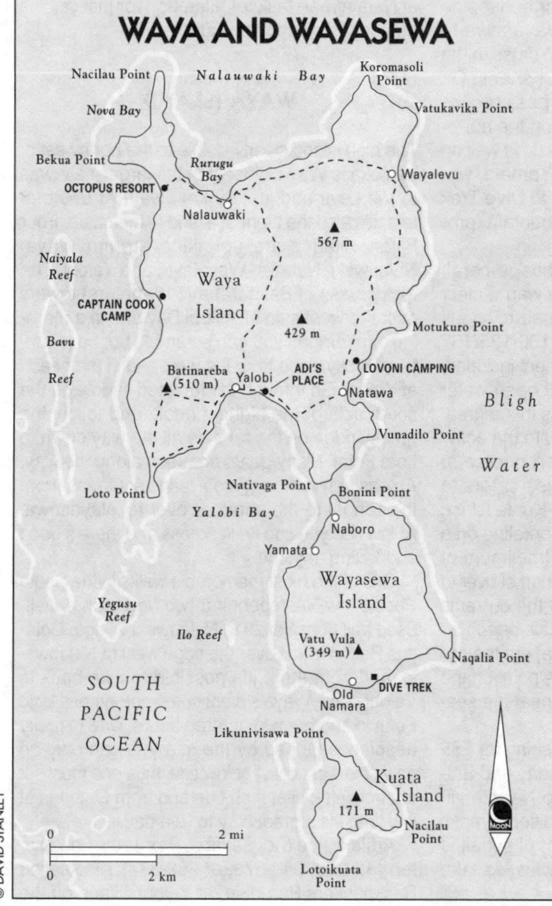



There's lots to see and do at Dive Trek with hiking and scuba diving the main activities. The most popular hike is to the top of Vatuvula, the fantastic volcanic plug hanging directly over the resort. The well trodden path circles the mountain and comes up the back, taking about 1.5 hours return excluding stops (a guide isn't really required). From the top of Vatuvula you get a sweeping view of the west side of Viti Levu, the Mamanucas, and the southern half of the Yasawa chain—one of the scenic highlights of the South Pacific. From Vatuvula you can trek northwest across the grassy uplands to another rock with a good view of Yalobi Bay (also known as Alacrity Bay).

The more ambitious can hike right around the island in four or five hours. Begin from Dive Trek just as the tide is starting to go out and travel counterclockwise to get over the hardest stretch first. Bush trails cut across the headlands to avoid coastal cliffs, but they're often hard to find, especially on the northeast side of the island. A sandbar links Wayasewa to Waya at low tide and it's possible to cross to the other island without removing your shoes. On your way around the island you'll pass two villages, Naboro and Yamata, both on the northwest side of Wayasewa, and if the tide is well on its way in by the time you get to Yamata, you should either look for a boat back to Dive Trek or ask about returning over the mountain (provided it's not too late).

The offshore reef features cabbage coral, whip coral, and giant fan corals in warm, clear waters teeming with fish, and scuba diving is well organized. Prices are F$65/100/135/157 for one/two/three/four tanks, equipment included, and Dive Trek's inexpensive PADI open-water certification course (F$330) makes this a great place to learn to dive. If you're new to the activity, try the "discover scuba" resort course at F$100. The resort's dive shop also caters to snorkelers with a snorkeling trip to Kuata Island at F$5 pp (minimum of five), or snorkeling on a reef halfway to Vomo at F$8 pp (minimum of six). With a buddy you could even snorkel over to Kuata, so long as you're aware of the currents (ask about this). There's a nice picnic beach on the side of Kuata facing Wayasewa, but the optimum snorkeling area is across the point on the southwest side. Look for the cave near the seagull rocks at the point itself.

Other activities include sunset fishing for F$5 pp (minimum of five), and on Tuesday and Saturday there's an organized visit to Naboro village for a kava ceremony and traditional *meke* entertainment (F$10 pp). Beach volleyball is every afternoon. No organized activities take place on Sunday.

Boat transfers from Lautoka depart Mon.-Sat. at 1300 (1.5 hours, F$40 pp one way). The boat leaves Dive Trek to return to Lautoka Mon.-Sat. at 0900. In both directions the boat fare includes bus transfers to/from Nadi/Lautoka hotels. Dive Trek also offers speedboat transfers to most other resorts in this area upon request: to Yalobi village on Waya Island at F$10 pp, to Octopus Resort F$20 pp, to Mana Island F$35 pp (three-person minimum).

You can book Dive Trek through **Rabua's Travel Agency** (tel./fax 724-364), Office No. 23, upstairs from the international arrivals concourse at Nadi Airport (ask for "Rambo"), or just call the number listed above. Budget

## WAYA ISLAND

The high island clearly visible to the northwest of Lautoka is Waya, closest of the larger Yasawas to Viti Levu and just 60 km away. At 579 meters, it's also the highest island in the chain. Four Fijian villages are sprinkled around Waya: Nalauwaki, Natawa, Wayalevu, and Yalobi. The rocky mass of Batinareba (510 meters) towers over the west side of Yalobi Bay and in a morning or afternoon you can scramble up the mountain's rocky slope from the west end of the beach at Yalobi. Go through the forested saddle on the south side of the highest peak, and follow the grassy ridge on the far side all the way down to Loto Point. Many goats are seen along the way. An easier hike from Yalobi leads southeast from the school to the sandbar over to Wayasewa. At low tide you can walk across and there's good snorkeling anytime.

One of the most memorable walks in the South Pacific involves spending two hours on a well-used trail from Yalobi to Nalauwaki village. Octopus Resort is just over the ridge west of Nalauwaki, and from there it's possible to hike back to Yalobi down Waya's west coast and across Loto Point in another two or three hours. Due to rocky headlands lapped by the sea you can only go down the west coast at low tide, thus one must set out from Yalobi at high tide and from Octopus at low tide. It's a great way to fill a day.

**Adi's Place** (Adi Sayaba, Box 1163, Lautoka; tel. 113-226, 650-573, or 962-377), also called Backpackers Paradise, at Yalobi village on the

## CAPTAIN WILLIAM BLIGH

In 1789, after being cast adrift by the mutineers on his HMS *Bounty,* Captain Bligh and 18 others in a seven-meter longboat were chased by two Fijian war canoes through what is now called Bligh Water. His men pulled the oars desperately, heading for open sea, and managed to escape the cannibals. They later arrived in Timor, finishing the most celebrated open-boat journey of all time. Captain Bligh did some incredible charting of Fijian waters along the way.

south side of Waya, is a small family-operated resort in existence since 1981. Although primitive, it makes a good hiking base with prices designed to attract and hold bare-budgeteers. The accommodations consist of one eight-bunk dorm at F$30 pp, a solid European-style house with three double rooms at F$40 pp, and camping space at F$20 pp. Lighting is by kerosene lamp. The rates include three meals but the food is variable with great meals served when Adi herself is present and little more than cabbage and rice at other times. If you've got a portable camp stove and a tent you can skip the meals and prepare your own food while paying F$9 pp to camp. Bring your own alcohol. It's right on one of the Yasawas' finest beaches, and you can lie in a hammock and observe village life (church on Sunday, kids going back and forth to school, etc.). Every Monday a cruise ship calls at Yalobi and the villagers put on traditional dances which Adi's guests can watch for F$5 per head. Scuba diving is not available here and you should not leave valuables unattended. If you haven't been able to reserve one of the more structured Yasawa resorts such as Dive Trek or Coral View, you should have no problem getting in here, but it shouldn't be your first choice. Adi's boat, the *Bula Tale,* departs Lautoka's Fisheries Wharf or the Neisau Marina for Yalobi daily except Sunday, charging F$35 pp each way for the two-hour trip. The boat usually stays overnight at Lautoka and leaves for Waya in the morning, returning to Lautoka in the afternoon, but this varies. Budget.

An even simpler budget place is **Lovoni Camping,** on a small rocky beach a 20-minute walk north of Natawa village on the east side of Waya. From Yalobi, it's a 30-minute hike across the ridge to Natawa. Lovoni is run by Adi's cousin Semi who had to rebuild everything after a hurricane in 1997. At last report there were two thatched *bures* at F$25 pp including meals and camping space. It's a place to hang out with some friendly people. Budget.

On a high white-sand beach in Likuliku Bay on northwestern Waya is **Octopus Resort Waya** (Box 1861, Lautoka; tel. 666-337, fax 666-210), run by Ingrid and Wolfgang Denk. Nalauwaki village is a 10-minute walk away over a low ridge. The four solidly constructed tin-roofed *bures* with private bath are F$68/88 single/double. Otherwise it's F$31 pp in a four-bed dorm, or F$22 pp to sleep in one of Octopus's set tents. If you bring your own tent it's also F$22 pp and there's an additional F$5 per tent fee to set it up (this unusual rate is part of a deliberate attempt to avoid overcrowding). Another two *bures* and a six-bed dorm may have gone up by the time you get there, but the Denks have no intention of expanding beyond that. Lunch and dinner are included in all rates. Drinks are served at their large restaurant/bar and a generator provides electricity in the public area each evening. Yachties are welcome to anchor offshore and use the facilities (meals can be ordered at F$4/12 for breakfast/dinner). When there's enough interest the Denks organize a *meke* (F$15 pp). Fishing trips are F$25 pp including lunch, but there's no scuba diving. Octopus is in a quiet, secluded location with some of Fiji's finest snorkeling right offshore (spectacular coral). It's one of the nicest backpacker resorts in the South Pacific—the equivalent of the upmarket Mamanuca resorts in almost everything but price. Reservations are essential as it's often full, and the most effective way to book is by fax as the phone connection doesn't always work. Allow ample time for this, and be persistent. Even then, readers have reported having their confirmed reservations canceled by Octopus at the last minute. Information may be available at the Cathay Hotel reception in Lautoka. Transfers depart Lautoka's Neisau Marina Monday at 1400 and Thursday at 1000, departing Waya for the return Monday and Wednesday at 0900 (F$40 each way).

## NAVITI ISLAND

Naviti, at 33 square km, is the largest of the Yasawas. Its king, one of the group's highest chiefs, resides at Soso, and the church there houses fine woodcarvings. On the hillside above Soso are two caves containing the bones of ancestors. Yawesa, the secondary boarding school on Naviti, is a village in itself. There are no accommodations for visitors.

## TAVEWA ISLAND

Tavewa is much smaller than Waya and twice as far from Lautoka, yet it's also strikingly beautiful with excellent bathing in the warm waters off a picture-postcard beach on the southeast side, and a good fringing reef with super snorkeling. Tall grass covers the hilly interior of this two-km-long island. Tavewa is in the middle of the Yasawas and from the summit you can behold the long chain of islands stretching out on each side with Viti Levu in the background. The sunsets can be splendid from the hill.

There's no chief here, as this is freehold land. In the late 19th century an Irishman named William Doughty married a woman from Nacula who was given Tavewa as her dowry. A decade or two later a Scot named William Bruce married into the Doughty family, and some time thereafter beachcombers called Murray and Campbell arrived on the scene and did the same, with the result that today some 50 Doughtys, Bruces, Murrays, and Campbells comprise the population of Tavewa. William Doughty himself died in 1926 at the ripe age of 77. Visit Auntie Lucy Doughty, the person who pioneered tourism to Tavewa back in the late 1970s, who lives next door to David Doughty's Place and sells books, maps, and postcards to visitors.

The islanders are friendly and welcoming; in fact, accommodating visitors is their main source of income. Most of their guests are backpackers who usually stay six nights, and most are sorry to leave. It's idyllic but bring along mosquito coils, toilet paper, candles, a flashlight (torch), bottled water, and a *sulu* to cover up. Be prepared for water shortages.

### Accommodations

In the budget to inexpensive category are three family-operated backpacker resorts on the east side of Tavewa. **Coral View Resort** (Box 3764, Lautoka; tel. 662-648) nestles in a cozy valley on a secluded beach with high hills on each side. It has six small thatched *bures* at F$66 double, four six-bunk dorm *bures* at F$30 pp, and mattresses in a large dormitory tent at F$25 pp. Camping with your own tent is F$22 pp. The new *bures* are F$80. There's no electricity in the *bures* but mosquito nets are supplied. You'll be lulled to sleep by the sound of the waves (unless you're in the two dorms near the noisy radio hut). Included are three generous meals (served promptly at 0800, 1200, and 1900) and one organized activity a day. Free boat trips are offered to Long Beach and Suntan Beach (both on Nacula Island), Honeymoon Island, and Blue Lagoon Beach. The excursion to Malakati village on Thursday morning or the boat trip to the Sawa-i-Lau caves requires a minimum of 10 people willing to pay F$20 to operate. Snorkeling gear is F$4 a day. In the evening a string band plays in the restaurant/bar and everyone sits around talking, drinking, or playing cards. Although there are lots of organized activities, Coral View is also a place where people come to relax and socialize, and most of the guests tend to be under 35. When the shuttle boat arrives from Lautoka all resort residents (including Snoopy the dog) line up on the beach to shake hands with new arrivals. Coral View tries to provide resort-style service (the staff wears matching uniforms), and Uncle Robert de Bruce keeps a close watch over everything from behind the scenes. Robert's son Don is captain of Coral View's 12-meter *Sabob III,* the fastest boat to Tavewa, which leaves Lautoka Wednesday at 1400 and on Tuesday and Saturday mornings, departing Tavewa for the return on Monday, Wednesday, and Friday mornings (2.5 hours, F$50 pp each way). Coral View bookings are handled at the reception of the Cathay Hotel in Lautoka, or at Coral View's Nadi Airport office (tel./fax 724-199) upstairs in the commercial arcade at arrivals. The airport office will give you a 15% discount if you book directly through them and stay at least four nights (the bare minimum you'd want to stay in any case).

The other main accommodation is **David's Place** (David and Kara Doughty, Box 10520, Nadi Airport; tel. 663-939), in a coconut grove near the small church on the island's longest beach. There are eight *bures* at F$66 double and two 10-bed dorms at F$30 pp (no electricity). Camping is F$22 pp with your own tent. David's *bures* are larger and more comfortable than those at Coral View. Since they started cutting

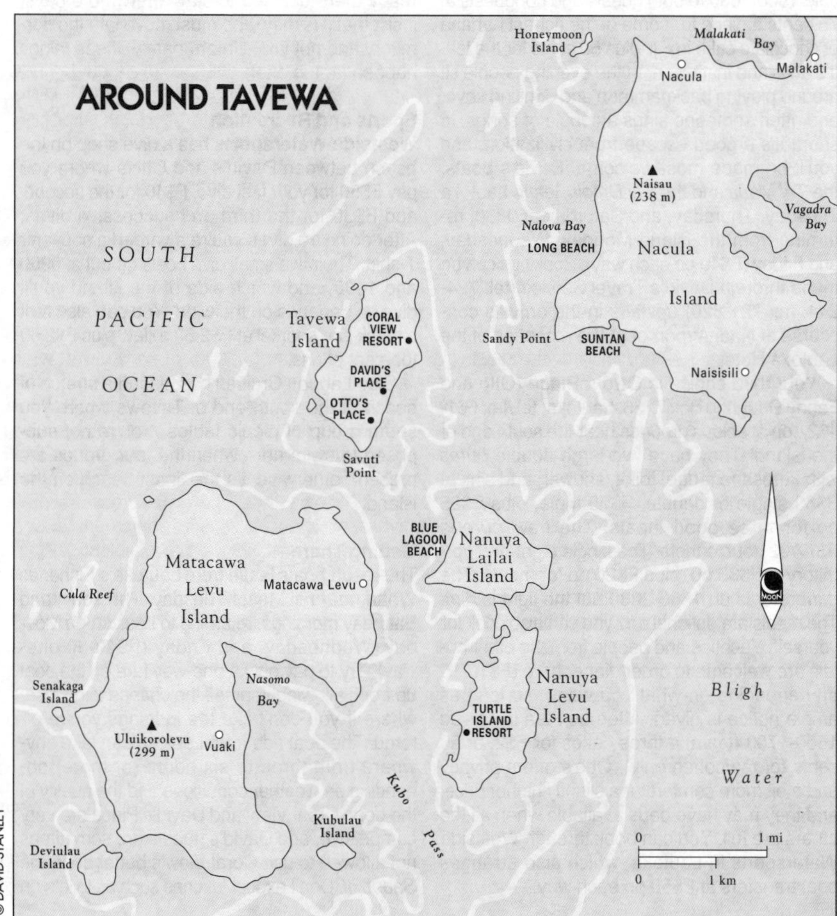

the grass the mosquito problem has declined, but the two communal toilets are sometimes inadequate. Three huge meals are included in the price with the Thursday *lovo* and Saturday barbecue part of the regular meal plan (opinions about the food vary). At David's you don't get the free trips provided at Coral View, but the optional tours are cheaper: F$12 for the cave trip and F$14 to visit Naisilisili village. David's solid new restaurant/bar with a concrete floor under the thatched roof serves as a hurricane shelter in time of need. David sells cold beer, soft drinks, and cigarettes here, and afternoon tea is available 1500-1630 to both guests and nonguests at 75 cents a piece for some of the richest banana or chocolate cake in Fiji, plus 50 cents for the tea. It's an island institution. In the evening people sit around playing backgammon and drinking kava, and often someone sings a couple of songs. In short, it's a good escape from civilization, and you'll be made most welcome. David's boats, the *Tai Maria* and the *Tai Dritolu,* leave Lautoka Tuesday, Thursday, and Saturday at 0830, returning from the island Monday, Wednesday, and Friday (F$40 pp each way). Bookings can be made through David's Travel Service (tel. 724-244, fax 721-820) upstairs in the arrivals concourse at Nadi Airport or at the reception of the Lautoka Hotel.

Your third choice is **Otto's Place** (Otto and Fanny Doughty, Box 7136, Lautoka; tel./fax 661-462), on spacious grounds near the south end of the island. They have two large double *bures* with kerosene fridge, toilet, shower, and sink at F$60 single or double, F$75 triple, plus F$25 pp for three good meals. The new *bure* is F$77/92 double/triple. The single eight-bed dormitory is F$30 pp, plus F$20 pp for meals. The generator is on 1800-2230 but the light is dim. The meals are optional and you can also cook for yourself. Yachties and people from the other hotels are welcome to order dinner here (F$10-15 pp depending on what you want), so long as ample notice is given. Afternoon tea is served 1500-1700 (tea and three cakes for F$2, or 50 cents for tea/coffee only). Otto's offers privacy and a bit more comfort for a slightly higher price, and they may have beds available when all the others are full. You can book through Westside Watersports in Lautoka, which also arranges boat transfers at F$50 pp each way.

Coral View caters more to the youth market while David's is fine for all ages. Pick Coral View if you want a lot of activities packed into a brief stay, David's if you want to relax. Be aware that bungalows on the island are in high demand and unless you have firm reservations you'll probably end up camping or staying in a dorm. If you definitely want a *bure* and nothing else, make this very clear when booking. Once on Tavewa, it may be difficult to extend your stay without taking somebody else's room. If you're still in Lautoka and hear that your prebooked room is no longer available because people already there decided to stay a few more days, insist that it is they who must move into the dormitory and not you. Unfortunately, these things happen far too often.

### Sports and Recreation

**Westside Watersports** has a dive shop on the beach between David's and Otto's where you pay F$50 for your first dive, F$40 for the second, and F$30 for the third and successive dives. After doing 10 dives you're awarded a souvenir T-shirt. Their two small dive boats go out at 0900 and 1400, and which side of the island you'll dive on depends on the wind. You can also rent a mask and snorkel at F$2.50 a day, plus F$2.50 for a set of fins.

Blue Lagoon Cruises has leased a stretch of beach at the south end of Tavewa where you see a group of picnic tables. You're not supposed to swim here when the tour groups are present, otherwise it's the finest beach on the island.

### Getting There

The resort boats leave from Lautoka's Fisheries Wharf near Fiji Meats Tuesday, Thursday, and Saturday mornings, returning to Lautoka on Monday, Wednesday, and Friday (F$40-50 one-way). Try to pay only a one-way fare on the boat up front, allowing yourself the chance to go elsewhere if you don't like the lodgings you're offered. The boat ride from Lautoka can take anywhere from three to six hours (or more) depending on weather conditions and the quality of the boat. Coral View and David's Place are very competitive, and David's guests are sometimes not allowed to use Coral View's better boat, the *Sabob III.* Don't expect luxuries such as toilets on these boats, so limit how much you drink before boarding. Also limit what you eat, or take seasickness pills if you're a poor sailor (a trip on one of the smaller boats can be frightful in rough weather). Be prepared to wade ashore at Tavewa.

## NANUYA LEVU ISLAND

In 1972 an eccentric American millionaire named Richard Evanson bought 200-hectare Nanuya Levu Island in the middle of the Yasawa Group for US$300,000. He still lives there, and his **Turtle Island Lodge** (Box 9317, Nadi Airport; tel. 663-889 or 660-922, fax 665-220) has gained a reputation as one of the South Pacific's ultimate hideaways. Only 14 fan-cooled, two-room *bures* grace Turtle, and Evanson swears there'll never be more.

Turtle is Tavewa at 20 times the price. The 28 guests (English-speaking mixed couples only, please) pay US$1,010 per couple per night plus 10% tax, but that includes all meals, drinks, and activities. You'll find the fridge in your cottage well stocked with beer, wine, soft drinks, and champagne, refilled daily, with no extra bill to pay when you leave. Sports such as sailing, snorkeling, scuba diving, canoeing, windsurfing, glass-bottom boating, deep-sea fishing, catamaraning, horseback riding, guided hiking, and moonlight cruising are all included in the tariff. Lodge staff will even do your laundry at no charge.

If you want to spend the day on any of the dozen secluded beaches, just ask and you'll be dropped off. Later someone will be back with lunch and a cooler of wine or champagne (or anything else you'd care to order over the walkie-talkie). Otherwise use the beach a few steps from your door. Meals are served at remote and romantic dine-out locations, or taken at the community table; every evening Richard hosts a small dinner party. He's turned down many offers to develop the island with hundreds more units or to sell out for a multimillion-dollar price. That's not Richard's style, and he's quite specific about who he *doesn't* want to come: "Trendies, jetsetters, obnoxious imbibers, and plastic people won't get much out of my place. Also, opinionated, loud, critical grouches and anti-socials should give us a miss." (Ringo Starr is said to be a regular here.)

Of course, all this luxury and romance has a price. Aside from the per diem, it's another US$750 per couple for roundtrip seaplane transportation to the island from Nadi. There's also a six-night minimum stay, but as nearly half the guests are repeaters that doesn't seem to be an impediment. (Turtle Island is off-limits to anyone other than hotel guests.) Turtle's success may be measured by its many imitators, including the Vatulele Island Resort, the Wakaya Club, Qamea Beach Club, Laucala Island, Kaimbu Is-

KARL PARTRIDGE

village house, Nacula village, Yasawa Islands

land, Nukubati Island Resort, and the Yasawa Island Resort.

Turtle Island has also set the standard for environmentally conscious resort development. Aside from planting thousands of trees and providing a safe haven for birds, Evanson has preserved the island's mangroves, cleverly erecting a boardwalk to turn what others may have considered an eyesore into a major attraction. And some of Evanson's guests do more than sun themselves. Every year since 1990 a group of California eye specialists has briefly converted Turtle Island into an unlikely clinic for dozens of Fijian villagers requiring eye surgery or just a recycled pair of prescription glasses, all for free.

Blue Lagoon Beach on neighboring **Nanuya Lailai Island** is used by cruise ship passengers and many yachts anchor just offshore. The snorkeling here is about the best in the area and boatloads of backpackers often arrive for a swim when the packaged tourists aren't around. You can tell the fish have been fed from the way they swim straight at you.

## SAWA-I-LAU ISLAND

On Sawa-i-Lau is a large limestone cave illuminated by a crevice at the top. There's a clear, deep pool in the cave where you can swim, and an underwater opening leads back into a smaller, darker cave (bring a light). A Fijian legend tells how a young chief once hid his love in this cave when her family wished to marry her off to another. Each day he brought her food until both could escape to safety on another island. Many cruise ships stop at this cave and the backpacker resorts on Tavewa also run tours. Yachties should present a *sevusevu* to the chief of Nabukeru village, just west of the cave, to visit. At last report Blue Lagoon Cruises wasn't visiting the cave anymore due to a dispute with the local chiefs over custom fees while Captain Cook Cruises did visit—this could change.

## YASAWA ISLAND

The Tui Yasawa, highest chief of the group, resides at Yasawairara village at the north end of Yasawa, northernmost island of the Yasawa group.

For many years the Fiji government had a policy that the Yasawas were "closed" to land-based tourism development, and it was only after the 1987 coups that approval was granted for the construction of **Yasawa Island Resort** (Box 10128, Nadi Airport; tel. 663-364, fax 665-044). This exclusive Australian-owned resort opened in 1991 on a creamy white beach on Yasawa's upper west side. Most of the resort's employees come from Bukama village, which owns the land.

The 16 thatched a/c *bures* with private baths consist of four duplexes at F$795 double, 10 deluxes at F$890, a two-bedroom unit at F$1,025, and a honeymoon unit at F$1,200, plus tax. Prices are reduced slightly in February and March. All meals are included, but unlike at most other resorts in this category, alcoholic drinks are *not.* Scuba diving and game fishing also cost extra. Guests arrive on a chartered flight (F$175 pp each way), which lands on the resort's private airstrip. Here you're met by a thatched six-wheel-drive truck called the "*bula* bus," seated on padded wooden benches in back, and carried to the resort. Children under 14 are only admitted during school holiday periods four times a year. To book, call only during local business hours, otherwise you'll get their machine. Luxury

M.G.L. DOMENY DE RIENZI

# KADAVU

This big, 50-by-13-km island 100 km south of Suva is the fourth largest in Fiji (411 square km). A mountainous, varied island with waterfalls plummeting from the rounded rainforested hilltops, Kadavu is outstanding for its vistas, beaches, and reefs. The three hilly sections of Kadavu are joined by two low isthmuses, with the sea biting so deeply into the island that on a map its shape resembles that of a wasp. Just northeast of the main island is smaller Ono Island and the fabulous Astrolabe Reef, stretching halfway to Suva. The birdlife is rich with species of honeyeaters, fantails, and velvet fruit doves found only here. The famous red-and-green Kadavu musk parrots may be seen and heard.

In the 1870s steamers bound for New Zealand and Australia would call at the onetime whaling station at Galoa Harbor to pick up passengers and goods, and Kadavu was considered as a possible site for a new capital of Fiji. Instead Suva was chosen and Kadavu was left to lead its sleepy village life; only today is the outside world making a comeback with the arrival of roads, planes, and a handful of visitors. Some 10,000 indigenous Fijians live in 60 remote villages scattered around the island.

## SIGHTS

The airstrip and wharf are each a 10-minute walk, in different directions, from the post office and hospital in the tiny government station of **Vunisea,** the largest of Kadavu's villages and headquarters of Kadavu Province. Vunisea is strategically located on a narrow, hilly isthmus where Galoa Harbor and Namalata Bay almost cut Kadavu in two.

The longest sandy beach on the island is at **Drue,** an hour's walk north from Vunisea. Another good beach is at **Muani** village, eight km south of Vunisea by road. Just two km south of the airstrip by road and a 10-minute hike inland is **Waikana Falls.** Cool spring water flows over a 10-meter-high rocky cliff between two deep pools, the perfect place for a refreshing swim

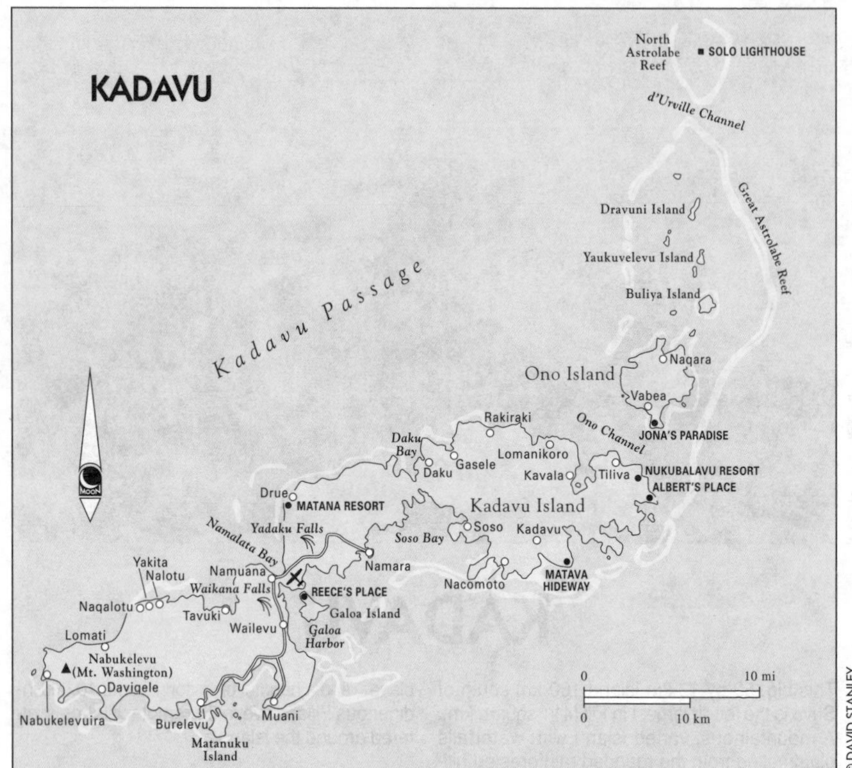


on a hot day. A second falls six km east of Vunisea is even better.

The women of **Namuana** village just west of the airstrip can summon **giant turtles** up from the sea by singing traditional chants to the *vu* (ancestral spirits) Raunidalice and Tinadi Caboga. On a bluff 60 meters above the sea, the garlanded women begin their song, and in 15 minutes a large turtle will appear. This turtle, and sometimes its mates, will swim up and down slowly offshore just below the overhanging rocks. For various reasons, the calling of turtles is performed very rarely these days.

### West of Vunisea

A road crosses the mountains from Namuana to **Tavuki** village, seat of the Tui Tavuki, paramount chief of Kadavu. A couple of hours west on foot is the **Yawe District,** where large pine tracts have been established. In the villages of Nalotu, Yakita, and Naqalotu at Yawe, traditional Fijian **pottery** is still made. Without potter's wheel or kiln, the women shape the pots with a paddle and fire them in an open fire. Sap from the mangroves provides a glaze.

Another road runs along the south coast from Vunisea to **Nabukelevuira** at the west end of Kadavu. There's good **surfing** at Cape Washington in this area but you'll need a boat and it's strongly suggested that you present a *sevusevu* to the village chief before engaging in the activity. Unfortunately, the villagers have become rather hostile to surfers who turn up unannounced and pay no heed to local customs.

The abrupt extinct cone of **Nabukelevu** (Mt. Washington) dominates the west end of Kadavu and petrels nest in holes on the north side of the mountain. It's possible to climb Nabukelevu (838 meters) from Nabukelevuira. There's no trail—you'll need a guide to help you hack a way.

### The Great Astrolabe Reef

The Great Astrolabe Reef stretches unbroken for 30 km along the east side of the small islands north of Kadavu. One km wide, the reef is unbelievably rich in coral and marinelife, and because it's so far from shore, it still hasn't been fished out. The reef surrounds a lagoon containing 10 islands, the largest of which is 30-square-km Ono. The reef was named by French explorer Dumont d'Urville, who almost lost his ship, the *Astrolabe,* here in 1827.

There are frequent openings on the west side of the reef and the lagoon is never over 10 fathoms deep, which makes it a favorite of scuba divers and yachties. The Astrolabe also features a vertical drop-off of 10 meters on the inside and 1,800 meters on the outside, with visibility up to 75 meters. The underwater caves and walls here must be seen to be believed. However, the reef is exposed to unbroken waves generated by the southeast trades and diving conditions are often dependent on the weather. Surfing is possible at Vesi Passage (boat required).

Many possibilities exist for ocean kayaking in the protected waters around Ono Channel and there are several inexpensive resorts at which to stay. Kayak rentals may not be available, thus one should bring along a folding kayak on the boat from Suva. Several companies mentioned in this book's main introduction offer kayaking tours in Kadavu.

## ACCOMMODATIONS

### Around Vunisea

Manueli and Tamalesi Vuruya run **Biana Accommodation** (Box 13, Vunisea; tel. 336-010), on a hill overlooking Namalata Bay near the jetty at Vunisea. The six rooms are F$30/55 single/double including breakfast, plus F$5 each for a real Fijian lunch or dinner (or you can cook). They ask that you call ahead before coming. Budget.

**Reece's Place** (Bill and Serima Reece, Box 6, Vunisea, Kadavu; tel. 336-097), on tiny Galoa Island just off the northwest corner of Kadavu, was the first to accommodate visitors to Kadavu, and it's still the least expensive place to stay around Vunisea station. It's a 15-minute walk from the airstrip to the dock, then a short launch ride to Galoa itself (F$6 pp return). There are 18 beds in three Fijian *bures* and three two-room houses at F$15 pp, and a F$9 five-bed dormitory. Pitch your tent for F$6 pp. Unless you have a camp stove, cooking your own food is not possible, but Serima is an excellent cook and three ample meals can be had for F$17 pp. There could be minor water problems. They use an electric generator in the evening. The view of Galoa Harbor from Reece's Place is excellent,

DAVID STANLEY

*Shoppers from outlying villages headed for Kadavu's market land on this beach near Vunisea. The hiking trails of Kadavu vie with untouched beaches such as this one in "downtown" Vunisea.*

and there's a long beach nearby, but the snorkeling in the murky water is poor. For F$8 pp (minimum of four), you can ride to the Galoa Barrier Reef, where the snorkeling is vastly superior. Scuba diving (F$35/60 one/two tanks plus F$15 for equipment) and PADI certification courses (F$280) are offered. They'll also take you surfing on the Great Astrolabe. Bill has spent many years overseas and is an entertaining guy with considerable knowledge of Fijian culture, local natural history, medicinal plants, etc. If you're there on Sunday, consider attending the service in the village church to hear the wonderful singing. Call ahead to check prices and availability. Shoestring.

A much more upscale operation is **Matana Beach Resort** (Box 8, Vunisea, Kadavu; tel. 311-780, fax 303-860) at Drue, six km north of Vunisea. The two oceanview *bures* on the hillside are F$200/330 single/double, while the six larger beachfront units are F$220/370/495/580 single/double/triple/quad, three meals included (three-night minimum stay, children under 12 not accepted). Boat transfers from Vunisea airport are also part of the package. Sunsets over Mt. Washington from the bar's open terrace can be spectacular. Matana caters almost exclusively to scuba divers who've booked from abroad with **Dive Kadavu.** The morning two-tank boat dive is F$130, and if they have a minimum of four people they'll do a one-tank afternoon dive for F$75 (the same applies at night). Their PADI open-water certification course is F$495. This whole operation meets the highest international standards. Windsurfers, sea kayaks, and paddle-boards are free. The snorkeling off Matana's golden beach is good, and the fantastic Namalata Reef is straight out from the resort. To snorkel from the dive boat is F$30. Premium.

### On North Kadavu

**Albert's Place** (Albert and Ruth O'Connor, c/o P.O. Naleca, Kadavu; tel. 336-086), at Lagalevu at the east end of Kadavu, is similar to Reece's Place but more remote. Each of the 10 small *bures* has a double and a single bed, coconut mats on the floor, and a kerosene lamp for light at F$22 pp (share twin) or F$12 pp in a six-bed dorm. Camping is F$9 pp. The units share rustic flush toilets and cold showers with plenty of running water (except during droughts), and everything is kept fairly clean. Mosquito nets and coils are supplied.

Meals cost another F$30 pp for all three, and Ruth O'Connor and her daughter Ramona serve huge portions. Their meals are exceptional, consisting of fresh fish, lobster, chicken curry, or seafood soup, and they bake their own bread daily. If you wish to do your own cooking, ask about this when booking, and bring your own stove and food, as little is available in Michel and Jesse's small store on the premises. There are several lovely waterfalls nearby where you can swim, and in the evening everybody sits around the kava bowl and swaps stories. As there are never more than 20 guests here at a time, it gets very chummy. The snorkeling right off Albert's beach is excellent, and scuba with **Naiqoro Divers** (run by Ezra with the help of Albert's sons Bruce and Julian) is F$50/70 for one/two tank boat dives, plus F$15 a day for equipment. Shore dives are F$10 a tank if you have your own gear. The equipment is new, the prices good, and these guys know their waters.

The easiest way to get there from Suva is by boat on the *Gurawa* or *Bulou-ni-Ceva,* which will bring you directly to Albert's Place or to Kavala Bay (a good hour west of Albert's on foot). Albert will pick you up at Vunisea Airport at F$55 for the first one or two plus F$25 for each additional person for the two-hour boat ride (these prices are fixed, so don't bother bargaining). Be sure to let him know you're coming. It's wise to allow plenty of time coming and going, so plan a stay at Albert's Place early on in your visit to Fiji so you don't have to be in a big rush to leave. People rave about this property—just don't expect luxuries like electricity at those prices! Budget.

The **Nukubalavu Adventure Resort** (Box 11522, Suva; tel. 520-089, fax 308-686) faces a two-km beach on the north side of Kadavu, between Albert's and Kavala Bay. Originally a backpacker camp, the resort has been upgraded and two-week dive vacationers are now the target market. With electricity, hot water, and private baths installed, rates for the five standard *bures* are F$50/75/105 single/double/triple, while the four deluxe units cost F$86/120/155. The 12-bed dorm is F$25 pp. The three-meal package is another F$60. Add 10% tax to all rates, plus another 5% if you pay by credit card. Scuba diving costs F$65/125/335 one/two/six tanks for boat dives or F$85 for night dives, plus F$25 for equipment rental, and a PADI certification course is offered at F$400. Snorkeling from the boat is F$25 including gear. The gorgeous Great Astrolabe Reef is only a five-minute boat ride away, and Nukubalavu claims to have purchased the exclusive right to dive on 50 different sites there! In any case, it's cheaper here than at the Matana Resort, though they don't have the same kind of boats available. The Nukubalavu launch can pick you up at Vunisea airport (F$35 pp each way with a two-person minimum), or come on by boat, which will drop you directly at the resort. (Incidentally, there's intense rivalry between Nukubalavu and Albert's Place, so take whatever you hear from one side or the other with a grain of salt.) Bookings are handled by their Suva office (tel. 314-554) on the 2nd floor of Pacific House, Butt and MacArthur Streets. Inexpensive.

Not to be confused with the Matana Resort is a newer resort called **Matava, The Astrolabe Hideaway** (Mark O'Brien, Box 63, Vunisea; tel. 336-098, fax 336-099), a 30-minute walk east of Kadavu village and almost opposite tiny Waya Island. The beach in front of Matava is rather muddy and shallow but the snorkeling off Waya is fine. Organized snorkeling trips are F$12, plus $8 if you need a mask and snorkel. There are three thatched *bures* with private bath at F$68 single or double, four doubles with shared bath at F$35, and two quads at F$45. The quads are also used as five-bed dorms at F$15 pp, or you can camp at F$8 pp. A deluxe oceanview *bure* with private bath is F$90 double. The meal plan is F$30 pp. Add 10% tax to all rates at Matava. Scuba diving is available at F$40/75/350 for one/two/10 tanks, plus F$20 for equipment. Night dives are F$50. PADI open-water certification is F$350. Kayaks, canoes, and windsurfers are for rent at F$10 a day. They'll pick you up from Albert's Place at F$10 pp, or charge F$22 pp each way for boat transfers from the airport. Budget to inexpensive.

### Accommodations on Ono

**Jona's Paradise Resort** (Box 15447, Suva; tel. 315-889, fax 315-992), at Vabea at the southern tip of Ono Island, offers accommodation in five traditional beach *bures* at F$65/110/150 single/double/triple, or camping at F$30 pp (minimum stay three nights). Children under 12 are welcome at F$25 in the parents *bure* or F$15 in a tent. All prices include three tasty meals but you might bring a few snack foods with you. It's a small, family-style resort with a steep white-sand beach, great snorkeling (hundreds of clownfish in crystal-clear water). Dive Kadavu has recently opened a base at the resort (see the Matana Beach Resort listing above for scuba rates). Boat trips are F$65/100 per half/full day, and you can also go hiking in the hills. Husband Jona is the best fisherman around (expect fresh fish every day and mud crab occasionally), wife Ledua is a super cook, young son Veita is an expert guide, and grandfather Villame is a master builder. One reader called this place "the image of paradise." The ferries *Gurawa* and *Bulou-ni-Ceva* drop passengers here once or twice a week, or you can arrange to be collected at Vunisea airport (F$50 pp each way). In Suva, book stays at Jona's at Global Air Services (tel. 315-889), 3 Ellery Street. Otherwise call Dive Kadavu. Budget.

A Canadian company plans to build a new 50-*bure* upmarket hotel called the **Yaukuve Vacation Resort** on Yaukuvelevu Island in the Astrolabe Lagoon north of Ono.

## OTHER PRACTICALITIES

Vunisea has no restaurants, but a coffee shop at the airstrip opens mornings, and two general stores sell canned goods. A woman at the market serves tea and scones when the market is open, Tues.-Saturday. Buy *waka* at the coop store for formal presentations to village hosts.

No banks are to be found on Kadavu, so change enough money before coming (and don't leave it unattended in your room or tent). Occasional carriers ply the 78 km of roads on Kadavu, but no buses.

## GETTING THERE

**Air Fiji** arrives from Suva twice a day (F$92) and **Sunflower Airlines** has daily flights from Nadi (F$126). Be sure to reconfirm your return flight immediately upon arrival. Only Reece's

Place meets all flights—boat pickups by the resorts on north Kadavu and Ono must be prearranged. The speedboats to north Kadavu are usually without safety equipment or roofs and in rough weather everything could get wet. There's no road from Vunisea to north Kadavu.

Boats arrive at Vunisea from Suva about twice a week, calling at villages along the north coast. The MV *Gurawa* of **Whippy's Shipping Co.** (tel. 311-507 or 340-015) leaves Suva for Ono and northern Kadavu Friday at 0600 (F$40 pp), returning to Suva on Saturday morning. Ask if lunch is included in the fare. The MV *Bulou-ni-Ceva* of the **Kadavu Shipping Co.** (tel. 311-766) also plies between Suva and Kadavu once or twice a week. Take seasickness precautions before boarding. For details turn to "Transportation" in the Suva section.

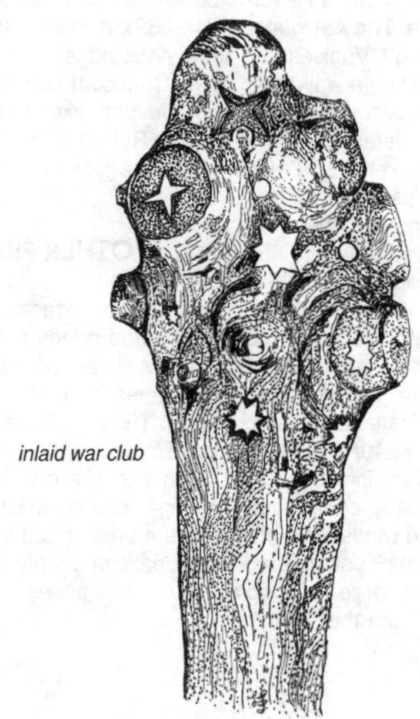

inlaid war club

LOUISE FOOTE

SALVATORE CASA

# THE LOMAIVITI GROUP

The Lomaiviti (or central Fiji) Group lies in the Koro Sea near the heart of the archipelago, east of Viti Levu and south of Vanua Levu. Of its nine main volcanic islands, Gau, Koro, and Ovalau are among the largest in Fiji. Lomaiviti's climate is moderate, neither as wet and humid as Suva, nor as dry and hot as Nadi. The population is mostly Fijian, engaged in subsistence agriculture and copra making.

The old capital island, Ovalau, is by far the best known and most visited island of the group, and several small islands south of Ovalau on the way to Suva bear popular backpackers' resorts. Naigani also has a tourist resort of its own, but Koro and Gau are seldom visited, due to a lack of facilities for visitors. Ferries ply the Koro Sea to Ovalau, while onward ferries run to Vanua Levu a couple of times a week.

# OVALAU ISLAND

Ovalau, a large volcanic island just east of Viti Levu, is the main island of the Lomaiviti Group. Almost encircled by high peaks, the Lovoni Valley in the center of Ovalau is actually the island's volcanic crater and about the only flat land. The crater's rim is pierced by the Bureta River, which escapes through a gap to the southeast. The highest peak is 626-meter Nadelaiovalau (meaning, the top of Ovalau), behind Levuka. Luckily Ovalau lacks the magnificent beaches found elsewhere in Fiji, which has kept the package-tour crowd away, and upmarket scuba divers have many better places to go, so it's still one of the most peaceful, pleasant, and picturesque historic places to visit in the South Pacific.

## LEVUKA

The town of Levuka on Ovalau's east side was Fiji's capital until the shift to Suva in 1882. Founded as a whaling settlement in 1830, Levuka became the main center for European traders in Fiji, and a British consul was appointed in 1857. The cotton boom of the 1860s brought new settlers, and Levuka quickly grew into a boisterous town with over 50 hotels and taverns along Beach Street. Escaped convicts and debtors fleeing creditors in Australia swelled the throng, until it was said that a ship could find the reef passage into Levuka by following the empty gin bottles floating out on the tide. The honest traders felt the need for a stable government, so in 1871 Levuka became capital of Cakobau's Kingdom of Fiji. The disorders continued, with extremist elements forming a "Ku Klux Klan," defiant of any form of Fijian authority.

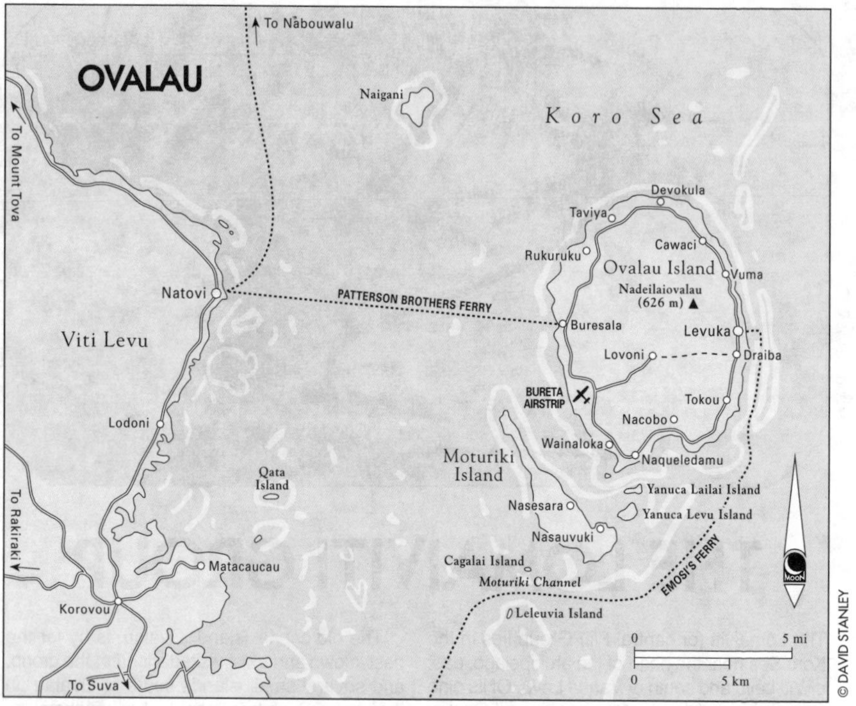

On 10 October 1874, a semblance of decorum came as Fiji was annexed by Great Britain and a municipal council was formed in 1877. British rule soon put a damper on the wild side of the blackbirding. Ovalau's central location seemed ideal for trade, and sailing boats from Lau or Vanua Levu could easily enter the port on the southeast trades. Yet the lush green hills that rise behind the town were to be its downfall, as colonial planners saw that there was no room for the expansion of their capital, and in August 1882 Gov. Sir Arthur Gordon moved his staff to Suva. Hurricanes in 1888 and 1895 destroyed much of early Levuka, with the north end of town around the present Anglican church almost flattened, and many of Levuka's devastated buildings were not replaced.

Levuka remained the collection center for the copra trade right up until 1957, but the town seemed doomed when that industry, too, moved to a new mill in Suva. But with the establishment of a fishing industry in 1964 Levuka revived, and today it's is a minor educational center, the headquarters of Lomaiviti Province, and a low-impact tourist center. There's a public electricity supply.

The false-fronted buildings and covered sidewalks along Beach Street give this somnolent town of 4,000 mostly Fijian or part-Fijian inhabitants a 19th-century, Wild West feel. From the waterfront, let your eyes follow the horizon from right to left to view the islands of Gau, Batiki, Nairai, Wakaya, Koro, and Makogai, respectively. Levuka's a perfect base for excursions into the mountains, along the winding coast, or out to the barrier reef a kilometer offshore.

It's customary to say "Good morning," *"Bula,"* or simply "Hello" to people you meet while strolling around Levuka, especially on the backstreets, and the locals have been rather put off by tourists who failed to do so. This is one of the little adverse effects of tourism, and a very unnecessary one at that.

## SIGHTS

Near Queen's Wharf is the old Morris Hedstrom store, erected by Percy Morris and Maynard Hedstrom in 1880s, great-granddaddy of today's Pacific-wide Morris Hedstrom chain. The store closed when the lease expired in 1979 and the building was turned over to the National Trust for Fiji. In 1981 the facility reopened as the **Levuka Community Center** (tel. 440-356; closed Sunday; admission F$2) with a museum and library, where cannibal forks vie with war clubs and clay pots for your attention. The many old photos of the town in the museum are fascinating and a side door leads into Patterson Gardens, a pleasant place to sit and take in the scene.

Stroll north along Levuka's sleepy waterfront to the **Church of the Sacred Heart,** erected by French Marist priests who arrived in 1858. The church's square clock tower was added in 1898 to commemorate the first priest, Father Breheret. The green neon cross on the stone tower lines up with another green light farther up the hill to guide mariners into port. Go through the gate behind the church to the formidable **Marist Convent School** (1892), originally a girls school operated by the sisters and still a primary school.

Totogo Lane leads north from the convent to a small bridge over Totogo Creek and the **Ovalau Club** (1904), adjoining the old **Town Hall** (1898), also known as Queen Victoria Memorial Hall, and the **Masonic Lodge** (1913), founded as "Little Polynesia" in 1875.

Recross the bridge and follow Garner Jones Road west up the creek to the **Levuka Public School** (1879), the birthplace of Fiji's present public educational system. Before WW I the only Fijians allowed to attend this school were the sons of chiefs. Other Levuka firsts include Fiji's first newspaper (1869), first Masonic Lodge (1875), first bank (1876), and first municipal council (1877).

Continue straight up Garner Jones Road for about 10 minutes, past the lovely colonial-era houses, and you'll eventually reach the source of the town's water supply, from which there's a good view. The path to **The Peak** branches off to the left between the steel water tank and the gate at the end of the main trail. It takes about an hour to scale The Peak, preferably with the guidance of some of the local kids.

DAVID STANLEY

*view of Levuka as seen from Gun Rock*

As you come back down the hill, turn left onto Church St. and follow it around to **Navoka Methodist Church** (1862). From beside this church mount the 199 steps to **Mission Hill** and Delana Methodist High School, which affords fine views. The mission school formed here by Rev. John Binner in 1852 was the first in Fiji.

### North of Levuka

On a low hill farther north along the waterfront is the **European War Memorial,** which recalls British residents of Levuka who died in WW I. Before Fiji was ceded to Britain, the Cakobau government headquarters was situated on this hill. **Holy Redeemer Anglican Church** (1904) beyond has period stained-glass windows.

Follow the coastal road north from Levuka to a second yellow bridge, where you'll see the **old Methodist church** (1869) on the left. Ratu Seru Cakobau worshipped here and in the small cemetery behind the church is the grave of the first U.S. consul to Fiji, John Brown Williams (1810-1860). For the story of Williams's activities, see "History and Government" in the main introduction. Across the bridge and beneath a large *dilo* tree is the tomb of an old king of Levuka. The large house in front of the tree is the residence of the present Tui Levuka.

Directly above is **Gun Rock,** which was used as a target in 1849 to show Cakobau the efficacy of a ship's cannon so he might be more considerate to resident Europeans. The early Fijians had a fort atop the Rock to defend themselves against the Lovoni hill tribes. Ask permission of the Tui Levuka (the "Roko") or a member of his household to climb Gun Rock for a splendid view of Levuka. If a small boy leads you up and down, it wouldn't be out of place to give him something for his trouble.

Continue north on the road, round a bend, pass the ruin of a large concrete building, and you'll reach a cluster of government housing on the site of a cricket field where the Duke of York (later King George V) played in 1878.

There's a beautiful deep pool and waterfall behind **Waitovu** village, about two km north of Levuka. You may swim here, but please don't skinny-dip; this is offensive to the local people and has led to confrontations in past. Since they're good enough to let you use this idyllic spot (which they own), it's common courtesy to respect their wishes (and to avoid arriving on a Sunday).

At Cawaci, a 30-minute walk beyond the Ovalau Holiday Resort, is a small white mausoleum (1922) high up on a point with the tombs of Fiji's first and second Catholic bishops, Bishop Julien Vidal and Bishop Charles Joseph Nicholas. The large coral stone church (1897) of **St. John's College** is nearby. This is the original seat of the Catholic Church in Fiji and the sons of the Fijian chiefs were educated here from 1894 onwards.

### South of Levuka

The **Pacific Fishing Company** tuna cannery (Box 41, Levuka; tel. 440-005, fax 440-400) is south of Queen's Wharf. A Japanese cold-stor-

*The Provincial Council meeting place at Levuka is built to resemble a traditional Fijian chief's* bure.

DAVID STANLEY

age facility opened here in 1964, the cannery in 1975. After sustaining losses for four years, the Japanese company involved in the joint venture pulled out in 1986, turning the facility over to the government, which now owns the cannery. In 1989 a F$2 million state-of-the-art can-making factory opened alongside the cannery, and major improvements to the wharf, freezer, storage, and other facilities were completed in 1992. The plant is supplied with albacore tuna caught in Kiribati and Solomons waters by Taiwanese longline fishing boats, and with skipjack and yellowfin by pole-and-line ships of the government-owned Ika Corporation. For both environmental and quality-control reasons, fish caught with nets are not accepted here. Most of the F$50 million worth of canned tuna produced each year is marketed in Britain by Sainsbury and John West, and in Canada by B.C. Packers. A thousand residents of Ovalau have jobs directly related to tuna canning and the government has heavily subsidized the operation to keep it going.

A little farther along is the **Cession Monument,** where the Deed of Cession, which made Fiji a British colony, was signed by Chief Cakobau in 1874. The traditional *bure* on the other side of the road was used by Prince Charles during his 1970 visit to officiate at Fiji's independence. It's now the venue of provincial council meetings.

One of Fiji's most rewarding hikes begins at Draiba village, a kilometer south of the Cession Monument. A road to the right just after a small bridge and before four single-story apartment blocks, marks the start of the 4.5-hour hike through enchanting forests and across clear streams to **Lovoni** village. Go straight back on this side road till you see an overgrown metal scrapyard on your right, near the end of the road. Walk through the middle of the scrapyard and around to the right of a decrepit tin-roofed building. The unmarked Lovoni trail begins at the foot of the hill, just beyond this building.

The Lovoni trail is no longer used by the locals and requires attentiveness to follow, so consider Epi's Midland Tour if you're not an experienced hiker. Be sure to reach Lovoni before 1500 to be able to catch the last bus back to Levuka. In 1855 the fierce Lovoni tribe, the Ovalau, burned Levuka, and they continued to threaten the town right up until 1871 when they were finally captured during a truce and sold to European planters as laborers. In 1875 the British government allowed the survivors to return to their valley, where their descendants live today.

If you forgo this hike and continue on the main road, you'll come to an old **cemetery** a little south of Draiba. A few kilometers farther is the **Devil's Thumb,** a dramatic volcanic plug towering above **Tokou** village, one of the scenic highlights of Fiji. Catholic missionaries set up a printing press at Tokou in 1889 to produce gospel lessons in Fijian. In the center of the village is a sculpture of a lion made by one of the early priests. It's five km back to Levuka.

**Wainaloka** village on the southwest side of Ovalau is inhabited by descendants of Solomon Islanders from the Lau Lagoon region who were blackbirded in Fiji over a century ago.

### Sports and Recreation

**Ovalau Divers** (Box 145, Levuka; tel. 440-095) operates out of Cafe Levuka. They offer diving on seven shipwrecks around Levuka at F$55/80 for one/two dives.

Most of the hotels (including the Royal) will arrange boats for reef snorkeling at F$6 pp, or for fishing at F$8 pp, upon prior notice. At high tide the river mouth near the Royal Hotel is an extremely popular swimming hole for the local kids (and some tourists). The rest of the day locals cool off by just sitting in the water fully dressed.

## ACCOMMODATIONS

There's a good choice of budget places to stay around Levuka (and thankfully no luxury resorts). The **Colonial Inn** (Box 50, Levuka; tel. 440-057), on Convent Road, has six double rooms above their restaurant at F$15/25 single/double, and dorm beds at F$10 pp, a cooked breakfast included. There's no hot water. Shoestring.

Another good bet is the **Old Capital Inn** (tel. 440-013) on Beach Street. The 15 fan-cooled rooms cost the same as rooms at Colonial Inn (where guests from both places take their breakfast). A separate cottage with cooking facilities is F$20/28/35 single/double/triple—good value. The quality of the beds in the dorm section here is poor, but a cool breeze blowing in from the east keeps the mosquitoes away. Budget.

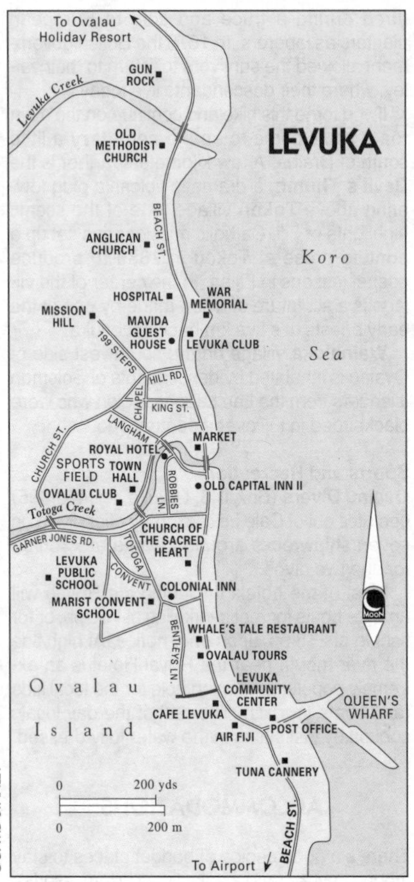


**Mavida Guesthouse** (Box 4, Levuka; tel. 440-477) on Beach Street, which has been functioning since 1869, is Fiji's oldest guesthouse. This old-fashioned English bed and breakfast owned by Patterson Brothers Shipping occupies a spacious colonial house on the waterfront near the Levuka Club. The 12 rooms are F$16/28 single/double, or F$9 in the dormitory (F$12 if you want a mosquito net), a cooked breakfast included. You can order an excellent dinner here. It's worth asking to see the room beforehand as all are different, and their nicest rooms go for F$30 double. Ask for a mosquito net. Unfortunately the Patterson Brothers bus which parks directly in front of the guesthouse every night cancels out some of the flavor. Budget.

For the full Somerset Maugham flavor, stay at the 15-room **Royal Hotel** (Box 47, Levuka; tel. 440-024, fax 440-174). Originally built in 1852 and rebuilt by Captain David Robbie in 1913 after a fire in the 1890s, this is Fiji's oldest regular hotel, run by the Ashley family since 1927. In the lounge, ceiling fans revolve above the rattan sofas and potted plants, and the fan-cooled rooms upstairs with private bath and minifridge are pleasant, with much-needed mosquito nets provided. Each room is in a different style. It's F$18/28/33 single/double/triple in the main building. There are also three a/c rooms with shared cooking facilities in a garden building at F$55 double, plus one large family cottage capable of accommodating 11 persons in five rooms at F$77 for the unit. The most deluxe accommodations are the two new self-catering cottages facing Beach St., which go for F$77 double. The 11-bed dormitory near the bar is F$10 pp. Checkout time is 1000, but you can arrange to stay until 1500 by paying another 50% of the daily rate (no credit cards accepted). Hotel staff will do your laundry for F$5. Everybody loves this place, but don't order dinner (F$8) as the food isn't highly rated. The bar, beer garden, snooker tables, dart boards, and videos are strictly for guests only. The colonial atmosphere and anachronistic prices make it about the best value in Fiji. Budget to inexpensive.

The **Sailor's Home** (Ovalau Tours and Transport, Box 149, Levuka; tel. 440-611, fax 440-405) is a restored 1870s house with two rooms at F$99 single or double (children under 12 free). There's a fully equipped kitchen and this old colonial house might just be the nicest place to stay in Fiji. Moderate.

### Around the Island

A good choice for families is the **Ovalau Holiday Resort** (Stephen and Rosemary Diston, Box 113, Levuka; tel. 440-329, fax 440-019) on a rocky beach at Vuma, four km north of Levuka (taxi F$5). *Bures* are F$22/35/45 single/double/triple, or pay F$8 pp in the dorm. Camping is F$5 pp, with the use of the dorm facilities. Cooking facilities, fridge, and hot showers are provided, and there's the Bula Beach Bar in a converted whaler's cottage. Given sufficient advance notice the restaurant does some fine home cooking. Though often dry, the swimming pool is the only one on Ovalau and the snorkeling around here is good. It's a nice place for an afternoon at the beach even if you prefer to stay in Levuka. Budget.

Ovalau Tours and Transport (Box 149, Levuka; tel. 440-611, fax 440-405) books accommodations at **Devokula village** at the north end of Ovalau, 11 km from Levuka. Guests sleep on mats under mosquito nets in one of seven authentic Fijian *bures* at F$99/155 single/double including all meals and activities. If you're willing to share the *bure* with other visitors it's F$55 pp. The only concession to the modern world here are the flush toilets and showers, otherwise it's the full Fijian experience. Transfers to Devokula are F$10 pp from Levuka or F$25 pp from the airport (minimum of two). Moderate to Expensive.

On the northwest side of Ovalau, 20 km from Levuka, is **Rukuruku Holiday Resort** (Box 112, Levuka; no phone). At last report the National Bank was foreclosing and the whole operation seemed to be on the verge of ruin. You can still camp for F$8 pp with some services provided, and dormitory-style accommodations are available at F$15-20 pp including breakfast. A rundown "deluxe *bure*" is also on offer, but at F$75 double plus 10% tax it's not worth it. The generator is often on the blink and they're usually out of beer. Basic groceries can be purchased in the adjacent Fijian village. The black-sand beach is only so-so, but the snorkeling out on the reef is good, and there's a natural freshwater swimming pool in the river adjacent to the resort. A vanilla plantation and beautiful verdant mountains cradle Rukuruku on the island side. This place has potential and attempts have been made to sell the property over the internet. Meanwhile, make sure they're still open before heading that way.

## FOOD

Few of the guesthouses in Levuka provide cooking facilities, but a half dozen small restaurants face Beach Street. All of these places are patronized mostly by foreigners, and prices are higher than what you may have paid in Suva or Lautoka, but with luck you'll enjoy some superior meals. In fact, many visitors seem to spend most of their time hopping from restaurant to restaurant.

**Cafe Levuka** (tel. 440-095), opposite the Community Center, has F$6 dinner specials daily until 2000. It's a good place to find out what's happening around town over coffee and cakes. Their fruit pancakes are great for breakfast.

**Kim's Restaurant** (tel. 440-059), also known as Pak Kum Loong, upstairs in a building near Court's Furniture Store, has a selection of Chinese dishes for under F$5. It's a good place to come for lunch weekdays as several inexpensive dishes are kept in a glass warmer at the entrance (meals ordered from the menu are individually prepared). You can dine on their breezy front terrace with a view of the waterfront.

The **Whale's Tale Restaurant** (tel. 440-235) on Beach Street is a favorite for its real home cooking at medium prices. A cooked breakfast with coffee will be F$6.60, buttered pasta for lunch costs F$5.50, and the three-course dinner special with a choice from among five main plates is F$10. They're fully licensed so you can get a beer with your meal, and their specially percolated coffee is the best in town. They sell bags of kava, Fijian handicrafts, and lovely tapa greeting cards.

The **Sea Site Restaurant** (tel. 440-553), a bit north of Whale's Tale, is basic, overpriced, and not recommended.

The **Colonial Inn** (tel. 440-057), on Convent Road, has an all-you-can-eat dinner Sunday at 1830 (F$7). There's a good selection of items in their buffet, and cold beer is available.

## ENTERTAINMENT

Despite the Members Only sign, you're welcome to enter the **Ovalau Club** (tel. 440-102), said to be the oldest membership club in the South Pacific. You'll meet genuine South Seas characters here, and the place is brimming with atmosphere. Ask the bartender to show you the framed letter from Count Felix von Luckner, the WW I German sea wolf. Von Luckner left the letter and some money at the unoccupied residence of a trader on Katafaga Island in the Lau Group, from which he took some provisions. In the letter, Count von Luckner identifies himself as

Max Pemberton, an English writer on a sporting cruise through the Pacific.

A good place for sunsets is the **Levuka Club** (tel. 440-272) on Beach Street, which has a nice backyard with picnic tables beside the water. It's less visited by tourists and a better choice than the Ovalau Club if you only want a quick beer.

## SERVICES AND INFORMATION

### Services

The **Westpac Bank** (tel. 440-346) and the **National Bank** (tel. 440-300) on Beach Street change traveler's checks.

Cafe Levuka will wash, dry, and fold your laundry within three hours for F$6.

Public toilets are available across the street from the National Bank.

### Information

The Tourist Information Desk at the Levuka Community Center (tel. 440-356) should have information on the offshore island resorts and various land tours around Ovalau.

Lisa at the Whale's Tale Restaurant (tel. 440-235) will be happy to give you her frank opinion of the offshore resorts—invaluable when planning a trip. Cafe Levuka (tel. 440-095) maintains a "Tourist Information Book" containing current information about almost every aspect of travel around Ovalau. The restaurant staffs are probably the people most likely to give you a straight answer to any question you may have about Levuka. Cafe Levuka also runs a one-for-one book exchange.

## TRANSPORTATION

**Air Fiji** (tel. 440-139), across the street from the Levuka Community Center, has two or three flights a day between Bureta Airport and Suva (F$54). Sunflower Airlines has an office next to Ovalau Tours on Beach St., but no flights from Ovalau at present. The Ovalau Tours minibus from Levuka to the airstrip is F$3 pp (a taxi will run F$17).

Inquire at **Patterson Brothers** (tel. 440-125), beside the market on Beach Street, about the direct ferry from Ovalau to Nabouwalu, Vanua Levu, via Natovi. The connecting bus departs Levuka Mon.-Sat. at about 0500. At Nabouwalu, there's an onward bus to Labasa, but bookings must be made in advance (F$51 straight through).

The bus/ferry/bus service between Suva and Levuka was discussed previously under "Transportation" in the Suva section. Two competing services are available, each taking just under five hours right through, and costing around F$24. The Patterson Brothers combination involves an express bus from Levuka to Buresala daily except Sunday at 0500, a 45-minute ferry ride from Buresala to Natovi, then the same bus on to Suva (change at Korovou for Lautoka). Bicycles are carried free on the ferry. The other choice is the *Emosi Express* leaving Queen's Wharf, Levuka, at 0900 on Monday, Wednesday, and Friday to Bau Landing, then a minibus to Suva (arriving at 1400). Southbound you can get off in Nausori and connect with the Sunbeam Transport bus to Lautoka at 1400. Inquire at the Old Capital Inn. From Levuka, Emosi's boat is more conveniently timed and there's a brief visit to Leleuvia Island, where free stopovers are possible. Advance bookings are required on the Patterson Brothers ferry/bus service, but not on Emosi's boat. Use a different service each way for a scenic circle trip from Suva.

Both taxis and carriers park across the street from the Church of the Sacred Heart in Levuka. Due to steep hills on the northwest side of Ovalau, there isn't a bus right around the island. Carriers leave Levuka for Rukuruku village Mon.-Fri. at 0745, 1145, and 1700, Saturday at 1145 and 1430 (F$1.50) along a beautiful, hilly road. During the school holidays only the 1145 trip may operate. Occasional buses and carriers also go to Lovoni (F$1). There's no service on Sunday.

### Tours

**Epi's Midland Tour** is a guided hike to Lovoni that departs Levuka Mon.-Sat. around 1000 (F$15 pp including lunch). You hike over and return by truck (or you can just go both ways by truck if you don't wish to walk). The route is steep and rugged footwear is essential. At Lovoni you can go for a swim in the river or meet the village chief. Epi is an enthusiastic young guy very knowledgeable about forest plants and there have been very good reports about his tour. His reservations books are at the Royal Hotel reception and at Cafe Levuka. Recommended.

**Ovalau Tours and Transport** (Box 149, Levuka; tel. 440-611, fax 440-405) operates a day tour to Devokula village. It's an intensive short course in Fijian culture with a kava presentation, handicraft demonstration, and many village activities explained. There's time to snorkel, and a traditional lunch is included in the F$25 pp price (minimum of six). The same company has a "tea and talanoa" program (F$25 for one or F$17.50 pp for two) which arranges for visitors to meet local residents in their own homes and gardens for tea and conversation. It's not at all "touristy" and you may end up revisiting your host as a friend outside the organized format. Ovalau Tours' historical town walking tour is F$15 for one or F$10 pp for two or more. Ask about sea kayaking, trekking, and diving tours.

If you wish to organize your own tour, it costs F$50 for the vehicle to hire a small carrier or taxi around the island.

## ISLANDS OFF OVALAU

### Yanuca Lailai Island

It was on tiny Yanuca Lailai Island, just off the south end of Ovalau, that the first 463 indentured Indian laborers to arrive in Fiji landed from the ship *Leonidas* on 14 May 1879. To avoid the introduction of cholera or smallpox into Fiji, the immigrants spent two months in quarantine on Yanuca Lailai. Later Nukulau Island off Suva became Fiji's main quarantine station.

It's possible to stay on Yanuca Lailai at **Lost Island Resort** (Box 131, Levuka). *Bure* accommodations cost F$26 double, camping F$12 pp, and three meals a day are another F$14 (F$7 for the *lovo* special). Reef tours from Lost Island are possible, and transfers from Levuka F$5 pp each way. It's also possible to visit on a day-trip from Levuka at F$20 pp, lunch included. For information contact Levi through the Tourist Information Desk at the Levuka Community Center (tel. 440-356). Budget.

### Moturiki Island

Small outboards to Moturiki Island depart Naqueledamu Landing most afternoons. The finest beaches are on the east side of Moturiki. Camping is officially discouraged, but possible.

### Caqalai Island

Caqalai (pronounced "Thanggalai") is owned by the Methodist Church of Fiji, which operates a small backpackers' resort on this palm-fringed island. The 12 *bures* are F$25 pp (triple occupancy), or camp for F$20 pp, three good meals included. You can use the communal fridge. It's primitive but adequate, and the island and people are great. Dress up for Sunday service in the village church. There's good snorkeling all around the island and you can wade to Snake Island, where banded sea snakes congregate. Information should be available at Cafe Levuka (boat from Levuka Monday, Wednesday, and Friday mornings at F$10 pp each way). Those already staying on Caqalai can make shopping trips to Levuka at F$5 return. Budget.

Reader Philip R. Marshall of Playa del Rey, California, sent us this:

> *Caqalai is not for every tourist. It's very small, taking about 10 minutes to walk around, and has simple unhygienic facilities. The one outhouse-style toilets must be flushed with buckets of seawater. Bathing is accomplished in a small shed with brackish water handpumped into buckets. Electricity is generated only during dinner hours, if the generator works (it did briefly on only one of my three nights there). On the positive side, the people are wonderfully friendly hosts, with music and kava in the evenings, but there is little to do. The snorkeling is fairly good in the vicinity (bring your own gear). I think Caqalai might appeal to people who have not spent much time on islands, who would enjoy a rough Gilligan's Island experience.*

### Leleuvia Island

Emosi Yee Show of Levuka's Old Capitol Inn runs a small backpacker resort (Box 15212, Suva; tel. 301-584) on Leleuvia, a lovely isolated 17-hectare reef island with nothing but coconut trees, fine sandy beaches, and a ramshackle assortment of tourist huts scattered across the island. Accommodations run F$15 pp in the dorm, F$20/30 single/double in a thatched hut, F$30/40 in a wooden bungalow, or F$12 pp if you camp. Water is in short supply on Leleuvia, and bathing is with a bucket of brackish water. Food is extra and meals are served a la carte with the most expensive thing on the menu costing F$6. The small shop sells candy, cake, and drinks. The owners send as many people as they can to Leleuvia, and it can get *very* crowded (pick Caqalai instead if you'd rather do your own thing).

Leleuvia is popular among backpackers who like to drink beer and party a lot (live Fijian music in the evening), so don't come expecting a rest. Actually, it sort of depends on who is on the island at the time. Sometimes it's great fun with lots of neat, congenial people, but other times the scene is dominated by "groupies," and newcomers are excluded. One reader called it "a Boy Scout holiday camp." Peace returns around 2230 when the generator switches off and everyone falls asleep.

Plenty of activities are laid on, especially reef trips by boat (F$5 pp) and scuba diving (F$55/80 one/two tanks on the same day), and on Sunday they'll even take you to church! For a nominal amount they'll drop you off on one-tree "Honeymoon Island." Leleuvia is the only Lomaiviti resort offering scuba diving, and the resident instructors have taught diving to quite a few guests. This isn't surprising because at F$340, it's one of the least expensive PADI open-water certification courses available in Fiji (this price only applies if several people are taking lessons at the same time). Many backpackers learn to dive at Leleuvia before going to Taveuni where such courses are almost F$100 more expensive. If you just want a taste of diving try their resort course. The snorkeling is also excellent though the sea is sometimes cold. Chances are, you'll love Leleuvia.

Getting there is easy on the *Emosi Express* from Levuka at 0900 Monday, Wednesday, and Friday. From Suva, you can catch the bus at 35 Gordon St. daily at 1200 and arrive via Bau Landing (F$35 roundtrip). Leleuvia is a free stopover on all of Emosi's regular trips between Levuka and Suva. Day-trips to Leleuvia from Levuka with lunch (F$22) are also offered. All bookings should be made through the Old Capital Inn in Levuka, or at Emosi Ferry Service (tel. 313-366), 35 Gordon St., Suva. Budget.

### Naigani

Naigani, 11 km off Viti Levu, is a lush tropical island near Ovalau at the west end of the Lomaiviti Group. It's just the right size for exploring on foot, with pristine beaches and only one Fijian village in the southwest corner.

**Naigani Island Resort** (Box 12539, Suva; tel. 300-925 or 312-069, fax 300-539 or 302-058), also known as Mystery Island Resort, offers 11 comfortable two-bedroom fan-cooled villas at F$218 for up to five people. Six of the villas have double rooms attached which go for F$165 double by themselves. When rented together the entire three-bedroom, six-person unit goes for F$250. During the off season mid-September to March (excepting Christmas) prices drop about F$20 per villa, and you can often obtain discounts as high as 50% by booking direct when things are slow (drop into the Suva office). Unfortunately the cooking facilities have been removed from the units and you're now required to take the meal plan, which is F$55 pp for three meals. There's a swimming pool with water slide. Some nonmotorized water sports are free, but fishing trips are charged extra. A nine-hole par-27 golf course is available. The daily minibus/launch connection from Suva at 1030 is F$60 roundtrip, and bookings can be made at their Suva office (tel. 312-069) at 22 Cumming St., 2nd Floor. From Levuka, call them up and arrange to be collected by the speedboat at Taviya village on the northwest side of Ovalau (accessible on the Rukuruku truck) at F$15 pp each way. Premium.

# OTHER ISLANDS OF THE LOMAIVITI GROUP

### Makogai

Makogai shares a figure-eight-shaped barrier reef with neighboring Wakaya. The anchorage is in Dalice Bay on the northwest side of the island. From 1911 to 1969 this was a leper colony staffed by Catholic nuns and many of the old hospital buildings still stand. Some 4,500 patients sheltered here including many from various other Pacific island groups. In the patients' cemetery on Makogai is the grave of Mother Marie Agnes, the "kindly tyrant" who ran the facility for 34 years. Both the British and French governments honored her with their highest decorations, and upon retiring at the age of 80 she commented that "the next medal will be given in heaven." Also buried here is Maria Filomena, a Fijian sister who working at the colony from its inception. After contracting leprosy in 1925 she joined her patients and continued serving them for another 30 years. Today Makogai is owned by the Department of Agriculture, which runs an experimental sheep farm here, with some 2,000 animals. A new breed obtained by crossing British and Caribbean sheep bears little wool and is intended as a source of mutton.

### Wakaya

A high cliff on the west coast of Wakaya is known as Chieftain's Leap, for a young chief who threw himself over the edge to avoid capture by his foes. In those days a hill fort sat at Wakaya's highest point so local warriors could scan the horizon for unfriendly cannibals. Chief Cakobau sold Wakaya to Europeans in 1840, and it has since had many owners. In 1862 David Whippy set up Fiji's first sugar mill on Wakaya.

The German raider Count Felix von Luckner was captured on Wakaya during WW I. His ship, the *Seeadler,* had foundered on a reef at Maupihaa in the Society Islands on 2 August 1917. The 105 survivors (prisoners included) camped on Maupihaa, while on 23 August von Luckner and five men set out in an open boat to capture a schooner and continue the war. On 21 September 1917 they found a suitable ship at Wakaya. Their plan was to go aboard pretending to be passengers and capture it, but a British officer and four Indian soldiers happened upon the scene. Not wishing to go against the rules of chivalry and fight in civilian clothes, the count gave himself up and was interned at Auckland as a prisoner of war. He later wrote a book, *The Sea Devil,* about his experiences.

In 1976 Canadian industrialist David Harrison Gilmour bought the island for US$3 million, and in 1990 he opened **The Wakaya Club** (Robert Miller, Box 15424, Suva; tel. 440-128, fax 440-406), with eight spacious cottages at US$1,275 double, all-inclusive (three-night minimum stay). Children under 16 are not accommodated. The snorkeling here is superb, and there's scuba diving, a nine-hole golf course, and an airstrip for charter flights (F$1,200 roundtrip per couple from Nadi). As you might expect at these prices (Fiji's highest!), it's all very tasteful and elegant—just ask Bill Gates, Pierce Brosnan, Carol Burnett, Michelle Pfeiffer, or Burt Reynolds. It's a hideaway for the rich and famous rather than a social scene. A third of Wakaya has been subdivided into 100 parcels, which are available as homesites at US$550,000 and up; red deer imported from New Caledonia run wild across the rest. Luxury.

### Batiki

Batiki has a large interior lagoon of brackish water surrounded by mudflats. Four Fijian villages are on Batiki and you can walk around the island in four hours. Waisea Veremaibau of Yavu village on the north side of the island takes guests at F$15 pp a day. Fine baskets are made on Batiki. Due to hazardous reefs, there's no safe anchorage for ships.

### Nairai

Seven Fijian villages are found on this 336-meter-high island between Koro and Gau. The inhabitants are known for their woven handicrafts. Hazardous reefs stretch out in three directions, and in 1808 the brigantine *Eliza* was wrecked here. Among the survivors was Charles Savage, who served as a mercenary for the chiefs of Bau for five years until falling into the clutches of Vanua Levu cannibals.

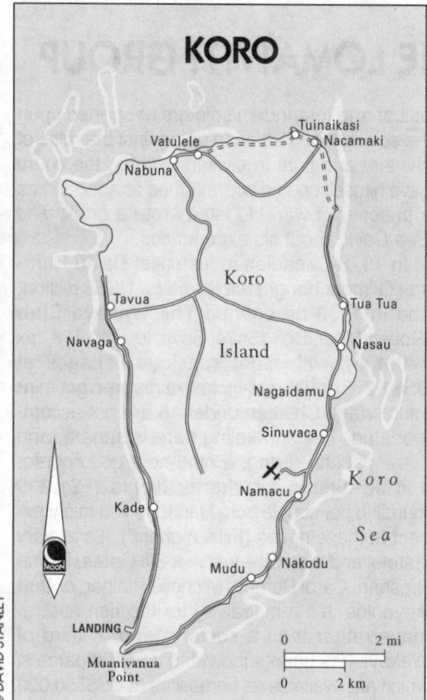


© DAVID STANLEY

## Koro

Koro is an eight-by-16-km island shaped like a shark's tooth. A ridge traverses the island from northeast to southwest, reaching 561 meters near the center. High jungle-clad hillsides drop sharply to the coast. The top beach is along the south coast between Mundu and the lighthouse at Muanivanua Point. Among Koro's 14 large Fijian villages is **Nasau,** the government center with post office, hospital, and schools.

The road to **Vatulele** village on the north coast climbs from Nasau to the high plateau at the center of the island. The coconut trees and mangoes of the coast are replaced by great tree ferns and thick rainforest.

At **Nacamaki** village, in the northeast corner of Koro, turtle calling is still practiced. The caller stands on Tuinaikasi, a high cliff about a kilometer west of the village, and repeats the prescribed words to bring the animals to the surface. The ritual does work, although the turtles are becoming scarce and only one or two may appear. If anyone present points a finger or camera at a turtle, they quickly submerge. Actually, it's not possible to photograph the turtles, as magic is involved—the photos wouldn't show any turtles. Anyway, you're so high above the water you'd need the most powerful telephoto lens just to pick them out. (One reader wrote in to report that no turtles have appeared since 1987, due to the killing of a shark by a local villager.)

The track south between Nacamaki and Tua Tua runs along a golden palm-fringed beach. There's a cooperative store at **Nagaidamu** where you can buy *yaqona* and supplies. Koro kava is Fiji's finest. A 30-minute hike up a steep trail from the coop brings you to a waterfall and idyllic swimming hole. Keep left if you're on your own (taking a guide would be preferable).

Koro has an unusual inclined **airstrip** on the east side of the island near Namacu village. You land uphill, take off downhill. Air Fiji can bring you here from Suva four times a week (F$104), and several carriers meet the flights.

The twice weekly **Consort Shipping Line** ferry *Spirit of Free Enterprise* plying between Suva and Savusavu/Taveuni ties up to the wharf near Muanivanua Point. The "Sofe" calls northbound on early Wednesday and Sunday mornings; the southbound trips stop at Koro late Monday and Thursday nights. The fare to/from Suva is F$25/44 deck/cabin one-way.

There are no hotels on Koro or Gau, so you'll have to stay with locals or ask permission to camp. On both islands your best bet is to wait till you meet someone from there, then ask them to write you a letter of introduction to their relatives back home on the island. It's always better to know someone before you arrive. Make it clear you're willing to pay your own way, then don't neglect to do so.

## Gau

Gau is the fifth-largest island in Fiji, with 16 villages and 13 settlements. There's a barrier reef on the west coast, but only a fringing reef on the east. A hot-spring swimming pool is close to the P.W.D. depot at **Waikama.** From Waikama, hike along the beach and over the hills to **Somosomo** village. If you lose the way, look for the creek at the head of the bay and work your way up it until you encounter the trail. There's a bathing pool in Somosomo with emerald green water.

A road runs from Somosomo to **Sawaieke** village, where the Takalaigau, high chief of Gau, resides. The remnants of one of the only surviving pagan temples *(bure kalou)* in Fiji is beside the road at the junction in Sawaieke. The high stone mound is still impressive.

It's possible to climb **Mt. Delaico** (760 meters), highest on the island, from Sawaieke in three or four hours. The first hour is the hardest. From the summit is a sweeping view. MacGillivray's Fiji petrel, a rare seabird of the albatross family, lays its eggs underground on Gau's jungle-clad peaks. Only two specimens have ever been taken: one by the survey ship *Herald* in 1855, and a second by local writer Dick Watling in 1984.

The coop and government station (hospital, post office, etc.) are at **Qarani** at the north end of Gau. Two ships a week arrive here from Suva on an irregular schedule, but there is no wharf so they anchor offshore. The wharf at **Waikama** is used only for government boats.

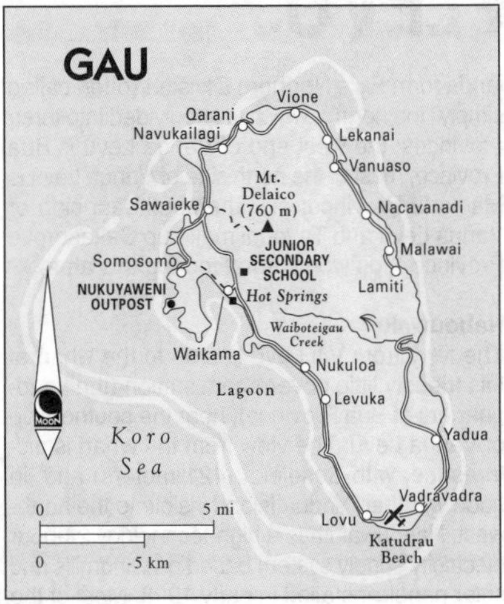

There are a number of waterfalls on the east coast, the most impressive are behind **Lekanai** and up Waiboteigau Creek, both an hour's walk off the main road. The "weather stone" is on the beach, a five-minute walk south of **Yadua** village. Bad weather is certain if you step on it or hit it with another stone.

No guesthouses are on Gau, but the driver of the carrier serving the airstrip may be willing to arrange village accommodations. Have your *sevusevu* ready and also contribute F$15 pp a day, at least. The airstrip is on Katudrau Beach at the south end of Gau. The five weekly flights to/from Suva on Air Fiji are F$76 each way.

Due to open in late 1999 is a wilderness luxury lodge called the **Nukuyaweni Outpost** (Kevin Wunrow, Bay of Angels, Private Mail Bag, Suva; tel./fax 448-112), on a point a couple of km southwest of Somosomo. It's rather different than other exclusive resorts around Fiji as it has been designed as a sort of artists' hideaway. There's a "creation station" with everything a Picasso might desire, and a state-of-the-art recording studio is to be added a kilometer up the beach so visiting musicians can combine business with pleasure. Therese Wunrow is a veteran of the Seattle Symphony Orchestra and her harp serenades the dinner crowd as the sun sets over the horizon pool. Nukuyaweni's eight beachfront cottages with private grotto showers cost F$1,300 double including meals, drinks, taxes, and all activities (minimum stay four nights). There are also two deluxe cottages with private pools at F$1,750 double (seven-night minimum). Children under 16 are not admitted to this "Sanctuary for the Romantic Soul." The resort bar and library is up in the trees. Great snorkeling is available off their beach, and there's extraordinary diving in Nigali Passage, just 10 minutes away by boat (large schools of big fish and manta rays). Construction was still underway as this book went to press, so check their website for current information.

SALVATORE CASA

# VANUA LEVU

Though only half as big as Viti Levu, 5,556-square-km Vanua Levu ("Great Land") has much to offer. The transport is good, the scenery varied, the people warm and hospitable, and far fewer visitors reach this part of Fiji than heavily promoted Nadi/Sigatoka/Suva. Fijian villages are numerous all the way around the island—here you'll be able to experience real Fijian life, so it's well worth making the effort to visit Fiji's second-largest island.

The drier northwest side of Vanua Levu features sugarcane fields and pine forests, while on the damper southeast side copra plantations predominate, with a little cocoa around Natewa Bay (the biggest bay in the South Pacific). Toward the southeast the scenery is more a bucolic beauty of coconut groves dipping down toward the sea. Majestic bays cut into the island's south side, and one of the world's longest barrier reefs flanks the north coast. There are some superb locations here just waiting to be discovered, both above and below the waterline.

Fiji Indians live in the large market town of Labasa and the surrounding cane-growing area; most of the rest of Vanua Levu is Fijian. Together Vanua Levu, Taveuni, and adjacent islands form Fiji's Northern Division (often called simply "the north"), which is subdivided into three provinces: the west end of Vanua Levu is Bua Province; most of the north side of Vanua Levu is Macuata Province; and the southeast side of Vanua Levu and Taveuni make up Cakaudrove Province. You won't regret touring this area.

### Nabouwalu

The ferry from Viti Levu ties up to the wharf at this friendly little government station (the headquarters of Bua Province), near the southern tip of Vanua Levu. The view from the wharf is picturesque, with Seseleka (421 meters) and, in good weather, Yadua Island visible to the northwest. Nabouwalu has a high-technology 24-hour electricity supply system based on windmills and solar panels installed in early 1998. Most of the 600 residents of this area are indigenous Fijians.

No hotels exist at Nabouwalu, but the lovely **Government Resthouse,** up on the hillside above Nabouwalu, has two rooms with shared cooking facilities at F$10 pp. Try to make advance reservations with the district officer, Bua, in Nabouwalu (tel. 836-027). Upon arrival, you

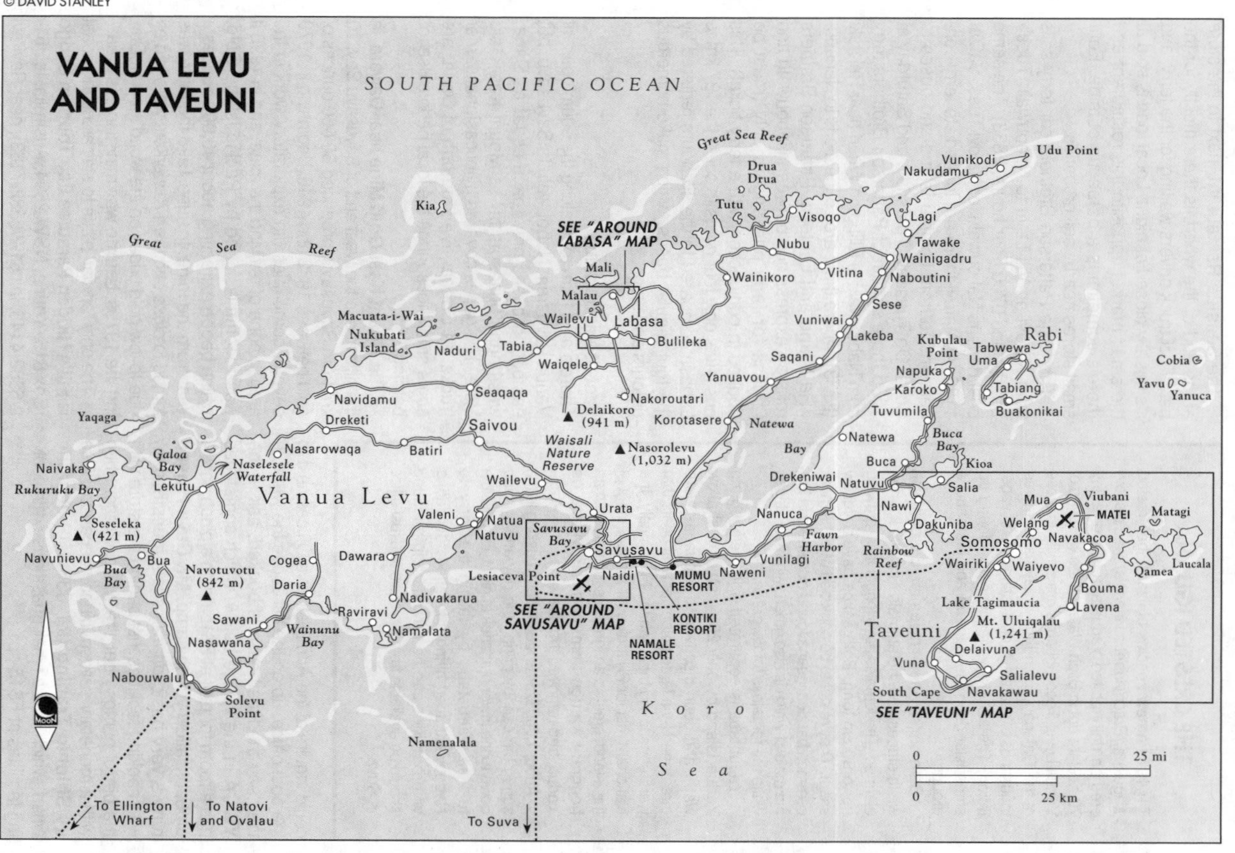
VANUA LEVU
AND TAVEUNI
SOUTH PACIFIC OCEAN
Great Sea Reef
Great Sea Reef
Udu Point
Vunikodi
Nakudamu
Drua
Drua
Tutu
Visoqo
Kia
Lagi
Tawake
Wainigadru
Naboutini
SEE "AROUND
LABASA" MAP
Nubu
Vitina
Wainikoro
Mali
Malau
Sese
Macuata-i-Wai
Nukubati
Island
Wailevu
Labasa
Bulileka
Vuniwai
Lakeba
Naduri
Tabia
Waiqele
Saqani
Kubulau
Point
Tabwewa
Uma
Rabi
Cobia
Yavu
Yanuca
Navidamu
Seaqaqa
Nakoroutari
Yanuavou
Napuka
Karoko
Tabiang
Buakonikai
Yaqaga
Dreketi
Saivou
Delaikoro
(941 m)
Korotasere
Natewa
Tuvumila
Nasarowaqa
Batiri
Waisali
Nature
Reserve
Nasorolevu
(1,032 m)
Natewa
Bay
Buca
Bay
Galoa
Bay
Naselesele
Waterfall
Buca
Kioa
Naivaka
Drekeniwai
Natuvu
Salia
Rukuruku Bay
Lekutu
Wailevu
Vanua Levu
Nawi
Mua
Viubani
Urata
Valeni
Natua
Natuvu
Nanuca
Dakuniba
Welang
MATEI
Matagi
Seseleka
(421 m)
Savusavu
Bay
Savusavu
Fawn
Harbor
Somosomo
Navakacoa
Navunievu
Bua
Cogea
Dawara
Vunilagi
Rainbow
Reef
Wairiki
Waiyevo
Qamea
Laucala
Bua
Bay
Navotuvotu
(842 m)
Lesiaceva Point
Naidi
MUMU
RESORT
Naweni
Daria
Nadivakarua
Bouma
SEE "AROUND
SAVUSAVU" MAP
Lake Tagimaucia
Lavena
Raviravi
KONTIKI
RESORT
Sawani
Wainunu
Bay
Namalata
Mt. Uluiqalau
(1,241 m)
Nasawana
NAMALE
RESORT
Taveuni
Delaivuna
Vuna
Nabouwalu
Salialevu
South Cape
Navakawau
Solevu
Point
Koro
SEE "TAVEUNI" MAP
Namenalala
Sea
0
25 mi
0
25 km
To Ellington
Wharf
To Natovi
and Ovalau
To Suva

## THE CRESTED IGUANA

In 1979 a new species of lizard, the crested iguana *(Brachylophus vitiensis),* was discovered on uninhabited Yaduataba Island, a tiny 70-hectare dot in Bligh Water off the west end of Vanua Levu. These iguanas are similar to those of the Galapagos, and they may have arrived thousands of years ago on floating rafts of vegetation. The same species was later found on some islands in the Yasawa and Mamanuca groups.

Both sexes are shiny emerald green with white stripes and the animals turn black when alarmed. The females have longer tails, growing up to 90 cm long. Both sexes have a yellow snout. They're not to be confused with the more common banded iguana found elsewhere in Fiji, the male of which is also green with white stripes while the female is totally green.

Yaduataba is separated from neighboring Yadua Island by only 200 meters of shallow water and upon discovery the iguanas were threatened by a large colony of feral goats that were consuming their habitat. Fortunately, the National Trust for Fiji took over management of the island, created an iguana sanctuary with an honorary warden from the Fijian village on Yadua, and removed the goats.

About 1,000 lizards are present, basking in the sun in the canopy during the day and coming down to the lower branches at night. It's possible to visit Yaduataba by taking the ferry to Nabouwalu, then hiring a local boat to Yadua where guides can be arranged. Information should be available from the National Trust office in Suva.

could inquire at the Administrative Offices next to the post office, up on the hill above the wharf. If they say the Resthouse is booked, ask at the **YWCA** in the village below, which sometimes has a room for rent at F$15 pp. In a pinch, they'll probably allow you to camp. **Mr. Gaya Prasad** runs a very basic *dharamshala* (guesthouse) with cooking facilities just behind the store with the petrol pumps near the wharf. Present him with a monetary *sevusevu* upon departure. Also try **Shlomo Trading** (tel. 836-050) near the wharf, which runs a small guesthouse with cooking facilities at F$15 pp.

The **Seaside Restaurant,** next to the store at the end of the wharf, is there mostly for the benefit of truck drivers waiting for the ferry, and it's usually closed at night. Local food is sold at the small market opposite this restaurant and there's sometimes a barbecue outside. Four small stores nearby sell groceries.

The large Patterson Brothers car ferry sails from Natovi on Viti Levu to Nabouwalu Tues.-Sat. around 0700 (four hours, F$33). The same boat departs Nabouwalu for Natovi Tues.-Sat. at 1130. At Natovi there are immediate ferry connections to/from Ovalau Island and buses to Suva. On Tuesday, Thursday, and Saturday at 1030 there's a direct Patterson Brothers ferry from Nabouwalu to Ellington Wharf near Rakiraki (F$33), where there are connections to Nananu-i-Ra Island and Lautoka. Patterson Brothers runs an express bus between Nabouwalu and Labasa for ferry passengers only (must be booked in conjunction with a ferry ticket). This bus takes only four hours to cover the 137 km to Labasa compared to the six hours required by the four regular buses, which make numerous detours and stops.

### East of Nabouwalu

There's a 141-km road along the south coast of Vanua Levu from Nabouwalu to Savusavu, but eastbound buses only reach as far as Daria, westbound buses as far as Mount Kasi Gold Mine. The gap is covered by occasional carrier trucks. At Cogea, five km north of Daria, are some small hot springs the local people use for bathing.

The **Mount Kasi Gold Mine** near Dawara, in the hills above the west end of Savusavu Bay, 70 km from Savusavu, produced 60,000 ounces of gold between 1932 and 1946. Beginning in 1979 several companies did exploratory work in the area in hope of reviving the mine, and in 1996 it was recommissioned by Pacific Island Gold, which began extracting about 40,000 ounces a year from the mine. In June 1998 the mine was forced to close and the 170 workers were laid off due to low gold prices on the world market. During the 1970s, bauxite was mined in this area.

The only "official" place to stay along this coast is **Fiji's Hidden Paradise Eco Tourism Lodge** (Box 815, Young, NSW 2594, Australia; tel. 61-2/6382-4146, fax 61-2/6382-7163), near Raviravi

*Dillon's fight with the Fijians*

village, about 10 km south of Mount Kasi. The three *bures* are about F$120 pp including meals. Lighting is by kerosene lamp. People come here to experience the people and land while retaining a bit of privacy. There's hiking, birdwatching, snorkeling, and cultural exchange with the villagers. Airport transfers from Savusavu are F$100 each way per car. In Savusavu, information should be available from Eco Divers or Sea Fiji Travel. Moderate.

### The Road to Labasa

The twisting, tiring north coast bus ride from Nabouwalu to Labasa takes you past Fijian villages, rice paddies, and cane fields. The early sandalwood traders put in at **Bua Bay.** At Bua village on Bua Bay is a large suspension bridge and the dry open countryside west of Bua stretches out to Seseleka (421 meters).

About 13 km west of Lekutu, at Galoa Bay on the north side of the narrow neck of land that joins the Naivaka Peninsula to the main island, is **Dillon's Rock.** In September 1813 a party of Europeans took refuge here after being ambushed during a raid on a nearby village. After witnessing Swedish mercenary Charles Savage being killed and eaten by enraged Fijian warriors after he descended to negotiate a truce, Peter Dillon of the *Hunter* and two others managed to escape to their boat by holding muskets to the head of an important chief and walking between the assembled cannibals. (In 1826 Dillon earned his place in Pacific history by discovering relics from the La Pérouse expedition on Vanikolo Island in the Solomons, finally solving the mystery of the disappearance in 1788 of that famous French contemporary of Captain Cook.)

About five km north of Lekutu Secondary School, one km off the main road (bus drivers know the place), is Fiji's most accessible yet least known waterfall, the **Naselesele Falls.** This is a perfect place to picnic between bus rides, with a nice grassy area where you could camp. The falls are most impressive during the rainy season, but the greater flow means muddy water, so swimming is better in the dry season. There's a large basalt pool below the falls, and since nobody lives in the immediate vicinity, you'll probably have the place to yourself. Much of this part of the island has been reforested with pine.

Farther east the road passes a major rice-growing area and runs along the **Dreketi River,** Vanua Levu's largest. A rice mill at Dreketi and citrus project at Batiri are features of this area. The pavement begins near the junction with the road from Savusavu. In the Seaqaqa settlement area between Batiri and Labasa, about 60 square km of native land were cleared and planted with sugarcane and pine during the 1970s.

# LABASA

Labasa is a busy Indian market town that services Vanua Levu's major cane-growing area. It's Fiji's fourth-largest town, with 25,000 inhabitants, four banks, and the Northern Division and Macuata Province headquarters. Vanua Levu's only sugar mill is here. Labasa was built on a delta where the shallow Labasa and Oawa rivers enter the sea; maritime transport is limited to small boats. Large ships must anchor off Malau, 11 km north, where Labasa's sugar harvest is loaded. Labasa's lack of an adequate port has hindered development.

Other than providing a good base from which to explore the surrounding countryside and an excellent choice of places to spend the night, Labasa has little to interest the average tourist. That's its main attraction: since few visitors come, there's adventure in the air, good food in the restaurants, and fun places to drink for males (a bit rowdy for females). It's not beautiful but it is real, and the bus ride that brings you here is great. This truly is the "friendly north."

Gabriel Teoman of Erl, Austria, sent us this:

*After reading your remarks, I headed straight for Labasa upon arrival in Fiji and ended up spending a month there, moving back and forth between Sikhs in town, Indian sugarcane farmers in the surroundings, and Fijian villagers in the interior. It was there where I got introduced into both Fiji-Indian and Fijian culture, where I experienced a genuinely Fijian* yaqona *ceremony and a* meke, *got treated to both a Sikh and a Hindu wedding, made lots of friends, and saw people living up to the image of the "friendly north." Even though almost all of Fiji was superb, those weeks remain special.*

If your time is very limited but you want to see a lot, catch a morning flight from Suva or Nadi to Labasa, then take an afternoon bus on to Savusavu, the nicest part of the trip. Otherwise stay in Savusavu and see Labasa on a long day-trip.

## SIGHTS

Labasa has an attractive riverside setting with one long main street lined with shops and restaurants. The park along the riverside near the Labasa Club is quite pleasant.

The **Labasa Sugar Mill,** beside the Oawa River two km east of town, opened in 1894. At the height of the crushing season from May to December there's usually a long line of trucks, tractors, and trains waiting to unload cane at the mill—a most picturesque sight. From the road here you get a view of **Three Sisters Hill** to the right.

Anyone with an interest in archaeology should take the two-km minibus ride to **Wasavula** on the southern outskirts of Labasa. Parallel stone platforms bearing one large monolith and several smaller ones are found among the coconut trees to the east of the road. This site (Fiji's first "national monument") is not well known, so just take the bus to Wasavula, get off, and ask. A small gift (F$2) should be given to anyone who shows you around. The Fijian villager who does so will assure you that the monoliths are growing in size!

### Around Labasa

The **Snake Temple** (Naag Mandir) at Nagigi, 12 km northeast of Labasa, contains a large rock shaped like a cobra that—as at Wasavula—Hindu devotees swear is growing. Frequent buses pass Naag Mandir.

On the way back to Labasa from Nagigi ask to be dropped at Bulileka Road, just before the sugar mill. Here you can easily pick up a yellow and blue bus to the **hanging bridge,** a suspension footbridge at Bulileka, six km east of Labasa. Get off the Bulileka bus at Boca Urata where it turns around. The hanging bridge is 150 meters down the road from the place (ask). Cross the bridge and continue through the fields a few hundred meters to the paved road where you can catch another bus back to Labasa. The main reason for coming is to see this picturesque valley, so you may wish to walk part of the way back.

The **Waiqele hot springs** are near a Hindi temple called Shiu Mandir about four km beyond Labasa airport, 14 km southwest of town (green and yellow Waiqele bus). Again, the only reason to come is to see a bit of the countryside.

You can get a view of much of Vanua Levu from the telecommunications tower atop **Delaikoro** (941 meters), 25 km south of Labasa, farther down the same road past the airport. Only a 4WD vehicle can make it to the top.

Farther afield is the **Floating Island** at Kurukuru, between Nakelikoso and Nubu, 44 km northeast of Labasa (accessible on the Dogotuki, Kurukuru, and Lagalaga buses).

At Udu Point, Vanua Levu's northeasternmost tip, a **Meridian Wall** has been built to mark the spot where the 180-degree meridian and international dateline cut across the island. Both sunset and sunrise can be observed from the wall, and great crowds are expected to welcome the millennium here at midnight on 31 December 1999.

If you're a surfer, ask about hiring a boat out to the **Great Sea Reef** north of Kia Island, 40 km northwest of Labasa.

### Sports and Recreation

The **Municipal Swimming Pool** (tel. 816-387), just before the hospital, is the place to cool off. Admission is F$1.10. A snack bar adjoins the pool and the Friendly North Inn's nice open bar is only a short walk away.

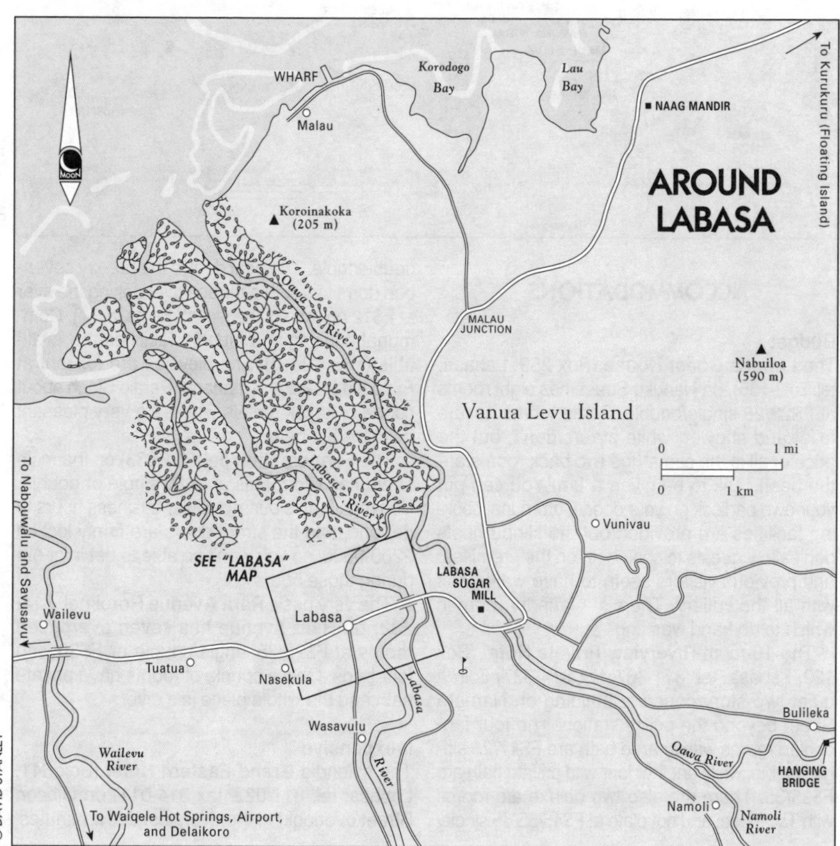

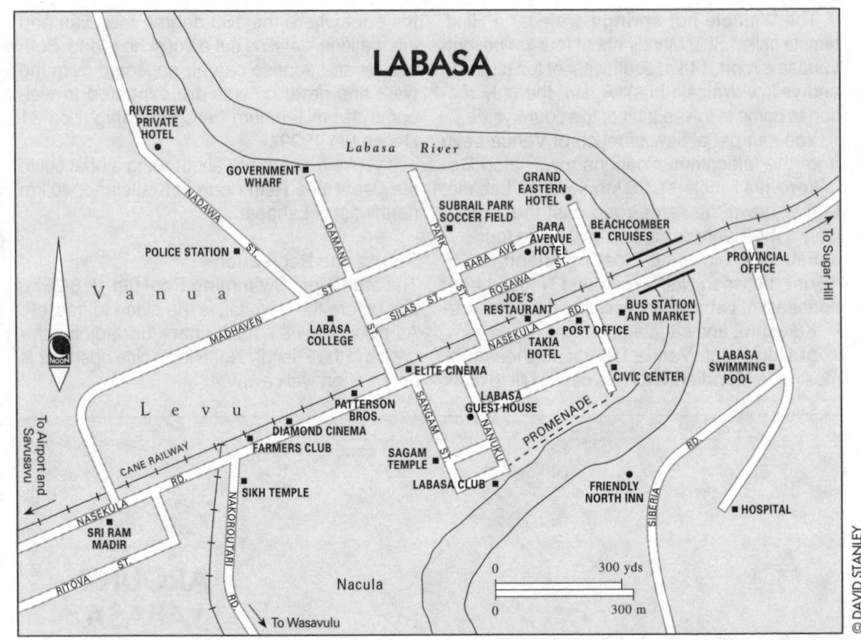


## ACCOMMODATIONS

### Budget

The **Labasa Guest House** (Box 259, Labasa; tel. 812-155), on Nanuku Street, has eight rooms at F$23/28 single/double. Some rooms have a toilet and shower, while others don't, but the price of all is the same (the two back rooms are the best). Ask to be given a fan. You can put your own padlock on your door. Communal cooking facilities are provided but the Hindu hosts don't allow guests to cook beef on the premises, and previous visitors seem to have walked off with all the cutlery. There's a laundry room in which to do hand washing.

The 10-room **Riverview Private Hotel** (Box 129, Labasa; tel. 811-367, fax 814-337) is in a quiet two-story concrete building on Namara Street beyond the police station. The four fan-cooled rooms with shared bath are F$17/25 single/double, while another four with private bath are F$25/35. There are also two deluxe a/c rooms with TV, fridge, and hot plate at F$45/55/65 single/double/triple. The best deal is the breezy seven-bed dormitory with a terrace overlooking the river at F$12 pp (one of the nicest dorms in Fiji). Communal cooking and laundry facilities are available (F$5 a load), and bicycles are for rent at F$10 a day. Ask the manager Pardip Singh about canoe or kayak rentals. There's a very pleasant riverside bar here.

The **Farmers Club** (tel. 811-633) on the main street has two rooms at F$20 single or double. You must arrive during regular business hours to get one, and the street doors are firmly locked 2200-0800, so you won't be able to get in or out during those hours.

The very basic **Rara Avenue Hotel** (tel. 814-232) on Rara Avenue has seven overpriced rooms at F$20/25 single/double or F$30 with four beds. Only a couple of rooms have private bath and the whole place is a dive.

### Inexpensive

The splendid **Grand Eastern Hotel** (Box 641, Labasa; tel. 811-022, fax 814-011) on Gibson Street overlooking the river, just a few minutes' walk from the bus station, reopened in late 1997 after a complete renovation and is now one of Fiji's top hotels. The 10 standard rooms with terraces in the wing facing the river are F$95/115 double/triple, while the larger deluxe rooms facing the swimming pool are F$115/135. There are also four suites upstairs in the main two-story building, each capable of accommodating a family of up to five at F$155 double plus F$20 per additional person (children under 12 free). All rooms have a/c, fridge, and private bath. The Grand Eastern's atmospheric dining room and bar retain much of the colonial flavor of the original hotel despite modernization.

The high-rise **Takia Hotel** (Box 7, Labasa; tel. 811-655, fax 813-527), at 10 Nasekula Rd. next to the post office, above the shopping area in the middle of town, has seven fan-cooled rooms at F$45/55 single/double, 26 a/c rooms at F$65/75, and one family suite at F$80/90, all with private bath. The fan rooms are along the corridor between the disco and the bar and will only appeal to party animals on Thursday, Friday, and Saturday nights (free admission to the disco for hotel guests).

A better medium-priced place is the **Friendly North Inn** (Box 1324, Labasa; tel. 811-555, fax 816-429) on Siberia Road opposite the hospital, about a kilometer from the bus station (F$1.50 by taxi). The 10 a/c rooms with TV and fridge are F$55/65 single/double, plus F$10 extra for private cooking facilities (you may be granted free access to a communal kitchen if you ask). Opened in 1996, it's just a short walk from the municipal swimming pool, and the Inn's large open air bar is a very pleasant place for a beer.

### Offshore Resorts

The luxury-category **Nukubati Island Resort** (Jenny Leewai-Bourke, Box 1928, Labasa; tel. 813-901, fax 813-914) sits on tiny Nukubati Island, one km off the north shore of Vanua Levu, 40 km west of Labasa. The six spacious fan-cooled beach bungalows are F$1,100 double including meals (emphasis on seafood) and activities, with a five-night minimum stay. Children are not allowed, and alcoholic beverages are extra. It's F$550 a day to hire the resort's sport-fishing boat. Access is by speedboat or 4WD vehicle from Labasa (free for guests).

**Mavuva Island Resort** (Box 4010, Labasa; tel. 816-401, fax 816-400), on another tiny island eight km northeast of Nukubati, offers luxurious two-story beach houses, each with its own courtyard containing a private saltwater swimming pool, at F$3,950 per couple for seven nights including all meals, some activities, and transfers from Nadi. The property is still being developed and furnished houses can be purchased for F$185,000, with the possibility of leasing the building back to the resort management for public rental while reserving three weeks a year for personal occupancy at no cost. Owners may operate small businesses on the island. (This listing is for information purposes only and not an endorsement.)

## FOOD AND ENTERTAINMENT

### Food

**Joe's Restaurant** (tel. 811-766; Mon.-Sat. 0600-2200), upstairs in a building on Nasekula Road, has an inexpensive fast-food area, and a more upmarket "wine and dine" section where you can order beer. Both are very popular, and the Chinese food served here puts Labasa's ubiquitous chow mein houses to shame.

Simple Fijian, Chinese, and Indian meals are available for under F$3 at many places along Nasekula Road, including the **Moon's Restaurant** (tel. 813-215), next to Elite Cinema, and the **Wun Wah Cafe** (tel. 811-653), across from

### VIDI VIDI

Vidi vidi is a game similar to billiards except that the ball is propelled by a flick of the finger rather than the tap of a cue. Two or four players position themselves around a rectangular "cram board" with holes in the four corners. The eight or nine brown balls are placed in the center of the board and the players try to knock them into the holes using a striker ball. The red "king ball" must go in last and if a player knocks it in prematurely all the balls he had previously sunk must come out and be knocked in again. Originally played in India, vidi vidi was brought to Fiji by Indian immigrants.

the post office. Breakfast is hard to order in Labasa, although several places along the main street will serve buttered scones and coffee.

For Indian food try the **Isalei Restaurant** (tel. 811-490; closed Sunday), on Sangam Avenue, or the **Govinda Vegetarian Restaurant** (tel. 811-364), next to Sunflower Airlines on Nasekula Road, which specializes in Indian *thali* meals.

### Entertainment

**Elite Cinema** (tel. 811-260) has films in English and Hindi and there's an evening show, while the **Diamond Cinema** (tel. 811-471) is closed at night.

This is a predominantly Indian town so most of the nightlife is male oriented. The **Labasa Club** (tel. 811-304) and the **Farmers Club** (tel. 811-633) both serve cheap beer in a congenial atmosphere. Couples will feel more comfortable at the Labasa Club than at the Farmers, and there's a nice terrace out back facing the river and two large snooker tables. The bar upstairs at the Farmers Club is a bit more sedate (and perhaps less colorful) than the one downstairs (both open daily 1000-2200).

The pub upstairs in the **Takia Hotel** (tel. 811-655) is a safe, fun place to drink, even though the bartenders are enclosed in a cage! There's also a disco at the Takia open Thursday, Friday, and Saturday 2030-0100 (admission F$4).

Indian **firewalking** takes place once a year sometime between June and October at Agnimela Mandir, the Firewalkers Temple at Vunivau, five km northeast of Labasa.

## OTHER PRACTICALITIES

### Services and Information

The ANZ Bank is opposite the bus station, and the Westpac Bank is farther west on Nasekula Road.

There's a **public library** (tel. 812-617; weekdays 0900-1300/1400-1700, Saturday 0900-1200) in the Civic Center near Labasa Bus Station. **Public toilets** are adjacent to the library.

### Health

The **Northern District Hospital** (tel. 811-444), northeast of the river, is available 24 hours a day in emergencies.

Less serious medical problems should be taken to a private doctor, such as Dr. Hermant Kumar of **Kumar's Medical Center** (tel. 814-155) on Jaduram St. near the Labasa Guest House. Nearby on Nanuku Street toward Nasekula Road is a private **dentist,** Dr. Ashwin Kumar Lal (tel. 814-077).

## TRANSPORTATION

**Air Fiji** (tel. 811-188) has service five or six times a day between Labasa and Suva (F$138). **Sunflower Airlines** (tel. 811-454), at the corner of Nasekula Road and Damanu St., flies direct to Nadi (F$180) four times a day, to Suva (F$148) twice daily, and to Taveuni (F$82) three times a week.

To get to the airport, 10 km southwest of Labasa, take a taxi (F$7) or the green and yellow Waiqele bus. Sunflower Airlines has a bus based at the airport that brings arriving passengers into town free of charge, but departing passengers must find their own way from Labasa to the airport. Air Fiji's bus takes passengers to/from the airport at 50 cents pp (when operating).

**Patterson Brothers** (tel. 812-444, fax 813-460) has an office near Sunflower Airlines on Nasekula Road where you can book your bus/ferry/bus ticket through to Suva via Nabouwalu and Natovi (10 hours, F$43). This bus leaves Labasa at 0600 daily except Sunday and Monday, and passengers arrive in Suva at 1715. There's also a direct bus/boat/bus connection from Labasa to Lautoka via Ellington Wharf (near Nananu-i-Ra Island) on Tuesday, Thursday, and Saturday, and another service straight through to Levuka. Ask about the through bus/boat service from Labasa to Taveuni via Natuvu, departing Labasa Monday, Wednesday, Friday, and Saturday at 0630 (six hours, F$16.20).

**Beachcomber Cruises** (tel. 811-492), in an office in the seafood warehouse next to the Grand Eastern Hotel, books passage on the car ferry MV *Adi Savusavu.* Their through bus/boat ticket to Suva via Savusavu is F$39/47 economy/first class (or F$5 less for the boat only).

**Consort Shipping Line** (tel. 811-144, fax 814-411) has an office at the Government Wharf at the north end of Damanu Street where you can book passage on the *Spirit of Free Enterprise* from Savusavu to Suva.

To be dropped off on Kia Island on the Great Sea Reef, negotiate with the fishing boats tied up near the Labasa Club. Village boats from Kia and Udu Point sometimes unload at the Government Wharf on the other side of town.

There are four regular buses a day (at 0630, 1030, 1300, and 1430) to Nabouwalu (210 km, F$7), a dusty, tiring six-hour trip. Another four buses a day (at 0700, 0900, 1200, and 1500) run from Labasa to Savusavu (94 km, three hours, F$4.35), a very beautiful ride on an excellent paved highway over the Waisali Saddle between the Korotini and Valili mountains and along the palm-studded coast. Take the early bus before clouds obscure the views. Latchman Buses Ltd. (tel. 814-390) also has an express bus departing Labasa for Savusavu daily at 0700 (two hours, F$4.55).

Rental cars are available from **Budget Rent A Car** (tel. 811-999) at Niranjans Mazda dealership on Zoing Place up Ivi St. from opposite the Jame Mosque at Nasekula west of town. **Avis** (tel. 811-688) is at Asco Motors behind the Shell service station at Nasekula at the west entrance to Labasa. Obtaining gasoline outside the two main towns is difficult, so tank up.

# SAVUSAVU

Savusavu is a picturesque little town opposite Nawi Island on Savusavu Bay. The view from here across to the mountains of southwestern Vanua Levu and down the coast toward Nabouwalu is superlatively lovely. In the 1860s Europeans arrived to establish coconut plantations. They mixed with the Fijians, and even though business went bust in the 1930s, their descendants and the Fijian villagers still supply copra to a coconut oil mill, eight km west of Savusavu, giving this side of Vanua Levu a pleasant agricultural air. The urban population of 5,000 is almost evenly split between Fiji Indians and indigenous Fijians with many part-Fijians here too.

Savusavu is Vanua Levu's main port, and cruising yachts often rock at anchor offshore, sheltered from the open waters of Savusavu Bay by Nawi Island. The surrounding mountains and reefs also make Savusavu a well-protected hurricane refuge. The diving possibilities of this area were recognized by Jean-Michel Cousteau in 1990 when he started using Savusavu as the base for his Project Ocean Search. Access to good snorkeling is difficult, however, as the finest beaches are under the control of the top-end resorts and most other shore access is over extremely sharp karst. Although much smaller than Labasa, Savusavu is the administrative center of Cakaudrove Province and has three banks. In the past few years tourism has taken off around Savusavu, with new resorts springing up all the time, though the town is far from being spoiled.

## Sights

The one main street through Savusavu consists of a motley collection of Indian and Chinese shops, parked taxis, loitering locals, and the odd tourist. The **Copra Shed Marina** is like a small museum with map displays and historical photos, information boards, and most of Savusavu's tourist services. Color photos of all yachts that have visited recently are displayed in the office next to the notice board. In front of the marina is a stone dated 1880 which is said to be from Fiji's first copra mill.

Visit the small **hot springs** boiling out among fractured coral below the Hot Springs Hotel. Residents use the springs to cook native vegetables; bathing is not possible. These and smaller hot springs along the shore of Savusavu Bay remind one that the whole area was once a caldera.

For a good circle trip, take a taxi from Savusavu past the airport to **Nukubalavu** village (six km, F$5), at the end of road along the south side of the peninsula. From here you can walk west along the beach to the Cousteau Fiji Islands Resort on **Lesiaceva Point** in about an hour at low tide. Try to avoid cutting through the resort at the end of the hike as the Cousteau management disapproves. From Lesiaceva it's six km by road back to Savusavu.

For some mountain hiking ask one of the Labasa buses to drop you at the entry kiosk to the **Waisali Nature Reserve** established by the National Trust for Fiji in 1991, about 40 km northwest of Savusavu. This 116-hectare reserve protects one of Vanua Levu's last unexploited tropical rainforests with native species such as the *dakua, yaka,* and *kuasi* well represented. Viewpoints offer sweeping views and a nature trail leads to a waterfall where you can swim.

### Sports and Recreation

**Eco Divers** (Box 264, Savusavu; tel. 850-122, fax 850-344) at the Copra Shed Marina offers scuba diving, snorkeling, dinghy hire, sailing, village visits, waterfall tours, and guided hiking. They charge F$94 for a two-tank boat dive, or F$380 for a PADI open-water certification course. Snorkeling from the boat is F$15 pp if four people go, F$25 pp for two people (two hours). Eco Divers and the Cousteau Fiji Islands Resort use 21 of the same buoyed dive sites off southern Vanua Levu. Ocean kayak rental is F$10/25 for one/three hours in a single-person kayak or F$15/35 in a double. They also rent mountain bikes at F$7/12 a half/full day and sailing catamarans at F$15 an hour. Eco Divers arranges 10-tank, seven-night diving/accommodation packages beginning at F$474 pp (double occupancy). Three-night guided kayak tours around northwestern Savusavu Bay are also offered.

## ACCOMMODATIONS

### In Savusavu Town

We've arranged this accommodation section beginning at Savusavu Bus Station and working west through town to Lesiaceva Point, then east along the coast.

The **Copra Shed Marina** (Box 262, Savusavu; tel. 850-457, fax 850-344) has a self-catering apartment upstairs in the marina for rent at F$55 a night for up to three people (long term rates available). It's a great deal, but call ahead to reserve. Inexpensive.

Hari Chand's **Hidden Paradise Guest House** (Box 41, Savusavu; tel. 850-106), just beyond Morris Hedstrom, has six rather hot wooden rooms at F$15/23/32 single/double/triple with fan and shared bath, F$28 double in twin beds, in-

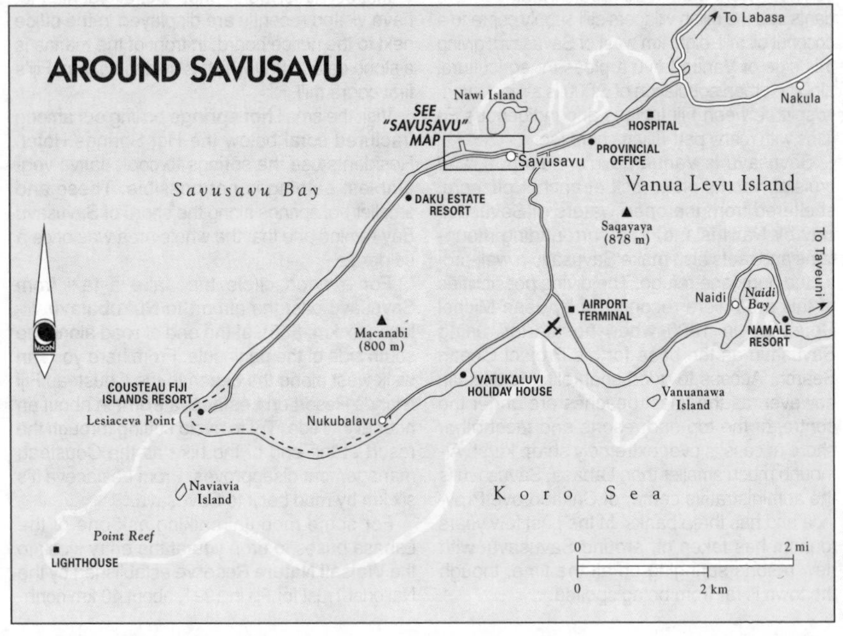

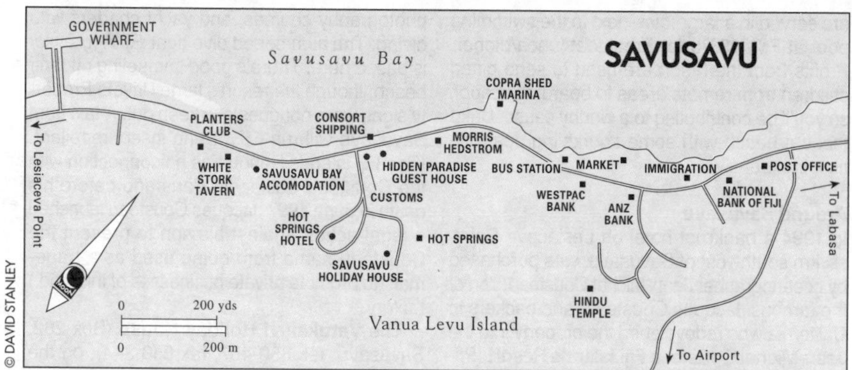


cluding a hearty English breakfast. Cooking and washing facilities are provided, and it's clean and friendly—don't be put off by the plain exterior. You'll be well protected by iron grills, fences, and watch dogs. The Indian restaurant here is very inexpensive, but pork, beef, and booze are banned. A member of the Chand family may offer to show you around the Hindu temple up on the hill, if you ask. Checkout time is 0900. Shoestring.

The **Hot Springs Hotel** (Box 208, Savusavu; tel. 850-195, fax 850-430), on the hillside overlooking Savusavu Bay, is named for the nearby thermal springs and steam vents. The 48 rooms, all with balconies offering splendid views, begin at F$120 single or double with fan, F$180 with a/c. There's no beach nearby, but the swimming pool terrace is pleasant. This former Travelodge is a convenient, medium-priced choice, and the hotel bar is open daily including Sunday. Catch the sunset here at happy hour (1700-1900) and ask about the buffet dinner laid out on Saturday nights. Just below the hotel they have a budget annex with a high sloping roof called the **Diver's Den** with four tiny single rooms, one room with two beds, and another with three beds. All beds can be converted into upper/lower bunks doubling the capacity. The Den is used mostly by Eco Divers scuba groups, which pay F$20 pp, and it's often fully booked. Budget to inexpensive.

David Manohar Lal's six-room **Savusavu Holiday House** (Box 65, Savusavu; tel. 850-149), also known as "David's Place," is just behind the Hot Springs Hotel. Five rooms with shared bath cost F$18/24/28 single/double/triple and one four-person family room is F$30. The seven-room dorm is F$15 pp, while camping is F$9/15 single/double. Stay over a week and you'll get 10% off and free laundry service. All rates include a cooked breakfast and there's a well-equipped kitchen. David's a delightful character to meet and also a strict Seventh-Day Adventist, so no alcoholic beverages are allowed on the premises. A cacophony of dogs, roosters, and the neighbor's kids will bid you good morning. It's often full with people from Eco Divers—call ahead. Shoestring.

**Savusavu Bay Accommodation** (Box 154, Savusavu; tel. 850-100), above Sea Breeze Restaurant on the main street, has five standard rooms with bath at F$18/23 single/double, four a/c rooms at F$40 single or double, and one large four-person family room at F$50. Cooking facilities are provided, and on the roof of this two-story concrete building is a terrace where travelers can wash and dry their clothes or just sit and relax. Many of the rooms are rented on a long-term basis, and the atmosphere is not as nice as in the places previously mentioned. Beware of a misleading sign outside reading The Hidden Paradise, which is intended to cause confusion with a competitor just down the street. Such are the petty politics of small town life. Shoestring.

The Anglican Diocese of Polynesia operates the **Daku Estate Resort** (Box 18, Savusavu; tel. 850-046, fax 850-334), one km west of the ferry landing. The six *bures* with fan and fridge (but no cooking) go for F$66/100/122 single/double/triple. Five larger four-person villas with fully equipped kitchens rent for F$88/110/132. Meals are served in a large *bure* next to the swimming pool at F$9/13/20 for breakfast/lunch/dinner. Profits from the resort are used to send gifted children from remote areas to boarding school, so you'll be contributing to a worthy cause. Daku faces a beach with some snorkeling possibilities. Inexpensive.

## Around Savusavu

In 1994 a bankrupt hotel on Lesiaceva Point, six km southwest of Savusavu, was purchased by oceanographer Jean-Michel Cousteau, son of the famous Jacques Cousteau, and backers in California who redeveloped the property into the **Jean-Michel Cousteau Fiji Islands Resort** (Private Bag, Savusavu; tel. 850-188, fax 850-340). This stylish resort recreates a Fijian village with 18 authentic-looking thatched *bures.* Garden accommodations, transfers, and all meals begin at F$590/790/990 single/double/triple, plus 10% tax. The rooms have fans but no a/c, telephones, or cooking facilities. The restaurant is built like a towering pagan temple and nonguests wishing to dine there *must* reserve. Free activities include sailing, kayaking, and fishing. The snorkeling off their beach is pretty good (ask about "split rock"). In addition, Gary Alford's outstanding onsite dive operation, "L'Aventure Cousteau," offers scuba diving (F$77/139 for one/two tanks plus gear), PADI/TDI scuba instruction, underwater photography courses, and yacht charters with diving. The high-speed dive boat *Fiji Aggressor* is based here. There's good snorkeling off their beach, though the resort's large Private Property signs warn nonguests to keep out. A taxi from Savusavu will run F$5. Bring insect repellent. (The Fiji Islands Resort has no connection with the Cousteau Society in Paris and before his death in June 1997 Jacques Cousteau launched a legal action against his son to prevent the Cousteau name from being used as a trademark to promote private businesses of this kind.) Luxury.

The **Vatukaluvi Holiday House** (Box 262, Savusavu; tel. 850-457, fax 850-344), on the south side of the peninsula, one km west of Savusavu airport, accommodates four people at F$55 for the whole breezy house (or F$330 for two weeks). Cooking facilities and fridge are provided, and there's good snorkeling off the beach. Ask for Geoff Taylor, vice-commodore of the Savusavu Yacht Club. A taxi to Vatukaluvi will cost F$3 from the airport, F$5 from Savusavu. Inexpensive.

The most upmarket place around Savusavu is **Namale Resort** (Box 244, Savusavu; tel. 850-435, fax 850-400), a working copra plantation founded in 1874, on a white-sand beach nine km east of Savusavu. The superb food and homey atmosphere amid exotic landscapes and re-

*Fijian schoolgirls smile for the camera at Savusavu, Vanua Levu.*

JOHN PENISTEN

freshing white beaches make this one of Fiji's most exclusive resorts. The 10 thatched *bures* are F$930/1,122 single/double per night including gourmet meals and drinks. The mosquito nets over the beds, ceiling fans, and louvered windows give the units a rustic charm. Airport transfers and all activities other than scuba diving are free (F$136 plus tax for a two-tank dive). Namale caters only to in-house guests—there's no provision for sightseers who'd like to stop in for lunch. Children under 12 are also banned. Luxury.

At last report, Kontiki Resort, 15 km east of Savusavu on the Hibiscus Highway, was closed due to legal complications although it could eventually reopen under new management.

Vanua Levu's only real backpacker camp, **Mumu Resort** (Rosie Edris, Box 240, Savusavu; tel. 850-416), 18 km east of Savusavu, occupies on the site of the spiritual home of Radini Mumu, a legendary queen of Fiji. The seven *bures* are F$45 single or double, the four bunkhouse rooms F$35 single or double, and the four-person "dream house" F$60. There's also a six-bed dorm at F$12 pp, and you can camp for F$4 pp. Communal cooking facilities are available, and Mumu's kitchen serves tasty Fijian and European dishes at budget prices. Mumu is surrounded by the Koro Sea on three sides, and two small uninhabited islands nearby are easily accessible. Although the scenery is good, the snorkeling is poor with a very long swim over a shallow flat before reaching a snorkelable area. Unfortunately Mumu has gone downhill in recent years and maintenance has been neglected. Beware of their dogs. A taxi here from Savusavu should be F$12, a bus around F$1, but call ahead unless you're planning to camp. Budget.

Ms. Collin McKenny from Seattle runs the **Lomalagi Resort** (Box 200, Savusavu; tel. 816-098, fax 816-099) in a coconut plantation a 15-minute walk from Nasinu village on Natewa Bay. It's up Salt Lake Road three km off the Hibiscus Highway, about 25 km from Savusavu airport. The six deluxe self-catering hillside villas are F$700-800 double including tax and transfers (children not admitted). The optional meal plan including a bottle of wine with dinner is another F$175 per couple. Two artificial waterfalls drop into the S-shaped saltwater swimming pool. Luxury.

### Namenalala Island

**Moody's Namenalala Island Resort** (Private Mail Bag, Savusavu; tel. 813-764, fax 812-366), on a narrow high island southwest of Savusavu in the Koro Sea, is one of Fiji's top hideaways. Hosts Tom and Joan Moody ran a similar operation in Panama's San Blas Islands for 15 years until June 1981, when they were attacked by Cuna Indians who shot Tom in the leg and tried to burn the resort. The media reported at the time that the Indians had been scandalized by hotel guests who smoked marijuana and cavorted naked on the beach, but Joan claims it was all part of a ploy to evict foreigners from San Blas to cover up drug-running activities.

In 1984, after a long search for a replacement, the couple leased Namenalala from the Fiji government, which needed a caretaker to protect the uninhabited island from poachers. Their present resort occupies less than 10% of Namenalala's 45 hectares, leaving the rest as a nesting ground to great flocks of red-footed boobies, banded rails, and Polynesian starlings. Giant clams proliferate in the surrounding waters within the 24-km Namena Barrier Reef, and from November to March sea turtles haul themselves up onto the island's golden sands to lay their eggs. The corals along the nearby drop-offs are fabulous and large pelagic fish glide in from the Koro Sea.

Each of the Moody's six bamboo and wood hexagonal-shaped *bures* are well tucked away in the lush vegetation to ensure maximum privacy. Illuminated by romantic gas lighting, each features a private hardwood terrace with 270-degree views. Alternative energy is used as much as possible to maintain the atmosphere (though there is a secret diesel generator used to do the laundry and recharge batteries).

The cost to stay here is F$484/610 single/double, including all meals. The food is excellent, thanks to Joan's firm hand in the kitchen and Tom's island-grown produce. The ice water on the tables and in the *bures* is a nice touch, but they don't sell liquor so bring your own.

This resort is perfect for birdwatching, fishing, and snorkeling, and scuba diving is available at F$60 per tank (certification card required). The soft corals at Namenalala are among the finest in the world. If you want a holiday that combines unsullied nature with interesting characters and a certain elegance, you won't go wrong here. A Turtle Airways seaplane from Nadi will run F$400 per couple if booked through the resort. Moody's closes from 1 March to 1 May every year. Luxury.

## FOOD AND ENTERTAINMENT

### Food

The **Captain's Table** (tel. 850-511; open Mon.-Sat. 0830-2100, Sunday 1100-2100) at the Copra Shed Marina is a yachtie hangout claiming to offer "the best pizza on Vanua Levu," which isn't saying a lot when you think about it. Most of Savusavu's hip young locals show up here eventually and in the evening the outdoor seating on the wharf is nice. Pick up a newspaper at the Bula Bookstore out front and enjoy a leisurely read while waiting for your order to arrive.

Several simple places around town offer basic meals of varying quality. The **New Ping Ho Cafe** (tel. 850-300), opposite the municipal market, accommodates vegetarians and everyone else with substantial portions of good food at decent prices. It's one of the few places open for dinner (1800-2100) and all the local expats eat here. (Ping Ho ran the bakery at the Mount Kasi Gold Mine during the 1930s and his descendants continue to operate the restaurant.)

The **A1 Restaurant** (tel. 850-153) near the bus station has Indian curries, but some of the cheapest curries in town are served at the **Sun Sang Cafe** (tel. 850-106) at Hidden Paradise Guest House. Also try the **Harbor Cafe** next to the Shell service station below the Hot Springs Hotel for Indian dishes.

The **Sea Breeze Restaurant** (tel. 850-100) below Savusavu Bay Accommodation serves mostly Chinese dishes, and the portions are large. It's open Sunday for lunch and dinner—cheaper than the New Ping Ho Cafe, but not as pleasant.

The biggest market at Savusavu is early Saturday morning. Free public toilets are behind the market.

### Entertainment

The **Light Ship Theater** next to A1 Restaurant shows action videos for F$1 admission.

Drinkers can repair to the **Planters Club** (tel. 850-233; Mon.-Thurs. 1000-2200, Friday and Saturday 1000-2300, Sunday 1000-1800) toward the wharf—the place is never out of Fiji Bitter. The weekend dances at the club are local events. Despite the Members Only sign outside, visitors are welcome. It's a vintage colonial club even without the colonists.

The **White Stork Tavern,** next to the Planters Club, is a rough public bar open Mon.-Sat. 1100-2100. If there's a dance on Friday and Saturday they'll stay open until 0100.

## OTHER PRACTICALITIES

### Services and Information

The ANZ Bank, National Bank, and Westpac Bank all have branches at Savusavu.

The **Bula Bookshop** (Hans, Box 265, Savusavu; tel./fax 850-580), at the Copra Shed Marina, has Suva newspapers and tasty ice cream sticks, plus postcards, T-shirts, and souvenirs. They sell Fijian nautical charts from March to October only. This is the local DHL Express agent.

**Sea Fiji Travel** (Box 264, Savusavu; tel. 850-345, fax 850-344), in the Copra Shed Marina, specializes in scuba diving and adventure travel.

### Yachting Facilities

The **Copra Shed Marina** (Box 262, Savusavu; tel. 850-457, fax 850-344) near the bus station allows visiting yachts to moor alongside at F$10 a day, or pay F$3 a day for an offshore hurricane mooring. Anchorage and use of the facilities by the whole crew is F$28 a week. You can have your laundry done for F$7 (wash and dry). The **Savusavu Yacht Club** (Box 3, Savusavu; tel. 850-561, fax 850-344) is based here.

Yachts can clear Fiji customs here. Arriving yachts should contact the Copra Shed Marina over VHF 16. The customs office (where yachties must report after the quarantine check) is next to the Shell service station below the Hot Springs Hotel. After clearing quarantine and customs controls, yachties can proceed to the Immigration Department, across the street from the Hot Bread Kitchen, a bit east of the market. If you check in after 1630 or on weekends or holidays there's an additional F$39 charge on top of the usual F$33 quarantine fee.

### Health

The **District Hospital** (tel. 850-437; open 0830-1600) is two km east of Savusavu on the road to Labasa (taxi F$2).

Dr. Joeli Tali's **Savusavu Private Health Center** (tel. 850-721; Mon.-Thurs. 0830-1600, Friday 0830-1400) is between the National Bank and the post office.

## TRANSPORTATION

**Air Fiji** (tel. 850-538), next to the post office, flies into Savusavu twice daily from Suva (F$118) and Taveuni (F$82). **Sunflower Airlines** (tel. 850-141), in the Copra Shed Marina, has flights to Savusavu twice daily from Nadi (F$180) and Taveuni (F$82). The airstrip is beside the main highway, three km east of town. Local buses to Savusavu pass the airport about once an hour, or take a taxi for F$2.

The **Consort Shipping Line Ltd.** (tel. 850-443, fax 850-442), opposite the Shell service station below the Hot Springs Hotel, runs the large car ferry MV *Spirit of Free Enterprise* from Suva to Savusavu (14 hours, F$32 deck, F$55 cabin). The ferry leaves Suva northbound Tuesday and Saturday nights, and Savusavu southbound Monday and Thursday nights. Northbound the Tuesday voyage continues to Taveuni, and between Savusavu and Suva the "Sofe" calls at Koro.

**Beachcomber Cruises** (tel. 850-266, fax 850-499), at the Copra Shed Marina, runs the 65-meter car ferry MV *Adi Savusavu* from Savusavu direct to Suva Wednesday and Sunday at 2000, and to Natovi with a bus connection to Suva Saturday at 0700 (F$34/42 economy/first class).

**Patterson Brothers Shipping** (tel. 850-161), at the Copra Shed Marina, operates the bus/boat connection to Taveuni via Natuvu, which should depart Savusavu Mon.-Sat. at 0900 (four hours, F$12.70).

Buses from Savusavu to Buca Bay and Napuka leave at 1030, 1300, 1430, and 1600 daily except Sunday (three hours, F$3.41).

Regular buses leave Savusavu for Labasa at 0730, 0930, 1300, and 1530, Sunday at 0930 and 1530 only (92 km, three hours, F$4.35). This ride is easily the most scenic in Fiji. The Latchman express bus to Labasa (two hours; F$4.55) departs Savusavu daily at 1430. There's also a bus that takes a roundabout route via Natewa Bay between Savusavu and Labasa, departing both ends at 0900 (F$8.45)—a scenic ride through an area seldom seen by tourists. Other Natewa Bay buses may finish their runs at Yanuavou or Wainigadru.

Buses leave Savusavu for Lesiaceva Point at 0715, 1200, and 1600 (54 cents). For more information on buses headed south or east of Savusavu, call Vishnu Holdings at tel. 850-276.

Numerous taxis congregate at Savusavu market; they're quite affordable for short trips in the vicinity.

**Avis Rent A Car** (tel. 850-911) has an office at the Hot Springs Hotel in Savusavu. **Budget Rent A Car** (tel. 850-700) is in the same office as Air Fiji next to the post office.

**Eco Divers** (tel. 850-122) at the Copra Shed Marina offers a variety of day tours, including a village tour (F$20), plantation tour (F$20), Labasa tour (F$90), and a Waisali Reserve tour (F$40). They only need two participants to run a tour.

# BUCA BAY AND RABI

## ALONG THE HIBISCUS HIGHWAY

This lovely (if dusty) coastal highway runs 75 km east from Savusavu to Natuvu on Buca Bay, then up the east side of Vanua Levu to the Catholic mission station of **Napuka** at the end of the peninsula. Old frame mansions from the heyday of the 19th-century planters can be spotted among the palms, and offshore you'll see tiny flowerpot islands where the sea has undercut the coral rock. Buca Bay is a recognized "hurricane hole," where ships can find shelter during storms. Prime Minister Rabuka hails from **Drekeniwai** village on Natewa Bay, one of the largest bays in the South Pacific.

Large red prawns inhabit a saltwater crevice in the center of a tiny limestone island off **Naweni** village between Savusavu and Buca Bay. The villagers believe the prawns are the spirit Urubuta and call them up by singing:

*Keitou oqo na marama ni vuna*
*keitou mai sara Urubuta*
*I tuba i tuba e*
*I tuba i tuba e*

The island is accessible on foot at low tide, but a *sevusevu* must first be presented to the chief of Naweni for permission to visit (no photos). Your local guides will also expect compensation. Ask to be shown the weather stone on the beach and, perhaps, a second pool of prawns on the other side of the village.

There are petroglyphs *(vatuvola)* on large stones in a creek near **Dakuniba** village, 10 km south of Natuvu (no bus service). Look for a second group of rock carvings a couple of hundred meters farther up the slope. The figures resemble some undeciphered ancient script.

The **Buca Bay Resort** (Natuvu, Buca Bay; tel. 880-370), also known as Natuvu Plantation, next to the ferry wharf at Natuvu, is run by Jack and Pam Cobelens. They have two rooms with shared bath at F$55 double, one with private bath at F$66, a regular *bure* at F$55, a family *bure* at F$88, and a six-bed dorm at F$17 pp (campers F$10 per tent). The staff serves meals upon request and the dorm has cooking facilities and a fridge. A swimming pool and library are available. Yachties are welcome to anchor off the resort and use the facilities. Activities in this area include a hike to Tagici Peak, birdwatching (the rare orange flame dove inhabits the upper forest), and the scenic three-hour afternoon bus ride to Napuka and back (Mon.-Sat. at 1300). Budget.

Buses to Savusavu leave Buca Bay at 0530, 0800, and 1600 (75 km, three hours, F$3.41). The ferry *Grace* leaves Natuvu for Taveuni weekdays at 0800 (F$5) and to use it you must sleep at Buca Bay. The Patterson Brothers barge *Yaubula* departs Natuvu for Taveuni Mon.-Sat. at 1100 (F$7.70, cars and vans F$50). It's a beautiful boat trip but it can be rough if the wind is up.

### Vanaira Bay

In 1998 the **Vanaira Bay Backpackers** (Douglas Thompson, Box 77, Waiyevo, Taveuni; tel. 880-017, fax 880-033) opened on the bay of that name at the east end of Vanua Levu directly across Somosomo Strait from Taveuni. The only access is by boat from Taveuni at F$20 pp return (or F$30 pp to Buca Bay). *Bure* accommodations are F$50 double, dorm beds F$15 pp, or you can camp for F$8 pp. Meals are F$5 each. It's an electricity-free hideaway with snorkeling and hiking possiblitities. Equipment rentals include kayaks at F$8 an hour, windsurfers F$10, and a Hobie cat at F$25. Libby Lesuma at Club Coco, next to the National Bank in Waiyevo on Taveuni, acts as their booking agent. There's a boat over from Waiyevo every Friday afternoon. Budget.

## KIOA

The Taveuni ferry passes between Vanua Levu and Kioa, home of some 300 Polynesians from Vaitupu Island, Tuvalu (the former Ellice Islands). In 1853 Captain Owen of the ship *Packet* obtained Kioa from the Tui Cakau, and it has since operated as a coconut plantation. In 1946 it was purchased by the Ellice islanders, who were facing overpopulation on their home island.

The people live at **Salia** on the southeast side of Kioa. The women make baskets for sale to tourists, while the men go fishing alone in small outrigger canoes. If you visit, try the coconut toddy *(kaleve)* or more potent fermented toddy *(kamanging)*. The Patterson Brothers ferry *Yaubula* often stops briefly at Kioa on its way to Taveuni.

## RABI

In 1855, at the request of the Tui Cakau on Taveuni, a Tongan army conquered some Fijian rebels on Rabi. Upon the Tongans' departure a few years later, a local chief sold Rabi to Europeans to cover outstanding debts, and before WW II the Australian firm Lever Brothers ran a coconut plantation here. In 1940 the British government began searching for an island to purchase as a resettlement area for the Micronesian Banabans of Ocean Island (Banaba) in the Gilbert Islands (present Kiribati), whose home island was being ravaged by phosphate mining. At first Wakaya Island in the Lomaiviti Group was considered, but the outbreak of war and the occupation of Ocean Island by the Japanese intervened. Back in Fiji, British officials decided Rabi Island would be a better homeland for the Banabans than Wakaya, and in March 1942 they purchased Rabi from Lever Brothers using £25,000 of phosphate royalties deposited in the Banaban Provident Fund.

Meanwhile the Japanese had deported the Banabans to Kusaie (Kosrae) in the Caroline Islands to serve as laborers, and it was not until December 1945 that the survivors could be brought to Rabi, where their 4,500 descendants live today. Contemporary Banabans are citizens of Fiji and live among Lever's former coconut plantations at the northwest corner of the island. The eight-member Rabi Island Council administers the island.

Rabi lives according to a different set of rules than the rest of Fiji; in fact, about all they have in common are their monetary, postal, and educational systems, kava drinking (a Fijian implant), and Methodism. The local language is Gilbertese and the social order is that of the Gilbert Islands. Most people live in hurricane-proof concrete-block houses devoid of furniture, with personal possessions kept in suitcases and trunks. The cooking is done outside in thatched huts.

Alcoholic beverages are not allowed on Rabi, so take something else as gifts. On Friday nights the local *maneaba* in Tabwewa village rocks to a disco beat and dancing alternates with sitting around the omnipresent kava bowl, but on Sunday virtually everything grinds to a halt. Another charming feature: adultery is a legally punishable offense on Rabi.

The island reaches a height of 472 meters and is well wooded. The former Lever headquarters is at Tabwewa, while the abandoned airstrip is near Tabiang at Rabi's southwest tip. Rabi's other two villages are Uma and Buakonikai. At Nuku between Uma and Tabwewa is a post office, Telecom office, clinic, handicraft shop, and general store. The hill behind the Catholic mission at Nuku affords a fine view. Motorized transport on Rabi consists of two or three island council trucks plying the single 23-km road from Tabwewa to Buakonikai weekdays and Saturday mornings (60 cents each way). Enjoy another fine view from the Methodist church center at Buakonikai. The islanders fish with handlines from outrigger canoes.

Up on the hillside above the post office at Nuku is the four-room **Rabi Island Council Guest House.** This colonial-style structure is the former Lever Brothers manager's residence and is little changed since the 1940s except for the extension now housing the dining area and lounge. View superb sunsets from the porch. One of the rooms is reserved for island officials; the rest are used mostly by contract workers. Other guests pay F$55 pp a night, which includes three meals. The facilities are shared (no hot water) and the electric generator operates 1800-2200 only—just enough time to watch a video (the library next to the court house rents *Go tell it to the judge,* a documentary about the Banaban struggle for compensation). Inexpensive.

Considering the limited accommodations and the remoteness of Rabi, it's important to call the **Rabi Island Council** (tel. 811-666, extension 31, fax 813-750) for guesthouse bookings and other information before setting out. You could also ask at the office of the **Rabi Council of Leaders** (Box 329, Suva; tel. 303-653, fax 300-543), 1st Floor, Banaba House, Pratt Street (above Hare Krishna Restaurant), Suva, but they'll probably only refer you to the island council. Foreign currency cannot be changed on Rabi and even Fijian bills larger than F$10 may be hard to break. Insect repellent is not sold locally.

To get there catch the daily Napuka bus at 1030 from Savusavu to Karoko. A chartered speedboat from Karoko to the wharf at Nuku on the northwest side of Rabi costs F$45 each way, less if people off the Napuka bus are going over anyway. The Patterson Brothers ferry *Yaubula* between Natuvu and Taveuni calls at Rabi about once a month depending on cargo, usually leaving Natuvu at 1100 on a Tuesday or a Thursday (any Patterson Brothers office should know). Two small trading vessels call at the jetty at Nuku on alternate Saturday mornings and they'll usually take you back to Karoko for F$5.

## THE BANABANS

The Banaban people on Rabi are from Banaba, a tiny, six-square-km raised atoll 450 km southwest of Tarawa in the Gilbert Islands. Like Nauru, Banaba was once rich in phosphates, but from 1900 through 1979 the deposits were exploited by British, Australian, and New Zealand interests in what is perhaps the best example of a corporate/colonial rip-off in the history of the Pacific islands.

After the Sydney-based Pacific Islands Company discovered phosphates on Nauru and Banaba in 1899 a company official, Albert Ellis, was sent to Banaba in May 1900 to obtain control of the resource. In due course "King" Temate and the other chiefs signed an agreement granting Ellis's firm exclusive rights to exploit the phosphate deposits on Banaba for 999 years in exchange for £50 a year. Of course, the guileless Micronesian islanders had no idea what it was all about.

As Ellis rushed to have mining equipment and moorings put in place, a British naval vessel arrived on 28 September 1901 to raise the British flag, joining Banaba to the Gilbert and Ellice Islands Protectorate. The British government reduced the term of the lease to a more realistic 99 years and the Pacific Phosphate Company was formed in 1902.

Things ran smoothly until 1909, when the islanders refused to lease the company any additional land after 15% of Banaba had been stripped of both phosphates and food trees. The British government arranged a somewhat better deal in 1913, but in 1916 changed the protectorate to a colony so the Banabans could not withhold their land again. After WW I the company was renamed the British Phosphate Commission (BPC), and in 1928 the resident commissioner, Sir Arthur Grimble, signed an order expropriating the rest of the land against the Banabans' wishes. The islanders continued to receive their tiny royalty right up until WW II.

On 10 December 1941, with a Japanese invasion deemed imminent, the order was given to blow up the mining infrastructure on Banaba, and on 28 February 1942 a French destroyer evacuated company employees from the island. In August some 500 Japanese troops and 50 laborers landed on Banaba and began erecting fortifications. The six Europeans they captured eventually perished as a result of ill treatment, and all but 150 of the 2,413 local mine laborers and their families were eventually deported to Tarawa, Nauru, and Kosrae. As a warning the Japanese beheaded three locals and used another three to test an electrified anti-invasion fence.

Meanwhile the BPC decided to take advantage of this situation to rid itself of the island's original inhabitants once and for all to avoid any future hindrance to mining operations. In March 1942 the commission purchased Rabi Island off Vanua Levu in Fiji for £25,000 as an alternative homeland for the Banabans. In late September 1945 the British returned to Banaba with Albert Ellis the first to step ashore. Only surrendering Japanese troops were found on Banaba; the local villages had been destroyed.

Two months later an emaciated and wild-eyed Gilbertese man named Kabunare emerged from three months in hiding and told his story to a military court:

> ***We were assembled together and told that the war was over and the Japanese would soon be leaving. Our rifles were taken away. We were put in groups, our names taken, then marched to the edge of the cliffs where our hands were tied and we were blindfolded and told to squat. Then we were shot.***

Kabunare either lost his balance or fainted, and fell over the cliff before he was hit. In the sea he came to the surface and kicked his way to some rocks, where he severed the string that tied his hands. He crawled into a cave and watched the Japanese pile up the bodies of his companions and toss them into the sea. He stayed in the cave two nights and, after he thought it was safe, made his way inland, where he survived on coconuts until he was sure the Japanese had left. Kabunare said he thought the Japanese had executed the others to destroy any evidence of their cruelties and atrocities on Banaba.

As peace returned the British implemented their plan to resettle all 2,000 surviving Banabans on Rabi, which seemed a better place for them than their mined-out homeland. The first group arrived on Rabi on 14 December 1945, and in time they adapted to their mountainous new home and traded much of their original Micronesian culture for that of the Fijians. There they and their descendants live today.

During the 1960s the Banabans saw the much better deal Nauru was getting from the BPC, mainly through the efforts of Hammer DeRoburt and the "Geelong Boys," who were trapped in Australia during the war and thus received an excellent education and understanding of the white people's ways. Thanks to this the Nauruan leadership was able to hold its own against colonial bullying, while the Banabans were simply forgotten on Rabi.

In 1966 Mr. Tebuke Rotan, a Banaban Methodist minister, journeyed to London on behalf of his people to demand reparations from the British for laying waste to their island, a case that would drag on for nearby 20 bitter years. After some 50 visits to the Foreign and Commonwealth offices, he was offered (and rejected) £80,000 compensation. In 1971 the Banabans sued for damages in the British High Court. After a lengthy litigation, the British government in 1977 offered the Banabans an *ex gratia* payment of A$10 million, in exchange for a pledge that there would be no further legal action.

In 1975 the Banabans asked that their island be separated from the rest of Kiribati and joined to Fiji, their present country of citizenship. Gilbertese politicians, anxious to protect their fisheries zone and wary of the dismemberment of the country, lobbied against this, and the British rejected the proposal. The free entry of Banabans to Banaba was guaranteed in the Kiribati constitution, however. In 1979 Kiribati obtained independence from Britain and mining on Banaba ended the same year. Finally, in 1981 the Banabans accepted the A$10 million compensation money, plus interest, from the British, though they refused to withdraw their claim to Banaba. The present Kiribati government rejects all further claims from the Banabans, asserting that it's something between them and the British. The British are trying to forget the whole thing.

For more information on Rabi and the Banabans see *On Fiji Islands,* by Ronald Wright.

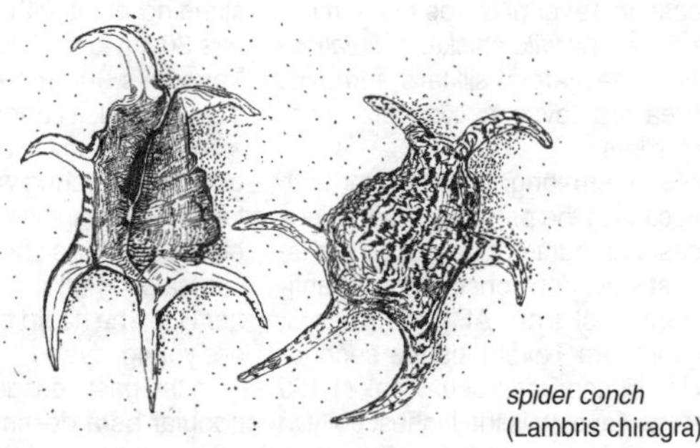

LOUISE FOOTE

*spider conch*
(Lambris chiragra)

SALVATORE CASA

# TAVEUNI

Long, green, coconut-covered Taveuni is Fiji's third-largest island. It's 42 km long, 15 km wide, and 470 km square in area. Only eight km across the Somosomo Strait from Vanua Levu's southeast tip, Taveuni is known as the Garden Island of Fiji because of the abundance of its flora. Around 60% of the land is tropical rainforest and virtually all of Fiji's coffee is grown here. Its surrounding reefs and those off nearby Vanua Levu are some of the world's top dive sites. The strong tidal currents in the strait nurture the corals, but can make diving a tricky business for the unprepared. Because Taveuni is free of the mongoose, there are many wild chickens, *kula* lorikeets, parrots, honeyeaters, silktails, ferntails, and orange-breasted doves, making this a special place for birders.

The island's 16-km-long, 1,000-meter-high volcanic spine causes the prevailing trade winds to dump colossal amounts of rainfall on the island's southeast side, and considerable quantities on the northwest side. At 1,241 meters, Uluiqalau in southern Taveuni is the second-highest peak in Fiji, and Des Voeux Peak (1,195 meters) in central Taveuni is the highest point in the country accessible by road. The European discoverer of Fiji, Abel Tasman, sighted this ridge on the night of 5 February 1643. The almost inaccessible southeast coast features plummeting waterfalls, soaring cliffs, and crashing surf. The 12,000 inhabitants live on the island's gently sloping northwest side. The bulk of the population is Fijian but Indians run most of the shops, hotels, buses, and taxis.

The deep, rich volcanic soil nurtures indigenous floral species such as *Medinilla spectabilis,* which hang in clusters like red sleigh bells, and the rare *tagimaucia (Medinilla waterousei),* a climbing plant with red-and-white flower clusters 30 cm long. *Tagimaucia* grows only around Taveuni's 900-meter-high crater lake and on Vanua Levu. It cannot be transplanted and blossoms only from October to December. The story goes that a young woman was fleeing from her father, who wanted to force her to marry a crotchety old man. As she lay crying beside the lake, her tears turned to flowers. Her father took pity on her when he heard this and allowed her to marry her young lover.

In the past decade Taveuni has become very popular as a destination for scuba divers and those in search of a more natural vacation area

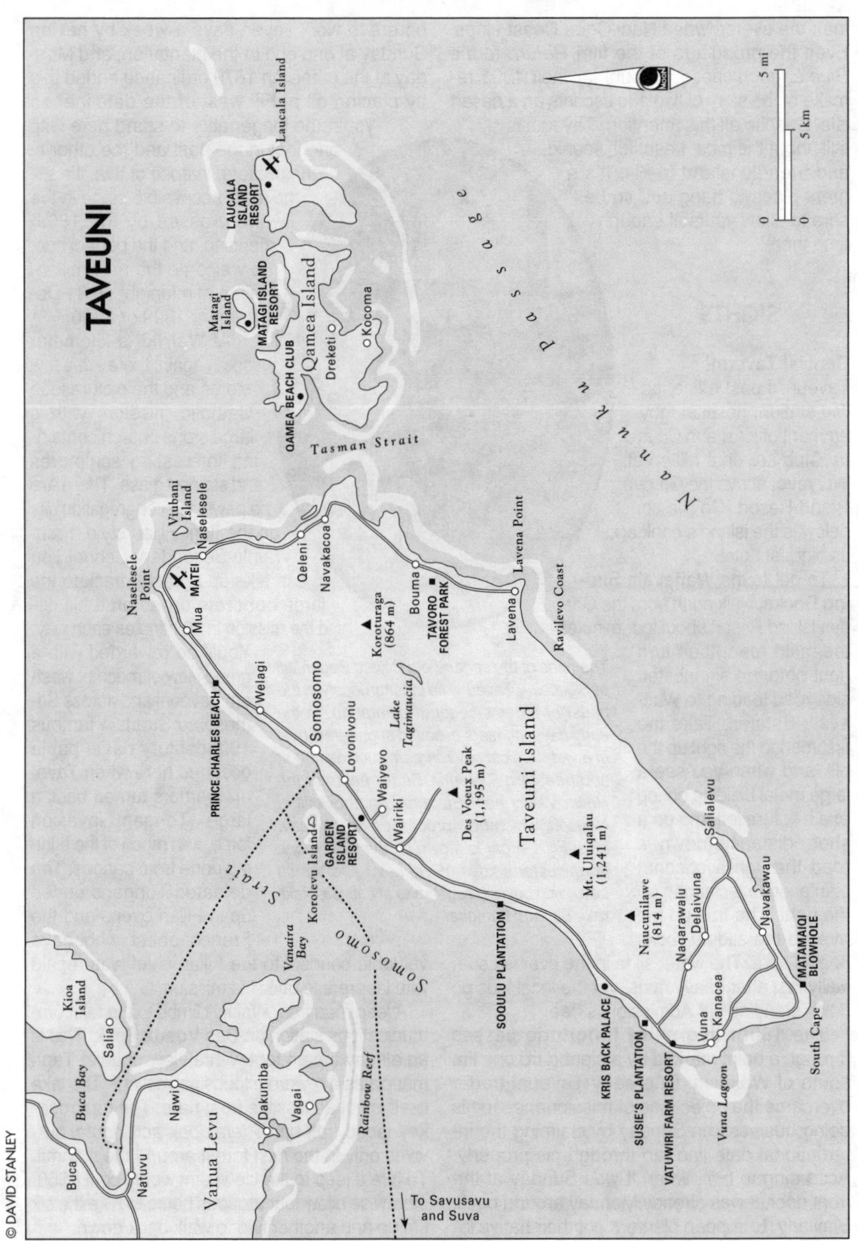
TAVEUNI
Laucala Island
LAUCALA ISLAND RESORT
Matagi Island
MATAGI ISLAND RESORT
Qamea Island
QAMEA BEACH CLUB
Dreketi
Kocoma
Tasman Strait
Viubani Island
Naselesele Point
Naselesele
MATEI
Mua
Qeleni
Navakacoa
Welagi
Koroturaga (864 m)
Bouma
TAVORO FOREST PARK
Lavena Point
Lavena
Ravilevo Coast
Nanuku Passage
PRINCE CHARLES BEACH
Somosomo
Lovonivonu
Lake Tagimaucia
Waiyevo
Des Voeux Peak (1,195 m)
Taveuni Island
GARDEN ISLAND RESORT
Wairiki
Korolevu Island
Mt. Uluiqalau (1,241 m)
Salialevu
Navakawau
Delaivuna
Naqarawalu
Naucunilawe (814 m)
SOQULU PLANTATION
MATAMAIQI BLOWHOLE
Kanacea
Vuna
KRIS BACK PALACE
SUSIE'S PLANTATION
VATUWIRI FARM RESORT
Vuna Lagoon
South Cape
Somosomo Strait
Vanaira Bay
Kioa Island
Salia
Buca Bay
Nawi
Dakuniba
Vagai
Rainbow Reef
Buca
Natuvu
Vanua Levu
To Savusavu and Suva
0 5 mi
0 5 km
MOON
© DAVID STANLEY

than the overcrowded Nadi/Coral Coast strips. Even the producers of the film *Return to the Blue Lagoon* chose Taveuni for their 1991 remake of the story of two adolescents on a desert isle. Despite all this attention, Taveuni is still about the most beautiful, scenic, and friendly island in Fiji. It's a great place to hang out, so be sure to allow yourself enough time there.

## SIGHTS

### Central Taveuni

Taveuni's post office, police station, hospital, government offices, and Country Club are on a hilltop at **Waiyevo,** above the Garden Island Resort. On the coast below is the island's bank and its biggest hotel.

To get to the **Waitavala Sliding Rocks,** walk north from the Garden Island Resort about four minutes on the main road, then turn right onto the signposted side road leading to Waitavala Estates. Take the first road to the right up the hill, and when you see a large metal building on top of a hill, turn left and go a short distance down a road through a coconut plantation to a clearing on the right. The trail up the river to the sliding rocks begins here. The water slide in the river is especially fast after heavy rains, yet the local kids go down standing up! Admission is free.

The **180th degree of longitude** passes through a point marked by a signboard one km south of Waiyevo. One early Taveuni trader overcame the objections of missionaries to his doing business on Sunday by claiming the international date line ran through his property. According to him, when it was Sunday at the front door, it was already Monday around back. Similarly, European planters got their native laborers to work seven days a week by having Sunday at one end of the plantation, and Monday at the other. An 1879 ordinance ended this by placing all of Fiji west of the dateline, so you're no longer able to stand here with one foot in the past and the other in the present. In spite of this, it's still the most accessible place in the world crossed by the 180th meridian, and the perfect spot to welcome the new millennium at midnight on 31 December 1999 or 2000.

DAVID STANLEY

*The ruins of the century-old Bilyard Sugar Mill at Salialevu, Taveuni, lie incongruously in the midst of today's coconut plantation. In the early days, planters believed sugar grew best in a wet, tropical environment such as that at southeastern Taveuni. Sugar fields in the Rewa Valley near Suva fed another mill at Nausori, which now processes rice. Today, all of Fiji's sugar is grown on the sunny, dry, northwestern sides of Viti Levu and Vanua Levu, with bustling sugar mills at Labasa, Rakiraki, Ba, and Lautoka.*

At **Wairiki,** a kilometer south again, there are a few stores and the picturesque Catholic mission, with a large stone church containing interesting sculptures and stained glass. There are no pews: the congregation sits on the floor Fijian style. From Wairiki Secondary School you can hike up a tractor track to the large **concrete cross** on a hill behind the mission in 30 minutes each way. You'll be rewarded with a grand view of much of western Taveuni and across Somosomo Strait. A famous 19th-century naval battle occurred here when Taveuni warriors turned back a large Tongan invasion force, with much of the fighting done from canoes. The defeated Tongans ended up in Fijian ovens and the French priest who gave valuable counsel to the Fijian chief was repaid with laborers to build his mission.

A jeep road from Wairiki climbs to the telecommunications station on **Des Voeux Peak.** This is an all-day trip on foot with a view of Lake Tagimaucia as a reward (clouds permitting). The lake itself is not accessible from here. The rare monkey-faced fruit bat *(Pteralopex acrodonta)* survives only in the mist forest around the summit. To hire a jeep to the viewpoint would cost F$60, otherwise allow four arduous hours to hike the six km up and another two to walk back down.

One of the only stretches of paved road on Taveuni is at Soqulu Plantation or "Taveuni Estates" (tel. 880-044), about eight km south of Waiyevo. This ill-fated condo development features an attractive golf course by the sea, tennis courts, and a bowling green, plus street signs pointing nowhere, empty roads, sewers, and 30 unfinished condominiums built by an undercapitalized real estate speculator who badly miscalculated Taveuni's potential for Hawaii-style residential development.

**Southern Taveuni**

Transportation to the south end of Taveuni is spotty with bus service from Somosomo Mon.-Sat. at 0800, 1200, and 1600 only. Since the 1600 bus spends the night at Vuna and doesn't return to Somosomo until the next morning, the only way to really see southern Taveuni is to also spend the night there. If this isn't possible, the roundtrip bus ride leaving Somosomo at 0800 and around noon is still well worth doing.

The bus from Somosomo runs south along the coast to Susie's Plantation, where it turns inland to Delaivuna. There it turns around and returns to the coast, which it follows southeast to Navakawau via South Cape. On the way back it cuts directly across some hills to Kanacea and continues up the coast without going to Delaivuna again. Southeast of Kanacea there is very little traffic.

A hike around southern Taveuni provides an interesting day out for anyone staying at Susie's Plantation or one of the other nearby resorts. From Susie's a road climbs east over the island to **Delaivuna,** where the bus turns around at a gate. The large Private Property sign here is mainly intended to ward off miscreants who create problems for the plantation owners by leaving open cattle gates. Visitors with sense enough to close the gates behind themselves may proceed.

You hike one hour down through the coconut plantation to a junction with two gates, just before a small bridge over a (usually) dry stream. If you continue walking 30 minutes down the road straight ahead across the bridge you'll reach **Salialevu,** site of the Bilyard Sugar Mill (1874-96), one of Fiji's first. In the 1860s European planters tried growing cotton on Taveuni, turning to sugar when the cotton market collapsed. Later, copra was found to be more profitable. A tall chimney, boilers, and other equipment remain below the school at Salialevu.

After a look around, return to the two gates at the bridge and follow the other dirt road southwest for an hour through the coconut plantation to **Navakawau** village at the southeast end of the island. Some of Fiji's only Australian magpies (large black-and-white birds) inhabit this plantation.

Just east of South Cape as you come from Navakawau is the **Matamaiqi Blowhole,** where trade wind-driven waves crash into the unprotected black volcanic rocks, sending geysers of sea spray soaring skyward, especially on a southern swell. The viewpoint is just off the main road.

At **Vuna,** lava flows have formed pools beside the ocean, which fill up with fresh water at low tide and are used for washing and bathing. Tuesday around 1500 the local butcher dumps the week's offal into the sea near here and the sharks go into a feeding frenzy.

**Northern Taveuni**

**Somosomo** is the chiefly village of Cakaudrove and the seat of the Tui Cakau, Taveuni's "king"; the late Ratu Sir Penaia Ganilau, last governor general and first president of Fiji, hailed from here. The two distinct parts of the village are divided by a small stream where women wash their clothes. The southern portion is the island's commercial center with several large Indian stores and a couple of places to stay. Pacific Transport has its bus terminus here.

The northern part of Somosomo is the chiefly quarter with the personal residence of the Tui Cakau on the hill directly above the bridge (no entry). Beside the main road below is the large hall built for the 1986 meeting of the Great Council of Chiefs. Missionary William Cross, one of the creators of today's system of written Fijian, who died at Somosomo in 1843, is buried in the attractive new church next to the meeting hall. There's even electric street lighting in this part of town!

The challenging trail up to lovely **Lake Tagimaucia,** 823 meters high in the mountainous interior, begins behind the Mormon church at Somosomo. The first half is the hardest. You'll need a full day to do a roundtrip, and a guide (F$20) will be necessary as there are many trails to choose from. You must wade for half an hour through knee-deep mud in the crater to reach the lake's edge. Much of the lake's surface is covered with floating vegetation, and the water is only five meters deep.

**Eastern Taveuni**

There are three lovely waterfalls in **Tavoro Forest Park and Reserve** (admission F$5), just south of Bouma on the northeast side of Taveuni. From the information kiosk on the main road it's an easy 10-minute walk up a broad path along the river's right bank to the lower falls, which plunge 20 meters into a deep pool. You can swim here, and change rooms, toilets, picnic tables, and a barbecue are provided. A well-constructed trail leads up to a second falls in about 30 minutes, passing a spectacular viewpoint overlooking Qamea Island and Taveuni's northeast coast. You must cross the river once, but a rope is provided for balance. Anyone in good physical shape can reach this second falls with ease, and there's also a pool for swimming. The muddy, slippery trail up to the third and highest falls involves two river crossings with nothing to hold onto, and it would be unpleasant in the rain. This trail does cut through the most beautiful portion of the rainforest, and these upper falls are perhaps the most impressive of the three, as the river plunges over a black basalt cliff, which you can climb and use as a diving platform into the deep pool. The water here is very sweet.

Tavoro Forest Park was developed with well-spent New Zealand aid money at the request of the villagers themselves, and all income goes to local community projects. In 1990 an agreement was signed putting the area in trust for 99 years and the forest park was established a year later. Eventually a trail will be cut from Tavoro right up to Lake Tagimaucia, but this awaits the creation of suitable overnight accommodations at Bouma and additional outside funding. For the time being visitors are allowed to sleep on mats in the park information kiosk at F$5 per head; otherwise it might be possible to camp or stay with the locals.

Bouma is easily accessible by public bus daily except Sunday. If you depart Waiyevo or Somosomo on the 0800 bus, you'll have about three and a half hours to see the falls and have a swim before catching the 1400 bus back to Waiyevo. This second bus does a roundtrip to Lavena, six km south (the 0800 bus finishes at Bouma), and it's worth jumping on for the ride even if you don't intend to get off at Lavena.

At Lavena the New Zealand government has financed the **Lavena Coastal Walk,** which opened in May 1993. The information kiosk where you pay the F$5 admission fee is right at the end of the road at Lavena and, when space is available, it's possible to sleep on one of the four mattresses on the floor upstairs in the kiosk at F$5 pp. There's no store here but the villagers will prepare meals for you at F$3 each. Otherwise, bring groceries and cook your own behind the kiosk—protect the food from mice. Lighting is by kerosene lamp, and mosquito coils are essential (the flies are a nuisance too). Additional accommodation may be available by the time you get there, and this is urgently required as it's not possible to visit Lavena as a day-trip by public bus (taxis charge F$50 return to bring you here). Buses depart Lavena for Somosomo Mon.-Sat. at 0600 and 1400, Sunday at 0800. The beach at Lavena is agreeable (be careful with the currents if you snorkel). The film *Return to the Blue Lagoon* was filmed here.

From the information kiosk at Lavena you can hike the five km down the Ravilevo Coast to **Wainibau Falls** in about an hour and a half. The last 30 minutes is a scramble up a creek bed, and during the rainy season you may have to wade or swim. Two falls here plunge into the same deep pool and diving off either is excellent fun (allow four hours there and back from Lavena with plenty of stops). It's also possible to visit the falls by motorboat, which can be arranged at the kiosk. A boat to Wainibau Falls is F$50 for up to three persons or F$15 pp for groups of four to six. If you also want to see **Savulevu Yavonu Falls,** which plummet off a cliff directly into the sea, you must pay F$75 for up to three people or F$25 pp for up to six. Intrepid ocean kayakers sometimes paddle the 20 km down the back side of Taveuni, past countless cliffs and waterfalls. Be on the lookout for native birds.

## SPORTS AND RECREATION

Taveuni and surrounding waters have become known as one of Fiji's top diving areas. The fabulous 32-km Rainbow Reef off the south coast of eastern Vanua Levu abounds in turtles, fish, overhangs, crevices, and soft corals, all in 5-10 meters of water. Favorite dive sites here include Annie's Bommie, Blue Ribbon Eel Reef, Cabbage Patch, Coral Garden, Jack's Place, Jerry's Jelly, Orgasm, Pot Luck, The Ledge, The Zoo, and White Sandy Gully. At the Great White Wall, a tunnel in the reef leads past sea fans to a magnificent drop-off and a wall covered in awesome white soft coral. Beware of strong currents in the Somosomo Strait.

Way back in 1976, Ric and Do Cammick's **Dive Taveuni** (c/o Postal Agency, Matei; tel. 880-441, fax 880-466) pioneered scuba diving in this area, discovering and naming most of the sites now regularly visited by divers. They cater mostly to small groups that have prebooked from abroad.

Also squarely aimed at the package tour market is the **Rainbow Reef Aqua-club** (Nigel and Carol Douglas, tel./fax 880-660) based across the road at Maravu Plantation. They offer two-tank morning dives to the outer reef walls provided at least four divers sign up. The live-aboard dive boat *Matangi Princess II* is based here. (Aqua-club is the new kid on the block at Taveuni and they seem to have deliberately chosen their name to create confusion with Rainbow Reef Divers run by Aqua-Trek at the Garden Island Resort. Such are the petty politics of outer island life.)

Walk-in divers are welcome at **Aquaventure** (c/o Postal Agency, Matei; tel./fax 880-381), run by Tania de Hoon, which has its base on the beach beside Beverly Campground, walking distance from most of the places to stay on northern Taveuni. They charge F$99 for two tanks, plus F$17 for gear (F$429 for 10 dives). Night dives are F$66. When appropriate, snorkelers are taken along at F$33 pp including gear. Their five-day NAUI certification course costs F$479 including six dives (or F$110 for an introductory dive).

**Rainbow Reef Divers** (Glenn Dziwulski, Box 1, Waiyevo; tel. 880-286, fax 880-288) at the Garden Island Resort caters mostly to divers who've prebooked from the States. The daily two-tank dives are F$165 plus gear (no one-tank dives), night dives F$96, and PADI scuba certification costs F$660 (a one-tank "discover scuba course" is F$148). You'll find cheaper dive shops but Rainbow's facilities are first rate.

Budget-minded divers should check out **The Dive Center** (Box 69, Taveuni; tel./fax 880-125), run by Vuna Reef Divers at Susie's Plantation, which offers boat dives on the Rainbow Reef at F$50/85 for one/two tanks (plus F$15 extra for gear). The Center's four-day PADI scuba certification courses (F$370) usually begin on Monday and Susie's makes a perfect base for these activities.

**Nok's Dive Center** (Box 22, Taveuni; tel. 880-246, fax 880-072), at Kris Back Palace north of Susie's, offers diving at F$55/88/400 for one/two/10 dives, plus F$11 a day for gear. Night dives are F$66. Snorkelers can go along in the boat at F$10 pp although some dive sites are not really suitable for snorkeling (ask). The four-day PADI certification course costs F$385, otherwise it's F$88 for a "baptism." Nok's dives the Great White Wall.

Offshore dive resorts such as Matangi Island and Qamea Beach Club receive mostly upscale divers who have booked from outside Fiji, and accommodations there are much more expensive than those on Taveuni.

**Little Dolphin Sports** (tel. 880-130), opposite Bhulabhai & Sons Supermarket, near the east end of the airstrip, rents paddle boats (F$15 a day), a three-person outrigger canoe (F$12/30 an hour/day), and snorkeling gear (F$8 a day). It's run by an Australian named Scott who is a mine of information. He'll ferry you out to a nice snorkeling spot on Honeymoon Island at F$10 pp return.

Adjacent to Aquaventure is **Ringgold Reek Kayaking** (tel. 880-083) with lots of two-person fiberglass kayaks for rent. It's run by Kenny Madden who lives up the hill.

The dive shop at the Garden Island Resort rents kayaks at F$5.50 an hour or F$22 a day.

## ACCOMMODATIONS

### Shoestring

Just north of Prince Charles Beach, a bit over one km south of the airport, are two of Taveuni's two best-established campgrounds. **Beverly's Campground** (tel. 880-684), run by Bill Madden, is a peaceful, shady place, adjacent to the hallowed sands of Maravu Plantation's beach. It's F$6 pp in your own tent, or F$8 pp to sleep in a small set tent, F$9 pp in a large set tent. The toilet and shower block is nearby. Cooking facilities (one-time charge of F$2 for gas) are available, but bring groceries (Bill provides free fresh fruit daily). The kitchen shelter by the beach is a nice place to sit and swap traveler's tales with the other guests. The clean white beach is just seconds from your tent.

A few hundred meters south is **Lisi's Campground & Cottages** (c/o Postal Agency, Matei; tel. 880-194), in a small village across the road from a white-sand beach. It's F$6 pp to camp, or F$10 pp in two small *bures.* A cottage with fridge goes for F$15/25 single/double. An unlit shower/toilet block is reserved for guests. Primitive cooking facilities are available in a *bure,* and your friendly hosts Mary and Lote Tuisago serve excellent Fijian meals at reasonable prices. Drawbacks include noise from the generator and throng of children running around, and the whole place is messy and dirty. Horseback riding can be arranged here.

A friendly Indian family runs **Kool's Accommodation** (Box 10, Waiyevo; tel. 880-395), just south of Kaba's Motel at Somosomo. The six rooms in two long blocks facing the eating area are F$15/20 single/double, and cooking facilities are provided (but no fridge). As the price may suggest, it's basic but a good bet for those on the lowest of budgets.

**Sunset Accommodation** (Box 15, Taveuni; tel. 880-229), on a dusty corner near the wharf at Lovonivonu, has two basic rooms behind a small store at F$15/20 single/double. Again, this is mostly a low-budget place to crash.

**Kris Back Palace** (Box 22, Taveuni; tel. 880-246, fax 880-072), between Soqulu Plantation and Susie's Plantation in southern Taveuni, is on a beautiful stretch of rocky coastline with crystal clear snorkeling waters. You can count on a good place to pitch your tent (F$7 for the first person in the tent and F$4 for the second). The two thatched two-bed *bures* are F$30 double, and there's also a five-bed dormitory *bure* at F$11 pp. The friendly managers will allow you to pick fruit at no cost in their plantation, and a three-meal deal is F$18 or you can cook your own. Scuba diving is available.

### Budget

The Petersen family runs a backpackers hangout called the **Tovu Tovu Resort** (tel. 880-560, fax 880-722) at Matei just east of Bhulabhai & Sons Supermarket. It's across the road from a rocky beach with murky water, and guests often walk the two km to Prince Charles Beach to swim. The two front *bures* capable of sleeping three are self-catering at F$67/72 single/double. Just behind are another two *bures* with private bath but no cooking at F$56/62, and up the hill is a large dormitory *bure* with a communal kitchen at F$15 pp. A budget *bure* with shared bath is F$25 double. You can also camp at F$6 per tent. The tin roofs are covered with thatch to keep them cool. The three-meal plan is F$25 pp and the restaurant terrace is a nice place to sit and socialize. Bicycles rent for F$15 a day.

**Niranjan's Budget Accommodation** (c/o Postal Agency, Matei; tel. 880-406) is just a five-minute walk east of the airport. The four rooms in the main building, each with two beds, fridge, fan, and cooking facilities, go for F$45/55/65 single/double/triple. Niranjan's also has an annex called **Airport Motel** two doors away, with four cheaper rooms with shared bath at F$44 double. The electric generator is on 1800-2200.

Brenda Petersen (tel. 880-171) who runs the airport snack bar can arrange rooms in the family house, the third driveway south of the airport on the inland side. Brenda's mother Margaret charges F$40 pp including all meals.

**Bibi's Hideaway** (Box 80, Waiyevo; tel. 880-443), about 500 meters south of the airport, has something of the gracious atmosphere of the neighboring properties without the sky-high prices. One room in a two-room cottage is F$30 single or double, while a larger family unit is F$70. The film crew from *Return to the Blue Lagoon* stayed here for three months, and with the extra income the owners built a deluxe *bure* with a picture window, which is F$50. All three units have access to cooking facilities and fridge, and you can pick fruit off their trees for free. Bibi's is located on lush, spacious grounds, and James, Victor, and Agnes Bibi will make you feel right at home. It's an excellent medium-priced choice if you don't mind being a bit away from the beach.

The original budget hotel on Taveuni was **Kaba's Motel & Guest House** (Box 4, Taveuni; tel. 880-233, fax 880-202) at Somosomo, which charges F$27/38/50 single/double/triple in one of four double rooms with shared facilities in the guesthouse. The cooking facilities are very good. The newer motel section is F$45/55/80 for one of the six larger units with kitchenette, fridge, fan, phone, and private bath. The water is solar-heated, so cold showers are de rigueur in overcast weather (ask for a discount in that case). Kaba's Supermarket is just up the street. No check-ins are accepted after 1800. Somosomo is a convenient place to stay for catching buses, but at night there's nothing much to do other than watch the BBC on TV.

**Andrew's Place** (Box 71, Waiyevo; tel./fax 880-241) is at Soqulu, a F$5 taxi ride south from Waiyevo. The five rooms are in a 120-year-old plantation house at F$40/50 single/double (meals F$5/8/15 breakfast/lunch/dinner). The Soqulo Golf Course is only a four-minute walk away (green fees F$20). Soqulo doesn't rent clubs but your Australian host Andrew Coghill will loan you a set, just bring your own balls. There's great snorkeling across the road, and Andrew can arrange hiking, birdwatching, and horse riding.

**Susie's Plantation Resort** (Box 69, Waiyevo; tel./fax 880-125), also known as Nomui Lala, just north of Vuna Point at the south end of Taveuni, offers peace and quiet amid picturesque rustic surroundings, at the right price. The 10 rooms in the plantation house are F$30/40 single/double with shared bath, or F$50/55 with private bath. Two simple seaside *bures* rent for F$55 double, and a larger family *bure* costs F$60. A place in the six-bed dorm is F$15, and camping is F$10 pp (tolerated but not encouraged). You can cook your own food (a well-stocked grocery store is at Vatuwiri Farm, a 10-minute walk south). Otherwise meals are available in the restaurant, housed in the oldest missionary building on the island (nonguests welcome). Electricity is available only during the dinner hours. This atmospheric resort right on the ocean has its own resident diving instructor, who leads daily trips to the Great White Wall and Rainbow Reef. The PADI scuba certification course offers a great opportunity to learn how to dive, but even if you're not a diver, you'll enjoy the superb snorkeling right off their rocky beach or at nearby Namoli Beach (better at low tide, as the current picks up appreciably when the tide comes in). Horseback riding can be arranged.

In 1998 **Vuna Lagoon Lodge** (Adi Salote Samanunu, Box 55, Waiyevo; tel./fax 880-627) opened on the Vuna Lagoon near Vuna village, a kilometer south of Vatuwiri Farm. Rooms here are F$30 double with shared bath or F$50 with private bath. Dorm beds cost F$15. Cooking facilities are provided or you can order meals. Wastes dumped by the local butcher into the sea nearby may have attracted sharks to this area and you should make inquiries before snorkeling. This place is run by the same people as Vakaviti Motel on the Coral Coast and information will be available there.

### Inexpensive

**Tuvununu Paradise Garden Inn** (c/o Postal Agency, Matei; tel. 880-465), 700 meters east of Naselesele village in northern Taveuni, offers eight rooms in a large wooden building overlooking Viubani Island at F$45/65 single/double, or F$20 pp in the dorm. The tidal flat in front of the inn is beautiful but not ideal for swimming, and at last report the Tuvununu was closed.

**Little Dolphin Sports** (tel. 880-130), less than a kilometer east of the airport, has an airy, two-story bungalow with cooking facilities called the "treehouse". At F$75 a night it's good value.

Several expatriate residents of the airport area have built nice little bungalows next to their homes or fixed up rooms in their personal residences that they rent to tourists. For instance, Audrey of **Audrey's Cafe** (tel. 880-039), half a km east of the airport, has a cottage at F$100 (children not admitted). An old steam tractor stands rusting under a coconut tree across the street. A few hundred meters west is **Coconut Grove Beachfront Cottages** (c/o Postal Agency, Matei; tel. 880-328), where Ronna Goldstein has three fan-cooled rooms with bath, one next to the restaurant at F$88/110 single/double and another below the beachfront terrace at F$110/132. The separate "Mango" bungalow with cooking facilities is F$132/154. (Guests in the other two rooms must use the restaurant. This is no hardship though as the food is especially good here.) Your stay here could depend on how well you get along with Ronna. At both Audrey's and Ronna's, it's important to call ahead to check availability as the rooms are often full. Use the card phone at the airport for this purpose (Air Fiji sells phone cards).

**Karin's Garden** (tel. 880-511, fax 880-511), almost opposite Bibi's Hideaway 500 meters south of the airport, has two bungalows for F$75 that overlook the same coast as overpriced Dive

Taveuni next door. You can cook and there's a restaurant on the premises.

The **Vatuwiri Farm Resort** (c/o Postal Agency, Vuna; tel./fax 880-316) at Vuna Point, a kilometer south of Susie's Plantation, offers the possibility of staying on an authentic working farm established in 1871 by James Valentine Tarte. The family's history was the subject of a 1988 novel by Daryl Tarte. Today the Tartes produce beef, vanilla, and copra, and rent three small cottages to tourists for F$120 double a night. Three good meals are F$60 pp extra. The rocky coast here is fine for snorkeling, and horseback riding is available. The Tarte family is congenial and this is perhaps your best chance to stay on a real working farm in Fiji.

### Moderate

The **Garden Island Resort** (Box 1, Waiyevo; tel. 880-286, fax 880-288) is by the sea at Waiyevo, three km south of Somosomo. Formerly known as the Castaway, this was Taveuni's premier (and only) hotel when it was built by the Travelodge chain in the 1960s. In 1996 the scuba operator Aqua Trek USA purchased the property and upgraded the facilities. The 30 a/c rooms in an attractive two-story building are F$132/168/198 single/double/triple, or F$30 pp in the two four-bed dorms. Air conditioning is F$15 extra but the ceiling fan should suffice. The buffet meal plan is F$75 pp, and eating by the pool is fun. There's no beach, but the Garden Island offers a restaurant, bar, evening entertainment, swimming pool, excursions, and water sports. Snorkeling trips are arranged twice a day to Korolevu Island and a large dive shop is on the premises. It's a nice place in which to hang out if you like large hotels. It's also convenient for sightseeing, entertainment, and transport.

### Luxury

Directly opposite the airport terminal is the **Garden of Eden Villa,** a large three-bedroom house capable of accommodating six people at F$700 a night including meals (minimum stay one week). If you can afford those bucks you can also afford to call the manager, Peter Madden (tel. 880-252), long distance from anywhere in the world and question him about what he's offering. Who knows, he may even throw in his 11-meter cruiser *Purple Haze!* Set on a bluff above the sea, this place is a favorite retreat of Fiji's president and other VIPs.

About 600 meters south of the airport are two of Taveuni's most exclusive properties. **Maravu Plantation Resort** (Jochen Kiess, c/o Postal Agency, Matei; tel. 880-555, fax 880-600) is a village-style resort on a real 20-hectare copra-making plantation. It has 10 comfortable *bures* with ceiling fans from F$340/440/540 single/double/triple plus tax but including meals, transfers, horseback riding, bicycles, and some other activities. Up to two children under 14 can stay free, paying only for their meals (F$50-100 per day per child). A *meke* is held weekly. There's a bar and swimming pool on the landscaped grounds. Airport transfers are F$6.

Almost across the street from Maravu Plantation is the deluxe **Dive Taveuni Resort** (Ric and Do Cammick, c/o Postal Agency, Matei; tel. 880-441, fax 880-466), formerly known as Ric's Place, patronized by an eclectic mix of scuba divers, fisherfolk, and honeymooners who arrive on prepaid packages. The five standard *bures* are F$360 pp, including meals, tax, and transfers. In addition, the clifftop honeymoon *bure* is F$1,180 double all inclusive, while the oceanfront suite is F$996 double. No alcohol is sold here, so bring your own. Dive Taveuni doesn't cater to people who stroll in unannounced. Stunning sunsets can be observed from the open terrace dining area and the swimming pool added in 1997 was designed to merge scenically with the sea on the horizon. They're closed in February and March.

Taveuni still doesn't have a public electricity supply but most of the places to stay have their own generators, which typically run 1800-2100 only.

## OTHER PRACTICALITIES

### Food

**Kumar's Restaurant** (tel. 880-435; Mon.-Sat. 0700-2000), 200 meters south of the National Bank in Waiyevo, is the cheapest regular restaurant on the island with surprisingly good curries in the F$3 range. Recommended.

Several stalls in the fish market opposite the Garden Island Resort serve cheap picnic table meals. The **Waci-Pokee Restaurant** (no phone;

open weekdays 0800-2000, Saturday 0800-1300 and 1700-2000, Sunday 1200-1430 and 1700-2000), next to the National Bank in Waiyevo, serves reasonable Chinese and local meals for around F$5. The thatched **Cannibal Cafe** directly behind the Waci-Pokee dispenses alcoholic beverages, local authorities permitting. A piece of chocolate cake is under a dollar but their slogan is "we'd love to have you for dinner." Enter through the restaurant or circle around the adjacent store.

Several of the one-unit accommodation places near the airport serve more upmarket meals, including Ronna Goldstein's **Coconut Grove Cafe** (tel. 880-328). The setting is lovely with a terrace overlooking the sea and the food is first rate, at prices to match. Ronna will be able to tell you anything you want to know about Taveuni. A similar scene revolves around **Audrey's Cafe** (daily 1000-1800), run by an American woman at Matei, a bit east of Ronna's. Audrey offers afternoon tea to guests who also enjoy the great view from her terrace, and she has various homemade goodies to take away. **Mrs. Lal's Curry Place** (tel. 880-705), between Ronna's and Audrey's, is cheaper with spicy Indian meals at F$7.50 a serve.

The **Vunibokoi Restaurant** (tel. 880-560), at the Tovu Tovu Resort east of Bhulabhai & Sons Supermarket at Matei, has a terrace where nonguests can order medium-priced meals prepared by Mareta, formerly of the Coconut Grove Cafe.

### Groceries

Those staying on the northern part of the island will appreciate the well-stocked **Bhulabhai & Sons Supermarket** (tel. 880-462) at the Matei Postal Agency between the airport and Naselesele village. Their generous ice cream cones are almost worth a special trip. Bhulabhai & Sons is closed on Sunday but a smaller Indian store 100 meters east will sell to you through the side window that day.

The variety of goods available at **Kaba's Supermarket** (tel. 880-088) in Somosomo is surprising, and a cluster of other small shops is adjacent. Small grocery stores also exist at Wairiki and Waiyevo. The only well-stocked grocery store in southern Taveuni is at Vatuwiri Farm, a kilometer south of Susie's Plantation.

### Entertainment

The **180 Meridian Cinema** at Wairiki shows mainly violence and horror films at 1930 on weekends.

The **Taveuni Country Club** (tel. 880-133), next to the police station up the hill at Waiyevo, is a safe, local drinking place. It's open Thurs.-Sat. only.

The only tourist-oriented nightlife on Taveuni are what's offered at the **Garden Island Resort** (tel. 880-286) which stages a *meke* and *lovo* Tuesday at 1830 (F$22 pp), but only when enough paying guests are present. **Maravu Plantation Resort** (tel. 880-555) also offers a weekly *meke* (reservations necessary).

### Services

Traveler's checks can be changed at the **National Bank** (tel. 880-433; Mon.-Thurs. 0930-1500, Friday 0930-1600) near the Garden Island Resort at Waiyevo.

**Club Coco** (Box 75, Waiyevo; tel. 880-017, fax 880-033), next to the National Bank in Waiyevo, sells local clothing, handicrafts, books, maps, and souvenirs, and manager Libby Lesuma can help with your travel and accommodations bookings.

A haircut from the barber next to Kaba's Motel in Somosomo is F$2/3 for men/women.

## TRANSPORTATION

### Getting There

Matei Airstrip at the north tip of Taveuni is serviced twice daily by **Air Fiji** (tel. 880-062) from Suva (F$150) and Savusavu (F$82), and by **Sunflower Airlines** (tel. 880-461) from Nadi (three a day, F$222), Suva (daily, F$150), and Savusavu (twice daily, F$82). Sunflower also arrives from Labasa (F$82) three times a week. Flights to/from Taveuni are often heavily booked. You get superb views of Taveuni from the plane: sit on the right side going up, the left side coming back. Krishna Brothers (tel. 880-504) in Somosomo is the agent for Air Fiji. Sunflower doesn't have an agent on Taveuni and to book you must call Matei Airport at 880-461.

**Consort Shipping** operates the weekly *Spirit of Free Enterprise* service from Suva to Taveuni via Koro and Savusavu (23 hours, F$34/68

*car ferry,* Spirit of Free Enterprise, *at Taveuni*

DAVID STANLEY

deck/cabin). This ferry departs Suva northbound Tuesday at 2100, and leaves Taveuni southbound Thursday at noon. The Consort agent, Ian Simpson (tel. 880-261), is at the fish market opposite the Garden Island Resort.

The **Beachcomber Cruises** car ferry *Adi Savusavu* departs Taveuni for Savusavu and Suva Wednesday at noon. It takes five hours to reach Savusavu, and after a three-hour stop continues to Suva, where it arrives at 0730 Thursday morning (F$38/44 economy/first class). The agent is Raj's Fruits and Vegetables (tel. 880-591), next to the Hot Bread Kitchen in Somosomo.

**Patterson Brothers** operates the barge *Yaubula* between Taveuni and Natuvu at Buca Bay on Vanua Levu, leaving Taveuni Mon.-Sat. at 0900 (two hours, F$7.70), leaving Natuvu at 1100. They also carry cars and vans for F$50. Through boat/bus tickets with a bus connection at Natuvu are available to Savusavu Mon.-Sat. (four hours, F$12.70) and to Labasa Monday, Wednesday, Friday and Saturday (six hours, F$16.20). The Patterson Brothers agent is Lesuma Holdings (tel. 880-036) in the back of the store next to the National Bank. Try to buy your combined boat/bus ticket at the Patterson Brothers office a day before, otherwise get one on the ferry itself as you board (arrive an hour before departure and be fast at holiday times as the 60-seater bus does fill up, unlike the 100-passenger ferry which always has space available). Coffee and snacks are sold on board the barge.

The small passenger boat *Grace* departs Taveuni for Natuvu Mon.-Fri. at 0545 (two hours, F$5), with regular bus connections to Savusavu (F$3). If you miss the bus connection, you'll have to wait around at Buca Bay all day for another bus to Savusavu (Public buses run from Natuvu to Savusavu only in the early morning and at 1600). If no bus is around, you should be able to find a carrier, but expect a rough trip. Information on the *Grace* is available from Mr. Latchman Prasad (tel. 880-134) who lives opposite Kaba's Supermarket in Somosomo.

If you arrive by boat at Taveuni, you could disembark at any one of three places. Some small boats from Vanua Levu transfer their passengers to the beach at Waiyevo by outboard. The large ferries from Suva tie up at a wharf a kilometer north of Waiyevo. There's another wharf called the "Korean Wharf" at Lovonivonu village, a kilometer north again, midway between Waiyevo and Somosomo, and this is usually used by the Vanua Levu ferries and other smaller cargo boats.

### Getting Around

Mon.-Sat. **Pacific Transport** (tel. 880-278) buses leave Waiyevo and Somosomo northbound to Bouma (F$2) at 0800, 1200, and 1600; southbound to Vuna (F$2) they also leave at 0800, 1200, and 1600. The northbound 0800 bus turns around at Bouma, but the 1200 and 1600 buses carry on to Lavena (F$2). Both of the 1600 buses stop and spend the night at their turn-around points, Lavena and Navakawau, heading back to Somosomo the next morning at 0600 (at 0800 on Sunday). Sunday service is very infrequent, although there are buses to Bouma and Vuna at 1600. Check the current schedule carefully as soon as you arrive and beware of buses leaving a bit early. The buses begin their journeys at the Pacific Transport garage at Somosomo, but they all first head south to Waiyevo hospital to pick up passengers.

One of Taveuni's biggest drawbacks is the extremely dusty road up the northwest coast, which makes it very unpleasant to walk anywhere between Wairiki and the airport when there's a lot of fast traffic passing. This combined with rather expensive taxi fares and sporadic buses make getting around rather inconvenient. Taveuni's minibus taxis only operate on a charter basis and don't run along set routes picking up passengers at fixed rates. The taxi fare from the wharf to Somosomo is F$2; from the airport to Somosomo it will be F$10. In general, the taxi fare will be about 10 times the corresponding bus fare.

You could hire a minibus taxi and driver for the day. Write out a list of everything you want to see, then negotiate a price with a driver. Otherwise, save money by using the buses for long rides and taxis for shorter hops. Rental cars are not available.

## OFFSHORE ISLANDS

### Qamea Island

Qamea (pronounced "Nggamea") Island, just three km east of Taveuni, is the 12th-largest island in Fiji. It's 10 km long with lots of lovely bays, lush green hills, and secluded white-sand beaches. Land crabs *(lairo)* are gathered in abundance here during their migration to the sea at the beginning of the breeding season in late November or early December. The birdlife is also rich, due to the absence of the mongoose. Outboards from villages on Qamea land near Navakacoa village on the northeast side of Taveuni. The best time to try for a ride over is Thursday or Friday afternoons. Vatusogosogo, one of six villages on Qamea, is inhabited by descendants of blackbirded Solomon islanders.

The **Qamea Beach Club Resort** (Jo Ann Koss, c/o Postal Agency, Matei; tel. 880-220, fax 880-092), on the west side of Qamea, has 11 thatched *bures* at F$620 single, double, or triple, and one split-level villa at F$730 (children under 13 not admitted). All units have a ceiling fan, minibar, and hammock-equipped deck. The meal plan is F$170 pp a day, served in a tall central dining room and lounge designed like a *burekalau* (temple). Activities such as snorkeling, sailing, windsurfing, village tours, and hiking are included in the basic price, but fishing and scuba diving are extra (18 of Fiji's top dive sites are nearby). The snorkeling right off Qamea's 400 meters of fine white sands is superb and there's also a freshwater swimming pool. The 30-minute bus/boat transfer from Taveuni airport is F$140 pp return. Luxury.

### Matangi Island

Matangi is a tiny horseshoe-shaped volcanic island just north of Qamea, its sunken crater forming a lovely palm-fringed bay. The island is privately owned by the Douglas family, which has been producing copra on Matangi for five generations and still does. In 1988 they diversified into the hotel business.

**Matangi Island Resort** (Noel Douglas, Box 83, Waiyevo; tel. 880-260, fax 880-274), 10 km northeast of Taveuni, makes no bones about serving as a base for scuba divers and some of the top dive sites in the world are close at hand. Matangi also caters to families and couples looking for a quiet holiday, and the deluxe treehouse *bure,* perched 10 meters up in an almond tree, is popular among honeymooners (F$464 pp). Other guests are accommodated in 10 neat thatched *bures* well spaced among the coconut palms below Matangi's high jungly interior. It's F$368 pp including all meals and boat transfers from Taveuni, and most guests are on packages prebooked from abroad. Luxury.

### Laucala Island

Laucala Island, which shares a barrier reef with Qamea, was depopulated and sold to Europeans in the mid-19th century by the chief of Taveuni, after the inhabitants sided with Tongan chief Enele Ma'afu in a local war. Today it's owned by Steven Forbes, son of the late multimillionaire businessman and New York publisher Malcolm Forbes, who is buried on the island. In 1972 Malcolm Forbes bought 12-square-km Laucala from the Australian company Morris Hedstrom for US$1 million. He then spent additional millions on an airstrip, wharf, and roads, and on replacing the thatched *bures* of the 300 Fijian inhabitants with 40 red-roofed houses with electricity and indoor plumbing. Forbes's former private residence stands atop a hill overlooking the native village, the inhabitants of which make copra.

In 1984, six years prior to his death in 1990, Forbes opened his island to affluent tourists who now stay in seven *bures*, each with living room, bar, and kitchen. The housekeepers prepare guests' breakfasts in their cottages; other meals can be taken in the plantation house, in Forbes's house, at the beachside barbecue area, or as a picnic anywhere on the island. The price is F$475 pp per night (four-night minimum stay), including all meals, "a reasonable supply" of liquor, sports, scuba diving, and deep-sea fishing. The charter flight from Nadi to Laucala Island is F$198 pp each way. Rick West, the resident general manager of **Fiji Forbes Inc.** (Box 41, Waiyevo; tel. 880-077, fax 880-099), is the only chief on Laucala. We've heard good things about this resort from people in a position to know. Luxury.

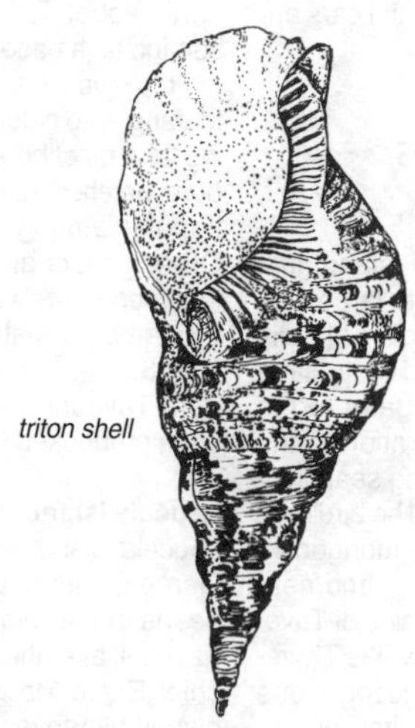
triton shell

LOUISE FOOTE

SALVATORE CASA

# THE LAU GROUP

Lau is by far the most remote part of Fiji, its 57 islands scattered over a vast area of ocean between Viti Levu and Tonga. Roughly half of them are inhabited. Though all are relatively small, they vary from volcanic islands to uplifted atolls to some combination of the two. Tongan influence has always been strong in Lau, and due to Polynesian mixing the people have a somewhat lighter skin color than other Fijians. The westward migrations continue today: over 40,000 Lauans live on Viti Levu and under 13,000 on their home islands. Historically the chiefs of Lau have always had a political influence on Fiji far out of proportion to their economic or geographical importance.

Vanua Balavu (52 square km) and Lakeba (54 square km) are the largest and most important islands of the group. These are also the only islands with organized accommodations, and Vanua Balavu is the more rewarding of the two. Once accessible only after a long sea voyage on infrequent copra-collecting ships, four islands in Lau—Lakeba, Vanua Balavu, Moala, and Cicia—now have regular air service from Suva. Occasional private ships also circulate through Lau, usually calling at five or six islands on a single trip, but they only offer deck passage. No banks are to be found in Lau and it's important to bring sufficient Fijian currency.

Few of these islands are prepared for tourism, so it really helps to know someone. But contrary to what is written in some guidebooks, individual tourists *do not* require a special permit or invitation to visit Lau—you just get on a plane and go. (Cruising yachties do need a permit.) Since the best selection of places to stay is on Vanua Balavu, that's the logical place to head first. Words like pristine, untouched, and idyllic all seem to have been invented for Lau, and the unconditional friendliness of the local people is renowned. This is one area where you don't need to worry about bumping into a McDonald's!

# NORTHERN LAU

## VANUA BALAVU

The name means the "long land." The southern portion of this unusual, seahorse-shaped island is mostly volcanic, while the north is uplifted coral. This unspoiled environment of palm-fringed beaches backed by long grassy hillsides and sheer limestone cliffs is a wonderful area to explore. Varied vistas and scenic views are on all sides. To the east is a 130-km barrier reef enclosing a 37 by 16 km lagoon. The Bay of Islands at the northwest end of Vanua Balavu is a recognized hurricane shelter. The villages of Vanua Balavu are impeccably clean, the grass cut and manicured. Large mats are made on the island and strips of pandanus can be seen drying before many of the houses.

In 1840 Commodore Wilkes of the U.S. Exploring Expedition named Vanua Balavu and its adjacent islands enclosed by the same barrier reef the Exploring Isles. In the days of sail, Lomaloma, the largest settlement, was an important Pacific port. The early trading company Hennings Brothers had its headquarters here. The great Tongan warlord Enele Ma'afu conquered northern Lau from the chiefs of Vanua Levu in 1855 and made Lomaloma the base for his bid to dominate Fiji. A small monument flanked by two cannons on the waterfront near the wharf recalls the event. Fiji's first public botanical garden was laid out here over a century ago, but nothing remains of it. History has passed Lomaloma by. Today it's only a big sleepy village with a hospital and a couple of general stores. Some 400 Tongans live in Sawana, the south portion of Lomaloma village, and many of the houses have the round ends characteristic of Lau. Fiji's current president, Ratu Sir Kamisese Mara, was born in Sawana.

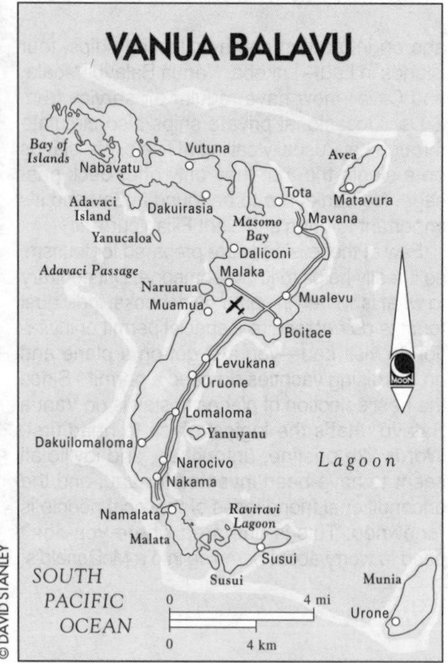


© DAVID STANLEY

### Sights

Copra is the main export and there's a small coconut oil mill at **Lomaloma.** A road runs inland from Lomaloma, up and across the island to **Dakuilomaloma.** From the small communications station on a grassy hilltop midway there's an excellent view.

Follow the road south from Lomaloma three km to **Narocivo** village, then continue two km beyond to the narrow passage separating Vanua Balavu and Malata islands. At low tide you can easily wade across to **Namalata** village. Alternatively, work your way around to the west side of Vanua Balavu, where there are isolated tropical beaches. There's good snorkeling in this passage.

A guide can show you **hot springs** and **burial caves** among the high limestone outcrops between Narocivo and Namalata. This can be easily arranged at Nakama, the tiny collection of houses closest to the cliffs, upon payment of a nominal fee. Small bats inhabit some of the caves.

Rent a boat to take you over to the **Raviravi Lagoon** on Susui Island, the favorite picnic spot near Lomaloma for the locals. The beach and

CAROLYN FOTOFILI

Moana's Guesthouse

snorkeling are good, and spelunkers can check out the cave. **Munia Island** is a privately owned coconut plantation where paying guests are accommodated in two *bures.*

### Events

A most unusual event occurs annually at Masomo Bay, west of **Mavana** village, usually around Christmas. For a couple of days the Mavana villagers, clad only in skirts of *drauniqai* leaves, enter the waters and stir up the muddy bottom by swimming around clutching logs. No one understands exactly why, and magic is thought to be involved, but this activity stuns the *yawa,* or mullet fish, that inhabit the bay, rendering them easy prey for waiting spears. Peni, the *bete* (priest) of Mavana, controls the ritual. No photos are allowed. A Fijian legend tells how the *yawa* were originally brought to Masomo by a Tongan princess.

### Accommodations

Mr. Poasa Delailomaloma (tel. 895-060) and his brother Laveti operate a charming traditional-style resthouse in the middle of Lomaloma village. A bed and all meals cost F$30 pp. Budget.

In Sawana village a short walk away from Poasa's is **Moana's Guesthouse** (Box 11, Lomaloma; tel. 895-006), run by Tevita and Carolyn Fotofili with the help of little daughter Moana. It's F$30 pp including all meals to share an oval-ended Tongan-style house with a three-bedded dorm and double room. Both places make perfect bases from which to explore the island, and you get a feel for village life while retaining a degree of privacy. The Fotofilis are planning to build some beach *bures* and a campground a km from the village, so call and ask. Budget.

You can also stay at Joe and Hélène Tuwai's **Nawanawa Estate** (Box 20, Lomaloma), a km from Daliconi village near the airport on the northwest side of the island. There's no phone but you can try announcing your arrival by writing them a letter as soon as you've booked your flight. They meet all flights and can accommodate 10 persons on the estate. In the unlikely event that they were full, something else could be arranged. The Tuwais charge F$40 pp including meals (children under 10 F$20). You'll share their attractive colonial-style home with solar electricity (no generator noise), and aside from hiking, snorkeling, and fishing, you can ask to be dropped on a deserted island for a small charge. Boat trips to the Bay of Islands are also possible. All three places above accept cash only. Budget

In 1994 Ratu Sir Kamisese Mara, paramount chief of the Lau Group, opened the **Lomaloma Resort** (Box 55, Lomaloma; tel. 895-091, fax 895-092) on tadpole-sized Yanuyanu Island just off Lomaloma. The seven round-ended *bures* (or *fales*) furnished in the traditional style catered mostly to upmarket scuba divers and cost F$276/450 single/double including all meals. In 1998 the Lomaloma Resort was closed and it was still not known when/if they would reopen.

### Getting There

**Air Fiji** flies to Vanua Balavu three times a week from Suva (F$150). The flights are heavily booked, so reserve your return journey before leaving Suva. A bus runs from the airstrip to Lomaloma. After checking in at the airstrip for departure you'll probably have time to scramble up the nearby hill for a good view of the island. Boat service from Suva is only every couple of weeks.

Several carriers a day run from Lomaloma north to Mualevu, and some carry on to Mavana.

## OTHER ISLANDS OF NORTHERN LAU

After setting himself up at Lomaloma on Vanua Balavu in 1855, Chief Ma'afu encouraged the establishment of European copra and cotton plantations, and several islands are freehold land to this day. **Kanacea,** to the west of Vanua Balavu, was sold to a European by the Tui Cakau in 1863, and the Kanacea people now reside on Taveuni. **Mago** (20 square km), a copra estate formerly owned by English planter Jim Barron, was purchased by the Tokyu Corporation of Japan in 1985 for F$6 million.

**Naitauba** is a circular island about 186 meters high with cliffs on the north coast. Originally owned by Hennings Brothers, in 1983 it was purchased from TV star Raymond Burr by the California spiritual group Johannine Daist Communion for US$2.1 million. Johannine Daist holds four-to-eight-week meditation retreats on Naitauba for longtime members of the communion. The communion's founder, Baba Da Free John, the former Franklin Albert Jones, who attained enlightenment in Hollywood in 1970, lives on the island.

There's a single Fijian village and a gorgeous white-sand beach on **Yacata Island.** Right next to Yacata and sharing the same lagoon is 260-hectare **Kaimbu Island,** which was owned by the Rosa family from 1872 to 1969, when it was purchased by fiberglass millionaires Margie and Jay Johnson. In 1987 the Johnsons opened a small luxury resort on the island, and although they sold Kaimbu to an undisclosed buyer in 1996, their son Scott stayed on as manager together with wife Sally of the Taveuni Cammick clan. **Kaimbu Island Resort** (Kaimbu Island Postal Agency; tel. 880-333, fax 880-334) consists of only three spacious octagonal guest cottages renting at F$1,990 per couple per day plus tax (minimum stay seven nights—children not accommodated). A private party of six can hire the entire island at F$5,000 a day. The price includes gourmet meals, drinks, snorkeling, sailing, windsurfing, sportfishing, scuba diving, and just about anything else you desire. The chartered flight from Suva or Taveuni to Kaimbu's central airstrip is another F$990 pp return. Add 10% tax to all rates. Bookings are handled by **Kaimbu Island Associates** (Box 10392, Newport Beach, CA 92658, U.S.A.; tel. 1-800/473-0332, fax 1-949/644-5773; e-mail: kaimbu @earthlink.net). Don't bother calling the Fiji number outside local business hours as you'll only get their answering machine. Luxury.

**Vatu Vara** to the south, with its soaring interior plateau, golden beaches, and azure lagoon, is privately owned and unoccupied much of the time. The circular, 314-meter-high central limestone terrace, which makes the island look like a hat when viewed from the sea, gives it its other name, Hat Island. There is reputed to be buried treasure on Vatu Vara.

**Katafaga** to the southeast of Vanua Balavu was at one time owned by Harold Gatty, the famous Australian aviator who founded Fiji Airways (later Air Pacific) in 1951.

**Cicia,** between Northern and Southern Lau, receives Air Fiji flights from Suva (F$138) twice a week. Five Fijian villages are found on Cicia,

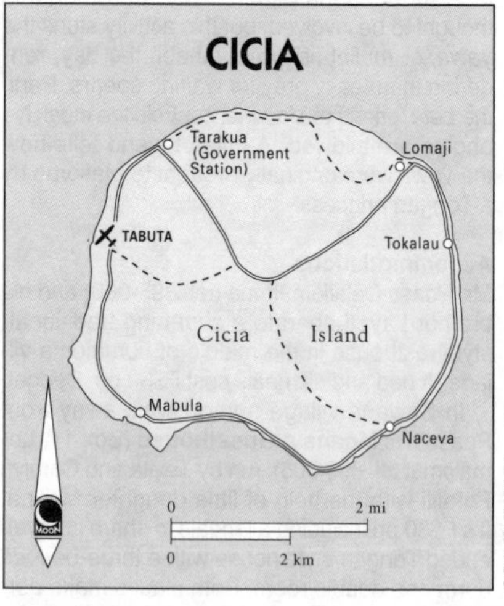

and much of the 34-square-km island is covered by coconut plantations. Fiji's only black-and-white Australian magpies have been introduced to Cicia and Taveuni.

**Wailagi Lala,** northernmost of the Lau Group, is a coral atoll bearing a lighthouse, which beckons to ships entering Nanuku Passage, the northwest gateway to Fiji.

# SOUTHERN LAU

## LAKEBA

Lakeba is a rounded volcanic island reaching 215 meters. The fertile red soils of the rolling interior hills have been planted with pine, but the low coastal plain, with eight villages and all the people, is covered with coconuts. To the east is a wide lagoon enclosed by a barrier reef. In the olden days, the population lived on Delai Kedekede, an interior hilltop well suited for defense.

The original capital of Lakeba was Nasaqalau on the north coast, and the present inhabitants of Nasaqalau retain strong Tongan influence. When the Nayau clan conquered the island, their paramount chief, the Tui Nayau, became ruler of all of Southern Lau from his seat at Tubou. During the 1970s and 1980s Ratu Sir Kamisese Mara, the present Tui Nayau, served as prime minister of Fiji.

### Sights

A 29-km road runs all the way around Lakeba. From the Catholic church you get a good view of **Tubou,** an attractive village and one of the largest in Fiji, with a hospital, wharf, several stores, and the Lau provincial headquarters. Tubou was originally situated at Korovusa just inland, where the foundations of former houses can still be seen. Farther inland on the same road is the forestry station and a nursery.

The Tongan chief Enele Ma'afu (died 1881) is buried on a stepped platform behind the Provincial Office near Tubou's wharf. In 1847 Ma'afu arrived in Fiji with a small Tongan army ostensibly to advance the spread of Christianity, and by 1855 he dominated eastern Fiji from his base at Vanua Balavu. In 1869 Ma'afu united the group into the Lau Confederation and took the title Tui Lau. Two years later he accepted the supremacy of Cakobau's Kingdom of Fiji, and in 1874 he signed the cession to Britain. Alongside Ma'afu is the grave of Ratu Sir Lala Sukuna (1888-1958), an important figure in the development of indigenous Fijian self-government. David Cargill and William Cross, the first Methodist missionaries to arrive in Fiji, landed on the beach just opposite the burial place on 12 October 1835. Here they invented the present system of written Fijian.

### Coconut Factory

Four km west of Tubou is the coir (husk fiber) and coconut oil factory of the **Lakeba Cooperative Association** at Wainiyabia. Truckloads of coconuts are brought in and dehusked by hand. The meat is then removed and sent to the copra driers. Coconut oil is pressed from the resulting copra and exported in drums. The dry pulp remaining after the extraction is bagged and sold locally as feed for pigs. The husks are flattened and soaked, then fed through machinery that separates the fiber. This is then made into twine, rope, brushes, and doormats, or it is bundled to be used as mattress fiber. Nothing is wasted. Behind the factory is Wainiyabia Beach, one of the most scenic on Lakeba.

### Nasaqalau and Vicinity

The finest limestone caves on the island are near the coast on the northwest side of Lakeba, 2.5 km southwest of Nasaqalau. **Oso Nabukete** is the largest; the entrance is behind a raised limestone terrace. You walk through two chambers before reaching a small, circular opening about one meter in diameter, which leads into a third chamber. The story goes that women attempting to hide during pregnancy are unable to pass through this opening, thus giving the cave its name, the "Tight Fit to the Pregnant" Cave.

Nearby is a smaller cave, **Qara Bulo** ("Hidden Cave"), which one must crawl into. Warriors used it as a refuge and hiding place in former times. The old village of Nasaqalau was located on top of the high cliffs behind the caves at Uluni-koro. The whole area is owned by the Nautoqumu clan of Nasaqalau, and they will arrange for a guide to show you around for a fee. Take a flashlight and some newspapers to spread over the openings to protect your clothing.

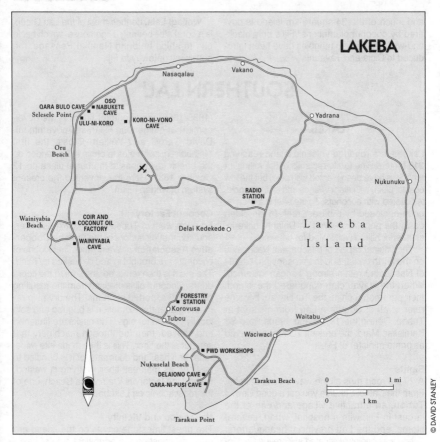

Each October or November the Nasaqalau people perform a shark-calling ritual. A month before the ritual, a priest *(bete)* plants a post with a piece of tapa tied to it in the reef. He then keeps watch to ensure that no one comes near the area, while performing a daily kava ceremony. When the appointed day arrives, the caller wades out up to his neck and repeats a chant. Not long after, a large school of sharks led by a white shark arrives and circles the caller. He leads them to shallow water, where all but the white shark are formally killed and eaten.

### East of Tubou

Two less impressive caves can be found at Tarakua, southeast of Tubou. **Qara-ni-pusi** has a small entrance, but opens up once you get inside. **Delaiono Cave** is just below a huge banyan tree; this one is easier to enter and smaller inside.

The number one beach near Tubou is **Nukuselal,** which you can reach by walking east along the coastal road as far as the P.W.D. workshops. Turn right onto the track, which runs along the west side of the compound to Nukuselal Beach.

### Into the Interior

Many forestry roads have been built throughout the interior of Lakeba. You can walk across the island from Tubou to Yadrana in a couple of hours, enjoying excellent views along the way. A radio station operates on solar energy near the center of the island. **Aiwa Island,** which can be seen to the southeast, is owned by the Tui Nayau and is inhabited only by flocks of wild goats.

### Accommodations

Mr. Kefoni Qica (c/o Lau Provincial Office, Tubou, Lakeba) runs a budget guesthouse at Tubou offering rooms with shared bath at F$20 pp bed and breakfast, plus F$6 each for lunch and dinner. To let him know you're coming, call the Lau Provincial Office from a post office (card telephones don't work for this call and the postal clerk must dial the call for you) and leave a message. The locals at Tubou concoct a potent homebrew *(uburu)* from cassava.

### Getting There

**Air Fiji** flies to Lakeba three times a week from Suva (F$150). A bus connects the airstrip to Tubou, and buses run around the island four times weekdays, three times daily weekends.

## OTHER ISLANDS OF SOUTHERN LAU

Unlike the islands of northern Lau, many of which are freehold and owned by outsiders, the isles of southern Lau are communally owned by the Fijian inhabitants. This is by far the most remote corner of Fiji. In a pool on **Vanua Vatu** are red prawns similar to those of Vatulele and Vanua Levu. Here the locals can summon the prawns with a certain chant.

**Oneata** is famous for its mosquitoes and tapa cloth. In 1830 two Tahitian teachers from the London Missionary Society arrived on Oneata and were adopted by a local chief who had previously visited Tonga and Tahiti. The men spent the rest of their lives on the island, and there's a monument to them at Dakuloa village.

**Moce** is known for its tapa cloth, which is also made on Namuka, Vatoa, and Ono-i-Lau. **Komo** is famous for its handsome women and dances *(meke),* which are performed whenever a ship arrives. Moce, Komo, and Olorua are unique in that they are volcanic islands without uplifted limestone terraces.

The **Yagasa Cluster** is owned by the people of Moce, who visit it occasionally to make copra. Fiji's finest *tanoa* are carved from *vesi* (ironwood) at **Kabara,** the largest island in southern Lau. The surfing is also said to be good at Kabara, if you can get there.

**Fulaga** is known for its woodcarving; large outrigger canoes are still built on Fulaga, as well as on **Ogea.** Over 100 tiny islands in the Fulaga lagoon have been undercut into incredible mushroom shapes. The water around them is tinged with striking colors by the dissolved limestone, and there are numerous magnificent beaches. Yachts can enter this lagoon through a narrow pass.

**Ono-i-Lau,** far to the south, is closer to Tonga than to the main islands of Fiji. It consists of three small volcanic islands, remnants of a single crater, in an oval lagoon. A few tiny coral islets sit on the barrier reef. The people of Ono-i-Lau make the best *magi magi* (sennit rope) and *tabu kaisi* mats in the country. Only high chiefs may sit on these mats. Ono-i-Lau formerly had air service from Suva, but this has been suspended.

### The Moala Group

Structurally, geographically, and historically, the high volcanic islands of Moala, Totoya, and Matuku have more to do with Viti Levu than with the rest of Lau. In the mid-19th century

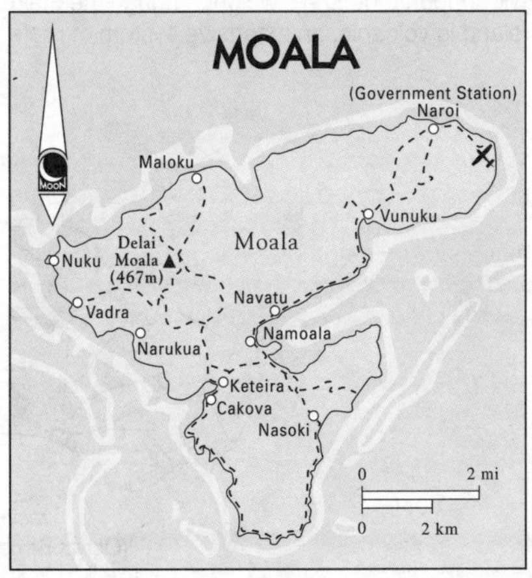

*Matuku Island, Moala Group*

ROBERT KENNINGTON

they were conquered by the Tongan warlord Enele Ma'afu, and today they're still administered as part of the Lau Group. All three islands have varied scenery, with dark green rainforests above grassy slopes, good anchorage, many villages, and abundant food. Their unexplored nature yet relative proximity to Suva by boat make them an ideal escape for adventurers. No tourist facilities of any kind exist in the Moala Group.

Triangular **Moala** is an intriguing 68-square-km island, the ninth largest in Fiji. Two small crater lakes on the summit of Delai Moala (467 meters) are covered with matted sedges, which will support a person's weight. Though the main island is volcanic, an extensive system of reefs flanks the shores. Ships call at the small government station of Naroi, also the site of an airstrip that receives **Air Fiji** flights four times a week from Suva (F$136).

**Totoya** is a horseshoe-shaped high island enclosing a deep bay on the south. The bay, actually the island's sunken crater, can only be entered through a narrow channel known as the Gullet, and the southeast trades send high waves across the reefs at the mouth of the bay, making this a dangerous place. Better anchorage is found off the southwest arm of the island. Five Fijian villages are found on Totoya, while neighboring **Matuku** has seven. The anchorage in a submerged crater on the west side of Matuku is one of the finest in Fiji.

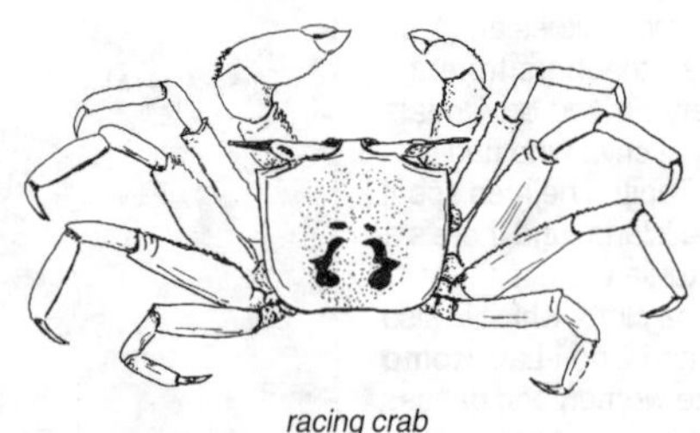

LOUISE FOOTE

*racing crab*
(Octypode ceratophthalma)

SALVATORE CASA

# ROTUMA

This isolated six-by-14-km volcanic island, 600 km north of Viti Levu, is surrounded on all sides by more than 322 km of open sea. There's a saying in Fiji that if you can find Rotuma on a map it's a fairly good map. The climate is damp and hot.

In the beginning Raho, the Samoan folk hero, dumped two basketfuls of earth here to create the twin islands, joined by the Motusa Isthmus, and installed Sauiftoga as king. Tongans from Niuafo'ou conquered Rotuma in the 17th century and ruled from Noa'tau until they were overthrown.

The first recorded European visit was by Captain Edwards of HMS *Pandora* in 1791, while he was searching for the *Bounty* mutineers. Christianity was introduced in 1842 by Tongan Wesleyan missionaries, followed in 1847 by Marist Roman Catholics. Their followers fought pitched battles in the religious wars of 1871 and 1878, with the Wesleyans emerging victorious. Escaped convicts and beachcombers also flooded in but mostly succeeded in killing each other off. Tiring of strife, the chiefs asked Britain to annex the island in 1881, and it has been part of Fiji ever since. European planters ran the copra trade from their settlement at Motusa until local cooperatives took over.

Rotuma is run like a colony of Fiji, with the administration in the hands of a district officer responsible to the district commissioner at Levuka. Decisions of the 15-member Rotuma island council are subject to veto by the national government. Some 2,800 Rotumans presently inhabit the island, and another 4,600 of their number live in Suva. The light-skinned Polynesian Rotumans are easily distinguished from Fijians. The women weave fine white mats. Fiji's juiciest oranges are grown here and Rotuma kava is noted for its strength.

## SIGHTS

Ships arrive at a wharf on the edge of the reef, connected to Oinafa Point by a 200-meter coral causeway, which acts as a breakwater. There's a lovely white beach at **Oinafa.** The airstrip is to the west, between Oinafa and Ahau, the government station. At **Noa'tau** southeast of Oinafa is a coop store; nearby, at **Sililo,** visit a hill with large

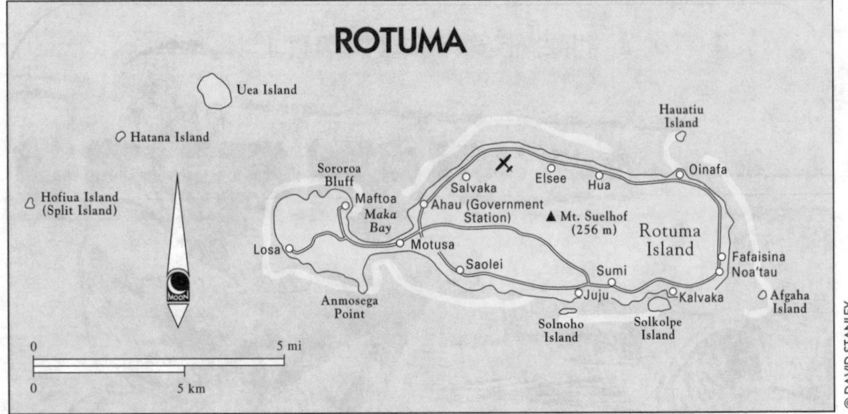


stone slabs and old cannons scattered about, marking the burial place of the kings of yore. Look for the fine stained-glass windows in the Catholic church at **Sumi** on the south coast. Inland near the center of the island is Mt. Suelhof (256 meters), the highest peak; climb it for the view.

**Maftoa** across the Motusa Isthmus has a cave with a freshwater pool. In the graveyard at Maftoa are huge stones brought here long ago. It's said four men could go into a trance and carry the stones with their fingers. **Sororoa Bluff** (218 meters) above Maftoa should also be climbed for the view. Deserted **Vovoe Beach** on the west side of Sororoa is one of the finest in the Pacific. A kilometer southwest of Sororoa is **Solmea Hill** (165 meters), with an inactive crater on its north slope. On the coast at the northwest corner of Rotuma is a natural **stone bridge** over the water.

**Hatana,** a tiny islet off the west end of Rotuma, is said to be the final resting place of Raho, the demigod who created Rotuma. A pair of volcanic rocks before a stone altar surrounded by a coral ring are said to be the King and Queen stones. Today Hatana is a refuge for seabirds. **Hofiua** or Split Island looks like it was cut in two with a knife; a circular boulder bridges the gap.

## PRACTICALITIES

### Accommodations

Few organized accommodations exist on Rotuma. Many Rotumans live in Suva, however, and if you have a Rotuman friend he/she may be willing to send word to his/her family to expect you. Ask your friend what you should take along as a gift. Although the National Bank of Fiji (tel. 891-023) has a small branch at Ahau on Rotuma, you should change enough money for all local expenditures before leaving Suva.

**Rotuma Island Backpackers** (Box 83, Rotuma; tel. 891-290) is operated by Vani Marseu of Motusa village who asks F$15 per couple to pitch a tent.

### Getting There

**Sunflower Airlines** (tel. 891-084) flies to Rotuma from Suva twice weekly (F$376). From Nadi the fare is F$428. **Kadavu Shipping** (tel. 311-766) operates the ship *Bulou-ni-ceva* from Suva to Rotuma once a month (two days, F$90/140 deck/cabin each way). Ask around Walu Bay for other ships from Suva.

# RESOURCES

## GUIDEBOOKS

Hammick, Anne. *Ocean Cruising on a Budget.* Camden, Maine: International Marine Publishing, 1991. Hammick shows how to sail your own yacht safely and enjoyably over the seas while cutting costs. Study it beforehand if you're thinking of working as crew on a yacht.

*Health Information for International Travel.* "The Yellow Book" is an excellent reference published annually by the Centers for Disease Control and Prevention, U.S. Public Health Service. Available from the Superintendent of Documents, Box 371954, Pittsburgh, PA 15250-7954, U.S.A. (tel. 1-202/512-1800, www.cdc.gov/travel/index.html)

Levy, Neil. *Micronesia Handbook.* Chico: Moon Travel Handbooks 1997. Covers the North Pacific countries of Nauru, Kiribati, the Marshall Islands, the Federated States of Micronesia, the Republic of Palau, Guam, and the Northern Marianas in the same manner as the book you're reading.

*Pacific Travel Fact File.* A reliable annual guide to upmarket accommodations all across the Pacific with exact prices listed. Travel agents will find it invaluable. Copies can be ordered from Box 622, Runaway Bay, Queensland 4216, Australia (fax 61-7/5537-9330, www.pacifictravel.com.au).

Ryan, Paddy. *The Snorkeler's Guide to the Coral Reef.* Honolulu: University of Hawaii Press, 1994. An introduction to the wonders of the Indo-Pacific reefs. The author spent 10 years in Fiji and knows the country well.

Schroeder, Dirk. *Staying Healthy in Asia, Africa, and Latin America.* Chico: Moon Travel Handbooks, 1995. Order a copy of this book produced by Volunteers in Asia if you want to acquire basic, practical knowledge of tropical medicine.

Schütz, Albert J. *Suva: A History and Guide.* Sydney: Pacific Publications, 1978. This slim volume is all you need to get to know the city.

Stanley, David. *South Pacific Handbook.* Chico: Moon Travel Handbooks, 1999. Covers the entire South Pacific in the same manner as the book you're reading. *Tahiti Handbook* by the same author also includes the Cook Islands.

## DESCRIPTION AND TRAVEL

Amadio, Nadine. *Pacifica: Myth, Magic, and Traditional Wisdom from the South Sea Islands.* New York: Harper Collins, 1993. Based on an Australian television series, this lavishly illustrated book deals with many of the classic themes and stories of the South Pacific. If your library has it, check it out.

Craig, Glen, and Paul Geraghty. *Children of the Sun.* Glen Craig Publishing, Box 212, Gympie 4570, Australia. Published in 1996, this photo book available at the Fiji Visitors Bureau office in Suva is like one big Fiji family picture album in glorious color.

Gravelle, Kim. *Romancing the Islands.* Suva: Graphics Pacific, 1995. In these 42 stories ex-American Fiji resident Kim Gravelle shares a quarter century of adventures in the region. A delightfully sympathetic look at the islands and its characters. Copies can be ordered from the author at Box 12975, Suva, Fiji Islands (US$25 postpaid).

Sahadeo, Muneshwar, et al. *Holy Torture in Fiji.* Suva: Institute of Pacific Studies, 1974. Rituals involving knives, oil, and fire; covers resistance to pain, the function of the ordeals, and other manifestations of religious devotion by Fiji Indians.

Siers, James. *Fiji Celebration.* New York: St. Martin's Press, 1985. Primarily a color-photo, coffee-table book, this also provides a good summary of the history of Fiji.

Stephenson, Dr. Elsie. *Fiji's Past on Picture Postcards.* Suva: Fiji Museum, 1997. Some 275 old postcards of Fiji from the Caines Jannif collection.

Theroux, Paul. *The Happy Isles of Oceania.* London: Hamish Hamilton, 1992. The author of classic accounts of railway journeys sets out with kayak and tent to tour the Pacific.

*Traditional Handicrafts of Fiji.* Suva: Institute of Pacific Studies, 1997. The significance and history of Fijian handicrafts.

Wibberley, Leonard. *Fiji: Islands of The Dawn.* New York: Ives Washburn, Inc., 1964. A masterful mixture of history and travel.

Wright, Ronald. *On Fiji Islands.* New York: Penguin Books, 1986. Wright relates his travels to Fijian history and tradition in a most pleasing and informative way.

## GEOGRAPHY

Crocombe, Ron. *The South Pacific: An Introduction.* Suva: Institute of Pacific Studies, 1989. A collection of lecture notes covering a wide range of topics from one of the region's leading academics.

Derrick, R.A. *The Fiji Islands: Geographical Handbook.* Suva: Government Printing Office, 1965. Derrick's earlier *History of Fiji* (1946) was a trailblazing work.

Donnelly, Quanchi, and Kerr. *Fiji in the Pacific: A History and Geography of Fiji.* Australia: Jacaranda Wiley, 1994. A high school text on the country.

Oliver, Douglas L. *The Pacific Islands.* Honolulu: University of Hawaii Press, 1989. A newer edition of the classic 1961 study of the history and anthropology of the entire Pacific area.

Ridgell, Reilly. *Pacific Nations and Territories.* A high school geography text that provides an overview of the region and also focuses on the individual islands. *Pacific Neighbors* is an elementary school version of the same book, written in collaboration with Betty Dunford. Both are published by Bess Press, 3565 Harding Ave., Honolulu, HI 96816, U.S.A. (tel. 1-800/910-2377 or 1-808/734-7159, fax 1-808/732-3627, www.besspress.com).

## NATURAL SCIENCE

Clunie, Fergus, and Pauline Morse. *Birds of the Fiji Bush.* Suva: Fiji Museum, 1984.

Lebot, Vincent, Lamont Lindstrom, and Mark Marlin. *Kava—the Pacific Drug.* Yale University Press, 1993. A thorough examination of kava and its many uses.

Martini, Frederic. *Exploring Tropical Isles and Seas.* Englewood Cliffs, N.J.: Prentice-Hall, 1984. A fine introduction to the natural environment of the islands now unfortunately out of print.

Mayr, Ernst. *Birds of the Southwest Pacific.* Rutland, VT: Charles E. Tuttle Co., 1978. Though poor on illustrations, this paperback reprint of the 1945 edition is still an essential reference list for birders.

Merrill, Elmer D. *Plant Life of the Pacific World.* Rutland, VT: Charles E. Tuttle Co., 1981. First published in 1945, this handy volume is still a useful reference.

Mitchell, Andrew W. *A Fragile Paradise: Man and Nature in the Pacific.* London: Fontana, 1990. Published in the U.S. by the University of Texas Press under the title *The Fragile South Pacific: An Ecological Odyssey.* Andrew Mitchell, an Earthwatch Europe deputy director, utters a heartfelt plea on behalf of all endangered Pacific wildlife in this brilliant book.

Watling, Dick. *Mai Veikau: Tales of Fijian Wildlife.* Suva: Fiji Times, 1986. A wealth of easily digested information on Fiji's flora and fauna. Copies are available in Fiji bookstores.

Zug, George R. *The Lizards of Fiji.* Honolulu: Bishop Museum Press, 1991. A comprehensive survey of the 23 species of Fijian lizards.

## HISTORY

Crocombe, Ron. *The Pacific Islands and the USA.* Suva: Institute of Pacific Studies, 1995. A comprehensive study of almost every aspect of the relationship from the 18th century to the present day. Crocombe's account of the self-serving manipulations practiced by a succession of U.S. officials over the years should chasten Americans still unwilling to come to terms with their country as just another imperialistic colonial power.

Clunie, Fergus. *Yalo i Viti.* Suva: Fiji Museum, 1986. An illustrated catalog of the museum's collection with lots of intriguing background information provided.

Denoon, Donald, et al. *The Cambridge History of the Pacific Islanders.* Australia: Cambridge University Press, 1997. A team of scholars examines the history of the inhabitants of Oceania from first colonization to the nuclear era. While acknowledging the great diversity of Pacific peoples, cultures, and experiences, the book looks for common patterns and related themes, presenting them in an insightful and innovative way.

Derrick, R.A. *A History of Fiji.* Suva: Government Press, 1950. This classic work by a former director of the Fiji Museum deals with the period up to 1874 only.

Gravelle, Kim. *Fiji's Times: A History of Fiji.* Suva: Fiji Times, 1979. An entertaining anthology of accounts originally published in the *Fiji Times.*

Howard, Michael C. *Fiji: Race and Politics in an Island State.* Vancouver: University of British Columbia Press, 1991. Perhaps the best scholarly study of the background and root causes of the Fiji coups.

Lal, Brij V. *Broken Waves: A History of the Fiji Islands in the 20th Century.* Honolulu: University of Hawaii Press, 1991. Lal is a penetrating writer who uses language accessible to the layperson.

Lal, Brij V. *Power and Prejudice: The Making of the Fiji Crisis.* Wellington: New Zealand Institute of International Affairs, 1988.

Mara, Ratu Sir Kamisese. *The Pacific Way: A Memoir.* Honolulu: University of Hawaii Press, 1997. Personal observations and reminiscences by the man who did so much to shape modern Fiji.

Ravuvu, Asesela. *The Facade of Democracy: Fijian Struggles for Political Control 1830-1987.* Suva: Institute of Pacific Studies, 1991. European politics, colonial rule, the Indian threat, multiculturalism, and cultural insensitivity—factors in the 1987 coups as seen by a Fijian nationalist.

Robertson, Robert T., and Akosita Tamanisau. *Fiji—Shattered Coups.* Australia: Pluto Press, 1988. The first detailed analysis to emerge from Fiji of events that shook the South Pacific. Robertson, a history lecturer at the University of the South Pacific until expelled by Rabuka, and his wife Tamanisau, a reporter with the *Fiji Sun* until Rabuka closed down the paper, wrote the book secretly in Fiji and smuggled out the manuscript chapter by chapter. A military raid on their Suva home failed to uncover the book in preparation.

Routledge, David. *Matanitu: The Struggle for Power in Early Fiji.* Suva: Institute of Pacific Studies, 1985. A revealing source of historical/anthropological background on the divisions within Fiji that led to the 1987 coup.

Scarr, Deryck. *Fiji: A Short History.* Honolulu: University of Hawaii Press, 1984. A balanced look at Fijian history from first settlement to 1982. Scarr also wrote *Fiji, Politics of Illusion: The Military Coups in Fiji* published in 1988.

Sutherland, William. *Beyond the Politics of Race: An Alternative History of Fiji to 1992.* Canberra: Research School of Pacific Studies, 1992. William Sutherland was Dr. Bavadra's personal secretary.

Usher, Sir Leonard, *Letters From Fiji: 1987-1990.* Suva: Fiji Times, 1993. A collection of letters written to Queen Elizabeth about the events unfolding in Fiji. A sequel covers the years 1990-1994.

Wallis, Mary. *Life in Feejee: Five Years Among the Cannibals.* First published in 1851, this book is the memoir of a New England sea captain's wife in Fiji. It's a charming, if rather gruesome, firsthand account of early European contact with Fiji and has some fascinating details of Fijian customs. You'll find ample mention of Cakobau, who hadn't yet converted to Christianity. Reprinted by the Fiji Museum, Suva, in 1983, but again out of print. A rare South Seas classic!

Wallis, Mary. *The Fiji and New Caledonia Journals of Mary Wallis, 1851-1853.* Suva: Institute of Pacific Studies, 1994. This reprint of the sequel to *Life in Feejee* offers many insights, and the editor, David Routledge, has added numerous notes.

## PACIFIC ISSUES

Crocombe, Ron, ed. *Land Tenure in the Pacific.* Suva: Institute of Pacific Studies, 1987. Twenty specialists contributed to this basic study of customs, equality, privilege, colonization, productivity, individualism, and reform.

*Culture and Democracy in the South Pacific.* Suva: Institute of Pacific Studies, 1992. A major book presenting essays and poetry about freedom by 16 Pacific writers.

Dé Ishtar, Zohl, ed. *Daughters of the Pacific.* Melbourne: Spinifex Press, 1994. A stirring collection of stories of survival, strength, determination, and compassion told by indigenous women of the Pacific. The stories relate their experiences, and the impact on them by nuclear testing, uranium mining, neo-colonialism, and nuclear waste dumping.

Emberson-Bain, 'Atu, ed. *Sustainable Development or Malignant Growth? Perspectives of Pacific Island Women.* Suva: Marama Publications, 1994. Contains valuable background information of the regional environment. Emberson-Bain's *Labour and Gold in Fiji* (Cambridge University Press, 1994) is also useful.

Ernst, Manfred. *Winds of Change.* Suva: Pacific Conference of Churches, 1994. A timely examination of rapidly growing religious groups in the Pacific islands and unequaled source of information on contemporary religion in the South Pacific.

Jalal, Patricia Imrana. *Law for Pacific Women: A Legal Rights Handbook.* This 700-page book is essential reading for anyone planning an extended stay in Cook Islands, Fiji, Samoa, Solomon Islands, Tuvalu, or Vanuatu. Order from the Fiji Women's Rights Movement, Box 14194, Suva, Fiji Islands (tel. 679/313-156, fax 679/313-466).

Robie, David, ed. *Tu Galala: Social Change in the Pacific.* Wellington: Bridget Williams Books, 1992. In this book, Robie has collected a series of essays examining the conflicting influences of tradition, democracy, and westernization, with special attention to environmental issues and human rights.

## SOCIAL SCIENCE

Colpani, Satya. *Beyond the Black Waters: A Memoir of Sir Sathi Narain.* Suva: Institute of Pacific Studies, 1996. Having migrated from southern India with his family, Sir Sathi Narain (1919-1989) became a leader in the construction industry and an influential figure in the country's life.

Lifuka, Neli, edited and introduced by Klaus-Friedrich Koch. *Logs in the Current of the Sea: Neli Lifuka's Story of Kioa and the Vaitupu Colonists.* Canberra: Australian National University, 1978. The troubled story of the purchase in 1946 and subsequent settlement of Kioa Island off Vanua Levu by Polynesians from Tuvalu, as told by one of the participants.

Norton, Robert. *Race and Politics in Fiji.* St. Lucia, Queensland: University of Queensland Press, 1990. A revised edition of the 1977 classic. Norton emphasizes the flexibility of Fijian culture, which was able to absorb the impact of two military coups without any loss of life.

Prasad, Shiu. *Indian Indentured Workers in Fiji.* Suva: South Pacific Social Studies Association, 1974. Describes the life of laborers in the Labasa area.

Ravuvu, Asesela. *Development or Dependence: The Pattern of Change in a Fijian Village.*

Suva: Institute of Pacific Studies, 1988. Highlights the unforeseen negative impacts of development in a Fijian village.

Ravuvu, Asesela. *The Fijian Ethos.* Suva: Institute of Pacific Studies, 1987. An in-depth study of Fijian ceremonies.

Ravuvu, Asesela. *Vaka i Taukei: The Fijian Way of Life.* Suva: Institute of Pacific Studies, 1983. A definitive study of kinship, houses, food, life-cycles, land, spirits, personality, values, and administration.

Roth, G. Kingsley. *Fijian Way of Life.* 2nd ed. Melbourne: Oxford University Press, 1973. A standard reference on Fijian culture.

Sahlins, Marshall D. *Moala: Culture and Nature on a Fijian Island.* Ann Arbor: University of Michigan Press, 1962. The results of a thorough study carried out in 1954 and 1955.

## LANGUAGE AND LITERATURE

Capell, A. *A New Fijian Dictionary.* Suva: Government Printer, 1991. A Fijian-English dictionary invaluable for anyone interested in learning the language. Scholars have a generally low opinion of this work which contains hundreds of errors, but it is readily available. Also see C. Maxwell Churchward's *A New Fijian Grammar.*

Griffen, Arlene, ed. *With Heart and Nerve and Sinew: Post-coup writing from Fiji.* Suva: Marama Club, 1997. An eclectic collection of responses to the coups and life in Fiji thereafter.

Hereniko, Vilsoni, and Teresia Teaiwa. *Last Virgin in Paradise.* Suva: Institute of Pacific Studies, 1993. The Rotuman Hereniko has written a number of plays, including *Don't Cry Mama* (1977), *A Child for Iva* (1987), and *The Monster* (1989).

Kikau, Eci. *The Wisdom of Fiji.* Suva: Institute of Pacific Studies, 1981. This extensive collection of Fijian proverbs opens up a window of understanding Fijian society, culture, and philosophy.

Michener, James A. *Return to Paradise.* New York: Random House, 1951. Essays and short stories. Michener's *Tales of the South Pacific,* the first of over 30 books, opened on Broadway in 1949 as the long-running musical *South Pacific.* This writer's ability to gloss over the complexities of life explains his tremendous popularity, and the predictable stereotypes in his one-dimensional South Seas tales perpetuate the illusory myth of the island paradise. Michener's portrayal of Fiji Indians in his story "The Mynah Birds" borders on outright racism.

Pillai, Raymond. *The Celebration.* Suva: South Pacific Creative Arts Society, 1980. A collection of short stories in which the heterogeneous nature of Fiji Indian society is presented by an accomplished narrator.

Schütz, A.J. *Say It In Fijian.* Sydney: Pacific Publications, 1979. An entertaining introduction to the language. Another text by Schütz, *The Fijian Language,* is published by the University of Hawaii Press.

Subramani. *South Pacific Literature: From Myth to Fabulation.* Suva: Institute of Pacific Studies, 1992. This academic study of island writers up to 1985 provides a useful reference for students of Pacific literature. Unlike expatriates such as Michener who view the South Pacific through European eyes, Subramani's writers put the islanders at the center of their narratives. Subramani's book is only interesting when read in conjunction with the works themselves.

Veramu, Joseph C. *Moving Through the Streets.* Suva: Institute of Pacific Studies, 1994. A fast-moving novel providing insights into the lifestyles, pressures, and temptations of teenagers in Suva. Veramu has also written a collection of short stories called *The Black Messiah* (1989).

Wendt, Albert, ed. *Nuanua: Pacific Writing in English Since 1980.* Honolulu, University of Hawaii Press, 1995. This worthwhile anthology of contemporary Pacific literature includes works by 10 Fijian writers including Prem Banfal, Sudesh Mishra, Satendra Nandan, and Som Prakash.

## REFERENCE BOOKS

Connell, John, et al. *Encyclopedia of the Pacific Islands.* Canberra: Australian National University, 1999. Published to mark the 50th anniversary of the Pacific Community, this important book combines the writings of 200 acknowledged experts on the physical environment, peoples, history, politics, economics, society, and culture of the South Pacific.

Douglas, Ngaire and Norman Douglas, eds. *Pacific Islands Yearbook.* Suva: Fiji Times. Despite the title, a new edition of this authoritative sourcebook has come out about every four years since 1932. Although a rather dry read, it's still the one indispensable reference work for students of the Pacific islands.

*The Far East and Australasia.* London: Europa Publications. An annual survey and directory of Asia and the Pacific. Provides abundant and factual political and economic data; an excellent reference source.

Fry, Gerald W., and Rufino Mauricio. *Pacific Basin and Oceania.* Oxford: Clio Press, 1987. A selective, indexed Pacific bibliography, which actually describes the contents of the books, instead of merely listing them.

Gorman, G.E., and J.J. Mills. *Fiji: World Bibliographical Series, Volume 173.* Oxford: Clio Press, 1994. Critical reviews of 673 of the most important books about Fiji.

Jackson, Miles M., ed. *Pacific Island Studies: A Survey of the Literature.* Westport: Greenwood Press, 1986. In addition to comprehensive listings, there are extensive essays that put the most important works in perspective.

Snow, Philip A., ed. *A Bibliography of Fiji, Tonga, and Rotuma.* Coral Gables, FL: University of Miami Press, 1969.

## BOOKSELLERS AND PUBLISHERS

Many of the titles listed above are out of print and not available in regular bookstores or from www.amazon.com. Major research libraries should have a few, otherwise write to the specialized antiquarian booksellers or regional publishers listed below for their printed lists of hard-to-find books on the Pacific. Sources of detailed topographical maps or navigational charts are provided in the following section.

Antipodean Books, Box 189, Cold Spring, NY 10516, U.S.A. (tel. 1-914/424-3867, fax 1-914/424-3617, www.antipbooks.com, e-mail: antipbooks@highlands.com). They have a complete catalog of out-of-print and rare items.

Bibliophile, 24 Glenmore Rd., Paddington, Sydney, NSW 2021, Australia (tel. 61-2/9331-1411, fax 61-2/9361-3371, www.ozemail.com.au/~susant, e-mail: susant@ozemail.com.au). An antiquarian bookstore specializing in books about Oceania. View their extensive catalog on line.

Bishop Museum Press, 1525 Bernice St., Honolulu, HI 96817-0916, U.S.A. (tel. 1-808/848-4135, fax 1-808/848-4132, www.bishop.hawaii.org/bishop/press). They have an indexed list of books on the Pacific; a separate list of "The Occasional Papers" lists specialized works.

Book Bin, 228 S.W. Third St., Corvallis, OR 97333, U.S.A. (tel. 1-541/752-0045, fax 1-541/754-4115, e-mail: pacific@bookbin.com). Their indexed mail-order catalog, *Hawaii and Pacific Islands,* lists hundreds of rare books and they also carry all the titles of the Institute of Pacific Studies in Suva. If there's a particular book about the Pacific you can't find anywhere, this is a place to try.

Books of Yesteryear, Box 257, Newport, NSW 2106, Australia (tel./fax 61-2/9918-0545, e-mail: patbooks@ozemail.com.au). Another reliable source of old, fine, and rare books on the Pacific.

Books Pasifika, Box 68-446, Newtown, Auckland 1, New Zealand (tel. 64-9/303-2349, fax 64-9/377-9528, www.ak.planet.gen.nz/pasifika, e-mail: books@pasifika.co.nz). Besides being a major publisher, Pasifika Press is one of New Zealand's best sources of mail order books on Oceania, including those of the Institute of Pacific Studies.

Bushbooks, Box 1370, Gosford, NSW 2250, Australia (tel. 61-2/4323-3274, fax 61-2/9212-2468, e-mail: bushbook@ozemail.com.au). An Australian source of the publications of the Institute of Pacific Studies in Suva.

Cellar Book Shop, 18090 Wyoming Ave., Detroit, MI 48221, U.S.A. (tel./fax 1-313/861-1776, http://members.aol.com/cellarbook, e-mail: cellarbook@aol.com). Their catalog, *The 'Nesias' & Down Under: Some Recent Books,* includes a wide range of books on the Pacific.

Empire Books, Colin Hinchcliffe, 12 Queens Staith Mews, York, YO1 6HH, United Kingdom (tel. 44-1904/610679, fax 44-1904/641664, e-mail: colin@empires.demon.co.uk). An excellent source of antiquarian or out-of-print books, maps, and engravings.

Institute of Pacific Studies, University of the South Pacific, Box 1168, Suva, Fiji Islands (tel. 679/313-900, fax 679/301-594, e-mail: ips@usp.ac.fj). Their catalog, *Books from the Pacific Islands,* lists numerous books about the islands written by the Pacific islanders themselves. Some are rather dry academic publications of interest only to specialists, so order carefully. USP centers all across the region sell many of these books over the counter. For internet access to the catalog, see the University Book Centre listing below.

International Marine Publishing Co., Box 548, Black Lick, OH 43004, U.S.A. (tel. 1-800/262-4729, fax 1-614/759-3641, www.pbg.mcgraw-hill.com/im). Their catalog, *Boating Books,* includes all the books you'll ever need to teach yourself how to sail. They also have books on sea kayaking.

Michael Graves-Johnston, Bookseller, Box 532, London SW9 0DR, United Kingdom (tel. 44-171/274-2069, fax 44-171/738-3747). Sells antiquarian books only.

Pan Pacifica, 4662 Sierra Dr., Honolulu, HI 96816, U.S.A. (fax 1-808/739-2326, www.PanPacifica.com, e-mail: panpac@lava.net). A source of recent official publications and research-level documents from museums and universities. Their primary clients are large research libraries.

Peter Moore, Box 66, Cambridge, CB1 3PD, United Kingdom (tel. 44-1223/411177, fax 44-1223/240559). The European distributor of books from the Institute of Pacific Studies of the University of the South Pacific, Fiji. Moore's catalog also lists antiquarian and secondhand books.

Serendipity Books, Box 340, Nedlands, WA 6009, Australia (tel. 61-8/9382-2246, fax 61-8/9388-2728, www.merriweb.com.au/serendip). The largest stocks of antiquarian, secondhand, and out-of-print books on the Pacific in Western Australia. Free catalogs are issued regularly.

South Pacific Regional Environment Program, Box 240, Apia, Samoa (tel. 685/21-929, fax 685/20-231, www.sprep.org.ws). They have a list of specialized technical publications on environmental concerns.

University Book Centre, University of the South Pacific, Box 1168, Suva, Fiji Islands (tel. 679/313-900, fax 679/303-265, www.usp.ac.fj/~bookcentre). An excellent source of books written and produced in the South Pacific itself. Check out their site.

University of Hawaii Press, 2840 Kolowalu St., Honolulu, HI 96822, U.S.A. (tel. 1-888/847-7377 or 1-808/956-8255, fax 1-808/988-6052, www2.hawaii.edu/uhpress). Their *Hawaii and the Pacific* catalog is well worth requesting if you're trying to build a Pacific library.

## MAP PUBLISHERS

*Defense Mapping Agency Catalog of Maps, Charts, and Related Products: Region VIII, Oceania.* National Ocean Service, Distribution Division, 6501 Lafayette Ave., Riverdale, MD 20737-1199, U.S.A. (tel. 1-301/436-6990, fax 1-301/436-6829, www.noaa.gov). A complete index and order form for nautical charts of the Pacific. The National Ocean Service also distributes nautical charts of American Samoa put out by the National Oceanic and Atmospheric Administration (NOAA).

Fiji Hydrographic Office. (Marine Department, Suva, Fiji; tel. 315-266, fax 303-251). Fiji's publisher of navigational charts. Their U.S.

agents are Captains Nautical Supplies (2500-15th Ave. West, Seattle, WA 98119, U.S.A.; tel. 1-206/283-7242, fax 1-206/281-4921) and Pacific Map Center (560 N. Nimitz Highway, Suite 206A, Honolulu, HI 96817, U.S.A.; tel. 1-808/545-3600, fax 1-808/545-1700).

International Maps. Hema Maps Pty. Ltd., Box 2660, Logan City, Queensland 4114, Australia (tel. 61-7/3290-0322, fax 61-7/3290-0478, www.hemamaps.com.au). Maps of the Pacific, Fiji, Solomon Islands, Vanuatu, and Samoa.

Lands and Surveys Department. (Plan and Map Sales, Government Buildings, Suva, Fiji; tel. 211-395, fax 304-037). The main publisher of topographical maps of Fiji with a 1:50,000 series covering most of the country.

## PERIODICALS

*Asia & Pacific Viewpoint.* Department of Geography, Victoria University of Wellington, Box 600, Wellington, New Zealand (tel. 64-4/472-1000, fax 64-4/495-5127, www.blackwell publishers.co.uk). Three times a year; annual subscription US$42. A scholarly journal concerned with the systematic, regional, and theoretical aspects of economic growth and social change in the developed and developing countries.

*Banaba/Ocean Island News.* Stacey M. King, Box 149, Miami, Queensland 4220, Australia (tel./fax 61-7/5576-3035, www.ion.com.au/~banaban, e-mail: banaban@ion.com.au, A$15 a year in Australia, A$20 elsewhere). This lively newsletter covers virtually everything relating to the Banabans of Fiji and Kiribati.

*Ben Davison's In Depth.* Box 1658, Sausalito, CA 94966, U.S.A. A monthly consumer protection-oriented newsletter for serious scuba divers. Unlike virtually every other diving publication, *In Depth* accepts no advertising or free trips, which allows Ben to tell it as it is.

*Centre for South Pacific Studies Newsletter.* Centre for South Pacific Studies, University of New South Wales, Kensington, NSW 2052, Australia (tel. 61-2/9385-3386, fax 61-2/9313-6337, e-mail: J.Lodewijks@unsw.EDU.AU). A useful publication that catalogs scholarly conferences, events, activities, news, employment opportunities, courses, scholarships, and publications across the region.

*Commodores' Bulletin.* Seven Seas Cruising Assn., 1525 South Andrews Ave., Suite 217, Fort Lauderdale, FL 33316, U.S.A. (tel. 1-954/463-2431, fax 1-954/463-7183, www.ssca.org, e-mail: SSCA1@ibm.net; US$53 a year worldwide by airmail). This monthly bulletin is chock-full of useful information for anyone wishing to tour the Pacific by sailing boat. All Pacific yachties and friends should be Seven Seas members!

*The Contemporary Pacific.* University of Hawaii Press, 2840 Kolowalu St., Honolulu, HI 96822, U.S.A. (www2.hawaii.edu/uhpress, e-mail: uhpjourn@hawaii.edu, published twice a year, US$35 a year). Publishes a good mix of articles of interest to both scholars and general readers; the country-by-country "Political Review" in each number is a concise summary of events during the preceding year. The "Dialogue" section offers informed comment on the more controversial issues in the region, while recent publications on the islands are examined through book reviews. Those interested in current topics in Pacific island affairs should check recent volumes for background information.

*Environment Newsletter.* The quarterly newsletter of the South Pacific Regional Environment Program, Box 240, Apia, Samoa (tel. 685/21-929, fax 685/20-231, www.sprep.org.ws). Back issues can be viewed on their website.

*Europe-Pacific Solidarity Bulletin.* Published monthly by the European Center for Studies Information and Education on Pacific Issues, Box 151, 3700 AD Zeist, the Netherlands (tel. 31-30/692-7827, fax 31-30/692-5614, www.antenna.nl/ecsiep, e-mail: ecsiep@antenna.nl).

*German Pacific Society Bulletin.* Dr. Friedrich Steinbauer, Feichtmayr Strasse 25, D-80992 München, Germany (tel. 49-89/151158, fax 49-89/151833). At DM 90 a year, Society membership is a good way for German speakers to keep in touch. News bulletins in English and German are published four to six times a year, and study tours to various Pacific destinations are organized annually.

*Globe Newsletter.* The Globetrotters Club, BCM/Roving, London WC1N 3XX, United Kingdom. This informative travel newsletter, published six times a year, provides lots of practical information on how to tour the world "on the cheap." This is *the* club for world travelers.

*Islands Business.* Box 12718, Suva, Fiji Islands (tel. 679/303-108, fax 679/301-423, e-mail: subs@ibi.com.fj; annual airmailed subscription A$35 to Australia, NZ$55 to New Zealand, US$45 to North America, US$55 to Europe). A monthly newsmagazine with in-depth coverage of political and economic trends in the Pacific. It's more opinionated than *Pacific Islands Monthly* and even has a gossip section that is an essential weather vane for anyone doing business in the region. In the December 1995 issue "Whispers" accurately forecast the devaluation of the Fiji dollar two years later. Travel and aviation news gets some prominence, and subscribers also receive the informative quarterly magazine *South Pacific Tourism.*

*Journal of Pacific History.* Division of Pacific and Asian History, RSPAS, Australian National University, Canberra, ACT 0200, Australia (tel. 61-2/6249-3140, fax 61-2/6249-5525, http://coombs.anu.edu.au/Depts/RSPAS/PAH/index.html). Since 1966 this publication has provided reliable scholarly information on the Pacific. Outstanding.

*Journal of Pacific Studies.* School of Social and Economic Development, University of the South Pacific, Box 1168, Suva, Fiji Islands (tel. 679/314-900, fax 679/301-487). Focuses on regional developments from a social sciences perspective.

*Journal of the Polynesian Society.* Department of Maori Studies, University of Auckland, Private Bag 92019, Auckland, New Zealand (tel. 64-9/373-7999, extension 7463, fax 64-9/373-7409, www2.waikato.ac.nz/ling/PS/journal.html). Established in 1892, this quarterly journal contains a wealth of material on Pacific cultures past and present written by scholars of Pacific anthropology, archaeology, language, and history.

*Pacific Affairs.* University of British Columbia, Suite 164, 1855 West Mall, Vancouver, B.C. V6T 1Z2, Canada (tel. 1-604/822-6508, fax 1-604/822-9452, www.interchange.ubc.ca/pacifaff, quarterly). Each issue contains four new articles and 50 book reviews, although most are oriented toward Asia.

*Pacific Islander.* KIN Publications, 558 E. Double St., Carson, CA 90745, U.S.A. (tel. 1-310/549-0920, fax 1-310/830-0711, e-mail: DPouesi@aol.com; US$22 for six issues). Daniel Pouesi's lively tabloid newspaper serving the Fijian, Samoan, and Tongan communities on the U.S. west coast.

*Pacific Islands Monthly.* Box 1167, Suva, Fiji Islands (tel. 679/304-111, fax 679/303-809, www.pim.com.fj, e-mail: fijitimes@is.com.fj; annual subscription A$40 to Australia, A$45 to New Zealand, US$40 to North America, and A$60 to Europe). Founded in Sydney by R.W. Robson in 1930, *PIM* is the granddaddy of regional magazines. In June 1989 the magazine's editorial office moved from Sydney to Suva and it's now part of the same operation that puts out *The Fiji Times.* Sadly, star columnists Roman Grynberg and David North recently left the magazine.

*Pacific Magazine.* Box 25488, Honolulu, HI 96825, U.S.A. (tel. 1-808/377-5335, fax 1-808/373-3953, www.pacificmagazine.com; every other month; US$15 a year surface mail, US$27 airmail to the U.S., US$39 airmail elsewhere). This business-oriented newsmagazine, published in Hawaii since 1976, will keep you up-to-date on what's happening in the South Pacific and Micronesia. The format is built around brief news reports on people and events rather than the longer background articles one finds in the other regional magazines.

*Pacific News Bulletin.* Pacific Concerns Resource Center, Box 803, Glebe, NSW 2037, Australia (tel./fax 61-2/9571-9039, e-mail: pacificnews@bigpond.com; A$15 a year in Australia, A$30 a year elsewhere). A 16-page monthly newsletter with up-to-date information on nuclear, independence, environmental, and political questions.

*Pacific Studies.* Box 1979, BYU-HC, Laie, HI 96762-1294, U.S.A. (tel. 1-808/293-3665, fax 1-808/293-3664, websider.byuh.edu/departments/ips, e-mail: robertsd@byuh.edu, quarterly, US$30 a year). Funded by the Polynesian Cultural Center and published by Hawaii's Brigham Young University.

*Pacifica.* Quarterly journal of the Pacific Islands Study Circle (John Ray, 24 Woodvale Ave., London SE25 4AE, United Kingdom, http://dspace.dial.pipex.com/jray/pisc.html, e-mail: jray@dial.pipex.com). This philatelic journal is exclusively concerned with stamps and the postal history of the islands.

*Pacifica Review.* The Institute for Peace Research, La Trobe University, Bundoora, Victoria 3083, Australia (tel. 61-3/9479-2676, fax 61-3/9479-1997; twice a year, A$25/35 local/overseas). A journal focusing on peace, security, and global change in the Asia Pacific region.

*Review.* Box 12095, Suva, Fiji Islands (Box 12095, Suva; fax 679/301-930, e-mail: review@is.com.fj). A monthly news magazine with excellent coverage of business and politics in Fiji.

*South Sea Digest.* Box 4245, Sydney, NSW 2001, Australia (tel. 61-2/9288-1708, fax 61-2/9288-3322, A$150 a year in Australia, A$175 overseas). A private newsletter on political and economic matters, published every other week. It's a good way of keeping abreast of developments in commerce and industry.

*Surf Report.* Box 1028, Dana Point, CA 92629, U.S.A. (tel. 1-949/496-5922, fax 1-949/496-7849, www.surfermag.com; US$35 a year). Each month this newsletter provides a detailed analysis of surfing conditions at a different destination (the last report on Fiji was issue 7#12). Back issues on specific countries are available, including a 14-issue "South Pacific Collection" at US$50. This is your best source of surfing information by far, and the same people also put out the glossy *Surfer Magazine* (US$25 a year).

*Tok Blong Pasifik.* South Pacific Peoples Foundation of Canada, 1921 Fernwood Road, Victoria, BC V8T 2Y6, Canada (tel. 1-250/381-4131, fax 1-250/388-5258, www.sppf.org, e-mail: sppf@sppf.org; C$25 a year in Canada, US$25 elsewhere). This lively quarterly of news and views focuses on regional environmental, development, human rights, and disarmament issues.

*Washington Pacific Report.* Fred Radewagen, Box 26142, Alexandria, VA 22313, U.S.A. (tel. 1-703/519-7757, fax 1-703/548-0633, e-mail: piwowpr@erols.com; published twice a month, US$164 a year domestic, US$189 outside U.S. postal zones). An insider's newsletter highlighting U.S. interests in the insular Pacific.

*WorldViews.* 1515 Webster St., No. 305, Oakland, CA 94612, U.S.A. (tel. 1-510/451-1742, fax 1-510/835-9631, www.igc.org/worldviews, e-mail: worldviews@igc.org; subscription US$25 to the U.S. and Canada, US$45 overseas). A quarterly review of books, articles, audiovisual materials, and organizations involved with development issues in the third world.

# OTHER RESOURCES

## DISCOGRAPHY

Fanshawe, David, ed. *Exotic Voices and Rhythms of the South Seas* (EUCD 1254). Cook Islands drum dancing, a Fijian *tralala meke,* a Samoan *fiafia,* a Vanuatu string band, and Solomon Islands panpipes selected from the 1,200 hours of tapes in the Fanshawe Pacific Collection. Order from Fanshawe One World Music (Box 574, Marlborough, Wilts, SN8 2SP, United Kingdom (tel./fax 44-1672/520211).

Linkels, Ad, and Lucia Linkels, eds. *Tautoga* (PAN 2097CD). The songs and dances of Rotuma, Fiji, recorded on the island in 1996. It's believed the *tautoga* dance arrived from Tonga in the 18th century. This PAN Records compact disc forms part of the series "Anthology of Pacific Music" and an extensive booklet explaining the music comes with the record. Music stores can order through Arhoolie, 10341 San Pablo Ave., El Cerrito, CA 94530, U.S.A. (tel. 1-510/525-7471, fax 1-510/525-1204).

*Music of Marginal Polynesia* (VICG 5276). In the series "World Sounds" produced by Victor Entertainment, Inc., Tokyo, Japan, and distributed in the U.S. by JVC Music, Inc., 3800 Barham Blvd., Ste. 305, Los Angeles, CA 90068, U.S.A. (tel. 1-213/878-0101, fax 1-213/878-0202). The music of Fiji, Wallis and Futuna, and Tuvalu, recorded 1977-85.

## USEFUL INTERNET SITES

**Air Pacific**
www.fijiislands.org/airlines/airpac.htm
The site provides access to Air Pacific's schedules, fares, air passes, flight seasons, offices, and route map. It's a great help in pricing a trip.

**Astral Travel**
www.island.to/astral.htm
An online brochure with blurbs about most of Fiji's top resorts but no prices. You can check Air Pacific and Sunflower Airlines flights and fares here. Nice features are the "legends of Fiji" pages, the color photos, and the Fijian music available in real audio.

**Come Meet the Banabans**
www.ion.com.au/~banaban/index.htm
All you ever wanted to know about the Banabans of Rabi Island and links that lead to interesting places.

**Dived and Gone to Heaven!**
www.naia.com.fj
A prerequisite for scuba divers, Nai'a Cruises' well-designed site provides lots of useful information on diving, lovely photos, and even a few videos. Prices are mentioned and abundant links are provided.

**Fiji For Less**
www.fiji4less.com
A must for the low-budget traveler, Fiji For Less gives exact prices at a few of Fiji's least expensive hotels and resorts with online bookings available. Their transfer/bed "Bula Fiji Starter Packs" are exceptional value if saving money is a priority.

**Fiji Government Official Site**
http://fiji.gov.fj
Although a bit stodgy, it's well worth perusing this site to taste the image local politicians and bureaucrats try to present to the world. The press releases are often edifying.

**Fiji Reservations & Travel**
www.fiji-islands.com
Also accessible at www.fijireservations.com, this online travel agency provides lots of good information on kayaking, surfing, and diving tours, resort packages, cruises, and house rentals. The section on purchasing land in Fiji is intriguing even if you're not a buyer.

**Fiji Visitors Bureau**
www.bulafiji.com
A mirror image of www.FijiIslands.org and

www.fijifvb.gov.fj, this site is used by Fiji's national tourist office to disseminate information about accommodations, activities, rentals, airlines, events, and the like. An e-mail directory and tourism-related links are provided.

**Internet Fiji**
www.internetfiji.com
Internet Fiji's well organized site offers weekly news bytes from *The Fiji Times,* a clean message board, and worthwhile links to government, business, real estate agencies, news sources, sporting bodies, and more.

**Internet Services**
www.is.com.fj
Telecom Fiji's complete user directory, the place to check if any of the phone, fax, or e-mail addresses in this book don't work. Links are provided to other directories worldwide. The same people run www.fiji-online.com with links to all websites in Fiji, plus international organizations involved in the islands.

**Matangi Island Resort**
www.matangiisland.com
One of the most appealing resort sites, the "tales of Fiji" in the culture pages are fun to read. It all makes you want to go there—until you see the prices.

**The Fiji Village**
www.fijivillage.com
More than any other, radio station FM 96's site gives you an authentic taste of Fiji with daily news bulletins, sports, shopping, and even audio clips from their English, Hindi, and Fijian stations. It seems designed for a local audience, which is great.

**Olsen Currency Converter**
www.oanda.com
Quick quotes on most international currencies, including the Fiji dollar.

**Netilus Destination: Oceania**
www.netilus.com
Another scuba diving must see, Netilus covers diving in Fiji, Tonga, and the Solomons with lots of nice photos and handy links.

**Pacific Islands Internet Resources**
www2.hawaii.edu/~ogden/piir/index.html
Michael R. Ogden's vast catalog of South Pacific links.

**Pacific Islands Monthly**
www.pim.com.fj
A salutary source of news and comment with about eight feature articles a month summarized.

**Pacific Islands Report**
http://pidp.ewc.hawaii.edu/PIReport
All the latest news from the islands posted daily Monday to Friday.

**Rob Kay's Fiji Guide**
www.fijiguide.com
The original author of Lonely Planet's Fiji guide offers a variety of travel information and tips not found elsewhere. Kay's links are also different and good.

**The Pacific Forum**
www.pacificforum.com/kavabowl/index.html
The Kava Bowl features a variety of chat rooms or forums where people from all across the Pacific add their often frivolous comments.

**The Weather Underground**
www.wunderground.com
Weather Underground's "Islands" section provides detailed two-day weather reports on 13 places around Fiji, plus worldwide hurricane tracking. For historical weather data on Suva, go to "International Weather" at www.weatherpost.com.

**University of the South Pacific**
www.usp.ac.fj
The university's site is surprisingly dull with lots of in-your-face information about their own bureaucratic structures. Its redeeming feature is the abundance of hot links, especially under the News & Events heading.

## WEBSITE DIRECTORY

Air Fiji, Suva: www.airfiji.net

Air New Zealand: www.airnz.co.nz

Air Pacific, Nadi: www.bulafiji.com/airlines/airpac/htm

Air Pacific, Nadi: www.fijiislands.org/airlines/airpac.htm

Air Promotion Systems, Los Angeles: www.pacificislands.com

Applied Geoscience Commission, Suva: www.sopac.org.fj

Aquaventure, Taveuni: www.aquaventure.org

Aqua-Trek, Nadi: www.aquatrek.com

Astral Travel, California: www.island.to/astral.htm

Avis Rent A Car, Nadi: www.avis.com.fj

Banaban Society, Australia: www.ion.com.au/~banaban

Canada 3000 Airlines: www.canada3000.com

Captain Cook Cruises, Nadi: www.captcookcrus.com.au

Communications Fiji Ltd., Suva: www.fijivillage.com

Cousteau Fiji Islands Resort, Savusavu: www.jmcfir.com

Crystal Divers, Nananu-i-Ra: www.crystaldivers.com

Department of Information, Suva: http://fiji.gov.fj

Dive Taveuni, Taveuni: www.divetaveuni.com

Fiji Aggressor, Hawaii: www.pac-aggressor.com

Fiji For Less, Suva: www.fiji4less.com

Fiji Reservations & Travel, Hawaii: www.fijireservations.com

Fiji Reservations & Travel, Hawaii: www.fiji-islands.com

Fiji Television Ltd., Suva: www.fijitv.com.fj

Fiji Trade & Investment Board, Suva: http://computech.ftib.org.fj

Fiji Travel, Los Angeles: www.fijitravel.com

Fiji Visitors Bureau, Suva: www.bulafiji.com

Fiji Visitors Bureau, Suva: www.fijifvb.gov.fj

Fiji Visitors Bureau, Suva: www.FijiIslands.org

Fish-Eye Bicycle Tours: www.fisheye.co.nz

Forum Secretariat, Suva: www.forumsec.org.fj

Garden Island Resort, Taveuni: www.aquatrek.com

Hidden Paradise Eco Lodge, Savusavu: www.geko.net.au/~mal

Hot Springs Hotel, Savusavu: www.HotSpringsHotel.com

Integral Multimedia & Communications, Suva: www.ifiji.com

International Telecommunications, Suva: www.fintel.com.fj

Internet Fiji, Suva: www.internetfiji.com

Internet Services, Suva: www.fiji-online.com

Island Hoppers, Nadi: www.helicopters.com.fj

Jacks Handicrafts, Nadi: www.jacks.handicrafts.com.fj

Last Call Cyber Cafe: http://members.tripod.com/~thelastcall

Lomalagi Resort, Savusavu: www.lomalagi.com

Maravu Plantation Resort, Taveuni: www.maravu.com

Marlin Bay Resort, Beqa: www.marlinbay.com

Matangi Island Resort, Taveuni: www.matangiisland.com

Ministry of Mineral Resources, Suva: www.mrd.gov.fj

Mocambo Hotel, Nadi: www.shangri-la.com

Nai'a Cruises, Lami: www.naia.com.fj

Navini Island Resort, Mamanucas: www.navinifiji.com.fj

Nukubati Island Resort, Labasa: www.nukubati.com

Nukuyaweni Outpost, Gau: www.bayofangels.com

Outrigger Hotels, Fuji: www.pacificinfoweb.com

Pacific Islands Monthly, Suva: www.pim.com.fj

Pacific Magazine, Honolulu: www.pacificmagazine.com

Philatelic Bureau, Suva: www.stampsfiji.com

Ra Divers, Nananu-i-Ra: www.radivers.com.fj

Rainbow Reef Aqua-club, Taveuni: www.Rainbowreef.com

Rainbow Reef Divers, Taveuni: www.aquatrek.com

Rolle Realty Ltd., Suva: www.fiji-online.com/rolle

Sea Fiji Travel, Savusavu: www.sni.net/dive

Sea Sports Ltd., Sigatoka: www.ida.net/users/davefx/Seasport.htm

Seven Seas Cruising Association, U.S.A.: www.ssca.org

Shangri-La's Fijian Resort, Nadi: www.shangri-la.com

Sonaisali Island Resort, Nadi: www.sonaisali.com.fj

South Seas Private Hotel, Suva: www.fiji4less.com

Subsurface Fiji, Lautoka: www.internetfiji.com/subsurface

Sunflower Airlines, Nadi: www.fiji.to

Taveuni Development Co., Suva: www.fijirealestate.com

Telecom Fiji, Suva: www.is.com.fj

Toberua Island Resort, Suva: www.toberua.com

Tourism Council of the South Pacific, Suva: www.tcsp.com

Treasure Island Resort, Mamanucas: www.treasure.com.fj

Turtle Island Lodge, Yasawas: www.turtlefiji.com

University Book Centre, Suva: www.usp.ac.fj/~bookcentre

University of the South Pacific, Suva: www.usp.ac.fj

Vatulele Island Resort, Nadi: www.vatulele.com

Victory Inland Safaris, Nadi: www.victory.com.fj

Yasawa Island Resort, Yasawas: www.yasawaislandresort.com

## E-MAIL DIRECTORY

Air Fiji, Suva: airfiji@is.com.fj

Air Pacific, Nadi: airpacific@is.com.fj

Air Promotion Systems, Los Angeles: jpfm@itr-aps.com

Adventure Fiji, Nadi: rosiefiji@is.com.fj

American Express/Tapa International, Suva: tapa@is.com.fj

Anchorage Beach Resort, Lautoka: tanoahotels@is.com.fj

Aquaventure, Taveuni: aquaventure@is.com.fj

Aqua-Trek, Nadi: aquatrek@is.com.fj

Avis, Nadi: aviscarsfj@is.com.fj

Beachcomber Island, Lautoka: beachcomber@is.com.fj

Bedarra House, Sigatoka: bedarrahouse@is.com.fj

Beqa Divers, Pacific Harbor: divefiji@is.com.fj

Blue Lagoon Cruises, Lautoka: blc@is.com.fj

Captain Cook Cruises, Nadi: captcookcrus@is.com.fj

Cathay Hotel, Lautoka: cathay@fiji4less.com

Centra Resort Pacific Harbor: centrapacharb@is.com.fj

Centra Suva Hotel, Suva: centrasuva@is.com.fj

Coconut Grove Cottages, Taveuni: coconutgrove@is.com.fj

Communications Fiji, Suva: fv@fm96.com.fj

Consort Shipping Line, Suva: consortship@is.com.fj

Copra Shed Marina, Savusavu: coprashed@is.com.fj

Cousteau Fiji Islands Resort, Savusavu: fiji4fun@is.com.fj

Crystal Divers, Nananu-i-Ra: crystaldivers@is.com.fj

Daily Post, Suva: postman@is.com.fj

Daku Estate Resort, Savusavu: daku@is.com.fj

Department of Information, Suva: info@fiji.gov.fj

Dive Kadavu, Kadavu: divekadavu@is.com.fj

Dive Taveuni, Taveuni: divetaveuni@is.com.fj

Dominion International Hotel, Nadi: dominionint@is.com.fj

Eco Divers, Savusavu: ecodivers@is.com.fj

Fiji Aggressor: fijiaggressor@is.com.fj

Fiji Dive Operators Assn., Savusavu: diveoperators@is.com.fj

Fiji For Less: info@fiji4less.com

Fiji Museum, Suva: fijimuseum@is.com.fj

Fiji Recompression Chamber Facility: recompression@is.com.fj

Fiji Reservations and Travel, Hawaii: fiji@maui.net

Fiji Times, Suva: fijitimes@is.com.fj

Fiji Trade & Investment Board, Suva: ftibinfo@ftib.org.fj

Fiji Visitors Bureau, Nadi: fvbnadi@is.com.fj

Fiji Visitors Bureau, Suva: infodesk@fijifvb.gov.fj

First Landing Resort, Lautoka: firstland@is.com.fj

Forum Secretariat, Suva: info@forumsec.org.fj

Garden Island Resort, Taveuni: aquatrek@is.com.fj

Grand Eastern Hotel, Labasa: grest@is.com.fj

Greenpeace Pacific Campaign, Suva: greenpeace@is.com.fj

Hidden Paradise Eco Lodge, Savusavu: mal@geko.net.au

Hideaway Resort, Korolevu: hideaway@is.com.fj

Hot Springs Hotel, Savusavu: hotspringshotel@is.com.fj

Islands Business Magazine, Suva: subs@ibi.com.fj

Jacks Handicrafts: jacks@is.com.fj

Jona's Paradise Resort, Ono: divekadavu@is.com.fj

Kaba's Motel, Taveuni: kaba@is.com.fj

Kaimbu Island Associates, California: kaimbu@earthlink.net

Kaimbu Island Resort, Northern Lau: kaimbu@is.com.fj

Khan's Rental Cars, Nadi: rehnuma@is.com.fj

The Last Call Restaurant, Lautoka: thelastcall@is.com.fj

Lomalagi Resort, Savusavu: lomalagi@is.com.fj

Mana Island Resort, Mamanucas: mana@is.com.fj

Maravu Plantation Resort, Taveuni: maravu@is.com.fj

Marlin Bay Resort, Beqa: marlinbay@is.com.fj

Matamanoa Sunrise Resort, Mamanucas: matamanoa@is.com.fj

Matana Beach Resort, Kadavu: divekadavu@is.com.fj

Matangi Island Resort, Matangi: info@matangiisland.com

Matava Astrolabe Hideaway, Kadavu: matava@suva.is.com.fj

Mocambo Hotel, Nadi: mocambo@is.com.fj

Mollie Dean Cruises, Lami: sere@is.com.fj

Musket Cove Resort, Mamanucas: musketcovefiji@is.com.fj

Musket Cove Yacht Charters, Mamanucas: musketcovefiji@is.com.fj

Nadi Bay Motel, Nadi: nadibay@is.com.fj

Naigani Island Resort, Lomaiviti: naigani@is.com.fj

Nai'a Cruises, Lami: naia@is.com.fj

Namale Resort, Savusavu: namale@is.com.fj

Namotu Island Resort, Nadi: namotu@is.com.fj

Navini Island Resort, Mamanucas: naviniisland@is.com.fj

Naviti Resort, Korolevu: naviti@is.com.fj

Nukubalavu Resort, Kadavu: nukubalavu@is.com.fj

Nukubati Island Resort, Labasa: nukubati@is.com.fj

Nukuyaweni Outpost, Gau: outpost@bayofangels.com

Otto's Place, Tavewa: westside@is.com.fj

Ovalau Tours and Transport, Levuka: otttours@is.com.fj

Pacific Concerns Resource Center, Suva: pcrc@is.com.fj

Pacific Islands Monthly, Suva: fijitimes@is.com.fj

Plantation Island Resort, Mamanucas: plantation@is.com.fj

Qamea Beach Club Resort, Qamea: qamea@is.com.fj

Ra Divers, Nananu-i-Ra: radivers@is.com.fj

Raffles Gateway Hotel, Nadi: gaby@is.com.fj

Rainbow Reef Aqua-club, Taveuni: rainbowreef@juno.com

Rainbow Reef Divers, Taveuni: aquatrek@is.com.fj

Rakiraki Hotel, Rakiraki: tanoahotels@is.com.fj

Reef Resort, Korotogo: reefresort@is.com.fj

Research Pacific, Suva: info@researchpacific.com

Review Magazine, Suva: review@is.com.fj

Rivers Fiji, Pacific Harbor: riversfiji@is.com.fj

Rosie The Travel Service, Nadi: rosiefiji@is.com.fj

Rosie's Deluxe Apartments, Nadi: rosiefiji@is.com.fj

Sandalwood Inn, Nadi: sandalwood@is.com.fj

Saweni Beach Apartments, Lautoka: saweni@fiji4less.com

Scubahire, Suva: divefiji@is.com.fj

Sea Fiji Travel, Savusavu: seafijidive@is.com.fj

Seashell Cove Resort, Nadi: seashell@is.com.fj

Sea Sports Ltd., Sigatoka: seasports@is.com.fj

Seven Seas Cruising Association, U.S.A.: SSCA1@ibm.net

Shangri-La's Fijian Resort: fijianresort@is.com.fj

Sheraton Fiji Resort, Nadi: kmutton@is.com.fj

Sheraton Vomo Island Resort: sheratonvomo@is.com.fj

Shotover Jet, Nadi: shotoverjet@is.com.fj

Skylodge Hotel, Nadi: tanoahotels@is.com.fj

Sonaisali Island Resort, Nadi: sonaisali@is.com.fj

South Sea Cruises, Nadi: southseaturtle@is.com.fj

South Seas Private Hotel, Suva: southseas@fiji4less.com

Subsurface Fiji, Lautoka: subsurface@is.com.fj

Sunflower Airlines, Nadi: sunair@is.com.fj

Suva Apartments, Suva: fasanoc@is.com.fj

Tanoa Apartments, Nadi: tanoahotels@is.com.fj

Tanoa International Hotel, Nadi: tanoahotels@is.com.fj

Tavarua Island Resort, Nadi: tavarua@is.com.fj

Thrifty Rent a Car, Nadi: rosiefiji@is.com.fj

Toberua Island Resort, Suva: toberua@is.com.fj

Tokatoka Resort Hotel, Nadi: tokatokaresort@is.com.fj

Tokoriki Sunset Resort, Mamanucas: tokoriki@is.com.fj

Tourism Council of the South Pacific, Suva: spice@is.com.fj

Tourist Information Center, Nadi: hostelsfiji@is.com.fj

Travel Inn, Suva: travelinn@fiji4less.com

Travelers Beach Resort, Nadi: beachvilla@is.com.fj

Tropical Dive, Taveuni: princessii@juno.com

Tubakula Beach Resort, Korotogo: tubakula@fiji4less.com

Turtle Airways, Nadi: southseaturtle@is.com.fj

Turtle Island Lodge, Yasawas: turtle@is.com.fj

Vatukaluvi Holiday House, Savusavu: coprashed@is.com.fj

Vatulele Island Resort: vatulele@is.com.fj

Vatulele Island Resort: vatu@magna.com.au

Victory Inland Safaris, Nadi: touristinfofj@is.com.fj

Wadigi Island Lodge, Mamanucas: wadigiisland@is.com.fj

Wakaya Club, Lomaiviti: wakaya@is.com.fj

Waterfront Hotel, Lautoka: tanoahotels@is.com.fj

Westside Watersports, Lautoka: westside@is.com.fj

Yasawa Island Resort, Yasawas: yasawaisland@is.com.f

# GLOSSARY

***adi***—the female equivalent of Ratu

**AIDS**—Acquired Immune Deficiency Syndrome

**archipelago**—a group of islands

**atoll**—a low-lying, ring-shaped coral reef enclosing a lagoon

***balabala***—tree fern

***balawa***—pandanus, screw pine

***balolo***—in Fijian, a reef worm *(Eunice viridis)*

**bareboat charter**—chartering a yacht without crew or provisions

**bark cloth**—see *tapa*

**barrier reef**—a coral reef separated from the adjacent shore by a lagoon

**bêche-de-mer**—sea cucumber; an edible sea slug

***bete***—a traditional priest

***bilibili***—a bamboo raft

***bilo***—a kava cup

**blackbirder**—A 19th-century European recruiter of island labor, mostly ni-Vanuatu and Solomon Islanders taken to work on plantations in Queensland and Fiji.

**Bose vaka-Turaga**—Great Council of Chiefs

**Bose vaka-Yasana**—Provincial Council

**breadfruit**—a large, round fruit with starchy flesh, often baked in the *lovo*

***bula* shirt**—a colorful Fijian aloha shirt

***buli***—Fijian administrative officer in charge of a *tikina;* subordinate of the roko tui

***bure***—a village house

**BYO**—Bring Your Own (an Australian term used to refer to restaurants that allow you to bring your own alcoholic beverages)

**caldera**—a wide crater formed through the collapse or explosion of a volcano

**cassava**—manioc; the starchy edible root of the tapioca plant

**chain**—an archaic unit of length equivalent to 20 meters

**ciguatera**—a form of fish poisoning caused by microscopic algae

**coir**—coconut husk sennit used to make rope, etc.

**confirmation**—A confirmed reservation exists when a supplier acknowledges, either orally or in writing, that a booking has been accepted.

**copra**—dried coconut meat used in the manufacture of coconut oil, cosmetics, soap, and margarine

**coral**—a hard, calcareous substance of various shapes, composed of the skeletons of tiny marine animals called polyps

**coral bank**—a coral formation over 150 meters long

**coral head**—a coral formation a few meters across

**coral patch**—a coral formation up to 150 meters long

**cyclone**—Also known as a hurricane (in the Caribbean) or typhoon (in Japan). A tropical storm that rotates around a center of low atmospheric pressure; it becomes a cyclone when its winds reach force 12 or 64 knots. At sea the air will be filled with foam and driving spray, the water surface completely white with 14-meter-high waves. In the Northern Hemisphere, cyclones spin counterclockwise, while south of the equator they move clockwise. The winds of cyclonic storms are deflected toward a low-pressure area at the center, although the "eye" of the cyclone may be calm.

***dalo***—*see* taro

**deck**—Australian English for a terrace or porch

**Degei**—the greatest of the pre-Christian Fijian gods

**desiccated coconut**—the shredded meat of dehydrated fresh coconut

**direct flight**—a through flight with one or more

stops but no change of aircraft, as opposed to a nonstop flight

***drua***—an ancient Fijian double canoe

**dugong**—a large plant-eating marine mammal; called a manatee in the Caribbean

**EEZ**—Exclusive Economic Zone; a 200-nautical-mile offshore belt of an island nation or seacoast state that controls the mineral exploitation and fishing rights

**endemic**—native to a particular area and existing only there

**ESCAP**—Economic and Social Commission for Asia and the Pacific

**expatriate**—a person residing in a country other than his/her own; in the South Pacific such persons are also called "Europeans" if their skin is white, or simply "expats."

**FAD**—fish aggregation device

**fissure**—a narrow crack or chasm of some length and depth

**FIT**—foreign independent travel; a custom-designed, prepaid tour composed of many individualized arrangements

**fringing reef**—a reef along the shore of an island

**GPS**—Global Positioning System, the space age successor of the sextant

**guano**—manure of seabirds, used as a fertilizer

**guyot**—a submerged atoll, the coral of which couldn't keep up with rising water levels

**HIV**—Human Immunodeficiency Virus, the cause of AIDS

**hurricane**—*see* cyclone

***ivi***—the Polynesian chestnut tree *(Inocarpus edulis)*

**jug**—a cross between a ceramic kettle and a pitcher used to heat water for tea or coffee in Australian-style hotels

***kai***—freshwater mussel

***kaisi***—a commoner

**kava**—a Polynesian word for the drink known in the Fijian language as *yaqona* and in English slang as "grog." This traditional beverage is made by squeezing a mixture of the grated root of the pepper shrub *(Piper methysticum)* and cold water through a strainer of hibiscus-bark fiber.

**knot**—about three kilometers per hour

***kokoda***—chopped raw fish and sea urchins marinated with onions and lemon; called *sashimi* in Japanese

***koro***—village

***kumala***—sweet potato *(Ipomoea batatas)*

***kumi***—stenciled tapa cloth

**lagoon**—an expanse of water bounded by a reef

***lali***—a hollow log drum hit with a stick

***Lapita* pottery**—pottery made by the ancient Polynesians from 1600 to 500 B.C.

**LDS**—Latter-day Saints; the Mormons

**leeward**—downwind; the shore (or side) sheltered from the wind; as opposed to windward

**live-aboard**—a tour boat with cabin accommodation for scuba divers

**LMS**—London Missionary Society; a Protestant group that spread Christianity from Tahiti (1797) across the Pacific

***lolo***—coconut cream

***lovo***—an underground, earthen oven (called an *umu* in the Polynesian languages); after A.D. 500 the Polynesians had lost the art of making pottery, so they were compelled to bake their food rather than boil it.

***magiti***—feast

**mahimahi**—dorado, Pacific dolphinfish (no relation to the mammal)

**mana**—authority, prestige, virtue, "face," psychic power, a positive force

**mangrove**—a tropical shrub with branches that send down roots forming dense thickets along tidal shores

**manioc**—cassava, tapioca, a starchy root crop

***masa kesa***—freehand painted tapa

***masi***—*see* tapa

***mata ni vanua***—an orator who speaks for a high chief

**matrilineal**—a system of tracing descent through the mother's familial line

***meke***—traditional song and dance

**Melanesia**—the high island groups of the western Pacific (Fiji, New Caledonia, Vanuatu, Solomon Islands, Papua New Guinea); from *melas* (black)

**Micronesia**—chains of high and low islands mostly north of the Equator (Carolines, Gilberts, Marianas, Marshalls); from *micro* (small)

**mynah**—an Indian starlinglike bird *(Gracula)*

**NAUI**—National Association of Underwater Instructors

**NGO**—Nongovernment organization

**NFIP**—Nuclear-Free and Independent Pacific movement

**overbooking**—the practice of confirming more seats, cabins, or rooms than are actually available to insure against no-shows

**Pacific rim**—the continental landmasses and large countries around the fringe of the Pacific

**PADI**—Professional Association of Dive Instructors

***palusami***—a Samoan specialty of coconut cream wrapped in taro leaves and baked

**pandanus**—screw pine with slender stem and prop roots. The sword-shaped leaves are used for plaiting mats and hats.

**parasailing**—a sport in which participants are carried aloft by a parachute pulled behind a speedboat

**pass**—a channel through a barrier reef, usually with an outward flow of water

**passage**—an inside passage between an island and a barrier reef

**patrilineal**—a system of tracing descent through the fathers familial line

**pawpaw**—papaya

**pelagic**—relating to the open sea, away from land

**Polynesia**—divided into Western Polynesia (Tonga and Samoa) and Eastern Polynesia (Tahiti-Polynesia, Cook Islands, Hawaii, Easter Island, and New Zealand); from *poly* (many)

**punt**—a flat-bottomed boat

**Quonset hut**—a prefabricated, semicircular, metal shelter popular during WW II; also called a Nissan hut

**rain shadow**—the dry side of a mountain, sheltered from the windward side

***rara***—a grassy village square

***ratu***—a title for Fijian chiefs, prefixed to their names

**reef**—a coral ridge near the ocean surface

***roko tui***—senior Fijian administrative officer

**roti**—a flat Indian bread

**sailing**—the fine art of getting wet and becoming ill while slowly going nowhere at great expense

***salusalu***—garland, lei

**scuba**—self-contained underwater breathing apparatus

**SDA**—Seventh-Day Adventist

**self-contained**—a room with private facilities (a toilet and shower not shared with other guests); as opposed to a "self-catering" unit with cooking facilities; the brochure term "ensuite" means the bathroom is shared

**sennit**—braided coconut-fiber rope

***sevusevu***—a presentation of *yaqona*

**shareboat charter**—a yacht tour for individuals or couples who join a small group on a fixed itinerary

**shifting cultivation**—a method of farming involving the rotation of fields instead of crops

**shoal**—a shallow sandbar or mud bank

**shoulder season**—a travel period between high/peak and low/off-peak seasons

**SPARTECA**—South Pacific Regional Trade and Economic Cooperation Agreement; an agreement that allows certain manufactured goods from Pacific countries duty-free entry to Australia and New Zealand

**SPREP**—South Pacific Regional Environment Program

**subduction**—the action of one tectonic plate wedging under another

**subsidence**—geological sinking or settling

**sulu**—a saronglike wraparound skirt or loincloth

**symbiosis**—a mutually advantageous relationship between unlike organisms

***tabu***—taboo, forbidden, sacred, set apart, a negative force

***tabua***—a whale's tooth, a ceremonial object

***takia***—a small sailing canoe

***talanoa***—to chat or tell stories

***tanoa***—a special wide wooden bowl in which *yaqona* (kava) is mixed; used in ceremonies in Fiji, Tonga, and Samoa

**tapa**—a cloth made from the pounded bark of the paper mulberry tree *(Broussonetia papyrifera).* It's soaked and beaten with a mallet to flatten and intertwine the fibers, then painted with geometric designs; called *siapo* in Samoan, *masi* in Fijian.

***tapu*—see** tabu

**taro**—a starchy elephant-eared tuber *(Colocasia esculenta),* a staple food of the Pacific islanders; called *dalo* in Fijian

***tavioka***—tapioca, cassava, manioc, arrowroot

***teitei***—a garden

**tiki**—a humanlike sculpture used in the old days for religious rites and sorcery

***tikina***—a group of Fijian villages administered by a *buli*

**timeshare**—part ownership of a residential unit with the right to occupy the premises for a certain period each year in exchange for payment of an annual maintenance fee

**TNC**—transnational corporation (also referred to as a multinational corporation)

**trade wind**—a steady wind blowing toward the equator from either northeast or southeast

**trench**—the section at the bottom of the ocean where one tectonic plate wedges under another

**tridacna clam**—eaten everywhere in the Pacific, its size varies between 10 centimeters and one meter

**tropical storm**—a cyclonic storm with winds of 35 to 64 knots

**tsunami**—a fast-moving wave caused by an undersea earthquake

***tui***—king

***turaga***—chief

***turaga-ni-koro***—village herald or mayor

***vakaviti***—in the Fijian way

**vigia**—a mark on a nautical chart indicating a dangerous rock or shoal

**VSO**—Volunteer Service Overseas, the British equivalent of the Peace Corps

***waka***—whole kava roots

**windward**—the point or side from which the wind blows, as opposed to leeward

**yam**—the starchy, tuberous root of a climbing plant

***yaqona***—*see* kava

***yasana***—an administrative province

**zories**—rubber shower sandals, thongs, flip-flops

# CAPSULE FIJIAN VOCABULARY

Although most people in Fiji speak English fluently, mother tongues include Fijian, Hindi, and other Pacific languages. Knowledge of a few words of Fijian, especially slang words, will make your stay more exciting and enriching. Fijian has no pure *b, c,* or *d* sounds as they are known in English. When the first missionaries arrived, they invented a system of spelling, with one letter for each Fijian sound. The reader should be aware that the sound "mb" is written *b,* "nd" is *d,* "ng" is *g,* "ngg" is *q,* and "th" is *c.*

*Au lako mai Kenada.*—I come from Canada
*au la o*—Vanua Levu version of *barewa*
*au lili*—affirmative response to *au la o* (also *la o mai)*
*Au ni lako mai vei?*—Where do you come from?
*Au sa lako ki vei?*—Where are you going?

*barewa*—a provocative greeting for the opposite sex
*bula*—a Fijian greeting

*Daru lako!*—Let's go!
*dua*—one
*dua oo*—said by males when they meet a chief or enter a Fijian *bure*
*dua tale*—once more

*e rewa*—a positive response to *barewa*

*io*—yes

*kana*—eat
*kauta mai*—bring
*kauta tani*—take away
*kaivalagi*—foreigner
*koro*—village
*Kocei na yacamu?*—What's your name?
*lailai*—small
*lako mai*—come
*lako tani*—go
*levu*—big, much
*lima*—five
*loloma yani*—please pass along my regards

*maleka*—delicious
*magimagi*—coconut rope fiber
*magiti*—feast
*marama*—madam
*mataqali*—a clan lineage
*moce*—goodbye

*Na cava oqo?*—what is this?
*Nice bola.*—You're looking good.
*ni sa bula*—Hello, how are you? (can also say *sa bula* or *bula vinaka;* the answer is *an sa bula vinaka)*
*ni sa moce*—good night
*ni sa yadra*—good morning

*phufter*—a gay male (a disrespectful term)

*qara*—cave

*rewa sese*—an affirmative response to *barewa*
*rua*—two

*sa vinaka—it's okay*
sega—no, none
*sega na leqa*—you're welcome
*sota tale*—see you again

*talatala*—reverend
*tabu rewa*—a negative response to *barewa*
*tolu*—three
*tulou*—excuse me
*turaga*—sir, Mr.

*va*—four
*vaka lailai*—a little, small
*vaka levu*—a lot, great
*vaka malua*—slowly

*vaka totolo*—fast
*vale*—house
*vale lailai*—toilet
*vanua*—land, custom, people
*vinaka*—thank you
*vinaka vakalevu*—thank you very much
*vu*—an ancestral spirit
*wai*—water
*yalo vinaka*—please
*yadra*—good morning
*yaqona*—kava, grog

# CAPSULE HINDI VOCABULARY

*aao*—come
*accha*—good
*bhaahut julum*—very beautiful (slang)
*chota*—small (male)
*choti*—small (female)
*dhanyabaad*—thank you
*ek aur*—one more
*haan*—yes
*hum jauo*—I go (slang)
*jalebi*—an Indian sweet
*jao*—go
*kab*—when
*kahaan*—where
*kahaan jata hai*—where are you going?
*kaise hai?*—how are you?
*khana*—food
*kitna?*—how much?
*kya*—what
*laao*—bring
*maaf kijye ga*—excuse me
*nahi*—no
*namaste*—hello, goodbye
*pani*—water
*rait*—okay
*ram ram*—same as *namaste*
*roti*—a flat Indian bread
*seedhe jauo*—go straight
*theek bhai*—I'm fine
*yeh kia hai*—what's this?
*yihaan*—here

# ACCOMMODATIONS INDEX

# INDEX

## GOLF



G



H



I



## HIKING/CLIMBING



*Many resorts also offer hiking. See the* Accommodations Index *for resort listings.*

## KAYAKING

## Q



## R



### RIVER RUNNING





## S

## SCUBA DIVING/SNORKELING



*Many resorts also offer scuba and snorkeling. See the* Accommodations Index *for resort listings.*



## SURFING

**Y**



## YACHTING





## PLEASE HELP US

Well, you've heard what *we* have to say, now we want to hear what *you* have to say! How did the book work for you? Your experiences were unique, so please share them. Let us know which businesses deserve a better listing, what we should warn people about, and where we're spot on. It's only with the help of readers like yourself that we can make *Fiji Handbook* a complete guide for *everyone*. The address is:

David Stanley
c/o Moon Travel Handbooks
5855 Beaudry Street
Emeryville, CA 94608, USA
(e-mail: travel@moon.com)

## ABOUT THE AUTHOR

Three decades ago, David Stanley's right thumb carried him out of Toronto, Canada, onto a journey that has so far wound through 171 countries, including a three-year trip from Tokyo to Kabul. His travel guidebooks to the South Pacific, Micronesia, Alaska, Eastern Europe, and Cuba opened those areas to budget travelers for the first time.

During the late 1960s, David got involved in Mexican culture by spending a year in several small towns near Guanajuato. Later he studied at the universities of Barcelona and Florence, before settling down to get an honors degree (with distinction) in Spanish literature from the University of Guelph, Canada.

In 1978 Stanley linked up with future publisher Bill Dalton, and together they wrote the first edition of *South Pacific Handbook.* Since then, Stanley has gone on to write additional definitive guides for Moon Publications, including *Fiji Handbook* and *Tahiti Handbook,* and early editions of *Alaska-Yukon Handbook* and *Micronesia Handbook.* He wrote the first three editions of Lonely Planet's *Eastern Europe on a Shoestring* as well as their guide to *Cuba.* His books have informed a generation of budget travelers.

Stanley makes frequent research trips to the areas covered in his guides, jammed between journeys to the 73 countries and territories worldwide he still hasn't visited. In travel writing David Stanley has found a perfect outlet for his restless wanderlust.

MOON TRAVEL HANDBOOKS
title list
atlas
order
links
.com EMAIL
MOON TRAVEL HANDBOOKS
DISCOVER THE DIFFERENCE
ECUADOR HANDBOOK
WHAT'S NEW
ATLAS
Excerpts and updates from our flagship series
ROAD TRIP USA
ROAD TRIP USA
The award-winning webguide to travel off the beaten path
THE PRACTICAL NOMAD
The definitive guide to independent travel, including expert advice on international airfares.
TRAVEL MATTERS
Our online news magazine: stories, contests and features

## LOSE YOURSELF IN THE EXPERIENCE, NOT THE CROWD

For more than 25 years, Moon Travel Handbooks have been the guidebooks of choice for adventurous travelers. Our award-winning Handbook series provides focused, comprehensive coverage of distinct destinations all over the world. Each Handbook is like an entire bookcase of cultural insight and introductory information in one portable volume. Our goal at Moon is to give travelers all the background and practical information they'll need for an extraordinary travel experience.

The following pages include a complete list of Handbooks, covering North America and Hawaii, Mexico, Latin America and the Caribbean, and Asia and the Pacific. Please check our Web site at **www.moon.com** for current prices and editions, or see your local bookseller.

"An in-depth dunk into the land, the people and their history, arts, and politics."

—***Student Travels***

"I consider these books to be superior to Lonely Planet. When Moon produces a book it is more humorous, incisive, and off-beat."

—***Toronto Sun***

"Outdoor enthusiasts gravitate to the well-written Moon Travel Handbooks. In addition to politically correct historic and cultural features, the series focuses on flora, fauna and outdoor recreation. Maps and meticulous directions also are a trademark of Moon guides."

—***Houston Chronicle***

"Moon [Travel Handbooks] . . . bring a healthy respect to the places they investigate. Best of all, they provide a host of odd nuggets that give a place texture and prod the wary traveler from the beaten path. The finest are written with such care and insight they deserve listing as literature."

—***American Geographical Society***

"Moon Travel Handbooks offer in-depth historical essays and useful maps, enhanced by a sense of humor and a neat, compact format."

—***Swing***

"Perfect for the more adventurous, these are long on history, sightseeing and nitty-gritty information and very price-specific."

—***Columbus Dispatch***

"Moon guides manage to be comprehensive and countercultural at the same time . . . Handbooks are packed with maps, photographs, drawings, and sidebars that constitute a college-level introduction to each country's history, culture, people, and crafts."

—***National Geographic Traveler***

"Few travel guides do a better job helping travelers create their own itineraries than the Moon Travel Handbook series. The authors have a knack for homing in on the essentials."

—**Colorado Springs *Gazette Telegraph***

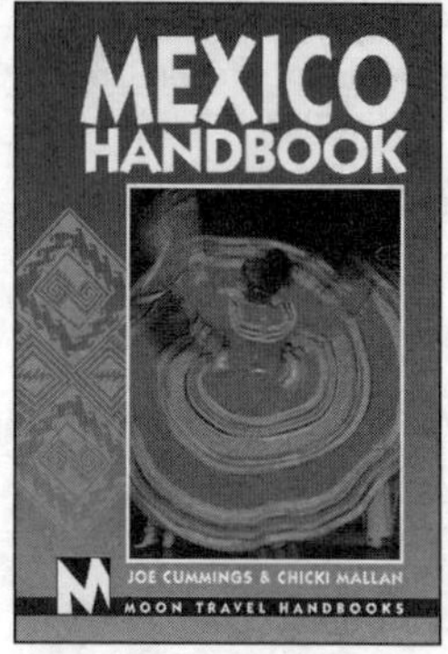


## MEXICO

**"These books will delight the armchair traveler, aid the undecided person in selecting a destination, and guide the seasoned road warrior looking for lesser-known hideaways."**

**—*Mexican Meanderings* Newsletter**

**"From tourist traps to off-the-beaten track hideaways, these guides offer consistent, accurate details without pretension."**

***—Foreign Service Journal***

| | |
|---|---|
| **Archaeological Mexico** | **$19.95** |
| Andrew Coe | 420 pages, 27 maps |
| **Baja Handbook** | **$16.95** |
| Joe Cummings | 540 pages, 46 maps |
| **Cabo Handbook** | **$14.95** |
| Joe Cummings | 270 pages, 17 maps |
| **Cancún Handbook** | **$14.95** |
| Chicki Mallan | 240 pages, 25 maps |
| **Colonial Mexico** | **$18.95** |
| Chicki Mallan | 400 pages, 38 maps |
| **Mexico Handbook** | **$21.95** |
| Joe Cummings and Chicki Mallan | 1,200 pages, 201 maps |
| **Northern Mexico Handbook** | **$17.95** |
| Joe Cummings | 610 pages, 69 maps |
| **Pacific Mexico Handbook** | **$17.95** |
| Bruce Whipperman | 580 pages, 68 maps |
| **Puerto Vallarta Handbook** | **$14.95** |
| Bruce Whipperman | 330 pages, 36 maps |
| **Yucatán Handbook** | **$16.95** |
| Chicki Mallan | 400 pages, 52 maps |

**"Beyond question, the most comprehensive Mexican resources available for those who prefer deep travel to shallow tourism. But don't worry, the fiesta-fun stuff's all here too."**

***—New York Daily News***

## LATIN AMERICA AND THE CARIBBEAN

**"Solidly packed with practical information and full of significant cultural asides that will enlighten you on the whys and wherefores of things you might easily see but not easily grasp."**

***—Boston Globe***

| | |
|---|---|
| **Belize Handbook** | **$15.95** |
| Chicki Mallan and Patti Lange | 390 pages, 45 maps |
| **Caribbean Vacations** | **$18.95** |
| Karl Luntta | 910 pages, 64 maps |
| **Costa Rica Handbook** | **$19.95** |
| Christopher P. Baker | 780 pages, 73 maps |
| **Cuba Handbook** | **$19.95** |
| Christopher P. Baker | 740 pages, 70 maps |
| **Dominican Republic Handbook** | **$15.95** |
| Gaylord Dold | 420 pages, 24 maps |
| **Ecuador Handbook** | **$16.95** |
| Julian Smith | 450 pages, 43 maps |
| **Honduras Handbook** | **$15.95** |
| Chris Humphrey | 330 pages, 40 maps |
| **Jamaica Handbook** | **$15.95** |
| Karl Luntta | 330 pages, 17 maps |
| **Virgin Islands Handbook** | **$13.95** |
| Karl Luntta | 220 pages, 19 maps |

## NORTH AMERICA AND HAWAII

**"These domestic guides convey the same sense of exoticism that their foreign counterparts do, making home-country travel seem like far-flung adventure."**

***—Sierra Magazine***

| | |
|---|---|
| **Alaska-Yukon Handbook** | **$17.95** |
| Deke Castleman and Don Pitcher | 530 pages, 92 maps |
| **Alberta and the Northwest Territories Handbook** | **$18.95** |
| Andrew Hempstead | 520 pages, 79 maps |
| **Arizona Handbook** | **$18.95** |
| Bill Weir | 600 pages, 36 maps |
| **Atlantic Canada Handbook** | **$18.95** |
| Mark Morris | 490 pages, 60 maps |
| **Big Island of Hawaii Handbook** | **$15.95** |
| J.D. Bisignani | 390 pages, 25 maps |
| **Boston Handbook** | **$13.95** |
| Jeff Perk | 200 pages, 20 maps |
| **British Columbia Handbook** | **$16.95** |
| Jane King and Andrew Hempstead | 430 pages, 69 maps |

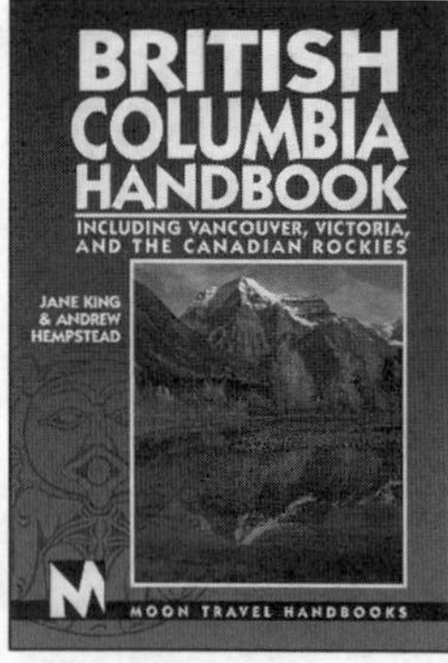

| | | | |
|---|---|---|---|
| **Canadian Rockies Handbook** | Andrew Hempstead | 220 pages, 22 maps | **$14.95** |
| **Colorado Handbook** | Stephen Metzger | 480 pages, 46 maps | **$17.95** |
| **Georgia Handbook** | Kap Stann | 380 pages, 44 maps | **$17.95** |
| **Grand Canyon Handbook** | Bill Weir | 220 pages, 10 maps | **$14.95** |
| **Hawaii Handbook** | J.D. Bisignani | 1,030 pages, 88 maps | **$19.95** |
| **Honolulu-Waikiki Handbook** | J.D. Bisignani | 360 pages, 20 maps | **$14.95** |
| **Idaho Handbook** | Don Root | 610 pages, 42 maps | **$18.95** |
| **Kauai Handbook** | J.D. Bisignani | 320 pages, 23 maps | **$15.95** |
| **Los Angeles Handbook** | Kim Weir | 370 pages, 15 maps | **$16.95** |
| **Maine Handbook** | Kathleen M. Brandes | 660 pages, 27 maps | **$18.95** |
| **Massachusetts Handbook** | Jeff Perk | 600 pages, 23 maps | **$18.95** |
| **Maui Handbook** | J.D. Bisignani | 450 pages, 37 maps | **$15.95** |
| **Michigan Handbook** | Tina Lassen | 360 pages, 32 maps | **$15.95** |
| **Montana Handbook** | Judy Jewell and W.C. McRae | 490 pages, 52 maps | **$17.95** |
| **Nevada Handbook** | Deke Castleman | 530 pages, 40 maps | **$18.95** |
| **New Hampshire Handbook** | Steve Lantos | 500 pages, 18 maps | **$18.95** |
| **New Mexico Handbook** | Stephen Metzger | 360 pages, 47 maps | **$15.95** |
| **New York Handbook** | Christiane Bird | 780 pages, 95 maps | **$19.95** |
| **New York City Handbook** | Christiane Bird | 300 pages, 20 maps | **$13.95** |
| **North Carolina Handbook** | Rob Hirtz and Jenny Daughtry Hirtz | 320 pages, 27 maps | **$14.95** |
| **Northern California Handbook** | Kim Weir | 800 pages, 50 maps | **$19.95** |
| **Ohio Handbook** | David K. Wright | 340 pages, 18 maps | **$15.95** |
| **Oregon Handbook** | Stuart Warren and Ted Long Ishikawa | 590 pages, 34 maps | **$17.95** |

| | |
|---|---|
| **Pennsylvania Handbook** | **$18.95** |
| Joanne Miller | 448 pages, 40 maps |
| **Road Trip USA** | **$24.00** |
| Jamie Jensen | 940 pages, 175 maps |
| **Road Trip USA Getaways: Chicago** | **$9.95** |
| | 60 pages, 1 map |
| **Road Trip USA Getaways: Seattle** | **$9.95** |
| | 60 pages, 1 map |
| **Santa Fe-Taos Handbook** | **$13.95** |
| Stephen Metzger | 160 pages, 13 maps |
| **South Carolina Handbook** | **$16.95** |
| Mike Sigalas | 400 pages, 20 maps |
| **Southern California Handbook** | **$19.95** |
| Kim Weir | 720 pages, 26 maps |
| **Tennessee Handbook** | **$17.95** |
| Jeff Bradley | 530 pages, 42 maps |
| **Texas Handbook** | **$18.95** |
| Joe Cummings | 690 pages, 70 maps |
| **Utah Handbook** | **$17.95** |
| Bill Weir and W.C. McRae | 490 pages, 40 maps |
| **Virginia Handbook** | **$15.95** |
| Julian Smith | 410 pages, 37 maps |
| **Washington Handbook** | **$19.95** |
| Don Pitcher | 840 pages, 111 maps |
| **Wisconsin Handbook** | **$18.95** |
| Thomas Huhti | 590 pages, 69 maps |
| **Wyoming Handbook** | **$17.95** |
| Don Pitcher | 610 pages, 80 maps |

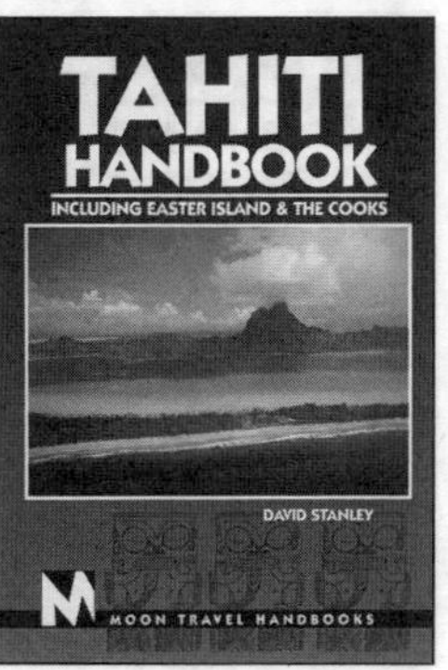


## ASIA AND THE PACIFIC

**"Scores of maps, detailed practical info down to business hours of small-town libraries. You can't beat the Asian titles for sheer heft. (The) series is sort of an American Lonely Planet, with better writing but fewer titles. (The) individual voice of researchers comes through."**

***—Travel & Leisure***

| | |
|---|---|
| **Australia Handbook** | **$21.95** |
| Marael Johnson, Andrew Hempstead, and Nadina Purdon | 940 pages, 141 maps |
| **Bali Handbook** | **$19.95** |
| Bill Dalton | 750 pages, 54 maps |
| **Fiji Islands Handbook** | **$14.95** |
| David Stanley | 350 pages, 42 maps |
| **Hong Kong Handbook** | **$16.95** |
| Kerry Moran | 378 pages, 49 maps |

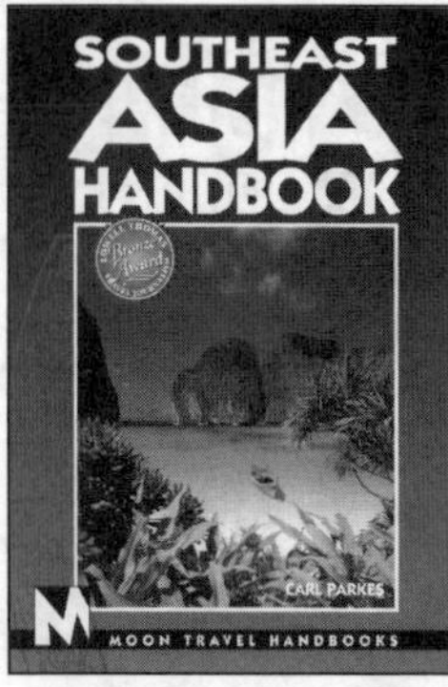

| | |
|---|---|
| **Indonesia Handbook** | **$25.00** |
| Bill Dalton | 1,380 pages, 249 maps |
| **Micronesia Handbook** | **$16.95** |
| Neil M. Levy | 340 pages, 70 maps |
| **Nepal Handbook** | **$18.95** |
| Kerry Moran | 490 pages, 51 maps |
| **New Zealand Handbook** | **$19.95** |
| Jane King | 620 pages, 81 maps |
| **Outback Australia Handbook** | **$18.95** |
| Marael Johnson | 450 pages, 57 maps |
| **Philippines Handbook** | **$17.95** |
| Peter Harper and Laurie Fullerton | 670 pages, 116 maps |
| **Singapore Handbook** | **$15.95** |
| Carl Parkes | 350 pages, 29 maps |
| **South Korea Handbook** | **$19.95** |
| Robert Nilsen | 820 pages, 141 maps |
| **South Pacific Handbook** | **$24.00** |
| David Stanley | 920 pages, 147 maps |
| **Southeast Asia Handbook** | **$21.95** |
| Carl Parkes | 1,080 pages, 204 maps |
| **Tahiti Handbook** | **$15.95** |
| David Stanley | 450 pages, 51 maps |
| **Thailand Handbook** | **$19.95** |
| Carl Parkes | 860 pages, 142 maps |
| **Vietnam, Cambodia & Laos Handbook** | **$18.95** |
| Michael Buckley | 760 pages, 116 maps |

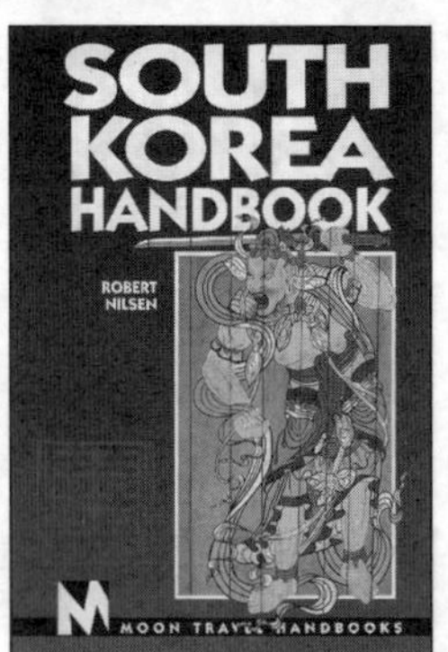


## OTHER GREAT TITLES FROM MOON

**"For hardy wanderers, few guides come more highly recommended than the Handbooks. They include good maps, steer clear of fluff and flackery, and offer plenty of money-saving tips. They also give you the kind of information that visitors to strange lands—on any budget—need to survive."**

***—US News & World Report***

| | |
|---|---|
| **Moon Handbook** | **$10.00** |
| Carl Koppeschaar | 150 pages, 8 maps |
| **The Practical Nomad: How to Travel Around the World** | **$17.95** |
| Edward Hasbrouck | 580 pages |
| **Staying Healthy in Asia, Africa, and Latin America** | **$11.95** |
| Dirk Schroeder | 230 pages, 4 maps |

# U.S.~METRIC CONVERSION

| | | |
|---|---|---|
| 1 inch | = | 2.54 centimeters (cm) |
| 1 foot | = | .3048 meters (m) |
| 1 yard | = | 0.914 meters |
| 1 mile | = | 1.6093 kilometers (km) |
| 1 km | = | .6214 miles |
| 1 fathom | = | 1.8288 m |
| 1 chain | = | 20.1168 m |
| 1 furlong | = | 201.168 m |
| 1 acre | = | .4047 hectares |
| 1 sq km | = | 100 hectares |
| 1 sq mile | = | 2.59 square km |
| 1 ounce | = | 28.35 grams |
| 1 pound | = | .4536 kilograms |
| 1 short ton | = | .90718 metric ton |
| 1 short ton | = | 2000 pounds |
| 1 long ton | = | 1.016 metric tons |
| 1 long ton | = | 2240 pounds |
| 1 metric ton | = | 1000 kilograms |
| 1 quart | = | .94635 liters |
| 1 US gallon | = | 3.7854 liters |
| 1 Imperial gallon | = | 4.5459 liters |
| 1 nautical mile | = | 1.852 km |

To compute celsius temperatures, subtract 32 from Fahrenheit and divide by 1.8. To go the other way, multiply celsius by 1.8 and add 32.

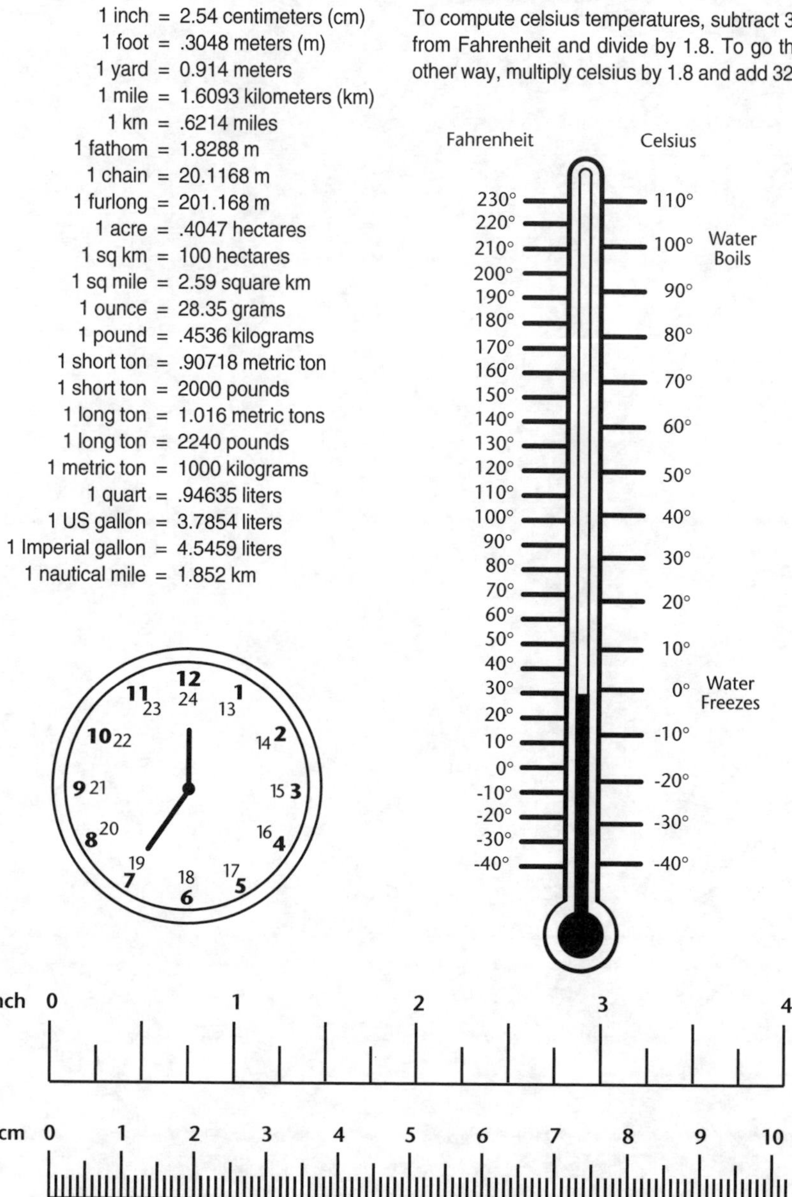

Readers interested in [illegible] *Tok Blong Pasifik*, [illegible] magazine in [illegible] informed [illegible] environment, human rights and development issues in the Pacific Islands, published quarterly by the South Pacific Peoples Foundation [illegible] and learn about [illegible]

South Pacific Peoples Foundation
[illegible] Fernwood Road
Victoria, BC, V8T 2Y6, CANADA
Tel 250 381 4131
Fax 250 388 5258
Email: [illegible]
Website: [illegible]

---

☐ Yes, I'd like to subscribe to *Tok Blong Pasifik* magazine
☐ Individual ([illegible])
☐ Student ($15.00)
☐ Organization ([illegible])

Enclose [illegible] cheque in Canada or US [illegible] for other countries).

Please print

Name: ______________________________

Address: ______________________________

______________________________

Postal Code __________ Country __________

Tel: ______________________________

Email: ______________________________

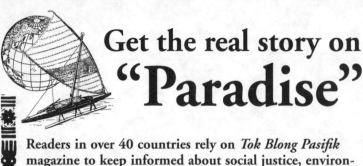